WORLD CIVILIZATIONS

THE GLOBAL EXPERIENCE
Volume 1

FOURTH EDITION

PETER N. STEARNS
George Mason University

MICHAEL ADAS
Rutgers University

STUART B. SCHWARTZ
Yale University

MARC J. GILBERT
North Georgia College & State University

PEARSON
Longman

New York San Francisco Boston
London Toronto Sydney Tokyo Singapore Madrid
Mexico City Munich Paris Cape Town Hong Kong Montreal

Vice President and Publisher: Priscilla McGeehon
Acquisitions Editor: Erika Gutierrez
Development Manager: Lisa Pinto
Development Editor: Barbara Conover
Supplements Editor: Kristi Olson
Media Editor: Patrick McCarthy
Executive Marketing Manager: Sue Westmoreland
Production Manager: Eric Jorgensen
Project Coordination, Text Design, and Electronic Page Makeup: Electronic Publishing Services Inc., NYC
Cover Designer/Manager: Wendy Ann Fredericks
Cover Art: Rank badge. Choson Dynasty. Colored silk and gold paper, thread on figured silk. 1600–1700 © Victoria
    & Albert Museum, London/Art Resource, NY
Photo Researcher: Jullie Chung, Photosearch, Inc.
Publishing Services Manager: Al Dorsey
Printer and Binder: Von Hoffmann Corporation
Cover Printer: Coral Graphic Services, Inc.

For permission to use copyrighted material, grateful acknowledgment is made to the copyright holders on pp. C-2–C-3, which are hereby made part of this copyright page.

The Library of Congress has cataloged Volume 1 as follows:
World civilizations : the global experience / Peter N. Stearns ... [et al.].--4th ed.
        p. cm.
    Includes bibliographical references and index.
    ISBN 0-321-16425-3
    1. Civilization--History. 2. Civilization--History--Sources. I. Stearns, Peter N.

CB69.W666 2003
909--dc22   2003058028

Please visit us at http://www.ablongman.com

ISBN
0-321-16425-3 (SVE version)
0-321-18280-4 (Volume 1)
0-321-18281-2 (Volume 2)
0-321-19447-0 (AP Edition)

1 2 3 4 5 6 7 8 9 10— VH— 06 05 04 03

BRIEF CONTENTS

PART I

THE ORIGINS OF CIVILIZATIONS   2

PART II

THE CLASSICAL PERIOD IN WORLD HISTORY   70

PART III

THE POSTCLASSICAL ERA   244

DETAILED CONTENTS

PART I

The Origins of Civilizations   2

v

PART II

The Classical Period
in World History   70

PART III
The Postclassical Era   244

PART IV
The World Shrinks, 1450–1750   482

LIST OF MAPS

PREFACE

When we began to work on the first edition of *World Civilizations: The Global Experience* in the early 1990s, we did so out of the conviction that it was time for a world history textbook truly global in its approach and coverage and yet manageable and accessible for today's college students. Our commitment to that goal continues with this fourth edition. We seek to present a truly global history—one that discusses the evolution and development of the world's leading civilizations—and balances that coverage with examination of the major stages in the nature and degree of interactions among different peoples and societies around the globe. We view world history not as a parade of facts to be memorized or a collection of the individual histories of various societies, but rather as a study of historical events in a global context. The study of world history combines meaningful synthesis of independent development within societies with comparative analysis of the results of contacts between societies.

Several decades of scholarship in world history and in area studies by historians and other social scientists have yielded a wealth of information and interpretive generalizations. The challenge is to create a coherent and comprehensible framework for organizing all this information. Our commitment to world history stems from our conviction that students will understand and appreciate the present world by studying the myriad forces that have shaped that world and created our place within it. Furthermore, study of the past in order to make sense of the present will help them prepare to meet the challenges of the future.

Approach

The two principal distinguishing characteristics of this book are its global orientation and its analytical emphasis. This is a true *world* history textbook. It deals seriously with the Western tradition but does not award it pride of place or a preeminence that diminishes other areas of the world. *World Civilizations: The Global Experience* examines the histories of all areas of the world and all peoples according to their growing or waning importance. It also considers what happened across regions by examining cross-civilizational developments such as migration, trade, the spread of religion, disease, plant exchange, and cultural interchange. Civilizations or societies sometimes slighted in world history textbooks—such as the nomadic societies of Asia, Latin American societies, the nations of the Pacific Rim, and the societies of nonurban sedentary peoples—receive attention here.

Many world history textbooks function as factual compendia, leaving analytical challenge to the classroom. Our goal throughout this book has been to relate fact to interpretation while still allowing ample opportunity for classroom exploration. Our analytical emphasis focuses on how key aspects of the past and present have been shaped by global forces such as the exchange of technology and ideas. By encouraging students to learn how to assess continuity and change, we seek to help them relate the past to the present. Through analysis and interpretation students become active, engaged learners, rather than passive readers of the facts of historical events.

Periodization

This text pays a great deal of attention to periodization, an essential requirement for coherent presentation. *World Civilizations: The Global Experience* identifies six periods in world history, each period determined by three basic criteria: a geographical rebalancing among major civilizational areas, an increase in the intensity and extent of contact across civilizations (or, in the case of the earliest period, cross-regional contact), and the emergence of new and roughly parallel developments in most, if not all, of these major civilizations. The book is divided into six parts corresponding to these six major periods of world history. In each part, basic characteristics of each period are referred to in chapters that discuss the major civilizations in the Middle East, Africa, Asia, Europe, and the Americas, and in several cross-cutting chapters that address larger world trends. Part introductions identify the fundamental new characteristics of parallel or comparable developments and regional or international exchange that define each period.

After sketching the hunting-and-gathering phase of human existence, Part 1, The Origins of Civilizations, focuses on the rise of agriculture and the emergence of civilization in parts of Asia, Africa, Central America, and southeastern Europe—the sequence of developments that set world history in motion from the origin of the human species until about 3000 years ago.

Part 2, The Classical Period in World History, deals with the growing complexity of major civilizations in several areas of the world. During the classical period, civilizations developed a new capacity to integrate large regions and diverse groups of people through overarching cultural and political systems. Yet many regions and societies remained unconnected to the increasingly complex centers of civilization. Coverage of the classical period of world history, then, must consider both types of societies.

The Postclassical Era, the period covered in Part 3, saw the emergence of new commercial and cultural linkages that brought most civilizations into contact with one another and with nomadic groups. The decline of the great classical empires, the rise of new civilizational centers, and the emergence of a network of world contacts, including the spread of major religions, are characteristics of the postclassical era.

Developments in world history over the three centuries from 1450 to 1750 mark a fourth period in world history—the period covered in Part 4, The World Shrinks. The rise of the West, the intensification of global contacts, the growth of trade, and the formation of new empires define this period and separate it from the preceding postclassical period.

Part 5, Industrialization and Western Global Hegemony, 1750–1914, covers the period of world history dominated by the advent of industrialization in western Europe and growing European imperialism. The increase and intensification of commercial interchange, technological innovations, and cultural contacts all reflected the growth of Western power and the spread of Western influence.

The 20th Century in World History, the focus of Part 6, defines the characteristics of this period as the retreat of Western imperialism, the rise of new political systems such as communism, the surge of the United States and the Soviet Union, and a variety of economic innovations, including the achievements of Japan, Korea, and the Pacific Rim. Part 6 deals with this most recent period of world history and some of its portents for the future.

Themes

We make world history accessible to today's students by using several themes as filters for the vast body of information that constitutes the subject. These themes provide a perspective and a framework for understanding where we have come from, where we are now, and where we might be headed.

Commonalities Among Societies

World Civilizations: The Global Experience traces several key features of all societies. We look at the technologies people have developed—for humans were toolmaking animals from an early date—and at the impact of technological change on the physical environment. We examine social structure, including the inequalities between the two genders and among different social classes. We also detail the intellectual and cultural developments occurring within various societies. These three areas—technology and the environment, inequalities and reactions to inequalities, and intellectual and cultural development—are filters through which to examine any human society.

Contacts Between Civilizations

Large regional units that defined aspects of economic exchange, political institutions, and cultural values began to spring up more than 5000 years ago. These civilizations—that is, societies that generate and use an economic surplus beyond basic survival needs—created a general framework for the lives of most people ever since. But different regions had a variety of contacts, involving migration, trade, religious missionaries, exchanges of diseases and plants, and wars. Formal relations between societies—what we now call international relations—also were organized. Many aspects of world history can be viewed in terms of whether societies had regular connections, haphazard interchange, or some mix of the two.

Features

The features in *World Civilizations: The Global Experience* have been carefully constructed and honed over the course of four editions. Our aim has been to provide students with tools to help them learn how to analyze change and continuity.

Full-Color Design

The fourth edition of *World Civilizations: The Global Experience* is published once again in full color and in a large format. Full-color maps providing a global orientation help students easily recognize and distinguish geographical features and areas. Maps in the part and chapter introductions highlight major developments during each period and familiarize students with all areas of the world. Full-color photos help bring history to life.

Part Introductions

Part introductions define the characteristics of the period of world history covered in that part, examine parallel or comparable developments that occurred among different societies as well as the new kinds of global contacts that arose, and identify key themes to be explored in the chapters that follow. Part introductions give students a context for analyzing the content of each chapter as well as a framework for seeing how the chapters within a part relate to one another. Timelines summarize the major events of the chronological period covered.

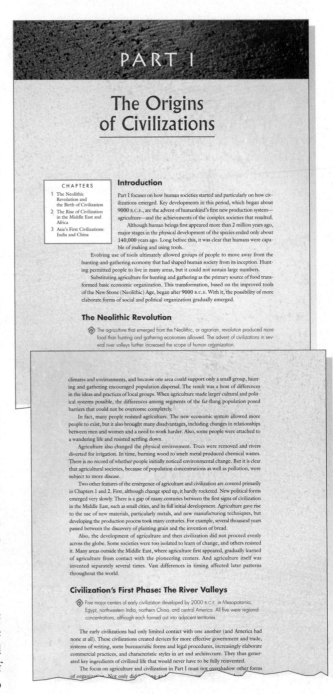

Chapter Introductions

Introductions to each chapter identify the key themes and analytical issues that will be examined in the chapter. The introduction to Chapter 9 on the spread of civilizations, for example, emphasizes that the encounters between the centers of civilization and the nomads and the clash between the great migratory waves and the settled societies have been as important in the diffusion of civilization among the world's peoples as was the spread of influence from centers such as Egypt, Rome, or Teotihuacan. The chapter begins with discussion of the basic issues debated over the spread of civilizations, such as whether early breakthroughs like agriculture were repeatedly reinvented or spread through contact and migration. This introduction gives the reader a context for understanding the similarities and differences among the diverse civilizations discussed in the chapter: sub-Saharan Africa, northern Europe, Japan, and the Pacific islands.

Timelines

Each part introduction begins with an extensive timeline that outlines the period under consideration. The timeline includes events in all the societies involved. Each chapter begins with a timeline that orients the student to the period, countries, and key events of the chapter.

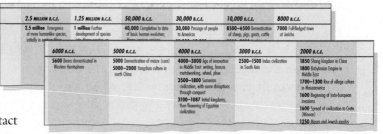

Section-Opening Focal Points

Focal point sections after each main chapter head give students a focus with which to understand the topic. In Chapter 29, on industrialization and imperialism, the first section of the chapter discusses how imperialism in Asia drew in the European powers of the time. The focal point in that section introduces the contrasts between colonizers who were willing to adopt the lifestyles of the people they sought to rule, such as the Dutch in Java, and those who imposed Westernization from early on, such as the British in India. This focus gives the reader a point of view with which to evaluate colonization during a particular era, not just a set of places, dates, and events to memorize.

Visualizing the Past

In most chapters, a *Visualizing the Past* feature asks students to deal with pictorial evidence, maps, or tables to interpret historical patterns. Text accompanying the illustrations provides a level of analysis, and a series of questions draws the students into providing their own analyses. In Chapter 3, for example, maps depicting three of the original centers of civilization—Egypt, Harappa, and China—make clear the key physical features these areas had in common as well as those that were unique. They encourage the reader to consider how these similarities and differences affected the course of civilized development.

Documents

Excerpts from original documents are included in *Document* boxes to give the reader contact with diverse voices of the past. We share a firm commitment to include social history involving women, the nonelite, and experiences and events outside the spheres of politics and high culture. Each document is preceded by a brief, scene-setting narration and followed by probing questions to guide the reader through an analysis of the document. In Chapter 24 on early Latin America, for example, the *Document* box presents a detailed statement not by the victor but by the vanquished: an educated bilingual Peruvian Indian who composed a memorial outlining the history of Peru under the Incas and reporting on later conditions under Spanish rule. The text and the drawings that accompany it offer a critical inside view of the workings of Spain's empire in America from a Native American point of view.

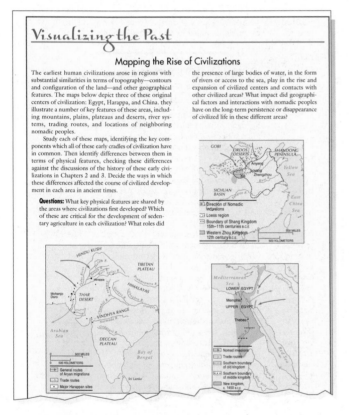

Visualizing the Past

Mapping the Rise of Civilizations

The earliest human civilizations arose in regions with substantial similarities in terms of topography—contours and configuration of the land—and other geographical features. The maps below depict three of these original centers of civilization: Egypt, Harappa, and China. they illustrate a number of key features of these areas, including mountains, plains, plateaus and deserts, river systems, trading routes, and locations of neighboring nomadic peoples.

Study each of these maps, identifying the key components which all of these early cradles of civilization have in common. Then identify differences between them in terms of physical features, checking these differences against the discussions of the history of these early civilizations in Chapters 2 and 3. Decide the ways in which these differences affected the course of civilized development in each area in ancient times.

the presence of large bodies of water, in the form of rivers or access to the sea, play in the rise and expansion of civilized centers and contacts with other civilized areas? What impact did geographical factors and interactions with nomadic peoples have on the long-term persistence or disappearance of civilized life in these areas?

Questions: What key physical features are shared by the areas where civilizations first developed? Which of these are critical for the development of sedentary agriculture in each civilization? What roles did

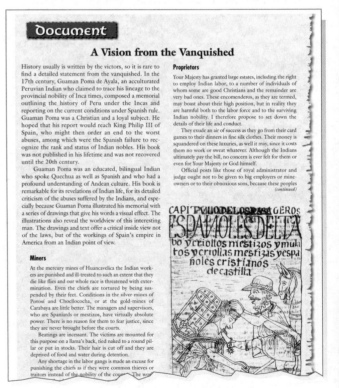

Document

A Vision from the Vanquished

History usually is written by the victors, so it is rare to find a detailed statement from the vanquished. In the 17th century, Guaman Poma de Ayala, an acculturated Peruvian Indian who claimed to trace his lineage to the provincial nobility of Inca times, composed a memorial outlining the history of Peru under the Incas and reporting on the current conditions under Spanish rule. Guaman Poma was a Christian and a loyal subject. He hoped that his report would reach King Philip III of Spain, who might then order an end to the worst abuses, among which were the Spanish failure to recognize the rank and status of Indian nobles. His book was not published in his lifetime and was not recovered until the 20th century.

Guaman Poma was an educated, bilingual Indian who spoke Quechua as well as Spanish and who had a profound understanding of Andean culture. His book is remarkable for its revelations of Indian life, for its detailed criticism of the abuses suffered by the Indians, and especially because Guaman Poma illustrated his memorial with a series of drawings that give his words a visual effect. The illustrations also reveal the worldview of this interesting man. The drawings and text offer a critical inside view not of the laws, but of the workings of Spain's empire in America from an Indian point of view.

Miners

At the mercury mines of Huancavelica the Indian workers are punished and ill-treated to such an extent that they die like flies and our whole race is threatened with extermination. Even the chiefs are tortured by being suspended by their feet. Conditions in the silver-mines of Potosí and Chocllococha, or at the gold-mines of Carabaya are little better. The managers and supervisors, who are Spaniards or mestizos, have virtually absolute power. There is no reason for them to fear justice, since they are never brought before the courts.

Beatings are incessant. The victims are mounted for this purpose on a llama's back, tied naked to a round pillar or put in stocks. Their hair is cut off and they are deprived of food and water during detention.

Any shortage in the labor gangs is made an excuse for punishing the chiefs as if they were common thieves or traitors instead of the nobility of the coun... The wor...

Proprietors

Your Majesty has granted large estates, including the right to employ Indian labor, to a number of individuals of whom some are good Christians and the remainder are very bad ones. These encomenderos, as they are termed, may boast about their high position, but in reality they are harmful both to the labor force and to the surviving Indian nobility. I therefore propose to set down the details of their life and conduct.

They exude an air of success as they go from their card games to their dinners in fine silk clothes. Their money is squandered on these luxuries, as well it may, since it costs them no work or sweat whatever. Although the Indians ultimately pay the bill, no concern is ever felt for them or even for Your Majesty or God himself.

Official posts like those of royal administrator and judge ought not to be given to big employers or mine-owners or to their obnoxious sons, because these peoples *(continued)*

In Depth Sections

Each chapter contains an analytical essay on a topic of broad application. The essay is followed by questions intended to probe student appreciation of the topic and suggest questions or interpretive issues for further thought. The *In Depth* section in Chapter 14, for example, which covers the Byzantine Empire, steps aside slightly from the discussion of Byzantium and Orthodox Europe to look at the question of where one civilization ends and another begins—a question still relevant today. How does one define states that sit between clearly defined civilizations and share some characteristics of each culture? The analytical argument in this section encompasses contested borders, mainstream culture, religion, language, and patterns of trade and looks more specifically at Poland, Hungary, and Lithuania, with elements of both western Europe and Russia in their cultures. The questions after the analysis prompt the reader to think about these difficult-to-define civilization border areas.

importance not only to the areas of civilization discussed in the chapter but also to the world as a whole. For example, in Chapter 18, this new summary section emphasizes that the spread of ideas, organizational models, and material culture from a common Chinese center spawned the rise of three distinct patterns of civilized development in Japan, Korea, and Vietnam. However, direct influences from other parts of the world were slight, because there was no sense that any other place had examples worth emulating. The intensity of interactions within the east Asian region generated a degree of isolation from the world beyond.

In Depth
Eastern and Western Europe: The Problem of Boundaries

Deciding where one civilization ends and another begins is not always easy, particularly when many political units and some internal cultural differences are involved. Defining the territory of the two related civilizations that developed in Europe is particularly difficult. A number of states sat, and still sit, on the borders of the two civilizations, sharing some characteristics of each. Furthermore, political disputes and nationalist attachments, fierce in this border territory of east central Europe during the past two centuries, make territorial definitions an emotional issue. So the question of defining Europe's civilizations is a particularly thorny case of a larger problem.

If a civilization is defined simply by its mainstream culture, then east and west Europe in the postclassical period divide logically according to Orthodox and Catholic territories (and use of the Cyrillic and Greek or of the Latin alphabets). By this reckoning, Poland, the Czech areas, and the Baltic states (these latter did not convert to Catholicism until the 14th century) are western, and Hungary is largely so. South Slavs are mainly but not entirely Orthodox, a regional division that can provoke recurrent violence. Russia and Ukraine are decidedly Orthodox in tradition. Religion matters. Poland and other Catholic regions have long maintained much more active ties with western Europe than Russia has. At the end of the postclassical period, a Czech religious dissenter, named Hus, even foreshadowed the later Protestant Reformation in his attacks on the Catholic church.

Politically, the case is more complicated. Poland, Hungary, and Lithuania formed large regional kingdoms at various times during and after the postclassical period. But these kingdoms were very loosely organized, much more so than the feu-

dal monarchies that were developing in western Europe. Exceptionally large aristocracies in Poland and Hungary (by western or by Russian standards) helped limit these states.

Trade patterns also did not closely unite Poland or Hungary with western Europe until much later, when the two regions were clearly different in economic structure. Also, Polish and Hungarian societies often shared more features with Russia than with western Europe.

Russian expansion later pulled parts of eastern Europe, including Poland, into its orbit, although it never eliminated strong cultural identities. It is also important to remember that borders can change. The Mongol invasions that swept through Russia also conquered Poland and Hungary, but the armies did not stay there. Part of the Ukraine was also free from direct Mongol control, which helped differentiate it from Russia proper. For two centuries, at the end of the postclassical period, the divisions within eastern Europe intensified. Since 1989, many east European countries have again achieved full independence from Russia, and they want to claim their distinctive pasts. Not an easy border area to characterize in terms of a single civilization, east central Europe has also been a victim of many conquests interspersed with periods of proud independence.

Questions: What were the main characteristics of Russian civilization as it first emerged in the postclassical period? In what ways did Poland, Hungary, and the Czech lands differ from these characteristics? Are there other civilization border areas, in the postclassical period or later, that are similarly difficult to define because of their position between two other areas?

NEW Global Connections

Each chapter ends with a new section—Global Connections—which reiterates the key themes and issues raised in the chapter and makes clear their

ttled on
clashed
into the
the Viet-
s proved
rces and
French
ate 18th
h of the
territory

s moved
noi, the
difficult
ting and
rs inter-
ns of the
and atti-
herners.
selves as
ir coun-
he Viet-
a as less
t. As the
outhern
manders
he north
ickering
he 16th
to chal-
mily that

ne were
the two

but from a distant land and religion about which the Vietnamese knew and cared nothing—France and the conversion-minded Roman Catholic church.

 GLOBAL CONNECTIONS: In the Orbit of China: The East Asian Corner of the Global System

The first millennium C.E. was a pivotal epoch in the history of the peoples of east Asia. The spread of ideas, organizational models, and material culture from a common Chinese center spawned the rise of three distinct patterns of civilized development in Japan, Korea, and Vietnam. In contrast to the lands of the nomadic peoples who had long been in contact with China from the north and west, each of these regions contained fertile and well-watered lowland areas that were suited to sedentary cultivation, which was essential to the spread of the Chinese pattern of civilized development. In fact, each provided an ideal environment for the cultivation of wet rice, which was increasingly replacing millet and other grains as the staple of China.

Common elements of Chinese culture, from modes of writing and bureaucratic organization to religious teachings and art, were transmitted to each of these three areas. In all three cases, Chinese imports, with the important exception of popular Buddhism, were all but monopolized by court and provincial elite groups, the former prominent in Japan and Korea, the latter in Vietnam. In all three cases, Chinese thought patterns and modes of social organization were actively and willingly cultivated by these local elites, who knew that they were the key to a higher level of d...

Further Readings

Each chapter includes several annotated paragraphs of suggested readings. Students receive reliable guidance on a variety of books: source materials, standards in the field, encyclopedic coverage, more readable general-interest titles, and the like.

On the Web

Each chapter ends with a list of annotated Web sites. Every effort has been made to find reliable, stable sites that are likely to endure. Even if some disappear, however, the annotations give students the key words necessary to search for similar sites.

Glossary

The comprehensive glossary is another feature that sets this book apart. It includes conceptual terms, frequently used foreign terms, and names of important geographic regions and key characters on the world stage. Much of world history will be new to most students, and this glossary will help them develop a global vocabulary.

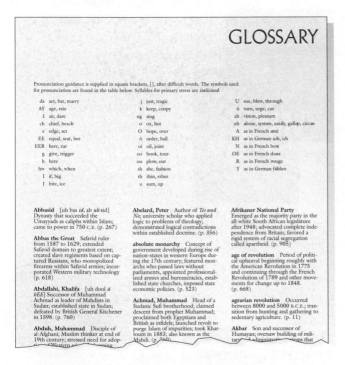

Organizational Changes to This Edition

In order to give the student a clearer chronological view of major world events, we have made a number of changes to both chapter order and topical organization within chapters.

Chapter 9, The Spread of Civilizations and the Movement of Peoples, now incorporates third edition Chapter 4, Nomadic Challenges and Sedentary Responses.

For reasons of chronology, the chapter on India's golden age, now Chapter 6, precedes the chapter on Rome and the Roman Empire, which is now Chapter 7.

Chapter 21 now emphasizes the world economy, rather than specifically stressing the importance of the West in the world.

The chapter on Africa and Africans in the age of the Atlantic slave trade, now Chapter 25, precedes the chapter on the Muslim empires, now Chapter 26. This facilitates connections with Chapter 24 on the Americas.

The text of a number of chapters within Part 6 has been heavily reorganized to give students a clearer view of major 20th-century events that affected the entire world: Chapter 33 now details World War I and the crisis of the European world order; Chapter 34, the world in the 1920s; Chapter 35, the decade of the Great Depression and the growth of authoritarian politics; and Chapter 36, World War II and the end of the European world order.

Chapter 40, Rebirth and Revolution, combines two third edition chapters relating to post–World War II events in China, Japan, Korea, and other countries of the Pacific Rim.

Chapter 41 has been extensively revamped to deal with globalization and its challenges as the leading themes of the 21st century.

Acknowledgments

Grateful acknowledgment is made to the following colleagues and reviewers, who made many useful suggestions during the development of this edition.

Sharlene Sayegh, California State University, Long Beach

J. Michael Allen, Brigham Young University, Hawaii Campus

David R. Smith, California State Polytechnic, Pomona

PETER N. STEARNS

MICHAEL ADAS

STUART B. SCHWARTZ

MARC JASON GILBERT

SUPPLEMENTS

For Qualified College Adopters

Companion Web site (www.ablongman.com/stearns)
Instructors can take advantage of the online course companion that supports this text. The instructor section of the Web site includes the instructor's manual, a list of instructor links, and downloadable images from the text.

Instructor's Resource Manual prepared by Norman Bennett of Boston University. The manual includes chapter summaries, discussion suggestions, critical thinking exercises, map exercises, primary source analysis suggestions, and term paper and essay topics. A special "Instructor's Tool Kit" by George Jewsbury of Oklahoma State University includes audiovisual suggestions.

Test Bank prepared by Denise Wright of the University of Georgia. A total of 2300 questions includes 50 multiple-choice questions and five essay questions per chapter. Each test is referenced by topic, type, and text page number.

TestGen-EQ Computerized Testing System. This easy-to-customize test generation software package presents a wealth of multiple-choice, true-false, short answer, and essay questions and allows users to add, delete, and print test items.

CourseCompass/BlackBoard/WebCT. Longman's extensive World History Content is available in CourseCompass, BlackBoard, and WebCT. All quickly and easily customizable for use with *World Civilizations*, the content includes primary sources, maps, and map exercises. Book specific testing is simply loaded. Ask your Longman representative for details.

Longman World History—Primary Sources and Case Studies (LongmanWorldHistory.com). The core of this Web site is its large database of thought-provoking primary sources, case studies, maps, and images—all carefully chosen and edited by scholars and teachers of world history. The contents and organization of the site encourage students to analyze the themes, issues, and complexities of world history in a meaningful, exciting, and informative way. Bundled at a deep discount to qualified college adopters, professors can visit the site for a free three-day trial.

The Historial Digital Media Archive CD-ROM. This new CD-ROM contains hundreds of images, maps, interactive maps, and audio/video clips ready for classroom presentation, or downloading into PowerPoint™, or any other presentation software. **Free to qualified college adopters.**

Map Transparencies to Accompany World Civilizations: The Global Experience, Fourth Edition. These text-specific transparencies are available to all adopters.

Discovering World History Through Maps and Views, Updated Second Edition, by Gerald A. Danzer, University of Illinois, Chicago, winner of the AHA's James Harvey Robinson Award for his work in developing map transparencies. This set of over 100 four-color transparency acetates is an unparalleled supplement that contains four-color historical reference maps, source maps, views and photos, urban plans, building diagrams, and works of art. The Update has been repackaged and comes in an easy-to-carry envelope rather than a bulky binder. The pedagogical material that currently appears on tabs throughout the binder will now be available **only** on supplements central. Instructions as to how to download these are located in the front of the transparency package. **Free to qualified college adopters**.

Historical Newsreel Video. This 90-minute video contains newsreel excerpts examining U.S. involvement in world affairs over the past 60 years. **Free to qualified college adopters.**

Longman-Penguin Putnam Inc. Value Packages. Students and professors alike will love the value and quality of the Penguin books offered at a deep discount when bundled with *World Civilizations: The Global Experience, Fourth Edition*, for qualified college adopters.

NEW Longman Atlas of World History. Featuring 52 carefully selected historical maps, this atlas provides comprehensive global coverage for the major historical periods, ranging from the earliest of civilizations to the present and including such maps as The Conflict in Afghanistan 2001, Palestine and Israel from Biblical Times to Present, and World Religions. Each map has been designed to be colorful, easy-to-read, and informative, without sacrificing detail or accuracy. In our global era, understanding geography is more important than ever. This atlas makes history—and geography—more comprehensible.

For the Student

Companion Web site (www.ablongman.com/stearns) The online course companion provides a wealth of resources for students using *World Civilizations*. Students can access chapter summaries, practice test questions, flash cards, and dozens of Web explorations.

Student Study Guide in two volumes, prepared by Theron Corse of Tennessee State University. Each volume includes chapter outlines, timelines, map exercises, multiple-choice practice tests, and critical thinking and essay questions.

World History Map Workbook, Second Edition, in two volumes. Volume 1 (to 1600) prepared by Glee Wilson of Kent State University. Each volume includes more than 40 maps accompanied by more than 120 pages of exercises. Each volume is designed to teach the location of various countries and their relationship to one another. Also includes exercises that enhance students' critical thinking abilities.

Documents in World History in two volumes: Volume 1, *The Great Tradition: From Ancient Times to 1500*; Volume 2, *The Modern Centuries: From 1500 to the Present,* edited by Peter N. Stearns, Stephan S. Gosch, and Erwin P. Grieshaber. This collection of primary source documents illustrates the human characteristics of key civilizations during major stages of world history.

Full-Color Longman Comparative World History Timeline. Free to qualified college adopters when packaged with the text, this fold-out, illustrated timeline provides a thorough and accessible chronological reference guide for world history. The timeline notes key events and trends in political and diplomatic, social and economic, and cultural and technological history.

Everything You Need to Know About Your History Course by Sandra Mathews-Lamb of Nebraska Wesleyan University. This guide helps students succeed in history courses by describing good techniques for taking notes, researching and writing papers; reading primary and secondary sources; reading maps, charts, and graphs; taking exams; learning from lectures; and using the textbook.

Mapping World History. This workbook was created for use in conjunction with *Discovering World History Through Maps and Views*. Designed to teach students to interpret and analyze cartographic materials as historical documents.

Research Navigator and Research Navigator Guide. Research Navigator is a comprehensive Web site comprised of three exclusive databases of credible and reliable source material for research and for

student assignments: (1) EBSCO's ContentSelec Academic Journal Database, (2) the *New York Times* Search by Subject Archive, and (3) "Best of the Web" Link Library. The site also includes an extensive help section. The Research Navigator Guide provides your students with access to the Research Navigator Web site and includes reference material and hints about conducting online research. **Free to qualified college customers when packaged.**

NEW Longman Atlas of World History. The 52 four-color maps of this atlas from Longman and Maps.com provides comprehensive global coverage for the major historical periods, ranging from the earliest of civilizations to the present. Each map has been designed to be colorful, easy-to-read, and informative, making history and geography more comprehensible.

ABOUT THE AUTHORS

Peter N. Stearns

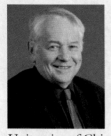

Peter N. Stearns is Provost and Professor of History at George Mason University. He received his Ph.D. from Harvard University, and, before moving to George Mason University, he taught at Rutgers University, the University of Chicago, and Carnegie Mellon, where he won the Robert Doherty Educational Leadership Award and the Elliott Dunlap Smith Teaching Award. He teaches world history and has for the past fifteen years. He currently serves as chair of the Advanced Placement World History Committee and also founded and is the editor of the *Journal of Social History*. In addition to textbooks and readers, he has written studies of gender and consumerism in a world history context. Other books address modern social and cultural history and include studies on gender, old age, work, dieting, and emotion. His most recent book in this area is *Anxious Parents: A History of Modern Childrearing in the United States.*

Michael Adas

Michael Adas is the Abraham Voorhees Professor of History and a Board of Governor's Chair at Rutgers University in New Brunswick, New Jersey. Over the past couple of decades his teaching has been focused on patterns and processes of global and comparative history. His courses on race and empire in the early modern and industrial eras and on world history in the 20th century have earned him a number of teaching prizes. In addition to texts on world history, Adas' writings have been devoted mainly to the comparative history of colonialism and its impact on the peoples and societies of Asia and Africa. Recent books include *Machines as the Measure of Men: Science, Technology and Ideologies of Western Dominance,* which won the Dexter Prize, and his forthcoming study of *Dominance by Design: Technological Imperatives and America's Civilizing Mission*. He is also currently writing a global history of the First World War.

Stuart B. Schwartz

Stuart B. Schwartz was born and educated in Springfield, Massachusetts, and then attended Middlebury College and the Universidad Autonoma de Mexico. He has an M.A. and Ph.D. from Columbia University in Latin American history. He taught for many years at the University of Minnesota and joined the faculty at Yale University in 1996. He has also taught in Brazil, Puerto Rico, Spain, France, and Portugal. He is a specialist on the history of colonial Latin America, especially Brazil, and is the author of numerous books, notably *Sugar Plantations in the Formation of Brazilian Society* (1985), which won the Bolton Prize for the best book in Latin American History. He is also the author of *Slaves, Peasants and Rebels* (1992), *Early Latin America* (1983), and *Victors and Vanquished* (1999). He has held fellowships from the Guggenheim Foundation and the Institute for Advanced Study (Princeton). For his work on Brazil he was recently decorated by the Brazilian government. He continues to read widely in the history and anthropology of Latin America, Africa, and early modern Europe.

Marc Jason Gilbert

Marc Jason Gilbert is a Professor of History at North Georgia College & State University. He is also a University System of Georgia Board of Regents Distinguished Professor of Teaching and Learning and codirector of that system's programs in India and southeast Asia. He received his Ph.D. in history from UCLA in 1978, where he built his own program in world history out of a mixture of more traditional fields. He was a founding member of the World History Association and one of its initial officers. More than a decade ago, he founded the Southeastern World History Association, a regional affiliate of the World History Association, of which he continues to serve as Executive Director. He has codirected two Summer Institutes for Teaching AP World History. He has attempted to bring global dimension to south and southeast Asian history in numerous articles and books, such as *How the North Won the Vietnam War.*

PROLOGUE

The study of history is the study of the past. Knowledge of the past gives us perspective on our societies today. It shows different ways in which people have identified problems and tried to resolve them, as well as important common impulses in the human experience. History can inform through its variety, remind us of some human constants, and provide a common vocabulary and examples that aid in mutual communication.

The study of history is also the study of change. Historians analyze major changes in the human experience over time and examine the ways in which those changes connect the past to the present. They try to distinguish between superficial and fundamental change, as well as between sudden and gradual change. They explain why change occurs and what impact it has. Finally, they pinpoint continuities from the past along with innovations. History, in other words, is a study of human society in motion.

World history is not simply a collection of the histories of various societies but a subject in its own right. World history is the study of historical events in a global context. It does not attempt to sum up everything that has happened in the past. It focuses on two principal subjects: the evolution of leading societies and the interaction among different peoples around the globe.

The Emergence of World History

Serious attempts to deal with world history are relatively recent. Many historians have attempted to locate the evolution of their own societies in the context of developments in a larger "known world": Herodotus, though particularly interested in the origins of Greek culture, wrote also of developments around the Mediterranean; Ibn Khaldun wrote of what he knew about developments in Africa and Europe as well as in the Muslim world. But not until the 20th century, with an increase in international contacts and a vastly expanded knowledge of the historical patterns of major societies, did a full world history become possible. In the West, world history depended on a growing realization that the world could not be understood simply as a mirror reflecting the West's greater glory or as a stage for Western-dominated power politics. This hard-won realization continues to meet some resistance. Nevertheless, historians in several societies have attempted to develop an international approach to the subject that includes, but goes beyond, merely establishing a context for the emergence of their own civilizations.

Our understanding of world history has been increasingly shaped by two processes that define historical inquiry: debate and detective work. Historians are steadily uncovering new data not just about particular societies but about lesser-known contacts. Looking at a variety of records and artifacts, for example, they learn how an 8th-century battle between Arab and Chinese forces in central Asia brought Chinese prisoners who knew how to make paper to the Middle East, where their talents were quickly put to work. And they argue about world history frameworks: how central European actions should be in the world history of the past 500 years, and whether a standard process of modernization is useful or distorting in measuring developments in modern Turkey or China. Through debate come advances in how world history is understood and conceptualized, just as the detective work advances the factual base.

What Civilization Means

Humans have always shown a tendency to operate in groups that provide a framework for economic activities, governance, and cultural forms—beliefs and artistic styles. These groups, or societies, may be quite small—hunting-and-gathering bands often numbering no more than 60 people. World history usually focuses on somewhat larger societies, with more extensive economic relationships (at least for trade) and cultures.

One vital kind of grouping is called civilization. The idea of civilization as a type of human society is central to most world history, though it also generates debate and though historians are now agreed that it is not the only kind of grouping that warrants attention. Civilizations, unlike some other societies, generate surpluses beyond basic survival needs. This in turn promotes a variety of specialized occupations and heightened social differentiation, as well as regional and long-distance trading networks. Surplus production also spurs the growth of cities and the development of formal states, with some bureaucracy, in contrast to more informal methods of governing. Most civilizations have also developed systems of writing.

Civilizations are not necessarily better than other kinds of societies. Nomadic groups have often demonstrated great creativity in technology and social relationships, as well as promoting global contacts more vigorously than settled civilizations sometimes did. And there is disagreement about exactly what defines a civilization—for example, what about cases like the Incas where there was not writing?

Used carefully, however, the idea of civilization as a form of human social organization, and an unusually extensive one, has merit. Along with agriculture (which developed earlier), civilizations have given human groups the capacity to fundamentally reshape their environments and to dominate most other living creatures. The history of civilizations embraces most of the people who have ever lived; their literature, formal scientific discoveries, art, music, architecture, and inventions; their most elaborate social, political, and economic systems; their brutality and destruction caused by conflicts; their exploitation of other species; and their degradation of the environment—a result of changes in technology and the organization of work.

ARCTIC OCEAN

GREENLAND

ICELAND

Arctic Circle

Yukon R.

60°N
BERING
SEA

GULF OF
ALASKA

HUDSON
BAY

ALEUTIAN ISLANDS

ROCKY MOUNTAINS

NORTH
AMERICA

St. Lawrence R.

40°N

Mississippi R.

APPALACHIAN MTS.

PACIFIC
OCEAN

ATLANTIC
OCEAN

ATL
MTS

Tropic of Cancer

GULF OF
MEXICO

20°N

HAWAIIAN
ISLANDS

WEST INDIES

Niger

CARIBBEAN SEA

0° Equator

GUIANA
HIGHLANDS

Amazon R.

SOUTH
AMERICA

ANDES MOUNTAINS

BRAZILIAN
HIGHLANDS

20°S

ATACAMA
DESERT

Tropic of Capricorn

Paraná R.

PACIFIC
OCEAN

40°S

60°S

Antarctic Circle

80°S

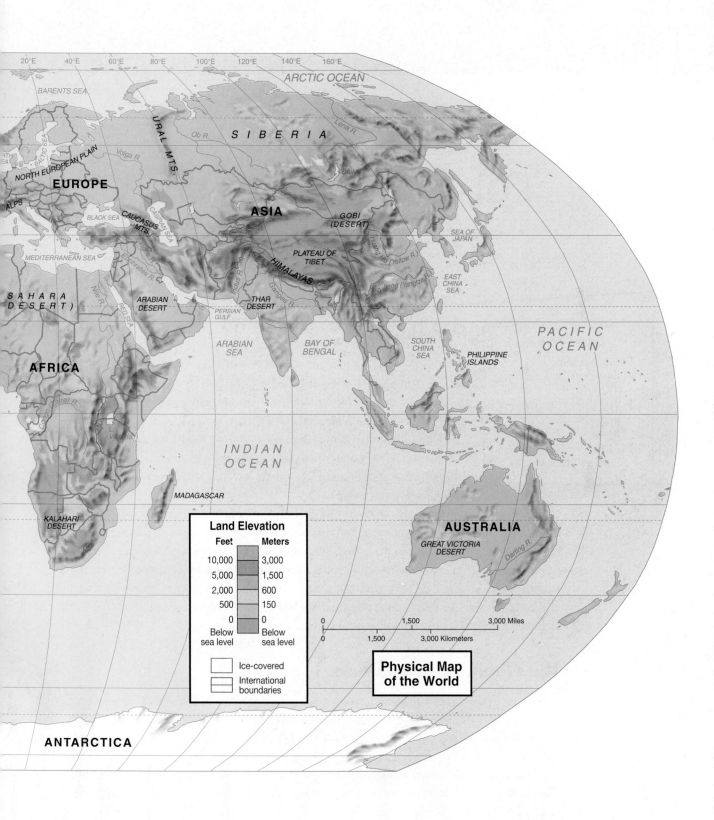

Physical Map of the World

PART I

The Origins of Civilizations

Introduction

Part I focuses on how human societies started and particularly on how civilizations emerged. Key developments in this period, which began about 9000 B.C.E., are the advent of humankind's first new production system—agriculture—and the achievements of the complex societies that resulted.

Although human beings first appeared more than 2 million years ago, major stages in the physical development of the species ended only about 140,000 years ago. Long before this, it was clear that humans were capable of making and using tools.

Evolving use of tools ultimately allowed groups of people to move away from the hunting-and-gathering economy that had shaped human society from its inception. Hunting permitted people to live in many areas, but it could not sustain large numbers.

Substituting agriculture for hunting and gathering as the primary source of food transformed basic economic organization. This transformation, based on the improved tools of the New Stone (Neolithic) Age, began after 9000 B.C.E. With it, the possibility of more elaborate forms of social and political organization gradually emerged.

The Neolithic Revolution

 The agriculture that emerged from the Neolithic, or agrarian, revolution produced more food than hunting and gathering economies allowed. The advent of civilizations in several river valleys further increased the scope of human organization.

Humankind had spread to all major continents and many island groups at least 15,000 years before agriculture was invented. Humans proved able to adapt to a wide variety of climates and environments, and because one area could support only a small group, hunting and gathering encouraged population dispersal. The result was a host of differences in the ideas and practices of local groups. When agriculture made larger cultural and political systems possible, the differences among segments of the far-flung population posed barriers that could not be overcome completely.

In fact, many people resisted agriculture. The new economic system allowed more people to exist, but it also brought many disadvantages, including changes in relationships between men and women and a need to work harder. Also, some people were attached to a wandering life and resisted settling down.

Agriculture also changed the physical environment. Trees were removed and rivers diverted for irrigation. In time, burning wood to smelt metal produced chemical wastes. There is no record of whether people initially noticed environmental change. But it is clear that agricultural societies, because of population concentrations as well as pollution, were subject to more disease.

Two other features of the emergence of agriculture and civilization are covered primarily in Chapters 1 and 2. First, although change sped up, it hardly rocketed. New political forms emerged very slowly. There is a gap of many centuries between the first signs of civilization in the Middle East, such as small cities, and its full initial development. Agriculture gave rise to the use of new materials, particularly metals, and new manufacturing techniques, but developing the production process took many centuries. For example, several thousand years passed between the discovery of planting grain and the invention of bread.

Also, the development of agriculture and then civilization did not proceed evenly across the globe. Some societies were too isolated to learn of change, and others resisted it. Many areas outside the Middle East, where agriculture first appeared, gradually learned of agriculture from contact with the pioneering centers. And agriculture itself was invented separately several times. Vast differences in timing affected later patterns throughout the world.

Civilization's First Phase: The River Valleys

 Five major centers of early civilization developed by 2000 B.C.E. in Mesopotamia, Egypt, northwestern India, northern China, and central America. All five were regional concentrations, although each fanned out into adjacent territories.

The early civilizations had only limited contact with one another (and America had none at all). These civilizations created devices for more effective government and trade, systems of writing, some bureaucratic forms and legal procedures, increasingly elaborate commercial practices, and characteristic styles in art and architecture. They thus generated key ingredients of civilized life that would never have to be fully reinvented.

The focus on agriculture and civilization in Part I must not overshadow other forms of organization. Not only did hunting-and-gathering economies persist, but nomadic herding was introduced. During the early civilization period and long after, interactions between nomadic societies and civilizations had important effects on world history.

2.5 MILLION B.C.E.	1.25 MILLION B.C.E.	50,000 B.C.E.	30,000 B.C.E.	10,000 B.C.E.	8000 B.C.E.
2.5 million Emergence of more humanlike species, initially in eastern Africa	**1 million** Further development of species into *Homo erectus*, an upright, tool-using human **600,000** Wide spread of species across Asia, Europe, Africa; development of fire use	**40,000** Completion to date of basic human evolution; *Homo sapiens sapiens* displaces other human species	**30,000** Passage of people to Americas **15,000–12,000** Domestication of dogs	**8500–6500** Domestication of sheep, pigs, goats, cattle **8500–3500** Neolithic Age; development of farming in Middle East	**7000** Full-fledged town at Jericho

Early civilizations did affect the balance between regional frameworks and wider contacts. Regional conditions, including geography, shaped particular patterns in each civilization. But civilizations also depended on contact, through trade and war, and their degrees of isolation varied considerably. It was in civilizations, finally, that new forms of social and gender inequality arose, shaping this vital human theme in new ways. Thus, most of this book's major themes are emphasized in this formative phase of world history.

Human agency is a challenge at this point in history. We do learn of individuals in the early civilizations, particularly kings and queens. Most of the big developments in the period—the invention of writing, the discovery of agriculture (almost certainly accomplished by women)—probably involved some combination of individual genius and accumulated adjustments by many people. Some developments must have been accidents, others responses to pressing problems such as changes in the food supply. The degree of explicit, conscious agency is shrouded in mystery.

The pioneering phase of civilization in Asia and parts of Europe and Africa lasted for many centuries, up to 2500 years. Yet, in part because of some widespread invasions, the early civilizations either ended or paused to regroup about 1000 B.C.E. This date signals a definable break between civilization's initial phase and a more mature phase.

Issues for Interpretation: Problems in Analyzing Early World History

The early phases of world history introduce key concepts, such as civilization, and vital early forms of what became separate civilized traditions. They also introduce issues that can be analyzed in dealing with the first millennia of agriculture.

Understanding the balance between technology and culture is one key issue. People in early societies increased their mastery over nature while producing a wide variety of styles of art and science. Both technology and culture involve important

6000 B.C.E.	5000 B.C.E.	4000 B.C.E.	3000 B.C.E.	2000 B.C.E.
5600 Beans domesticated in Western Hemisphere	**5000** Domestication of maize (corn) **5000–2000** Yangshao culture in north China	**4000–3000** Age of innovation in Middle East: writing, bronze metalworking, wheel, plow **3500–1800** Sumerian civilization, with some disruptions through conquest **3100–1087** Initial kingdoms, then flowering of Egyptian civilization	**2500–1500** Indus civilization in South Asia	**1850** Shang kingdom in China **1800** Babylonian Empire in Middle East **1700–1300** Rise of village culture in Mesoamerica **1600** Beginning of Indo-European invasions **1600** Spread of civilization to Crete (Minoan) **1250** Moses and Jewish exodus from Egypt

encounters between human society and its physical environments. Both must be considered in determining the characteristics of any civilization.

Comparison is another essential feature of analysis. The early civilizations all had to devise institutions and agricultural techniques. Although they had some characteristics in common, they also differed in political structure and cultural styles.

Interpreting heritage is another important issue for these first periods in world history. How much did later civilizations borrow from earlier examples, beyond basic techniques, and how much did they invent separately? Early civilizations introduced some techniques, including writing and the use of money, that have lasted to our own day, but by 1000 B.C.E. they had not yet spread to most areas of the world. Whether the early civilizations also set the tone for later, larger societies is open to greater debate. A recent argument that Egypt, as an African society, really provided basic institutions and ideas for Greek and later European culture is an effort to explore how much of the later shape of major civilizations was prepared during the long river valley phase.

Defining the close of the first period of world history is considerably tougher than identifying its origins and main features. The five main river valley civilizations met different fates. The first civilization in India almost completely disappeared, whereas the Chinese civilization that still exists is in some ways directly linked to its early river valley phase.

The early world history period also set some precedents that can be used in later analysis. Historians often draw analogies between the early periods of later civilizations and these first arrivals. Analogy applies particularly vividly to civilizations in the Americas, most of which arose somewhat later but are often compared with patterns in Egypt or Mesopotamia. The advent of agriculture invites comparison with the centuries of industrialization after about 1750, for these were two of the very few times when the human species fundamentally altered its framework for existence. The nature, causes, and limitations of the agrarian revolution of the late Neolithic period set patterns and raised questions that have helped us understand the much more recent Industrial Revolution. Because recent human history involves almost unprecedented alterations in basic living habits, we can only benefit from understanding comparable prior experiences.

CHAPTER 1

THE NEOLITHIC REVOLUTION AND THE BIRTH OF CIVILIZATION

Cave paintings discovered in Lascaux, France, in 1940—an example of which is shown here—probably served a ritualistic purpose for the Paleolithic artists who created them.

The starting point for exploring world history involves the modes of human organization that had developed by the end of the transition period between the **Paleolithic (Old Stone) Age** and the **Neolithic (New Stone) Age.** In this period, from roughly 12,000 to 8000 B.C.E., changes occurred in human organization and food production that made possible the food surpluses and new kinds of specialization that were essential to the first stirrings of civilized life in the 9th millennium B.C.E.

The rise of farming in the Neolithic Age (between roughly 8500 and 3500 B.C.E.) generally is seen as the source of the first truly revolutionary transformations in human history. Agriculture made the survival of the human species more secure. It gave humans a much greater capacity to change their environments to suit their needs. The most visible signs of this capacity were the spread of regularly cultivated fields and especially the development of towns. Human control over other animal species was evidenced by the growing herds of domesticated goats, sheep, and cattle that became important sources of food and materials for clothing and shelter. Trade between centers of settlement and production greatly increased contacts between different human groups, enhancing the innovation and increase of resources that were key features of the Neolithic Age. These changes also produced increasingly complex and stratified social systems and major shifts in relationships between men and women. Transformations of this sort occurred in all areas of the world where civilizations emerged in the last millennia B.C.E.

Human Life in the Era of Hunters and Gatherers

 During the Paleolithic (Old Stone) Age, *Homo sapiens*, one of several humanlike species, gained clear advantages over its rivals. Mental development, manual dexterity, and the tool making and languages these made possible were critical to this outcome. By 10,000 B.C.E., *Homo sapiens* had spread over much of the earth. Most human groups in this era supported themselves by **hunting and gathering,** but by the end of the Paleolithic Age, many peoples were experimenting with agriculture and permanent settlements.

By the late Paleolithic Age in 12,000 B.C.E., humans had evolved in physical appearance and mental capacity to roughly the same level as today. Our species, *Homo sapiens,* had been competing with increasing success for game and campsites with other humanlike creatures for nearly 100,000 years. *Homo sapiens'* large brain, critical to the survival of all branches of the genus *Homo*, was almost the same size as that of modern humans. As Figure 1.1 shows, the erect posture of Stone Age humans and related humanoids freed their hands. The combination of these free

LATE PALEOLITHIC	TRANSITION PHASE		NEOLITHIC AGE		METAL AGE	
18,000 B.C.E.	15,000 B.C.E.	10,000 B.C.E.	8000 B.C.E.	6000 B.C.E.	4000 B.C.E.	2000 B.C.E.
18,000–10,000 Central Russian mammoth bone settlements	**15,000–12,000** Domestication of dogs **10,500–8000** Natufian settlements	**8500** Domestication of sheep **8500–5000** Development of farming in the Middle East	**7500–6500** Domestication of pigs, goats, cattle **7000** Full-fledged town at Jericho **6250–5400** Çatal Hüyük at its peak	**5600** Beans domesticated **5000–2000** Yangshao culture in North China **5000** Domestication of maize (corn)	**4000–3000** Age of innovation in the Middle East: introduction of writing, metalworking, wheel, plow **3500** Llama domesticated **3500–2350** Civilization of Sumer **c. 3100** Rise of Egyptian civilization **2500–1500** Indus Valley or Harappan civilization in South Asia	**2000** Kotosh culture in Peru **c. 1766** Emergence of Shang kingdom in China **1700–1300** Rise of village culture in Mesoamerica **1000–500** Olmec civilization in Mesoamerica **400** Potatoes domesticated

hands with opposable thumbs and a large brain enabled different human species to make and use tools and weapons of increasing sophistication. These implements helped to offset the humans' marked inferiority in body strength and speed to rival predators, such as wolves and wild cats, as well as to many of the creatures that humans hunted. A more developed brain also allowed humans to transform cries and grunts into the patterned sounds that make up language. Language greatly enhanced the possibilities for cooperation and a sense of cohesion within the small bands that were the predominant form of human social organization. By the end of the Paleolithic Age, these advantages had made *Homo sapiens* a species capable of changing its environment.

Paleolithic Culture

No matter how much *Homo sapiens* had developed in physical appearance and brain capacity by around 12,000 B.C.E., its **culture,** with some exceptions, was not radically different from the cultures of rival human species such as the **Neanderthals,** who had died out thousands of years earlier. Fire had been mastered nearly a half million years earlier. Probably originally snatched from flames caused by lightning or lava flows, fire was domesticated as humans developed techniques to preserve glowing embers and to start fires by rubbing sticks and other materials together. The control of fire led to numerous improvements in the lives of Stone Age peoples. It made a much wider range of foods edible. This was particularly true of animal flesh, which was almost the

only source of protein in a culture without cows, goats, or chickens and thus lacking in milk, cheese, and eggs. Cooked meat, which was easier to digest, may also have been preserved and stored more effectively. This gave Stone Age peoples a buffer against the constant threat of starvation. In addition, fire was used to frighten off predatory animals and to harden wooden weapons and tools. Its light and warmth became the focal point of human campsites.

By the late Paleolithic Age, human groups survived by combining hunting and fishing with the gathering of wild fruits, berries, grains, and roots. They had created many tools, such as those shown in Figure 1.2, for these purposes. Tools of wood and bone have perished; surviving stone tools such as these are our main evidence of the technology of this age. Early tools, crafted by species from which humans evolved, have been found at sites well over 2 million years old. These early species made tools by breaking off the edges of stone cores to create crude points or rough cutting surfaces. By the late Paleolithic Age, their fully human descendants had grown much more adept at working stone. They preferred to chip and sharpen flakes broken off the core stone. These chips could be made into knife blades, arrow points, or choppers, which had a wide range of uses, from hunting and warfare to skinning animal carcasses and harvesting wild plants.

Early human groups also left behind impressive evidence of artistic creativity. The late Paleolithic was a period of particularly intense artistic production. Fine miniature sculpture, beads and other forms of jewelry, and carved bones have been found in abundance at

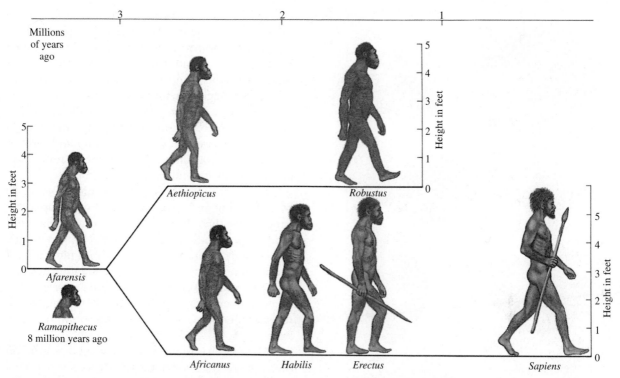

Figure 1.1 *As this artist's illustration shows, the humanoids' upright posture, which freed their hands, meant that over long periods of time Homo sapiens could develop tools and weapons. This meant that they became less fit for life in the tree canopy of forested areas. But their improving eyesight and ability to walk or run ever greater distances proved highly advantageous in the open grassland areas they came to prefer.*

sites dating from this period. But the most striking works that survive from this period are the cave paintings that have been discovered at dwelling sites in areas as diverse as southern France, the plains of Africa south of the Sahara, and the Middle East. Some of these paintings appear to have religious significance. They may have been intended to depict prominent deities or to promote fertility. Paintings at some sites may represent early counting systems or primitive calendars. Whatever their purpose, the art of the Old Stone Age suggests a sophisticated level of thinking. It also indicates that humans were becoming increasingly interested in expressing themselves artistically and in leaving lasting images of their activities and concerns.

The Spread of Human Culture

As Map 1.1 illustrates, the possession of fire and tools with which to make clothing and shelters made it possible for different human species to extend the range of their habitation far beyond the areas where they had originated. During the last Ice Age, which began about 2.5 million years ago and ended in 12,000 B.C.E., humans first moved northward from Africa into Europe and eastward from the present-day Middle East into central Asia, India, and east Asia. Neanderthals and other peoples related to humans were found across this zone as late as 35,000 B.C.E., and some archeologists claim that by then they may have begun to migrate across a land bridge into the continents we now call North and South America. Glaciation or increases in the size of the polar ice caps caused a significant drop in sea levels. The receding waters exposed land bridges from Siberia in northeast Asia to the New World and from southeast Asia to Australia. By around 12,000 B.C.E., human colonies were found in North and South America and in the south and west of Australia. Thus, by the late Paleolithic Age, groups of the *Homo sapiens* species had colonized all of the continents except Antarctica.

Figure 1.2 *Early human groups developed a variety of stone tools. The tools shown here include hand axes (top row), weapon points (second row from the top), scrapers for peeling off animal hides or working wood (third row from the top), and a hammerstone (lower left).*

Human Society and Daily Life at the End of the Paleolithic Age

Most human societies in the Paleolithic Age consisted of small groups that migrated regularly in pursuit of game animals and wild plants. But recent archeological research has shown that in some places, natural conditions and human ingenuity permitted some groups to establish settlements, where they lived for much of the year and in some cases for generation after generation. These settled communities harvested wild grains that grew in abundance in many areas. After surviving for centuries in this way, some of these communities made the transition to true farming by domesticating plants and animals near their permanent village sites.

The rejection of full-fledged agriculture by some groups and their reversion to migratory lifestyles cau-

tion us against seeing farming as an inevitable stage in human development. There was no simple progression from hunting-and-gathering peoples to settled foraging societies and then to genuine farming communities. Rather, human groups experimented with different strategies for survival. Climatic changes, the availability of water for crop irrigation, dietary preferences, and procreation patterns affected the strategy adopted by a particular group. However, only groups involved in crop and animal domestication have proved capable of producing civilizations.

However successful a particular group proved to be at hunting and gathering, few could support a band larger than 20 to 30 men, women, and children. Dependence on migrating herds of game made these bands **nomads,** many of whom moved back and forth between the same forest and grazing areas year after year. These migration patterns meant that small numbers of humans needed a large land area to support themselves, so human population densities were very low.

Most of us imagine Stone Age peoples living in caves. But recent research suggests that most preferred to live on open ground. The migratory peoples who lived on hilltops or in forest clearings built temporary shelters of skins and leaves or grass thatching. Their flimsy campsites could be readily abandoned when movements of the herd animals they hunted or threats from competing bands prompted migration. Although it is likely that bands developed a sense of territoriality, boundaries were vague, and much conflict focused on rival claims to sources of game and wild foods.

Within each **band**, labor was divided according to gender. Men hunted and fished in riverine or coastal areas. Because they became skilled in the use of weapons in the hunt, it is also likely that men protected the band from animal predators and raids by other human groups. As the cave paintings featured in the Document section suggest, animal hunts were major events in the annual cycle of life in Paleolithic societies. Nearly all able-bodied men participated in the hunting parties, and women and children prepared and preserved the meat. Although women's roles were less adventuresome and aggressive than men's, they were arguably more critical to the survival of the band. Women gathered the foods that provided the basic subsistence of the band and permitted its survival in times when hunting parties were unsuccessful. Women also became adept in using medicinal plants, which were the only means Paleolithic peoples had to treat disease.

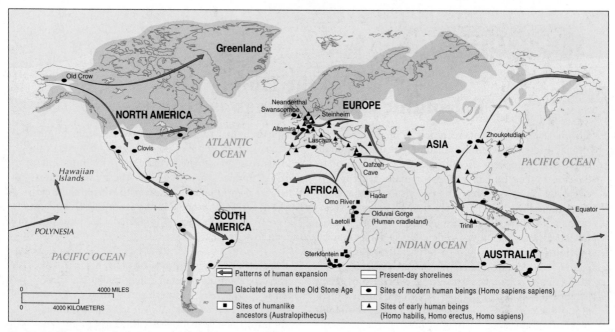

Map 1.1 *The Spread of Human Populations, c. 10,000 B.C.E.*

Settling Down: Dead Ends and Transitions

Although most humans lived in small hunting-and-gathering bands until well into the **agrarian revolution,** between 8500 and 3500 B.C.E., some prefarming peoples worked out a very different strategy of survival. They devised more intensive hunting-and-gathering patterns that permitted them to establish semipermanent and even permanent settlements and to support larger and more complex forms of social organization. Among the most spectacular Paleolithic settlements are those of central Russia. Apparently there was an abundance of large but slow woolly mammoths in that region some 20,000 years ago. These animals supplied meat that, when supplemented by wild plant foods gathered in the area, made it possible for local peoples to live in the same place throughout much of the year. Large numbers of mammoth bones found in what were in effect garbage pits at the settlement sites suggest how dependent they were on the mammoths. This reliance is equally vividly demonstrated by the extensive use of the bones of these huge mammals in building dwellings, such as that shown in Figure 1.3.

Remnants found in food storage pits and other artifacts from the central Russian settlements suggest that these people participated in trading networks with other peoples as far as 500 miles away in the area of the Black Sea. Burial patterns and differing degrees of bodily decoration also indicate clear status differences among the groups that inhabited the settlements. Mammoth bone communities lasted from about 18,000 to 10,000 B.C.E., when they suddenly disappeared for reasons that are still unknown.

Even more sophisticated than the central Russian settlements were those of the **Natufian complex,** which extended over much of present-day Palestine, Israel, Jordan, and Lebanon. Climate changes between 12,000 and 11,000 B.C.E. enabled wild barley and wheat plants to spread over much of this area. When supplemented with nuts and the meat of gazelles and other game, these wild grains were sufficient to support many densely populated settlements on a permanent basis. Between about 10,500 and 8000 B.C.E., the Natufian culture flourished. Population densities reached as high as six to seven times those of other early Neolithic communities. The Natufians developed sophisticated techniques of storing grain, and they devised pestles and grinding slabs to prepare it for meals. They built circular and oval stone dwellings that were occupied year round for centuries.

The evidence from housing layouts, burial sites, jewelry, and other artifacts indicates that, like the mammoth-hunting societies of central Russia, Natufian society was stratified. Clothing appears to have been used to distinguish a person's rank, and grand

Document

Tales of the Hunt:
Paleolithic Cave Paintings as History

The first historical events recorded by humans were the animal hunts, depicted in remarkably realistic and colorful cave paintings. Because writing would not be devised by any human group for many millennia to come, we cannot be certain of the meanings that those who created the paintings were trying to convey. Some of them may have been done purely for the sake of artistic expression. But others, which clearly depict animals in flight, pursued by human hunters, probably were painted to celebrate and commemorate actual incidents in particularly successful hunting expeditions. Their locations deep in cave complexes and the rather consistent choice of game animals as subject matter suggest that they also served a ritual purpose. Perhaps capturing the images of animals in art was seen as a way of assisting future hunting parties in the wild. In addition, it is possible that those who painted the animal figures hoped to acquire some of the strength and speed of the animals to improve their chances in the hunt and to ward off animals that preyed on the human hunters. Whatever their intentions, those who created these early works of art, such as the one shown in this Document, also created the first conscious historical accounts of the human experience.

Questions: Which interpretation of the meanings of the cave paintings outlined here makes the most sense to you? Why? How can we use what we know about Paleolithic societies to read these paintings for historical information? Are these paintings what we would consider works of art today? If so, why? If not, why not?

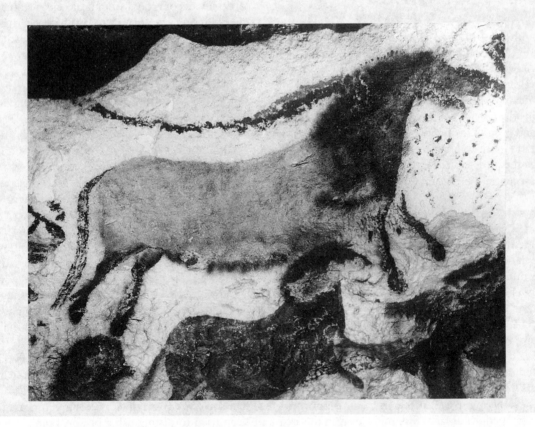

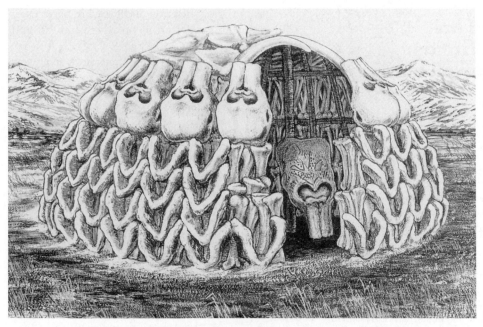

Figure 1.3 *This sketch of a reconstructed mammoth bone hut suggests the ingenuity of the design and construction of these single-room structures. The bones were covered by earth and branches to insulate the structures from the cold and rain. The large numbers of great mammoth skeletons that made up these shelters attest to the hunting skills and weapon-making ability of the central Asian peoples who built them.*

burial ceremonies marked the death of community chieftains. There is also evidence that Natufian society was **matrilocal** (young men went to live with their wives' families) and **matrilineal** (family descent and inheritance were traced through the female line). The fact that women gathered food crops in the wild may explain the power and influence they enjoyed in Natufian settlements.

The Natufian strategy for survival did not involve new tools or production techniques. It rested primarily on intensive gathering of wild grains and improvement of storage techniques. But the Natufians' concentration on a couple of grain staples, gazelle meat, and nuts rendered the culture vulnerable. After 9000 B.C.E., the climate of the region where the Natufian settlements were located grew more and more arid. The grains and game on which they depended were reduced or vanished from many locations. One thousand years later, all the Natufian sites had been abandoned.

A Precarious Existence

Until the late Paleolithic, advances in human technology and social organization were remarkably slow compared with the advances that have occurred since about 8000 B.C.E. Millions of years of evolution of the genus *Homo* had produced small numbers of humans, mostly scattered in tiny bands across six continents. On average, the lives of these humans were violent and short. They crouched around their campfires in constant fear of animal predators and human enemies. They were at the mercy of the elements and helpless in the face of injury or disease. They had a few crude tools and weapons; their nomadic existence reflected their dependence on the feeding cycles of migrating animals.

The smaller numbers of human groups that lived in permanent settlements had better shelters, a more secure food supply, and larger communities on which to draw in their relentless struggle for survival. But their lifestyles were precarious; their specialized hunting-and-gathering practices meant that shifts in grazing patterns or the climate could undermine their carefully developed cultures. Late Paleolithic humans had improved greatly on earlier versions of the species. But there was little evidence that within a few thousand years they would radically transform their environments and dominate all other forms of life.

Agriculture and the Origins of Civilization: The Neolithic Revolution

In the Neolithic (New Stone) Age, between roughly 8500 and 3500 B.C.E., some human societies, in different areas over much of the globe, crossed one of the great watersheds in human history. They mastered sedentary agriculture and domesticated animals, such as cattle, sheep, and horses, that would prove critical to human development. These innovations produced the food surpluses and rising populations that made possible the rise of genuine towns and the increasing specialization of occupations within human societies.

There was nothing natural or inevitable about the development of agriculture. Because plant cultivation involves more labor than hunting and gathering, we can assume that Stone Age humans gave up their former ways of life reluctantly and slowly. In fact, peoples such as the Bushmen of southwest Africa still follow them today. But between about 8000 and 3500 B.C.E., increasing numbers of humans shifted to dependence on cultivated crops and domesticated animals for their subsistence. By about 7000 B.C.E., their tools and skills had advanced sufficiently to enable cultivating peoples to support towns with more than 1000 people, such as Jericho in the valley of the Jordan River and Çatal Hüyük in present-day Turkey. By 3500 B.C.E., agricultural peoples in the Middle East could support sufficient numbers of nonfarmers to give rise to the first civilizations. As this pattern spread to or developed independently in other parts of the world, the character of most human lives and the history of the species were fundamentally transformed.

Because there are no written records of the transition period between 8500 and 3500 B.C.E., we cannot be certain why and how some peoples adopted these new ways of producing food and other necessities of life. Climatic changes associated with the retreat of the glaciers late in the last Ice Age (from about 12,000 B.C.E.) may have played an important role. These climatic shifts prompted the migration of many big game animals to new pasturelands in northern areas. They also left a dwindling supply of game for human hunters in areas such as the Middle East, where agriculture first arose and many animals were first domesticated. Climatic shifts also led to changes in the distribution and growing patterns of wild grains and other crops on which hunters and gatherers depended.

In addition, it is likely that the shift to sedentary farming was prompted by an increase in human populations in certain areas. This population growth may have been caused by changes in the climate and plant and animal life. It is also possible that population growth occurred because the hunting-and-gathering pattern reached higher levels of productivity. Peoples such as the Natufians found that their human communities could grow significantly as they intensively harvested grains that grew in the wild. As the population grew, more and more attention was given to the grain harvest, which eventually led to the conscious and systematic cultivation of plants and thus the **Neolithic revolution.**

The Domestication of Plants and Animals

The peoples who first cultivated cereal grains had long observed them growing in the wild and collected their seeds as they gathered other plants for their leaves and roots. In late Paleolithic times, wild barley and wheat grew over large areas in the present-day Middle East. Hunting-and-gathering bands in these areas may have consciously experimented with planting and nurturing seeds taken from the wild, or they may have accidentally discovered the principles of domestication by observing the growth of seeds dropped near their campsites.

However it began, the practice of agriculture caught on only gradually. Archeological evidence suggests that the first agriculturists retained their hunting-and-gathering activities as a hedge against the ever-present threat of starvation. But as Stone Age peoples became more adept at cultivating a growing range of crops, including various fruits, olives, and protein-rich legumes such as peas and beans, the effort they expended on activities outside agriculture diminished.

The earliest farmers probably sowed wild seeds, a practice that cut down on labor but sharply reduced the potential yield. Over the centuries, more and more care was taken to select the best grain for seed and to mix different strains in ways that improved crop yields and resistance to plant diseases. As the time needed to tend growing plants and the dependence on agricultural production increased, some roving bands chose to settle down, and others practiced a mix of hunting and **shifting cultivation** that allowed them to continue to move about.

Several animals may have been domesticated before the discovery of agriculture, and the two processes combined to make up the critical transformation in human culture called the Neolithic revolution. Different animal species were tamed in different ways that reflected both their own natures and the ways in which they interacted with humans. For example, dogs were originally wolves that hunted humans or scavenged at their campsites. As early as 12,000 B.C.E., Stone Age peoples, initially in east Asia, found that wolf pups could be tamed and trained to track and corner game. The strains of dogs that gradually developed proved adept at controlling herd animals such as sheep. Knowledge of dogs spread quickly over almost all inhabited areas—the later migrations to the Americas included Asian dogs—because they were so useful in hunting and herding. Docile and defenseless herds of sheep could be domesticated once their leaders had been captured and tamed. Sheep, goats, and pigs (which also were scavengers at human campsites) were first domesticated in the Middle East between 8500 and 7000 B.C.E. Horned cattle, which could run faster and were better able to defend themselves than wild sheep, were not tamed until about 6500 B.C.E.

Domesticated animals such as cattle and sheep provided New Stone Age humans with additional sources of protein-rich meat and, in some cases, milk. Animal hides and wool greatly expanded the materials from which clothes, containers, shelters, and crude boats could be crafted. Animal horns and bones could be carved or used for needles and other utensils. Because plows and wheels did not come into use until the Bronze Age, c. 4000–3500 B.C.E., when stone tools and weapons gave way to metal ones, most Neolithic peoples made little use of animal power for farming, transportation, or travel. However, there is evidence that peoples in northern areas used tamed reindeer to pull sleds, and those farther south used camels to transport goods. More importantly, Neolithic peoples used domesticated herd animals as a steady source of manure to enrich the soil and thus improve the yield of the crops that were gradually becoming the basis of their livelihood.

The Spread of the Neolithic Revolution

The greater labor involved in cultivation, and the fact that it did not at first greatly enhance peoples' secu-

rity or living standards, caused many bands to stay with long-tested subsistence strategies. Through most of the Neolithic Age, sedentary agricultural communities coexisted with more numerous bands of hunters and gatherers, migratory farmers, and hunters and fishers. Long after sedentary agriculture became the basis for the livelihood of the majority of humans, hunters and gatherers and shifting cultivators held out in many areas of the globe.

The domestication of animals also gave rise to **pastoralism,** which has proved to be the strongest competitor to sedentary agriculture as a way of life throughout most of the world. Pastoralism, or a nomadic herding way of life, has thrived in semiarid areas such as central Asia, the Sudanic belt south of the Sahara desert in Africa, and the savanna zone of east and south Africa. These areas could not support dense or large populations, but they have produced independent and hardy peoples. Nomads were well versed in the military skills needed to challenge more heavily populated agrarian societies. Horse-riding nomads who herded sheep or cattle have destroyed powerful kingdoms and laid the foundations for vast empires. The camel nomads of Arabia played critical roles in the rise of Islamic civilization. The cattle-herding peoples of central, east, and south Africa produced some of the most formidable preindustrial military organizations. Interactions between herding nomads and agricultural peoples would form a major theme in world history until about 500 years ago.

Those who adopted agriculture gained a more stable base for survival and increased in numbers. They also passed on their production techniques to other peoples. The spread of key crops can be traced on Map 1.2. Wheat and barley spread throughout the Middle East and to India. These crops also spread northward to Europe, where oats and rye were added later. From Egypt, the cultivation of grain crops and fibers, such as flax and cotton used for clothing, spread to peoples along the Nile in the interior of Africa, along the north African coast, and across the vast savanna zone south of the Sahara desert.

Agriculture in the African rainforest zone farther south evolved independently in the 2nd millennium B.C.E. and was based on root crops such as cassava and tree crops such as bananas and palm nuts. In northern China during the Neolithic Age, a millet-based agricultural system developed along the Huanghe or Yellow River basin. From this core region, it spread in the last millennium B.C.E. east toward the North China Sea and southward toward the Yangtze basin.

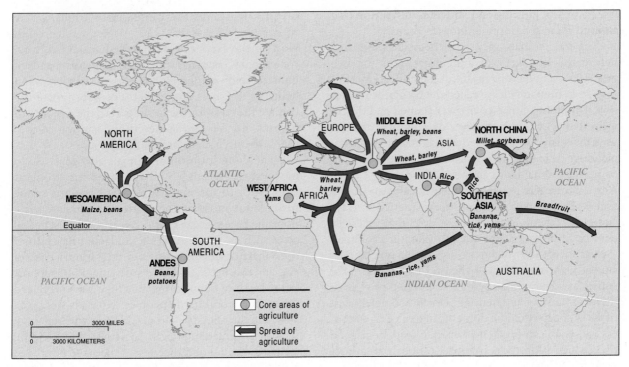

Map 1.2 *The Spread of Agriculture*

A later but independent agricultural revolution based on rice began in mainland southeast Asia sometime before 5000 B.C.E. and slowly spread north toward south China and west toward India and across the islands of southeast Asia. In the Americas, agrarian systems based on maize (corn), manioc, and sweet potatoes arose in Mesoamerica (Mexico and Central America today) and present-day Peru. Long before the arrival of Columbus in the Americas in 1492 C.E., these and other crops had spread through large portions of the continents of the Western Hemisphere, from the temperate woodlands of the North Atlantic coast to the rain forests of the Amazon region. Thus, varying patterns of agricultural production were disseminated on all the inhabited continents except Australia to nearly all the regions of the globe with sufficient rainfall and suitable temperatures.

The Transformation of Material Life

With the development of agriculture, humans began to transform more and more extensively the environments in which they lived. A growing portion of humans became sedentary farmers who cleared the lands around their settlements and controlled the plants that grew and the animals that grazed on them. The greater presence of humans was also apparent in the steadily growing size and numbers of settlements. These were found both in areas that humans had long inhabited and in new regions that farming allowed them to settle. This great increase in the number of sedentary farmers is primarily responsible for the leap in human population during the Neolithic Age. For tens of thousands of years before agriculture was developed, the total number of humans had fluctuated between an estimated 5 and 8 million. By 4000 B.C.E., after four or five millennia of farming, their numbers had risen to 60 or 70 million. Hunting-and-gathering bands managed to subsist in the zones between cultivated areas and continued to fight and trade with sedentary peoples. Areas devoted to pastoralism became even more important. But villages and cultivated fields became the dominant features of human habitation over much of the globe.

The sudden surge in invention and social complexity in the Neolithic Age marks one of the great turning points in human history. Increased reliance on sedentary cultivation led to the development of a wide variety of agricultural tools, such as digging sticks used to break up the soil, axes to clear forested areas, and the plow. Seed selection, planting, fertilization, and weeding techniques improved steadily. By the end of the Neolithic Age, human societies in several areas had devised ways to store rainwater and rechannel river water to irrigate plants. The reservoirs, canals, dikes, and sluices that permitted water storage and control represented another major advance in humans' ability to remake their environment.

More and better tools and permanent settlements gave rise to larger, more elaborate housing and community ritual centers. Houses usually were uniform in construction. Most of the early ones contained the features depicted in Figure 1.4, which shows an archeological reconstruction of a dwelling from the Neolithic Age. Building materials varied greatly by region, but sun-dried bricks, wattle (interwoven branches, usually plastered with mud), and

stone structures were associated with early agricultural communities. Seasonal harvests made improved techniques of food storage essential. At first, baskets and leather containers were used. But already in the early Neolithic Age, pottery, which protected stored foods better from moisture and dust, was known to several cultures in the Middle East.

Social Differentiation

The surplus production that agriculture made possible was the key to the social transformations that made up another dimension of the Neolithic revolution. Surpluses meant that farmers could exchange part of their harvest for the specialized services and products of craftspeople such as toolmakers and weavers. Human communities became differentiated

Figure 1.4 *Houses in early agricultural settlements, such as this one reconstructed at Skara Brae, usually included special storage areas. Most were centered on clay or stone hearths that were ventilated by a hole in the roof or built into the walls. There were also clearly demarcated and slightly raised sleeping areas, and benches along the walls. More dependable and varied food supplies, walls, and sturdy houses greatly enhanced the security and comfort of human groups. These conditions spurred higher birth rates and lowered mortality rates, at least in times when crop yields were high.*

by occupations. Full-time political and religious leaders emerged and eventually formed elite classes. But in the Neolithic Age, the specialized production of stone tools, weapons, and pottery was a more important consequence of the development of agriculture than the formation of elites. Originally, each household crafted the tools and weapons it needed, just as it wove its own baskets and produced its own clothing. Over time, however, families or individuals who proved particularly skilled in these tasks began to manufacture implements beyond their own needs and to exchange them for grain, milk, or meat.

Villages in certain regions specialized in producing materials that were in demand in other areas. For example, flint, which is extremely hard, was the preferred material for axe blades. Axes were needed for forest clearing, which was essential to the extension of cultivation in much of Europe. The demand was so great that villagers who lived near flint deposits could support themselves by mining the flint or crafting the flint heads and trading, often with peoples who lived far from the sources of production. Such exchanges set precedents for regional specialization and interregional trade.

It is difficult to know precisely what impact the shift to agriculture had on the social structure of the communities that made the transition. Social distinctions probably were heightened by occupational differences, but well-defined social stratification, such as that which produces class identity, was nonexistent. Leadership remained largely communal, although village alliances may have existed in some areas. It is likely that property in Neolithic times was held in common by the community, or at least that all households in the community were given access to village lands and water.

By virtue of their key roles as food gatherers in prefarming cultures, it can be surmised that women played a critical part in the domestication of plants. Nonetheless, there is evidence that their position declined in many agricultural communities. They worked the fields and have continued to work them in most cultures. But men took over tasks involving heavy labor, such as clearing land, hoeing, and plowing. Men monopolized the new tools and weapons devised in the Neolithic Age and later times, and they controlled the vital irrigation systems that developed in most early centers of agriculture. As far as we can tell, men also took the lead in taming, breeding, and raising the large animals associated with both farming and pastoral communities. Thus, although Neolithic art suggests that earth and fertility cults, which focused on feminine deities, retained their appeal (see Visualizing the Past), the social and economic position of women may have begun to decline with the shift to sedentary agriculture.

Visualizing the Past

Representations of Women in Early Art

The earliest writing system we know of was not introduced until around 3500 B.C.E. in the civilization of Sumer in Mesopotamia (see Chapter 2). Consequently, evidence for piecing together the history of human life in the Paleolithic and Neolithic ages comes mainly from surviving artifacts from campsites and early towns. Stone tools, bits of pottery or cloth, and the remains of Stone Age dwellings can now be dated rather precisely. When combined with other objects from the same site and time period, they give us a fairly good sense of the daily activities and life cycle of the peoples who created them.

As we have seen in the Document on cave paintings, of all the material remains of the Stone Age era, none provide better insights into the social organization and thinking of early humans than works of art. Much of what we know about gender relations, or the status of males and females and the interaction between them, has been interpreted from the study of the different forms of artistic expression of Stone Age peoples. The stone carvings and figurines reproduced here illustrate themes and impressions of women and their roles that recur in the art of many prehistoric cultures.

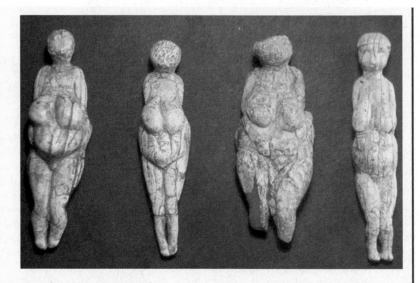

Some of the earliest rock carvings, such as the "Venus of Laussel" (c. 25,000 B.C.E.) shown here, depict robust pregnant women. Figurines similar to the Laussel Venus, which was found in the remains of a campsite at St.-Germain-en-Laye in France, are among the most common artifacts of early human cultures. At other early sites, including Çatal Hüyük, women are depicted both as goddesses and in a variety of social roles. As shown in the sketches of some of the many clay figurines found at Hacilar, another prehistoric town uncovered in what is today Turkey, women played many key roles in early human cultures. As in the Laussel Venus, voluptuous women predominate, and in many of the clay sculptures their roles in reproduction and nurturing are celebrated. But female figures in postures suggesting political authority, such as the woman shown sitting on what may have been a throne with animal heads, have also been found. Many of these statuettes may also have been intended to depict goddesses and have served as objects of worship. For example, some of the more intriguing female figures that have been found are those of older women accompanied by vultures, also reproduced here, that were painted on the walls of what appear to have been cult centers at Çatal Hüyük.

Questions: On the basis of the sample provided in these illustrations, which roles in early human society were closely associated with women? What do these representations tell us about the extent and sources of power exercised by women in prehistoric times? How do they compare to the roles of women in contemporary societies? Why might women have been seen as deities in these early societies, and what sort of requests might those who worshiped goddesses have made through their prayers and offerings?

The Idea of Civilization in World Historical Perspective

The belief that there are fundamental differences between civilized and "barbaric" or "savage" peoples is very ancient and widespread. For thousands of years the Chinese set themselves off from cattle- and sheep-herding peoples of the vast plains to the north and west of China proper, whom they saw as barbarians. To the Chinese, being civilized was cultural, not biological or racial. If barbarians learned the Chinese language and adopted Chinese ways—from the clothes they wore to the food they ate—they were regarded as civilized.

A similar pattern of demarcation and cultural absorption was found among the American Indian peoples of present-day Mexico. Those who settled in the valleys of the mountainous interior, where they built great civilizations, lived in fear of invasions by peoples they regarded as barbarous and called **Chichimecs,** meaning "sons of the dog." The latter were nomadic hunters and gatherers who periodically moved down from the desert regions of north Mexico into the fertile central valleys in search of game and settlements to pillage. The Aztecs were simply the last, and perhaps the most fierce, of a long line of Chichimec peoples who entered the valleys and conquered the urban-based empires that had developed there. But after the conquerors settled down, they adopted many of the religious beliefs and institutional patterns and much of the material culture of defeated peoples.

The word *civilization* is derived from the Latin word *civilis*, meaning "of the citizens." The term was coined by the Romans. They used it to distinguish between themselves as citizens of a cosmopolitan, urban-based civilization and the "inferior" peoples who lived in the forests and deserts on the fringes of their Mediterranean empire. Centuries earlier, the Greeks, who had contributed much to the rise of Roman civilization, made a similar distinction between themselves and outsiders. Because the languages of the non-Greek peoples to the north of the Greek heartlands sounded like senseless babble to the Greeks, they lumped all the outsiders together as *barbarians*, which meant "those who cannot speak Greek." As in the case of the Chinese and Aztecs, the boundaries between civilized and barbarian for the Greeks and Romans were cultural, not biological. Regardless of the color of one's skin or the shape of one's nose, it was possible for free people to become members of a Greek **polis**—city-state—or to become Roman citizens by

adopting Greek or Roman customs and swearing allegiance to the polis or the emperor.

Until the 17th and 18th centuries C.E., the priority given to cultural attributes (e.g., language, dress, manners) as the means by which civilized peoples set themselves off from barbaric ones was rarely challenged. But in those centuries, two major changes occurred among thinkers in western Europe. First, efforts were made not only to define the differences between civilized and barbarian but to identify a series of stages in human development that ranged from the lowest savagery to the highest civilization. Peoples such as the Chinese and the Arabs, who had created great cities, monumental architecture, writing, advanced technology, and large empires, usually won a place along with the Europeans near the top of these ladders of human achievement. Nomadic, cattle- and sheep-herding peoples, such as the Mongols of Central Asia, usually were classified as barbarians. Civilized and barbarian peoples were pitted against various sorts of **savages.** These ranged from the hunters and gatherers who inhabited much of North America and Australia to many peoples in Africa and Asia, whom the Europeans believed had not advanced beyond the most primitive stages of social and political development.

The second major shift in Western ideas about civilization began at the end of the 18th century but did not really take hold until a century later. In keeping with a growing emphasis in European thinking and social interaction on racial or biological differences, modes of human social organization and cultural expression were increasingly linked to what were alleged to be the innate capacities of each human *race*. Although no one could agree on what a race was or how many races there were, most European writers argued that some races were more inventive, moral, courageous, and artistic—thus more capable of building civilizations—than others. Of course, white (or Caucasian) Europeans were considered by white European authors to be the most capable of all. The hierarchy from savage to civilized took on a color dimension, with white at the top, where the civilized peoples clustered, to yellow, red, brown, and black in descending order.

Some authors sought to reserve all the attainments of civilization for whites, or peoples of European stock. As the evolutionary theories of thinkers such as Charles Darwin came into vogue in the late

1800s, race and level of cultural development were seen in the perspective of thousands of years of human change and adaptation rather than as being fixed in time. Nevertheless, this new perspective had little effect on the rankings of different human groups. Civilized whites were simply seen as having evolved much further than backward and barbaric peoples.

The perceived correspondence between race and level of development and the hardening of the boundaries between civilized and "inferior" peoples affected much more than intellectual discourse about the nature and history of human society. These beliefs were used to justify European imperialist expansion, which was seen as a "civilizing mission" aimed at uplifting barbaric and savage peoples across the globe. In the last half of the 19th century virtually all non-Western peoples came to be dominated by the Europeans, who were confident that they, as representatives of the highest civilization ever created, were best equipped to govern lesser breeds of humans.

In the 21st century much of the intellectual baggage that once gave credibility to the racially embedded hierarchies of civilized and savage peoples has been discarded. A number of 20th-century developments, including the revolt of colonized peoples and the crimes committed by the Nazis before and during World War II in the name of racial purification, discredited racist thinking. In addition, these ideas have failed because racial supremacists cannot provide convincing proof of innate differences in mental and physical aptitude between various human groups.

These trends, as well as research that has resulted in a much more sophisticated understanding of evolution, have led to the abandonment of rigid and self-serving 19th-century ideas about civilization.

Perhaps the best way to avoid the tendency to define the term with reference to one's own society is to view civilization as one of several human approaches to social organization rather than attempting to identify specific kinds of cultural achievement (e.g., writing, cities, monumental architecture). All peoples, from small bands of hunters and gatherers to farmers and factory workers, live in societies. All societies produce *cultures*: combinations of the ideas, objects, and patterns of behavior that result from human social interaction. But not all societies and cultures generate the surplus production that permits the levels of specialization, scale, and complexity that distinguish civilizations from other modes of social organization. All peoples are intrinsically capable of building civilizations, but many have lacked the resource base, historical circumstances, or desire to do so.

Questions: Identify a society you consider to be civilized. What criteria did you use to determine that it was civilized? Can you apply those criteria to other societies? Can you think of societies that might not fit your criteria and yet be civilizations? Do the standards that you and others use reflect your own society's norms and achievements rather than neutral, more universal criteria?

The First Towns: Seedbeds of Civilization

 By about 7000 B.C.E., techniques of agricultural production in the Middle East had reached a level at which it was possible to support thousands of people, many of whom were not engaged in agriculture, in densely populated settlements. In these and other Middle Eastern Neolithic settlements, occupational specialization and the formation of religious and political–military elite groups advanced significantly. Trade became essential for the community's survival and was carried on with peoples at considerable distances, perhaps by specialized merchants. Crafts such as pottery, metalworking, and jewelrymaking were highly developed.

Two of the earliest of these settlements were at Jericho, in what is today part of Palestine, and at Çatal Hüyük, in present-day southern Turkey. With populations of about 2000 and 4000 to 6000 people, respectively, Jericho and Çatal Hüyük would be seen today as little more than large villages or small towns. But in the perspective of human cultural development, they represented the first stirrings of urban life. Their ruling elites and craft specialists contributed to the introduction in the 4th millennium B.C.E. of critical inventions—such as the wheel, the plow, writing, and the use of bronze—that secured the future of civilized life as the central pattern of human history.

Jericho

Proximity to the Jordan River and the deep and clear waters of an oasis spring account for repeated human settlement at the place where the town of **Jericho** was built. By 7000 B.C.E., more than 10 acres were occupied by round houses of mud and brick resting on stone foundations. Most early houses had only a single room with mud plaster floors and a domed ceiling, but some houses had as many as three rooms. Entry to these windowless dwellings was provided by a single wood-framed doorway and steps down to the floor of the main room underground. Although there is no evidence that Jericho was fortified in the early stages of its growth, its expanding wealth made the building of walls for protection from external enemies necessary. The town was enclosed by a ditch cut into the rocky soil and a wall almost 12 feet high. The extensive excavation needed for this construction was impressive because the peoples who undertook it had neither picks nor shovels. The stones for the wall were dragged from a riverbed nearly a mile away. These feats suggest a sizable labor force that was well organized and disciplined.

When Jericho was rebuilt in later centuries, the wall reached a height of nearly 15 feet, and the fortifications included a stone tower at least 25 feet high. The area covered by the town increased. Round houses gave way to rectangular ones, entered through larger and more elaborately decorated wooden doorways. Houses were made of improved bricks and provided with plaster hearths and stone mills for grinding grain. They were also furnished with storage baskets and straw mats. Small buildings have been uncovered that were used as religious shrines during the later stages of the town's history.

Although Jericho's economy was based primarily on wheat and barley farming, there is considerable evidence of reliance on hunting and trade. Domesticated goats provided meat and milk, and gazelles and various marsh birds were hunted for their flesh, hides, and feathers. The town was close to large supplies of salt, sulfur, and pitch. These materials, which were in great demand during this era, were traded for obsidian, a dark, glasslike volcanic rock; semiprecious stones from Anatolia; turquoise from the Sinai; and cowrie shells from the Red Sea.

The ruins excavated at Jericho indicate that the town was governed by a distinct and powerful ruling group, which probably was allied to the keepers of the shrine centers. There were specialized artisans and a small merchant class. In addition to fertility figurines and animal carvings like those found at many other sites, the inhabitants of Jericho sculpted life-sized, highly naturalistic human figures and heads. These sculptures, which may have been used in ancestral cults, give us vivid impressions of the physical features of the people who enjoyed the wealth and security of Jericho.

Çatal Hüyük

The first community at **Çatal Hüyük** in southern Turkey was founded around 7000 B.C.E., somewhat later than the earliest settlements at Jericho. But the town that grew up at this site was a good deal more extensive than that at Jericho and it contained a larger and more diverse population. Çatal Hüyük was the most advanced human center of the Neolithic Age. At the peak of its power and prosperity, the city occupied 32 acres and contained as many as 6000 people. Its rectangular buildings, which were centers of family life and community interaction, were remarkably uniform and were built of mud-dried bricks. They had windows high in their walls and were entered from holes in their flat roofs. These entryways also served as chimneys. The presence of stored food in early towns such as Çatal Hüyük made the houses tempting targets for nomadic bands or rival settlements. For that reason they were increasingly fortified and, as Figure 1.5 illustrates, often quite ingeniously.

The standardization of housing and construction at Çatal Hüyük suggests an even more imposing ruling group than that found at Jericho. The many religious shrines at the site also indicate the existence of a powerful priesthood. The shrines were built in the same way as ordinary houses, but they contained sanctuaries surrounded by four or five rooms related to the ceremonies of the shrine's cult. The walls of these religious centers were filled with paintings of bulls and carrion eaters, especially vultures, suggesting fertility cults and rites associated with death. The surviving statuary indicates that the chief deity of the Çatal Hüyük peoples was a goddess.

The obvious importance of the cult shrines and the elaborate burial practices of the peoples of Çatal Hüyük reveal the growing role of religion in the lives of Neolithic peoples. The carefully carved sculptures

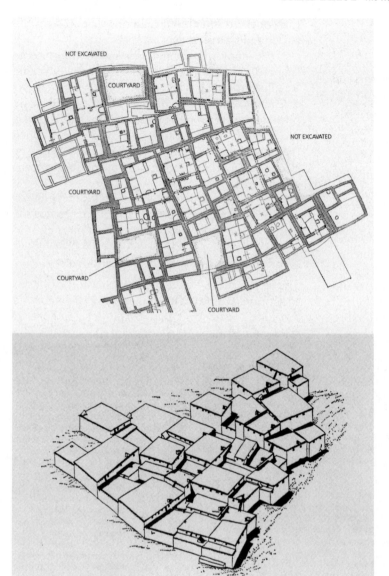

Figure 1.5 *This artist's reconstruction depicts the layout of living units in the town of Çatal Hüyük. It shows how the houses were joined together to provide fortification for the town. Movement within the settlement was mainly across the roofs and terraces of the houses. Because each dwelling had a substantial storeroom, when the outside entrances were barricaded, the larger complex of homes was transformed into a fortress.*

associated with the sanctuaries and the fine jewelry, mirrors, and weapons found buried with the dead attest to the high level of material culture and artistic proficiency of these town dwellers.

Excavations also reveal an economic base that was much broader and richer than that of Jericho. Hunting remained important, but the breeding of goats, sheep, and cattle vastly surpassed that associated with Jericho. Çatal Hüyük's inhabitants consumed a wide range of foods, including several grains, peas, berries, berry wine, and vegetable oils made from nuts. Trade was extensive with the peoples in the surrounding hills and also in places as distant as present-day Syria and the Mediterranean region. Çatal Hüyük was also a major center of production by artisans. Its flint and obsidian weapons, jewelry, and obsidian mirrors were some of the finest produced in the Neolithic Age. The remains of the town's culture leave little doubt that its inhabitants had achieved a civilized level of existence.

The 4th Millennium B.C.E.: Another Watershed

The level of specialization and political organization that developed in early towns, such as Jericho and Çatal Hüyük, proved critical to the invention and dissemination of new tools and production techniques during the 4th millennium B.C.E. The years from 4000 to 3000 B.C.E. saw a second wave of major transformations in human culture in the Middle East and nearby regions. During this transition era, the use of the plow significantly increased crop yields, and wheeled vehicles made it possible to carry more food and other raw materials over greater distances. Both developments meant that even larger populations could be supported and concentrated in particular locales. Although copper had been used for spear and axe heads for millennia, accident and experiment revealed that when copper was mixed with other metals such as tin, it formed bronze, a harder and more durable material. The bronze tools that resulted further enhanced agricultural production and contributed to the development of larger and more lethal military forces. Like agriculture earlier, the new technologies—the wheel, the plow, bronze—began to spread in Afro-Eurasia in the centuries after 3500 B.C.E.

As metalworking improved further, better tools and weapons facilitated the rise of more centralized and expansive states. These radically new political units, which were usually centered on fortified towns and cities, greatly increased contacts between farming and nomadic peoples in everything from war and conquest to trade and religious expression. Merchant groups in farming societies also nurtured trading networks that provided perhaps the first enduring linkages between the urban centers of different states and civilizations. New modes of transportation, state patronage and protection, and a growing inventory of products to exchange made it possible to extend these networks across continents in Afro-Eurasia. Cross-cultural exchanges became ever more complex and vital for the societies that participated in them. The development of writing, first in Mesopotamia and later in India, China, and other centers of agrarian production, greatly improved communications and exchange within both these commercial networks and regional state systems. Writing enhanced the power of the political elites, who directed efforts at imperial expansion. Writing also played a key role in the emergence of each of the transcultural religions that arose in the ancient and classical eras.

The innovative technologies and modes of agrarian production that were at the heart of the Neolithic Revolution became the basis for an unparalleled spread and increase of human societies, and made possible the cross-cultural connections and ongoing exchanges that are the focus of world history. Once these processes were in motion, only the most isolated of societies were immune to influences from the outside.

🌐 GLOBAL CONNECTIONS: The Neolithic Revolution as the Basis for World History

The combination of fundamental transformations in society and culture that we include in the Neolithic revolution were essential to the development of cross-cultural and interregional linkages between formerly dispersed and isolated human groups, and eventually to the rise of world history. The diffusion of agriculture from its initial locations, though gradual, shows how human contacts could spread new ideas and technologies. The spread of foodstuffs initially native to one area across various parts of Asia, Africa, and Europe was another facet of early connection among regions. Nomadic herding groups provided additional contacts, and some developments, like the domestication of dogs, spread both widely and fast. The development of sedentary agriculture meant that ever larger numbers of humans could be supported on much smaller amounts of land than was possible for either hunting-and-gathering or pastoral peoples. In the Neolithic transition, farming was also linked to the domestication of animals, such as cattle and sheep, which provided further staple foods for the human diet as well as materials for clothing and modes of transportation and warfare.

Pastoralism, which has proved the major alternative to sedentary agriculture through most of recorded history, was much more narrowly dependent on animal husbandry. As a consequence, it has been a good deal more constricted in the options it offered for human social and cultural development. In contrast to pastoralism or hunting and gathering, farming made it possible to concentrate growing numbers of humans in towns and later cities. Because agrarian societies could generate surplus food production, they could also support occupational specialization on the part of groups like full-time blacksmiths, traders, or potterymakers. Surpluses also facilitated the emergence of nonfarming elite groups, like priests or warriors, which governed ever larger and increasingly diverse concentrations of human populations.

Further Readings

Perhaps the fullest account of human prehistory available is Brian Fagan's *People of the Earth* (1998 ed.), which includes an extensive bibliography on prehistoric developments in virtually all regions of the world. A considerable literature has developed in recent years on early humans and the critical Neolithic transformations. John Mear's recent pamphlet on *Agricultural Origins in Global Perspective* (AHA, 2000) provides a concise and authoritative survey of this process in key regions over much of the globe. For other broad overviews that trace the archeological and historical discoveries that made it possible for us to understand these critical processes in the shaping of human history, see Robert J. Wenke's *Patterns in Prehistory* (1984) and C. Wesley Cowan and Patty Jo Watson, eds., *The Origins of Agriculture: An International Perspective* (1992).

For a clear discussion of debates on the Neolithic revolution and references to major authors and works, see Stephen K. Sanderson, *Social Transformations* (1995). Several of these works are of special relevance, despite their sometimes technical language and details, especially Donald O. Henry's *From Foraging to Agriculture* (1989), Douglas Price and James A. Brown, eds., *Prehistoric Hunter–Gatherers: The Emergence of Cultural Complexity* (1986), and Allen W. Johnson and Timothy Earle, *The Evo-lution of Human Societies: From Foraging to Agriculture* (1987). For the origins of agriculture in the often neglected Americas, see Stuart J. Fiedel, *Prehistory of the Americas* (1992 ed.). M. C. and H. B. Quennell's *Everyday Life in the New Stone, Bronze and Early Iron Ages* (1955) is difficult to top for an imaginative reconstruction of life in the Neolithic Age, although some of it is now dated. The most reliable treatment of technology in this era can be found in volume 1 of C. Singer et al., *A History of Technology* (1954). The most readable introduction to the earliest towns is in James Mellaart's *Earliest Civilizations of the Near East* (1965) and *The Neolithic of the Near East* (1975).

On the Web

Early human life forms, from Neanderthal to Homo sapiens, can be examined at http://www.members.iinet.net.au/~chawkins/heaven.htm. The dramatic findings at Olduvai Gorge made by the Leakey family that revolutionized knowledge about human prehistory and the continuing debate over human origins can be viewed at http://www.talkorigins.org/. Views of Chauvet, rich in cave paintings, can be found at http://www.culture.gouv.fr/culture/arcnat/chauvet/en/index.html. A virtual walk through an exhibit on human prehistory at http://users.hol.gr/~dilos/prehis/prerm5.htm also includes a discussion of the views of Darwin and others on human evolution, a gallery of art and artifacts, and an artist's reconstruction of Çatal Hüyük. The diaries of archeologists working at Çatal Hüyük are among the many features of the official Çatal Hüyük Web page at http://catal.arch.cam.ac.uk/catal/catal.html.

A virtual tour of the social life of early man in the Americas, including a glimpse of one of mankind's first fire starting matches, can be taken at http://pecosrio.com.

CHAPTER 2

THE RISE OF CIVILIZATION IN THE MIDDLE EAST AND AFRICA

This detail from Egyptian tomb art shows a husband and wife doing harvesting work. As dictated by patriarchal values, the husband takes the lead in work, the wife following to assist.

The central subject of this chapter is the nature of river valley civilization and its manifestations in two key places. The first full civilization emerged by 3500 B.C.E. in **Mesopotamia,** in the Tigris–Euphrates valley in the Middle East. By 3000 B.C.E., civilization developed along the Nile in Egypt. These early civilizations had several distinctive political and cultural features. Egypt's focus on the afterlife, for example, contrasted with Mesopotamian beliefs in people being buffeted by fate. Both civilizations generated a number of traditions that can still be found in civilizations around the Mediterranean, in parts of Europe, and even across the Atlantic.

By 1000 B.C.E., when new problems brought the river valley period to an end, both of these early civilizations had influenced other cultures in eastern Africa and southern Europe and additional centers in the Middle East. These smaller centers of civilization developed important innovations of their own.

Setting the Scene: The Middle East by 4000 B.C.E.

 Agricultural societies, long established in the Middle East, began to generate additional innovations around 4000 B.C.E. A series of new technologies, including metalwork, had huge implications for broader social changes.

Agriculture and the Rise of Civilization

Agricultural economies did not always generate civilization as a form of human organization. The transition was not quick anywhere, even where small regional centers like Jericho developed. But agriculture could encourage attention to more elaborate forms of government. Rules for defining agricultural property were one spur. Where irrigation systems were essential, as in the Middle East, cooperation among farmers had to be organized. Integration of hundreds of square miles around rivers in the Middle East or the Nile in Egypt was central to the emergence of civilization.

The series of new inventions, available in the Middle East by around 4000 B.C.E., more directly promoted civilizations. They helped create larger economic surpluses and more specialization of labor.

Innovation, Specialization, and Productivity

The first **potter's wheel** was invented around 6000 B.C.E. It allowed people to produce higher-quality ceramics, making food storage easier. A group of specialized manufacturing workers emerged to make pots to exchange for food produced by others.

The wheel was another Middle Eastern innovation, around 4000 B.C.E. Wheeled vehicles long remained slow, but they were vital to many monumental construction projects in which large blocks of stone were moved to the construction sites of temples; shipbuilding also improved gradually.

The introduction of bronze, again around 4000 B.C.E., allowed a greater variety of tools than could be made of stone or bone, and the tools were lighter and

7000 B.C.E.	4000 B.C.E.	3000 B.C.E.	2000 B.C.E.	1000 B.C.E.	1 C.E.
7000–4000 Spread of agriculture through most of Middle East **5000** Farming along Nile River **4000** Sumerians settle in Tigris–Euphrates valley	**3500** Early Sumerian alphabet **3100–2700** Initial kingdoms **3000** Introduction of bronze tools	**2700–2200** Old Kingdom period **2600** First great pyramid **2400–2200** Akkadian empire conquers Sumer **2052–1786** Middle Kingdom period; civilization to Upper Nile **2000** Phoenician state **2000** Gilgamesh epic written	**1800** Babylonian Empire; Hammurabi, 1796–1750 **1700** Hyksos invasion **1600** Minoan civilization (Crete) **1600** Possible settlement of Jews in southeast Mediterranean **1575–1087** New Kingdom period **1400–1200** Hittite Empire; use of iron **1250** Moses and Jewish exodus from Egypt **1100** Spread of use of iron **1000–970** Kingdom of Israel under King David **1000** Kush independent kingdom **1000** Indo-European invasion of Greece **1000** Spread of Phoenician settlements in western Mediterranean	**800** Beginning of writing of Bible **730** Kushite rule of Egypt **721** Assyrian invasion conquers northern Israel **665–617** Assyrian Empire **539** Persian Empire	**100** C.E. Decline of Kush and its capital Meroë **300** C.E. Rise of Axum (Ethiopia)

more quickly made. The Middle East was the first region to move from the Neolithic (stone tool) Age to the **Bronze Age** as people developed metal hoes, plows, and weapons. Again, new technology promoted further specialization as groups of artisans concentrated on metal production, exchanging their wares for food. Bronze technology also promoted more formal political structures because bronze weaponry gave organized armies new means of control. Use of bronze also necessitated trade: Middle Eastern traders ultimately found the components of bronze (copper and tin) in places as distant as Afghanistan and England. Along with irrigation, then, new technologies were the framework for the emergence of civilization with the rise of Sumerian society along the Tigris–Euphrates valley.

Civilization in Mesopotamia

 The first civilization emerged about 3500 B.C.E. It generated several features characteristic of most later civilizations, including writing, expanded cities, and a complex social structure. It had distinctive religious beliefs and artistic styles. Periodic invasions, leading to the rise and fall of empires, punctuated its history.

The Sumerians

Sumer, the first river valley civilization, used rivers but also feared them. Major floods occurred. Archeologists have found Sumerian cities where one city was built on top of an earlier one, separated by a layer of mud swept over in a flood. Mud tablets containing the first Sumerian "book" tell the story of how the gods decided to wipe out mankind with a flood. Only one man, with his family and animals, was saved. His name was not Noah, but Utnapishtim.

The first civilization arose in the northeastern section of what we now call the Middle East, along the great Tigris and Euphrates rivers that lead to the Persian Gulf. Between the northern hills and the deserts of the Arabian peninsula, running from the eastern Mediterranean coast to the plains of the Tigris and Euphrates, lies a large swath of arable land called the Fertile Crescent. The rivers overflow their banks in the spring, depositing fertile soil when they recede. Rainfall is scant, so as population pressure increased as a result of early agriculture, farming communities began to find ways to tame and use the rivers through irrigation ditches. With the improved tools of the Bronze Age, developments in the region were swift. The fertile Tigris–Euphrates region generated large food surpluses, promoting population growth and village expansion as well as increased trade and specialization. The region was vulnerable in one respect: It was so flat that it was open to invasion.

The final boost toward establishing civilization was provided by the **Sumerians,** a people who had migrated into the area from the north about 4000 B.C.E. They settled in an area of about 700 square miles, where they mixed with other local people in a pattern that has remained characteristic of the region. The Sumerians early developed centers of religion, pilgrimage, and worship. Well before 3000 B.C.E., many of these centers boasted elaborately decorated temples built of mud brick. Sumerians were impressed with the power of grim gods who, they believed, ultimately controlled human destiny. It was the Sumerians who introduced the first writing system, capping the developments that created Mesopotamian civilization.

Sumerian Political and Social Organization

Sumerian culture remained intact until about 2000 B.C.E. Its political organization was based on a series of tightly organized **city-states** in which an urban king, who claimed great authority, ruled the agricultural hinterland. In some cases, local councils advised the king. One of the functions of Sumerian city-states was to define boundaries, unlike the less formal territories of precivilized villages in the region. Each city-state helped regulate religion and enforce its duties. It also provided a system of courts for justice. Kings were warriors whose leadership of a trained army in defense and war remained vital in Sumerian politics, where fighting loomed large. Kings and priests controlled vast amounts of land. Slaves, who had been conquered in wars with nearby tribes, worked this land.

Sumerian political and social organization set up traditions that long endured in the region. City-state government established a tradition of regional rule, which sometimes yielded to larger empires but often returned as the principal organizational form. Many successor civilizations also relied on slave labor. The use of slaves and the lack of natural barriers to invasion help explain recurrent warfare, which was needed to supply labor in the form of captured slaves.

The Sumerians, aided by political stability and the use of writing, added to their region's economic prosperity. Farmers learned how to cultivate date trees, onions, and garlic. Oxen were used to pull plows and donkeys carried goods. Wheeled carts helped transport goods. The Sumerians introduced the use of fertilizer and adopted silver as a means of exchange for buying and selling. Major cities expanded—one city reached a population of over 70,000—with substantial housing units in rows of flat-roofed, mud-brick shops and apartments. More commonly, cities contained as many as 10,000 people. The Sumerians improved the potter's wheel, and the production of pottery expanded. Spurred by the increasing skill level and commercial importance of pottery, men began to take this trade away from women. The Sumerians also invented glass. Trade expanded to the lower Persian Gulf and to the western portion of the Middle East along the Mediterranean. By 2000 B.C.E., the Sumerians had trading contacts with India.

Sumerian Culture and Religion

Writing, the most important invention between the advent of agriculture and the age of the steam engine, was introduced about 3500 B.C.E. The Sumerian invention of writing was probably rather sudden. It was based on new needs for commercial, property, and political records, including a celebration of the deeds of proud local kings. Writing was preceded by the invention of clay cylinder seals on which little pictures of objects could be recorded. The earliest Sumerian writing evolved from those pictures, baked on clay tablets, which were turned into symbols and gradually transformed into phonetic elements. The early Sumerian alphabet, a set of symbols representing sounds, may have had as many as 2000 symbols derived from the early pictures. Soon writers began to use more abstract symbols to represent sounds, which allowed the Sumerians to reduce the alphabet to about 300 symbols. Figures 2.1 and 2.2 show an example of their writing and its translation. Sumerian writers used a wedge-shaped stick to impress the symbols on clay tablets. The resulting writing is called **cuneiform,** meaning "wedge shaped," and it was used for several thousand years in the Middle East for many different languages. Cuneiform writing was difficult to learn, so specialized scribes monopolized it. The Sumerians believed that every object in nature should have a separate name to ensure its place in the universe; knowing the name gave a person some power over the object. In other words, writing quickly took on religious purposes, allowing people to impose an abstract order over nature and the social world.

The Sumerians also steadily elaborated their culture, again using writing to advance earlier forms of expression. By about 2000 B.C.E., they wrote down the world's oldest story, the *Epic of Gilgamesh,* which went back at least to the 7th millennium B.C.E. in oral form. Gilgamesh, described as the ruler of a

Figure 2.1 *One of the early uses of writing involved marking property boundaries. This picture shows cuneiform writing on a Mesopotamian map from about 1300 B.C.E. The map focuses on defining the king's estate, with sections for priests and for key gods such as Marduk. In what ways did writing improve property maps?*

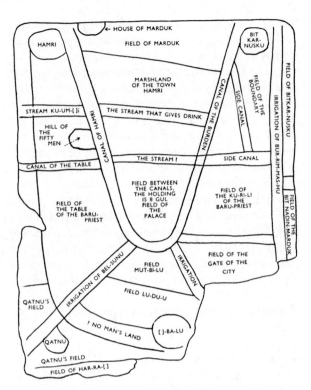

Figure 2.2 *A translation of the map shown in Figure 2.1.*

city-state, became the first hero in world literature. This was the epic that also described the great flood. The overall tone of the epic and of Sumerian culture (perhaps reflecting the region's often disastrous floods) was somber. Gilgamesh does great deeds but constantly bumps up against the iron laws of the gods, who ultimately control human destiny.

> The heroes, the wise men, like the new moon have their waxing and waning. Men will say, "Who has ever ruled with might and with power like Gilgamesh?" As in the dark month, the month of shadows; so without him there is no light. O Gilgamesh, this was the meaning of your dream. You were given the kingship, such was your destiny; everlasting life was not your destiny. …Gilgamesh, why do you search? The life you seek you will never find. When the gods created the world, they made death a part of human fate.

Along with early literature, Sumerian art and science developed steadily. Statues and painted frescoes

adorned the temples of the gods, and statues of the gods decorated homes. Sumerians sought to learn more about the movement of the sun and stars, thus founding the science of astronomy, and to improve their mathematical knowledge. The Sumerian system of numbers, based on units of 12, 60, and 360, is the one we use today in calculations involving circles and hours. Sumerian charts of major constellations have been used for 5000 years in the Middle East and, through later imitation, in India and Europe. In other words, Sumerians and their successors in Mesopotamia created patterns of observation and abstract thought about nature on which many later societies, including our own, still rely.

Religion played a vital role in Sumerian culture and politics. Gods were associated with various forces of nature. At the same time, gods were seen as having human form and many of the more disagreeable human characteristics. Thus, the gods often quarreled and used their power in selfish and childish ways, which made interesting stories but also created a fear that the gods might make life difficult. The gloomy cast of Sumerian religion also included an afterlife of suffering, an original version of the concept of hell.

Because gods were believed to regulate natural forces, such as flooding, in a region where nature was often harsh and unpredictable, they were more feared than loved. Priests' power derived from their responsibility for placating the gods through prayers, sacrifices, and magic. Priests became full-time specialists, running the temples and performing the astronomical calculations of the dates for normal flooding, which were needed to manage the irrigation systems. Each city had a patron god and erected impressive shrines to honor this god and other deities. Massive towers, called **ziggurats,** formed the monumental architecture for this civilization. Prayers and offerings to prevent floods and protect good health were a vital part of Sumerian life. **Animism**—the idea that a divine force lay behind and within natural objects such as rivers, trees, and mountains—was common among agricultural peoples. But specifically Sumerian religious beliefs about the creation of the earth by the gods from a chaos of water and about divine punishment through floods continue to influence Jewish, Christian, and Muslim cultures, all of which were born much later in the Middle East.

Sumerian activities in trade and war spread widely in the Middle East. Portions of the Gilgamesh tale appeared in later literature such as the Jewish Bible, which developed well to the west of Sumer. Even after Sumer itself collapsed, the Sumerian language was still used in religious schools and temples, showing the power of this early culture and its decidedly religious emphasis.

What Civilization Meant in Sumeria

Sumer's achievements illustrate the elements of civilization, outlined in the Prologue. Some historians seek a bare-bones definition: Civilizations had greater economic surpluses than other forms of society. This was certainly true of Sumer, which boasted a rich agriculture capable of supporting a minority of specialist workers plus priests and government officials.

The initial Mesopotamian civilization also can be used to flesh out a more elaborate definition, which other historians prefer. First, Sumerian civilization generated a clearly defined state, or government, replacing the much more loosely organized communities of previous agricultural societies. Second, civilization involved the creation of cities beyond scattered individual centers such as Jericho. The economy remained fundamentally agricultural, and at least 80 percent of all people still lived in the countryside (as was true in all civilizations until 200 years ago). But the cities were crucial in promoting trade, more specialized manufacture, and the exchange of ideas. At the same time, cities depended on a well-organized regional economy that could provide food for urban areas and on a government capable of running essential services such as a court system to handle disputes.

The Importance of Writing   Writing was another important feature of Sumerian and most other civilizations. While sophisticated societies can develop without writing, the new communication system had various consequences. Societies with writing can organize more elaborate records, including the lists essential for effective taxation. Writing is a precondition for most formal bureaucracies, which depend on standardized communication and the ability to maintain documentation. Societies with writing can record data and build on past discoveries, thus producing a more elaborate intellectual life. For example, it is no accident that, with writing, an early civilization such as Mesopotamia began to generate more formal scientific knowledge. Societies before the development of writing typically depended on poetic sagas to convey their value systems; the poetry was designed to aid in memorization. With writing, the importance of sagas such as the Gilgamesh epic continued, but the diversity of cultural expressions soon increased and other kinds of literature supplemented the long, rhymed epics.

Writing also promotes trade and manufacturing. Sumerian merchants used writing to communicate with their trading partners in places such as India. Written records helped preserve manufacturing knowledge. One of the first recorded uses of Sumerian writing was to transmit a beer recipe.

Writing also created new divisions within the population of early civilizations. Only a small minority of people—priests, scribes, and a few merchants—had time to master writing.

Civilization: Gains and Losses   There is often confusion between defining a society as a civilization and assuming that civilization produces a monopoly on higher values and controlled behavior. Civilization is not necessarily progress. In the first place, civilization brings losses as well as gains. As the Middle East moved toward civilization, distinctions based on social class and wealth increased. This was clearly the case in Sumer, where social structure ranged from slaves, who were treated as property, to powerful kings and priests. Civilizations typically have firmer class or caste divisions and greater separations between ruler and ruled than "simpler" societies. Civilizations often create greater inequalities between men and women than noncivilized societies do. Many early civilizations, including those of the Middle East, went to considerable lengths to organize the supposed inferiority of women on a more structured basis than ever before, treating women as the property of fathers or husbands.

Furthermore, noncivilized societies are often well regulated, with interesting, important cultures. Some noncivilized societies are particularly successful in avoiding anger and aggression in human dealings. In contrast, many civilized societies, including Sumerian society, value aggressive behavior and count warlike qualities as virtues. Civilizations do not even clearly promote human happiness.

However, the development of civilization did generate new technological and political capacities and increasingly elaborate and diverse artistic and intellectual forms. In this limited sense, the term **civilization** has meaning and legitimately commands the attention of most historians. Because of the power and splendor civilizations could attain, they tended to spread as other societies came under their influence or deliberately tried to imitate their achievements. However, early civilizations spread slowly because many peoples had no contact with them and because their disadvantages, such as greater social inequality, often seemed repellent.

Later Mesopotamian Civilization: A Series of Conquests

Later Mesopotamian civilization was recurrently unstable as one ruling people gave way to another invading force. The region's map (see the Visualizing the Past box) shows the geographic framework for this process. The Sumerians, themselves invaders of the fertile river valleys, did not set up a sufficiently strong and united political force to withstand pressures from outside, particularly when other peoples of the Middle East began to copy their key achievements.

The Akkadian Empire Shortly after 2400 B.C.E., a king from a non-Sumerian city in Mesopotamia, Akkad, conquered the Sumerian city-states and inaugurated the Akkadian Empire. Here, one king controlled a fairly large region while maintaining many Sumerian cultural and economic forms. This empire soon sent troops as far as Egypt and Ethiopia. Its first ruler, **Sargon I,** is the first clearly identified individual in world history. He unified the empire and integrated the city-states into a whole. He also added to Sumerian art a new style marked by the theme of royal victory (Figure 2.3). Professional military organization expanded because Sargon maintained a force

Figure 2.3 *This bronze head of Sargon, founder of the Akkadian dynasty, dates from about 2350 B.C.E. The elaborate metalwork displays the artistic talents acquired by leading craftsmen, evoking power and emotion appropriate to a major ruler.*

Visualizing the Past

Mesopotamia in Maps

The Mesopotamian civilizations steadily expanded from their roots in the fertile valley between the Tigris and Euphrates rivers throughout their centuries of existence. Reading the maps can help explain the nature of the civilizations in the region.

What do these maps suggest about the relationship between Mesopotamian civilizations and the topography of the Middle East? Does geography suggest reasons for invasion and political instability in this civilization center? Did later empires in the region have the same relationship to river valleys as did the earlier states? What might have caused the change? Why did even the larger empires not spread through the Arabian peninsula? What were the potential contacts between Mesopotamia and other river valley civilization centers? Why has the Middle East been so significant in European, African, and Asian history?

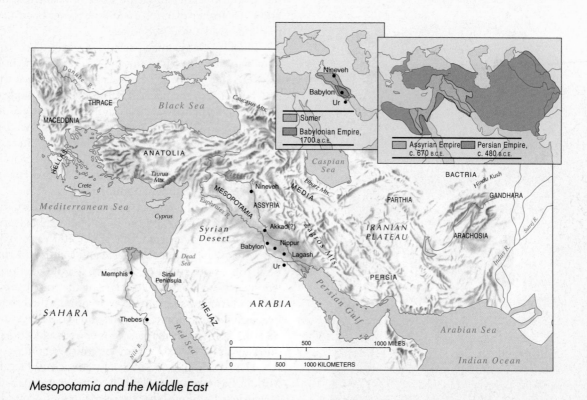

Mesopotamia and the Middle East

of 5400 troops. Extensive tax revenues supported his operations. The Akkadians were the first people to use writing for more than commercial and temple records, producing a number of literary works. Sargon's daughter Enheduanna, high priestess of the gods Nanna and An, left behind the first works of literature whose authorship can be attributed to a specific individual: two hymn cycles praising the gods and temples of Mesopotamia.

The Akkadian Empire lasted only 200 years and then was overthrown by another invading force. By this time, around 2000 B.C.E., kingdoms were springing up in various parts of the Middle East, and new invading groups added to the region's confusion.

The Babylonian Empire

Around 1800 B.C.E. the **Babylonian Empire** arose and again unified much of Mesopotamia. Large cities testified to the wealth and power of this new empire. This Babylonian empire was headed by **Hammurabi,** one of the great rulers of early civilized history (Figure 2.4). Hammurabi set up an extensive network of officials and judges and maintained a separate priesthood. He also codified the laws of the region to deal with a number of criminal, property, and family issues. At the same time, Sumerian cultural traditions were maintained and

Figure 2.4 *The stele of Hammurabi shows the king in front of the sun god, Shamash. Hammurabi's code of law is carved below this stele. What are the power implications of this presentation?*

elaborated. The famous Hammurabic code thus built on earlier codifications by Sumerian kings. The Document box shows what kinds of problems the code sought to regulate through laws.

Rulers such as Hammurabi claimed great power, often associating themselves with the gods. Artistic monuments celebrated rulers' power in a tradition that has continued ever since (even for rulers not seen as divine).

Babylonian culture did more than celebrate power. A poem expressed the continued pessimism and sobriety of the dominant beliefs: "I look about me and see only evil. My troubles grow and I cannot find justice. I have prayed to the gods and sacrificed, but who can understand the gods in heaven? Who knows what they plan for us? Who has ever been able to understand a god's conduct?"

Finally, Babylonian scientists extended the Sumerian work in astronomy and mathematics. Scholars were able to predict lunar eclipses and trace the paths of some of the planets. Babylonians also worked out useful mathematical tables and an algebraic geometry; they could figure out areas and volumes for many shapes, devise squares, and compound interest. The modern 60-minute hour and 360-degree circle arose from the Babylonian system of measurement applied to earlier Sumerian numbering systems.

Indeed, of all the successors of the Sumerians, the Babylonians constructed the most elaborate culture, although their rule lasted only about 200 years. The Babylonians expanded commerce and a common cultural zone, both based on growing use of cuneiform writing and a shared language. During the empire itself, new government strength showed in both the extensive legal system and the opulent public buildings and royal palaces. The rooftop gardens of trees and vines of one king dazzled visitors from the entire region.

The Babylonian empire fell by about 1600 B.C.E. Middle Eastern society had become so prosperous that it was beginning to attract recurrent waves of attack from nomadic peoples pressing in from central Asia, and few geographic barriers impeded the incursions. The invading **Hittite** people, one of the first of the Indo-European groups to enter in from central Asia, set up an empire of their own. The Hittites soon yielded, and a series of smaller kingdoms disputed the region for several centuries between about 1200 and 900 B.C.E.

Document

Hammurabi's Law Code

Hammurabi, as king of Babylon, united Mesopotamia under his rule from about 1800 to 1750 B.C.E. His law code, the earliest such compilation still in existence, was discovered on a stone slab in Iran in 1901 C.E. Not a systematic presentation, it was a collection of exemplary cases designed to set general standards of justice. The code provides vital insights into the nature of social relations and family structure in this ancient civilization. Examples of the Hammurabic code follow:

When Marduk commanded me to give justice to the people of the land and to let [them] have [good] governance, I set forth truth and justice throughout the land [and] prospered the people.

At that time:

If a man has accused a man and has charged him with manslaughter and then has not proved [it against] him, his accuser shall be put to death.

If a man has charged a man with sorcery and then has not proved [it against] him, he who is charged with the sorcery shall go to the holy river; he shall leap into the holy river and, if the holy river overwhelms him, his accuser shall take and keep his house; if the holy river proves that man clear [of the offense] and he comes back safe, he who has charged him with sorcery shall be put to death; he who leapt into the holy river shall take and keep the house of his accuser.

If a man has come forward in a case to bear witness to a felony and then has not proved the statement that he has made, if that case [is] a capital one, that man shall be put to death.

If he has come forward to bear witness to [a claim for] corn or money, he shall remain liable for the penalty for that suit.

If a judge has tried a suit, given a decision, caused a sealed tablet to be executed, [and] thereafter varies his judgment, they shall convict that judge of varying [his] judgment and he shall pay twelvefold the claim in that suit; then they shall remove him from his place on the bench of judges in the assembly, and he shall not [again] sit in judgment with the judges.

If a free person helps a slave to escape, the free person will be put to death.

If a man has committed robbery and is caught, that man shall be put to death.

If the robber is not caught, the man who has been robbed shall formally declare whatever he has lost before a god, and the city and the mayor in whose territory or district the robbery has been committed shall replace whatever he has lost for him.

If [it is] the life [of the owner that is lost], the city or the mayor shall pay one maneh of silver to his kinsfolk.

If a person owes money and Adad [the river god] has flooded the person's field, the person will not give any grain [tax] or pay any interest in that year.

If a person is too lazy to make the dike of his field strong and there is a break in the dike and water destroys his own farmland, that person will make good the grain [tax] that is destroyed.

If a merchant increases interest beyond that set by the king and collects it, that merchant will lose what was lent.

If a trader borrows money from a merchant and then denies the fact, that merchant in the presence of god and witnesses will prove the trader borrowed the money and the trader will pay the merchant three times the amount borrowed.

If the husband of a married lady has accused her but she is not caught lying with another man, she shall take an oath by the life of a god and return to her house.

If a man takes himself off and there is not the [necessary] maintenance in his house, his wife [so long as] her [husband is delayed] shall keep [herself chaste; she shall not] enter [another man's house].

If that woman has not kept herself chaste but enters another man's house, they shall convict that woman and cast her into the water.

If a son strikes his father, they shall cut off his forehand.

If a man has put out the eye of a free man, they shall put out his eye.

If he breaks the bone of a [free] man, they shall break his bone.

If he puts out the eye of a villain or breaks the bone of a villain, he shall pay one maneh of silver.

If he puts out the eye of a [free] man's slave or breaks the bone of a [free] man's slave, he shall pay half his price.

If a man knocks out the tooth of a [free] man equal [in rank] to him[self], they shall knock out his tooth.

If he knocks out the tooth of a villain, he shall pay one-third maneh of silver.

If a man strikes the cheek of a [free] man who is superior [in rank] to him[self], he shall be beaten with 60 stripes with a whip of ox-hide in the assembly.

If the man strikes the cheek of a free man equal to him[self in rank], he shall pay one maneh of silver.

(continued)

If a villain strikes the cheek of a villain, he shall pay ten shekels of silver.

If the slave of a [free] man strikes the cheek of a free man, they shall cut off his ear.

Questions: What can you tell from the Hammurabic code about the social and family structure of Mesopotamia? What is the relationship between law and trade? Why did agricultural civilizations such as Babylon insist on harsh punishments for crimes? What religious and magical beliefs does the document suggest? Using specific examples, show how interpreting this document for significant historical meaning differs from simply reading it.

Ancient Egypt

 Egyptian civilization formed by 3000 B.C.E. in northeastern Africa along the Nile River. The Egyptians benefited from trade and technological influence from Mesopotamia, but they produced a very different society and culture. Egypt's distinctive flavor showed in its rich art and massive monuments. More stable than Mesopotamia and protected from the main invasion route by the desert, Egyptian civilization flourished for more than 2000 years before beginning to decline about 1000 B.C.E.

On Being a God King

Early on, Egypt moved toward a strong kingship. Egyptian kings, ultimately called pharaohs, were seen as contacts between gods and people, and ultimately as gods themselves. Early kings were seen as manifestations of one god, Horus, and became another god, Osiris, after death. Pharaohs were often shown as huge figures in art, towering over their subjects. Their power also showed in the practice of burying servants with a dead pharaoh, so they could help him in the next life. But for all these claims, kings faced limits also. Popular writings often treated them irreverently, which means that it is hard to tell how much ordinary people believed the references to godhood. And priests often controlled the kings, insisting on elaborate rituals to which kings had to conform. Despite the big claims, it was not always clear who ruled—a situation not uncommon in world history.

Basic Patterns of Egyptian Society

Unlike Mesopotamia and the Middle East, where a river valley civilization ultimately spread throughout an entire region, Egyptian civilization from its origins to its decline focused on the Nile River and the deserts immediately around it. The Nile's steady flow is marked by predictable flood surges. This also gave a more optimistic cast to Egyptian culture. It could be seen as a source of never-failing bounty to be thankfully received rather than as a menacing cause of floods, as with Mesopotamian rivers.

Farming had been developed along the Nile by about 5000 B.C.E., but some time before 3200 B.C.E. economic development accelerated, in part because of growing trade with other regions, including Mesopotamia. This acceleration was the basis for the formation of regional kingdoms. Unlike Sumer, Egypt moved fairly directly from precivilization to large government units without passing through a city-state phase, although the first **pharaoh** (king), **Narmer,** had to conquer a number of petty local kings around 3100 B.C.E. Egypt always had fewer problems with political unity than Mesopotamia did, in part because of the unifying influence of the course of the Nile River. By the same token, however, Egyptian politics tended to be more authoritarian and centralized, for city-states in the Mesopotamian style, though often ruled by kings, also provided the opportunity for councils and other participatory institutions.

By 3100 B.C.E. Narmer, king of southern Egypt, conquered the northern regional kingdom and created a unified state 600 miles long (Map 2.1). This state was to last 3000 years. Despite some important disruptions, this was an amazing record of stability, even though the greatest vitality of the civilization was exhausted by about 1000 B.C.E. During the 2000-year span in which Egypt displayed its greatest vigor, the society went through three major periods of monarchy (the Old, the Intermediate, and the New Kingdoms), each divided from its successor by a century or two of confusion.

In all its phases Egyptian civilization was characterized by the strength of the pharaoh. The pharaoh was held to be descended from gods and he was attributed the power to ensure prosperity and control the rituals that ensured the regular flow of the Nile and the fertility derived from irrigation. Much Egyptian art was devoted to demonstrating the power and sanctity of the pharaoh. An extensive bureaucracy was recruited from the landed nobles and trained in writing and law. Governors were appointed for key regions and were responsible for supervising irrigation and arranging for the great public works that became a hallmark of Egyptian culture. Most Egyptians were peasant farmers who were closely regulated and heavily taxed.

Given the importance of royal rule and the belief that pharaohs were gods, it is not surprising that each of the main periods of Egyptian history was marked by some striking kings. Early in each dynastic period, where a new family line took power, leading pharaohs conquered new territories. Sometimes they pressed up the Nile River into present-day Sudan and once even moving up the Mediterranean coast of the Middle East. Late in Egyptian history one pharaoh, **Akhenaton,** tried to use his power to install a new one-god religion, replacing the Egyptian pantheon. This was a dramatic assertion of royal authority. As the god spoke only through Akhenaton, it suggested the end of priests' power. However, his effort failed against the powerful priesthood, and the controversy distracted him from military affairs, leading to some difficult wars. Historians debate whether his vision was simply a fascinating historical accident or has some larger significance about impulses toward a new kind of religious framework.

It was to commemorate their greatness that many pharaohs built the **pyramids** to house themselves and their family and staff after death, commanding work crews of up to 100,000 men to haul and lift the stones. The first great pyramid was built about 2600 B.C.E.; the largest pyramid followed about a century later, taking 20 years to complete and containing 2 million blocks of stone, each weighing 5.5 tons (Figure 2.5). These monuments were triumphs of human coordination, for the Egyptians were not particularly advanced technologically. They even lacked pulleys or other devices to hoist the huge slabs of stone that formed the pyramids. Recent aerial discoveries reveal that early Egyptians built at least one roadway to the stone quarries, but roads were not used during the age of the pyramids. Masses of workers rolled stones over logs and onto Nile barges

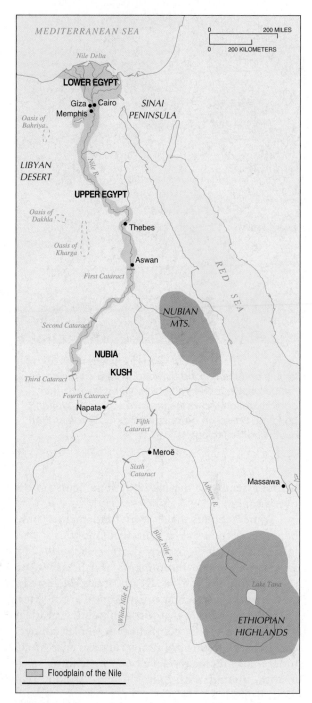

Map 2.1 *Egypt, Kush, and Axum, Successive Dynasties. As Egypt weakened, kingdoms farther up the Nile and deeper into Africa rose in importance.*

Figure 2.5   *The Sphinx of Giza, including ruins of its temple and the Second Pyramid, with a causeway running down to the Valley Temple on the left. The agglomeration shows the massive scale of Egyptian building, based on organization of labor rather than advanced technology.*

before assembling the massive monuments on the river's banks.

Some scholars have seen fundamental links between Egypt's stable, centralized politics and its fascination with an orderly death, which gave rise to massive funeral monuments and preservation through mummification. Death rituals suggested a concern with extending organization to the afterlife based on a belief that through politics, death as well as life could be controlled. A similar connection between strong political structures and careful funeral arrangements developed in Chinese civilization, though with quite different specific religious beliefs.

Egyptian Ideas and Art

Egyptian culture separated itself from Mesopotamia in several ways other than politics and monument building. The Egyptians did not adopt the Sumerian cuneiform alphabet, developing a hieroglyphic alpha-

bet instead. **Hieroglyphs,** more pictorial than the Sumerian cuneiform, were based on simplified pictures of objects abstracted to represent concepts or sounds. As in Mesopotamia, the writing system was complex, and its use was largely monopolized by the powerful priestly class. Egyptians ultimately developed a new material to write on, papyrus, made from strips of a plant pressed together. This was cheaper to make and to use than clay tablets or animal skins and allowed much more elaborate recordkeeping. Despite the elaborate writing system, Egypt did not generate the same kind of epic literary tradition found in the Middle East.

Egyptian achievements in astronomy were less advanced than those of Mesopotamia. However, the Egyptians were the first people to establish the length of the solar year, which they divided into 12 months, each with three 10-day weeks. The week was the only division of time not based on any natural cycles. The achievement of this calendar suggests Egyptians' concern about predicting the Nile floods and their ability in astronomical observation. The Egyptians also made important strides in medicine, including knowledge of a variety of drugs and some contraceptive devices. The Greeks later learned elements of Egyptian medical knowledge and passed the information on to later Middle Eastern and European civilizations. Geometry was also advanced.

The pillar of Egyptian culture was not science but religion, which was firmly established as the basis of a whole worldview. The Egyptian religion promoted the worship of many gods. Like early religions almost everywhere, it mixed magical ceremonies and beliefs with worship. The Egyptians were concerned with death and preparation for life in another world where— unlike the Mesopotamians—the Egyptians held that a happy, changeless well-being could be achieved. The care shown in preparing tombs and **mummifying** bodies, along with elaborate funeral rituals, particularly for the rulers and bureaucrats, was designed to ensure a satisfactory afterlife, although Egyptians also believed that favorable judgment by a key god, Osiris, was essential. Other Egyptian deities included a creation goddess, similar to other Middle Eastern religious figures later adapted into Christian veneration of the Virgin Mary, and a host of gods represented partially by animal figures. Egyptian art focused heavily on the gods, as Figure 2.6 suggests, but earthly and human scenes were portrayed as well in characteristic, stylized forms that lasted without great change for many centuries.

Figure 2.6 *A relief from the temple of Aten at Tel el-Amarna shows the pharaoh Akhenaton, Queen Nefertiti, and one of their daughters adoring the god Aten in the form of the sun's disk. Aten sends down tiny hands to accept the libations of the royal pair, showing the links the pharaohs claimed between divine power and their own authority.*

Continuity and Change

Stability was a hallmark of Egyptian culture. Given the duration of Egyptian civilization, there were surprisingly few basic changes in styles and beliefs. Egypt was fairly isolated, and this isolation helped preserve continuity. Change did occur occasionally. The invasions of Egypt from Palestine near the end of the Old Kingdom period (about 2200 B.C.E.) were distinct

exceptions to Egypt's usual self-containment. They were followed by attacks from the Middle East by tribes of Asian origin, which brought a period of division, chaos, and rival royal dynasties. But the unified monarchy was reestablished during the Middle Kingdom period. During this period Egyptian settlements spread southward into what is now the Sudan, toward what later became the African kingdom of Kush (see Map 2.1).

Another period of social unrest and invasion followed, ending in the final great kingdom period, the New Kingdom, about 1570 B.C.E. Trade and other contacts with the Middle East and the eastern Mediterranean, including the island of Crete, gained ground. These contacts spread Egyptian influences, notably in monumental architecture, to other areas. It was during the New Kingdom that Egyptians first instituted formal slavery. After about 1150 B.C.E., new waves of invasion, internal conspiracies, and disorganization, including strikes and social protest, brought fairly steady decline.

Egypt and Mesopotamia Compared

 By comparing the two first civilizations, we can highlight their differences as well as their important similarities.

Comparisons in politics, culture, economics, and society suggest that the two civilizations varied substantially because of largely separate origins and environments. The distinction in overall tone was striking, with Egypt more stable and cheerful than Mesopotamia not only in its beliefs about gods and the afterlife but in the colorful and lively pictures the Egyptians emphasized in their decorative art. The distinction in internal history was also striking: Egyptian civilization was far less marked by disruption than its Mesopotamian counterpart.

Egypt and Mesopotamia differed in many ways thanks to variations in geography, exposure to outside invasion and influence, and different beliefs. Despite trade and war, they did not imitate each other much. Egypt emphasized strong central authority, whereas Mesopotamian politics shifted more often over a substructure of regional city-states. Mesopotamian art focused on less monumental structures and embraced a literary element that Egyptian art lacked. Mesopotamians did not share the Egyptian concern for preparations for the afterlife, which motivated the great tombs and pyramids through which ancient Egypt and some of the pharaohs live on in human memory.

The economies differed as well. Mesopotamia generated more technological improvements because the environment was more difficult to manage than the Nile valley. Trade contacts were more wide-ranging, and the Mesopotamians gave considerable attention to a merchant class and commercial law.

Social differences between the two civilizations are less obvious because we have less information on daily life for this early period. It is probable, though, that the status of women was higher in Egypt than in Mesopotamia (where women's position seems to have deteriorated after Sumer (see the In Depth section). Egyptians paid great respect to women, at least in the upper classes, in part because marriage alliances were vital to the preservation and stability of the monarchy. Vivid love poetry indicated a high regard for emotional relations between men and women. Also, Egyptian religion included

more pronounced deference to goddesses as sources of creativity.

Differences were not the whole story, for as river valley civilizations Egypt and Mesopotamia shared important features. Both emphasized social stratification, with a noble, land-owning class on top and masses of peasants and slaves at the bottom. A powerful priestly group also figured in the elite. Although specific achievements in science differed, both civilizations emphasized astronomy and related mathematics and produced durable findings about units of time and measurement. Both Mesopotamia and Egypt changed slowly by more modern standards. Having developed successful political and economic systems, both societies tended strongly toward conservation. Change, when it came, usually was brought by outside forces (natural disasters or invasions).

Finally, both civilizations left important heritages in their regions and adjacent territories. Several smaller civilization centers were launched under the impetus of Mesopotamia and Egypt, and some would produce important innovations of their own by about 1000 B.C.E.

In Depth

Women in Patriarchal Societies

Most agricultural civilizations downgraded the status and potential of women, compared to the standards of hunting-and-gathering societies. Agricultural civilizations generally were **patriarchal;** that is, they were run by men and based on the assumption that men directed political, economic, and cultural life. Furthermore, as agricultural civilizations developed and became more prosperous and more elaborately organized, the status of women often deteriorated.

Individual families normally were patriarchal. The husband and father made the key decisions, and the wife gave humble obedience to this male authority. Patriarchal family structure rested on men's control of most or all property, starting with land. Marriage was based on property relationships, and it was assumed that marriage, and therefore subordination to men, was the normal condition for women. A revealing symptom of patriarchy in families was the fact that after marrying, a woman usu-

ally moved to the orbit (and often the residence) of her husband's family.

Characteristic patriarchal conditions developed in Mesopotamian civilization. Marriages were arranged for women by their parents, and a formal contract was drawn up. Early Sumerians may have given women greater latitude than they enjoyed later on: Their religion attributed considerable power to female sexuality, and their law gave women important rights so that they could not be treated as outright property. Still, in Sumerian law the adultery of a wife was punishable by death, whereas a husband's adultery was treated far more lightly—a double standard characteristic of patriarchalism. Mesopotamian societies after Sumerian times began to emphasize the importance of a woman's virginity at marriage and to require women to wear veils in public to emphasize their modesty. A good portion of Mesopotamian law (such as the Hammurabic code) was devoted to prescriptions for women, ensuring certain basic protections but clearly emphasizing limits and inferiority.

Patriarchal conditions varied from one agricultural civilization to another, however. Egyptian civilization gave women, at least in the upper classes, considerable credit and witnessed several powerful queens. Nefertiti, wife of Akhenaton, seems to have been influential in the religious disputes in this reign; artistic works, as in Figure 2.5, suggest her religious role. Some agricultural societies traced descendants from mothers rather than from fathers. This was true of Jewish law, for example. But even these matrilineal societies held women to be inferior to men; for example, Jewish law insisted that men and women worship separately, with men occupying the central temple space. These variations are important, but they usually operated within a basic framework of patriarchalism. It was around 2000 B.C.E. that an Egyptian writer, Ptah Hotep, put patriarchal beliefs as clearly as anyone in the early civilizations: "If you are a man of note, found for yourself a household, and love your wife at home, as it beseems. Fill her belly, clothe her back.... But hold her back from getting the mastery."

Why was patriarchalism so pervasive? As agriculture improved with the use of better techniques, women's labor, though still vital, became less important than it had been in hunting-and-gathering or early agricultural societies. This was particularly true in the upper classes and in cities, where men often took over the most productive work (craft production or political leadership, for example). The inferior position of women in the upper classes, relative to men, usually was more marked than in peasant villages, where women's labor remained essential.

Agriculture also promoted a higher birth rate than in hunting-and-gathering societies, where prolonged breastfeeding provided real birth control. Agricultural societies, needing more family labor, loosened these constraints, with children often born about two years rather than five years apart. This was a key pressure on women's domestic roles.

More generally, agricultural societies were based on concepts of property, beginning with the ways land was organized. Early law codes defined property relationships. It seemed essential in those circumstances for a man to know who his heirs were—that is, to try to make sure that he monopolized the sexual activities of his wife or wives. This situation helps account for the strong legal emphasis on women's sexual fidelity and the tendency to treat women as part of a man's property. Within this framework, it became possible to think of women as inferior and

partly ornamental, so that when groups achieved a certain prosperity they often tried to demonstrate it by further reducing the status of women. This pattern was very clear in Chinese civilization and operated also in India and later in western Europe. In sum, patriarchalism was a response to economic and property conditions in agricultural civilizations and could deepen over time.

Patriarchalism raises important questions about women themselves: Why did they put up with it? Many women internalized the culture of patriarchalism, holding that it was their job to obey and to serve men and accepting arguments that their aptitudes were inferior to those of men. But patriarchalism did not preclude some important options for women. In many societies, a minority of women could gain expression through religious tasks, such as prayer or service in ceremonies. These could allow them to act independently of family structures. Patriarchal laws defined some rights for women even within marriage, protecting them in theory from the worst abuses. Babylonian law, for example, gave women as well as men the right to divorce under certain conditions when the spouse had not lived up to obligations. Women could also wield informal power in patriarchal societies by their emotional hold over husbands or sons. Such power was indirect, behind the scenes, but a forceful woman might use these means to figure prominently in a society's history. Women also could form networks, if only within a large household. Older women, who commanded the obedience of many daughters-in-law and unmarried daughters, could shape the activities of the family.

Patriarchalism was a commanding theme in most agricultural civilizations from the early centuries onward. Its enforcement, through law and culture, was one means by which societies tried to achieve order. In many agricultural civilizations, patriarchalism dictated that boys, because of their importance in carrying on the family name and the chief economic activities, were more likely to survive: When population excess threatened a family or a community, female infants sometimes were killed as a means of population control.

Questions: How do you think most women reared in a patriarchal society would react to their conditions? What might cause differences in women's conditions in patriarchal societies? Why were upper-class women often more inferior to men in power than peasant women were?

Civilization Centers in Africa and the Eastern Mediterranean

Toward the end of the early civilization period, between 2000 and 1000 B.C.E., several partially separate centers of civilization sprang up on the fringes of the civilized world in Africa and the Middle East, extending into parts of southern Europe. Maps 2.1 and 2.2 illustrate this dispersion. These centers resulted in part from the expansion efforts of river valley pioneers, as in the Egyptian push southward during the New Kingdom period and the spread of Mesopotamian commerce. In the Middle East, separate societies emerged during the chaotic centuries after the collapse of the Hittite empire. They also had characteristics of their own that often had lasting significance.

Kush and Axum: Civilization Spreads in Africa

The kingdom of **Kush** is the first known African state other than Egypt. It sprang up along the upper (southern) reaches of the Nile, on the frontiers of Egyptian activity, where Egyptian garrisons were stationed from time to time. Early artistic work illustrates Kush's emergence, as in Figure 2.7. By 1000 B.C.E. it developed as an independent political unit, strongly influenced by Egyptian forms. By 730 B.C.E., as Egypt declined, Kush was strong enough to conquer its northern neighbor and rule it for several centuries. When this conquest was ended by Assyrian invasion from the Middle East, the Kushites began to push their frontiers farther south, gaining a more diverse African population and weakening the Egyptian influence. A new capital was established at Meroë by the 6th century.

Kushites became skilled in the use of iron and had access to African ore and fuel. The use of iron tools

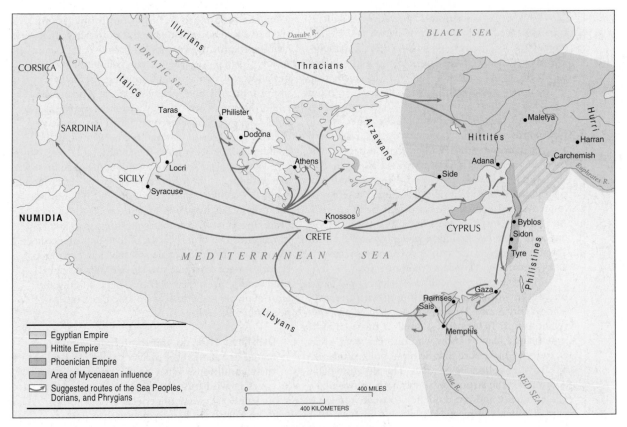

Map 2.2   *The Eastern Mediterranean, c. 1100 B.C.E. By the 12th century B.C.E. many smaller cultures had sprung up around the Mediterranean, such as those of the Mycenaeans and the Hebrews.*

Figure 2.7 *This tomb painting from about 1300 B.C.E. highlights black-skinned people from the rising kingdom of Kush, who interacted increasingly with Egyptian society and at one point controlled Egypt directly.*

extended the area that could be cultivated. Kushites developed a form of writing derived from Egyptian hieroglyphics that has not yet been fully deciphered. They established several significant cities. Their political organization, similar to Egypt's, emphasized a strong monarchy with elaborate ceremonies based on the belief that the king was a god. Kushite economic influence extended widely in sub-Saharan Africa. They traded extensively with people to the west and through this trade may have spread knowledge of ironmaking to much of the rest of Africa. The greatest period of the kingdom at Meroë lasted from about 250 B.C.E. to 50 C.E. By this time the kingdom was a channel for African goods—animal skins, ebony, ivory, gold, and slaves—into the Middle East and the Mediterranean. Many monuments were built during those centuries, including huge royal pyramids and an elaborate palace in Meroë, along with fine pottery and jewelry. Meroë began to decline from about 100 C.E. onward and was defeated by a kingdom to the south, **Axum,** about 300 C.E. Prosperity and extensive political and economic activity did not end in this region but extended into the formation of a kingdom in present-day Ethiopia.

The extent of Kush's influence is not entirely clear. Whether African peoples outside the upper Nile region learned much from Kush about political forms is unknown. There was little imitation of its writing, and the region of Kush and Ethiopia would long remain isolated from the wider stream of African history. Nevertheless, the formation of a separate society stretching below the eastern Sahara was an important step in setting the bases for technological and economic change in upper Africa. Although its achievements figure less prominently in later African development, Kush may have done for sub-Saharan Africa what Sumer achieved for the Middle East in setting up a wider process of civilization in motion.

Cultures in the Mediterranean Region

Smaller centers in the Middle East began to spring up after about 1500 B.C.E. Though dependent on the larger Mesopotamian culture for many ideas, these centers added important new elements and in some cases extended the hold of civilization westward to the Asian coast of the Mediterranean. They also added to the diversity of the Middle East, creating an array of identities that marked the region even under later conquerors, such as the Roman Empire and the sweeping religion of Islam. Several of these smaller cultures proved immensely durable and influenced other parts of the world.

The Hebrews and Monotheism   The most important of the smaller Middle Eastern groups were the Hebrews, who gave the world one of its most influential religions. The Hebrews were a Semitic people (a population group that also includes the Arabs). They were influenced by Babylonian civilization. They may have settled in the southeast corner of the Mediterranean about 1600 B.C.E., probably migrating from Mesopotamia and then developing agriculture. Some may have moved into Egypt, where they were treated as a subject people, although the first clear record of the Hebrews dates only to 1100 B.C.E. According to Jewish tradition, Moses led the Hebrews to Palestine in search of a homeland promised by God in the 13th century B.C.E. This was later held to be the central development in Jewish history. By 1100 B.C.E. the Jews began to emerge as a people with a self-conscious culture and some political identity. At most points, however, the Jewish state was small and weak, retaining independence only when other parts of the Middle East were disorganized. A few Jewish kings unified their people, but at many points the Jews were divided into separate regional states. Most of Palestine came under foreign domination from 722 B.C.E. onward, but the Jews were able to maintain their cultural identity and key religious traditions. A series of dynamic prophets elaborated Jewish beliefs and added to the rich religious literature.

The Jews' distinctive achievement was the development of a strong **monotheistic** religion. Early Jewish leaders may have emphasized a particularly strong creator god as the most powerful of many divinities, a hierarchy not common in animism. Such an emphasis encouraged a focus on the father God for prayer and loyalty. According to Mosaic tradition, this divinity, through the prophets, increasingly urged Jews to abandon the worship of all other gods and to receive from God the Torah (a holy law). Keeping this law would ensure divine protection and guidance, as illustrated in Figure 2.8. From this point onward Jews

Figure 2.8   *This Jewish wall painting, from a synagogue at Dura Europas (about 239 C.E.), reflects the artistic style of the Roman Empire. However, the scene is central to Jewish tradition, showing Abraham and the covenant of God, rejecting the apparatus of pagan idolatry symbolized by the material items of worship to the right.*

regarded themselves as a chosen people under God's special guidance.

The development of monotheism had a wide significance. In Jewish hands the concept of God became less humanlike and more abstract, a basic change not only in religion but in overall outlook. God had a power and a planning quality far different from the attributes of the traditional gods of the Middle East and Egypt. The gods, particularly in Mesopotamia, were whimsical and capricious; the Jewish god was orderly and just, and people could know what to expect if they adhered to God's rules. The link to ethical conduct and moral behavior was also central. Religion for the Jews was a system of life, not merely a set of rituals and ceremonies. God's laws were clearly spelled out in the Torah and other writings developed between the 9th and 2nd centuries B.C.E. The full impact of this religious transformation on Middle Eastern and Mediterranean civilization would come later, when Jewish ideas were taken up by the proselytizing faiths of Christianity and Islam. But the basic concept formed one of the legacies of the twilight period between the first great civilizations and the new cultures that arose in their place.

The impact of Jewish religion beyond the Jewish people was complex. The Jews saw God's guidance in all of human history, not simply their own. Ultimately all peoples would be led to God. But God's special pact was with the Jews, and little premium was placed on missionary activity or converting others to the faith. This limitation helps explain the intensity and durability of the Jewish faith. It also kept the Jewish people a minority within the Middle East, although at various points the religion was spread somewhat more widely by substantial conversions to Judaism.

The Minoans About 1600 B.C.E., a civilization developed on the island of Crete. This **Minoan** society traded widely with both Mesopotamia and Egypt and probably acquired many of its civilized characteristics from this exchange. For example, Minoan society copied Egyptian architectural forms and mathematics, although it developed important new artistic styles in the colossal palace built in the capital city, Knossos. The writing system was adapted from Egyptian hieroglyphics. Political structures similar to those of Egypt and the Mesopotamian empires emphasized elaborate bureaucratic controls complete with extensive recordkeeping under a powerful monarch. Minoan navies conquered parts of the Greek mainland; these conquests eventually led to the establishment of the first civilization there. Centered in the kingdom of Mycenae, this early Greek civilization developed a considerable capacity for monumental building and conducted important wars with city-states in the Middle East, including the famous conflict with Troy.

Civilizations in Crete and Greece were overturned by a wave of Indo-European invasions, culminating about 1000 B.C.E. Although the civilization that arose later to form classical Greece had somewhat separate origins, it built extensively on the memories of this first civilized society and on its roots in Egyptian and Mesopotamian achievements.

The Phoenicians Another distinct society grew up in the Middle East in what is now the nation of Lebanon. Around 2000 B.C.E. a people called the **Phoenicians** settled on the Mediterranean coast. Like the Minoans, they quickly turned to seafaring because their agricultural hinterland was not extensive. The Phoenicians improved on the knowledge they gained through their elaborate trading contacts with the major civilization centers. About 1300 B.C.E. they devised a simplified alphabet of only 22 letters based on the Mesopotamian cuneiform. The Phoenician alphabet served as ancestor to the Greek and Latin lettering systems. The Phoenicians also upgraded the Egyptian numbering system.

However, the Phoenicians were a merchant people, not vested in extensive cultural achievements. They advanced manufacturing techniques in several areas, particularly the production of dyes for cloth. Above all, for commercial purposes, they dispersed and set up colonies at several points along the Mediterranean. They benefited from the weakening of Egypt and the earlier collapse of Minoan society and its Greek successor because there were few competitors for influence in the Mediterranean by 1000 B.C.E. Phoenician sailors moved steadily westward, setting up a major trading city on the coast of north Africa at Carthage and lesser centers in Italy, Spain, and southern France. The Phoenicians even traded along the Atlantic coast of Europe and reached Britain, where they sought tin. By the 6th century B.C.E., Phoenicia collapsed in the wake of the Assyrian invasions of the Middle East, although several of the colonial cities, such as Carthage, long survived.

The Issue of Heritage

 Early civilizations unquestionably created a series of tools that would never have to be reinvented. Historians debate how much influence particular cultures or political patterns would have on societies that later built on the early civilizations.

For several centuries after about 1200 B.C.E., a series of invasions and migrations by Indo-European peoples from central Asia disrupted the civilization of the Middle East. These were hunters and herders. They introduced the use of iron, which soon would establish the basis for a new series of political units and wealthy economies. But for the moment there was some break in developments. The Indo-Europeans played down Mesopotamian and Egyptian beliefs about the divinity of kings, for example, preferring rulers selected by councils of military leaders. They brought in new religious ideas. They helped bring to a close the river valley civilization phase in the Middle East.

The accomplishments of the river valley civilizations would continue to have impact, even amid new patterns. The tools of civilization never had to be reinvented in the eastern Mediterranean and north Africa. Basic mathematics and science, the idea of writing, and key technologies persisted, to be used by later societies. Even a few words lasted, like the Sumerian *alsokol*, still visible in English as *alcohol*.

Cultural elements survived as well. The Jewish religion continued to thrive, and would later have wider influence. Musical instruments like harps, drums, and flutes, invented in early Mesopotamian civilization, as well as the development of the seven- and eight-tone scales, would influence the music of Greece and other societies. Egyptian architecture had wide impact, as did ideas of divine kingship.

Some historians have claimed even deeper conditioning. It has been argued that cultures under Mesopotamian influence, including Greece, Christianity, and Islam, emphasized a division between humanity and nature that was quite different from the cultural traditions of India, China, and sub-Saharan Africa. Instead of seeing people as part of a larger natural harmony, the Mesopotamian tradition saw humans as separate, with some antagonism to the forces of nature. Religions from this region have encouraged action and anxiety, in contrast to the tranquility urged in Indian religions.

Clearly, later civilizations in the Mediterranean built on the massive achievements of Mesopotamian and Egyptian societies. Historians debate the range of influence. But there were other formative civilization centers, whose heritage would also loom large in later world history in shaping major societies in Asia.

 GLOBAL CONNECTIONS: The Early Civilizations and the World

Mesopotamia and Egypt presented two different approaches to relationships outside the home region. Mesopotamia was flat, with few natural barriers to recurrent invasion from the north. Perhaps for this reason, Mesopotamian leaders thought in terms of expansion. Many conquering emperors expanded their territory, though within the Middle East. Many traders pushed outward, dealing either with merchants to the east or sending expeditions into the Mediterranean and beyond, and also to India. The Middle East's role as active agent in wider contact was clearly being established.

Egypt was not isolated, however, it was more self-contained. There was important trade and interaction along the Nile to the south, which brought mutual influences with the peoples of Kush and Ethiopia. Trade and influence also linked Egypt to Mediterranean islands like Crete, south of Greece. A few interactions, finally, occurred with Mesopotamia. But most Egyptians, including the leaders, thought of Egypt as its own world. There was less need or desire to learn of wider horizons. Correspondingly, ancient Egypt played less of a role as intermediary among regions than did Mesopotamia.

Further Readings

Two excellent studies can guide additional work on early civilization in Mesopotamia: C. L. Redman's *The Rise of Civilization: From Early Farmers to Urban Society in the Ancient Near East* (1988) and N. J. Nissen's *The Early History of the Ancient Near East, 9000–2000 B.C.* (1988). See also S. N. Kramer, *History Begins at Sumer* (1981); C. B. F. Walker, *Cuneiform* (1987); and H. W. F. Saggs, *Babylonians* (1995). Important studies of Egypt include T. G. H. James, *Ancient Egypt: The Land and Its Legacy* (1988); N. C. Grimal, *A His-*

tory of Ancient Egypt (1992), and Gay Robins, *Women in Ancient Egypt* (1993). See also Donald Redford, *Egypt, Canaan, and Israel in Ancient Times* (1995), and David O'Connor, *Ancient Nubia: Egypt's Rival in Africa* (1993). For an excellent study of non-Western science beginning with the Egyptians and Mesopotamians, see Dick Teresi, *Lost Discoveries: The Ancient Roots of Modern Science—From the Babylonians to the Maya* (2002). Two books deal with important special topics: M. Silver's *Economic Structures of the Ancient Near East* (1987) and T. Jacobsen's *The Treasures of Darkness: A History of Mesopotamian Religion* (1976). Two studies of Israel are J. Bright, *A History of Israel* (1981), and the first two volumes of W. D. Davies and L. Finkelstein, eds., *The Cambridge History of Judaism* (1984, 1987). For studies of Phoenicia and its role in world history, see N. K. Sanders, *The Sea Peoples* (1985), and M. E. Auber, *The Phoenicians and the West* (1996). On disruptions in the late Bronze Age, see Trude Dothan and Moshe Dothan, *People of the Sea: The Search for the Philistines* (1992). Martin Bernal's controversial *Black Athena* (1992) seeks to trace ancient African influences on the classical Western world but may best be employed as a window into the use and misuse of history by both Afrocentric and Eurocentric scholars.

On the Web

It is possible to make a virtual visit to the Mesopotamian cities of Ur (http://www.taisei.co.jp/cg_e/ancient_world/ur/aur.html) and Nippur (http://www.oi.uchicago.edu/OI/PROJ/NIP/PUB93/NSC/NSC.html), and to take virtual tours of key sites of Egyptian (http://www.ancientegypt.co.uk/menu.html) and

Kushite civilizations (http://www.nubianet.org/about/about_history6.html and http://www.thebritishmuseum.ac.uk/egyptian/bmsaes/issue1/welsby.html). A head-turning virtual walk through an Egyptian pyramid is offered at http://www.pbs.org/wgbh/nova/pyramid/explore/. The ancient civilizations of Persia can be viewed at http://www-oi.uchicago.edu/OI/MUS/PA/IRAN/PAAI/PAAI.html and http://www.crystalinks.com/iran.html. Ancient mathematical systems are examined http://www-groups.dcs.st-andrews.ac.uk/~history/Indexes/Babylonians.html and http://www-groups.dcs.st-andrews.ac.uk/~history/Indexes/Egyptians.html. Persepolis and ancient Iran receive close treatment in http://www-oi.uchicago.edu/OI/MUS/PA/IRAN/PAAI/PAAI.html and http://www.crystalinks.com/iran.html.

The Web offers an introduction to cuneiform (http://saturn.sron.nl/~jheise/akkadian/) and a tutorial in hieroglyphic writing (http://www.eyelid.co.uk/hiero1.htm and http://emuseum.mnsu.edu/prehistory/egypt/hieroglyphics/heiroglyphics.html) and also a closer look into one of humanity's first recorded literary productions, the Epic of Gilgamesh (http://www.wsu.edu/~dee/MESO/GILG.HTM).

The Web also offers insight into the life and/or royal art of the most significant rulers of the ancient world, including Narmer (http://www.crystalinks.com/narmer.html), Ahkenaton (http://sangha.net/messengers/akhenaton.htm), Nefertiti (http://sangha.net/messengers/nefertiti.htm), and Cyrus the Great (http://oznet.net/cyrus/).

CHAPTER 3

ASIA'S FIRST CIVILIZATIONS: INDIA AND CHINA

One of the mysterious seals from the Indus valley civilization. The figures at the top of the seal were characters from a system of writing that no one has been able to decipher. The long-horned bull that dominates the carved surface was to become revered and a symbol of the civilizations that followed.

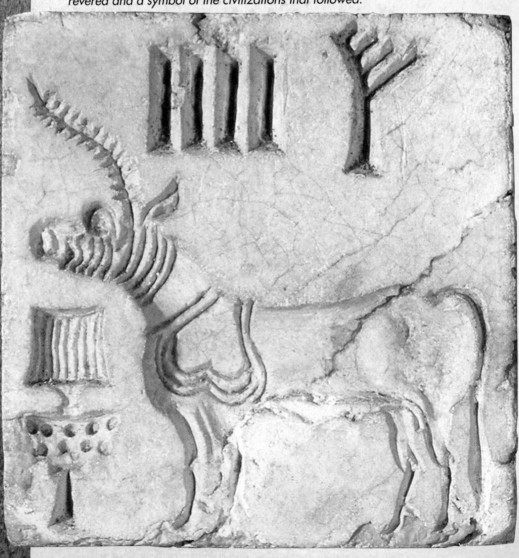

Like Sumer and Egypt in the Middle East and north Africa, civilizations first developed in east and south Asia near great river systems. The early sections of this chapter trace the rise and fall of **Harappan civilization** in India and the history of the nomadic peoples who supplanted the Harappans. Between about 1500 and 1000 B.C.E., as the great cities of the Indus region crumbled into ruins, nomadic Aryan migrants from central Asia moved into the fertile Indus plains and pushed into the Ganges River valleys to the east. It took these unruly, warlike peoples many centuries to build a civilization that rivaled that of the Harappans. By about 700 B.C.E., their priests had begun to orally preserve the sacred hymns and ritual incantations that had long been central to Aryan culture. In the centuries that followed, strong warrior leaders built tribal units into larger kingdoms.

The emergence of priestly and warrior elites signaled the beginning of a new pattern of civilization in south Asia. By the 6th century B.C.E., the renewal of civilized life in India was marked by the emergence of great world religions, such as Hinduism and Buddhism, and a renewal of trade, urban life, and splendid artistic and architectural achievements.

The initial development of civilization in China combined the material advances of Mesopotamian history with the continuity of Egyptian civilization. Civilization in China took shape about 1500 B.C.E. It emerged gradually out of Neolithic farming and potterymaking cultures that had long been present in the Yellow River region of east Asia. The establishment of the Shang kingdom at this time gave political expression to various civilizing trends. The appearance of a distinctive and increasingly specialized elite supported by the peasant majority of the Chinese people, the growth of towns and the first cities, the spread of trade, and the formulation of a written language all indicated that a major civilization was emerging in China.

The political dominance of the Shang came to an end in 1122 B.C.E. But under the new royal house of the Zhou, civilized development in China was enriched and extended as the Chinese people migrated east and south from their original Yellow River heartland. By the end of the Zhou era, which would last officially until 256 B.C.E., many of the central elements of Chinese civilization were firmly established. Some of those elements have persisted to the present day.

The Indus Valley and the Birth of South Asian Civilization

 In the 3rd millennium B.C.E., south Asia's first civilization, one of humankind's earliest, developed along the **Indus River** system in northwest India. Anchored by two

400,000 B.C.E.	8000 B.C.E.	4000 B.C.E.	3000 B.C.E.	2000 B.C.E.	1000 B.C.E.
400,000–350,000 Peking Man	8000–4000 Transition to sedentary agriculture; silk weaving	4000–2500 Spread of farming and villages in western India 4000 Yangshao	2500 Emergence of Harappan civilization 2200 Longshan	1766 Shang kingdom; writing develops 1600–1500 Beginning of Aryan nomadic migration 1600–1200 Collapse of the Harappan civilization 1122 Former or western Zhou kings	770 Later or eastern Zhou kings 700 Composition of the first of the sacred Vedas 600–500 Age of the Buddha, and Hindu–Buddhist rivalry 550–480 Age of Confucius

great cities, **Harappa** and **Mohenjo Daro**, the Indus civilization excelled in urban planning and irrigation. A combination of factors that we still do not fully understand led to the decline of the civilization in the mid-2nd millennium B.C.E. The contrary pressures of long periods of excessive flooding of the Indus and the gradual desertification of the northwest region gravely weakened Harappa's agricultural and urban base. In roughly the same time period, horse-riding, cattle-herding Indo-Europeans entered the Indian subcontinent in waves. Their incursions further weakened a civilization already in trouble, and they certainly contributed to its eventual disappearance from history until the mid-19th century C.E.

Great torrents of water from the world's highest mountain range, the **Himalayas,** carved out the vast Indus River system, which nurtured the first civilization in the Indian subcontinent (Map 3.1). As the rapidly running mountain streams reached the plains of the Indus valley, they branched out into seven great rivers, of which five remain today. These rivers converge midway down the valley to form the Indus River, which runs for hundreds of miles to the southwest and empties into the Arabian Sea.

The streams that flow from high in the Himalayas are fed by monsoon rains. Rain clouds are carried from the seas surrounding the Indian subcontinent by **monsoons**—seasonal winds—across the lowlands to the mountains, where, cooled and trapped, they release their life-giving waters. These summer, or wet, monsoons, which blow toward central Asia from the sea, are a critical source of moisture for the plains and valleys they cross before they reach the mountains. The streams from the mountains also carry rich soil to the plains, constantly enlarging them and allowing exten-

sive cultivation and dense human habitation. The Indus is only one of many river systems on the Indian subcontinent formed by melting snow and monsoon rains, but it was the first to nurture a civilization.

The lower Indus plains were a very different place in the 3rd millennium B.C.E. than they are today. Most of the region is now arid and desolate, crisscrossed by dried-up riverbeds. In Harappan times it was green and heavily forested. Game animals and pasturage for domesticated animals were plentiful. Long before the first settlements associated with the Harappan complex appeared, the plains were dotted with farm settlements. By at least 3000 B.C.E., these pre-Harappan peoples cultivated wheat and barley and had developed sophisticated agricultural implements and crop-growing techniques.

The pre-Harappan peoples knew how to make bronze weapons, tools, and mirrors, and they had mastered the art of potterymaking. Recurring motifs, such as bulls and long-horned cattle, on elaborately decorated bowls and storage urns suggest links to early agricultural communities in the Middle East. Pottery designs indicate that fish probably were a major source of food. The long-horned bull was a central image in the Harappan culture and remains important in Indian iconography (the art of pictorial representation). Pre-Harappan peoples in the Indus valley also carved many small figurines of women. These statuettes differ from those found in many other early cultures in the detailed attention given to hairstyles and jewelry.

The Discovery and Mystery of Harappa

In the late 1850s C.E., the British were building railroads through the Indus valley. In need of materials for the railbed, British engineers allowed their con-

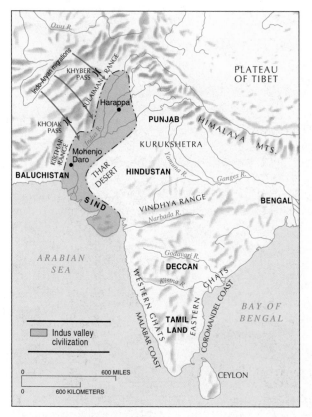

Map 3.1 *India in the Age of Harappa and the Early Aryan Migrations*

that made up the first civilization in south Asia. The evidence found so far indicates that Harappan civilization developed rapidly in the mid-3rd millennium B.C.E. It diverged sharply from the village cultures that preceded it in levels of material culture, scale, and organization. The civilization was apparently anchored on two capital cities: Harappa, in the north, on one of the five great rivers that forms the Indus, and Mohenjo Daro, 400 miles to the south, on the banks of the Indus proper.

The Great Cities of the Indus Valley

Though hundreds of miles apart, Harappa and Mohenjo Daro were remarkably similar in layout and construction (Figure 3.1). Both were built on a square grid pattern that was divided by main roads into 12 precisely measured segments. Each city was surrounded by walls, which extended a mile from east to west and one-half mile from north to south. The buildings and the city walls were made of standardized kiln-dried bricks. Coordinated construction on such a massive scale would have meant an autocratic government that could organize and supervise the daily tasks of large numbers of laborers.

The existence of a strong ruling class is also indicated by the presence of large, well-fortified citadels in each capital city. These citadels may have served as sanctuaries for the cities' populations in times of attack and as community centers in times of peace. The citadel at Mohenjo Daro included a very large building that may have been a palace. Both citadels contained what are believed to have been audience and assembly halls or places of worship as well as public bathing tanks. The elaborately decorated bath at Mohenjo Daro was surrounded by a cloister, which opened onto many small rooms that may have housed priests. Large granaries near each of the citadels suggest that the state stored grain for ceremonial purposes, times of shortage, and possibly the regulation of grain production and sale.

Although the main avenues were straight and about 30 feet wide, the lanes and paths in the cities' quarters were narrow and twisting. Brick houses of one to three stories were jumbled together in these areas, which must have been densely populated at the height of Harappan civilization. The layout of the houses was strikingly uniform; each consisted of a courtyard surrounded by rooms for sleeping, cooking,

struction workers to use bricks found in the dirt mounds of long-abandoned cities in the valley. A British general named Alexander Cunningham, later head of the Indian Archeological Survey, visited one of these sites in 1856. While there, he was given several artifacts. Some of these were soapstone seals imprinted with various carvings, including the figure of a bull and what appeared to be letters in an unknown script. Cunningham was convinced that the artifacts were of ancient origin and was intrigued by the strange script, which bore little resemblance to that of any of the languages then used in India. As head of the archeological survey, he took steps to ensure the full-scale excavation of what came to be recognized as one of the earliest and most mysterious human civilizations.

Decades of extensive digging at the original site and hundreds of other sites throughout the Indus valley uncovered a huge complex of cities and villages

Figure 3.1 *This artistic recreation of Mohenjo Daro conveys a sense of the impressive size and well-planned layout of the city. Note the fortified walls and gates and the fortresslike construction of the blocks of buildings within the city. As long as these great structures were maintained, they may have concealed the military vulnerability of Harappan civilization. When they fell into disrepair, Indus valley towns would have been open to assault and takeover by more warlike peoples migrating into the region.*

and, in the larger homes, receiving visitors. Entrance to the houses was gained through a long passageway from the street, which in combination with few windows may indicate a concern for security. Each home had a bathing area, in which Harappans apparently washed standing up by pouring jugs of water over their bodies. Each house was also equipped with a toilet, perhaps the first ever devised, that was connected by a drainage pipe to a citywide sewage system, which was among the best in the ancient world.

Harappan Culture and Society The great cities and many towns of the Harappan complex were supported by a rather advanced agricultural system based on the cultivation of wheat, rye, peas, and possibly rice. Cotton was widely cultivated, and numerous domesticated animals were reared. It is likely that irrigation systems were built to catch and control waters from the monsoon and the rivers, and that fish caught in the rivers were a dietary staple. Local goods were

carried by riverboats and ox carts, reproduced in clay models like those shown in Figure 3.2.

The cities of Harappa were major trading centers. Jade from China and precious jewels from what later became Burma have been unearthed at various Indus sites. Stone seals produced in the Indus region, such as those shown in Figure 3.3, have been found in the urban ruins of other ancient civilizations such as Sumer in Mesopotamia. In addition to realistic depictions of animals and human figures, the seals contain a complex writing system that no one has ever deciphered. The fact that Harappan merchants used large numbers of the seals to ensure that crates and urns were not opened during transport suggests that trade was highly developed in the Indus valley civilization.

Despite these overseas contacts, Harappan peoples appear to have been conservative and highly resistant to innovations introduced from the outside. They cast tools and weapons in bronze, but most of their implements were inferior to those of Mesopotamian peoples, with whom they had contact.

Figure 3.2 *This wheeled model clay cart, found during the excavation at Mohenjo Daro, tells us a good deal about the main mode of land transport used in south Asia's first civilization. Similar models have been found in almost all Indus valley settlements, and in some respects they resemble the ox-drawn, nearly solid-wheeled carts still used in India today.*

Their weapons were even more primitive and would have left them vulnerable to invasions by peoples more adept at warfare.

Harappan society appears to have been dominated by a powerful priestly class, which ruled from the citadel of each capital. The priests would have derived this control from their role as intermediaries between the Harappan populace and a number of gods and goddesses, who controlled fertility. Several of what are believed to be gods are depicted on seals, such as those in Figure 3.3. One of the recurring figures is a naked male figure with a horned head and a fierce expression. On some of the seals he is pictured in a crossed-legged posture of meditation similar to that later called the lotus position. This suggests that *yoga*, special techniques for exercise and postures for meditation, may have had its origin in the Harappan era. Numerous figurines of women, also naked except for a great deal of jewelry, have been found. These mother-goddesses appear to have been objects of worship for the common people, whereas the horned god was apparently favored by the priests and upper classes.

The obsession with fertility was also reflected in the worship of sacred animals, especially bulls, and in the large quantity of phallic-shaped objects that have been found at Harappan sites. Along with a handful of superbly carved figurines of male notables, dancing women or goddesses, and animals, these religious objects represent the height of artistic expression for the apparently practical-minded peoples of Harappa.

The uniformity and rigid ordering of Harappan culture would not have been possible without an extensive administrative class serving the priests. It is likely that members of this class and possibly wealthy mercantile families lived in the large two- and three-story houses. Characteristically, size, not decoration, set their dwellings off from those of artisans, laborers, and slaves.

The Slow Demise of Harappan Civilization It was once widely accepted that Harappan civilization was the victim of assaults by nomadic invaders eager to claim the rich Indus valley as pastureland for their cattle. A dramatic vision of a wave of "barbarian" invaders smashing Harappans' skulls made for good storytelling but bad history. Archeological investigations of recent decades demonstrate that Harappa declined gradually in the mid-2nd millennium B.C.E. The precise causes of that decline remain a matter of dispute.

It is likely that a combination of factors led to Harappa's decline. There is evidence of severe flooding at Mohenjo Daro and other sites. Short-term natural disasters, including severe earthquakes, may have compounded the adverse effects of long-term climatic changes. Shifts in the monsoon pattern and changes in temperature may have begun the process of desertification that eventually transformed the region into the arid steppe that it has been for most of recorded history. Rapid changes in pottery types suggest sudden waves of migrants into the region. It is possible that the Harappans were too weak militarily to prevent these incoming peoples from settling in or taking over their towns and cities. In many cases these centers of urban life had already been abandoned in response to natural calamities, particularly flooding. A marked decline in the quality of building and town planning indicates that the priestly elite was losing control.

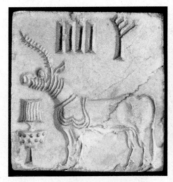

Figure 3.3 *A sample of the soft stone seals found at most Indus valley excavation sites and at trading centers from the Middle East to China. Like some modern languages, such as Arabic, the Harappan script was written and read from right to left. Like Chinese and ancient Egyptian, Harappan writing appears to have been pictographic, but no one has found a consistent pattern that would tell us what the symbols signified.*

Some of the migrants probably were bands of Aryan herders who entered the Indus region over an extended period of time rather than in militant waves. But the Aryan pastoralists may have consciously destroyed or neglected the dikes and canals on which the agrarian life of the Harappan peoples had once depended. Cattle raising would then have replaced crop cultivation, further undermining the economic basis of the civilization. That there was a good deal of violent conflict in this transition cannot be ruled out. Groups of skeletons with smashed skulls or in postures of flight from floods or foreign invaders have been found on the stairways at some sites. Thus, environmental changes and related administrative decline combined with the effects of nomadic migrations to undermine south Asia's first civilization.

Aryan Incursions and Early Aryan Society in India

While Harappan civilization was crumbling, new peoples were moving into the Indus valley. Of these migrants, those of Aryan descent gradually gained the upper hand. Beginning as a rowdy and fragmented warrior culture, the Aryans eventually built a sophisticated civilization on the Indian subcontinent. By the last centuries B.C.E., this new civilization had developed a written language, built sizeable cities, produced sophisticated art and literature, and was nurturing two of the great world religions, Hinduism and Buddhism.

Despite the claims of 19th- and 20th-century racist thinkers, the **Aryans** were not a race or distinct biological group. The term *Aryan* is a linguistic one. The Aryans were originally herders who spoke one variant of a group of related Indo-European languages and lived in the area between the Caspian and Black seas. For reasons probably related to climatic shifts and conflicts over grazing lands, these nomadic peoples began to migrate in large numbers from their homelands in the 3rd and 2nd millennia B.C.E. The first migrations were westward into Asia Minor and eventually Europe. The second waves were eastward toward Iran and the Indus valley.

The Aryans' mobility and military prowess made it possible for them to prevail over peoples who occupied the lands into which they moved. The remarkable extent of the area affected by their expansion is illustrated by the great variety and prominence of modern languages that belong to the Indo-European family. From the Celtic, Germanic, and Romance languages of western Europe and the Slavic tongues to the east, to the speech of the ancient Persians and modern Iranians and the **Sanskrit**-derived languages of north India, the ancient Indo-European invaders have left a lasting legacy. Despite millennia of separation and differing paths of cultural development on the part of Indo-European groups, the similarities among their widely dispersed languages remain striking. The word for *father*, for example, is *pater* in Latin, *vater* in German, and *pitar* in Sanskrit.

Aryan Warrior Culture

To the Aryan branch of the Indo-European nomads, the Indus and the valleys beyond were a paradise of lush, well-watered, and underpopulated grasslands and forests. After spreading across the Indus plains (and probably pushing the Harappan peoples farther south), the Aryans moved in waves of small bands to the southeast. There they entered the rich plains and valleys formed by the Ganges River system, which, as Map 3.1 illustrates, surpassed the great Indus complex in size. Like the Indus plains in earlier times, the Ganges region provided the combination of monsoon rains and great river systems that made civilized life possible. The Aryans took many centuries to approach the level of civilization achieved by the Harappan peoples. But the potential for agriculture was so obvious that herding bands began to settle down and cultivate lands cleared from the forests in the first generations after their arrival.

The Aryans in India did not develop writing until long after they entered the subcontinent. But we can learn a good deal about their way of life from the hymns they composed for religious-based animal sacrifices, entertainment, and historical chronicles. Transmitted orally for centuries by priests and bards, the hymns were written down in sacred books called the **Vedas** in the 6th century B.C.E.

The Vedic hymns describe the Aryan invaders as a restless and warlike people organized at first in tribes and later in small kingdoms. The tribes and kingdoms fought constantly among themselves, often over cattle and pasturelands, and warred with the indigenous peoples. The chief deity of the Aryans was **Indra,** the god of battle and lightning (Figure 3.4).

Figure 3.4 *The Aryan god of war, Indra, was considered king of the cosmos in early times. Later devotees of the religion we now call Hinduism gave Indra a lower status. But they continued to venerate him as ruler of the skies and the god of rain and thunder. This pattern typifies a tendency in early south Asian religions to identify particular deities with specific natural phenomena and powers.*

He was described as a colossal, hard-drinking warrior with a huge pot belly. Indra was revered as the smasher of dams and the destroyer of cities. The Aryans were superb horsemen who also used chariots in their wars. Their bows and arrows and metal-tipped spears were a good deal more effective than the weapons of the indigenous peoples. All together the Vedas describe the Aryans as a rowdy crew who were fond of beer and loved to gamble, race horses, and make war.

Except for their military hardware, early Aryan material culture represented a marked decline from the level reached during the Harappan period. Wood and thatch villages replaced stone and brick cities and towns. There is little evidence of interest in sculpture or painting, and thus it is unlikely that great works of art were produced. However, the

Aryans were extremely fond of music. They played flutes, harps, lutes, and a variety of cymbals and drums, and they delighted in singing and dancing. If the Vedic hymns are to be believed, they were also much addicted to gambling, particularly dice. One of the few secular early Vedic poems, "The Gambler's Lament," vividly captures the pleasures and pitfalls of the gamblers' den. One passage reminds the tempted youth that

> The dice are armed with hooks and piercing;
>
> they are deceptive, hot and burning.
>
> Like children they give and take again,
>
> they strike back at their conquerors.
>
> They are sweetened with honey through the magic they
>
> work on the gambler.

Gambling has remained a recurring theme in Indian religious and philosophical discourses throughout history. Allusions to fate as the throw of the dice can be found in philosophical writings. Dice games play pivotal roles in the plots of the great epics that later represented and shaped the great civilizations built by the descendants of the early Aryan invaders.

Aryan Society

When they entered the Indian subcontinent, the Aryan bands were divided into three main social groups: warriors, priests, and commoners. Conflict with the indigenous peoples added a fourth group: slaves, or serfs. Although social differences among the first three groups were pronounced, the dividing line between the freeborn Aryans and the enslaved population was particularly rigid. Apparently, there was also a physical dimension to the sharp division between the free and enslaved. The Aryans pictured themselves as light-skinned conquerors in a sea of dark-skinned **Dasas,** their name for the indigenous peoples. Attempts were made to prohibit **miscegenation**—sexual relations and procreation—between Aryans and Dasas. Marriages between the two groups were forbidden. Penalties were prescribed according to the respective ranks of the men and women who had sexual relations.

As the Aryans settled down, social divisions became more complex, with groups such as farmers, merchants, and artisans joining the ruling groups of warriors, priests, and herders. Social distinctions were further complicated by widespread miscegenation. Over the centuries, four broad varnas (social classes) developed: brahmans (priests), warriors, merchants,

Document

Aryan Poetry in Praise of a War-Horse

The following early Vedic hymn exults in the power of a great Aryan war-horse.

> Rushing to glory, to the capture of herds,
> Swooping down as a hungry falcon,
> Eager to be first, he darts amid the ranks of the chariots
> Happy as a bridegroom making a garland,
> Spurning the dust and champing at the bit.
> And the victorious steed and faithful,
> His body obedient to his driver in battle,
> Speeding on through the melee,
> Stirs up the dust to fall on his brows.

> And at his deep neigh, like the thunder of heaven,
> The foemen tremble in fear,
> For he fights against thousands, and none can resist him,
> So terrible is his charge.

Questions: In what ways does this poem convey the Aryans' delight in warfare? What does it tell us about the way they fought their battles and their attitudes toward the herd animals that were so central to their culture? How does it convey the Aryans' ideals of manliness, heroism, and loyalty, and what does it say about their attitudes toward death?

and farmers. Beneath them were the outcaste and untouchable descendants of the Dasas and other non-Aryan migrants.

The culture of the Aryan invaders placed great emphasis on physical strength, martial skills, and heroic exploits. Descent and inheritance were **patrilineal,** through the male line. Elder men monopolized authority within the household, although their mothers and wives could influence decisions behind the scenes. At marriage, brides left their own households and families and went to live with those of their husbands. Monogamous marriages were the norm, but **polygamy** (one husband with several wives) and **polyandry** (one wife with several husbands) are recounted in the Aryan epics.

Sizable dowries, or marriage payments, in the form of cattle, food, or precious objects were commonly given to the husband's family. In some cases, a prospective husband paid a bride-price to his wife-to-be's family. This practice suggests that female children had not yet become the economic burden that they have been considered through much of south Asian history. Nonetheless, sons were preferred to daughters because of the men's important family ritual functions and their key roles as warriors and priests. These positions were never held by women, nor were women allowed to be the chieftains of tribal bands or rulers of the kingdoms that developed in the early centuries of Aryan invasions.

Aryan Religion

The early Aryans were polytheists who worshiped a wide range of deities that physically resembled humans and had human emotions and needs. Like those of the ancient Greeks, each Aryan god and goddess had the power to assist supplicants in a particular aspect of their lives. Thus, there were gods or goddesses to whom devotees offered sacrifices for success in business (the goddess Lakshmi), the means to overcome obstacles in their lives (Ganesha, the elephant-headed god), and the good fortune to conceive children (the god Shiva and a number of female deities). The widespread worship of female deities may well have represented a carryover into Aryan culture of a prominent aspect of Harappan civilization. Nonetheless, like the human society that worshiped these deities, the Aryan pantheon was dominated by males, particularly gods relating to war, fire, and rain. Religious worship centered on animal sacrifices and ritual offerings of food designed to win specific favors

from individual deities. The major function of the Vedic priests was to perform these critical sacrifices, a role that later allowed them to amass great power.

In contrast to their Hindu and Buddhist descendants, there appears to have been little introspection among the early Aryans. The oldest Vedas consist mainly of songs, some quite beautiful, praising the various deities and giving incredibly detailed formulas for sacrifices. There is little speculation on issues that would later preoccupy Indian priests and philosophers, such as the purpose of creation, the fate of the dead, and the nature of the soul. There was no concept of reincarnation (rebirth) or the transmigration of the soul. Much as the ancient Greeks believed, evildoers went to the House of Clay after death, and the virtuous were rewarded in the World of the Fathers. But in an early hymn to Vishvakarman, the creator god, there is a vision of a primal essence and oneness that prefigures later Indian thinking:

> What was the germ primeval which the waters received
>
> where all the gods were seen together?
>
> The waters, they received that germ primeval
>
> wherein the gods were gathered all together.
>
> It rested set upon the unborn's navel,
>
> that One wherein abide all things existing.

In a later hymn, this explanation is questioned and the thinker speculates that it is impossible even for the god of creation to know why the universe came into being:

> None knoweth whence creation has arisen;
>
> And whether he has or has not produced it:
>
> He who surveys it in the highest heaven,
>
> He only knows, or haply he may know not.

Harappa's Fall and Aryan Dominance

During the early centuries of the Aryan migrations, which began around 1500 B.C.E., civilization disappeared from India. Pastoralism dominated Indian economic life as sedentary agriculture retreated with the fleeing Harappan peoples. A well-defined elite gave way to feisty chieftains chosen for their popularity among their warrior followers. A complex division of labor and responsibility gave way to highly egalitarian tribal societies that dominated sharply separated subject populations. State control and standardization were replaced by fractious warrior bands and political chaos.

With the spread of cultivation among the invading tribes and the growth of trade some centuries after the fall of Harappa, the basis for civilization again emerged. The small kingdoms that arose in the foothills of the Himalayas and the upper Ganges plains combined the ingredients that would give rise to India's great classical civilizations. These civilizations produced a succession of wealthy and far-flung empires; gave rise to two major religions, Hinduism and Buddhism, as well as a variety of lesser-known faiths; and produced splendid art, architecture, philosophy, and literature. But the new patterns of civilized life that developed in the last centuries B.C.E. diverged widely from those established by the Harappans. Although some Harappan symbols and beliefs were adopted by the Aryans and other invaders, Harappan civilization became little more than a memory.

A Bend in the River and the Beginnings of China

At about the time the Aryan invasions began in south Asia in the mid-2nd millennium B.C.E., early Chinese civilization was taking shape along the Huanghe, or Yellow River. Established by nomadic warrior peoples similar in many ways to the Aryans, the Shang phase of Chinese civilization lasted more than six centuries. In this era the vital irrigation systems that earlier inhabitants of the Yellow River basin had begun were greatly expanded and improved. The peoples of that region also developed a system of writing that has proved to be a critical source of identity, unity, and civilized development among the Chinese from Shang times to the present day.

Humanlike creatures as well as human beings have lived on the north China plain for hundreds of thousands of years. Peking man, one of the most famous hominids (two-legged primates) had campsites along the Fen River nearly 400,000 years ago, and several Paleolithic sites have been uncovered along the **Yellow River** where it arcs through the Ordos desert (Map 3.2). From Neolithic times (c. 8500–3500 B.C.E.) cultivating peoples gravitated to the lands that make up the base of the **Ordos bulge,** where conditions were suitable for sedentary agriculture and human settlement.

The region abounded in rich **loess,** a fine-grained, yellow-brown soil deposited by powerful winds from central Asia in prehistoric times. In places, this extremely fertile soil had built up over thousands of millennia to depths of over 300 feet. The Yellow River was named for the peculiar color of the soil that is washed into the river. Rich soil and the abundant supplies of water in areas near the Yellow River and its tributaries made the southern portions of the Ordos bulge and the areas eastward along the north China plain suitable for intensive grain cultivation and dense settlement. In addition, the region was shielded by mountains to the west and south but open to trade and migratory movements from the grasslands of the northwest.

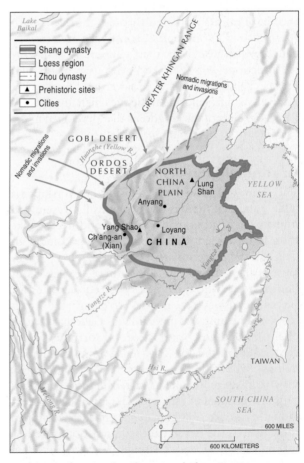

Map 3.2 *China in the Shang and Zhou Eras*

By 4000 B.C.E., human communities supported by sedentary agriculture were spread across the loess zone. These communities developed into two widely spread cultural complexes that laid the basis for the Shang dynasty and Chinese civilization. Both the Yangshao culture (c. 2500–2000 B.C.E.) and the Longshan culture (c. 2000–1500 B.C.E.) were based on very different mixes of agriculture and hunting. In the Yangshao period, hunting and fishing predominated, supplemented by foods supplied by shifting cultivation. By the Longshan period, the cultivation of grain—millet in particular—was the central preoccupation, and extensive farming made it possible for the inhabitants of the Yellow River region to support large, permanent villages surrounded by walls of stamped earth.

Increasingly elaborate irrigation systems were vital to the expanding agrarian base of society. The shallow bed of the river after it empties onto the plains of north China, and the large quantities of silt it carries, make it particularly treacherous in the spring. The melting snows of the Tibetan plateau and Kunlun mountains turn the river into a raging torrent capable of flooding large portions of the plains. From ancient times, controlling the river by building and maintaining great earthen dikes has been a major preoccupation of *peasants*—subsistence-oriented farmers—and the ruling classes.

These concerns may have given rise to China's first rulers and prompted a high level of community and intervillage cooperation. It is significant that one of the most abused of China's early and semimythical leaders was a man named Kun, who proved incapable of controlling a succession of great floods. His son, **Yu,** who devised an effective system of flood control, has been revered for millennia as one of the great monarchs of China's mythical golden age. When later thinkers such as Confucius searched China's past for leaders whose skill and virtue might be emulated in their own times, men such as Yu came readily to mind.

The Warrior Kings of the Shang Era

Semilegendary Chinese accounts tell us that Yu, the father of north China's great network of dikes and canals, also founded China's first kingdom, **Xia.** Because no archeological sites connected to Xia have been found, it is possible that the kingdom was purely the fabrication of later writers. But in the centuries before 1500 B.C.E., numerous small kingdoms had begun to emerge south of the Ordos bulge and east along the north China plain. Most of them were ruled by the nomadic tribal groups that continued to filter into the area from the north and west.

In this region of different ethnic and linguistic groups, a distinctive Chinese culture formed. Key features of this culture included its cooking vessels and cuisine, its reliance on cracked animal bones for divination, its domestication of the silkworm and use of silk fabrics for clothing, and its practice of ancestor worship. The form of ancestor worship followed also suggests that Chinese culture was already patrilineal. By 1500 B.C.E., one of the tribes in the Ordos region, the Shang, conquered most of the other tribes and established a kingdom that would lay the foundations of Chinese civilization.

Until recent decades we knew little more about the **Shang** than about their Xia predecessors. But extensive excavation of Shang sites at Anyang, Zhengzhou, and elsewhere have given us insights into many aspects of Shang culture and society. In some respects they were very much like those of the Aryans, who were conquering northern India during this same period. Like the Aryans, the Shang were warlike nomads. They fought on horseback and from chariots with deadly bronze weapons. Non-Shang subject peoples provided the foot soldiers that made up the bulk of their armies. Like those of Aryan India and Homeric Greece, Shang battles were wild clashes between massed soldiers that hinged on hand-to-hand combat between a few champions on each side. But unlike the Aryans and ancient Greeks, the Shang warriors were ruled by strong kings, who drew on their vassals' energies and military prowess to build an extensive empire.

The Shang monarch was seen as the intermediary between the Supreme Being, *Shangdi*, and ordinary mortals. His kingdom was viewed as the center of the world, and he claimed dominion over all humankind. Shang rulers directed the affairs of state and bore ritual responsibilities for the fertility of their kingdom and the well-being of their subjects. In the springtime, they participated in special ceremonies that included a symbolic mating with female fertility spirits. In times of drought and famine, Shang rulers, or perhaps designated surrogates, were obliged to perform ritual dances in the nude. The dancer—presumably the surrogate—was later burned alive to placate the spirits whose anger had caused the natural calamities.

Shang Society

Shang monarchs were served by a sizable bureaucracy in the capital city at Anyang and the surrounding areas. But most of the peasant and artisan populations of the kingdom were governed by **vassal retainers:** subordinate leaders serving the king and great lords and usually bound to them by personal ties. These officials were recruited from the former ruling families and the aristocratic classes of the many subordinate states. The vassals depended on the produce and labor of the commoners in these areas to support their families and military forces. In return for grants of control over varying numbers of peasants, warrior aristocrats collected tribute (usually in the form of agricultural produce), which went to support the monarch and his court. They supplied soldiers for the king's armies in times of war, and they kept the peace and administered justice among the peasants and townspeople.

Shang rulers and their families, servants, and noble retainers lived within walled towns in large compounds that housed **extended families.** These extended families consisted of several generations of the family patriarch's sons and grandsons and their wives. As in Aryan India, family life, at least among the upper classes, was dominated by the elder men in the household. At marriage, a woman went to live with her husband's family. Unswerving obedience was expected of both women and younger men. Within their own households and family spheres, patriarchs and husbands exercised absolute authority. Their commands were carried down the family hierarchy from elder to younger brother and from mother-in-law to young wife.

Judging from later social arrangements in China, the extended family pattern was widespread only among elite groups who had the resources to support large households with many servants. Ordinary peasants, who made up the great majority of the population, lived in modified **nuclear families:** households consisting of husband and wife, their children, and perhaps a grandmother or orphaned cousin. It is likely that peasant families were as male-dominated and patrilocal (the wife living in her husband's village) as those of the elite.

Peasants were in effect the servants of the nobles. By Shang times they were growing a wide range of crops, but their staple foods were millet, wheat, beans, and rice. They cultivated the land in the village in cooperative work teams using a variety of wooden hoes, spades, and crude plows. They lived in sunken houses of stamped earth and made offerings to local gods of the soil and hearth.

Although the peasants had limited opportunities for social and economic advancement, they were better off than most of the slaves who made up the lowest strata of society in the Shang era. It is likely that many of the artisans were slaves, but some were free and quite prosperous. This latter group probably was engaged in highly skilled crafts, such as weaving silk textiles and casting bronze. Artisan dwellings were located outside the walls of Shang towns, and some were surprisingly large and elaborate.

Shang Culture

Like the elites of many early civilizations, the Shang rulers and nobility were preoccupied with rituals, oracles, and sacrifices. In addition to the fertility functions of the ruler, the entire elite was involved in persuading spirits to provide good crops and large families. Shang artistic expression reached its peak in the ornately carved and expertly cast bronze vessels that were used to make these offerings. Offerings included fine grain, incense, wine, and animals, but Shang records also tell of water festivals at which ritual contests were waged between rival boats, each attempting to sink the other. Those aboard the losing craft drowned when it capsized, and they were offered up to the deities responsible for fertility and good harvests.

War captives and servants were buried with deceased Shang rulers and major officials. Like the pharaohs of ancient Egypt, the kings of Shang went to the otherworld accompanied by their wives, servants, and loyal retainers as well as their favorite horses, hunting dogs, war chariots, and weapons. Ancestral veneration grew into a cult of the royal clan that involved sacrifices of war captives, mass burials, and the construction of tombs for the emperors.

Concern for abundant harvests and victory in war led the Shang elite to put great stock in the predictions of shamans, or priests, who served as **oracles:** sacred people who could prophesy the future. As the bronze vessel in Figure 3.5 shows, much of Shang artistic expression went into producing the ritual objects used by the oracles. Warriors about to go into

Visualizing the Past

Mapping the Rise of Civilizations

The earliest human civilizations arose in regions with substantial similarities in terms of topography—contours and configuration of the land—and other geographical features. The maps below depict three of these original centers of civilization: Egypt, Harappa, and China. they illustrate a number of key features of these areas, including mountains, plains, plateaus and deserts, river systems, trading routes, and locations of neighboring nomadic peoples.

Study each of these maps, identifying the key components which all of these early cradles of civilization have in common. Then identify differences between them in terms of physical features, checking these differences against the discussions of the history of these early civilizations in Chapters 2 and 3. Decide the ways in which these differences affected the course of civilized development in each area in ancient times.

Questions: What key physical features are shared by the areas where civilizations first developed? Which of these are critical for the development of sedentary agriculture in each civilization? What roles did the presence of large bodies of water, in the form of rivers or access to the sea, play in the rise and expansion of civilized centers and contacts with other civilized areas? What impact did geographical factors and interactions with nomadic peoples have on the long-term persistence or disappearance of civilized life in these different areas?

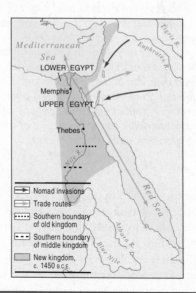

Figure 3.5 *This elaborately decorated bronze incense vessel from the Shang era, with its whimsical horse and catlike figure, shows the sophisticated artistic expression achieved very early in Chinese history. It also demonstrates a high level of metalworking ability, which carried over into Shang weapons and tools. Although the design of these ritual vessels often was abstract, mythical creatures such as dragons and sacred birds were deftly cast in bronzes that remain some of the great treasures of Chinese art.*

battle, officials embarking on long journeys, or families negotiating marriage alliances routinely consulted these oracles to ensure that their efforts would turn out well. This reliance on the shamans strongly influenced beliefs and behavior in the Shang era.

The actual procedures followed by the shamans who presided over these rituals gave rise to perhaps the single most important element in Chinese cul-ture: writing. Since pre-Shang times, Chinese oracles had based their predictions on readings taken from animal bones or tortoise shells (Figure 3.6). A bone or shell was drilled with a hole and seared with a red-hot iron poker. The bone or shell cracked, and the patterns of the cracks were interpreted by a shaman or priest. Over time the practice evolved of inscribing the bones and shells with painted designs that became part of the patterns the shamans read. These designs gradually were standardized and came to form the basis of a written Chinese language.

Like the hieroglyphics of the ancient Egyptians, early Chinese characters were pictographic. Thus, they readily conveyed the ideas they were intended to express. The original character for the sun, for example, was a circle with a dot in the center, the character for a tree was a single tree, and a forest was a set of three trees. Combinations of characters made it possible for the Chinese elite to convey increasingly complex ideas. The character for emperor, for example, combined elements of the **ideographs** for *king, heaven, earth,* and *harmony.*

Over time the number of characters has increased substantially. By the end of the Shang period, there were an estimated 3000 characters. A well-educated scholar in the modern era would need to master some 8000 characters. The way they are written has also changed significantly. Many characters have been simplified, and most have been stylized so that they are less pictographic. The bones or bronze vessels on which the characters were originally carved gradually gave way to bamboo slips, silk scrolls, and wooden plates, and they in turn were supplanted in the 1st century C.E. by paper (a critical Chinese invention). Assorted fine brushes and inks were developed to paint the characters, which themselves became a major mode of artistic expression in later periods.

Writing and Chinese Identity

Writing became the key to Chinese identity and the growth of civilization in China. The peoples of the loess region and the north China plain spoke a bewildering variety of languages, often unintelligible from one group to the next. They were surrounded by nomadic herders to the north and shifting cultivators to the south, whose contacts with and movements into the loess zone further complicated the linguistic muddle. But the use of increasingly standardized and sophisticated written characters provided the bond

Figure 3.6 *The written Chinese language began as symbols painted on bones that oracles used to predict the future. Like the hieroglyphics of the ancient Egyptians, early Chinese characters, such as those illustrated here, were pictographic. Over time they were simplified, stylized, and standardized, but an educated person had to memorize several thousand to be literate.*

that gave growing numbers of these loess zone peoples a common identity. This sense of identity was felt most keenly by the elite groups, who monopolized the use of the characters, but eventually it filtered down to the cultivating and artisan classes. With the persistence and growth of this identity, the Chinese people entered history for the first time.

The Decline of the Shang and the Era of Zhou Dominance

 By the 11th century B.C.E., the decentralized Shang political system had long been in decline. In the west of the multilingual kingdom, a newly arrived nomadic people, the **Zhou,** had set up a vassal state that originally recognized Shang rule. The Zhou are believed to have been Turkic-speaking peoples from central Asia. By the end of the 12th century B.C.E., the Zhou had openly seized power and established a dynasty that was to last until late in the 3rd century B.C.E. In the early Zhou period, a distinct class of scholar-administrators, the **shi,** began to emerge, and Chinese civilization expanded as far south as the Yangtze River.

In the early centuries of their reign, the Zhou rulers exercised more power than their Shang predecessors. Under **Wu,** the military commander who had defeated the Shang, and his brother, the Duke of Zhou, the empire was greatly expanded, especially to the east and south. Because the original Zhou capital at **Xian** was too far to the west to effectively control

these new areas, a second capital was built at **Loyang,** hundreds of miles to the east (Map 3.2). Wu and other early Zhou rulers governed their vast domains through a hierarchy of vassals, who were controlled to a much greater extent than had been the case under the Shang. Many of the most powerful vassals were relatives, fellow clansmen, or long-standing allies of the Zhou household. Thus, ties of kinship cemented their loyalty and obedience to the Zhou overlords. In turn, the vassals controlled lesser vassals further down the hierarchy, who were often their own subordinates or relatives.

In the early Zhou period, formal oaths of allegiance and regularized fief-granting procedures transformed the Shang vassal system into a more genuine feudal order. Here, as in later political systems of this type, **feudalism** stressed mutual obligation and benefits within the ruling clan. The Zhou rulers granted to their loyal warrior retainers *fiefs:* permission to extract revenue and services from peasant villages. In return, the favored vassals pledged their loyalty to the dynasty in a special ceremony in the ruler's palace. During the ceremony the new fiefholder was given a clump of earth, symbolizing the land and villages granted to him by the monarch. At the same time, a charter of his duties to his ruler and his rights as a fiefholder was presented to the assembled court.

Zhou monarchs had virtually no control over the fiefdoms beyond those in the central core regions. If a vassal stopped sending tribute to the capital or refused requests to muster troops for war or laborers for Zhou building projects, he was in effect declaring war and risking annihilation. As long as the Zhou overlords were strong, it was safer, and profitable enough, to pass on revenue to the court and to rally to the Zhou overlord's call to battle. But when the dynasty weakened, the flow of revenue from the vassals' domains dried up and their troops were increasingly used for wars between the feudal lords or in alliances against the Zhou rulers.

Changes in the Social Order

Two developments worked against the continuance of the feudal system. The first was the elaboration of an ideology that the Zhou rulers used to legitimize their rule. When King Wu overthrew the Shang dynasty, he claimed that the Shang had lost the **Mandate of Heaven,** and thus no longer deserved the allegiance of their vassals. The concept of the Mandate of Heaven provided a powerful rationale for the Zhou monarchs to strive to centralize authority. Wu charged that his successful bid for the throne was proof that the Zhou had the moral fiber and leadership potential to inherit the heavenly mandate the Shang had betrayed.

This appeal to a supernatural source of power was a common feature of preindustrial monarchies throughout the world, and it became a pillar of the political system in China. It also meant that the Zhou had established the principle that supreme political authority was granted by heaven, not by a ruler's vassals or the common people. This claim would greatly enhance the capacity of the Zhou and subsequent royal houses to rule as absolutist and authoritarian monarchs. But it also contained a potentially critical check on their powers, which was to be explored by Chinese social thinkers in the late Zhou era. If a ruler governed by virtue of the Mandate of Heaven, it was possible—as the Shang precedent clearly demonstrated—for a monarch and royal house to fail in their duties and lose the mandate. In that case, it was legitimate for their subjects to overthrow them and replace them with a new imperial house.

The second development working against the persistence of feudalism in China involved the emergence of an alternative to the military retainers who governed most of the empire. During the early Zhou era, the small corps of professional bureaucrats who had once served the Shang rulers began to grow in size and expertise. These administrators, who were the best-educated men in the empire, came to be known in the late Zhou period (c. 770–400 B.C.E.) as *shi*, or men of service. Their literacy and willingness to serve as scribes, clerks, advisors, and overseers won them a livelihood as administrators, both at the court and in the palaces of the fiefholders and their subordinate vassals. Some of these aspiring administrators were supported by grants of villages, but others, particularly those at the royal court, were paid regular salaries out of the imperial treasury. They performed a wide range of services that could be embarrassingly menial; some even had to cultivate small plots of land to supplement their meager salaries. Increasingly, however, they came to specialize in keeping records; running particular departments, such as public works or war; or organizing palace rituals and ceremonies. There is some evidence that even before the end of the early Zhou era in the mid-8th century B.C.E., the most favored of these administrators had begun to amass considerable influence as advisors to the ruler and powerful nobles.

New Patterns of Life

In the early Zhou era, the conquerors lived separately from the subjugated "black-haired people." This division appears to confirm the supposition that the Zhou were originally Turkic tribespeople with lighter hair and eye coloring than the peoples they found in the loess soil region and along the north China plain. In the twin capitals of Xian and Loyang, the Zhou and their servants lived in one side of the walled city, while peoples of other ethnic groups lived in the other.

Zhou vassals lived away from the capitals and resided in walled garrison towns. Each town was laid out on a rectangular grid with two main roads that crossed at a central square. Servants, artisans, and slaves lived in or near the garrison towns. Beyond them stretched the villages and tilled fields of the serfs who made up most of the empire's population. Their staple crops remained millet and wheat, but rice was widely cultivated in the eastern and southern portions of the Zhou domains.

The introduction of better farm implements (Figure 3.7) and the extension of the irrigation system contributed to higher levels of productivity. But much of the increase went to fill the coffers of the lords and the Zhou court rather than to the peasants themselves. The peasants were burdened by their lords' regular demands for labor on road, building, and irrigation projects. They were also obliged to feed and house the lords' retainers when they journeyed from the garrison towns. In times of war, the peasants marched on foot alongside the chariots and cavalry of the lords' army.

As time passed, the lords' demands grew more and more oppressive. A rare insight into the peasants'

Figure 3.7 *This carving from the Han era depicts a four-pronged hoe that was used to turn over the soil for cultivation. An earlier wooden hoe may have been the single most important tool of the Shang and Zhou eras. It was far more efficient for preparing sizable plots of land than simple digging sticks that had been used to poke holes in the soil to plant seeds. The hoe made Chinese agriculture much more productive and thus capable of supporting a larger population.*

plight is provided by a poem from the *Book of Odes* that was written in the late Zhou era:

Big rat, big rat,

Do not eat my millet!

Three years I have served you,

But you will not care for me.

I am going to leave you

And go to that happy land;

Happy land, happy land;

Where I will find my place.

Big rat, big rat,

Do not eat my sprouts!

Three years I have served you

But you give me no comfort.

I am going to leave you

And go to those happy fields;

Happy fields, happy fields;

Who there shall long moan?

Peasants at some distance from their lords' garrison towns appear to have been the best off. In fact, communications were so poor in many parts of the empire that local lords were content to leave peasant communities alone if they regularly supplied tribute and gifts on special occasions. The peasants in the outlying villages were, in effect, free farmers. However, the peasant lament just quoted probably more accurately captures the reality of life for most peasants in the Zhou period.

Migrations and the Expansion of the Chinese Core

Throughout the centuries of Zhou rule, both the area controlled by its vassals and the lands occupied by peoples who identified themselves as Chinese grew steadily. New agricultural tools and techniques of production stimulated population growth, which in turn led to the extension of cultivation into new areas along the north China plain and then southward along the coast. Periodic nomadic raids and, at times, lasting conquests pushed Chinese peasant migrants to the south and east.

Whatever their reasons for migrating, in the Zhou era hundreds of thousands of Chinese people moved down the Yellow River, into the Shandong peninsula, and then south across the flatlands to first the Huai and later the great Yangtze River basins (see Map 3.2). As they advanced, non-Chinese peoples, who were hunters and gatherers and shifting cultivators, fell back into the hills to the west of the great plains and then to the mountainous region south of the Yangtze. By the end of the Zhou era, Chinese civilization straddled the two great river systems—the Yellow and the Yangtze—that have been the heart of Chinese civilization for thousands of years. The basin of the Yellow River was securely Chinese, despite the continuing nomadic threat. The Yangtze had barely been reached, but the enormous agricultural potential of the rice-growing, monsoon-watered south had begun to be tapped.

Cultural Change in the Early Zhou Period

The Zhou influx into the loess heartland of early China strengthened the dominance of males within the family and in society. Perhaps the key roles played by males in ancestor veneration contributed to their increased authority. The cults of royal and familial ancestors became the centers of religious observance. Human sacrifice ended, but philosophical speculation remained minimal as increasingly elaborate rites and ceremonies developed around the worship of deceased members of the family, clan, and dynasty. Family patriarchs and monarchs monopolized these ceremonies designed to win the blessings of the ancestors or heaven, an abstract realm called **Tian.**

As in Aryan India, more and more stress was placed on the importance of performing these and other ceremonies flawlessly. An obsession with correctly performed rites led to the elite's more generalized concern with refined manners and proper decorum. The rough nomads had rapidly settled down to enjoy the amenities of the rich and powerful among the civilized.

The End of the Early or Western Zhou

By the 8th century B.C.E., Zhou power was in decline. Its control over its vassals had diminished dramatically, and several of the vassals' domains had grown powerful enough to openly challenge the overlordship of the dynasty. In 771 B.C.E., an allied group of northern nobles attacked Xian. The Zhou ruler was killed in battle, and in the months that followed, most of the western portions of the kingdom were lost to leaders of the vassal alliance or to nomadic invaders eager to take advantage of internal divisions among the Chinese. Retainers loyal to the Zhou managed to rescue a young prince and escort him safely to Loyang. The shift to the eastern capital marks the end of the early or western Zhou era.

A less powerful eastern Zhou kingdom survived for over five centuries more. The territory it controlled shrank to little beyond the capital and its immediate environs. Zhou vassals warred continuously, using the defense of the royal house to legitimize their attacks and conquests. Over time, successful lords annexed the holdings of defeated neighbors, and several rival kingdoms emerged in place of the fiefdoms that had existed in the early Zhou era. The growing chaos and widespread suffering that resulted prompted a reaction on the part of

In Depth

The Legacy of Asia's First Civilizations

In their size, complexity, and longevity, the first civilizations to develop in south Asia and China match, and in some respects surpass, the earliest civilizations that arose in Mesopotamia and Egypt. But the long-term impact of the Harappan civilization in the Indus

basin was strikingly different from that of the Shang and Zhou civilizations in north China. The loess zone and north China plain where the Shang and Zhou empires took hold became the center of a continuous civilization that was to last into the 20th century C.E. and, some historians would argue, to the present day. Although regions farther south, such as the Yangtze basin, would in some time periods enjoy political, economic, and cultural predominance within China, the capital and center of Chinese civilization repeatedly returned to the Yellow River area and the north China plain. By contrast, the Indus valley proved capable of nurturing a civilization that endured for more than a thousand years. But when Harappa collapsed, the plains of the Indus were bypassed in favor of the far more lush and extensive lands in the basin of the Ganges River network to the east. Although the Indus would later serve, for much shorter time spans, as the seat of empires, the core areas of successive Indian civilizations were far to the east and south.

The contrast between the fates of the original geographic centers of Indian and Chinese civilizations is paralleled by the legacies of the civilizations themselves. Harappa was destroyed, and it disappeared from history for thousands of years. Although the peoples who built the Indus complex left their mark on subsequent Indian culture, they did not pass on the fundamental patterns of civilized life that they had evolved. Their mother-goddess, yoga positions, and the dancing god of fertility endured. Some of their symbols, such as the swastika and the *lingam* (a phallic image, usually made of stone), were prominent in later artistic and religious traditions. The Harappans' tanks, or public bathing ponds, remain a central feature of Indian cities, particularly in the south. Their techniques of growing rice and cotton were preserved by cultivating peoples fleeing nomadic incursions and were later taken up by the newly arrived Indo-Aryan tribes.

Nearly everything else was lost. In contrast to the civilizations of Mesopotamia, which fell but were replaced by new civilizations that preserved and built on the achievements of their predecessors, much of what the Harappan peoples had accomplished had to be redone by later civilized peoples. The cities of the Indus civilization were destroyed, and comparable urban centers did not reappear in south Asia for more than a thousand years. The Harappans' remarkably advanced standards for measuring distance and weight ceased to be used. Their system of writing was forgotten, and when rediscovered it was celebrated as an intriguing but very dead language from the past. Harappan skills in community planning, sewage control, and engineering were meaningless to the nomadic peoples who took control of their homelands. The Harappan penchant for standardization, discipline, and state control was profoundly challenged by the brawl-

ing, independent-minded warriors who supplanted them as masters of the Indian subcontinent.

In contrast to the civilization of the Indus valley, the original civilization of China has survived nomadic incursions and natural catastrophes and has profoundly influenced the course of Chinese history. Shang irrigation and dike systems and millet and wheat cultivation provided the basis for the innovations and expansion of subsequent dynasties. Shang and Zhou fortified towns and villages surrounded with stamped earth walls have persisted as the predominant patterns of settlement throughout Chinese history. The founders of the Shang and Zhou dynasties have been revered by scholars and peasants alike as philosopher-kings who ought to be emulated by leaders at all levels. The Shang and Zhou worship of heaven and their veneration of ancestors have remained central to Chinese religious belief and practice for thousands of years. The concept of the Mandate of Heaven has been pivotal in Chinese political thinking and organization.

Above all, the system of writing that was originally formulated for Shang oracles developed into the key means of communication between the elites of the many peoples who lived in the core regions of Chinese civilization. The scholar-bureaucrats, who developed this written language and also profited the most from it, soon emerged as the dominant force in Chinese culture and society. Chinese characters provided the basis for the educational system and bureaucracy that were to hold Chinese civilization together through thousands of years of invasions and political crises.

The reasons for the differing legacies of Harappan and early Chinese civilizations are numerous and complex. But critical to the disappearance of the first and the resilience of the second were different patterns of interaction between the sedentary peoples who built early civilizations and the nomadic herders who challenged them. In India, the nomadic threat was remote—perhaps nonexistent—for centuries. The Harappan peoples were deficient in military technology and organization. When combined with natural calamities, the waves of warlike nomads migrating into the Indus region proved too much for the Harappan peoples to resist or absorb. The gap between the nomads' herding culture and the urban, agriculture-based Harappan civilization was too great to be bridged. Conflict between them may well have proved fatal to a civilization long in decline.

By contrast, the loess regions of northern China were open to invasions or migrations on the part of the nomadic herding peoples who lived to the north

(continued)

and west. Peoples from these areas moved almost continuously into the core zones of Chinese civilization. The constant threat posed by the nomads forced the peoples of the north China plain to develop the defenses and military technology needed to defend against nomadic raids or bids for lasting conquest. Contrasting cultures and ways of life strengthened the sense of identity of the cultivating peoples. The obvious nomadic presence prodded these same peoples to unite under strong rulers against the outsiders who did not share Chinese culture. Constant interaction with the nomads led the Shang peoples to develop a culture that was receptive to outside influences, social structures, and political systems. Nomadic energies reinvigorated and enriched the kingdoms of the Shang and the Zhou, in contrast to India, where they proved catastrophic for the isolated and far less adaptable peoples of the Indus valley civilization.

Questions: Compare the early civilizations of India and China with those of Sumer and Egypt. Which are more similar in terms of longevity? Which factors were critical in the failure of the Indus civilization to persist? Which best explain Chinese longevity? Are these the same as those that account for the long life of Egyptian civilization? Why did the Indus civilization have such a limited impact on subsequent civilizations in India, in contrast to Sumer and the other civilizations of Mesopotamia?

the shi bureaucrats, a reaction that would produce some of China's greatest thinkers and radically alter the course of Chinese civilization.

GLOBAL CONNECTIONS: Contrasting Legacies: Harappan and Early Chinese Civilizations

China, like the early civilizations of Mesopotamia, was one of the great sources of civilizing influences in human history as a whole. The area affected by ideas developed in China was less extensive than that to which the peoples of Mesopotamia gave writing, law, and their other great achievements. But contacts with China provided critical impetus for the development of civilization in Japan, Korea, and Vietnam. Writing and political organization were two areas in which the earliest formulations of Chinese civilization vitally affected other peoples. In later periods, Chinese thought and other modes of cultural expression such as art, architecture, and etiquette also strongly influenced the growth of civilized life throughout east Asia.

China's technological innovation was to have an impact on global civilization comparable to that of early Mesopotamia. Beginning with increasingly sophisticated irrigation systems, the Chinese have devised a remarkable share of humankind's basic machines and engineering principles. In the Shang and Zhou eras they also pioneered key processes such as silk manufacturing.

By contrast, because of the processes that saw it virtually disappear from Indian history for thousands of years, Harappan civilization did not have a lasting impact on the human experience as a whole. Traces of the oldest of the civilizations of south Asia, such as yogic practices, have spread worldwide, but more fundamental elements of the civilization, such as its remarkable urban planning and advanced sewage systems, have had no discernable impact on the development of city living in other regions and later times. Despite evidence of extensive commercial links between Harappa and neighboring civilizations in the Middle East, there is little to indicate that the latter were significantly affected by imports from the Indus region. The fact that Harappa proved much more vulnerable than early Chinese civilizations to natural calamities and climate change, as well as the infiltration of large numbers of nomadic herding peoples, goes far to account for the sharply contrasting global legacies of these two core regions of human civilization. Endurance and longevity not only provide more time for a civilized center to disseminate its ideas and material culture, but they also suggest to other peoples that borrowing might enhance their chances to build powerful, wealthy, and enduring civilizations of their own.

Further Readings

The best, brief introduction to the Indus valley civilization remains the relevant sections of A. L. Basham's *The Wonder That Was India* (1954). For the most authoritative, up-to-date and detailed coverage of all aspects of the civilization, see Gregory L. Possehl's *Indus Age: The Beginnings* (1999). For a sense of the state of archeological research and recent discoveries, see the sometimes technical essays in Possehl, ed.,

Harappan Civilization: A Contemporary Perspective (1982), and N. N. Bhattacharyya, *Ancient Indian History and Civilization: Trends and Perspectives* (1988). Earlier book-length studies that place Harappa in the context of Indian prehistory more generally include Stuart Piggot's *Prehistoric India* (1950) and Bridget and Stuart Allchin's *The Birth of Indian Civilization* (1968). Romilla Thapar's *History of India* (1966) has a superb chapter on Aryan culture and society. Interesting works that deal with social life and gender relations in the Vedic period include the textual analyses in Laurie L. Patton, ed., *Jewels of Authority: Women and Textual Tradition in Hindu India* (2002); C. Chakraborty's account of *Common Life in the Rigeveda and Atharvaveda* (1977); and the lively and contentious arguments in *Ancient India* (1969), by D. D. Kosambi. On ancient Indian political systems, see A. C. Pandey, *Government in Ancient India* (2000).

For ancient China, the most current interpretations can be found in the superb essays in Michael Loewe and Edward L. Shaughnessy, eds., *The Cambridge History of Ancient China: From the Origins of Civilization to 221 B.C.* (1999). For earlier accounts that are still readable and informative, see Wolfram Eberhard's *History of China* (1977 ed.) and the early portions of Michael Loewe's *Imperial China* (1965). More detailed (and technical) accounts of the formation of China through the early Zhou era include Kwang-chih Chang's *The Archeology of Ancient China* (1977) and *Shang Civilization* (1980); H. G. Creel's *The Origins of Statecraft in Ancient China* (1970); and Ping-ti Ho's *The Cradle of the East* (1975). K. C. Wu's *The Chinese Heritage* (1982) provides the fullest political history of the Shang and early Zhou eras, which can be supplemented by Roger Ames, *The Art of Rulership: A Study of Ancient Chinese Political Thought* (1994). The nomadic impact on the formation of China is treated mainly from the Chinese perspective by Nicola Di Cosmo, *Ancient China and Its Enemies* (2002). Early Chi-

nese cities are explored in Wu Liangyong, *A Brief History of Chinese City Planning* (1985), and early Chinese accomplishments in technology are surveyed in *China: 7000 Years of Discovery* (1983) compiled by the Chinese Scientific and Technological Museum, Beijing.

On the Web

An overview of early Indian history and culture may be found at http://www.historyofindia.com/ancfrm.html. Two principal cities of the Indus Valley, Harappa and Mohenjo Daro, can be visited virtually at http://www.harappa.com/welcome.html and http://www.harappa.com/indus/slideindex.html. The docks that carried their products to Sumer and beyond are examined at http://www.harappa.com/indus/slideindex.html, http://www.harappa.com/lothal/1.html, and http://www.itihaas.com/ancient/indus4.html. The evolution of the oldest of the Hindu scriptures, the Vedas and the *Upanishads*, are discussed at http://campus.northpark.edu/history/WebChron/India/Upanishads.html and at http://sanatan.intnet.mu/.

The Yellow River as the cradle of Chinese civilization is analyzed at http://www.cis.umassd.edu/~gleung/. Early Chinese oracle bones and their place in the evolution of writing are explored at http://acc6.its.brooklyn.cuny.edu/~phalsall/images/shnagbon.jpg. Images drawn from early Chinese history and culture can be viewed at http://www.chaos.umd.edu/history/ancient1.html and http://www.chinapage.com/chinese.html. Early Chinese ethical systems are discussed at http://www.san.beck.org/EC13-Chou.html. An introduction to Chinese history prior to the Chin dynasty (221 B.C.E.) is provided at http://asterius.com/china/ and http://www.chaos.umd.edu/history/ancient1.html.

PART II

The Classical Period in World History

Introduction

Between 1000 and 500 B.C.E., a classical period took shape in several centers of Asia, northern Africa, and southern Europe. These centers lasted until roughly the 5th century C.E. The classical civilizations built on the achievements of earlier river valley civilizations. Originating in China, India, and the Mediterranean, each major classical civilization overlapped one or more of the earlier centers geographically. But the pace of change stepped up in each classical center. The innovations were dramatic: Empires developed as a political form, and great thinkers and religious leaders drew traditional cultural elements together in striking new statements that were the basis for whole new cultures.

However, many regions and human societies were not connected to the classical centers. In these regions, important developments occurred during the classical period, yielding new civilizations, as in the Americas, or more advanced agricultural economies. In short, the world after 1000 B.C.E. divided into three main parts: one in which the roots of civilization were well established, another in which complex societies were first forming, and a third in which alternative forms of organization, built around nomadic economies, were consolidating. Coverage of the classical period must embrace all three major sectors. Civilization, nomadism, and contact—key themes in world history—all gained new dimensions during the classical period.

The Boundaries of Classical Civilizations

 Classical civilizations differed from their river valley ancestors in complexity. Their political institutions, commerce, and cultures became more elaborate. The classical civilizations also differed in geographic range: They extended over a much larger territory than the river valley societies had done, which meant a major expansion not only of civilization but of the need to integrate diverse regions and peoples.

The nature of the classical period can be described in two ways: by sketching the currents that set the new period in motion and those that drew it to a close, and by defining the distinctive characteristics of the classical civilizations.

No single event ushered in the classical period of history, which is one reason that pinning down a starting date is difficult. Nor were there dramatic technological breakthroughs of the sort that had prepared the rise of the first river valley civilizations, although the growing use of iron weaponry played a role. The classical period began soon after 1000 B.C.E.

One sign of the new era was the partial relocation of civilization centers: The heart of Indian civilization shifted from the Indus to the Ganges River valley as the Aryans cleared the dense forests of the northern Indian plains and spread cultivation. The expansion of China to the south had already begun in the early Zhou era, but it continued with the spread of Chinese culture and political forms into the Yangtze River valley and the mountain regions to the south and west. In the Middle East, a Persian state arose in Mesopotamia.

Geographic change was more dramatic in the eastern Mediterranean. From 800 B.C.E. onward, an important new center began to develop in Greece as the Indo-European invaders of the peninsula settled down. Greece used but greatly altered the scope of earlier cultural achievements from Crete, Mesopotamia, and Egypt, becoming a major source of innovation throughout the Mediterranean region.

The expansion of the civilization centers also brought new peoples into contact with civilization on the fringes of the great empires. During the classical period, nomadic groups in Europe and agricultural peoples outside China in eastern Asia began to learn what civilization was. Civilization had already moved into parts of sub-Saharan Africa through contacts with Egypt; some of the results fanned out into other parts of Africa south of the desert during the classical period. At the same time, the importance of interaction between nomadic groups and civilizations increased. Nomadic traders in central Asia played a vital role in international trade routes from eastern Asia to western Asia and Europe. Nomadic invasions periodically changed the face of civilizations themselves.

The end of the classical period, between the 3rd and 6th centuries C.E., was clearer than its beginning but hardly a unified event. Internal decay in the classical empires

5000 B.C.E.	2000 B.C.E.	1000 B.C.E.	750 B.C.E.	500 B.C.E.
5000 Early Japanese settlement	**2000** Germans settle in Denmark **1200–700** Vedas composed **1500–500** Polynesian migrations **1122–770** Initial Zhou kingdom	**1000** Germans expand southward **900** Maya begins **850–250** Chavin culture (Andes) **800** Rise of Greek city-states **800 B.C.E.–1000 C.E.** Bantu migration, sub-Saharan Africa **770–403** Later Zhou kingdom; beginning of China's classical period	**750–600** Meroë (Kush) rules Egypt **600** Zoroastrian religion in Iran **600** Legendary ruler in Japan **551–c. 233** Period of the great Chinese philosophers: Confucius, Laozi, Mencius, Legalists **550** Formation of Persian Empire **c. 542–483** Buddha	**500–449** Greek wars with Persia; Persia defeated **500–450** Beginnings of Roman republic **470–430** Height of Athenian culture; Socrates and Greek philosophical style **431 ff.** Peloponnesian Wars; decline of Greece **330** Alexander the Great **327–325** Alexander's invasion **322–185** Mauryan Empire **300–100** Hellenistic period **300 B.C.E.–900 C.E.** Height of Maya **264–140** Roman expansion in North Africa (Punic Wars) and eastern Mediterranean

combined with a new surge of invasions from central Asia to topple great states from China in the east to Rome in the west. The resultant reworking of civilization patterns was the trigger for yet another new period in world history after about 500 C.E.

The classical period thus was bounded at its beginnings by new sources of vigor and innovation, produced by adaptations in the original river valley centers after 1000 B.C.E., and at its end by huge dislocations caused by decay and invasion following a creative period stretching over a thousand years.

Regional Integration in the Classical Period

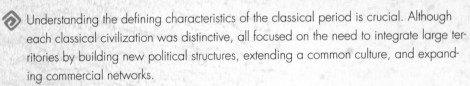 Understanding the defining characteristics of the classical period is crucial. Although each classical civilization was distinctive, all focused on the need to integrate large territories by building new political structures, extending a common culture, and expanding commercial networks.

In the economic sphere, classical civilizations created larger trading zones. The Mediterranean became a single economic region, first under Greek control and then under the imperial Romans. In this common market, local areas could maintain profitable specializations by trading with other Mediterranean areas. China helped link two major growing regions, one of wheat and millet and the other of rice, through rising internal trade. Indian trade, both from the Ganges region and through the efforts of seagoing merchants,

250 B.C.E.	1 C.E.	250 C.E.	500 C.E.	750 C.E.
221 Shi Huangdi proclaimed first emperor of China	**23–220** Later Han dynasty; invention of paper and compass	**300** Decline of Meroë	**451** First Hun invasions	**800–1300** Mississippian culture
202 B.C.E.–9 C.E. Initial Han dynasty; key technical developments of horse collar and water mill	**27** Augustus founds Roman Empire	**300** Spread of Buddhism	**476** Last Roman emperor in West	**900** Polynesians to New Zealand
200 B.C.E.–200 C.E. Greater Buddhist influence	**30** Crucifixion of Jesus	**300–400** Yamato claim imperial control of Japan	**527–565** Justinian Eastern emperor	**900–1200** Toltecs
133 ff. Decline of Roman republic	**88** Beginning of Han decline	**300–700** Rise of Axum; conversion to Christianity	**580 ff.** Spread of Buddhism in Japan	**1000** Height of kingdom of Ghana, Africa
100 Germans begin contact with Rome; Slavs migrate into eastern Europe	**106** Height of Roman territory	**300–900** Intermediate Horizon period (Andes)	**589–618** Sui dynasty	
	180 Beginning of decline of Rome	**300–1000** Second wave of Polynesian migrations to Hawaii	**600–647** Harsha's Empire	
	200–500 Nasca culture (Andes)	**312–337** Constantine; formation of Eastern Empire; adoption of Christianity	**618** Tang dynasty	
	200–700 Mochica culture (Andes)	**319–540** Gupta Empire	**700 ff.** Spread of Islam; trans-Sahara trade in Africa	
	200–1300 Anasazi in North America	**400** Chinese script imported		
	220 Last Han emperor deposed	**401 ff.** Large-scale Germanic invasions in Roman Empire		

fanned out through the subcontinent and across the Indian Ocean from the Red Sea in the west to the South China Sea in the east.

Cultural integration also was important in defining new civilization areas. Important cultural innovations emerged in the 6th and 5th centuries B.C.E. in all three classical centers and Persia. This cultural integration indicated a common need for a new definition of basic cultural values. Socratic philosophy and the great philosophical tradition in Greece, Confucianism and Daoism in China, and the spread of Zoroastrianism in Persia and Buddhism in India all emerged at roughly the same time, serving as major cultural orientations for these regions. The great classical works of Hindu philosophy also were written in this era. Basic classical styles in art and architecture also were shaped in this period and continued to define standard patterns. Hindu-derived art in India and classical Greco-Roman buildings in the West still shape artistic expression today.

Cultural changes provide one of the clearest opportunities to consider the impact of human agency, and many more creative individuals of the classical period can be examined by name than is true of the earlier civilizations. Major thinkers set new systems of thought in motion. But how much did they innovate? To what extent did they simply gather or record ideas that had accumulated as a result of more anonymous cultural activity? For example, Confucius explicitly stated that he was simply recording traditional wisdom. Furthermore, the uses of cultural systems often changed greatly after the original creative impulse. Buddhism retained some of the initial guidelines developed by Buddha himself, but it also shifted greatly as it became more popular and spread to wider areas.

Human agency was vital to the innovative qualities of the classical period, in political as well as cultural change, but it is not always easy to assess.

Cultural innovation was matched by dissemination through each civilization. Indian religious values spread through the subcontinent and moved steadily southward from centers along the northern rivers. Chinese philosophies and religions also spread among elites throughout the Middle Kingdom, building on the unified elite language, Mandarin. Greek language, art, and philosophy spread through the Mediterranean basin and the Middle East. The emergence of wide cultural zones defined by distinctive styles and systems of thought was a crucial development.

Finally, there was substantial political integration. Each of the three most durable centers of classical civilization formed huge regional empires for periods of several centuries. Persia, a fourth major center, also boasted a large empire for several centuries. The Chinese imperial system emerged as the fullest example of political integration. The ability to construct such large political units both reflected and promoted the other kinds of integration in each civilization.

Economic, cultural, and political integration meant that the great classical civilizations developed new abilities in internal communications, with enough shared language and shared technical systems to send messages over great distances. Road systems fanned out in classical China and in the great Indian and Roman empires. Bureaucracies and laws provided new unity as well, and military forces moved easily within each civilization.

The expansion of the largest civilizations allowed some important contacts among them. In addition to trade from China to the Mediterranean, even more important forms of cultural borrowing or diffusion arose in the classical period. India was particularly affected by cultural exchange from the Mediterranean region. More important was India's role in facilitating international trade and cultural influence as the economies of the classical civilizations reached their peaks in the first centuries C.E. Cross-civilization contacts were limited, however, and they did not shape the period as a whole. For example, elite Romans bought silk cloth made in China, but they did not know China directly; China was too distant, and regional traders divided the trading routes into separate segments. Nevertheless, a basic Afro-Eurasian framework was established that has steadily increased in size and importance to the present day.

There was even some movement toward more formal international relations, though only on a regional basis. Various local states sent emissaries to the Han emperor in eastern Asia. At the end of the period, Chinese students and merchants visited India to learn more about Buddhism. In the Mediterranean region, Greeks and then Romans exchanged emissaries with regional leaders, which helped coordinate the loose network of individual states that made up the Athenian and later the Roman Empire.

These massive empires and cultural networks gave the classical era an awe-inspiring majesty to later peoples. This accounts for use of the word *classical* to describe this period.

It was in this period that great monuments of thought, politics, and art were developed that provided foundations for most of humankind's later civilizations.

Each main classical civilization differed greatly from the others in culture, politics, and economic and social forms. The chapters that follow will encourage comparisons among them. At the same time, the general similarities among the classical civilizations must be emphasized as well, based on their expansion and efforts at integration, because they provide a common framework of analysis.

CHAPTER 4

UNIFICATION AND THE CONSOLIDATION OF CIVILIZATION IN CHINA

This bronze miniature of a horse and carriage demonstrates the high level of both artistic and technological proficiency that the Chinese had attained by the last centuries B.C.E. The elaborate harness and finely crafted wheels and axle were as refined as those of any world culture at that time.

The breakdown of the Zhou dynasty's ability to control its vassals in the 8th century B.C.E. led to a long period of political conflict and social turmoil throughout China. In both the Yellow and the Yangtze river basins, many states rose and fell, each seeking to replace the Zhou as the paramount power in east Asia. Internal conflicts left China vulnerable to outside invaders, and between the 8th and 3rd centuries B.C.E., nomadic peoples often raided the farming areas of the north China plain. Many of the nomads settled down and eventually assimilated the distinct culture that had been developing in the region since the age of the Shang warrior kings. Some of these invaders captured existing states; others established new dynasties that further intensified the already complex political maneuvers and wars for supremacy.

The yearning for unity and an end to civil strife appeared to be answered in the 3rd century B.C.E. by the emergence of the warrior strongman **Shi Huangdi**. By 221 B.C.E., Shi Huangdi's state of **Qin** had vanquished all its rivals, and he founded a new imperial dynasty that promised to bring an end to the centuries of strife. But Shi Huangdi proved to be a tyrant. His death in 210 B.C.E. was the signal for resistance throughout the empire to the rule of his less despotic and less capable son and his inner circle of advisors. A rapidly spreading revolt, led by two peasants, toppled the Qin dynasty in 207 B.C.E. and gave rise to its much longer-lived successor, the **Han.**

The Han era, which lasted, with a brief interruption, for more than 400 years, saw the consolidation of Chinese civilization. Unity was established in the old core regions, and Chinese political control was greatly extended in all directions. Perhaps more critically, the Han rulers founded the largest, most effective, and most enduring bureaucracy in the preindustrial world. They oversaw the development of the first civil service examinations and the professionalization of Chinese administration. These institutions helped build a sense of Chinese distinctiveness and identity that was reflected in later centuries by Chinese references to themselves as the "sons of Han." This identity proved critical to the survival of Chinese civilization in the centuries of war, foreign invasion, and internal division that returned when the Han dynasty collapsed in the early 3rd century C.E.

Philosophical Remedies for the Prolonged Crisis of the Later Zhou

 The political rivalries, warfare, and rebellions that arose from the long decline of the Zhou dynasty during the Warring States period prompted much debate over remedies for China's political and social ills. In the last centuries of the later or

1200 B.C.E.	600 B.C.E.	400 B.C.E.	200 B.C.E.	1 C.E.	200 C.E.
1122–770 Former or western Zhou kingdom 770–403 Later or eastern Zhou kingdom	551–c. 233 Period of the "hundred philosophers" (including Confucius, Laozi, Mencius, Sunzi, the Legalists) 403–222 Warring States period	c. 400–320 Era of Sunzi 221–207 Qin dynasty 221 Shi Huangdi proclaimed first emperor of China 221 Great Wall completed 202–195 Reign of Liu Bang (Gaozu emperor)	200 B.C.E.–9 C.E. Initial Han dynasty; development of the horse collar, stern-post rudder, and watermill 141–87 Reign of Han Wudi	23–220 Later Han dynasty; invention of paper and the compass 9–23 Interregnum of Wang Mang	2nd century Development of porcelain

eastern Zhou era, some of China's greatest thinkers, including Confucius and Laozi, tried in very different ways to restore order and social harmony. Blended together by later scholars and administrators, the teachings of these great philosophers were worked into the composite ideology that for millennia was central to civilized life in China.

The warfare that raged throughout China after the Zhou rulers lost power was a major setback for both the emerging bureaucratic elite and the ordinary people. Military skills and physical prowess were valued over the literary and ceremonial aptitudes of the shi. Local lords, whose kingdoms were constantly threatened by their neighbors, tended to concentrate power in their own hands. They put little stock in the council of men who stayed behind in the palace while they risked their lives in battle. The military leaders who wore trousers—which were widely adopted following the example of the horse-riding northern nomads—were contemptuous of the courtiers and administrators who wore robes and gowns. In most kingdoms, the power of the old aristocratic families was strengthened. This often occurred at the expense of the bureaucrats, who were reduced to little more than clerks and fawning courtiers of the local strongmen. Rituals were neglected, and court etiquette, which had been prized in the early Zhou era, was replaced by the rough manners of nomadic invaders. Many scholar-bureaucrats found themselves without political positions and were forced to work as village schoolteachers and local scribes.

With rulers concentrating on the survival of their kingdoms, most resources were devoted to warfare. Public works, including dikes, canals, and regional granaries, were neglected, and some fell into ruin. Marauding armies stole or destroyed the crops on which the peasants depended. Hard-pressed rulers taxed the farmers heavily and conscripted them to

transport military supplies and, increasingly, to fight in the wars of the late Zhou period. Armies spread disease and destruction throughout China. The impact of natural calamities was compounded by the breakdown of public works and social support systems.

Perhaps because most kingdoms depended on outside areas for at least some vital materials—such as iron, horses, and salt—trade continued to increase despite political fragmentation and social disruption. The introduction of copper money and the growing acceptance of private property favored the Chinese merchant class. By the end of the Zhou era, traders were growing wealthy by supplying courts, armies, and town populations and investing in land. Wealth and political connections brought these big traders considerable power. For example, a legendary merchant named Zu Kung was said to have saved one kingdom from destruction, strengthened two others, and caused the decline and fall of two more in the course of a single business trip. As trade and production by artisans increased, towns grew, particularly walled administrative centers. By the last centuries of the Zhou period, China could boast of several urban centers with hundreds of thousands of people. For many centuries to come, no other civilization could support cities of this size.

Confucius and the Restoration of the Shi

Threatened by the great power of the warrior overlords of rival kingdoms and the rising wealth and influence of the mercantile class, the aspiring shi, as the scholar-bureaucrats came to be called, found a champion in Kung Fuzi, or **Confucius,** as he is known in the West. Confucius was born in the mid-6th century B.C.E. into a poor shi family. Like many others, Confucius's father had lost his place at the local court. Young Confucius had to take jobs, such as accounting, that were considered demeaning for a young man of his education and abilities. He was an outspoken and opinionated person who often offended people by the brutally frank expression of his views. He had hoped for a high post in the state of Lu, near the present-day Shandong Peninsula (see Map 4.1), but having been passed over, he took to the road in search of the ideal ruler.

He never found his ideal, and he spent most of his life traveling from one kingdom to another. But during his travels he met many leaders and local shi, supported himself by teaching, and earned a reputation for wisdom. Soon Confucius had attracted a large following. Some traveled with him as loyal disciples; others promoted his ideas at the courts of local rulers and compiled his sayings in what would come to be known as the *Analects,* or collected sayings (thus, "Confucius says").

Confucius was frustrated in his search for an ideal king to serve and unable to test his ideas as an administrator and advisor. But he developed ethical princi-

ples and a view of the proper ordering of society that would shape Chinese civilization for the next 2500 years. He was not a religious teacher, like the Jewish prophets or the Buddha, but rather a social philosopher. Though ancestral veneration played a role, his thinking was focused on the earthly realm and the proper ways to arrange social relationships and achieve good government. He was obsessed with the need for order and harmony. He believed that they could come about only if Chinese rulers relied on the advice of wise and educated men. In Confucius's view, such men could be recruited only from among the shi.

Confucius was convinced that a small minority of superior men was destined by their talents and sense of duty to govern and set an example for the common people. In a revolutionary bit of thinking, he argued that these men (women were explicitly excluded) were superior not because of aristocratic birth but because of their education and training. Thus, superior men were made, not born. This

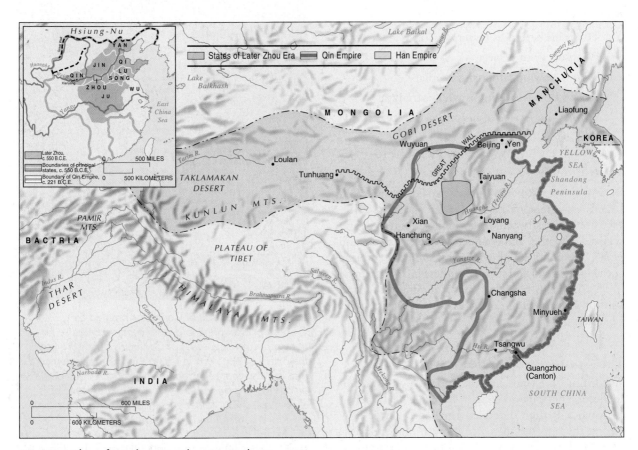

Map 4.1   *China from the Later Zhou Era to the Han Era*

meant that even a peasant could aspire to this exalted status. But most of the superior men were drawn from the elite classes, especially the old aristocracy and established shi households.

Confucian Thought and Social Ideals

There was a strong ethical dimension to Confucian thought. Confucius believed that superior men should be given power not to enrich or glorify themselves but to serve society. He stressed that the welfare of the common people must be paramount in the decisions of good emperors and their advisors. Confucius reasoned that in return for their rulers' concern and protection, the common people should respect, support, and acknowledge the superior status of their overlords. Social harmony depended on each person's accepting his or her allotted place and performing the tasks of his or her social station. Obedience and deference were owed to one's superiors and elders, to males from females, and to teachers from students. To Confucius, a good man is one who

> Treats his betters as betters,
>
> Wears an air of respect,
>
> Who in serving father and mother
>
> Knows how to put in his whole strength,
>
> Who in the service of his prince will lay down his life
>
> Who in intercourse with friends is true to his word.

According to Confucius, society was held together by personal ties of loyalty and obedience. Five links were stressed: three family links (father and son, elder brother and younger brother, husband and wife), one political link (ruler and subject), and one social link (friend and friend). If these links were honored, Confucius believed, only a minimum of intervention by the state in the lives of its subjects would be necessary.

The Confucian Gentleman

According to Confucius, the superior or educated man was a person of courage who made decisions on his own and then defended them no matter how strong the opposition. Once in positions of power, shi officials were to respect rulers but not be afraid to admonish them for errors in judgment or for neglecting the welfare of their subjects. A superior man—a term that became synonymous with membership in the shi class—controlled his emotions. He presented a calm and composed face to rivals, subordinates, and friends. He was well mannered and observed the proper rituals and forms of address and behavior, which varied depending on the social status of the person with whom he was interacting. As the portrait in Figure 4.1 demonstrates, succeeding generations of Chinese scholars and administrators venerated Confucius as the personification of the well-centered, highly accomplished shi gentleman.

Above all, the shi gentleman was a generalist rather than a specialist. He strove to be equally

Figure 4.1 *A portrait of Confucius painted by a Chinese prince in the mid-18th century. Because no contemporary likenesses of Confucius have survived, the artists of each era in China's long history depicted him in ways that reflected the tastes and needs of the elites then in power. Here, for example, Confucius is shown as a wise, fatherly member of the scholar-gentry class, with official headgear and robes of office. In less stable and prosperous times, he might be sketched as a stern teacher bent on restoring the moral fiber that the Chinese believed was essential to social harmony.*

accomplished at running a government department, directing the repair of irrigation works, composing poetry, or painting the plum blossoms in his garden. He earned power and status as a moral exemplar, not for performing specific tasks. Confucius thought that with such men in charge of China, war and social strife would be brought under control forever.

The Heirs of Confucius

During his lifetime and after his death in the early 5th century B.C.E., Confucius had many disciples who spread his teachings and debated over their interpretation. The most important division arose between the followers of **Mencius** (Meng Ko) and those of **Sunzi,** who lived in the 3rd and 2nd centuries B.C.E. Mencius assumed that humans were inclined to be good and thus ought to be ruled in such a way that their goodness could develop to the fullest extent. His egalitarian thinking stressed the consent of the common people as the basis for political power. It provided the philosophical underpinnings for the long-standing Chinese belief that the people had the right to rise up and overthrow incompetent or oppressive rulers.

Sunzi rejected Mencius's basic assumption. He argued that humans were inclined to be lazy and evil. He concluded that a strong, authoritarian government was necessary to curb their selfish desires and their capacity to harm each other. Sunzi believed that humans could be improved through strong laws and education, but he did not agree that the people were the ultimate source of political power. The ideas of both thinkers and those of Confucius continued to influence intellectual discourse in China for millennia. But in the short term, the views of Sunzi, bolstered by the arguments of later political philosophers known as the **Legalists,** were the most influential.

Daoist Alternatives

A very different cure for China's ills in the late Zhou era was offered by the recluse and philosopher **Laozi** (often called Lao Tsu in popular Daoist texts). Laozi's life history has been obscured by fantastic legends, including those relating that his mother was pregnant with him for decades and that when he was born he was an old man with a white beard. Whatever his actual background, Laozi developed into a thinker who had little use for government or absolute ethical prescriptions. As a solution for the sufferings brought on by human greed and ambition, Laozi recom-

mended a retreat into nature. Through the contemplation of nature, he believed, the individual could become attuned with the **Dao:** the cosmic force and source of all creation. Laozi stressed nonaction over political power and self-examination over the mastery of others. He taught,

It is wisdom to know others.

It is enlightenment to know one's self.

The conqueror of men is powerful.

The master of himself is stronger.

It is wealth to be content.

It is willful to force one's way on others.

Although much of Laozi's message concerned withdrawal from the world, he could not resist giving advice to those who remained in society, particularly the rulers of China's many kingdoms. He chastised them for enjoying war and the excessive pursuit of pleasure in their palaces while the mass of the population went hungry. He wrote,

When the court is arrayed in splendor,

The fields are full of weeds,

And the granaries are bare.

Laozi exhorted rulers and men of affairs to cultivate the virtues of patience, selflessness, and concern for the welfare of all creatures. He argued that these virtues were consistent with the nature of the Dao. Like Confucius, he believed that wise rulers and honest administrators made for happy and peaceful kingdoms. But Laozi differed from Confucius in his views on how a good ruler was to be nurtured and what qualities he possessed. Unlike Confucius, who viewed a strong state and sound society as the primary goals, Laozi saw them as temporary concerns that were of little relevance to the wise man in search of the hidden meanings of creation and human life.

Like Confucius, Laozi had many disciples in his own lifetime and in later centuries. His poetic sayings were interpreted by these followers in widely varying ways. Some held to his original emphasis on withdrawal from the world, communion with nature, and meditation. Others mixed his ideas with magic, eroticism, and a search for a concoction that would bring immortality to those who drank it. The meditative followers had the greatest appeal to the shi elite and courtiers of later ages. These elite disciples drew on Daoist ideas to enhance their sensitivity to art and the natural world and to satisfy their interest

Document

Teachings of the Rival Chinese Schools

The brief passages quoted here are taken from the writings of Confucius, Mencius, Sunzi, and Laozi. Identify the author of each passage and explain why you believe it was written by the person you chose.

I take no action and the people are reformed.
I enjoy peace and people become honest.
I do nothing and people become rich.
I have no desires and people return to the good and simple life.

The gentleman cherishes virtue; the inferior man cherishes possessions.
The gentleman thinks of sanctions; the inferior man thinks of personal favors.

The nature of man is evil; his goodness is acquired.
His nature being what it is, man is born, first, with a desire for gain.
If this desire is followed, strife will result and courtesy will disappear.

Keep your mouth closed.
Guard your senses.
Temper your sharpness.
Simplify your problems.
Mask your brightness.
Be at one with the dust of the earth.
This is primal union.

Personal cultivation begins with poetry, is made firm with rules of decorum, and is perfected by music.

When it is left to follow its natural feelings, human nature will do good. That's why I say it is good. If it becomes evil, it is not the fault of man's original capability.

Questions: Which of these ideas are most compatible? Which of them could best be called religious? Which are most secular? Which philosophers propose ideas that are best suited to people who want to build a strong and unified political order?

---

in questions about the supernatural. The masses, on the other hand, were attracted by the magical solutions to everyday problems emphasized by conjurers and charlatans with rather dubious claims to being Laozi's disciples.

The Triumph of the Qin and Imperial Unity

By the end of the 5th century B.C.E., the long wars had reduced the number of states striving to supplant the house of Zhou. The failure of larger states, such as Ju and Wu based in the Yangtze River valley, to conquer the kingdoms of the north China plain in the preceding centuries left only seven main rivals and the rump kingdom that was still ruled by the descendants of the Zhou dynasty. In the 4th and 3rd centuries B.C.E., one of these kingdoms, the westernmost state of the Qin dynasty, grew steadily more powerful at the expense of its rivals. At the end of the 3rd century, the Qin warlord, Shi Huangdi, defeated his rivals and unified China under Qin rule. Once in power, Shi Huangdi strove to build a highly centralized state and invested heavily in grandiose

public works projects. His excesses in both efforts led to revolts against his weaker successor and the replacement of his short-lived but pivotal dynasty by the Han.

Like the original Zhou dynasty, the Qin rulers were of nomadic origins. The warriors of Qin had served as the defenders of the western boundaries of the Zhou empire in earlier centuries. As a backward land ruled by "barbarians," Qin was the object of ridicule by the rulers and administrators of states to the east, who considered themselves more civilized. Ambassadors and travelers from eastern states, such as Wei and Lu, complained of the crude living quarters in the Qin capital, the gross manners found even at court, and the disregard for ceremony in the affairs of state. They failed to note the innovations in the kingdom of Qin that eventually gave it greater political and military power than all of its rivals combined.

The Transformation of a "Barbarian" Land

It is true that the Qin state lagged behind most of its rivals in the fine arts and refined etiquette. But from as early as the 5th century B.C.E., the rulers of Qin had initiated several critical social and political changes that greatly increased their ability to wage war against their snobbish rivals to the east and south. The Qin state had long supported experimentation with bronze and ironworking that had transformed toolmaking and weaponmaking in the Zhou era. To encourage peasants to adopt new tools and more productive cultivation techniques, the Qin freed them from bondage to local lords and allowed them to claim their own land. Over time, these measures substantially increased the resource base on which Qin political ambitions depended. Because freeing the peasants undermined the support of the vassal warriors, who had originally carried out local administration, the Qin attempted to build a regular bureaucracy supported by the dynasty and totally loyal to it. These efforts attracted migrant shi administrators, who were willing to put up with bad manners if well-paying positions were to be had.

Qin power and military prowess were also increased by the many wars the state fought, first to survive and later to conquer the rest of China. The Qin conscripted for military service the peasants it had freed and given land, making its armies larger than those of rival states. The superior bureaucracy of the Qin meant that its forces were better supplied and organized. The nomadic background of the Qin elite ensured an ample supply of able military leaders. It also made the Qin more receptive to military innovations than many of their adversaries. For example, they were one of the first states to use massed cavalry, which gave their armies mobility. Qin armies were also the first to adopt the crossbow, which came into widespread use in the late Zhou era. Good leadership and free peasants, who may have felt that they had more to fight for than the vassals and serfs of other kingdoms, made the Qin armies famous for their ferocity and speed.

The Legalist Sanction

From at least the 4th century B.C.E., the efforts of Qin rulers to break the power of their vassals were justified by the writings of several statesmen who came to be known collectively as the Legalists. The semilegendary Shang Yang, who served a Qin ruler of the mid-4th century B.C.E., was the founder of the Legalist school of political philosophy. In *The Book of Lord Shang*, he argued that the power of China's rulers should be absolute. Their major objective should be to enhance the strength and wealth of the state. Shang Yang argued that the people existed to serve the state, and he had little to say about the ruler's duty to promote their welfare. He believed that the main responsibility of the state with regard to the people was to enforce strict laws with harsh punishments for offenders. Although the ruler was absolute, even he should not be above the law. To drive this point home, Shang Yang once had the crown prince punished for breaking the law: The cheek of the prince's tutor was tattooed in retribution for the offense.

As Shang Yang discovered at the end of his life, he too was subject to the strict laws. When he fled the court after the death of the ruler who was his patron and protector, the aged statesman sought refuge at a roadside inn. But it was illegal for a traveler to stay at an inn without a permit, which Shang Yang did not have. The innkeeper, who faced death if he did not obey the law, turned out the old man. Shang Yang later led an unsuccessful rebellion, which resulted in his being tied to chariots and ripped apart in punishment.

Shi Huangdi, Emperor of China

Shi Huangdi, the "tiger" of Qin, was extremely receptive to the Legalist approach to government. A man of unbounded ambition, energy, and physical courage, he was also a megalomaniac who did not tolerate the slightest challenge to his rule. Because of complaints from his officials, he once had hundreds of shi buried alive. His solution to leaks of news from the palace was similarly harsh: When his disapproval of the overuse of carriages by his courtiers became known throughout the capital and no one would admit to repeating comments he had made in confidence, Shi Huangdi executed all who were present when he made the comments. When he was told that a chain of hills was blocking the critical wet monsoons, he had the trees on them cut down and their surface dyed red, the color associated with criminals in China.

By 221 B.C.E., Shi Huangdi had completed the work of his predecessors. He had defeated the last of rival states of the Qin and had unified China. To strengthen his hold over his vast domain, Shi Huangdi ordered all regional fortresses destroyed and the weapons of local warrior groups collected and melted down. Former states disappeared, and 36 provinces were created in their place. Vassal overlords and regional commanders were replaced by Qin bureaucrats. Surviving princes and aristocrats, as well as very wealthy merchants, were ordered to live in the capital at Xianyang, where Shi Huangdi's huge palace loomed over hundreds of others. The emperor's scribes developed a standard script and coinage, and weights and measures were unified throughout the empire.

Shi Huangdi's greatest passion was for building. His architects joined and expanded the walls that had been built by the northern kingdoms to keep out nomadic invaders, thus creating China's **Great Wall** (Figure 4.2). The Great Wall and other public works projects, such as canals and roadways, were constructed by millions of forcibly recruited peasant laborers; 700,000 were said to have been used to build the emperor's palace alone. Even Shi Huangdi's death did not put an end to his building projects. In preparing for his own burial, the emperor ordered the construction of a massive tomb at Mount Li, which was not uncovered until 1971. The army of clay soldiers and horses shown in Figure 4.3, which were buried in the Mount Li tomb with Shi Huangdi, provide a final testament to his megalomania and unchecked demands on his subjects.

The Collapse of a Tyrannical but Pivotal Regime

Shi Huangdi's building frenzy and the harsh rule of his Legalist administrators aroused resistance throughout the Qin's newly won empire. The shi were particularly angered by the repression of any ideas that challenged those of the Legalists. The early efforts at thought control by the Qin ruler culminated in a campaign to burn all but a handful of state-approved books. All works, except an official political history of China, Legalist texts, and works on technology, medicine, and astrology, were to be confis-

Figure 4.2   *When kept in good repair and supplied with sufficient numbers of soldiers, the high walls and broad battlements of the Great Wall were a formidable obstacle for nomads who sought to invade China. The wall was made by joining and extending several walls that had been built by regional kingdoms in north China before they were conquered by the Qin. Among the most impressive engineering triumphs of the ancient world, the wall ran for more than 1400 miles through and above the north China plain (see Map 4.1). For more than two millennia, it buffered the interaction between Chinese civilization and the nomadic peoples to the west and north of the Yellow River basin.*

Figure 4.3 *Hundreds of these clay warriors were found in the tomb of the first Chinese emperor, Shi Huangdi. Remarkably, each of the warriors has different facial features. Together with the clay horses also found in the tomb, these massed forces are striking evidence of the power of the founder of China's first, short-lived imperial dynasty. They also reflect his obsession with monumental building projects, a direct cause of the fall of the repressive Qin dynasty within a few years of Shi Huangdi's death.*

cated by state officials and destroyed. At this time, books were written by hand on bamboo strips that were then bound together. Their high cost and the small numbers of literate elite meant that books were scarce and easily located.

At the same time, the peasants were alienated by the Qin's endless demands for taxes and labor. In fact, Shi Huangdi's appetite for building projects was the immediate cause of the revolt that led to the abrupt collapse of the dynasty in 207 B.C.E., just three years after the emperor's death. The two peasants who began the revolt were conscripted to work on the Great Wall (see Figure 4.2). On the journey from their village to the construction site, they realized that they could not arrive on time. Because the typical penalty for arriving late for a labor assignment was death, the two men concluded that they had little to lose by rousing others to revolt. Their calls for resistance found a ready audience among the weary peasantry and angry shi elite. The revolt spread rapidly, and within months the Qin dynasty was toppled. Shi

Huangdi's son was murdered by a band of conspirators, and the emperor's huge palace was burned to the ground.

Although Qin rule over all of China lasted only a matter of decades, its short reign was a turning point in Chinese history. Shi Huangdi not only unified China but governed it with a centralized bureaucracy staffed by salaried officials. This meant that he was not dependent on unsteady and potentially hostile vassals, a dependency that had destroyed earlier dynasties. It also involved strengthening the shi, who increasingly provided the social and political bonds that would hold China together through times of crisis and foreign invasion.

The public works projects of the Qin provided the grid of roads and canals that made it possible for later dynasties to hold far-flung territories together. The construction of the Great Wall reinforced the long-standing division between the nomads of central and north Asia and the farmers to the south. Improved communication and a unified currency

In Depth

Sunzi and the Shift from Ritual Combat to "Real" War

The development of classical civilizations in the Middle East, Greece, China, and India greatly advanced the business of making war. Agricultural surpluses made it possible to support specialized fighters and military commanders. Population growth made for larger armies, which needed armor, weapons, and training. Horses, and in some areas camels and elephants, were raised to carry men into battle or pull war chariots. Advances in metalworking meant steadily improving weaponry, and fortification became a major concern for early engineers and architects. Warfare came to involve more soldiers, who fought for longer periods and suffered more casualties. Frontier defenses and military campaigns became primary concerns for those who ruled civilized states.

Despite advances in weaponry and training, at least for warrior elites, warfare in most early civilizations was a combination of ritual and chaos. Wars normally were not fought during harvest times, the winter, or the monsoon season. A ruler was expected to announce his intention to attack a neighboring kingdom well in advance. Before battle, the high priests of each ruler offered sacrifices to the gods. Their readings of various sorts of omens, not strategic considerations, determined the time and place of combat. Battles consisted primarily of formal duels between trained and well-armed warriors in the midst of confused collisions of masses of poorly trained and armed foot soldiers, who were usually slaves or forcibly recruited peasants. Though often fierce, the warriors' duels were regulated by codes of honor and fair play. For example, it was unseemly for a warrior to strike from behind or to strike when his opponent had fallen.

Duels between warrior champions were the set pieces of a battle. As the great epics of early civilizations, such as the Indian *Mahabharata* and the Greek *Iliad*, demonstrate, great warriors cut bloody swaths through the ranks of poorly prepared infantry and lesser fighters to get to each other and set up the hand-to-hand combats that normally determined the outcome of battle. The death of a commander, who was often the ruler of the kingdom at war or a renowned champion, meant the collapse of his forces and their chaotic flight from the field. Normally, the victorious army did not destroy or capture what remained of the opposing soldiers. The game had been played and won. The winners either retired with their booty to prepare for the next round or began negotiations to set the terms on which the defeated party would submit to their overlordship.

The Shang and early Zhou periods of Chinese history were filled with wars, most of which were fought according to this ritualized pattern. But by the late Zhou period, some commanders and thinkers had become highly critical of the indecisiveness and waste of the endless conflicts between the warring states. In the 4th century B.C.E., Sunzi, an advisor to one of the warring monarchs, responded to these concerns with a treatise, *The Art of War*, a classic of military theory. Sunzi proposed a vision of military conflict very different from the ritualized approach to war.

Sunzi argued that war was merely an extension of statecraft. Wars ought not to be games or macho contests for bragging rights; they ought to be fought only for ends that increased the territory, wealth, and power of the state. With these aims in mind, Sunzi insisted that speed was of the essence in warfare and that long wars burdened the subjects of the warring rulers and bred rebellions. He also urged that target kingdoms be captured swiftly and with as little damage as possible. Sunzi argued that war was a science, which should be the object of extensive study. Rather than brawny warriors, commanders ought to be men well versed in organization, strategy, and tactics. He proposed, and Chinese rulers set up, special schools to train officers in the art of war.

Sunzi's ideas transformed warfare in China. Rulers made every effort short of war to bring down their rivals. Bluffs, spies, threats, and saboteurs were used before armies were sent to war. Both before and after war was actually declared, substantial state resources and large bureaucracies were devoted to building and training armies and supplying them in the field. Sneak attacks were considered fair, and feints and ruses were regularly used by field commanders. Weather conditions and advantageous terrain determined the time and place of battle.

Psychological devices were strongly recommended. For example, techniques were used to make the enemy commanders angry and cause them to make foolish moves that might demoralize their armies. Discipline was needed, rather than individual heroics. This point was driven home by a ruler who had one of his commanders beheaded because the general's troops attacked ahead of schedule, despite the fact that this action was the key to victory. In combat, regular formations replaced mass brawls; soldiers fought as units under the direction of a chain of commanders. Good fighters were still valued, but now as unit leaders rather than accomplished duelists. The main object of battle became the destruction of the enemy's forces as quickly as possible.

Shi Huangdi's military and political successes demonstrated how effective warfare reorganized along the lines suggested by Sunzi might be. Halfway across the globe, the Greeks were independently developing comparable patterns of warfare. Ironically, this shift in approaches to warfare between the Greek city-states was occurring at about the same time the compilers of the *Iliad* were celebrating the contests of great heroes such as Achilles and Hector. In roughly the same era as Sunzi and Shi Huangdi, the tightly disciplined formations and training of smaller Greek armies culminated in Alexander the Great's unprecedented conquests.

But these successes did not put an end to ritual warfare between civilized peoples. Although Chinese armies tended to be organized and led according to the prescriptions of Sunzi and other theorists, the chivalric codes and battles centered on the duels of champions persisted. This was particularly true in societies that were dominated by warrior elites, such as those that later developed in India, Japan, Africa, Europe, and Mesoamerica. But conditions in the warring states and the genius of Sunzi had led to a radically new vision of what wars were about and how they were fought. The effects of this vision are still felt by civilized societies.

Questions: What were some of the major differences between ritual warfare and the new approach proposed by Sunzi? What are the main advantages and drawbacks of each approach? If you were an ancient ruler, which would you tell your military commanders to use? Why? What aspects of Chinese political systems and society contributed to the rise of this approach to warfare? Can you think of other civilizations that were able to build similar military systems?

enabled China's merchants to establish interregional markets and promoted the interdependence of very different geographic areas of the Chinese empire. Although the threat of a return to war and anarchy loomed briefly after the sudden collapse of the Qin, the foundations Shi Huangdi had laid for a centralized empire permitted another remarkable leader to establish a far milder and more lasting dynasty in China: the house of Han.

The Han Dynasty and the Foundations of China's Classical Age

The sudden collapse of the Qin Empire threatened to plunge China again into warfare and social strife. But one of the revolts against the Qin produced a leader, a man of peasant origins, who reunified China and founded a dynasty, the Han dynasty, that consolidated most of the key elements of Chinese civilization. The Han era was also a time of great creativity and innovation. The long peace saw the growth of great cities, the expansion of trade and the mercantile classes, and a new surge of inventiveness that greatly advanced artisan and peasant productivity.

The pent-up anger produced by a decade and a half of harsh state demands and repression flared into regional riots and rebellions throughout the former Qin territories. Vassal chiefs fought former Qin bureaucrats for local control, and some dreamed of founding a renewed empire. The unlikely winner of these many-sided contests for power was a man of peasant birth named **Liu Bang**. Liu Bang's early life hardly suggests that he would become the founder of one of China's longest-lived and most illustrious dynasties. In his youth Liu Bang was lazy, uneducated, and jobless. He was best known for his fondness for wine and women, tastes that remained pronounced throughout his life. In the years before the end of the Qin dynasty, Liu Bang, either because he had changed his shiftless ways or through clever maneuvers, had established himself as a village headman. In the confusion that followed the fall of the Qin, he built up a following of soldiers, ex-bureaucrats, and disgruntled peasants.

Liu Bang was not much of a military commander; in fact, legend has it that he lost all the battles he fought for control of China except the last one. But he did have a gift for picking able subordinates and allowing them to exercise their talents. His skill at mediating between quarrelsome followers allowed him to hold his motley armies together while the forces of his enemies dissolved in violent factional fights. In 202 B.C.E., after years of campaigning and negotiation, Liu Bang proclaimed himself the new emperor of China, thus founding the Han dynasty that would rule China, with a brief interruption, for the next 400 years.

The Restoration of Imperial Control

For a time it looked as though the new emperor, whose official name was Gaozu, would restore the system of vassalage that had formed the basis for royal administration in the Zhou era. He raised many of his followers to the ranks of the nobility, and he rewarded them, as well as existing lords who had supported his efforts to win the throne, with large estates. However, it soon became clear that even his once-loyal followers were not above using the domains they had been granted to build up independent bases of power that could eventually threaten the dynasty itself. In addition to this threat, Liu Bang's determination to establish a more centralized imperial administration was promoted by the shi officials who attached themselves to his cause during his struggle for power and after he became emperor. Perhaps because Liu Bang was illiterate, he came to rely heavily on his shi advisors even though he personally despised them. His efforts at bureaucratic centralization focused on enhancing their training and responsibilities.

Liu Bang's moves toward bureaucratic centralization were taken up by several strong and able rulers who succeeded him on the Han throne, most notably Han Wudi (140–87 B.C.E.). First, the larger fiefs granted to the highest nobles were broken up by a royal decree that required the domains of the vassals to be divided between all their sons at the time of their death rather than pass intact to their eldest son. At the same time, regular government appointees, especially regional governors and district magistrates, expanded their authority at the expense of local lords. In the time of Han Wudi, vassals were forbidden to bequeath their domains to heirs they had adopted. When a noble died without legitimate offspring, his estates were confiscated by the central government. Under a variety of pretexts, Han Wudi's administrators also seized the fiefs of many other vassals, who were then relegated to the status of commoners.

Han Expansion

The Han rulers used the impressive military might at their disposal to enlarge the empire and neutralize external threats. The most formidable of the external enemies were the **Hsiung-nu** nomads who lived north of the Great Wall. From the time of the first Han emperor, these skilled horsemen of Mongol descent had raided and looted territories south of the wall. Liu Bang attempted to buy them off by giving them presents and marrying one of his daughters to the highest Hsiung-nu chieftain. By the time of Han Wudi, it was clear that major expeditions would be necessary to put an end to the Hsiung-nu incursions. Han Wudi's forces defeated the nomads and annexed their pasturelands to the north and west of the Great Wall to the Han domains.

Han armies also expanded the empire to the east and south. In the east, the northern parts of Korea were conquered in 108 B.C.E. and were ruled by the Chinese for more than 400 years. Conquests in the south extended Chinese civilization into the mountainous interior and down the coast of the South China Sea to Vietnam. The many different ethnic groups who lived in these areas either submitted to Han rule and assimilated to Chinese civilization or, like the various branches of the T'ai-speaking peoples, migrated farther south into what later became Burma, Thailand, and Laos. The southernmost of the peoples who resisted Han rule were subjects of the kingdom the Chinese called Nam Viet. After many attempts, Han armies finally conquered this state and established control over the Vietnamese people in 111 B.C.E.

The Revenge of the Shi

The majority of the shi, who were followers of Confucius and his disciples, deeply resented the favoritism Shi Huangdi showed the Legalists. The fall of the Qin provided them an opportunity to strike back. At the urging of the Confucian school, Liu Bang and his successors banned the works of the Legalists, and members of the school were hounded from the court and in some cases killed. The harsh law codes of the Qin were replaced by the milder edicts of the Han. Legalist ideas were eventually blended into the mix of philosophies and religious beliefs that came to make up China's official ideology.

Confucianism in its varying forms soon became the dominant thought system in Chinese civilization. Its full ascendancy was delayed in the early Han era by the suspicions of rulers, such as Liu Bang, who strongly favored Daoism, and the rivalry of non-Confucian thinkers. But by the end of the 2nd century B.C.E., the shi scholar-officials and the Confucian ideas they championed had won prominence among the Chinese ruling classes that they would enjoy for much of the next 2000 years. A thorough knowledge of Confucian teachings became essential to employment and promotion in the Han government. This prerequisite for success in Han politics was institutionalized by the founding of an imperial university at the capital at Xian in 124 B.C.E. By the end of the Han era there were more than 30,000 students at this state-supported center.

Education, Examinations, and Shi Dominance

Although students at the imperial university were expected to master law and a choice of specialized fields, including history, astronomy, and music, all concentrated on memorizing and interpreting the Confucian classics. These were given even greater emphasis when formal examinations for government positions were established at the beginning of the last century B.C.E. The Chinese examination system marked the beginning of the first professional civil service in human history. At first, exams were confined to the upper levels of government, but local and regional exams were later established to identify and test local talent. Theoretically, any Chinese man could take them. But no one could hope to pass them without a proper education, and education was expensive. This meant that members of established shi families, the old aristocracy, and local landlord households had a clear advantage.

Each elite family supported the brightest of its sons. They were tutored at home as children and then enrolled in local schools, where they mastered the Chinese characters and the Confucian texts. On occasion a particularly bright child from a peasant household was adopted by a shi or landlord family and given the support he needed to do well on the exams and advance in the bureaucracy.

In general, people from the lower classes could not afford a proper education, but several examples are recounted by Chinese historians of enterprising farmers or merchants who rose to high administrative posts. In one instance at the end of the 2nd century B.C.E., a dismissed police official, who had resorted to pig breeding to support himself, in his later years so impressed the emperor with his responses to the examiners' questions that he was eventually given the post of imperial chancellor.

Opportunities for government positions were limited by the fact that only a small percentage of jobs were allotted by competitive examination. Although the Han rulers tried to put an end to hereditary rank, many political positions automatically passed from father to son. Many offices were appointive, and a man's chance of winning an office depended on personal links to the emperor or high officials who distributed the political spoils. Thus, in the Han era, few offices were earned by passing exams. However, the Han system nurtured a revolutionary idea: that administrative office and the exercise of political power ought to depend on personal merit and effort rather than birth alone.

The Emergence of the Scholar-Gentry

The growing influence of the shi in government was also felt in Chinese social life as a whole. In effect, three main social strata came to be recognized by those who wrote the official documents and histories: the literate shi, the ordinary but free subjects, and the underclass, called the "mean people." Within each of these large groupings there were important occupational and status divisions. For example, the shi ranged from the powerful families that served the imperial household to local tutors and petty clerks stationed in frontier provinces. The common people included groups that we would identify as separate classes. The majority were peasants, but even they varied greatly in wealth and social status. Some controlled large amounts of land, lived in extended family compounds, and tried to provide their sons with the education that would elevate the family to shi status.

Increasingly, local landlord families were linked by marriage or the success of their sons to the shi. This combination gave rise to a new class configuration, the **scholar-gentry**, who superseded the shi. As their dual label suggests, the scholar-gentry upheld their position through both landholdings in the rural areas and political posts in the bureaucracy, which was housed mainly in the towns. Families tended to maintain branches in both areas. Wealth from landholding was used to educate the brightest sons, who increased the family's fortunes by winning lucrative administrative positions. Well-placed family members in the town looked after the interests of their rural elders and cousins in such matters as tax quotas, military protection, and civil litigation. If bandits or nomads raided the area where the rural branch of the family lived, those family members could take refuge with their relatives in town. When towns were attacked by warring armies, the city dwellers fled to the country-side. This double base and mutual support made for remarkable durability. Some families played major roles in Chinese politics and society for centuries. Some lasted for thousands of years—far longer than any imperial dynasty.

In both town and country, scholar-gentry families lived in large walled compounds, such as that shown in Figure 4.4. These dwellings often had separate buildings for each unit of the extended family. Surviving clay figurines of gentry homes show that they were multistoried structures with stucco or

Figure 4.4 *Walls, strong gates, and numerous stories were prominent features of extended-family dwellings in the Han era, as this painted pottery model from the 1st century C.E. shows. Each family unit usually had its own rooms for sleeping. Cooking, eating, and bathing generally were done in spaces shared by all members of the household, excluding servants, who lived in separate parts of the family compound.*

wooden walls and tiled roofs. Most compounds included an inner garden, where children could play and their elders could chat and enjoy nature. In times of peace, scholar-gentry families lived the good life. Family granaries ensured a ready supply of good food, and household servants took care of tedious chores such as cleaning, cooking, and washing clothes. Male and female members of the family dressed in silks, which commoners, including merchants, were not permitted to wear (at least in public).

When a member of a scholar-gentry household who held an administrative position left the compound for work or a night on the town, he rode in a horse-drawn carriage like that shown in the wonderful stone rubbing in Figure 4.5. Like his clothing, the carriage was of a size and design that indicated his government rank. Both male and female members of the family enjoyed the deference of the common people. Merchants offered them their finest goods, servants scurried to do their bidding, and peasants bowed politely as they passed in their carriages. A commoner who forgot his place could expect to be chided by his peers or roughed up by the toughs that most gentry families employed to look after their safety.

Class and Gender Roles in Han Society

There is considerable evidence that women, particularly those from powerful scholar-gentry households, enjoyed more freedom and status in the Han era than they had in later periods of Chinese history. Because marriages, especially among the elite, were arranged with family alliances rather than romantic concerns in mind, young men had as little say in the choice of their future spouses as women. Although the woman's father paid a dowry to the family of his son-in-law, and she went to her husband's house to live, the young bride usually could rely on her powerful relatives to ensure that she was well treated in her new home. She was often allowed to take along her servants and even a sister as live-in companions. Widowed women were permitted to remarry, and all women participated in family ceremonies. Perhaps most important, women of upper-class families were often tutored in writing, the arts, and music. There were several important female poets in the Han era, and at least one prominent court historian was a woman.

Despite these promising trends, women at all social levels remained subordinated to men. Family

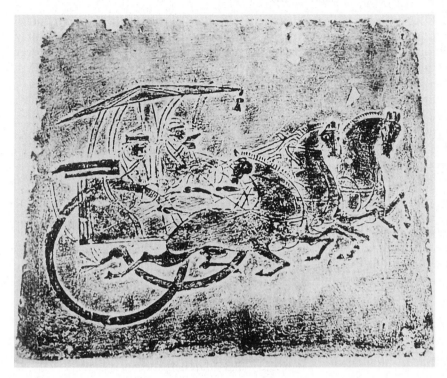

Figure 4.5 *The racing horses and decorated carriage shown on this rubbing from a stone carving from the later Han era suggest the confidence and opulence of the elite classes, who alone could afford such a vehicle. They also suggest that those who belonged to the elite classes could move about with considerable speed, if not comfort. The driver of the carriage would have been a servant who was specially trained to handle the spirited horses depicted here.*

households were run by the older men, and although women could inherit, male children normally received the greater share of family property. The following verse from the *Book of Poetry*, which indicates typical responses to the birth into an aristocratic family of a son and a daughter, clearly illustrates the preference for and consequent privileges of males:

Sons shall be born to him—

They will be put to sleep on couches;

They will be clothed in robes;

They will have scepters to play with;

Their cry will be loud.

(Hereafter) they will be resplendent with red
  knee-covers,

The (future) king, the princes of the land.

Daughters shall be born to him—

They will be put to sleep on the ground;

They will be clothed in wrappers;

They will have tiles to play with.

It will be theirs neither to do wrong nor to
  do good.

Only about the liquor and the food will they
  have to think,

And to cause no sorrow to their parents.

Political positions were reserved for men, although women could sometimes exert powerful influence from behind the throne. But this backstage control at the court merely confirmed the view of the Confucian scholars that women were unfit for politics. Their attitudes are bluntly set forth in the *Book of Poetry:*

A woman with a long tongue

Is a stepping-stone to disorder.

Disorder does not come down from Heaven—

It is produced by women.

Those from whom come no lessons, no
  instruction,

Are women and eunuchs.

Among the scholar-gentry, young married women were subjected to the demands and criticisms of domineering mothers-in-law. This was a lesser problem among the lower classes, where residence in extended households was not common. Nonetheless, women from peasant families were expected to cook, clean house, and work long hours in the fields. Some found social outlets and even a degree of financial independence working in the markets of nearby towns. But all were legally subordinated to their fathers and husbands. At all class levels, women were expected to marry, and whatever their individual talents, their most vital social function remained the bearing of children, preferably boys.

Peasant Life

Ordinary farmers held varying amounts of land, but few produced more than they needed to live and pay taxes. Moderately prosperous farmers sold their surplus to traders or their agents, or in a local market town. Most peasants who had a decent-sized plot of land lived well. But many peasants had little or no land of their own and were forced to work for landlords in order to earn a meager living. Peasants with plots that were too small to support their families complained to Han officials that they "did not have enough husks and beans to eat and [that] their coarse clothing was not in good condition." Those who worked the land of others as tenants or landless laborers were even more miserable. According to an official description, they "wore the coverings of oxen and horses and ate the food of dogs and pigs."

Key Chinese inventions, such as the shoulder collar (which permitted horses to pull greater loads) and the wheelbarrow, eased the work of farmers at all levels. Expanded irrigation networks, improved iron tools, and new cropping patterns allowed larger agricultural yields that were consumed mostly by upper-class groups and the town populations. Despite these advances, many of the poorest peasants continued to work the land with the simpler tools shown in the rubbing in Figure 4.6.

The existence of farmland in many areas, particularly the south, relieved population pressure and provided frontier outlets where hard-pressed laborers could clear land and start life anew. The losers in this process were the mainly non-Chinese ethnic groups who occupied these areas. Some peasants took to banditry in the rugged hill country or the forested zones that still existed in large parts of the Yellow and Yangtze river basins. Others scraped by as beggars in provincial towns or lived with vagabonds who traveled the roads of the empire in search of temporary employment or vulnerable merchants and country houses to rob. Many more peasants joined **secret societies** with colorful names such as the Red Eyebrows, which provided financial support in times of shortage and physical protection in case of disputes with other farmers or local notables.

The Han Capital at Xian

The urban growth that had been one of the most notable social developments in the late Zhou era continued in the Han period. The new capital city at Xian took on the basic features of Chinese imperial cities from that time forward. Laid out on a somewhat distorted grid, Xian had great roadways that gave access to and defined the main quarters of the city. Much of the city was protected by long earth and brick walls, with towers and gates at regular intervals. Estimates of Xian's population range from about 100,000, which probably includes only people living within the walls, to 250,000, which includes people living outside the walls and in neighboring villages.

The emperor lived in an inner or **forbidden city,** which only his family, servants, and closest advisors were permitted to enter. The inner city was an impressive complex of palaces, towers, and decorated gateways. Each palace included audience halls, banquet rooms, large gardens and fishponds, and luxurious living quarters for the emperor, his wife and concubines (women who lived in the palace as secondary wives or sexual partners for the emperors), and their children. To the west of Xian, beyond the city walls, a large pleasure garden was laid out for the imperial family. It included one of the earliest known zoos.

The forbidden city was surrounded by administrative buildings and the palaces of the most powerful aristocratic and scholar-gentry households. Under later dynasties, this zone became a distinct imperial city within the capital. Some of the imperial palaces and government buildings were made of stone or brick, but many were made of clay covered with brightly colored plaster. Most were roofed with the glazed tiles with upturned edges that would become characteristic of Chinese architecture in the following millennia.

Towns and Traders

The Han capital at Xian was only one of many imposing cities in China in this era. It is likely that

Figure 4.6 *A Han relief on a funeral tile found in the Chengdu region in Sichuan (eastern Han dynasty, 25 B.C.E.–221 C.E.). The hunting scene in a luxuriant landscape in the upper panel is linked with a scene (lower panel) of peasants working in the fields. Such illustrations enable historians to track the development of toolmaking and weaponmaking in ancient civilizations such as China. They also make it possible to study patterns of organization in agrarian and artisan production (for which direct evidence is sparse) as well as the leisure activities of officials and the landed elites.*

China was the most urbanized civilization in the world at this time—a fact that tells us much about the productivity of its agricultural sector. There were many towns with more than 10,000 people and several towns, such as Xian, with populations in the tens of thousands. Most towns were walled, and many were administrative centers dominated by the multistory residences and offices of imperial officials and scholar-gentry notables. But other towns grew up around mining and manufacturing centers, and many were centers of trade that continued to grow in the Han era.

This growth was greatly advanced by Han military expansion to the west and south. It resulted in the establishment of new overland trade routes into central Asia and south China. Overseas links were also established with northern Vietnam, the rest of southeast Asia, and the rich trading towns of coastal India.

Large mercantile firms controlled these long-distance trading networks. They grew wealthy from the transport and sale of bulk items, such as grain and horses, as well as from supplying the elite classes with exotic luxury items such as incense, fragrant woods, and rhinoceros horn, which when ground into an edible powder was believed to enhance male potency. Merchant families also made great fortunes by lending money and investing in mining, shipbuilding, sheep raising, and less legitimate enterprises such as gambling halls, brothels, and grave robbing.

Although the merchant classes became wealthier and more numerous, they found it increasingly difficult to translate their profits into political power or social status. Fearing their rivalry, the scholar-gentry induced successive Han rulers to issue laws that restricted merchant activities and privileges. Under most Han rulers, for example, merchants could not hold administrative posts, although they often exerted local influence. They were not allowed to own carriages, carry weapons, or wear silk clothing. Scholar-gentry writers consistently ranked merchants below the peasants in terms of their social usefulness, arguing that peasants produced food and essential services, whereas traders lived off the labor of others.

A Genius for Invention and Artisan Production

Long before the Han, the Chinese had displayed a special aptitude for invention and technological innovation. They had built massive irrigation systems, canal networks, and fortifications. They devised cropping techniques that for millennia were some of the most productive known to humanity. In the centuries of Han rule, however, their talent for invention reached new heights, and with it rose the excellence of their artisan production. There is little doubt that China was the most technologically innovative and advanced of all the classical civilizations.

At the level of the elite, the introduction of the brush pen and paper at the end of the 2nd century B.C.E. greatly facilitated the administrative work of the scholar-gentry and advanced their literary and artistic production. The Han Chinese also developed watermills to grind grain and power artisan workshops, and rudders and compasses to steer and guide ships (although in the Han era compasses were used primarily for divination; they were not used by sailors until the 9th century C.E.). They devised ingenious mining techniques to allow them to fully exploit the iron and copper resources that had become critical to warfare and domestic production. In the centuries of Han rule, silkmaking was carried to new levels of refinement, and techniques for making lacquerware and porcelain were pioneered, which allowed China to remain a leader in ceramics until well into the modern era.

All these advances promoted the growth of the artisan, manufacturing classes. Artisans tended to be clustered in special sectors of Chinese towns, but in some regions villages were devoted almost exclusively to crafts such as potterymaking or silk weaving. Skilled artisans were in high demand and probably had a higher living standard than most peasants, although the scholar-gentry accorded them a lower official social status. Again, the ideal and reality did not necessarily correspond, for some members of the artisan classes amassed wealth and were allowed to carry weapons, ride horses, and wear silk clothing.

The Arts and Sciences in the Han Era

Chinese art during the classical period was largely decorative. Careful detail and expert artistry were most valued. Artistic styles often reflected the precision and geometric qualities of the many symbols of Chinese writing, and calligraphy itself became a highly prized art form. Chinese painting was much less developed than it became under later Chinese dynasties. But the bronzes and ceramic figurines (Figure 4.7), bowls, and vases produced in this era set a very high standard for later Chinese artists. Important work was also done in jade and ivory carvings and woven silk screens.

In the sciences, the Chinese were more drawn to practical experimentation than theorizing. By 444 B.C.E., court astronomers had developed an accurate calendar based on a year of 365.5 days. Later astronomers calculated the movements of the planets Saturn and Jupiter and observed sunspots more than 1500 years before comparable observations were made in Europe. The main purpose of Chinese astronomy was to make celestial phenomena predictable, as part of a wider interest in ensuring harmony between heaven and earth. In astronomy and other areas, Chinese scientists steadily improved their instruments, even inventing a seismograph to register the strength of earthquakes. The Chinese were also active in medical research. They made great strides in diagnosing diseases and prescribing herbal remedies and other drugs to cure them. Recent evidence

Visualizing the Past

Capital Designs and Patterns of Political Power

The design and physical layout of the capital cities of early civilizations can tell us a great deal about the distribution of political power and social status in different centers of the ancient world. In addition, the configurations of these pivotal cities usually manifest religious beliefs and conceptions of the cosmic order in the ways they are oriented and physically constructed. Therefore, plans of the capital centers of ancient civilizations can be "read" like written texts to help us understand the early history of some of humankind's greatest civilizations. Reproduced below are schematic diagrams of some of the key features of the capital cities of three of the great early civilizations of Eurasia: from Xian in Han China, Athens in Greece, and Harappa in India. Study and compare these diagrams for what they tell us about the kinds of elite groups that exercised political power, social stratification, and thinking about the relationship between the supernatural and human rulers in each civ-

ilization for which they served as capitals. In thinking about these issues, you may want to refer to relevant sections in Chapters 3, 4, and 5.

Questions: Which social groups were the most powerful politically in each society? Was supreme power shared or concentrated in a single person? To what extent was each civilization bureaucratized? How prominent was military force in the exercise of power by the elites in each civilization? To what extent was political power legitimized by religious figures, ideas, and conceptions of the workings of the cosmos? To what degree did the rulers and political elites seek to separate themselves from the subject population, and what evidence could you use to determine this? In what ways would these capital centers compare and contrast with the physical layout of Washington, D.C., in the present day?

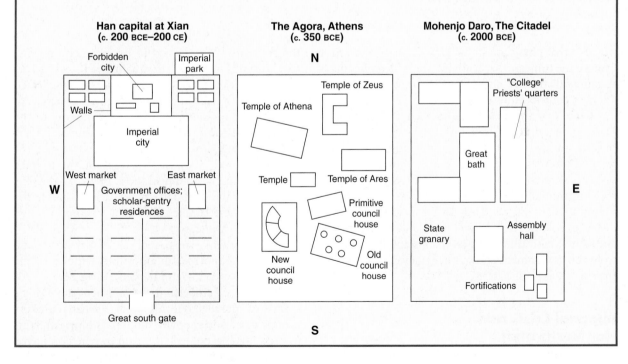

Figure 4.7   *A range of popular Chinese entertainments from the Han period are illustrated by this group of terra cotta figurines. Two musicians on the left happily accompany the dancers in the center, while two servants on the right appear to be sharing a bit of gossip. Such figurines provide invaluable evidence regarding the lives of ordinary people in classical China.*

suggests that physicians in the Han era had begun to explore the principles of acupuncture, which remains the most distinctive and one of the most beneficial Chinese contributions to medicine.

Chinese mathematics also stressed the practical. Daoism encouraged some interest in studying the orderly processes of nature, but most research focused on how things work. For example, Chinese scholars studied the mathematics of music in ways that promoted advances in acoustics. They also sought to work out standards for the measurement of distance, volume, and weight. This kind of scientific and mathematical learning won substantial backing from the government and was generally approved by the shi scholar-officials.

Imperial Crisis and Han Restoration

For more than two centuries the Han maintained their hold over a unified Chinese empire. But by the end of the 1st century B.C.E., problems centering on

the court itself threatened to bring an end to Han rule. After Han Wudi, the quality of the emperors declined markedly. Many of his successors neglected the duties of government and, like the monarchs of the late Shang and Zhou, indulged heavily in the pleasures of food, drink, and concubines. As the hold of the emperors over state affairs weakened, the powerful families of their wives sought to take charge of imperial administration. In 6 C.E., the only male heir of the Han dynasty was a small child, giving one of these families, the Wang, the opportunity to seize the throne.

With the initial support of the scholar-gentry and the general populace, an ambitious nephew of the Empress Dowager Wang named **Wang Mang** proclaimed himself emperor in 9 C.E. But Wang Mang's many well-intended reforms rapidly alienated the very groups that had originally supported him. Attempts to exert imperial control over land ownership angered the scholar-gentry. Government monopolies, which sent the price of food and other essentials soaring, led to widespread peasant unrest. In 23 C.E., the hapless

Wang Mang was overthrown, and the Han dynasty was restored.

The Later Han and Imperial Collapse

The later Han dynasty ruled a unified China for nearly 200 years. For a time the peace and prosperity of the former Han era returned. Internal rebels and nomad invaders were suppressed. The last centuries of the dynasty saw little of the innovation and creativity of the early centuries of Han rule. Inventions were improved, scholars commented on the works of earlier thinkers, the population of the empire continued to grow, and trading networks expanded. But major breakthroughs in government, the arts, and invention would have to wait for centuries and the next great dynasty, the Tang.

Politically, the later Han was a period of steady decline. Han rulers were plagued by struggles between factions at the court, which had been transferred from Xian eastward to the city of Loyang (Map 4.1). Challenges from the families of the emperors' wives continued, but they were complicated by the growing power of the **eunuchs:** men who had been castrated to make them reliable guardians of the emperor's wives and concubines. Although there were often many concubines in residence, they had no official status and their children normally could not inherit the throne. Some eunuchs were orphans, but many were sons of families who saw their recruitment into the eunuch corps at the palace as a sure way to financial security and political advancement.

Over the years, the number of eunuchs increased, and after the Han dynasty was restored, they gained substantially in power as palace administrators and inner advisors of the later emperors. In the last decades of Han rule, these emperors attempted to use the eunuchs to check the power of their wives' families. The three-way struggles that developed between the scholar-gentry, the families of the rulers' wives, and the eunuchs eventually ripped the court apart.

Divisions at the center of the empire weakened the emperor's ability to stop nomadic incursions and remedy the worsening conditions of the mass of the people. A weak imperial administration meant growing power for landlords and increasing autonomy for regional officials. Local notables pressed the peasantry that worked their lands for more taxes and higher rents. Secret societies spread like wildfire, and peasant uprisings broke out throughout the empire. Military commanders and regional lords seized power and fought against each other for the right to claim the Han throne.

The dynasty was not officially overthrown until 220 C.E., but decades earlier its power had been usurped. The end of the Han meant the return of the warring states and began nearly 400 years of division and turmoil that ended only with the rise of the Sui dynasty at the end of the 6th century C.E. (see Chapter 10).

 GLOBAL CONNECTIONS: Classical China and the World

The short-lived Qin dynasty and four centuries of Han rule established the basic components of a civilization that would last for thousands of years, making it the longest-lived in world history. As the achievements of the classical age demonstrate, China had also become one of the most creative and influential civilizations of all human history. The strength of its agrarian base has allowed China to carry about one-fifth of the total human population from the last centuries B.C.E. to the present day. The productivity of its peasants has made it possible for some of the world's largest cities to flourish in China, and nurtured one of history's largest and most creative elites. In China's classical age, the world's largest and for much of history its best run bureaucracy was established, and civil service exams were invented.

The Chinese also pioneered in the development of a whole range of basic technologies that were later disseminated over much of Eurasia and northern Africa. These ranged from paper and compasses, which created new possibilities for human communication and cross-cultural interaction, and water mills, which provided new sources of power and food processing, to porcelain, which elevated dining to unparalleled levels of elegance and opened up exciting possibilities for artistic expression. Over the centuries, beginning in this classical period itself, Chinese merchants and central Asian nomads disseminated these inventions over much of the globe, and have consequently contributed to technological transformations in societies as diverse as those found in Japan, Rome, the Middle East, and England.

Chinese influence was directly involved in the patterns of world trade that began to emerge during the classical centuries. China's production of silk was unusually high quality, and the product began to be valued elsewhere, in India, the Middle East, and even the distant Mediterranean during the Roman Empire. Trade in silk and other luxury products generated a network of roads through central Asia known collectively as the **Silk Roads.** Under the Han, the Chinese government actively encouraged this trade with regions to the west. Improved roads, both in China and in the Middle East, encouraged trade as well. One Chinese emissary, Zhang Qian, actually traveled to western India. Most trade along the silk roads was carried by nomadic merchants, and until well after the classical period no one seems to have traveled all the way from China to the Mediterranean or vice versa. But the trade was lively, spurring attention also to sea routes in the Indian Ocean. While we do not know the volume of goods involved, silk road trade was important enough to win considerable attention in upper-class and government circles, and it provided an initial framework on which global trading patterns would later elaborate.

China's role was greater still in the huge swath of territory from central Asia to the Pacific. Over much of central and east Asia, Chinese influence in political thought and organization, approaches to warfare, art and architecture, religion, and social norms was pervasive. For nearly two thousand years, China would serve as the "Middle Kingdom" for the diverse peoples of this vast area—the focus of their trade and the model for their often successful efforts to fashion their own variants of empire, prosperity and sophisticated lifestyles.

Further Readings

Good introductions to life in China in the classical age can be found in Wolfram Eberhard's *A History of China* (1977); Dun J. Li's *The Ageless Chinese* (1965); and E. Reischauer and J. K. Fairbank's *East Asia: The Great Tradition* (1960). *China's Civilization* (1976), by Arthur Cotterell and David Morgan, contains useful illustrations and incorporates more recent interpretations of developments in early China. Two works deal extensively with the life and reign of Shi Huangdi: Arthur Cotterell's *The First Emperor of China* (1981) and Li Yu-Ning's *The First Emperor of China* (1975).

A brief and clear introduction to Chinese thought is provided by Frederic Mote's *Intellectual Foundations of China* (1971). A much more detailed study that places Chinese thought in a comparative context can be found in Benjamin Schwartz's *The World of Thought in Ancient China* (1983). Michael Loewe's *Everyday Life in Early Imperial China* (1968) is excellent on Han society, as is the more detailed and scholarly work *Han Social Structure* (1972) by T'ung-Tsu Ch'u, which includes extensive quotations from Chinese texts and valuable insights into the position of women, merchants, artisans, and eunuchs. The shifting position of women is the focus of Bret Hinsch's *Women in Early Imperial China* (2002). A detailed survey of the archeological work done on Han sites and what they tell us about Han society is provided by Wang Shongshu's *Han Civilization* (1982). Michèle Pirazzoli-t'Serstevens's lavishly illustrated study *The Han Civilization of China* (1982) contains the most comprehensive, up-to-date, and readable overview of Han civilization available. Edmund Capon and William MacQuitty's *Princes of Jade* (1973) is less informative and reliable, but it also contains superb plates and illustrations.

The most authoritative and detailed account of science and technology in the Han and later dynastic periods can be found in Joseph Needham's multivolume study, *Science and Civilization in China* (1954–). Burton Watson's *Courtier and Commoner in Ancient China* (1974), which is a translation of portions of Ban Ku's *History of the Former Han*, includes examples and anecdotes that allow the student to gain a vivid sense of the day-to-day workings of Han society. China's trade and cultural exchanges with neighboring civilizations is treated insightfully in Xinru Liu, *Ancient India and Ancient China: Trade and Religious Exchanges, AD 1-600* (Delhi, 1988).

On the Web

The life of Confucius is addressed at http://www.confucius.org/intro/edbio.htm. A useful comparison between Confucius and Socrates is made at http://www.san.beck.org/C&S-Contents.html. Connections between Confucianism, Daoism, and Western philosophy are made at http://www.friesian.com/confuci.htm. These sites also offer extensive examinations of Confucian philosophy. Mencius' life is reviewed at http://www.san.beck.org/EC14-Confucian.html#4. The life of Laozi is reviewed at http://www.campus.northpark.edu/history/WebChron/China/LaoTse.CP.html, while the philosophy of Daoism is explored in an enjoyable, informal, and therefore Daoist way at http://www.his.com/~merkin/DaoBrief.html. The place of Legalist ruler Shi Huangdi's Qin dynasty and its impact on Chinese history is debated at http://emuseum.mnsu.edu/prehistory/china/early_imperial_china/qin.html. An analysis of his famous tomb can be found at http://www.utexas.edu/courses/wilson/ant304/biography/arybios98/smith-bio.html. A spectacular visual recreation of the tomb complex as it was at the time of its construction is offered at http://www.taisei.co.jp/cg_e/ancient_world/xian/axian.html

Take a virtual tour of later versions of the Great Wall at http://www.chinavista.com/travel/greatwall/greatwall.html and the imperial Forbidden City at http://www.chinavista.com/beijing/gugong/!start.html, which suggest the originals designed in earlier times. The value of such products, or lack of same, is analyzed in Sunzi's "Art of War" offered at http://www.swan.ac.uk/poli/texts/suntzu/arta.htm. The text itself is available at http://www.chinapage.com/sunzi-e.html and offered indexed by topic at http://acc6.its.brooklyn.cuny.edu/~phalsall/texts/artofwar.html.

CHAPTER 5

CLASSICAL GREECE AND THE HELLENISTIC WORLD

Vase art, with realistic figures from Greek legends surrounded by geometric designs, played a prominent role in Greece. In this myth, Hercules is bringing the Erymanthian boar back to Eurystheus, who is so frightened that he has hidden in a wine jar. The representation of emotion was more vivid than it had been in stylized Egyptian art.

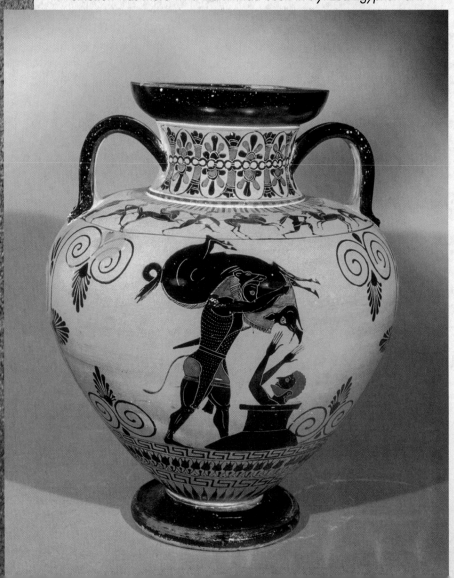

Beginning about 800 B.C.E. on the peninsula and islands of Greece and in the surrounding territory in the eastern Mediterranean, a second center of classical civilization began to take shape.

Greek politics and culture flourished until about 400 B.C.E., then began to decline. A military empire then emerged, initially forged by Alexander the Great, which set up what is called the **Hellenistic period. Hellenism** means "derived from the Greek." Under Alexander and then several regional kings, many Greek values and styles spread through the Middle East and much of northern Africa and southern Europe.

Although the Greeks often battled with each other, they had a proud sense of their own values and their differences from outsiders. Greeks thought foreigners sounded funny, making noises like "bar, bar, bar"—so they called them barbarians. The Greeks alternately attributed great events to the often whimsical actions of the gods and to human action. Individuals unquestionably produced the enduring art and political theory of Athens in the 5th century B.C.E., but what was special about the framework that produced these individuals? Here is a chance to discuss the role of human agency.

As in China, classical Greek civilization built on earlier regional civilizations, which had created elaborate monuments, developed a form of writing, and produced strong monarchies. Influenced by cultures in the Middle East and Egypt, civilization on the island of Crete and around Mycenae on the Greek mainland had expanded for several centuries after 2000 B.C.E. However, internal warfare and a wave of Indo-European invasions ended the first phase of civilization in this part of the Mediterranean by about 1100 B.C.E. Rich capital cities, including Mycenae, were abandoned. For a time agriculture itself deteriorated as some Greeks turned to nomadic life, and purely local governments predominated.

By 800 B.C.E., a full-fledged classical society began to take shape. Like the other classical societies, Greek civilization extended over a wide region, ultimately embracing a far larger area than any of the earlier cultures of the eastern Mediterranean. The Greeks produced less tidy political unities than the Chinese emperors had in their expansion, but their cultural and commercial outreach and periodic military forays affected a large portion of western Asia, northeastern Africa, and southern Europe. Many political traditions and cultural forms survived classical Greece itself, influencing later societies in the Mediterranean and beyond.

1600 B.C.E.	1200 B.C.E.	800 B.C.E.	600 B.C.E.	500 B.C.E.	400 B.C.E.	300 B.C.E.
1600 Indo-European invasions **1400** Kingdom of Mycenae; Trojan War	**1000–800** Greek "Dark Ages" after Dorian invasions	**800–700** Rise of Greek city-states and economy; Homeric epics, *Iliad* and *Odyssey*	**600–500** Spread of commercial agriculture; rise of social protest **550** Cyrus the Great forms Persian Empire **546–527** Pisistratus tyrant in Athens **525–456** Aeschylus launches tradition of dramatic tragedy	**500–449** Greek defeat of Persia; spread of Athenian Empire **470–430** Athens at its height: Pericles, Phidias, Sophocles, Socrates **431–404** Peloponnesian Wars	**399** Socrates condemned **384–322** Aristotle **359–336** Philip II of Macedon **338–323** Macedonian Empire; Alexander the Great	**300–100** Hellenistic period **250–126** Flourishing of Hellenistic astronomy and mathematics

A Revealing Fight

When Alexander the Great was campaigning in Persia, one night he had dinner with a boyhood friend, Cleitus, now one of his generals. They probably drank too much wine. Cleitus accused his commander of becoming a Persian. Alexander took this as a great insult and ran him through with a spear. This chapter will help you understand why Cleitus would say this and why Alexander would take offense. The story also says something about the personality of many conquerors.

The Persian Empire: Parallel Power in the Middle East

 As Greek civilization began to form, an important Persian empire developed, centered in the eastern portion of the Middle East. This empire, and several successor states, maintained separate political and cultural values. Ultimately less influential than Greek culture, the Persian tradition surfaced at many points in world history and still affects the nation of Iran today.

After the fall of the great Egyptian and Hittite empires in the Middle East by 1200 B.C.E., much smaller states predominated. Then new powers stepped in, first the Assyrians and then an influx of Iranians (Persians). A great conqueror emerged by 550 B.C.E. **Cyrus the Great** established a massive Persian Empire, which ran across the northern Middle East and into northwestern India (Figure 5.1). The new empire was the clearest successor to the great Mesopotamian states of the past, and Cyrus carefully tolerated traditional cultures. The Iranians advanced iron technology in the Middle East.

Persia was also the center of a major new religion. A religious leader, Zoroaster, revised the polytheistic religious tradition of the Sumerians by seeing life as a battle between two divine forces: good and evil. **Zoroastrianism** emphasized the importance of personal moral choice in picking one side or the other, with a Last Judgment ultimately deciding the eternal fate of each person. The righteous would live on in a heaven, the "House of Song," while the evil would be condemned to eternal pain. Zoroastrianism converted Persia's later emperors and added to the cultural richness of this civilization.

Later kings expanded Persian holdings. They were unable to defeat the Greeks, but they long dominated the Middle East, providing an extensive period of peace and prosperity. The empire even set up a postal service, probably the world's first. Ultimately, the Persian Empire was toppled by Alexander the Great, a Greek-educated conqueror. Persian language and culture survived in the northeastern portion of the Middle East, periodically affecting developments in the region as a whole.

Figure 5.1 *Using ceremonial styles similar to those of earlier Mesopotamia, the great Persian Empire celebrated its powerful kings. This wall relief is on the great ceremonial stairway leading to the royal audience hall of Darius and Xerxes.*

The rise of classical civilization in Greece was thus in competition with that in Persia. Greek achievements ultimately proved more influential—for example, Zoroastrianism faded in importance—but they were not unrivaled.

The Political Character of Classical Greece

Greek leaders valued an intense political life, and political forms—indeed, many of our terms, such as *politics* itself, come from the Greek heritage. Greek politics usually was localized. It emphasized no single kind of government organization. Rule by aristocrats was more characteristic, but periods of tyranny were also important. The Greeks also sketched a dynamic version of democracy.

A key spur to Greek civilization was a general revival of trade in the eastern Mediterranean. Trade allowed many Greek city-states (including Greek-dominated cities in Greece and Mediterranean Asia, particularly in what is now Turkey) to increase their wealth and their range of contacts. By 700 B.C.E., several Greek centers had trading connections around the Black Sea and in Egypt and southern Italy. Eco-nomic revival prompted population growth and social change in the Greek centers, which encouraged new political structures that challenged dominance by the owners of landed estates.

The Emergence of Greek Forms

Greek political systems evolved rapidly from the civilization's early days until a period of decline set in after a major internal war at the end of the 5th century B.C.E. In contrast, cultural development continued into the Hellenistic centuries, when the civilization's geographic range widened on the heels of Alexander the Great's conquests.

During the 8th century B.C.E., the Greeks adapted the Phoenician alphabet for writing their own language. This alphabet was easier to learn than any previous writing system. The advancement of literacy further stimulated trade by aiding in the exchange of commercial information and enhancing cultural life. At this point two great poems, the *Iliad* and the *Odyssey*, which focused on the legendary Mycenaean War with Troy, were written down, possibly by the poet Homer, to whom they were attributed, or by a larger group of writers gradually formalizing oral tradition. The Homeric achievement set forth definitions of the gods and human nature that profoundly shaped later Greek thinking. Soon after the Homeric epics were written, other writers in several cities, including the famous woman poet Sappho, began writing poems that ranged from military songs to lyric statements. A distinctive Greek art also began to emerge. Architects defined the shape of the Greek temple as an oblong building framed by pillars. Early Greek sculptors used Egyptian models. Later sculptors moved toward more realistic portrayals including full-profile figures. Geometric designs on pottery similarly yielded to more realistic scenes of human activities, reflecting the growing appreciation of human beauty and the central importance of human life.

The City-State as a Political Unit

Greek politics also took shape in the three centuries after 800 B.C.E. Greek government in this early period and thereafter revolved around the city-state, a regional government centered in a major city, embracing the surrounding agricultural land as well. These units could be tiny or large, like Sparta, one of the key city-states. Athens, the most famous city-state, was about the size of the state of Rhode Island; by the 5th century B.C.E., Athens had a population of roughly 250,000, of whom 100,000 lived in the city proper. The city-state government came naturally to Greece, partly because a mountainous terrain made larger connections difficult (Map 5.1). Many city-states were formed in a valley or bay, with a single city organizing the surrounding agricultural area. However, Greek settlements in other areas, such as the northern Middle East or southern Italy, also adopted the city-state form even when natural conditions did not require it. By 600 B.C.E., nearly 300 independent

Map 5.1 *The Greek World. Mountainous terrain encouraged local city-state politics, but access to the sea promoted expansion and commerce.*

cities had developed in Greece. Although the city-state form promoted frequent wars because no single unit predominated, it did encourage a political life of unusual intensity. This explains why the Greek word for city-state government—*polis* (plural *poleis*)—is the origin of our word *politics.*

Early Greek poleis were ruled mainly by land-owning aristocrats, mostly descendants of the Indo-European warrior class who were still responsible for most military activities. Free farmers were also citizens, supporting the government and often participating in periodic assemblies but not ruling directly. Councils played a vital role in the early Greek city-states, even when there was a single king or other ruler.

This system increasingly was challenged from about 700 B.C.E. onward. With the commercial expansion that began in the 8th century, aristocratic rule often was disputed. Some city-states escaped major contests, remaining largely agricultural; Sparta, for example, maintained a strong militaristic regime under aristocratic leadership. But in active trading centers, merchants and a growing urban manufacturing group chafed under aristocratic rule. Furthermore, in many areas agriculture itself changed. Landlords began to specialize in growing olives and grapes and in making cooking oil and wines. They began importing cheap grain from colonies in Asia, Egypt, and Sicily to provide basic foodstuffs. These imports squeezed out local independent farmers, widening the gulf between the rich and poor. The ideals of widespread citizenship were contradicted by these developments.

The result by the 6th century B.C.E. was growing social protest, pitting urban groups and dispossessed farmers against the aristocratic elite. One common outcome was a series of tyrants who won popular support against the aristocratic interest. These tyrants often developed public works and other activities that benefited the lower classes and the cities, while stifling aristocratic opposition. The idea of one-man rule contradicted traditions of community governance. Many reformers tried to restore earlier ideals of citizenship while dealing with the new social tensions. **Solon,** a reformer in Athens early in the 6th century, set up laws that would ease the burden of debts on the farmers by prohibiting slavery for such debts. The idea developed that laws could be written and revised, rather than being passed down unaltered from tradition; here was one source of new political interest and participation.

Other forces pressed for political change. Military activity increasingly involved larger numbers of citizens who formed tightly organized and well-coordinated lines of infantry. Naval forces in the port cities, such as Athens, depended on extensive recruitment of rowers. This development increased the need for strong bonds between citizens within the polis and gave new leverage to nonaristocrats. By 500 B.C.E., participation in public life became a widespread ideal in many poleis; it corresponded to the busy functions that grouped city dwellers together in the marketplace.

The dominant religion also supported this ideal of political unity and involvement. Each city-state had its own patron god or goddess, and regular rituals called forth prayer and ceremony on behalf of the city's well-being. These ceremonies included plays, choruses, sporting events, and religious exercises, all calling attention to the power and cohesion of the polis. In 399 B.C.E., the philosopher Socrates was condemned by a jury in Athens for corrupting his students by encouraging skepticism and doubt; he was given a choice between exile and death. He chose death because, as he said, the city had been the source of his character and he owed it obedience; better to die than to be apart.

The Rise of Democracy in Athens

After the period of greatest social tension, city-state governments continued to vary. Aristocratic councils returned in many places; Sparta had two kings to check each other, ruling on behalf of the military aristocracy. Generally, however, a democratic tendency gained ground by the 5th century, and here Athens proudly took the lead.

Athens had undergone a fairly standard, if highly dramatic, political evolution before its democratic flowering in the 5th century B.C.E. Solon's reforms expanded the citizenship rights of most men. Citizens could elect a council that monitored the aristocratic government. But these reforms did not prevent the rise of the tyrannical leader **Pisastratus,** who gained popular support against the traditional noble councils, ruling from 546 to 527 B.C.E. Pisastratus sponsored major new buildings and public works, which created new jobs, while dominating the major councils. Soon after his death, a new reform leader, **Cleisthenes,** reestablished a council, elected by all citizens, that prepared agendas for an assembly composed of the citizens themselves. Athens was ready to become the most powerful and most fully developed Greek democracy of the 5th century B.C.E.

Full-blown Athenian democracy, after a few additional reforms about 462 B.C.E., continued to depend on the popular assembly as sovereign authority. All decisions of state emanated from this body or had to be approved by it, and all citizens could debate or propose in assembly meetings. This was direct democracy—the word *democracy* comes from the Greek word for people, *demos*—rather than rule through elected representatives. Because the assembly met frequently, only a minority of citizens had time to attend regularly, and a few leading speakers usually predominated. Citizens also served as jurors in court trials, and every judicial decision could be appealed to a citizen board. Most officials were selected by lot on the grounds that any citizen could serve as an administrator. A few key officials—the generals and imperial treasurers—were elected, usually from the nobility, but the assembly could remove or punish them for faulty service. Terms of office were brief, to encourage popular control.

This was a democracy of a different sort from the version common in the contemporary world. It depended on the small size of the city-state and the intensive participation of its citizens. Furthermore, many adults were excluded from political rights. Women had no rights of political participation. Half of all adult males were not citizens in any sense, being slaves or foreigners. Even at its most democratic, the Athenian government was shaped by considerable aristocratic behind-the-scenes control. The Athenian leader **Pericles** guided Athens during its decades of

greatest glory after the mid-5th century, was an aristocrat who managed to direct affairs year after year through wise manipulation of political groups and his own prestige, even when he did not hold formal office. Many Athenians, and still more Greeks in city-states where democracy did not go as far, persisted in believing that real political virtue lay in aristocratic rule (*aristocracy* being derived from the Greek word *aristos,* or "rule of the best"). Sparta continued to represent the aristocratic alternative.

Athenian democracy rested far more directly on the public devotion and talent of citizens than modern democracies do. Pericles offered a classic definition of the democratic ideal:

> The administration is in the hands of the many and not of the few. But while the law secures equal justice to all alike in their private disputes, the claim of excellence is also recognized; and when a citizen is in any way distinguished he is preferred to the public service, not as a matter of privilege but as the reward of merit. Neither is poverty a bar, but a man may benefit his country whatever be the obscurity of his condition.

This was not an easy political system because of the expectations of responsible service to the state. Citizen juries handled trials of officials accused of serving badly. The names of politicians judged to be potential tyrants were scratched on *ostraka,* or pottery fragments, such as those pictured in Figure 5.2. If one name was listed often enough, the person was banished—ostracized—

Figure 5.2 *Ostraka from the Athenian Agora, 5th century B.C.E. Ostraka are votes to banish the people whose names are scratched on the potsherds; the names include Themistocles and his principal opponent, Aristeides.*

for 10 years. The ostraka shown here list the names of two political opponents in Athens's great war with Persia, Themistocles and Aristeides.

Ideals and reality could clash. Alcibiades (c. 450–404; Figure 5.3) was one ambitious official often accused of fatal mismanagement as Athens was locked in a life and death struggle with Sparta, Athens's bitter city-state rival, in the **Peloponnesian War.** Wealthy and handsome, this aristocrat had studied with Socrates and was related to Pericles. He saw war as an opportunity for personal glory, urging the democratic assembly to reject peace opportunities and then mounting an ill-timed effort to conquer Sicily to gain new power. Finally brought down by his opponents, he joined the Spartan attack on Athens. Later he regained popular favor in Athens and won a command in the navy. He fled when Athens lost, but the Spartans arranged to have him murdered. Historians have often used Alcibiades' case not just as an example of power hunger but as a warning about how democracies can choose dangerous leaders when they face crisis and when voters are lured by promises of easy gains.

By the end of the 5th century, when Athens plunged into a devastating war with Sparta, the polis demonstrated some of the weaknesses as well as the strengths of democracy. Ordinary citizens worked hard in the war, but the lower-class citizens, eager for government jobs and booty, often pressed for reckless expeditions that weakened the state in its military efforts and contributed substantially to ultimate defeat.

A Comparison of Greek and Chinese Political Styles

The Greek political approach involved intense emphasis on political virtue and responsibility. Participation in politics was part of the ideal life. This was true in aristocratic states as well as in the less typical democracies. This approach, with its concern for a sound political system, reflected some similarities with the values Confucianism emphasized in China. But in the decentralized atmosphere of Greek politics, a far larger array of political structures was tossed up than was true in China, with its greater emphasis on a single centralized system. Also, the Greeks placed more value on participation (including the idea of citizenship) than on hierarchy and obedience. There was more emphasis on formal preparation of law (a theme the Romans later extended) and far less emphasis on a bureaucracy and bureaucratic codes.

Greek Diplomacy and the Tensions of United Effort

During the four centuries when Greek political forms evolved, many city-states sent out additional colonies, which expanded exposure to Greek political values. Colonies helped relieve population pressure at home. They also provided vital grain supplies to the mainland while serving as markets for processed products, including wine, cooking oil, and manufactured goods. By the 5th century Greek colonies dotted the Mediterranean coast of present-day Turkey, the entire coastline of the Black Sea, and key points in northern Africa, Italy, and even southern France and Spain. Map 5.2 shows the key centers of the Greek colonial empire. By providing new wealth, colonies supported the political and cultural vigor of Greece.

At their best, from 750 to 420 B.C.E., the Greek city-states were capable of sufficient coordination to deal with a variety of general problems. They joined in regular celebrations such as the athletic competitions of the **Olympic games**, which grouped wrestlers and runners in often bitter (and occasionally rigged) competitions (Figure 5.4).

Figure 5.3 *Alcibiades was the handsome and greedy Athenian leader whose career and final failures affected the great war with Sparta.*

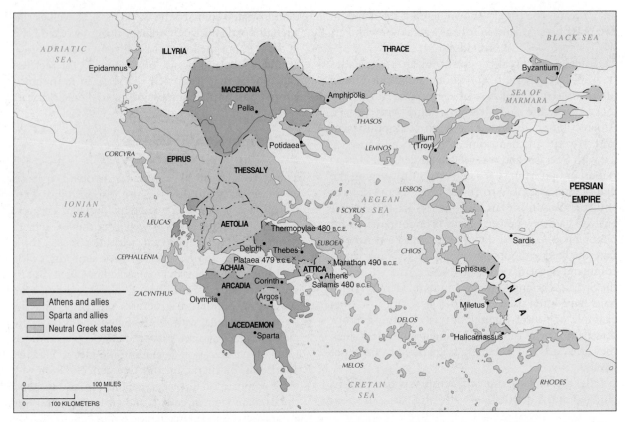

Map 5.2   *Greece and Greek Colonies of the World, c. 431 B.C.E. On the eve of the Peloponnesian War, Greek civilization had succeeded in spreading to key points around the Mediterranean world.*

They supported some common religious organizations, such as the **oracles at Delphi,** whose predictions and advice were widely sought.

More important was the collaboration that allowed Greece to defeat its most pressing outside enemy, the great empire of Persia. Soon after Cyrus the Great created the Persian Empire, he turned against wealthy Greek colonies along the Asian side of the Mediterranean and conquered them by about 540 B.C.E. Persian power became an obvious threat to the Greek mainland, impelling cooperation between Athens and Sparta, the most powerful city-states. In 499 B.C.E. the conquered Greek cities rebelled against the Persians and were aided by the Athenian navy. The rebellion failed, and the Persian kings (Darius I, then Xerxes) moved against Greece in punishment. In 480 B.C.E., a Persian army of 100,000 troops moved down the Greek peninsula, initially winning great success, and captured Athens, destroying much of the city. But the Athenian-led Greek fleet, which defeated the Persian navy and cut

off supplies, and then a Spartan-led force bested the Persian army. While Persia continued to dominate the Middle East, Greek independence was preserved. The greatest age of Greek politics and culture followed, including the perfection of Athenian political institutions and the Age of Pericles.

The **Persian Wars** provided some of the most dramatic moments in classical Greek history. In the battle at Thermopylae, 300 Spartans and a few thousand other Greek soldiers blocked a huge Persian army until they were betrayed by local Greeks and caught from behind. After the Greek military triumph at Marathon, a runner labored nearly 23 miles to bring news to Athens, collapsing after the word was passed.

In the years after Persia's defeat, Athens began to form an empire of its own. Athenian naval power helped organize an alliance of lesser Greek cities (see Map 5.2). This **Delian league** was headed by an Athenian admiral and its treasury was controlled by Athens. Increasingly, many cities became completely

Figure 5.4 *This statue of a discus thrower by the sculptor Myron shows the Greek love for athletics and the realistic but heroic style adopted for human figures by the classical Greek artists.*

integrating most new territory into a single political entity gained great attention. In contrast, city-states, even democracies such as Athens, tended to look on colonies as centers to exploit for wealth and supplies, paying less attention to durable regional linkages.

The Greek political structure was fragile. With so many different government units, division could easily override common purpose. Class separatism also produced animosity, with democrats and aristocrats glaring at each other both within and among the poleis. A new and bitter conflict between the leading states set the stage for declining political vigor within Greece itself.

Even warfare could go wrong. Greek soldiers, most of them farmers, fought shoulder to shoulder in units called phalanxes. Cooperation was key. As one observer put it, "Farming teaches a person to help others. In fighting enemies, each person needs the help of others." Unfortunately, things could get confused if a line was broken through. In a battle with Sparta in 424 this happened to the Athenians. Their vision hampered by heavy helmets, they began hacking at everything that moved, including each other.

Athens Versus Sparta

The growing imperial power of Athens attracted competition from Sparta, which had its own alliance system of land-based city-states. Competition for power in the Greek peninsula in the later 5th century B.C.E., with each side fearing that the other might gain a dominant position, was heightened by ideological conflicts that some historians have compared with the "cold war" struggles between the capitalist United States and the communist Soviet Union in the decades after World War II. Sparta stood for the old Greece before its alteration by extensive commerce and massive political change. Aristocratic rule had been transformed into a highly military regime in which boys were trained for battle and girls for the bearing of brave sons. Spartan militarism was designed to control a large force of near-slaves, who did the agricultural work. Use of money was discouraged by minting coins of unwieldy size. Discipline and control were the themes of Spartan society.

Unlike Sparta, Athens encouraged extensive trade and a vibrant, creative culture, and its democracy contrasted with the narrow aristocratic dominance of Sparta. Both sides were aware of their differences and intensely disliked the principles of the rival society. Both also drew allies from like-minded poleis. Sparta had unexpected advantages because its traditional

dependent on Athenian rule without having a voice in policy. The empire provided great resources for Athens, but its wealth complicated Athenian politics. The city grew to include increasing numbers of noncitizens, and the spoils of political office became increasingly attractive and highly contested. Politicians competed to find ways to spend money and curry popular favor. Many Athenians wondered whether authoritarian control of colonies based on military force and heavy tribute payment was compatible with free political life at home. Certainly this type of expansion was different from China's, where principles were widely admired, even by some aristocratic Athenians. The heavy-handedness of Athens's empire also drew hostility from many smaller cities.

For a few decades, around 450 B.C.E., an uneasy peace prevailed between the Greek rivals. Pericles, though aggressively proud of Athenian values, judged that Athenian welfare rested on a cautious foreign policy and peace with the Spartans. But in 435 B.C.E., a revolt in a colonial city-state, Corcyra, disrupted the precarious balance. Corcyra had been neutral between Athens and Sparta, but it had a large navy that now risked coming under the control of a Spartan ally. Athens insisted that Corcyra was under its protection, for it feared a rival navy, but this persuaded Sparta that Athens was power-hungry. War broke out in 431 B.C.E. when Spartan forces marched into Athenian territory.

In the resultant Peloponnesian War, the Athenian strategy was to let Sparta invade its countryside while relying on its fleet to maintain supplies and to raid the Spartan coast. But during the second year of the war, a massive plague broke out in Athens, ultimately killing one-third of the population, including Pericles. Grievances rose in Athens, and there was no longer a leader to provide consistent guidance. A victory over Spartan troops brought a chance for peace, but a warlike faction in Athens insisted on continuing the war, seeking to conquer new territory while wasting precious Athenian resources. The attempt to invade Sicily failed, costing Athens more than 200 ships, 4500 men, and the support of many allies. Finally, in 404 B.C.E., a Spartan general cut off the Athenian food supply, and the city had to surrender. Athens was deprived of its remaining ships, and the city walls were torn down. A political age came to an end, not only in Athens but in all of Greece.

The Hellenistic Period

 After a period of instability, a conquering empire took over Greece and then turned to further expansion in the Middle East and Egypt. Although the unitary empire did not survive its creator, Alexander the Great, a series of regional kingdoms persisted in the region for two centuries under considerable Greek influence. This Hellenistic period produced few political institutions of lasting importance, but it solidified Greek cultural achievements and expanded their geographic impact.

Spartan domination of Greece, after the collapse of Athens, did not work well. Periodic wars against the Persians and between key Greek states dominated the first half of the 4th century. By 355 B.C.E., Greece had returned to a setting of independent, disorganized city-states, many of them exhausted by decades of war and civil strife.

Macedonian Conquest

Into this power vacuum came a new force from the kingdom of **Macedon** on the northern borders of Greece. Macedonian conquests in turn opened a period of three centuries in which Greek culture spread widely in Egypt and far into western Asia. Greek city-states persisted in this new Hellenistic world, but they were no longer the dominant forms. In geography, politics, and to an extent culture, a new era opened in the 4th century B.C.E. The roots of the new order lay in the rise of a Macedonian dynasty, which conquered first Greece and then the Persian Empire within two generations.

The Kingdom of Macedon, to the north of Greece, was semibarbaric by Greek standards. Its residents spoke Greek, and Macedonian kings had long been interested in Greek culture. When **Philip II** (r. 359–336 B.C.E.) seized power, he strengthened the monarchy within Macedon and then turned his attention to the chaos of Greece. Skilled both as a general and as a diplomat, Philip soon developed a strong army that had more flexible tactics than the standard citizen force of the poleis. By seizing some northern Greek territory, he gained the resources to pay mercenary troops and peasant soldiers. Then he turned to the divided city-states of central Greece.

Despite warnings by insightful leaders, states such as Athens were no longer willing to make major sacrifices for self-defense. Philip also found allies in Greek statesmen who wanted a new unity, even if it was imposed from the outside. Finally, in 338 B.C.E., Philip won a decisive battle, aided by a cavalry charge led by his 18-year-old son Alexander. Macedon now ruled the bulk of Greece, and while the city-states retained their governments with rights of internal administration, Macedonian garrisons ensured tax tributes and loyalty to the new kingdom.

Alexander the Great

Philip's death left the next stage of Macedonian expansion to Alexander, who gained power at the age of 20 (Figure 5.5). **Alexander the Great,** eager to continue his father's conquest, turned to the target of the Persian Empire, still vast but now weakly ruled. In 334 B.C.E., Alexander moved into Asia with about 35,000 troops. Daring triumphs brought him control of the Persian side of the Mediterranean coast. Then, in 333 B.C.E., Alexander defeated the main Persian army led by its emperor in Syria (Map 5.3).

Persian efforts to sue for peace were ignored: Alexander wanted the whole empire and more. He moved into Egypt, now a weakened regional state, where he was greeted as pharaoh and son of a god. By 331 B.C.E., he entered Babylon and then seized the vast Persian treasury, as the Greeks and Macedonians gained revenge for the many Persian threats to their homeland. Alexander pressed into India, but he finally had to stop because his men refused to go farther.

Alexander planned a dazzling future for his new empire, hoping to merge Greek and Asian institutions and values and add further conquests. He founded many cities bearing his name, including **Alexandria** in Egypt. He spread Macedonian and Greek officials through his vast new Middle Eastern holdings. Alexander also encouraged intermarriage with Persian and other local women, a practice in which he himself set an example. Eager to promote a Hellenistic culture, he founded centers of scholarship in Greek learning, but he also recognized the need to accommodate various traditions in a multinational empire. Whether he could have succeeded in consolidating his unprecedented holdings, given his vision and organizational skills, cannot be known, for he died of a fever in Babylon at the age of 33.

Figure 5.5 *This bust of Alexander the Great is in the heroic style of Greek sculpture. The youthful emperor was one of the greatest conquerors in world history.*

Later Hellenistic States

Alexander's unexpected death quickly brought disunity to the new empire, though not an end to the Hellenistic enterprise. Quarrels among his successors allowed key generals to seize the major provinces as kings. Three major regional dynasties resulted: one in Egypt (the **Ptolemies**), which ended with the suicide of the famous queen, Cleopatra, in 31 B.C.E.; another in Mesopotamia (the **Seleucids**); and one in Macedonia and Greece (the **Antigonids**).

An important but short-lived kingdom, Bactria, in northwestern India, served as an unusual point of cultural exchange in the classical period. Indian artists used Greek themes, portraying even Buddha in Greek costume, and mathematical knowledge was exchanged. Greeks stationed in Bactria sometimes converted to Buddhism or Hinduism. These religions were not brought back to the Mediterranean, but Indian ideas of personal holiness had some impact on Hellenistic philosophy and may have influenced later religious life, including the rise of Christianity, in the region.

The major successor states enjoyed about 125 years of vigor and prosperity. Trade in Greek goods continued to flourish, and all the new kings encouraged commerce. Many Greeks moved toward the government jobs and merchant positions available in the Middle East. However, wealth centered on the city dwellers and the Hellenized upper classes (whether of Greek origin or not), while native peasants suffered from high taxes and the lack of adequate land. Internal divisions caused a decline in production,

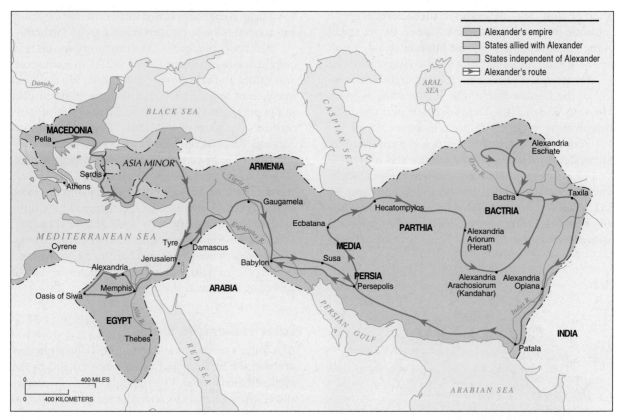

Map 5.3 *Alexander's Empire, c. 323 B.C.E., and the Hellenistic World*

and warfare between the kingdoms weakened the successor states and opened them to outside attack. In the 2nd century B.C.E. Rome moved actively into this vacuum, expanding its own empire.

The two centuries of Hellenism marked the end of the characteristically Greek political style. City-states continued to exist officially, and they maintained some functions even later under Roman control. But they no longer served as intense focal points because of the control exercised by foreign monarchs. Hellenistic politics centered on military empires.

Hellenism promoted wide exchanges. Contacts not only with India but also with the African kingdom of Kush had important effects, including expanded trade and some use of war elephants, the armored tanks of the classical era. Hellenistic leaders also generated innovations, particularly in science. The spread of Greek-derived culture, then, set a new framework for intellectual life in a large and diverse portion of the civilized world. This was Hellenism's most lasting legacy.

Creativity in Greek and Hellenistic Culture

 The genius of Greek civilization lay more obviously in various facets of culture than in politics. It was Greek culture that made the most lasting contributions of this civilization to the Mediterranean world, particularly in art and philosophy, and that served as the key linkage in the larger Hellenistic orbit of Alexander.

Religion, Philosophy, and Science

The Greeks did not create a major religion, and in this they differed from China and especially India. Greek ideas ultimately influenced great religions, particularly Christianity and to some degree Islam, but this came later. The characteristic Greek religion was derived from belief in the spirits of nature, elevated into a complex set of gods and goddesses who were seen as interfering in human life. The Greeks had a creator or father god, Zeus, who presided over an unruly assemblage of divinities whose functions ranged from regulating the daily passage of the sun (Apollo) or the oceans (Poseidon) to inspiring war or human love and beauty. Specific gods patronized other human activities such as metalworking, hunting, literature, and history. Regular ceremonies to the gods had real political importance, and many people sought the gods' aid in foretelling the future or ensuring a good harvest or good health. Stories of the gods' activities provided rich entertainment and could drive home lessons about appropriate moral behavior, including courage and humility. Homeric poets portrayed the Trojan War as guided by gods and goddesses in conflict, overseeing the struggle of mere mortals: "Thus the happy gods greatly augmented the clash of battle and made bitter strife break out everywhere."

This religion, passed down from earlier Indo-European experience, cemented community loyalties. However, it was not intensely spiritual. Interestingly, the basic Indo-European pantheon of gods was the same as that brought to India, which in both cases assumed human form (see Chapter 6). However, the Greek religion differed considerably from the more other-worldly Indian one. Greek religion tended toward a human-centered, worldly approach. Stories of the gods allowed illustration of human qualities, rather like large-scale soap operas; the gods could be jealous, sneaky, lustful, and powerful. Greek religion, like the Indian religion, helped engender an important literary tradition. In both religions, the gods provided good stories or served as vehicles for deeper inquiry into human passions and weaknesses. Greek gods were considered mainly in terms of what they could do for humankind and what they could reveal about human nature, rather than as representations of higher planes of spirituality or a divine experience.

The lack of spiritual passion in Greek religion failed to satisfy many ordinary workers and peasants, particularly when times were hard because of political chaos or economic distress. Popular "mystery" religions, which had more exciting rituals and promised greater spiritual insight, often swept through Greece with their secret ceremonies, a strong sense of fellowship, and greater focus on divine powers. The importance of mystery religions to some extent paralleled the role of Daoism in providing a contrast to more politically directed religion or philosophy, although none of the mystery religions won the currency or durability of Daoism in China.

Greek religion did not promote systematic thinking about nature or ethics. Hence, from at least the 6th century onward, many Greek thinkers attempted to generate philosophical systems that were separate from a primarily religious base. Their work also reflected the challenge of new contacts with Persian and other Middle Eastern cultural systems. The resultant attempt to understand humankind, society, and nature by rational observation and deduction became one of the hallmarks of Greek and Hellenistic culture. The approach was similar to that of Confucianism in China, but it had different specifics and a different and wider-ranging scope.

Many thinkers sought to generate ethical systems on the basis of rational definitions of right and wrong. **Socrates** (born in 465 B.C.E. and the tutor of Plato, who in turn would teach the philosopher Aristotle) urged people to consider the bases of right action in terms of rational reflection on goals and consequences. In contrast to earlier Middle Eastern traditions, he thus formulated secular criteria rather than devising rewards and punishments from an other-worldly system. **Aristotle,** the most important Greek philosopher, maintained this ethical system by stressing the importance of moderation in human behavior against the instability of political life in Athens and the excesses of the gods.

During the Hellenistic period, other ethical systems were devised. A group called the **Stoics** emphasized an inner moral independence, to be cultivated by strict discipline of the body and personal bravery. These ethical systems were major contributions in their own right, attracting many disciples and generating much literary debate; they were later blended with Christian religious thought.

Greek philosophy devoted much attention to defining appropriate political structures—not surprisingly, given the various Greek constitutional systems. The Athenian philosopher **Plato,** in the 5th century, devised an ideal government structure in which philosophers would rule. Most Greek political theory stressed the importance of balance between aristocratic principles and some popular contribution. Aristotle also discussed social topics such as slavery and the role and status of women, providing vigorous defenses for the inevitability and usefulness of slavery and for family structures that assumed women's inferiority.

A philosophy separate from official religion, though not necessarily hostile to it, also placed considerable emphasis on the powers of human thought. In Athens, Socrates encouraged his pupils to question received wisdom on the ground that the chief human duty was "the improvement of the soul." Socrates himself ran afoul of the Athenian government in the aftermath of the Peloponnesian War, for he seemed to be undermining political loyalty with his constant questions. But the Socratic principle of thinking things through by means of skeptical questioning, rather than assuming on the basis of authority or faith, became a recurrent strand in classical Greek thinking. Socrates' great pupil, Plato, suggested that human reason could approach an understanding of the perfect forms—the absolutely True, Good, and Beautiful—that he believed underlie nature.

Greek interest in rationality carried over to the underlying order of physical nature. The Greeks were not great scientists compared with the classical Chinese. Few new scientific findings came from Athens, although philosophers such as Aristotle collected large amounts of biological data. In mathematics, Greeks learned from earlier Egyptian findings and often studied in Egypt. The key Greek interest lay in speculation about nature's order. In practice, the Greek concern translated into theories about the motions of the planets and the organization of the elemental principles of earth, fire, air, and water, and into a great interest in mathematics as a means of understanding nature's patterns. Greek and later Hellenistic work in geometry was impressive, featuring the basic theorems of Pythagoras and Euclid's geometry.

Scientists in the Hellenistic period made some important contributions, especially in studies of anatomy; medical writings by Galen were not improved upon in the Western world for many centuries. The Hellenistic astronomer Ptolemy formalized an elaborate theory of the sun's motion around a stationary earth; this new Hellenistic theory contradicted much earlier Middle Eastern astronomy, which had recognized the earth's rotation. The idea of an earth-centered universe seemed to explain many observed phenomena, including eclipses, and this fact along with the reputation of Greek science ensured that Ptolemy's theory was long taken as fixed wisdom in Western thought.

Other Hellenistic scientists added more constructively to the observations about planetary motion. Archimedes (c. 287–212 B.C.E.) wrote about mathematics and the measurement of water power. He devised pulley systems to pump out flooded ships and fields and invented novel kinds of fortifications. Other Hellenistic scientists, dissecting the corpses of criminals, made important discoveries about digestion and the vascular system.

Literature and the Visual Arts

Despite the importance of the rationalist tradition, science and mathematics were far less important than art and literature in conveying key cultural values in Greek and Hellenistic culture. The official religion inspired artistic expression and justified the creation of temples, statues, and plays devoted to the glories of the gods. But the human-centered qualities of the Greeks also showed through, as artists emphasized realistic portrayals of the human form and poets and playwrights used the gods as vehicles for pondering the human condition.

All the arts received attention. Music and dance performances were vital parts of religious festivals, but their styles have not been preserved. Far more durable was the Greek interest in drama, for plays took a central role in this culture. Greek dramatists worked on both comedy and tragedy, making a formal division between the two that is still part of the Western tradition. (The Document box illustrates the two approaches.) On the whole, the Greeks placed greatest emphasis on tragedy. Their belief in human reason and balance also involved a sense that these virtues were precarious, so that a person could easily be ensnared in situations of powerful emotion and uncontrollable consequences. The Athenian dramatist **Sophocles,** for example, so insightfully portrayed the psychological flaws of his hero Oedipus that modern psychology long used the term *Oedipus complex* for potentially tragic attachments between a man and his mother. Another Athenian playwright, **Aristophanes,** used similar beliefs in the limitations of human experience to produce a sense of comedy, poking fun at human nature.

Greek literature contained a strong epic tradition as well, starting with the beautifully crafted tales of the *Iliad* and the *Odyssey*. By the 5th century B.C.E., interest in human affairs led to a new kind of formal historical writing: Herodotus tried to sort out fact from myth in dealing with various Mediterranean cultures, and Thucydides composed a vivid account of the Peloponnesian War.

Document

The Power of Greek Drama

This section consists of two passages, one by the great tragedian **Aeschylus** (525–456 B.C.E.), and one by Athens's leading writer of comedies, **Aristophanes** (c. 450–385 B.C.E.). Aeschylus' passage, from the play *Libation Bearers*, sees Orestes confront his mother, Clytemnestra, after having killed her lover and suspecting that she killed his father. Clytemnestra has learned what Orestes did and knows what is to come; she asks a slave:

Clytemnestra: Swift! Bring me an axe that can slay. I will know now if I am to win or lose. I stand here on the height of misery.

[Orestes enters with his companion Pylades.]

Orestes: It is you I seek. The other has had his fill. You love him—you shall lie in the same grave.

Clytemnestra: Stop—oh, my son. Look—my breast. Your heavy head dropped on it and you slept, oh, many a time, and your baby mouth where never a tooth was, sucked the milk and so you grew—

Orestes: Oh, Pylades, what shall I do? My mother— Awe holds me. May I spare?

Pylades: Where then Apollo's words and the dread compact? Make all men enemies but not the gods.

Orestes: Good counsel. I obey. You—follow me. I lead you where he lies to kill you there.

Clytemnestra: It seems, my son, that you will kill your mother.

Orestes: Not I. You kill yourself.

Clytemnestra: I am alive—I stand beside my grave. I hear the song of death.

[They go out and the Chorus sings that her fate is just.]

Lift up your head, oh, house. I see the light.

[The palace doors roll back. Orestes stands over the two dead bodies.]

Orestes: I am blameless of the one. He died the death adulterers must die. But she who planned this thing of horror against her husband by whom she had borne beneath her girdle the burden of children—what think you of her? Snake or viper was she? Her very touch would rot a man.

Chorus: Woe—woe—Oh, fearful, deeds!

Orestes: Did she do it or did she not? The proofs you know—the deed and the death. I am victor but vile, polluted.

Chorus: One trouble is here—another comes.

Orestes: Hear me and learn, for I know how it will end. I am borne along a runaway horse. My thoughts are out of bounds. Fear at my heart is leaping up. Before my reason goes—oh, you my friends, I say I killed my mother—yet not without reason—she was vile and she killed my father and God hated her—Look—look—women—there—there— black—all black, and long hair twisting like snakes. Oh, let me go.

Chorus: What fancies trouble you, O son, faithful to your father? Do not fear.

Orestes: No fancies. My mother has sent them. They throng upon me and from their eyes blood drips, blood of hate. You see them not? I—I see them. They drive me. I cannot stay.

[He rushes out.]

Chorus: Oh, where will this frenzy of evil end?

In Aristophanes' play *Plutus*, the author mocks what he sees as the reigning values of Athens. The passage begins with a slave asking his respectable-looking master why they are following a blind man:

Chremylus: I'll tell you why, straight out. Of all my slaves I know that you are the best, most constant—thief. Well—I have been a good, religious man, but always poor—no luck.

Slave: And so you have.

Chremylus: So then I want to ask—not for myself, I've pretty well shot all my arrows now—but for my son, my only son. I prayed that he might change his ways and turn into a scoundrel, wicked, rotten through and through, and so live happily ever after. The god replied, the first man I fell in with to follow.

Slave: Yes—Quite good. Of course, a blind man can see it's better nowadays to be a rotten scoundrel.

(continued)

[The man in front proves to be Wealth himself, not aware of his power because he is blind. The two others proceed to enlighten him.]

Chremylus: Why everything there is, is just Wealth's slave. The girls, now, if a poor man comes along, will they look at him? But just let a rich one, and he can get a deal more than he wants.

Slave: Oh, not the sweet, good, modest girls. They never would ask a man for money.

Chremylus: No? What then?

Slave: Presents—the kind that cost a lot—that's all.

Chremylus: Well, all the voting's done for Wealth of course. You man our battleships. You own our army. When you're an ally, that side's sure to win. Nobody ever has enough of you. While all things else a man can have too much of—of love.

Slave: Of loaves.

Chremylus: Of literature.

Slave: Of candy.

Chremylus: Of fame.

Slave: Of figs.

Chremylus: Of manliness.

Slave: Of mutton.

Questions: What were the purposes of comedy and tragedy in classical Athens? How does Aeschylus's passage move toward a starkly tragic view? How is a truly tragic situation for a person defined? What values might have led an Athenian audience to enjoy a satire such as that by Aristophanes? Are the Greek ideas of comedy and tragedy suggested in the passage different from American definitions today?

In the visual arts, the emphasis of classical Mediterranean civilization lay in sculpture, architecture, and ceramics. In Athens' brilliant 5th century B.C.E.—the age of Pericles, Socrates, Sophocles, Aristophanes, and many other intensely creative figures—sculptors such as Phidias developed unprecedented skill in realistic portrayals of the human form, from lovely goddesses to muscled warriors and athletes.

Greek architecture from the 8th century B.C.E. onward emphasized monumental construction, square or rectangular in shape, with columned porticoes. As Figure 5.6 shows, the Greeks devised three distinct styles for their massive buildings, each more ornate than the last: the **Doric, Ionic,** and **Corinthian.** They invented what Westerners and others in the world today still regard as classical architecture, although the Greeks themselves were influenced by Egyptian and Cretan models. Greece provided abundant stone for ambitious temples, markets, and other public buildings. Many of these structures were filled with products of the sculptors' workshops. They were also brightly painted, although over the centuries the paint faded so that later imitators came to think of the classical as involving plain stone.

Classical Mediterranean art and architecture were intimately linked with the society that produced them. Because of the formal role of classical styles in later societies, it is tempting to attribute a stiffness to Greek art that was not present in the original. Greek structures were built to be used. Temples and marketplaces were part of daily urban life. Classical art was also flexible, according to need. Classical dramas were not merely examples of high art performed in front of a cultural elite. Indeed, Athens lives in the memory of many intellectuals not only because of the creativity of its writers and philosophers but also because of the large audiences for plays by authors such as Sophocles. Thousands of people gathered in the big hillside theaters of Athens and other cities for the new plays and the music and poetry competitions that entertained while honoring the gods (see Figure 5.7).

The Principles of Greek Culture

Overall, Greek and Hellenistic cultural achievement rested on four major principles. First, the interest in formal political theory, with a strong emphasis on debating the merits of different constitutional structures and assuming that government forms could be planned, obviously reflected the distinctive political atmosphere of Greece. Although Greek politics faced frequent crises, Greek ideas had wide influence on later civilizations.

Second, art and sculpture glorified human achievement, starting with a celebration of the beauties of the ideal human form, which was used also to represent the gods.

Figure 5.6 *Varied column designs marked the progression of Greek architecture from the square Doric simplicity of the Parthenon (left), through Ionic (the outer columns in image at right), to the more ornate Corinthian (center column in image at right).*

Third, drama, philosophy, and art stressed the importance of human striving. Although ethical philosophers stressed moderation, Greeks' fascination with human energy and striving was different from the more consistent restraint urged in secular Chinese thought.

Fourth, the philosophical and scientific tradition emphasized the use of logic in understanding the natural world.

Greek culture also harbored a tension between the educated elite and the common masses. Plays and other art forms were widely shared. Some great thinkers stemmed from ordinary ranks, such as Socrates, a stonemason by trade. But Greek philosophy was closed to most ordinary people and, unlike in China, there was no particular effort to persuade ordinary people to participate in the values of the elite.

Hellenistic Culture During and After Alexander

Greek art and sculpture continued to dominate Hellenistic output, and the commercial wealth of the early Hellenistic kingdoms encouraged a vast amount of new building and decoration. Although no new styles emerged, there was some movement toward more sentimental, emotional statuary.

Hellenistic intellectuals concentrated on developing new knowledge in science and mathematics.

Alexander and the Hellenistic dynasty in Egypt encouraged this work, and the expansion of cultural exchange in the Mediterranean in the Middle East also favored new research. Hellenistic thinkers thus preserved Greek scientific achievements and added significant new elements. Their work provided most of the scientific learning available to the Western world for almost 2000 years. It also set a durable basis for scientific research in the Middle East and northern Africa. Astronomical charts and maps improved greatly, despite Ptolemy's confusion about the earth as the center of the universe. Geography also improved, and one scientist was able to calculate the circumference of the earth within 200 miles. At the same time, interest in astrology and magic increased.

Patterns of Greek and Hellenistic Society

Greek and Hellenistic society mirrored many standard social features of an agricultural economy. These included a large peasantry but also a land-owning aristocracy, and dependence on commerce combined with suspicion of it. Patriarchal family structures predominated. Distinctive features included slavery and a slightly greater ambivalence about women than was true in classical China.

Figure 5.7 *Greek dramas were staged in this theater of Dionysus. This magnificent outdoor facility was nestled in a hillside, with the stage at the base of seating risers sculpted in stone. The location of the theater reflected its important public functions.*

Economic and Social Structure

The economic and social structure of classical Greece, including the colonies it sent out around the Mediterranean, had many features in common with other agricultural civilizations. It particularly resembled other civilizations in which an invading, warlike group settled down to agriculture. Thus, although 8th-century Greece clearly depended on farming, it had an aristocracy based on ownership of large estates and special claims to military service. At the same time, many farmers were independent, owning their plots of land and claiming some political and social status, just as tribal soldiers had once done. But—again in a common pattern—the Greek economy evolved, particularly as trade rose and cities grew. Social structure became more complex, and inequalities widened in many ways, as with the growth of slavery.

However, there were also distinctive features in the Greek pattern. Because mainland Greece was so rocky and mountainous—a terrain unsuited to grain growing—many city-states came to depend heavily on seagoing trade and colonies. (The Visualizing the

Past box focuses on economic and social aspects of Greek trade.) Colonization and frequent wars produced many opportunities to seize slaves, and classical Mediterranean society was more dependent on slavery than were Indian or Chinese civilizations in the same period. Likewise, while Greeks developed many craft products, they paid less attention to improving manufacturing technology than China and India did. Slavery played a key role in this nontechnological focus, along with Greek concern for science as a philosophical system rather than as a collection of useful data. One Hellenistic scholar refused to write a handbook on engineering because "the work of an engineer and everything that ministers to the needs of life is ignoble and vulgar."

Aristocratic dominance in Greek society showed in the ambiguous position of merchants. Greece progressively became involved with trade, but aristocratic suspicion of merchant values persisted, particularly among conservatives, who opposed change in favor of traditional austerity. Sparta, which had unusually fertile land, tried to downplay trade

In Depth

Defining Social History

Over the past 30 years, historians have argued about the proper focus of their work. Should history focus on great achievements by major individuals? Or should social history, with its wider definition of significance, guide our view of the past?

Until fairly recently, many historians wrote as if the principal elements of the past that were worth recapturing involved formal politics—the changes in the structure of the state, the rise and fall of major political leaders, and wars and intellectual life. How the masses of people lived was relevant as it affected taxation levels (and thus what political leaders could do), political protest, and military service. New inventions or big changes in the economic or social system, such as an increase of slavery, could figure in. But the detailed work of the historian focused on charting and explaining what the leading statesmen and thinkers were doing.

Often, the key legacies of a major time period or civilization seem to lie in its dominant political forms, artistic styles, and religious concepts. Thus in classical Greece, political and intellectual achievements not only commanded great attention at the time, at least in the upper classes, but also contributed greatly to later societies after the Greek and Hellenistic ages had ended. We may well look to Pericles, Socrates, or the great sculptor Phidias for example and inspiration.

Yet modern historical research does not begin or end with the doings of the greatest statesmen and thinkers. The newer field of social history, which has gained momentum in the United States and elsewhere over the past 40 years, increasingly defines a wider agenda. Social historians do not deny the significance of political structures or philosophical systems, but they argue that history also consists of the doings of ordinary people: family activities, death, disease, work, and leisure. For social historians, the past is much larger than was once believed. It includes many groups of people besides the elite: women, peasants and artisans, children and youth. Social historians integrate great ideas with the beliefs of large numbers of people about how the universe worked or what the good life was. They combine attention to political forms with an understanding of the social structures and problems that helped generate these forms.

Think of how these issues apply to classical Greece. Judgments of Greece clearly vary, depending on whether slaves or farmers or aristocrats are the focus. What happens when women's conditions are considered, as well as men's?

Social historians do not always have an easy time fleshing out their topics. Ordinary people did not conveniently describe their beliefs for posterity the way thinkers such as Aristotle and Confucius did. Particularly for early and classical civilizations, when records have been lost and most people were illiterate, it is not easy to characterize work and family values.

Partly for this reason, many world histories until recently focused on formal governments and intellectual history alone. One world historian leaves ordinary people out simply because, in his view, only the groups that produce major milestones are worth attending to; the supporting cast is irrelevant. Another world historian once argued that the lives of ordinary people changed little, at least during the long reign of agriculturally based civilizations, so there is little to know about them in comparison with the obvious ups and downs of governments and artistic styles. Yet social history, for all its complexity, continues to gain ground, determining much of the subject matter of world history, for three major reasons.

First, the history of long-ignored groups and topics helps us understand these same topics in societies today. It is just as important to have a historical perspective on women's roles, and to see how they changed and varied in the past, as it is to understand how Greek leaders were chosen. At certain times, work, women's roles, or family forms may change only gradually, even amid lively political developments. But the reverse may also be true, and there is no question that social historical change can be charted and assessed.

Second, patterns and changes in social history intimately affect the ways governments and intellectuals function, and the reverse is true as well. In classical civilizations, such as China and Greece, a vast gulf often separated wealthy, literate aristocrats or bureaucrats from ordinary peasants or slaves. Yet governments had to be organized in such a way as to keep ordinary people contented or repressed (or they had to contend with protest). Confucianism tried to deal with this issue; Greek city-state governments experimented almost constantly with systems that would preserve a class structure yet provide enough harmony for political life. One key way to grasp a civilization or the causes of change is

(continued)

to talk about how formal institutions and intellectual styles related to the masses of people and the basic structures of life.

Finally, ordinary people and the structures they were involved with could leave legacies, just as intellectual and political leaders did. Later periods or societies would thus build on earlier patterns of work, ways to treat children, or definitions of slavery.

Among the social sciences during the past 30 years, social history has proved to be one of the most fruitful sources of new knowledge and analysis. The result is a redefinition of the past and of the kinds of questions to raise about how societies function.

Questions: What are some of the key problems of social history? What would a social historian emphasize in discussing the major features of classical Chinese civilization? Besides knowing about Greek and Hellenistic political development and intellectual styles, what would the social historian try to pinpoint in summing up this classical civilization?

altogether. Its deliberately cumbersome coinage discouraged commerce, and aristocratic estate owners directed a semislave population of farm workers. Even in bustling Athens, most merchants were foreigners, mainly from the Middle East. Overall, merchants held higher status in the classical Mediterranean than in Confucian China, but their standing was less firm than in India (see Chapter 6).

Rural Life and Agriculture

Most of the population of the Greek and Hellenistic world was rural, even though the elaborate, important political and cultural activities occurred in cities. Rural peoples preserved distinctive rituals and beliefs. Many Greek farmers annually gathered for a spring passion play to celebrate the recovery of the goddess of fertility from the lower world. This event was seen as a vital preparation for planting and also hinted at the possibility of life after death—a prospect important to many people who endured a life of hard labor and poverty. Many free farmers played a vital role in the early politics of the Greek city-states.

At the same time, large landlords tried to force these farmers to become tenants or laborers or to join the growing urban lower class. Class tension was encouraged by special features of Greek agriculture. As Greek society advanced, there was a natural tendency to specialize in cash crops, such as olives for cooking oil and grapes for wine, that could be sold widely. Grain was imported from areas more appropriate to its production: parts of the northern Middle East, Sicily, and northern Africa. However, changing to olive and grape cultivation was expensive: Grapevines and olive trees did not begin to yield fruit for five years. To convert to olives and grapes,

farmers went into debt and often failed; aristocratic estate owners with more abundant resources converted more successfully, taking over the land of failed farmers.

Mediterranean agriculture thus became unusually market oriented, designed to produce goods for sale. Traditional grain-growing continued in key regions, such as Thessaly in Greece. However, in comparison with other agricultural civilizations, fewer farmers produced simply for their own needs, except in the early period before civilization fully developed. Imports of basic foods were more extensive here than in India or China. This was one obvious spur to the empire: to try to ensure access to adequate grain supplies. Greek expansion pushed out mainly toward sources of grain in Sicily and around the Black Sea. Greek pottery designs, revealing much about everyday life, also show other kinds of raw materials exports from the colonies, including materials for making textiles.

Market agriculture gained further momentum in the Hellenistic kingdoms. Vast estates spread out in Egypt and the Middle East, requiring specialized banks and financial agents. Elements of this capitalistic agriculture affected Mediterranean history later under both the Roman Empire and Arab rule. The system also helped generate the surpluses needed for spreading Hellenistic culture and its urban monuments.

Slavery and Production

Slavery was an important ingredient of the classical Mediterranean economy. Philosophers such as Aristotle produced elaborate justifications of the need for slavery in a proper society: Without slaves, how would aristocrats learn what must be learned to maintain culture or have the time to cultivate political virtue?

Visualizing the Past

Commerce and Society

Greek commerce expanded along with the colonies. In this painting on the interior of the Arkesilas Cup, dating from 560 B.C.E., the king of Cyrene, a Greek colony in northern Africa, is shown supervising the preparation of hemp or flax for export. What does the picture suggest about the nature and extent of social hierarchy? How can costumes be used in this kind of assessment? What is the king most concerned with? What kinds of technology are suggested? Can you think of other types of evidence to use in analyzing this kind of colonial commercial economy?

Slaves were acquired mainly as a result of wars, more frequent in the Mediterranean world than in China and India. Athenians used slaves for household service and as workers in their vast silver mines, which hastened the progress of Athens's empire and commercial operations. Sparta used **helots,** or unfree labor, extensively for agricultural work. The Spartan system relied less on prisoners taken from war, for it was imposed by Indo-European conquerors over previous residents in the area. Of the approximately 270,000 people in 5th-century Athens, 80,000 to 100,000 were slaves, whereas helots in Sparta outnumbered their masters by nearly 10 to 1. In cities such as Athens some slaves enjoyed considerable independence and could earn money on their own. Manumission, or freeing, of valued slaves was common. Yet slave systems also needed extensive military controls.

Greek slavery had its ambiguities, often based on the personal qualities of specific slaves. For example, Pasion began his life as an Athenian slave, but his owner freed him. By his death in 370 B.C.E. he was a respected businessman, owning a bank and a shield factory. And he had many slaves himself. Late in his life he turned his holdings over to a slave he had freed, and his will stated that after his death the man should marry his widow and become guardian to his sons. Of course, this was not a typical story; it would have been far less likely to occur in the Athenian mines (Pasion seems to have been a domestic slave) or in Sparta.

Men, Women, and Social Divisions

Greek society emphasized the importance of a tight family structure, with husband and father firmly in control. Women had vital economic functions, particularly in farming and artisan families. A woman with a strong personality could command a major place within a household, and a free woman's responsibility for family possessions was protected by law. But in law and culture, women were held inferior. Even the activities of free women were directed toward their husbands' interests. The rape of a free woman, though a crime, was a lesser offense than seducing her, because seduction meant winning her affections away from her husband. Families burdened with too many children sometimes put infant girls to death. Pericles stated common beliefs about women when he said, "For a woman not to show more weakness than is natural to her sex is a great glory, and not to be talked about for good or for evil among men." He also thought that women's bodies showed that they were "failed men." On the other hand, the oppression of women was probably less severe in this civilization than in China, for many Greek women were active in business and controlled a substantial minority of urban property.

Although Greek culture represented women abundantly as goddesses and as powerful figures in drama, often with revered powers, and celebrated the female form as well as the male form in art, the real cultural status of women was low. Aristotle argued that women provided only an abode for a child developing before birth, claiming that male seed alone contained the full germ of the child. This is why he also thought that women's bodies showed that they were "failed men." Marriages were arranged by a woman's father; husbands could divorce wives at will, whereas women had to go to court. Adultery was tolerated for men but was grounds for divorce in the case of women. Within upper-class households, where women had vital functions including the supervision of domestic slaves, men entertained their guests in separate rooms. Women did join together in festivals such as the three-day Thesmophoria in Athens, when they went to a great encampment to perform rituals designed to promote the fertility of the land.

However, women's daily duties focused on the home. Upper-class men consorted with slave and noncitizen women more often than with their wives. Men also spent time mentoring young adolescent boys, and there is evidence of sexual relations between them. The training of female children was left to older women in the household.

Interestingly, conditions for citizen women improved somewhat in the Hellenistic period. Artists and playwrights began to show more interest in women and their conditions. Women in Hellenistic cities appeared more freely in public, and some aristocratic women gained new functions (in forming cultural clubs, for example). Several queens exercised great power, often ruling harshly. Cratesiclea, the mother of a Hellenistic king in Sparta, willingly served as a hostage to help form an alliance with a more powerful state; she reputedly said, "send me away, wherever you think this body of mine will be most useful to Sparta." More widely, Hellenistic women began to take an active role in commerce, although they still could not own property.

A Complex Legacy

Classical Greece and its Hellenistic successors lasted for about 600 years. Although major political and social changes took place during this span, some durable characteristics also developed.

Greece's political legacy obviously lay more in the realm of ideas than in enduring political institutions such as China's emperor and bureaucracy, although the next leading Mediterranean city-state, Rome, copied some Greek structures. On the whole, Greek art and philosophy formed the most lasting contributions of this classical civilization. But, partly because they did not generate a major religion, Greek contributions to a lasting popular culture were more limited than was true in China or India.

A final complexity in dealing with classical Greece (and then Rome) involves its relationship to contemporary North Americans. For most North Americans, Greece is the first phase of their own classical past. The framers of the Constitution of the United States were very conscious of Greek precedents. Designers of public buildings in the United States have copied Greek and Roman models. The Western educational tradition has long invited elaborate explorations of the Greco-Roman past as part of the standard intellectual equipment for the educated person.

Yet this important legacy is complicated. In the first place Greeks had no special monopoly in science or political innovation. They were actually inferior to India and China in production technology. Furthermore, Greek ideas did not flow smoothly into a Western tradition (indeed, they had far more initial impact on the Middle East, which was where Greeks tended to look when they thought of spreading their key achievements). Important revivals and modifications had to occur before the Greek approach to science had fruitful impact on western Europe many centuries later. Democracy did not clearly spread from Greece at all, except that its example could be used by later advocates, whose passions had very different sources, as additional justification.

GLOBAL CONNECTIONS: Greece and the World

Like other classical civilizations, and notably China, classical Greeks had a definite sense of the inferiority of the non-Greek world, which they indiscriminately called barbarian. Some Greek city states, like Sparta, were quite closed to outside influences. But overall, the Greeks were also a trading and expansionist people. They set up Greek colonies in various parts of the Mediterranean. They traded even more widely, and relied heavily on foreigners for part of this trade. Some Greeks were immensely curious about other peoples and their habits. The historian and traveler Herodotus (484–425) talked enthusiastically about customs very different from his own, though he was also capable of believing wild exaggerations about how some people lived.

Greek outreach was obviously extended by Alexander the Great, who did not have such a keen belief in Greek superiority. Alexander forged important new contacts between the eastern Mediterranean, the rest of the Middle East, and even western India. He even hoped to extend his system into China, but obviously this did not occur. The system did not last, but the interest in setting up stronger links with Asia remained an important concern. The Greek world, in other words, was a Mediterranean world, looking eastward primarily, though also to northeastern Africa.

Further Readings

The archeology, arts, and culture of ancient Persia are addressed in J. Curtis, *Ancient Persia* (1989). On the Persian Empire, see J. M. Cook, *The Persian Empire* (1983). Two good surveys on classical Greece are K. Dover's *The Greeks* (1981) and Nancy Demand's *A History of Ancient Greece* (1996); both have bibliographies. An older study on Greek culture is extremely solid: H. D. F. Kitto's *The Greeks* (1957). On Hellenism, M. M. Austin, *The Hellenistic World from Alexander to the Roman Conquest* (1981); Peter Green, ed., *Hellenistic History and Culture* (1993); P. Green, *Alexander to Actium: The Historical Evolution of the Hellenistic Age* (1990); and Joseph Roisman, ed., *Alexander the Great* (1995), are excellent introductions. Works on key special topics are Oswyn Murray, *Early Greece* (1993), and Frank Frost, *Greek Society* (3rd ed., 1987). On Greek intellectual life, see W. Burkert's *Greek Religions* (1985), and G. E. R. Lloyd's *The Revolutions of Wisdom: Studies in the Claims and Practices of Ancient Greek Science* (1987). Particular features of Greek society are treated in Moses Finley's *Slavery in the Ancient World* (1972), an exciting study; Sarah Pomeroy, *Goddesses, Whores, Wives, and Slaves: Women in Classical Antiquity* (1975); R. Just, *Women in Athenian Law and Life* (1988); Yvon Garlan, *Slavery in Ancient Greece* (1988); and Victor Hanson, *The Western Way of War: Infantry Battle in Classical Greece* (1989). On politics, Donald Kagan's *Western Heritage* (1991) deals with a key issue.

An excellent way to approach Greek history is through documents from the period itself. See Herodotus, *The Histories* (trans. de Selincourt) (1972), M. Crawford, ed., *Sources for Ancient History* (1983), and M. R. Lefkowitz and M. B. Fant, eds., *Women's Life in Greece and Rome: A Source Book in Translation* (1982).

Though it deals with a later period, key social features of the region are explored in F. Braudel's classic *The Mediterranean and the Mediterranean World* (2 vols., 1972).

On the Web

A fine site linking Greek texts, geography, and art is http://www.perseus.tufts.edu/. Daily life in ancient Greece is explored at http://members.aol.com/Donnclass/Greeklife.html. The world of Greco-Roman women, from their private life to legal status, is examined at http://www.bbc.co.uk/schools/landmarks/ancientgreece/athens/women.shtml and http://dmoz.org/Society/People/Women/History/Ancient/Greece/. Some of the leading personalities of Classical Greek and Hellenistic times are illuminated at Web sites, including those devoted to Aristophanes (http://www.imagi-nation.com/moonstruck/clsc13.htm), Sophocles (http://www.imagi-nation.com/moonstruck/clsc1.htm), Socrates (http://www.san.beck.org/SOCRATES1-Life.html), Philip II (http://www.historyofmacedonia.org/AncientMacedonia/PhilipofMacedon.html), Alexander the Great (http://www.historyofmacedonia.org/AncientMacedonia/AlexandertheGreat.html), Cleopatra (http://womenshistory.about.com/cs/cleopatrabios/), and Plato's life and times (http://plato-dialogues.org/life.htm and http://plato.evansville.edu/life.htm).

The monumental architecture and the art of Greece are introduced at http://www.ancientgreece.com/art/art.htm. For a virtual tour of the acropolis of Athens and the Parthenon, http://www.in-athens.com/archeological/acropolis.htm. The lasting influence of these ancient buildings can be seen at a study of classical Greek themes in modern American architecture at http://ah.bfn.org/a/DCTNRY/vocab.html. The Minoan palaces of ancient Crete can be visited at http://dilos.com/region/crete/minoan_pictures.html. Greek religion is explored at http://www.museum.upenn.edu/Greek_World/religion.html. The Zoroastrianism of the Persian Empire is examined at http://www.zoroaster.net/indexe.htm and http://www.avesta.org/avesta.html. The historic Amber trade route began at this time and can be toured at http://www.cichw.net/amber.html and http://www.american.edu/ted/AMBER.HTM.

CHAPTER 6

RELIGIOUS RIVALRIES AND INDIA'S GOLDEN AGE

The cave temples carved out of solid stone at Ajanta in central India provide dramatic testimony to the religious fervor that swept through south Asia in the age of the Buddha and the Hindu revival.

After the long period of disruption following Harappa's fall around 1500 B.C.E., a new civilization arose in India. India became the third great center of classical civilization, along with the Mediterranean and Middle East (Greece, Persia, Rome) and China. The new foundations for Indian civilization were laid between 1500 and 500 B.C.E. by the nomadic Aryan invaders who were moving into India during the centuries when Harappa collapsed. By the end of this period, fairly large states, ruled by kings who claimed divine descent, controlled much of the fertile farmland of the Ganges River plains. The settlement of this vast area came at the cost of clearing the great forests that once covered it. As in northwest India earlier (see Chapter 3) and in the Mediterranean somewhat later, cultivation and forest clearing contributed to significant shifts in broader climatic patterns.

Ritual divisions and restrictions on intermarriage between different social groups grew more rigid as an increasingly complex social hierarchy became a pervasive force in Indian life. Above all, the Vedic priests, or brahmans, emerged as the dominant force in Indian society and culture. As the brahmans' power peaked, however, forces were building in Indian society that threatened to alter the course of civilized development in south Asia. By the 6th century B.C.E., many religious seers and dissenting philosophers wanted to move beyond the rituals associated with sacrifices to the gods and were weary of the power-seeking and materialism of the priestly class. The most successful of these thinkers, the **Buddha,** founded one of the great world religions—a religion that for centuries provided a powerful challenge to the brahmans and many of the ancient Vedic beliefs and practices.

In the centuries that followed, the rivalry between Buddhists and brahmans played a major role in shaping gender relationships and the nature of social hierarchies as a whole in south Asia. The Buddha's teachings also contributed to the establishment of India's first genuine empire. Beginning in the late 4th century B.C.E., the rulers of a local dynasty in eastern India, the Mauryas, began to build what would become the largest empire in premodern India. The Mauryan Empire was short-lived, however. When it collapsed, it was followed by another round of nomadic invasions through the Himalayan passes in the northwest, and the subcontinent was again fragmented politically. But in the early 4th century C.E., there arose in north India a powerful new dynasty, the Gupta, that was committed to reasserting the brahmans' dominance. The Gupta rulers' patronage of the religion we now know as Hinduism reaffirmed the position of the brahmans as high priests and political advisors. It also led to an age of splendid Hindu achievement in architecture, painting, sculpture, philosophy, literature, and the sciences.

1600 B.C.E.	1200 B.C.E.	700 B.C.E.	500 B.C.E.	300 B.C.E.	100 C.E.	300 C.E.
1600–1000 Period of Aryan invasions **c. 1500** Fall of Harappan civilization	**1200–700** Sacred Vedas composed	**700–c. 550** Era of unrivaled brahman dominance **c. 542–483** Life of the Buddha	**327–325** Alexander the Great's invasion **322–298** Chandragupta Maurya rules **322–185** Time of the Mauryan Empire	**c. 300** Kautilya's *Arthashastra* is written **268–237** Ashoka is emperor of India **200 B.C.E.–200 C.E.** Period of greatest Buddhist influence **170–165** Yueh-chi invasions **c. 150** Indo-Greek invasions	**1–105** Kushana Empire in the northwest	**319–540** Gupta Empire **405** Fa-hsien's (Fa-xian's) pilgrimage **541** First Hun invasion **606–647** Harsha's Empire

The Age of Brahman Dominance

 Over most of the areas in India where the Aryans settled, religious leaders or brahmans became the dominant force after about 1500 B.C.E. In this era, earlier patterns of social stratification rigidified into a religiously sanctioned hierarchy of social groups, based in part on occupational differences, that the peoples of south Asia called *jatis*. In recent centuries this mode of social stratification has also come to be known by the name the Portuguese gave to it, the **caste system.** The caste system was dominated by brahmans and regional warrior groups, which shared political power and the highest status. By about 500 B.C.E., several major challenges to this social order had emerged. The most enduring and serious of these proved to be Buddhism.

The forces that made for the renewal of civilization in south Asia after the fall of Harappa were initially centered not on the great plains of the Ganges and Indus river systems but in the foothills of the Himalaya Mountains (see Map 6.1). Tribes of Aryan warrior-herders settled in the lush valleys of the cool hills. The hills provided abundant pasturage for their herds of horses and cattle. The wooded valleys proved easier to clear for farming than the rainforest-covered plains along the Ganges and its tributaries. In the hill regions, single Aryan tribes or confederations of tribal groups developed small states—in many ways similar to those in Homeric Greece—that were based on a combination of sedentary agriculture and livestock breeding. The territories of most of these states extended no farther than the hills surrounding a single large valley or several adjoining valley systems. Most of the states were republics ruled collectively by a council of the free warrior elite. Individual leaders were usually called kings, even though their offices and powers more closely resembled those of tribal chieftains. They were elected or removed from office by a vote of the warriors' councils.

The hill republics were well suited to the preservation of traditional Aryan values and lifestyles. Wars between the numerous hill states were frequent, as were feuds and cattle raids. Thus, the warrior elites were kept busy at activities that brought them wealth and honor. The republics nurtured the spirit of independence that had been strong among the invading Aryan tribes as well as hostility toward those who tried to concentrate political authority in the hands of a single ruler.

The warrior elites were also careful to keep the power of the brahmans in check, and the hill cultures fostered a healthy skepticism toward the priests and the gods they worshiped. In one early hymn the brahmans, chanting their prayers, are compared to croaking frogs gathered about a pond in the rainy season. Given these trends, it is not surprising that the hill regions were major centers of religious reform from the 6th century B.C.E. onward. One of the greatest religious reformers of all time, the Buddha, was from one of these republics, as were the founders of several other, less well-known Indian religions such as Jainism.

The Kingdoms of the Gangetic Plains

As Aryan settlement spread in the last millennium B.C.E. from the Indus region and Himalayan foothills

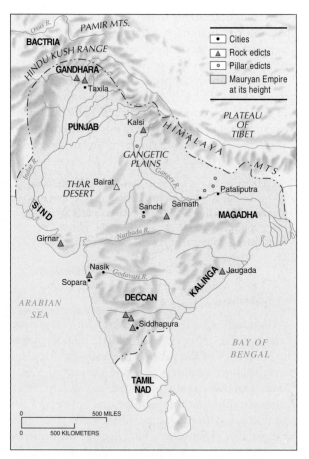

Map 6.1   India at the Time of Ashoka

internal social conflicts. In popular epics and philosophical tracts, rulers were taught to revere the brahmans and follow their advice, to patronize public works, and to rule in ways that promoted the welfare of their people. Ideally, kings were supposed to be hard-working, honest, and accessible to all subjects. There are even passages in the ancient texts that justify the violent overthrow of evil rulers.

It is highly unlikely that monarchs who lived up to all these high ideals would have survived the court intrigues and the assaults of rival rulers that were common in the era of brahman dominance. In fact, the sources from this period suggest a darker side to kingship that may have been closer to the realities of the age. Kings lived in constant fear for their thrones and lives. They were threatened by internal rivals, including their own sons, and by neighboring monarchs. A ruler's survival depended on the extensive use of spies and informers, a strong and loyal palace guard, and his courage and skill as a military commander.

Sources of Brahman Power

Although most rulers of the kingdoms on the Ganges plains were members of the warrior elite, brahmans living at the court centers often exercised more real power. Their positions as the educators of the princes who would someday rule and as the chief advisors to the kings themselves made them influential figures in the ruling circles. Like that of the scholar-gentry in China, their literacy in a society where few could read or write made the brahmans obvious candidates for administrative positions, from heads of bureaucratic departments to judges and tax collectors. In addition, only the brahmans knew how to perform the sacred rituals that were essential to crowning a new king. They alone knew the rites that conferred divine status on a monarch, and without divine status a ruler's legitimacy was in doubt. Once the ruler was installed, brahman astrologers foretold his future and regulated his daily schedule, telling him when to make war or mate with his wives.

As the brahmans' pivotal role in court ceremonies and prophecy indicates, their power and prestige were linked to their capacity to mediate between the gods and humans. The key function of the priests of the early Aryan invaders was to offer sacrifices to the gods and spirits (Figure 6.1), who often intervened in human affairs. By the 7th and 6th centuries B.C.E., the sacrifices themselves had become more powerful than the gods to whom they were offered.

to vast plains of the Ganges River system (see Map 6.1), republics and religious skeptics gave way to kings and powerful brahman priests. The hilly regions were divided into a patchwork of rival kingdoms. By contrast, in the lowland plains rulers were also drawn from the warrior elite, but they held power in their own right rather than deriving it from selection by warrior councils. Except for their influential brahman advisors, there were no formal checks on the kings' power. Many kings claimed descent from divine ancestors, and their thrones normally were inherited by their sons. All considered themselves to be the supreme war leaders, chief judges, and protectors of the peoples in their domains.

As these roles suggest, the powers and privileges these kings enjoyed were justified by the duties they performed and the services they provided for their subjects. As contemporary writings stress, they were expected to protect their kingdoms from invaders and

Figure 6.1 *Perhaps the most frequently depicted Indian religious image is the god Shiva as the celestial dancer, here portrayed in a south Indian bronze. The position of the god's hands and the objects held in them each represent a different aspect of his power, which may be simultaneously creative and destructive. His left hand closest to his head, for example, is held in the posture of reassurance, and the left hand furthest away holds a drum, which signifies time. His right foot crushes the demon of ignorance, which seems to want to be destroyed by the illustrious god.*

By this time it was widely believed that if the sacrifice was done correctly, the god had no choice but to grant the wish of the petitioner. Thus, a king could ensure victory, a peasant village sufficient rainfall, or a barren woman fertility if the proper ceremony was conducted flawlessly. Only the brahmans were able to perform the ceremony and allowed to read the sacred texts where the prayers and instructions for various types of sacrifices were set forth.

Only a small percentage of the brahmans in a given kingdom served as advisors at the court or as state administrators. Many were the personal priests or physicians of wealthy high-caste families; most were village priests, schoolteachers, and wandering ascetics. Some were alchemists, sorcerers, or even charlatans, living off the gullibility of the masses, who

believed in their ability to tell fortunes and cast magic spells. But all brahmans, from the palaces of kings to the most remote villages, were privileged beings, exempt from taxes and protected from injury by the harsh punishments imposed on those who dared to assault them. The following passage is from one of the ancient religious texts written by the brahmans. Not surprisingly, it warns that not even kings were considered exempt from the horrible fate that befell those who harmed a brahman.

> Whenever a king, fancying himself mighty, seeks to devour a Brahman, [his] kingdom is broken up.
> [Ruin] overflows that kingdom as water swamps a leaky boat;
> Calamity smites that country in which a priest is wronged.
> Even trees … repel, and refuse their shade to, the man who claims a right to the property of a Brahman.

In addition to the power exercised by the brahmans and the services they provided, religion shaped the daily lives of the peoples of south Asia through the ethical prescriptions found in the sacred Vedas. These texts were orally compiled and systematically transmitted by the brahman priests between 1200 and 900 B.C.E. In the last centuries B.C.E., the Vedas were written in Sanskrit, which became the standard and scholarly language of India, akin to Greek and Latin in the West. From the chants and ritual formulas of the early Vedas, the texts were increasingly devoted to religious and philosophical speculation and moral prescriptions. This highly religious culture provided the context for further changes as Indian civilization moved to even greater complexity.

An Era of Widespread Social Change

The rise of kings and increasing brahman dominance were only two of the many social changes that occurred as full civilization took shape for the second time in Indian history. Around the court centers of the lowland kings, towns, such as that in Figure 6.2, grew up as servant, artisan, and merchant groups catered to the needs of the rulers, their courtiers, and often large numbers of brahman advisors and administrators. Along the Ganges and other rivers, towns developed that were devoted to trade or the specialized manufacture of key products such as pottery, tools, and cotton textiles. With the increase in commerce and specialized production, merchants and

Figure 6.2 *Like many of the larger Indian towns, the one portrayed in this artist's recreation (based on classical Indian stone sculptures from the last centuries B.C.E.) depicts an Indian city that has walls, a moat, and multistoried buildings constructed mainly of intricately carved wood. In an age of political division and warfare, fortifications provided essential protection for urban centers, and villages were often surrounded by mud walls. As the army emerging from the city gates in the drawing suggests, elephants were a central element in Indian warfare in this era.*

artisans became established as distinct social groups. The great wealth of the larger trading houses allowed the merchants to win a prominent place in the Indian social hierarchy, which became both more complex and more rigid in this era.

Another social stratum that assumed major importance in this period was the peasantry. As farming replaced herding as the basis for the economies of the lowland kingdoms, peasants came to make up a large percentage of India's population. Mud-walled farming villages spread across the plains of northern India, although throughout the classical era they continued to be dwarfed in most places by massive rain forests. Irrigation networks and new agricultural tools steadily increased productivity and hence the ability to support ever larger numbers of nonfarming specialists. Most peasants grew staples such as rice, millet, and wheat, but some villages specialized in cotton, plants for dyes such as indigo, and luxury crops such as sugar cane.

The Caste System

The class division in India between warriors, priests, and commoners that made up the tribal social order of the early Aryan invaders had changed radically over the centuries. New social groups, such as merchants and peasants, were added to these broad social categories (**varnas**), and each was subdivided into occupational subgroups (jatis) or castes for the purpose of general analysis. These smaller groupings were particular to different regions in south Asia. They were arranged in a hierarchy according to the degree to which the tasks each group performed were considered polluting, particularly at the highest and lowest levels. Those who dealt with human waste or slaughtered animals, for example, were regarded as extremely defiling, whereas scholars and wandering holy men who avoided physical labor and refused to eat animal flesh were revered for their purity.

At the top of the caste pyramid were the brahman, warrior, and merchant groups, who made up only a small minority of the total population. The bulk of the population belonged to peasant and artisan subgroups, which made up most of the central and lower layers of the caste hierarchy. Beneath the peasants and artisans were the **untouchables,** who performed the most despised tasks in Indian society, including removing human waste from towns and villages, sweeping the streets, and tanning leather hides. The Indians' reverence for cows, which may have been present in Harappan society, and their aversion to dead animals made the latter occupation particularly polluting. Even the untouchables were divided into caste subgroups, with sweepers looking down on manure handlers, who in turn despised leatherworkers.

Over the centuries, the boundaries between caste groups hardened. In addition to occupation, a caste's position in the Indian social hierarchy was distinguished by its diet and by the caste groups with which its members could dine or exchange food. A caste's status also determined the social groups with which its members were allowed to intermarry and whether they were permitted to read the Vedas. Only members of castes belonging to the three highest varnas (brahmans, warriors, and merchants) were allowed to read the sacred texts. **Rama,** perhaps the greatest Indian cultural hero, was celebrated in the great epic the *Ramayana* for cutting off the head of a peasant holy man who recited hymns from the Vedas while hanging upside down from a tree.

Enforcing Social Divisions

A person was born into a caste group and could not change his or her caste status. Over long periods of time, a caste group could collectively rise or fall in status, but individuals were tied to the fortunes of their caste. Refusal to accept the duties and status of the caste into which one was born could lead to beatings and other forms of physical abuse. If the rebellious person continued to violate caste laws, he or she would be ostracized or outcast. This penalty normally meant certain death because no one, including a member of the outcast's own family, was allowed to pay him or her for labor or offer food, drink, or other services.

In addition to local sanctions, the caste system was upheld by Indian rulers and the belief that it was supernaturally ordained. One of the chief duties of a righteous monarch was to preserve the caste hierar-

chy and ensure that people at each level carried out the tasks and behaved in the manner appropriate to their rank. Ideally, the caste system allowed a harmonious exchange of products and services at all levels of Indian society. For example, peasants provided food for the brahmans, who saw to their religious and ritual needs, and for the warriors, who defended them from bandits and foreign invaders. Of course, high-caste groups, particularly brahmans and warriors, enjoyed a disproportionate share of wealth and power. But except in times of severe natural calamity or social crisis, even the lowliest untouchables were guaranteed a livelihood, however meager.

The caste position and career determined by a person's birth were called one's **dharma,** or life path, in a particular existence. The concept of transmigration of the soul helped to explain why some were given the enviable dharma of a brahman and others were consigned to untouchable status. In the Vedic era, it was widely accepted that a person's soul existed through many human lives and was transferred from one body to another after death. In each of its lives, the soul accumulated varying amounts of merit and demerit, depending on the actions of the person in whose body it dwelled. The sum of these merits and demerits at any given point in time made up one's **karma** (the fruits of one's behavior and actions in previous lives). A soul's karma determined the caste that the soul would be born into in its next **reincarnation.** Thus, a person who was born as a brahman had a soul that had built up a large surplus of merit; a person born as a sweeper was paying the penalty for the sins of his or her past lives.

One of the greatest sins was to violate one's dharma—to refuse the duties and status attached to the caste into which one was born. The only way to ensure a better situation in the next rebirth was to accept one's situation in the present and fully perform the tasks one was allotted. Thus, the concepts of the transmigration of the soul and reincarnation explained the inequities of the caste system and provided a religious rationale for accepting one's place in the caste hierarchy.

The Family and the Changing Status of Women

Some of our best insights into family life and gender relationships in this era are provided by the two great Indian epics, the *Mahabharata* and the *Ramayana.*

In Depth

Inequality as the Social Norm

The Indian caste system is perhaps the most extreme expression of a type of social organization that violates the most revered principles on which modern Western societies are based. Like the Egyptian division between a noble and a commoner and the Greek division between a freeperson and a slave, the caste system rests on the assumption that humans are inherently unequal and that their lot in life is determined by the families and social strata into which they are born. The caste system, like the social systems of all other classical civilizations, presumed that social divisions were fixed and stable and that people ought to be content with the station they had been allotted at birth.

These assumptions directly contradict some of the West's most cherished current beliefs. They run counter to one of the most basic organizing principles of modern Western culture, rooted in a commitment to equality of opportunity. This principle is enshrined in European and American constitutions and legal systems, taught in Western schools and churches, and proclaimed in Western media. The belief in human equality, or at least equality of opportunity, is one of the most important ideas that modern Western civilization has exported to the peoples of Africa, Asia, and Latin America.

The concept of equality rests on two assumptions. The first is that a person's place in society should be determined not by the class or family into which he or she is born but by personal actions and qualities. The second is that the opportunity to rise—or fall—in social status should be open to everyone and protected by law. Some of our most cherished myths reflect these assumptions: that anyone can aspire to be president of the United States, for example, or that an ordinary person has the right to challenge the actions of the politically and economically powerful. Of course, equality is a social ideal rather than something any human society has achieved. No one pretends that all humans are equal in intelligence or talent, and there are important barriers to equality of opportunity.

What is just and natural for modern societies would have been incomprehensible in the classical age. In fact, most human societies through most of human history have been organized on assumptions that are much closer to those underlying the Indian caste system than to those underlying modern Western norms. Ancient Egyptians or Greeks, or for that matter medieval Europeans or early modern Chinese, believed that career possibilities, political power, and social privileges should be set by law according to the position of one's family in the social hierarchy. The Indian caste structure was the most complex of the systems by which occupations, resources, and status were allotted. But all classical civilizations had similar social mechanisms that determined the obligations and privileges of members of each social stratum.

In some ways, classical Chinese and Greek societies provided exceptions to these general patterns. In China, people from lowly social origins could rise to positions of great status and power, and well-placed families could fall on hard times and lose their gentry status. But "rags to riches" success stories were the exception rather than the rule, and mobility between social strata was limited. In fact, Chinese thinkers made much of the distinctions between the scholar-gentry elite and the common people.

Although some of the Greeks, particularly the Athenians, developed the idea of equality for all citizens in a particular city-state, most of the people of these societies were not citizens, and many were slaves. By virtue of their birth the latter were assigned lives of servitude and drudgery. Democratic participation and the chance to make full use of their talents were limited to the free males of the city-states.

In nearly all societies, these fixed social hierarchies were upheld by creation myths and religious beliefs that proclaimed their divine origins and the danger of punishment if they were challenged. Elite thinkers stressed the importance of the established social order to human peace and well-being; rulers were duty bound to defend it. Few challenged the naturalness of the hierarchy itself; fewer still proposed alternatives to it. Each person was expected to accept his or her place and to concentrate on the duties and obligations of that place rather than worry about rights or personal desires. Males and females alike were required to subordinate their individual yearnings and talents to the needs of their families, clans, communities, or social superiors. In return for a person's acceptance of his or her allotted place in the hierarchy, he or she received material sustenance and a social slot. Of course, these benefits were denied to people who fought the system. They were outcast or exiled, physically punished, imprisoned, or killed.

(continued)

Questions: What arguments did the thinkers of the classical civilizations of Greece, China, and India use to explain and justify the great differences in social status and material wealth? How did those who belonged to elite groups justify their much greater status, wealth, and power compared to the peasants, artisans, and servants who made up most of the population? Why did people belonging to these subordinate social strata, including oppressed groups such as slaves and untouchables, accept these divisions? Comparing these modes of social organization with the ideals of your own society, what do you see as the advantages and drawbacks of each?

Although these tales of war, princely honor, love, and social duty were not written down until the last centuries B.C.E., they were related in oral form long before. They suggest that by the middle centuries of the last millennium B.C.E., the extended family was increasingly regarded as the ideal. Those who could support such large households, which normally meant only the highest caste groups, gathered all the male members of a given family and their wives and children under the same roof. At times up to four generations, from great-grandparents to their great-grandsons and great-granddaughters, lived together in the same dwelling or family compound.

Although these arrangements limited privacy and often led to family quarrels, they also provided a high degree of security and human companionship. Lower-caste groups such as peasants and artisans rarely could afford to support extended households. As a consequence, most Indian families were nuclear families, made up of parents and their children, with perhaps a widowed grandparent sharing their dwelling.

Somewhat contradictory visions of the positions and roles of women emerge from the epics, which suggest that attitudes toward women may have been in flux. On one hand, women were seen as weak, passionate, frivolous, and fond of gossip and slander. Female demons in the *Ramayana* were jealous temptresses and vengeful jilted lovers. Within the family, women remained clearly subordinated to men. Although youths were expected to obey and honor their mothers, parental veneration was focused on the father, to whom complete obedience and loyalty were expected. Wives were instructed to be attentive to their husbands' needs and ready to obey their every command. Rama's wife, Sita, was chosen for her beauty and absolute devotion to her husband. When he was forced into exile in the forest, she followed without question or complaint. When she was carried off to Sri Lanka by the demon Ravanna, Rama raced to defend her honor and his own. Having rescued her after a mighty battle with Ravanna and his evil minions, Rama refused to take her back because he suspected that she may have been raped while in captivity. Only when she proved her virtue by walking unscathed through a fire would he accept her again as his wife. Throughout both epics, the fate of women was controlled by men, be they gods, demons, or mortal humans.

On the other hand, some passages in the epics and other sources from this period indicate that in certain ways women had greater freedom and opportunities for self-expression than was true in the last centuries B.C.E. Women in the epics often were depicted as strong-willed and cunning. Sita and Draupadi, two of the wives of the five Pandava brothers who were the heroes of the *Mahabharata*, displayed remarkable courage and strength of character during their ordeals. Contemporary sources mention women who were renowned scholars of the sacred Vedic texts, which later they were not even permitted to read. Women in this era also made their mark as teachers, poets, musicians, and artists, although the last two activities were not highly esteemed. Like their brothers, girls from high-caste families were allowed to undergo the special ceremonies that celebrated their twice-born or exalted status—an honor boys continued to enjoy that gradually died out for young women. Women were even famed for their skills in the martial arts, as the amazon (female warrior) palace guards of several monarchs demonstrated.

The End of an Era

Roughly 1000 years after the first Aryan tribes entered India, a new civilization had come into being that was very different from the Harappan complex it replaced. Sedentary agriculture was well established and was productive enough to support a variety of specialized elites, true cities, extensive trade, and nonagrarian artisan manufacturers. In the caste system, the Indians had developed perhaps the most complex scheme of social stratification and labor division in human history. They had also made notable accomplishments in philosophical and religious speculation and artistic creativity. Although most of the artworks were done in wood and thus have perished over time, the profound thought of the age has been transmitted through the ages in extensive Sanskrit texts such as the Vedas and the great Indian epics. Some of the most sublime speculation about the supernatural and the meanings of human existence is contained in the portions of the *Mahabharata* called the *Bhagavad Gita*, or "Song Divine." In the following passage, the god Krishna counsels Arjuna, one of the great warriors of the epic, as he prepares for battle.

> To action alone hast thou a right and never at all to its fruit; let not the fruits of action be thy motive; neither let there be in thee any attachment to inaction.
> Fixed in yoga, do thy work, O winner of wealth [Arjuna], abandoning attachment, with an even mind in success and failure, for evenness of mind is called yoga....
> The wise who have united their intelligence [with the Divine], renouncing the fruits which their action yields and freed from the bonds of birth, reach the sorrowless state.

However, these great achievements of the brahmanic age were only a prelude to the religious, philosophical, and artistic creativity that occurred in south Asia in the last centuries B.C.E. The absolute and increasingly self-serving dominance of the brahmans, the succession of petty wars between the kings they advised, and the religious bankruptcy displayed by the sacrificial cults all prompted major challenges. These challenges and the brahman responses to them both remade and enriched Indian civilization in the millennium between 500 B.C.E. and 500 C.E.

Religious Ferment and the Rise of Buddhism

The 6th and 5th centuries B.C.E. were a time of great social turmoil and philosophical speculation throughout Eurasia. In China, Confucius and Laozi proposed very different views of the proper organization of human society and purposes of life. In Persia, Zoroaster founded a new religion, while the prophets Ezekiel and Isaiah strove to improve the Hebrews' understanding of their single, almighty God. In Greece, the writings of Thales and Pythagoras laid the basis for unprecedented advances in philosophy, the sciences, and mathematics. India too was caught up in this transcontinental trend of social experimentation and intellectual probing.

Indian reformers questioned the brahmans' dominance and the value of the sacrifices on which it ultimately rested. They sought alternatives to the caste system as the basis for India's social order. They posed questions about the nature of the universe and the end of life that the Vedic thinkers had debated for centuries, and they often came up with very different answers. Some experimented with new techniques of meditation and self-mortification; others promoted new religions that would free the masses from what were viewed as the oppressive teachings of the brahmans. One holy man and thinker, the Buddha, did all of these things and in the process made the most globally influential religious and philosophical breakthroughs of an age of remarkable intellectual ferment.

The Making of a Religious Teacher

Accounts of the Buddha's life are so cluttered with myths and miracles that it is difficult to know what kind of man he actually was and what sort of message he originally preached. We are fairly certain that he lived from the mid-6th century to the second decade of the 5th century B.C.E. He was born into one of the warrior clans of the hill states south of the Himalayas (see Map 6.1), where, as we have seen, the rule of kings and the hold of the brahmans was weak. Buddhist traditions hold that he was the son of the local ruler who was haunted by a prophecy made by a religious seer at the time of the Buddha's birth. The seer predicted that the child would someday refuse his father's throne and become a wandering *ascetic* (a person who renounces the pleasures of the material world).

To prevent this, the king confined his son to the palace grounds and provided him with every imaginable human pleasure and comfort. But as he approached manhood the prince grew curious about the world beyond the palace gardens and walls. With the aid of a trusted servant, the Buddha ventured forth into the nearby countryside, where he encountered for the first time illness, old age, death, and a wandering ascetic. Unsettled by these encounters with human suffering, the prince became moody and withdrawn. Finally, as the holy man had predicted, he renounced all claims to succeed his father as king and set off with a group of wandering ascetics to meditate and ponder the many questions posed by his discoveries beyond the palace walls.

In the wilderness, the Buddha experimented with the many ways Indian **gurus,** or religious teachers, had devised to reach a higher understanding of the nature of humanity and the supernatural world. He did yogic exercises, fasted almost to death, chanted sacred prayers for days on end, and conversed with every seer he encountered. Discouraged by his failure to find the answer to the questions that had driven him to take up the life of a wandering ascetic, and exhausted by the self-punishment he had inflicted, the Buddha collapsed, legend has it, under a huge tree. Saved from death by the care of a young girl, the Buddha turned to meditation in his search for understanding. Ultimately, by disciplining his mind and body, he achieved enlightenment, which rested on his discovery of what Buddhists came to call the Four Noble Truths.

The central issue for the Buddha was the problem of suffering, which he believed all living things experience because all living things and the objects to which they are attached are impermanent. The moment we are born we begin to die, he reasoned. People whom one loves or befriends may turn indifferent or hostile or simply move away; love and friendship are inevitably ended by death. The goals to which humans devote their lives, such as fame and wealth, are empty and, once attained, can easily be lost. These attachments to the illusory and impermanent things of the world are the source of suffering.

One can escape suffering only by ceasing to desire the things of the world and realizing that even one's sense of self is part of the illusion. This realization, or enlightenment, can be achieved by following the eight-step process that includes right action, thinking, and meditation. Once enlightenment has been attained, the individual is released from suffering because she or he is free from desire and attachment. He or she has attained **nirvana**—not heaven in the Christian sense, but simply an eternal state of tranquility.

Having attained enlightenment, the Buddha, because of his great compassion for all living creatures, set out to spread his message to all humanity (and, Buddhist legends relate, to the creatures of the forest). He became the most successful of the numerous seers and gurus who traveled through the hill and lowland kingdoms in this era, challenging the teachings of the brahmans and offering alternative modes of worship and paths to salvation. The Buddha soon gained a great following, which ranged from exalted monarchs to humble sweepers and included both men and women. As he feared, his followers turned his teachings into an organized religion. What had probably begun as a starkly pessimistic and antiworldly vision of existence, without gods or the promise of an everlasting paradise, became one of the great salvationist faiths of all human history.

The Emergence of Buddhism as a Religion

After his death (again as he feared), the Buddha—often in the form of lifelike sculptures such as that in Figure 6.3—was worshiped as a deity. His most faithful disciples became monks who devoted their lives to spreading his message and achieving nirvana. They held conferences in which they tried to compile authoritative collections of his teachings and the traditions concerning his life. Not surprisingly, disagreements over points of doctrine and meaning arose at these sessions. These disputes led to the formation of rival schools of monks, who vied with each other, the brahmans, and other sects to build a popular following.

Over time, the rival schools created elaborate philosophical systems. But in their efforts to attract a broader following, the monks stressed more accessible aspects of what had become a new religion. They offered miraculous tales of the Buddha's life, which included traditions that his mother had been a virgin and that he had been visited by revered scholars from afar soon after his birth. In the popular mind, nirvana became equated with heaven. Graphic visions of heavenly pleasures and the tortures of hell became central features of popular Buddhism. The Buddha was worshiped as a savior who returned periodically to help the faithful find the way to heaven. Although within the monastic communities Buddhist monks continued their emphasis on meditation and the achievement of nirvana, laypeople were encouraged to perform good deeds that would earn enough merit for their souls to go to one of the Buddhist heavens after death.

The Buddhist Challenge

Many philosopher-ascetics criticized the religious beliefs and caste system that the brahmans had estab-

Figure 6.3 *This beautifully detailed sandstone statue of the Buddha meditating in a standing position was carved in the 5th century C.E. Note the nimbus, or halo, which was common in later Buddhist iconography. The calm radiated by the Buddha's facial expression suggests that he has already achieved Enlightenment. As Buddhism spread throughout India and overseas, a wide variety of artistic styles developed to depict the Buddha himself and key incidents of his legendary life. The realism and stylized robes of the sculpture shown here indicate that it was carved by artists following the conventions of the Indo-Greek school of northwestern India.*

lished. But none was as successful at winning converts as the Buddha and the many monastic orders committed to his teachings. The monks and monastic organizations provided a viable alternative to the brahman priesthood as centers of scholarship, education, and religious ritual, and often directly opposed the beliefs that the brahmans championed. Although the Buddha retained the ideas of karma and reincarnation, he rejected the Vedas as divinely inspired teachings that ought to be accepted as the ultimate authority on all issues. He ridiculed the powers the brahmans claimed for their sacrifices and the gods for whom they were intended. He favored introspection and self-mastery over ritual. In so doing, he struck at the very heart of the brahmans' social and religious dominance.

The Buddha rejected the lifestyles of both the brahmans who had become addicted to worldly power and the brahman ascetics who practiced extreme forms of bodily mortification. He tried to do away with the caste system, an aim that gave his teachings great appeal among the untouchables and other groups. The Buddha also accepted women as his followers and taught that they were capable of attaining nirvana. These opportunities were institutionalized in Buddhist monastic organizations, which normally included provisions for communities of nuns. The evidence we have suggests that monastic life became a fulfilling career for women in many parts of India. This outlet proved doubly meaningful in an era when educational and other occupational opportunities for women were declining, and upper-caste women in particular were increasingly confined to the home.

The Greek Interlude

The intellectual and social ferment that swept northern India in the 6th century B.C.E. was intensified by political upheavals touched off by the invasion of northwestern India by Alexander the Great. This was an important, though unusual case of direct contact between two civilization areas during the classical period. In 327 B.C.E. Alexander's armies crossed the Hindu Kush into India, thus beginning his last major campaign of conquest. It was a rousing success. His greatly outnumbered armies won a series of battles against the peoples living in the upper Indus valley. As in his Persian campaigns, Alexander's well-trained troops proved more than a match for the war chariots, archers, and cavalry of his Indian adversaries.

Once the surprise wore off, his veteran soldiers also proved able to cope with the war elephants that had frightened their horses in early battles.

Victory stirred Alexander's passion for further conquests. But his soldiers, weary of endless battles and fearful of the stiffening resistance of Indian princes in an exotic and very distant land, refused to go farther east. After much debate, Alexander agreed to lead his forces out of India. Those who survived an epic march through the desert wastes to the north and west of the Indus River returned to Persia in 324 B.C.E. Alexander's death a year later left his Indian conquests to be fought over by the commanders who divided up his empire.

Although several Greek rulers controlled territory in India's northwest for decades after Alexander's invasion, the impact of his campaign was largely indirect. It stimulated trade and cultural exchange between India and the Mediterranean region. Of particular importance were the flow of Greek astronomical and mathematical ideas to India and the impact of Indian thinking on religious movements in the Mediterranean. Greek Stoicism and the mystery religions that swept the eastern Mediterranean in the centuries around the birth of Christ owe much to Indian philosophical influences. In the arts, the combination of Indian and Greek styles led to an Indo-Greek school of sculpture that was both distinctive and influential in shaping approaches to the depiction of the Buddha. As Figure 6.3 illustrates, Indian motifs were blended with Greek physical features and artistic techniques.

The Rise of the Mauryas

Appropriately, the most lasting effects of Alexander's invasion were military and political. The defeats suffered by the kingdoms in the northwest created a political vacuum that was soon filled by the ablest of the regional lords, **Chandragupta Maurya** (322–298 B.C.E.). After some initial setbacks, Chandragupta, whose original base was on the Ganges plain in the vicinity of the present-day state of Bihar, embarked on a sustained campaign to build a great empire. After conquering much of the northwest and driving the Greek successors of Alexander out of India, his armies began to conquer the kingdoms of the Ganges plain that would later form the heartland of the **Mauryan** Empire (see Map 6.1).

As Chandragupta's empire grew, the folksy atmosphere of earlier localized court centers gave way to a new imperial style. He reigned from an elaborately carved and decorated palace set in large and well-tended gardens. Adopting the Persian example, Chandragupta proclaimed himself an absolute emperor and on state occasions sat on a high throne above hundreds of his splendidly attired courtiers. He was guarded by a special corps of amazons, and elaborate precautions were taken to safeguard his life. The food Chandragupta ate was first tasted by servants to ensure that it was not poisonous. There were hollow pillars in which to hide palace spies, secret passages to enable the king to move about the palace undetected, and an obligatory bath and frisking for all who entered. Chandragupta built a standing army that Greek writers estimated (overly generously) at 500,000, and he tried with some success to replace regional lords with his own administrators.

All of these safeguards were consistent with the recommendations set forth in a treatise on statecraft, the *Arthashastra,* that dominated political thinking during Chandragupta's reign and in the centuries that followed. The *Arthashastra* bore a much greater resemblance to Sunzi's *Art of War* than to Plato's *Republic.* Attributed to **Kautilya,** an astute advisor to Chandragupta Maurya, the work is actually a compilation over many generations of the political theory and practical advice of several authors. In great detail, Kautilya and his fellow political strategists described the techniques a ruler must use to attain and hold power. Spies disguised as beggars, barbers, and even holy men should be stationed everywhere in a king's own domains and those of his enemies. Crime and internal dissent must be punished harshly. The authors of the *Arthashastra* sanctioned the removal of rival rulers by bribery and assassination (for which specially trained prizefighters were recommended) and by using traitors to undermine resistance in neighboring kingdoms. Like Sunzi in China, they scorned the notion of chivalrous warfare.

With such advice, it is little wonder that Chandragupta and his successors rapidly conquered a vast empire that included all of south Asia but the southern tip (see Map 6.1). Chandragupta's son and successor, Bindusara, extended the Mauryan Empire to the east along the Ganges plains and far to the south of the subcontinent. Little is known about Bindusara, but he was apparently a highly cultured man. He once requested wine, figs, and a philosopher as presents from one of the Greek rulers in western Asia. He received the wine and figs, but not the philosopher because, as the ruler informed him, the Greeks did not trade in philosophers. Bindusara's son, **Ashoka,** completed the conquests begun by his father and grandfather, and in his long reign from 268 to 232 B.C.E., northern India enjoyed unprecedented political unity, prosperity, and cultural splendor.

Ashoka's Conversion and the Flowering of Buddhism in the Mauryan Age

In the early years of his rule, Ashoka showed little of the wisdom and tolerance that set off his reign as one of the great periods in Indian history. He won his throne only after a bloody struggle in which he eliminated several brothers. According to contemporary Buddhist sources, which are intent on depicting Ashoka before his conversion in the worst possible light, he was both bad-tempered and impetuous. One often-cited example of Ashoka's brutal excesses was his insistence that a woman from his harem be put to death for telling him that he was ugly. He also delighted in conquest, at least until he witnessed the horrible sufferings that were caused by his conquest of Orissa in eastern India. That experience, and regret for his earlier brutality, led to his conversion to Buddhism.

From the time of his conversion onward, Ashoka strove to serve his people and promote their welfare. He ceased to enlarge his domains by conquest, used his revenues to build roads, hospitals, and rest houses, and sought to reduce the slaughter of animals in his kingdom by encouraging vegetarianism. His attempts to curb the slaughter of cows, either for sacrifices or for food, were particularly important. These efforts, in conjunction with a long-standing reverence for cattle that reached back to the Harappa era, contributed to the sacred status that this animal long ago attained in Indian civilization. Because Ashoka's edicts were aimed at restricting animal sacrifices, they aroused the anxiety of the brahmans, who saw them as a threat to the rituals that were vital to their dominance in Indian society.

The influence of Buddhism on Ashoka's personal life spilled over into his state policy. Drawing on the Buddhist concept of a righteous world ruler spreading peace and good government, Ashoka attempted to build an imperial bureaucracy that would enforce his laws and sanctions against war and animal slaughter. Although his efforts to establish meaningful control by a centralized administration met with some success, they also aroused opposition. The brahmans, resenting their displacement as political advisors and administrators by Ashoka's bureaucrats, tried to stir up local resistance. Warrior families that had once ruled the small states also sought to retain control over local politics. They waited for signs of dynastic weakness in the hope of reviving their lost kingdoms.

Imperial Patronage and Social Change

Several social groups gained from Ashoka's attempts to recast Indian society in a Buddhist mold. Seeing in Buddhism an advantageous alternative to the caste system, merchants and artisans supported Ashoka's efforts. They generously patronized orders of Buddhist monks, which increased greatly in wealth and membership. Women also had good reasons to support the Buddhist alternative. Their position within the family was strengthened under Buddhist law. In addition, the monastic life gave them opportunities for achievement and self-expression as nuns, scholars, and artists.

One of the chief signs of the Buddhist surge under Ashoka and his successors was the spread of great monastery complexes throughout the subcontinent. Most of the monasteries were made of wood and thus were lost in fires or destroyed by later invaders. But the Buddhist architectural legacy was preserved in the great stone shrines, or **stupas,** that were built to house pieces of bone or hair and personal possessions that were said to be relics of the Buddha (Figure 6.4). Most of the freestanding stupas were covered mounds of dirt surrounded by intricately carved stone gateways and fences.

Another major effect of Ashoka's dedication to Buddhism resulted from his efforts to spread the faith beyond the Indian subcontinent. He sent missions, including one led by one of his sons, to Sri Lanka to the south and to the Himalayan kingdoms and the steppes of central Asia to the north. Establishing Buddhism in each region was critical because converted rulers and monks in these areas were instrumental in spreading the religion to much of the rest of Asia. From Sri Lanka Buddhism was carried to

Figure 6.4 *The great Buddhist stupa at Sanchi in central India. Stupas were built to house relics of the Buddha, and they became major sites of pilgrimage. The intricate carved gates and railing surrounding the stupa related incidents from the Buddha's life or displayed symbols associated with his teachings. The great dome that covered the dirt mound that formed the core of the stupa often was painted white, and it struck approaching pilgrims as a great cloud floating on the horizon.*

Burma, Java, and many other parts of southeast Asia. From Nepal and central Asia it was carried into Tibet, China, and the rest of east Asia.

Ashoka's Death and the Decline of the Mauryas

Ashoka's bold experiments in religious and social change and the empire that he and his forebears had established did not long survive his death. Weaker rulers followed him to the throne. The empire was first divided between rival claimants within the Maurya household and then pulled apart by internal strife and local lords, who attempted to reestablish the many kingdoms that had been absorbed into the empire. By 185 B.C.E., the Mauryan Empire had disappeared. Political fragmentation returned to the subcontinent, and new warrior invaders compounded the rapidly growing divisions. Although some of these conquerors built substantial empires and were devoted to the continued spread of Buddhism, none of them could match Ashoka in power and resolution.

Brahmanical Recovery and the Splendors of the Gupta Age

 Across the Indian subcontinent in the centuries between the fall of the Mauryas and the rise of the Guptas in the late 3rd century C.E., Buddhism and Hinduism vied, largely peacefully, for the patronage of Indian rulers and the support of the Indian masses. By the time of the founding of the Gupta Empire in the 4th century C.E., it was clear that the brahmans could meet the Buddhist challenge. Gupta patronage fortified the brahman revival, which produced one of India's most glorious ages of philosophical and artistic creativity and social sophistication.

Even in the centuries immediately after the fall of the Mauryan dynasty, when the influence of Buddhism in Indian society was at its height, patterns had developed that rendered it vulnerable to a brahman counteroffensive. Over time, Buddhist monks became more and more concentrated in huge monasteries.

Visualizing the Past

The Pattern of Trade in the Ancient Eurasian World

The period of Mauryan rule coincided with a great expansion in trade between the main centers of civilization in Eurasia and Africa. In the centuries that followed, a permanent system of exchange developed that extended from Rome and the Mediterranean Sea to China and Japan. The trading networks that made up this system included both those established between ports connected by ships and sea routes and those consisting of overland exchanges transmitted along the chain of trading centers that crossed central Asia and the Sudanic region of Africa. By the last centuries B.C.E., this far-flung trading system included much of the world as it was known to the peoples of the Eastern Hemisphere.

Some products produced at one end of the system, such as Chinese silks and porcelains, were carried the entire length of the network to be sold in markets at the other edge, in Rome, for example. As a general rule, products carried over these great distances tended to be high-priced luxury goods such as spices and precious jewels. But most of the exchanges, particularly in bulk goods such as metal ores or foodstuffs, were between adjoining regions. The ports of western India, for example, carried on a brisk trade with those in the Red Sea and Persian Gulf, while trading centers in southeast Asia supplied China with forest products and other raw materials in exchange for the many items manufactured by China's highly skilled artisans. Although
(continued)

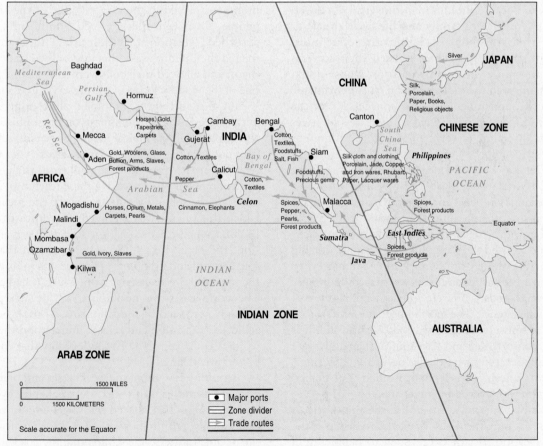

Eurasian and African Trading Goods Routes, c. 300 B.C.E. to 300 C.E.

some merchants and seamen, particularly the Chinese and Arabs, could be found in ports far from their homelands, most confined their activities within regional orbits, such as the Arabian Sea, the Persian Gulf, or the South China Sea.

The map on the preceding page provides an overview of this great trading network in the age of the classical civilizations, roughly the 3rd century B.C.E. to the 3rd century C.E. It shows the main centers of production, the goods exported overland and overseas, and the main directions of trade in these products. In each of the main sectors participating in the system, key ports, inland trading centers, and the products produced in different regions are shown.

Questions: Which civilizations or areas in the global trading network were the main centers for the production of finished products, such as cloth and pottery? What major centers supplied raw materials, such as forest products or foods? Which areas and port centers strike you as key points of convergence for the various types of trade? What advantages would these areas enjoy? Why were luxury goods likely to be transported the greatest distances? Why were bulk goods, especially foods, usually shipped only short distances, if at all? What were the advantages and disadvantages of sea and land transport? Besides trade goods, what other things might be transmitted through the trading networks? How great a role do you think the trading system played in the development of global civilization?

Increasingly isolated from village and urban life, the monks grew obsessed with fine points of philosophy that often had little or no relevance to ordinary believers. Because Buddhism in India had not developed a sequence of family and life cycle rituals or folk festivals, the monks had little occasion to interact with the people. They focused their services more and more on wealthy patrons, whose donations supported the monasteries. This support made the daily rounds to collect alms unnecessary for the monks in many areas and led to luxurious lifestyles and lax discipline at some of the more prominent Buddhist centers.

While the Buddhist monks became more remote from the Indian populace, the brahmans strove to make changes in belief and worship that would make Hinduism more appealing to ordinary people. They played down the need for grand and expensive sacrifices and stressed the importance of personal worship and small, everyday offerings of food and prayers to the gods. Increasing emphasis was placed on intense devotion to gods, who were seen as manifestations of one divine essence. The most important of these gods included **Shiva** (see Figure 6.1) and **Vishnu** and their female consorts Kali and Lakshmi. Certain gods were especially revered by particular occupational groups, such as Ganesh, the elephant-headed, pot-bellied deity who was favored by merchants.

Temples sprang up to house the multitude of statues that were the focus for popular worship of the gods. Devotional cults were open to people at all caste levels, sometimes including the untouchables. Women also were allowed to participate, at times, as cult poets and singers. In addition, the brahmans multiplied or enriched special festivals and rites of passage, such as child-naming celebrations, weddings, and funerals. These occasions enlarged the role the brahmans played in the everyday life of the Indian people. Over centuries, revived Hinduism simply absorbed salvationist Buddhism. The brahmans treated the Buddha as another god of the Hindu pantheon and allowed their followers to worship him as one of the worldly forms of the preserver god Vishnu.

At the elite level, brahman philosophers and gurus placed increasing emphasis on the sophisticated and sublime philosophical ideas associated with the later books of the Vedas, the *Upanishads.* Not heaven or hell but the release of the soul from the endless cycle of rebirths was stressed in these teachings. Moderate asceticism and meditation were the means by which this release was achieved. In contrast to the Buddha, who preached that the soul itself was an illusion, the orthodox Hindu schools taught that the soul was real and its ultimate purpose was to fuse with the universal divine essence from which it had come. The world was *maya*, or illusion, only because it was wrongly perceived by most humans. Those who had achieved realization and release understood that the world was an extension of a single reality that encompassed everything.

In addition to monastic weaknesses and brahman reforms, Buddhism in India was weakened by economic changes that altered the social circumstances that had favored the new religion. Most critical was the decline of the Rome–China trading axis with the fall of the Han Empire in the 3rd century C.E. Not only did this undermine the position of the merchant groups that had been major patrons of Buddhism, but it also made large-scale traders more and more dependent on local kings and warrior households, which remained the chief allies of the brahmans.

The damage done to Buddhism by the loss of the mercantile classes was compounded by the collapse of the Mauryan and later Buddhist empires, which had been the monastic orders' supreme source of patronage. Their eventual replacement by the **Guptas,** who were enthusiastic supporters of the brahmans and Hinduism, all but sealed the fate of Buddhism in India. Its demise was gradual and only occasionally hastened by violent persecution. But centuries of rule by the Guptas in north India and Hindu kingdoms in the south left only pockets of Buddhist strength, which decayed over time.

The Gupta Empire

In the last decades of the 3rd century C.E., a family of wealthy landholders in the eastern Ganges plains infiltrated the court of the local ruler and seized his throne. Through a succession of clever alliances and timely military victories, the Gupta family built an empire that by the end of the 4th century C.E. extended across most of northern India (Map 6.2). The Guptas' domains were not nearly as extensive as those of the Mauryas, and they had far less control over the regional lords and villages than the Mauryas had, particularly under Ashoka. The Gupta rulers never tried to build a genuine bureaucracy or regulate affairs at the local level. Their empire was in fact a massive tributary edifice in which former kings were left to rule in the name of the Guptas, and regional warrior elites were autonomous governors of all but the empire's heartlands in the Ganges basin.

The Guptas were content to be acknowledged as supreme overlords and to draw tribute from the many vassals under their rule. Weak control from the center meant that local lords periodically revolted or squabbled among themselves. Although internal warfare continued, it was at a lower level than in the centuries after the fall of the Mauryas. Until the 5th century, foreign invaders were kept beyond the Himalayas and internal conflicts were short and localized. Gupta dominance brought more than two and a half centuries of peace and prosperity to much of north India.

A Hindu Renaissance

From the outset, the Guptas had been staunch defenders of Hinduism and patrons of the brahmans.

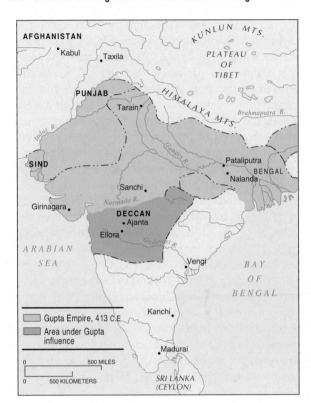

Map 6.2 *The Gupta Empire*

With the family's rise to power, the brahmans' roles as sanctifiers of and advisors to kings were fully restored. Buddhist monks were increasingly confined to their monasteries, which, lacking the patronage of the imperial court, had to depend on wealthy local merchants or landowners for support. The brahmans' roles as gurus, or teachers, for the princes of the imperial court and the sons of local notables also became entrenched. Brahmans regained the aura of mystery and supernatural power that they had enjoyed in the Vedic age. In *The Signet Ring of Rakshasa,* one of the great dramas produced in the Gupta epoch, King Chandragupta prostrates himself at the feet of his teacher and advisor, Chanyaka. The ruler lavishes presents on brahmans linked to the court and relies on their stratagems to thwart his adversaries. With their power base and sources of patronage restored, brahman priests, poets, scholars, and patrons of the arts became the driving force behind an era of splendid achievement in literature, music, art, architecture, and the natural sciences.

The most dramatic expressions of the Hindu resurgence were the great temples that rose above the rapidly growing urban centers, both within the Gupta domains and in the independent kingdoms in the far south (Figure 6.5). In many cases the temples themselves provided the impetus for urban growth. Merchants, artisans, servants, and laborers migrated to the towns where the temples were located to serve the growing numbers of pilgrims who journeyed to the sacred sites. The intricately carved stone gateways and sanctuary towers proclaimed the majesty of the Hindu gods and goddesses. In eastern India and elsewhere, the temple towers teemed with sculptures of deities and friezes of their exploits; with animals, which were often the vehicles or manifestations of major gods or goddesses; and with humans engaged in all manner of activities, including sexual intercourse.

Hindu art stressed symbolism rather than accurate representation, which was so highly valued by the ancient Greeks. The sculpture and the god or goddess it depicted stood for something else, including creation (Brahma), destruction (Shiva), fertility (Lakshmi), and death (Kali as Durga). In fact, the temple complexes as a whole were massive **mandalas,** or cosmic diagrams, measured precisely and laid out according to established conventions.

Achievements in Literature and the Sciences

Although written languages had developed in India before the rise of the Gupta dynasty, the Gupta reign initiated one of the great ages of Indian literary achievement. In the Gupta period and the centuries that followed, many of the great classics of Sanskrit, the sacred and classical Indian language, and Tamil, one of the major languages of the south, were written. The poet Kalidasa, who is acknowledged as the greatest Sanskrit author, lived in a period when Gupta power was at its height. In the "Cloud Messenger" and numerous other poems, he provided vivid pictures of life in the Gupta age. In the following passage, for example, the clouds bringing the monsoon rains pass over a town where the poet exclaims,

> Your body will grow fat with the smoke of incense from open windows where women dress their hair.
>
> You will be greeted by palace peacocks, dancing to welcome you, their friend.
>
> If your heart is weary from travel you may pass the night above mansions fragrant with flowers
>
> Whose pavements are marked with red dye from the feet of lovely women.

Figure 6.5 *An approaching pilgrim's view of the temple towers in the city of Madurai in south India. Like medieval cathedrals and Islamic mosques, these great structures attest to the intense faith and devotion associated with the Hindu resurgence of the early centuries* C.E.

In addition to poetry and drama, Hindu scholars in the classical era wrote treatises on the nature of time, space, and causality. These works contain arguments that have much in common with the findings of modern science on many issues. In fact, the era of the Hindu revival was a time of great Indian achievement in mathematics and the sciences. In addition to advances in geometry and algebra that were made independently of the work in these fields by the Greeks, Indian thinkers calculated the circumference of the globe and the value of pi with remarkable accuracy. They also used the concept of zero, devised decimals, and, most critically, formulated the system of numbers that virtually all human societies use today. We in the West call these numbers "Arabic" because it was through Arab merchants and scholars that they came to be known and used in Europe from the 10th century C.E. onward. In the Gupta age and afterward, the Indians also made major breakthroughs in medicine. They developed hospitals, surgical techniques, and sophisticated treatments for a variety of illnesses.

Intensifying Caste and Gender Inequities

As the brahmans recovered their social dominance, the caste hierarchy they had long promoted became the backbone of the Indian social system. Caste divisions grew even more complex and came to vary significantly between different areas in the subcontinent. Styles of dress increasingly distinguished members of each varna, and the restrictions on untouchables and other low-caste groups grew harsher and more pervasive. In some areas, for example, untouchables traveling on roadways between towns had to clap sticks together or continually shout that they were on the road to warn high-caste groups that they were in danger of being polluted. If a brahman or merchant was seen approaching, the untouchable was required to leave the road and pass by through the fields at a distance. The untouchables were not allowed to use any wells but their own or to worship in the temples used by other caste groups. Even their living quarters were segregated from the rest of the towns and rural villages.

Like the untouchables, women at all caste levels suffered a further reduction of their status and restriction of career outlets. They were no longer allowed to read the sacred Vedas, although a few remained prominent in the devotional cults. Hindu law declared that women were legally minors, subject to the supervision and protection of their fathers, husbands, and (if widowed) sons. Except for their personal clothing and jewelry, women were not allowed to inherit property. The fact that family fortunes could pass only from father to son and that large dowries were required to arrange marriages with suitable spouses meant that girls were increasingly seen as an economic liability. In some regions where dowry amounts were highly inflated, female infants were killed to save families from financial ruin.

Women were tied to the home, their lives run by men. As the passage quoted in the Document box indicates, a young woman was raised to defer to her husband and to respond to his every wish. Marriages were primarily a means of establishing alliances between families. They were arranged with the groom having little say and the bride none. Child marriages were not uncommon among the upper castes. Young girls left the familiar surroundings of their own homes to live with their husbands' families. In their new households, they were at the mercy of their mothers-in-law, who could be caring and reassuring but, if the literature from this and later periods is any gauge, were very often bossy and critical. A young girl's place in the new household depended almost wholly on her ability to bear sons, who would care for her in old age. A woman whose husband died before she bore him a son was doomed to a lonely life in the remote corners of the family compound. Even widows who bore sons were not to be envied. They were not allowed to remarry or go out alone lest they defile the memory of their deceased husbands.

Other than marriage, few avenues were open to women. A single woman was regarded as an economic liability and a blot on her family's honor. As the Buddhist monasteries shrank in numbers and size, the possibility of becoming a nun diminished. Only by becoming a courtesan, accomplished in all the arts including sexual intercourse, could a woman establish some degree of independence. Courtesans, who are sometimes celebrated in the literature of this period, could become well educated, acquire wealth, and find outlets for their talents. They were far above the despised common prostitutes in status, but they could not hope to have social respectability or raise families of their own. Unlike married women, whose husbands were duty bound to support them, courtesans depended on the tastes and whims of men, who dominated all aspects of interaction between the sexes in the Gupta age.

Document

A Guardian's Farewell Speech to a Young Woman About to Be Married

One of the great plays written during the Hindu revival of the early centuries C.E. was *Shakuntala*, by Kalidasa. The play is a Cinderella-style tale about a beautiful young woman, Shakuntala, who is loved by a king, and the travails she must endure before they are happily united. In the following exchange, as Shakuntala sets out to join her husband at his palace, she is instructed by her guardians (the hermits Kashyapa and Gautami) on the proper behavior for a young wife, in a manner that recalls the famous speech by Polonius to his son, Laertes, in Shakespeare's *Hamlet*.

Kashyapa: Now you Shakuntala. Respect your superiors,

Be friendly toward the ladies of the palace.

Never be angry with your husband, no matter what happens.

Be polite with the maids;

In everything be humble.

These qualities make a woman; those without them are black sheep in their families.

What is your opinion, Gautami?

Gautami: A bride needs nothing more. Remember his advice, Shakuntala.

Shakuntala: How will I ever manage in the palace? I feel so lost. I belong here, Father.

Kashyapa: Don't worry, my child; you are privileged.

You will be his great wife;

He is noble and great.

You will give him a son, as the East gives us light.

The pain of separation will then pass.

Questions: What does this conversation tell you about gender relationships and marriage in classical India? What does it say about attitudes toward women? How do these relationships and attitudes compare with those found in China and Greece in this era? How do they compare with those in our own society?

The Pleasures of Elite Life

Although women were limited in career options and largely confined to the home, life for those of the upper castes had its rewards, at least once a woman had established her place in her husband's family by having sons. Well-to-do families lived in large compounds set in gardens filled with flowering plants and colorful birds. They were waited on by servants and entertained at periodic festivals and in their own compounds by swings, games such as chess and pachisi (both of which the Indians invented), and wandering musicians. They dressed in silks and fine cottons and enjoyed one of the world's great cuisines. When they ventured away from the family compound, the very wealthy were carried in litters borne by servants and given the place of honor to which their caste entitled them.

Men from the upper castes were particularly privileged. They were expected to experience the four stages of the ideal Hindu life that were firmly established in this era for men only. In their youth they were to work hard as students, but many diversions and pleasures were available to the fashionable sons of well-to-do families. Many of these pastimes are described in the famous *Kamasutra* by Vatsayana, who lived in the Gupta era. Though often dismissed as little more than a glorified sex manual, Vatsayana's work contains detailed instructions on virtually all aspects of the life of the wealthy young man. There are recommendations for grooming and hygiene, discussions of good etiquette in various situations, advice on the best way to select a wife, and, of course, instructions in making love to either a witty and knowledgeable courtesan or one's future wife. There was a double standard: Young men were expected to come to marriage knowledgeable in the ways of love, but young women who were not virgins were disgraced and unmarriageable.

The student was expected in the second stage of life to become a householder and, ideally, a faithful husband. Preserving or adding to the family fortune was a major task in this phase of life, and bearing sons to perform one's funeral rites and continue the family line was essential. At some point in middle age, the householder was supposed to bid farewell to his family and go off to the forest to join the hermits in meditation. In his final years, the upper-caste man was expected to enter the fourth stage of life by becoming a wandering holy man, completely dependent on the charity of others. Few men actually advanced beyond the householder stage. But the fact that the sequence had become the social ideal indicates that Indian religion and society could readily accommodate scholarship and worldly pursuits, bodily denial, and meditation as valid paths to self-fulfillment.

Lifestyles of the Ordinary People

For most Indian peasants, artisans, and sweepers at the lower levels of the caste system, the delights of upper-caste youths or the life of a wandering holy man were unattainable. Most Indians lived lives of hard work, if not sheer drudgery. Most knew no deference from others but rather spent their lives bowing to and serving their caste superiors. At the lower-caste levels, women were somewhat freer in their ability to move about the town and countryside and buy and sell in the local marketplace. But they had no servants to perform their many household chores and had to do backbreaking farming tasks, such as weeding fields or transplanting rice.

There were, of course, small pleasures. Even low-caste groups could attend temple festivals, watch dances (Figure 6.6) and dramatics performed in the open air, and risk their meager wages in dice games or betting on roosters specially bred to fight with each other. In an age when India was one of the most fertile and productive regions on the earth, it is probable that all but the untouchables lived as well as ordinary people did anywhere in the world.

The Indian economy continued to grow in the Gupta period, despite the decline of long-distance trade with China and Rome. Leadership in international commerce increasingly shifted to the trading cities on the east and west coasts and the southern seaports. Strong trading links were maintained with kingdoms in Sri Lanka and throughout southeast Asia, which were strongly influenced by Indian cultural exports. In fact, India became the pivot of the great Indian Ocean trading network that stretched from the Red Sea and Persian Gulf in the west to the South China Sea in the east—a position it maintained

Figure 6.6   *Stylized sculptures depicting young women from the Hindu temple at Khajuraho in eastern India. These figures represent a standardized form of feminine beauty in south Asian culture: large breasts, small waist, and ornate jewelry. The profusion of jewelry was already in evidence in the Harappan figurines that are believed in many cases to be goddesses. The stylized physical features may have reflected the well-conditioned figures of female dancers. In the Gupta era, these highly trained professionals were a prominent feature of major court centers and large temple complexes, such as the one at Khajuraho.*

until the age of European overseas expansion after the 16th century C.E. India was known by the time of the Guptas as a land of great wealth as well as the home of many religions. A Chinese Buddhist, Fa-hsien, on a pilgrimage to India, exclaimed,

> The people are many and happy. They do not have to register their households with the police. There is no death penalty. Religious sects have houses of charity where rooms, couches, beds, food, and drink are supplied to travelers.

Gupta Decline and a Return to Political Fragmentation

For nearly 250 years, the Guptas managed to hold together the collection of vassal kingdoms that they passed off as an empire. Signs of future danger appeared in the northwest with the first of the probes across the Himalayas by the nomadic Huns from central Asia in the early 5th century C.E. Preoccupied by the growing threat on their northern frontier, the later Gupta rulers failed to crush resistance from their vassals and challenges from states to the south of the Gupta domains. By the middle of the century, Gupta efforts to hold back repeated assaults by greater and greater numbers of Hun invaders were faltering. With the death of **Skanda Gupta,** the last of the truly able Gupta monarchs, a flood of nomadic invaders broke into the empire. Their pillaging and widely dispersed assaults finished off what remained of Gupta military might, and the empire dissolved into a patchwork of local kingdoms and warring states. From the mid-7th century until the establishment of the Delhi Sultanate in the early 13th century, northern India was divided and vulnerable to outside invasions.

 ## GLOBAL CONNECTIONS: India and the Wider World

No classical civilization was more open to outside influences than that of the Indian subcontinent. And none was more central to cross-cultural exchanges in the centuries that ushered in what we have come to label the Common Era (C.E.) of world history. The brahman-dominated, caste-ordered civilization that flourished at the end of Vedic era and later under the Guptas produced some of humanity's most sublime art and philosophy; important breakthroughs in mathematics, the sciences, and technology; prosperous urban centers; and a population that has been second only to that of China through much of human history.

The period dominated by the Mauryas in between saw the rise of Buddhism, one of a handful of truly world religions. In this era and the age of the Guptas that followed, Buddhism was but one of numerous components of Indian civilization that were exported to China and east Asia, across the steppes of central Asia, throughout most of southeast Asia, and as far west as the Mediterranean.

In mainland and island southeast Asia, the impact of Indian civilization was especially critical. Indian merchants played a key role in trade with these regions, and other influences followed. Indian religions and epics, art and architecture, and concepts of kingship sparked the rise of centralized states and complex societies that culminated in great civilizations, such as those centered at Angkor Wat in Cambodia and the kingdom of Majapahit in central Java. In the Mediterranean, Indian influences were felt in areas as diverse as artistic techniques, philosophies such as Stoicism, and religious ideas that significantly affected Christianity. Central to all of these developments was the fact that in the centuries that witnessed the flowering of Indian civilization under the Mauryas and Guptas, the coastal areas of the Indian subcontinent became, and would remain for millennia, one of the core areas of an ever expanding trading network that would eventually encompass most of the Eastern Hemisphere. Indian manufactured goods, such as cotton textiles and bronze statuary, soon became some of the most coveted commodities in this system of exchange. Indian merchants and sailors would carry them throughout the Indian Ocean and to the emporiums of the silk roads that dominated overland trade beyond the Himalaya Mountains. Indian religions, artwork, scientific discoveries, and epic literature came to enrich, and at times spur major transformations in, civilizations over much of the known world.

Further Readings

Perhaps the most readable introductions to life and society in India's classical age can be found in A. L. Basham's *The Wonder That Was India* (1963) and Jeannine Auboyer's *Daily Life in Ancient India* (1961). The works of Romilla Thapar, especially her *Ashoka and the Decline of the Mauryas* (1997 ed.), are the best on the political history of the era. Her more general *A History of India* (1966) is very detailed and quite technical—certainly a challenge for the beginner. On the Guptas the most comprehensive recent work is Ashvini Agrawal's *Rise and Fall of the Imperial Guptas* (1989). Fine narrative histories of all aspects of Indian civilization in this period can be found in the appropriate chapters of *The History and Culture of the Indian People* (1964), eds. R. C. Majumdar, A. K. Majumdar, and D. K. Ghose. One of the best works on the position of women and social life more generally is Pandharinath Prabhu's *Hindu Social Organization* (1940). On the development of the caste system, see B. R. Kamble, *Caste and Philosophy in Pre-Buddhist India* (1979). A wide range of other aspects of ancient Indian culture is covered in the fine essays in A. L. Basham's *A Cultural History of India* (1975).

Superb introductions to various branches of Indian religious and philosophical thinking, with well-selected portions of the appropriate texts, can be found in S. Radhakrishnan and Charles Moore, eds., *A Source Book in Indian Philosophy* (1967) and Ainslee Embree (ed.), *Sources of Indian Tradition Volume 1: from the Beginning to 1800* (2nd ed., 1988). Of the many books on Buddhism, Trevor Ling's *The Buddha* (1973) is one of the more accessible, but needs to be supplemented with recent research, many of the findings of which are explored in Jonathan S. Walters, *Finding Buddhists in Global History* (1998). S. Radhakrishnan's *Hindu View of Life* (1927) provides a useful insider's view of Hindu religious beliefs and social organization. Heinrich Zimmer's *Philosophies of India* (1956), though somewhat dated, remains a good place to begin exploring the riches and diversity of Indian mythology and religious thinking. Benjamin Rowland's *The Art and Architecture of India* (3rd rev. ed., 1970) is the most objective and comprehensive work available in English on Indian art; and J. C. Harle's *Gupta Sculpture* (1974) provides an introduction to some of the glories of the Gupta age. For a taste of Indian literature in the classical period, there are English translations of the *Ramayana* and the *Mahabharata* and P. Lal's fine translations of *Great Sanskrit Plays* (1957).

On the Web

The grandeur of the Mahabharata is examined at http://web.utk.edu/~jftzgrld/MBh1Home.html, while the art and global reach of the Ramayana can be explored in depth through text and maps at http://www.maxwell.syr.edu/maxpages/special/Ramayana and at http://www.askasia.org/frclasrm/lessplan/l000054.htm. The rituals associated with Hindu prayers as well as that faith's major tenets are illuminated at http://www.asia.si.edu/education/pujaonline/puja/homes.html, while a user-friendly glimpse into the form and practice of Hindu worship is provided at http://www.asia.si.edu/education/pujaonline/puja/exhibit.html.

The life of Buddha is explored at http://www.miami.edu/phi/bio/Buddha/bud-life.htm and viewed through art and architecture at http://ias.berkeley.edu/orias/visuals/buddha/life.html. Alexander the Great's brief sojourn in India is the subject of a mock ancient newspaper article at http://www.itihaas.com/ancient/alex.html. An Indian view critical of both this campaign and also of the bias of Western writers who have addressed it is offered in an article entitled "Alexander the Ordinary" at http://www.itihaas.com/ancient/1.html.

The man who is considered to be India's first imperial ruler, Chandragupta Maurya, is the subject of study at http://www.itihaas.com/ancient/chandra.html, http://campus.northpark.edu/history/WebChron/India/Chandragupta.html, and http://www.itihaas.com/ancient/samudragupta.html. His grandson, Ashoka, was arguably one of the world's greatest monarchs, as seen at http://www.csuchico.edu/~cheinz/syllabi/asst001/spring98/Ashoka.htm. Ashoka discusses his life and empire in an inspired interview featured at http://www.itihaas.com/ancient/ashoka.html. His famous edicts are illuminated at http://www.cs.colostate.edu/~malaiya/ashoka.html.

One the ancient world's finest philosophers of government, Kautilya, is discussed at http://www.sscnet.ucla.edu/southasia/History/Ancient/Kautilya.html, while the text of his political manual, the Arthashastra, is offered at http://www.mssc.edu/projectsouthasia/history/primarydocs/Arthashastra/. Democracy as practiced in ancient India is analyzed at http://www.nipissingu.ca/department/history/muhlberger/histdem/indiadem.htm. Daily life in ancient India is explored at http://members.aol.com/Donnclass/Indialife.html.

CHAPTER 7

ROME AND ITS EMPIRE

This Roman painting features a young woman in an unusual role, as a student of the early Greek poet Sappho.

This chapter deals with the final center of the classical Mediterranean based around Rome. Rome began its main development well after Greece, India, and China. It benefited from important trade with India and along the silk roads. However, its connections with Greece was richer still. Rome preserved and extended many features of Greek and Hellenistic politics, culture, and economic organization. Rome also had a distinct tone and history which is why separate treatment of the final 700 years of classical experience in the Mediterranean is needed. Greece and Rome together produced the larger heritage of classical Mediterranean civilization. Rome also expanded the classical zone to the west, in Europe and northern Africa alike.

The earliest phases of Roman history occurred while Greece and then Alexander and his successors held center stage to the east. It was during the 5th century B.C.E. that a new city-state near the middle of the Italian peninsula began to define a separate existence. Soon Rome took on the trappings of a regional civilization, complete with its own language and an alphabet derived from the Greek alphabet. Roman influence in Italy gradually expanded, making the Italian peninsula a focus of activity in the western Mediterranean.

In the 3rd century B.C.E., Rome twice defeated the north African city-state of Carthage. These wars not only made Rome supreme in the west but also involved it in the affairs of the declining Hellenistic kingdoms. By the mid-2nd century B.C.E., Rome ruled Greece and the eastern Mediterranean directly, although it never penetrated fully into the Middle East's heartland. The Romans' massive empire flourished for four centuries and then limped through another 250 years in decline, an achievement in political organization and durability that the Greeks had never attained. Consequently, the fall of the Roman Empire about 476 C.E. was far more dramatic than the more gradual evolution of Greece and the Hellenistic world.

Discussion of Roman society must highlight the issue of regional contacts, for Rome's vast holdings brought interaction among an unusual range of areas. Christianity, spreading through most of these areas, ultimately added a vital new religious ingredient to contacts in the Mediterranean world. Rome's trade network was wider than the Greeks', though based on similar exchanges. It had major impact on economic organization not only in Italy but also northern Africa. Rome's military ventures also led to widespread capture of slaves, which for a time was very important. Rome's success brought complex contacts with more nomadic peoples, who played a significant role in the later stages of empire.

500 B.C.E.	**300 B.C.E.**	**100 B.C.E.**	**1 C.E.**	**100 C.E.**	**200 C.E.**
500–450 Beginnings of Roman republic; Twelve Tables of Law **400** Rome completes control of central Italy	**264–146** Rome's Punic Wars **167** Rome begins conquest in eastern Mediterranean **146–133** Decline of Roman republic **133–121** Gracchus brothers' reform attempts **107 ff.** Increasing power of generals **106–43** Cicero	**70–19** Vergil **46** Julius Caesar dictator **44** Assassination of Caesar **27** Augustus Caesar; rise of Roman Empire	**c. 30** Crucifixion of Jesus **35** Paul converts to Christianity	**101–106** Under Trajan, Rome's greatest territory **180** Death of Emperor Marcus Aurelius; beginning of decline of empire	**313** Constantine legalizes Christianity **476** Fall of Rome

Finally, the Roman Empire served as a breeding ground for one of the great religious changes in world history: the advent of Christianity. Christianity did not spring directly from the mainstream principles of Greco-Roman civilization, but it did use many of these principles selectively. (In its spread and church structure, it depended heavily on what Rome had achieved.)

A Foundation Story

Roman mythology argued that the city was founded by two brothers, Romulus and Remus, who had been orphaned and were nursed and raised by wolves. Many city statues showed a nursing wolf ready to take care of the two brothers, providing a vivid symbol for Rome itself. Why would this be an attractive story about the city's beginnings? What qualities does it imply for the supposed founders?

The Development of Rome's Republic

 Building on the foundations of classical Mediterranean civilization, Rome early established firm political institutions, checking aristocratic control through some popular voice. Rome also quickly began its pattern of expansion, first in Italy and then beyond. Tensions between expansion and established political values formed the key theme of Roman history by the 2nd century B.C.E. as the republic was wracked by a series of crises.

Etruscan Beginnings and the Early Republic

The people of Rome were Indo-Europeans who migrated to Italy beginning about 1000 B.C.E. They gradually adopted agriculture and, by about 800 B.C.E., gained some contact with Greek settlements farther south. Rome was ruled for a time by the **Etruscans,** who provided powerful kings and organized tightly knit armies skilled in the use of horses and war chariots. The Etruscans imposed a strong government, but about 510 B.C.E., the local Roman aristocracy rebelled and gradually devised a constitution carefully crafted to avoid tyrannical control. The Romans developed a *republic*—a state without a king—because they had found monarchy contrary to the public good (*res publica*). By this time the Romans had also adapted the Greek alphabet to form their own Latin alphabet, which remains in use throughout western Europe and the Americas today.

The constitution of the early **Roman republic** favored the aristocracy. Aristocrats staffed the powerful **Senate,** which advised on policy and selected magistrates (Figure 7.1). But lower-class citizens gained bly in which the wealthy predominated. This basic political structure successfully balanced various interests but resembled many Greek city-states in depending heavily on the aristocratic voice. It lasted for several centuries as Rome moved from a small local state to the center of a growing empire.

The early Roman economy also resembled that of Greece about three centuries before. Aristocrats controlled large estates, but there were many grain-growing farmers, who were also independent citizens capable of military service. By introducing early the idea of written law (which placed some check on arbitrary aristocratic actions) and by allowing popular assemblies and elected officials to give some voice alongside the aristocratic Senate, the Roman republic constructed more explicit balances than most of the early Greek city-states had done. More than the Greeks, the Romans emphasized patron-client (**clientage**) relationships by which landlords would aid and protect lesser citizens in return for loyalty and work.

Rome's diplomatic and military directions departed even more markedly from the patterns of the early Greek poleis because there were fewer social tensions to distract the government and because no successful city-state rivals managed to restrain the dynamic newcomer.

The Expansion of Rome

Rome developed a solid army based on the service of citizen-farmers; though not as rigidly organized as Sparta, Rome stressed discipline and self-sacrifice within the framework of a largely agricultural economy. However, Rome was not as sheltered from outside attack by natural boundaries as many of the Greek poleis had been. It faced challenges from other areas in Italy, including a league of city-states to the north. Rome dealt with these challenges, from 496 B.C.E. onward, through a combination of alliances and military attacks. By about 400 B.C.E. it had gained control over the whole of central Italy. A second wave of expansion, toward the southern end of the peninsula, began about 360 B.C.E., gradually winning over rival tribes by means of superior military organization and tight control over allied states.

Scholars have debated why Rome became so expansionist. Some point to a general greed and aggressiveness, others to the specific political system in which consuls had only a year in office in which to gain glory through military victories. Romans themselves usually argued that they were acting in self-defense,

Figure 7.1 *This statue of a Roman patrician—the class that made up the Senate—comes from the time of the empire. The family patriarch, clad in his toga, holds busts of his two sons.*

some voice. As in Greece, citizenship gave some people definite legal and political rights. At about 450 B.C.E., a law code was written to protect the property holdings of ordinary people and facilitate commerce. Soon, the ordinary citizens, or **plebeians,** won the right to elect their own representatives, the **tribunes.** However, it was the Senate that continued to serve as the center of Roman political life. The two chief executives, or **consuls,** were elected by an annual assem-

and certainly each acquisition prompted new argument for further expansion to protect the territory against attack. Ultimately, other motives developed, such as the quest for slaves, that made continued expansion essential.

Roman success depended heavily on its military organization. Roman infantry units, the famous **legions,** were disciplined and flexible fighting forces trained never to give up. They gave Rome a reputation for being able to bounce back from defeats through a persistent will to win. In contrast to the Greek phalanx, Roman legions lined up in three columns. This provided backups for the first line and also made enemy breakthroughs less likely. The legions' military virtues were memorialized in art, as Figure 7.2 reveals.

The Roman military was supported by the rich agricultural economy of central Italy, which provided an abundant population base, and each wave of expansion increased the military and economic resources available. Once established, Roman rule proved flexible, although it provoked some resentment. Beginning in 338 B.C.E, Rome began to grant elites in some conquered areas Roman citizenship, which reduced the likelihood of rebellion. In other cases, Rome allowed local governments to persist. Only in a few cases did colonies depend only on garrisons of Roman soldiers to keep order, although civilian and military settlements did extend the reach of Roman culture.

Expansion into southern Italy made Rome a rival of the former Phoenician colony, **Carthage,** for control of the western Mediterranean. Carthage, located in northern Africa in the modern nation of Tunisia, had a substantial navy and was quick to see the threat from Roman control over Sicily. A series of **Punic Wars** (*Punic* from the Roman word for *Phoenician*) began in 264 B.C.E. Rome developed its own navy for the first time; both Carthage and Rome generated new allies and colonies in Spain as competition escalated. During the Second Punic War the great Carthaginian general **Hannibal** brought a large army to Italy, including 50 war elephants. But gradually the Romans wore Carthage down. In the Third Punic War (146 B.C.E.) the Romans decided to kill or enslave every inhabitant of Carthage. Insisting "Carthage must be destroyed" Romans also spread salt around the city so nothing could grow. Rome now had a significant overseas empire, including much of Spain and substantial parts of northern Africa held either outright or through allied states.

Figure 7.2 *The tombstone of a Roman centurion, Marcus Favonius Facilis (i.e., easy or skillful), son of Marcus, of the tribe of Pollia, centurion of the 20th Legion, highlights his military dress and demeanor.*

As Map 7.1 demonstrates, Rome's growing power also drew the new empire toward the eastern Mediterranean, partly to defeat Carthaginian allies such as Macedon and partly because rival states in the region appealed for help. The collapse of the Hellenistic kingdoms left a vacuum of power in this region that Rome was called to fill. From 167 B.C.E. onward the Romans began to conquer Macedonia and Greece, and they soon set up a protectorate over the Asian coast of the Mediterranean as well as Egypt.

The Results of Expansion

The republic often was brutal in its treatment of the areas conquered outside Italy. Opponents of Roman

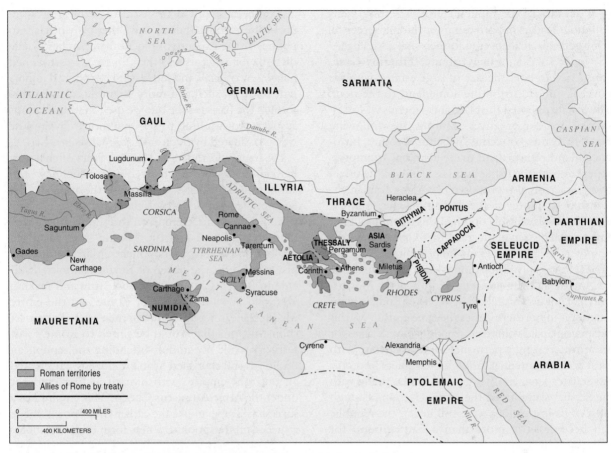

Map 7.1 *The Expansion of the Roman Republic, 133 B.C.E. By the end of the Punic Wars, Rome dominated much of the Mediterranean world.*

rule in Greece were punished severely; much booty and many prisoners were taken. The conquest of Spain during the 2nd century B.C.E. produced repeated atrocities. Imperial expansion changed Roman society and politics, to the dismay of traditionalists. New trade and wealth enriched the upper classes, creating larger gaps between rich and poor and making it increasingly difficult to manage Rome's balanced constitution. Aristocrats exploited many farmers who could not compete with cheap grains imported from Sicily and later northern Africa. Central Italy, like Greece before it, turned into a grape and olive region, highly commercial and organized mainly in large estates. Adding to social complexity was the rise of an important business class, which also helped the state to collect taxes. Slavery also increased as a result of military conquests. Many slaves worked in households or craft production, even tutoring Roman children, but bands of slaves were used in

mining and on the great agricultural estates. Scholars generally believe that at least 2 million people passed through slavery in Italy during the 2nd and 1st centuries B.C.E.

The Crisis of the Republic

What was happening around Rome closely resembled earlier patterns in Greece, where social and economic tensions produced political unrest. But the Roman crisis was in many ways greater because the expanding empire created so many new opportunities for the upper classes to gain new lands and increase their supply of slaves. Dispossessed farmers flooded into the city of Rome. This began a process that would push the city's population past 1 million, much of it consisting of poor, irregularly employed laborers. The result of these changes was a deep class conflict between popular leaders and aristocrats during the final decades of the republic. In this setting many ambitious leaders in both camps, including successful army generals, maneuvered for personal advantage.

In 133 B.C.E., a new tribune, **Tiberius Gracchus,** tried to limit the size of large estates, with the government redistributing some land to the poor. The Senate opposed the plan, and Tiberius was assassinated by conservatives. During the following decades, **Gaius Gracchus,** Tiberius' brother, introduced land reforms and made a special attempt to appeal to both the rising business class and the urban poor. Gracchus also proposed extending Roman citizenship to more of the Italian people, but the Roman masses selfishly opposed this dilution of their authority. The Senate decreed that Gracchus was to be put to death; a servant helped him fall on his sword. Political rivalries and violence continued.

In 107 B.C.E., a successful army general, **Marius,** who had put down a rebellion in one of Rome's client kingdoms in northern Africa, became consul. Marius began using paid volunteers from the lower classes for his army, creating a permanent military group with great political potential through their ability to coerce the Senate. Then another general, **Sulla,** siding with the Senate, slaughtered the Marius faction. Though most of its institutions were still intact, the republic had become little more than a battleground for opposing ambitions.

In 77 B.C.E., another general, Pompey, came to the fore. Like his predecessors, he enhanced his power by winning new conquests, first in Spain and then in the Middle East. His success, plus renewed civil war at home, prompted the Senate to give him special powers. A middle-class political leader, **Cicero,** eloquently pleaded for a return to republican balance, arguing against the generals and popular demagogues, but he was not heeded. Pompey joined with other generals, including **Julius Caesar,** to form a new government that could override the Senate. Caesar, who won considerable support from the Roman lower classes, pursued his own goals by winning new territory across the Alps in Gaul (present-day France). He then defied Pompey and the Senate by bringing his troops back to Italy and taking over the government in 49 B.C.E. Effectively, Caesar's victory in the ensuing civil war ended the republic.

Caesar made few formal changes in government institutions. The Senate, which was packed with Caesar's men, still existed and debated, but its acts were a sham because of Caesar's control of the army. Caesar brought more Italians and other provincials into politics at the expense of old Roman families. Made dictator for 10 years and then for life, Caesar named many new officials and judges and introduced important reforms, such as a more scientific calendar that formed the basis for the one we use today. Caesar was suspected of wanting to set up a monarchy, and he was assassinated by traditionalist senators in 44 B.C.E.

Caesar's death led to 13 more years of civil war; his cause was defended by his grandnephew and adopted son Octavian, who fought the armies of the Senate. Octavian soon took the name *Caesar,* which would come to mean emperor. In a series of wars, particularly in Egypt and the Middle East, Octavian finally won out. His last opponents, Marc Antony and his wife, Cleopatra, queen of Egypt, committed suicide in 31 B.C.E, ending the civil strife and making Octavian absolute master of Rome and the entire Mediterranean world. Octavian then crafted a new set of institutions that would be suited to Rome's vast territory while not unduly offending the republican traditions still cherished by many citizens. He created an outright empire, with himself as first emperor under the name **Augustus Caesar.** This empire was a success as Rome, unlike the earlier Greek poleis, made a successful transition to a new form of government.

Roman Culture

 As Rome struggled with its political crisis, a major cultural transformation was taking place that merged earlier Roman values and the Latin language with the impressive heritage of Greek and Hellenistic learning.

Roman intellectual life was never as vibrant as that of 5th-century Athens, in part because Roman writers and artists were so eager to adopt Greek forms. But Rome had its own strengths, while preserving and modifying many Greek cultural achievements.

The Range of Roman Art

Greek artistic styles and literary influence increasingly shaped Roman upper-class life, from the 2nd century into the days of the empire, although as the Document box reveals, the result was a raging cultural controversy over what Roman values should be. Many

Document

Rome and a Values Crisis

Rome's increasing contact with the eastern Mediterranean, particularly Greece, brought important debates about culture. Many conservatives deplored Greek learning and argued that it would corrupt Roman virtue. Cicero, a leading politician in the Senate and a major Latin writer, here defends Greek literature, using Hellenistic justifications of beauty and utility. Cicero played a major role in popularizing Greek culture during the 1st century B.C.E. His comments also reflect the concerns that Greek culture inspired a source of change.

Do you think that I could find inspiration for my daily speeches on so manifold a variety of topics, did I not cultivate my mind with study, or that my mind could endure so great a strain, did not study provide it with relaxation? I am a votary of literature, and make the confession unashamed; shame belongs rather to the bookish recluse, who knows not how to apply his reading to the good of his fellows, or to manifest its fruits to the eyes of all. But what shame should be mine, gentlemen, who have made it a rule of my life for all these years never to allow the sweets of a cloistered ease or the seductions of pleasure or the enticements of repose to prevent me from aiding any man in the hour of his need? How then can I justly be blamed or censured, if it shall be found that I have devoted to literature a portion of my leisure hours no longer than others without blame devote to the pursuit of material gain, to the celebration of festivals or games, to pleasure and the repose of mind and body, to protracted banqueting, or perhaps to the gaming-board or to ballplaying? I have the better right to indulgence herein, because my devotion to letters strengthens my oratorical powers, and these, such as they are, have never failed my friends in their hour of peril. Yet insignificant though these powers may seem to be, I fully realize from what source I draw all that is highest in them. Had I not persuaded myself from my youth up, thanks to the moral lessons derived from a wide reading, that nothing is to be greatly sought after in this life save glory and honour, and that in their quest all bodily pains and all dangers of death or exile should be lightly accounted, I should never have borne for the safety of you all the brunt of many a bitter encounter, or bared my breast to the daily onsets of abandoned persons. All literature, all philosophy, all history, abounds with incentives to noble action, incentives which would be buried in black darkness were the light of the written word not flashed upon them. How many pictures of high endeavor the great authors of Greece and Rome have drawn for our use, and bequeathed to us, not only for our contemplation, but for our emulation! These I have held ever before my vision throughout my public career, and have guided the workings of my brain and my soul by meditating upon patterns of excellence.

But let us for the moment waive these solid advantages; let us assume that entertainment is the sole end of reading; even so, I think you would hold that no mental employment is so broadening to the sympathies or so enlightening to the understanding. Other pursuits belong not to all times, all ages, all conditions; but this gives stimulus to our youth and diversion to our old age; this adds a charm to success, and offers a haven of consolation to failure. In the home it delights, in the world it hampers not. Through the night watches, on all our journeying, and in our hours of country ease, it is an unfailing companion.

If anyone thinks that the glory won by the writing of Greek verse is naturally less than that accorded to the poet who writes in Latin, he is entirely in the wrong. Greek literature is read in nearly every nation under heaven, while the vogue of Latin is confined to its own boundaries, and they are, we must grant, narrow. Seeing, therefore, that the activities of our race know no barrier save the limits of the round earth, we ought to be ambitious that whithersoever our arms have penetrated there also our fame and glory should extend; for the reason that literature exalts the nation whose high deeds it sings, and at the same time there can be no doubt that those who stake their lives to fight in honour's cause find therein a lofty incentive to peril and endeavor. We read that Alexander the Great carried in his train numbers of epic poets and historians. And yet, standing before the tomb of Achilles at Sigeum, he exclaimed, "Fortunate youth, to have found in Homer an herald of thy valor!" Well might he so exclaim, for had the *Iliad* never existed, the same mound which covered Achilles' bones would also have overwhelmed his memory.

Questions: What kind of objections to Greek learning is Cicero arguing against? Which of his arguments had the most lasting appeal to those who were reshaping Roman culture? Can you think of similar debates about foreign culture in other times and places in history? How would you use this document to reconstruct the debate Cicero was participating in and why it seemed important?

Source: Cicero, *Pro Archia Poeta*. Translated by N. H. Watts. Loeb Classical Library. Cicero, Pro Archia (Harvard University Press, 1965), 12–14, 16, 23–24.

aristocratic families were educated by Greek slaves, who as tutors had considerable independence and in a few cases produced important literary and historical works of their own. Imitation of Greece was aided by the similarity between Roman and Greek religions in which essentially the same gods and goddesses merely had different names. Rome's literary creativity was less impressive than that of the Greeks, partly because Greek authors were so widely read. The Roman poet **Vergil** picked up the Greek epic tradition and linked Roman history and mythology with the great stories of the *Iliad* and the *Odyssey* in his work the *Aeneid*. Roman poets and biographers also were active, shaping the Latin language and providing stylistic models. Roman sculptors worked mainly in the Greek tradition, producing busts of great men and statues and scenes of heroic grandeur. Rome also developed active painters, who produced lively (and sometimes pornographic) decorations for the houses of the wealthy.

Greek influence and the practical issues of politics in an increasingly complex society prompted creativity in many other areas, although science advanced little beyond the compilation of Greek material into textbooks. Roman leaders valued skill in oratory, and they advanced discussions of the arts of rhetoric. Ethical philosophy received much attention. Hellenistic schools, including Stoicism, won many converts because Roman leaders were eager to develop arguments for moral behavior that had strong logical support. Writers such as Cicero discussed the joys and sorrows of human life, urging moderation and a dedication to the public good.

Roman architecture benefited as the city's wealth grew. Again, Greek styles provided primary inspiration, with the Romans preferring more ornate designs for columns and arches, as Figure 7.3 illustrates. But Rome added its own genius to Greek architecture, mainly through engineering advances that allowed larger structures to be built. Huge stadiums, public baths, temples, massive aqueducts to carry water to cities, great stretches of paved road, and huge port facilities began to appear in the later republic. Urban Romans, both men and women, delighted in bath pavilions that featured pools of hot and cold water, often in ornate surroundings. Baths, along with stadiums, began to appear not only in Rome but in cities throughout the empire, as a means of displaying power and attracting Roman colonists. Roman ability to construct elaborate arches, which

Figure 7.3 *These columns surround the Arch of Titus near the Colosseum in Rome. The use of decorative styles that originated in classical Greece was a central feature of Roman public design. Roman buildings became steadily more massive and monumental, surpassing the Greek originals.*

allowed buildings to carry great structural weight, was unsurpassed anywhere in the world. Under Augustus, statues, fountains, and temples to the gods spread through Rome, making the city the showcase of the new empire, with a population of 1 million. Massive monuments, in styles adapted from the Greeks, were built from England in the north to the desert fringes of northern Africa, from Spain to present-day Hungary and Romania, and down the Middle Eastern coast of the Mediterranean.

Of course not all Roman architecture was of such splendor. Many plebeians in Rome and other cities lived in *insulae*, crowded, unstable apartment buildings. After a fire in 64, new measures were introduced to make the insulae more comfortable and fire-resistant. The buildings now had to abide by maximum height limits and to be constructed at least partially from fireproof stone, not just wood. The government made more efforts to maintain the public water system, so that water was accessible to all.

Major Themes in Roman Literature

Prosperity and greater stability during the reign of Augustus and his successors brought growing attention to other cultural activities. Many writers praised the new imperial house, but poets such as **Horace** combined this loyalty with humor and creative skill in adapting Greek poetic meters to the Latin language. Horace, initially a republican, shifted his support to Augustus; his odes were lyrical poems, many of them praising the emperor and his family. Another poet, **Ovid,** stressed the growing sensuality of the aristocracy in his writing on the arts of love. Exiled by the emperor for downplaying family values, he also wrote about the Roman religion and translated Greek nature stories. Historians such as **Livy** wrote elaborate accounts of Rome, linking the empire to the republican past.

Vergil's great epic poem the *Aeneid* was dedicated to the glories of Augustus and his empire:

> Now fix your sight, and stand intent, to see
>   your Roman race, and Julian progeny.
>
> There mighty Caesar waits his vital hour,
>
> Impatient for the world, and grasps his
>   promised power.
>
> Africa and India shall his power obey;
>
> He shall extend his propagated sway beyond
>   the solar year, without the starry way…
>
> But Rome! 'tis thine alone, with awful sway,
>
> To rule mankind, and make the world obey,
>
> Disposing peace and war, thy own majestic way.

After the cultural surge of the late republic and early empire, which was spurred by the assimilation of Greek forms, Roman cultural activity declined somewhat. Intellectual life continued, but it stressed preservation, imitation, textbook summaries, and education of the upper classes. Well before the empire began to deteriorate politically, mainstream literary and artistic vitality began to decline. Only the new religious inspiration of Christianity generated new uses for Latin and Greek literary skill, philosophy, and art.

The Institutions of Empire

 Augustus and his successors had to create new policies to hold Rome's expanding empire together. Republican values were not forgotten, but the importance of military administration and effective laws gained ground. However, Rome did not follow China's pattern in developing an elaborate bureaucracy or an integrating political culture.

Imperial Rule

Rome's rule of its growing empire rested heavily on tolerance and cohesion through law. Local governments, including the old Greek city-states, gained autonomy as the harsh colonial policies of the republic were revised. Some whole kingdoms, as in parts of northern Africa, were preserved, although they were required to obey Roman foreign policy and obtain permission for any new succession to the throne. This policy of tolerance greatly facilitated Roman control, for an elaborate bureaucratic apparatus was not needed. Only much later, in different circumstances, did lack of centralization prove to be a disadvantage. At the same time, Rome maintained small military garrisons in most areas and large outposts in newly conquered or threatened regions. Army generals doubled as provincial governors in such cases, which allowed them to build regional power, even to the point of challenging the emperor back in Rome. In only a few cases, such as the forced dissolution of the independent Jewish state in 63 C.E. after a major local rebellion, did the Romans take over distant areas completely.

Augustus and His Successors

In building an imperial government after his final victory in 31 B.C.E., Octavian talked sincerely about the validity of republican virtues and the importance of discipline and family virtues. He also retained many of the agencies of the republic, including the Senate, while weakening most of them by installing his own supporters, who were in full control. Symbolizing the transition, in 27 B.C.E. the Senate voted to grant Octavian the title *Augustus,* a word often applied to gods and appropriate to an office that dominated the state. The emperor thus controlled the apparatus of government, making major appointments and military decisions and establishing new laws and policies.

Augustus set about consolidating his new regime by instituting moral reforms, banning mystery religions, and insisting on adherence to traditional Roman ceremonies. He revised the law to strengthen family stability while encouraging people to have children by ruling that women with at least three children could gain new rights. Augustus launched an ambitious new building program in Rome, which brought new jobs to the Roman masses and new entertainments as well. Augustus also tried to regularize control over the provinces. He relied heavily on his army of 250,000 men, giving them abundant rewards for long service and loyalty. He maintained the earlier policy of allowing local autonomy to accompany military strength while encouraging the development of Romanized colonies in many provinces, particularly in northern Africa and western Europe.

The empire Augustus created maintained its basic organizational structure for about two centuries. Incompetent emperors were common in this period, in part because no clear lines of succession were established. Effectively, the army controlled basic power, which worked well when a strong emperor held the army's loyalty but badly when an emperor lost command of the troops. Succession battles among rival generals were common. By 96 C.E., emperors began to reduce these problems by adopting their own successors. This practice yielded a series of five good emperors who brought Rome to its greatest power. The best of the early emperors tried to maintain Augustus's careful balance between real authority and the appearance of respect for political tradition and law. For example, Emperor Claudius wanted to marry his niece, which was illegal. He might have ignored the law, but instead he changed it so that any Roman man could marry a niece.

Government and Expansion

The Roman imperial state maintained a fairly standard set of functions. Regulation of commerce was essential to the Roman state's efforts to ensure vital stocks of grain from Egypt, Sicily, and northern Africa. A large official staff was needed to oversee food supplies and prices for huge cities such as Rome. Public works in the form of roads and harbors facilitated military transport as well as commerce, and government-sponsored amenities such as public baths and stadiums attracted public loyalty and helped recruit Roman settlers for such distant provinces as Britain. The building of aqueducts to carry water to cities was another major state activity. All these public works and regulations took substantial tax revenues.

Government-supported religious ceremonies continued, but there was little attempt to impose this religion on all subjects, and various other religions, including the worship of the Egyptian goddess Isis, usually were tolerated. Only Jews and, later, Christians found the state's claim to primary loyalty unacceptable, and only they drew Roman reprisals; the Roman government tolerated Jewish monotheism but reacted fiercely to Jewish revolt. Even the later Roman emperors, who promoted the idea that the emperor himself was a god, normally were tolerant of other religions, inconsistently attacking Christianity because of the Christians' refusal to place the state first in their devotion.

Expansion continued during the early empire. The emperor **Trajan** adopted an aggressive foreign policy in 101–106 C.E. The boundaries of the empire were pressed to the greatest extent ever; fortifications were built in northern England and along the Rhine and Danube rivers, signaling the inclusion of much of western Europe in the new geography of Mediterranean civilization. The empire also reached deeper into the Middle East, with new provinces in Armenia, Assyria, and Mesopotamia (Map 7.2). But the expense of maintaining the vast boundaries placed growing burdens on the imperial economy. A turn from expansion to defense, though probably inevitable, led to a voluntary withdrawal under Trajan's successor, Hadrian, west of the Euphrates.

By 180 C.E., the empire had reached a pinnacle of power that would quickly turn to descent. Foreign policy became defensive, building walls and trying to finance border garrisons to keep invaders out. The later Roman Empire, though still capable of impressive achievements, was enmeshed in a pattern of gradual decline, which in turn was part of the general collapse of the classical world.

Roman Law

Rome's greatest political contribution lay in its legal system. Although local laws applied to many areas of the empire, Roman law provided a general system, open to citizens in any part of the empire. The law also facilitated commerce. Roman jurists carefully thought through general principles, building one of the most extensive legal systems anywhere in the world.

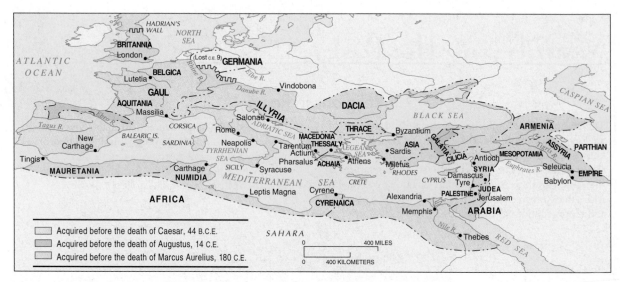

Map 7.2   *The Roman Empire from Augustus to 180 C.E. The empire expanded greatly in its first centuries, but such far-flung colonies proved impossible to maintain, both militarily and economically. How do the size and location of the empire compare with the earlier expansion of the republic?*

The law focused heavily on protecting private property and family stability. It let the state determine fairness in some areas that had previously been open to decisions by families and landlords. A minority of people throughout the empire were allowed citizenship and full access to this law. **Paul,** a key figure in early Christianity and born a Jew, was proud of being a Roman citizen. Principles of Roman law would be revived in other societies later on.

Useful law, plus regional tolerance and some access to citizenship, promoted loyalty and allowed Rome to maintain its empire in considerable peace for several centuries. This achievement was more impressive than the initial conquests.

The Evolution of Rome's Economic and Social Structure

Several basic features of Roman economic and social development closely paralleled earlier patterns in Greece. A local agricultural economy that yielded two social groups—aristocracy and free farmers—became increasingly complex as a result of urban and commercial growth.

As earlier in the Greek city-states, a class of merchants expanded during the final centuries of the republic. Many merchants were foreigners, for Romans did not take well to seafaring and built clumsy boats that hugged the shores. Traders from Greece and the Middle East played a vital role. But a native business group expanded as well, and its prestige was higher than that of its counterpart in classical Greece had been. Merchants gained political voice in the Roman Senate in the later days of the republic, although they never matched aristocratic prestige. Rome and other imperial cities also developed large artisan and shopkeeper groups and a large, sometimes troubling, propertyless lower class.

Rome's family structure resembled that of classical Greece and all the major classical civilizations that tended toward strong central government. The family structure was firmly patriarchal. Artistic representations of the family pressed this point. Roman law stipulated that "the husband is the judge of his wife. If she commits a fault, he punishes her; if she has drunk wine, he condemns her; if she has been guilty of adultery, he kills her." Later, however, husbands' power was modified by the need for approval by a family court including members of both families. Here was a key contribution of Roman law. If divorced because of adultery, a Roman woman lost one-third

Visualizing the Past

Religions in Rome

The Temple of Isis, in Rome, was designed in the style of an Egyptian Temple (Horus, at Edou). Its date is not known, but Emperor Domitian added embellishments to the structure in 95 C.E. The Egyptian style (the temple was the same length as its counterpart in Edou) was mixed with some Roman elements. It included statues, fountains, and representations of the Nile and Tiber rivers.

Questions: What Egyptian and Roman styles were merged in this building? Why would an emperor not only tolerate but patronize a temple devoted to an Egyptian goddess? What does the temple suggest about Rome's religious policy?

of her property and had to wear a special garment that set her apart like a prostitute. The oppression of women was less severe in Rome than in Greece and China, however. As wives and mothers, many aristocratic Roman women wielded political power, if only through their husbands. Women freely appeared in public and attended major entertainments; some were educated, though rarely as well as men in the same class. However, inequality between men and women increased again in the empire's final stages.

Slavery in Rome

Improvement was not the watchword where social inequality was concerned. The spread of Roman slav-ery contributed further to the decline of free farmers and to the unusual militarism of Rome in the late republic and early empire. Slave revolts, though not common, required a military presence. Displaced Italian farmers increasingly sought a longer-term career in the military, where they could earn pay and have some chance to acquire property as veterans. Most obviously, military expansion was a vital source of additional slaves, for the Roman slave population did not reproduce itself. This was an obvious contrast to China and India, where an expansionist foreign policy was not a central issue in labor supply. Not surprisingly, slavery brought tension to the Roman world, both between slaves and their masters and between different segments of the free population.

For example, in 61 C.E., the city prefect of Rome was murdered by one of his slaves. Custom dictated that every one of the 400 slaves in the household be executed in retribution. The injustice of killing so many innocent people sparked a riot. In the end the Senate decided to go through with the execution, but the emperor had to line soldiers along the entire route on which the condemned slaves passed.

Roman slavery must be interpreted subtly, however. Being a slave was not necessarily the worst condition possible. Some people sought slavery as a way to get into a richer household or even to escape the countryside for the city. Many would have agreed that being a free rural worker was often worse than being a slave. Partly this reflected widespread poverty; economic security could seem preferable to freedom. It also reflected the variable conditions of slavery. Many slaves, again particularly in cities, had great latitude and interesting work. Many could buy or gain freedom. As in other forms of historical inequality, it is important not to impose contemporary standards on the complexity of the past.

But slavery itself could change, and it had social as well as personal consequences in Rome. As Roman agriculture became increasingly commercialized from the 2nd century B.C.E. onward, slavery spread steadily. Many new slaves were used for manual labor, and large supplies of these slaves were brought in from Spain and later Britain and Germany, the Slavic lands of the northern Balkans, and Africa. Slaves worked the mines and quarries under brutal conditions. They also increasingly staffed the large estates, along with some paid laborers and tenant farmers. Far more than in earlier Greece, the Roman economy became dependent on slave labor; grain supplies and other agricultural products relied on this labor. This pattern foreshadowed the use of slaves on commercial estates in the Americas from the 16th century onward, where slave labor provided the production on which the economy depended, but it was unusual in the classical world.

Finally, the extensive use of slaves at Rome's high point helps explain the stagnant production technology in manufacturing and agriculture. The Romans displayed real engineering genius in their buildings, roads, and city design, but they paid little attention to techniques of food supply or manufacturing. Estate agriculture and government organization of ports and markets, not production methods, took center stage, with abundant slave labor as a vital component. A few engine designs were sketched, but merely as exercises; there was no interest in building or using them. Some manufacturing operations used waterwheels for power, and there is evidence that these spread in the 2nd century C.E. Still, there were few new inventions.

A further result was an ongoing lag behind the economies of India and China in sophisticated manufacturing. The Roman upper classes eagerly bought silks and other processed goods that came from Asia, arriving at the Mediterranean by the overland silk roads through the Middle East. In return, the Romans offered exotic African animals, skins, and gold, not products they made.

Rome's Economic Structure

The empire was not joined in a single economic and social pattern. The social arrangements characteristic of Italy were not uniform through the Roman empire. The environmental impact of Rome's agricultural needs varied as well. Rome established vigorous cities in Spain, France, and England and populated them with the families of soldiers, who married local women, and with colonists. Only gradually and incompletely, however, did estate agriculture spread to Europe north of the Mediterranean. Many local farmers continued to practice subsistence agriculture and even hunting. The gap between new, Romanized cities and the rural people, who were usually ignorant of Latin as well as illiterate, was often wide. In parts of northern Africa, Romans urged a ruthless policy of economic exploitation. Peasants in Egypt and in other parts of northern Africa were pressed to produce grain for sale in the Italian markets, and large estates quickly predominated. Ultimately, production pressure had devastating environmental results in this region, as desert conditions expanded. During the Roman Empire period and thereafter, agricultural exploitation was so intense that the resulting soil exhaustion and desert conditions have not been reversed to this day. A third distinctive region was the portion of the empire in Greece and western Asia, where more active commerce and larger merchant groups maintained pre-Roman traditions and wielded greater wealth than existed in much of the western empire.

Because of the divisions of classical Mediterranean society, by region as well as class and gender, no easy generalizations about overall social achievement can be made. An 18th-century English historian

In Depth

The Classical Civilizations in Comparative Perspective

The three great classical civilizations lend themselves to a variety of comparisons. The general tone of each differed from the others, ranging from India's otherworldly strain to China's emphasis on government centralization, although it is important to note the varieties of activities and interests and the changes that occurred in each of the three societies. Basic comparisons include several striking similarities. Each classical society developed empires. Each relied primarily on an agricultural economy. Greco-Roman interest in secular culture bears some resemblance to Confucian emphasis in China, although in each case religious currents remained as well. But Greco-Roman political values and institutions differed from the Confucian emphasis on deference and bureaucratic training. Greek definitions of science contrasted with those of India and China, particularly in the emphasis on theory. Several focal points can be used for comparison.

Each classical civilization emphasized a clear social hierarchy, with substantial distance between elites and the majority of people who did the manual and menial work. This vital similarity between the civilizations reflected common tensions between complex leadership demands and lifestyles and the limited economic resources of the agricultural economy. Groups at the top of the social hierarchy judged that they had to control lower groups carefully to ensure their own prosperity. Each classical society generated ideologies that explained and justified the great social divisions. Philosophers and religious leaders devoted great attention to this subject.

Within this common framework, however, there were obvious differences. Groups at the top of the social pyramid reflected different value systems. The priests in India, the bureaucrats in China, and the aristocrats in Greece and the Roman republic predominated. The status of merchants varied despite the vital role commerce played in all three civilizations.

Opportunities for mobility varied also. India's caste system allowed movement within castes, if wealth was acquired, but little overall mobility. This was the most rigid classical social structure because it tied people to their basic social and occupational position by birth. China's bureaucratic system allowed a very small number of talented people from below to rise on the basis of education, but most bureaucrats continued to come from the landed aristocracy. Mediterranean society, with its aristocratic emphasis, limited opportunities to rise to the top, but the importance of acquired wealth (particularly in Rome) gave some nonaristocrats important economic and political opportunities. Cicero, for example, came from a merchant family. Various classes also shared some political power in city-state assemblies; the idea of citizens holding basic political rights across class lines was unusual in classical civilizations.

Each classical civilization distinctively defined the position of the lowest orders. India's untouchables performed duties culturally evaluated as demeaning but often vital. So did China's "mean people," who included actors. As Greece and then Rome expanded, they relied heavily on the legal and physical compulsions of slavery to provide menial service and demanding labor. Greece and Rome gave unusual voice to farmers when they maintained their own property but tended to scorn manual labor itself, a view that helped justify slavery. Confucianism urged deference but offered praise for peasant work.

Finally, each classical civilization developed a different cultural glue to help hold its social hierarchy together. Greece and Rome left much of the task of managing the social hierarchy to local authorities; community bonds, as in the city-states, were meant to pull different groups into a sense of common purpose. They also relied on military force and clear legal statements that defined rights according to station. Force and legal inequalities played important roles in China and India as well, but there were additional inducements. India's Hinduism helped justify and sustain the hierarchy by promising rewards through reincarnation for those who submitted to their place in any given existence. Chinese Confucianism urged general cultural values of obedience and self-restraint, creating some agreement—despite varied religions and philosophies—on the legitimacy of social ranks by defining how gentlemen and commoners should behave. Chinese and Indian social structures lasted longer than those of Greece and Rome.

In no case did the social cement work perfectly; social unrest surfaced in all the classical civilizations, as in major slave rebellions in the Roman country-side or peasant uprisings in China. At the same time, the rigidity of classical social structures gave many common people some leeway. Elites viewed the masses as being so different from themselves that they did not try to revamp all their beliefs or community institutions.

Questions: Why did the classical civilizations seem to need radical social inequalities? What was the relationship between wealth and social position in each classical civilization? If India used religion to compensate for social inequalities, what did China and the Mediterranean use?

characterized the high point of the Roman Empire before 180 C.E. as the period in human history "during which the condition of the human race was most happy or prosperous." This is doubtful, given the technological accomplishments of China and India. And certainly many slaves, women, and poor farmers might have disagreed, even in the Mediterranean world itself. Furthermore, Mediterranean society, like most classical civilizations, was massively split between upper-class and urban populations and the rural majority. Many farmers continued to work largely as their ancestors had, with similar tools and similar poverty, untouched by the doings of the great or the bustle of the cities, except when wars swept over their lands.

The Origins of Christianity

 The early history of Christianity, ultimately one of the great world religions, is also part of the history of the Roman Empire. Early Christianity benefited from the sheer size of the empire and copied aspects of its organization. At the same time, Christianity represented a new value system that could be accommodated only after many struggles and adjustments on both sides.

In the initial decades of the Roman Empire, at the eastern end of the Mediterranean, a new religion, Christianity, emerged. Much of the impetus for this new religion rested in issues in the Jewish religion, including a long-standing belief in the coming of a Messiah and rigidities that had developed in the Jewish priesthood. Whether or not Christianity was created by God, as Christians believe, the early stages of the religion focused on cleansing the Jewish religion of stiff rituals and haughty leaders. It had little to do with Roman culture at first. Christianity arose in a remote province and appealed particularly to poor people.

Life and Death of Jesus

Christianity originated with **Jesus of Nazareth,** a Jewish prophet and teacher who was regarded as the son of God by his disciples (Figure 7.4). Jesus preached in Israel during the time of Augustus, urging a purification of the Jewish religion that would free Israel and establish the kingdom of God on earth. He urged a moral code based on love, charity, and humility, and he asked the faithful to follow his lessons, abandoning worldly concerns. Many disciples believed that a final judgment day was coming on which God would reward the righteous with immortality and condemn sinners to everlasting hell.

Jesus won many followers among the poor. He also roused suspicion among the upper classes and the leaders of the Jewish religion. These people helped persuade the Roman governor, already concerned about unrest among the Jews, that Jesus was a dangerous agitator. As a result, Jesus was put to death, crucified along with common criminals, about 30 C.E. His followers believed that he was resurrected on the third day after his death, proof that he was the son of God. This belief helped the further spread of the religion among Jewish communities in the Middle East, both within the Roman Empire and beyond. As they realized that the Messiah was not immediately returning to earth to set up the Kingdom of God, the disciples of Jesus began to fan out, particularly around the eastern Mediterranean, to spread the new religious message.

Initially, converts were Jewish by birth and followed the basic Jewish law. However, their belief that Christ was divine as well as human roused hostility among other Jews. When one early convert, Stephen,

Figure 7.4   *This sarcophagus, or tomb, from the 4th century shows Christ and the apostles in typical Roman dress.*

was stoned to death, many disciples left Israel and traveled throughout western Asia.

Christianity Gains Converts and Religious Structure

Gradually over the next 250 years, Christianity won many converts. By the 4th century C.E., about 10 percent of the residents of the Roman Empire were Christian, and the new religion had also made converts elsewhere in the Middle East and in **Ethiopia.** As it spread Christianity connected increasingly with larger themes in Roman history. With its appeal to the poor, Christianity was well positioned to reflect social grievances in an empire of increasing inequality. Slaves, dispossessed farmers, and poor city dwellers found hope in a religion that promised rewards after death. Christianity also answered cultural and spiritual needs—especially but not exclusively among the poor—left unmet by mainstream Roman religion and culture. Roman values had stressed political goals and ethics suitable for life in this world. They did not join

peoples of the empire in more spiritual loyalties, and they did not offer many emotionally satisfying rituals. As the empire consolidated, reducing direct political participation, a number of highly emotional religions spread from the Middle East and Egypt. These religions offered rituals charged with excitement and mystery. Worship of divinities such as Mithra and Isis, derived from earlier belief systems, attracted some Romans with rites of sacrifice and a strong sense of religious community. Christianity, though far more than a mystery religion, had some of these qualities and won converts on this basis as well. Christianity gained ground in part because of features of Roman political and cultural life.

The spread of Christianity also benefited from some of the positive qualities of Rome's empire. Political stability and communication over a wide area aided missionary efforts, and the Roman example helped inspire the government forms of the growing Christian church. At the same time, separate church institutions were essential since that state seemed unreliable for Christians—a key contrast to Islam later on. Early Christian communities regulated them-selves, but with expansion more formal government was introduced, with **bishops** playing a role like that of Rome's provincial governors. Bishops headed churches in regional centers and supervised the activ-ities of other churches in the area. Bishops in politi-cally powerful cities, including Rome, gained particular authority. Roman principles also helped move what initially had been a religion among Jews to a genuinely cosmopolitan stance. Under the lead-ership of Paul, converted to Christianity about 35 C.E., Christian missionaries began to move away from insisting that adherents of the new religion must fol-low Jewish law. Rather, in the spirit of Rome and Hel-lenism, the new faith was seen as universal, open to all whether or not they followed Jewish practices in diet, male circumcision, and so on.

Paul's conversion to Christianity proved vital. Paul was Jewish, but he had been born in a Greek city and was familiar with Greco-Roman culture. He helped explain basic Christian beliefs in terms Greeks and Romans could grasp, and he preached in Greece and Italy as well as the Middle East. Paul created Christian theology as a set of intellectual principles that followed from, but generalized, the message of Jesus. Paul also modified certain initial Christian impulses. Jesus himself drew a large number of women followers, but Paul stressed women's subor-dination to men and the dangers of sexuality. It was Paul's emphasis on Christianity as a universal religion, requiring abandonment of other religious beliefs, and his related use of Greek—the dominant language of the day throughout the eastern Mediterranean—that particularly transformed the new faith.

Relations with the Roman Empire

Gradually, Christian theological leaders made further contact with Greco-Roman intellectual life. They began to develop a body of Christian writings beyond the Bible messages written by Jesus' disciples. By the 4th century C.E., Christian writings became the most creative cultural expressions in the Roman Empire, as theologians explained issues in the new religion and related it to Greek philosophy and Roman ethics. Ironically, as the Roman Empire was in most respects declining, Christianity produced an outpouring of complex thought and often elegant use of language. The *Confessions* of St. **Augustine** were thoroughly Christian but reflected Latin classical style and Greek philosophical concepts. Christianity thus not only

redirected Roman culture but also preserved many earlier literary and philosophical achievements.

Adherents of the new religion did clash with Roman authorities. Christians, who like Jews put their duties to God first, would not honor the emperor as a god. They also seemed to reject the authority of the state in other spheres. Several early emperors, including Nero, persecuted Christians, killing some and driving their worship underground. Persecution was not constant, however, which helps explain why the religion continued to spread. It resumed only in the 3rd century, when several emper-ors tried to use religious conformity and new claims to divinity as a way of cementing loyalty to a declin-ing state. Roman beliefs, including periodic tolerance, helped shape a Christian view that the state had a legitimately separate but subordinate sphere; Western Christians often cited Christ as saying, "Render unto Caesar that which is Caesar's, and unto God that which is God's."

The full story of early Christianity goes beyond the history of Rome, and we will turn to it again in Chapter 10. Christianity had more to do with open-ing a new era in the history of the Mediterranean region than with shaping the later Roman Empire. Yet important connections did exist that explain fea-tures of Christianity and later Roman history.

The Decline of Rome

 Rome began to decline after about 180 CE. Symptoms were gradual, including loss of terri-tory and economic reversals. Ultimately, Rome was periodically invaded and the empire finally collapsed.

Well before Christianity became a major factor in Mediterranean life, the Roman Empire began to show important signs of decay. Its political and social framework became increasingly vulnerable. Defend-ing the borders of the empire and maintaining gov-ernment was costly, and tax revenues began to decline. Further expansion of the empire became impossible after 117 C.E. because the government could not afford the troops needed to keep order in more distant provinces and because pressures from border groups, particularly the Germanic tribes in central Europe, began to increase. Yet without expan-sion, the necessary rewards for the armies became more difficult to obtain. Other economic disruptions followed from regional changes. The Italian economy, for example, began to suffer by the 3rd century C.E. as Spanish- and French-grown wine cut into local profits, reducing prosperity and tax revenues at the empire's core. Disruptions of this sort forced new, more subsistence-oriented economic arrangements. Slavery declined. More estates turned into local economic and political units rather than commercial operations as connections that had cemented the empire began to come apart. The empire also suffered from devastating epidemics, possibly the result of contacts with unfamiliar diseases from south Asia, that killed off much of the population.

The Classical Mediterranean Heritage

By preserving and extending Greek culture and political ideas, and adding its own achievements in law and empire and in monumental architecture, Rome helped create a lasting heritage from the classical Mediterranean world. The great achievement of course was sheer expansion, from the Atlantic Ocean deep into the Middle East. This meant that the Greco-Roman heritage would have wide geographic impact, for centuries to come.

At the same time, however, the Mediterranean heritage was not passed on smoothly. Parts of the heritage, including the capacity to unite the Mediterranean world, were lost entirely after Rome's decline. Rome and Greece were remembered with the same reverence as classical China or India. But their legacy was more selective, and its transmission proved more complex as Rome's imperial structure faltered.

GLOBAL CONNECTIONS: Rome and the World

During the early centuries of Rome's development, its leaders were quite conscious of a wider Mediterranean world. Rome's expansion reflected this awareness of powerful competitors. The wars with Carthage brought Rome into contact, and ultimate victory, with a powerful state in north Africa. Roman leaders were also alert to the influence of Greek culture in the eastern Mediterranean. Some feared elaborate Greek art and lifestyles as a distraction from pure Roman virtue, but even more were drawn to the benefit of further incorporating Greek culture. The movement toward the east drew Rome into interaction with many Middle Eastern peoples, as far as Persia.

At the height of the empire, Rome seemed to have created its own world. There was trade on the fringes of the empire. On the northern border in Europe, Germanic tribes learned about the empire through trade and occasional fighting. This helped some decide, ultimately, that they wanted to move into the empire directly. Trade also occurred with other parts of Africa, particularly in the northeast. Wealthy Romans were also quite aware of luxury goods from Asia, particularly Chinese silks, though they knew almost nothing of China itself. The goods were brought to the Mediterranean by nomadic merchants. Some Roman merchants visited India in search of trading opportunities. But the big focus in Rome was internal development in a territory that clearly surpassed any empire ever established in the area. Tolerant of local diversities, Romans also built the same kinds of monuments and amenities in Asia, Africa, and Europe—a testimony to their confidence in the validity of their own styles and to their sense that there was little to learn beyond the borders they directly controlled.

Further Readings

Two solid surveys with bibliographies are K. Christ's *The Romans: An Introduction to Their History and Civilization* (1984) and M. Grant's *The World of Rome* (1990). On Rome's early history, see H. H. Scullard's *A History of the Roman World 753–146 B.C.* (1961). Excellent analyses of the basic features of Roman cultural and social life are M. Grant's *A Social History of Greece and Rome* (1992) and P. Garnsey and R. Saller's *The Roman Empire: Economy, Society and Culture* (1987). See also R. MacMullen's *Roman Social Relations 50 B.C. to A.D. 284* (1981). A bold quantitative study is R. Duncan-Jones' *The Economy of the Roman Empire* (1982). On slavery, the best recent works are K. Hopkins' *Conquerors and Slaves, Slaves and Masters in the Roman Empire* (1987) and K. R. Bradley and W. Philips Jr.'s *Slavery from Roman Times to the Early Transatlantic Trade* (1985). On women, see S. Dixon, *The Roman Mother* (1989); J. F. Gardner, *Women in Roman Law and Society* (1986); and Elaine Fanthum and others, *Women in the Classical World: Image and Text* (1994). Florence DuPont's *Daily Life in Ancient Rome* (1999 ed.) examines Roman ideas of space and time and of honor as well as family relations and social divisions.

For war and diplomacy, see Y. Garlan's *War in the Ancient World* (1975); E. N. Luttwak's *The Grand Strategy of the Roman Empire* (1976); Susan Raven's *Rome in Africa* (1993); and Stephen Dyson's *The Creation of the Roman Frontier* (1985).

Collections of source materials include M. Crawford, ed., *Sources for Ancient History* (1983), and C. Fornara, *Translated Documents of Greece and Rome* (1977). J. Boardman, J. Griffin, and O. Murray, *The Oxford History of the Roman World* (1990), and T. Cornell and J. Mathews, *Atlas of the Roman World* (1982) are useful reference guides to Roman civilization.

The rise and spread of Christianity are treated in two outstanding studies: R. MacMullen's *Christianizing the Roman Empire* (1984) and Peter Brown's *The World of Late Antiquity, A.D. 150–750* (1971). Brown has also written several more specialized studies on early Christianity in the West.

On the Web

It is possible to take a virtual flight over the ancient city of Rome and visit computer-generated reconstructions of its most famous buildings, including the Forum, at http://www.taisei.co.jp/cg_e/ancient_world/rome/arome.html. It is possible to experience the Roman world through its architecture (http://harpy.uccs.edu/roman/html/romarch.html) and technology (http://www.unc.edu/courses/rometech/public/content/art_

handbook.html and http://www.bbc.co.uk/history/ancient/romans/tech_01.shtml.

The ancient Roman city of Pompeii may also be visited at http://www.iath.virginia.edu/pompeii/forummap.html. The role of the volcano Vesuvius in shaping human history is explored at http://volcano.und.nodak.edu/vwdocs/volc_images/img_vesuvius.html and its link to http://www.westnet.com/~dobran/publ.html, which examines such disasters as a force in world history.

The organization of the Roman army is discussed at http://members.tripod.com/~S_van_Dorst/reparmy.html. The women of the Roman Empire are the focus of http://dominae.fws1.com/ and http://www.stoa.org/diotima/. The men of Rome have their day at Web sites devoted to Julius Caesar (http://www.vroma.org/~bmcmanus/caesar.html, which includes a link to historians' judgments of his career), Pompeii (http://www.hadrians.com/rome/romans/emperors/emperor_hadrian.html), and Tiberius Gracchus (http://www.gracchus.esmartweb.com/). The home of the quintessential Roman poet Horace, his life, art, and the world in which he lived is beautifully presented at http://www.humnet.ucla.edu/horaces-villa/. Links to the homepage of a well-known, if somewhat controversial, group of scholars who study Jesus of Nazareth as a historical figure can be found at http://www.valpo.edu/home/faculty/fniedner/Jesuspage.html.

CHAPTER 8

THE PEOPLES AND CIVILIZATIONS OF THE AMERICAS

The great pyramids of classic Maya cities such as this one at Tikal demonstrate the architectural skills of the builders and the ability of the Maya states to mobilize labor.

In 1839 a young and adventurous American named John Lloyd Stephens, accompanied by Frederick Catherwood, a young English artist, set out to explore reports of ancient cities buried in the rain forest of Central America. Stephens was an experienced traveler who had seen Egypt and parts of the Middle East, and he wished to examine once and for all the idea that something like the civilizations of the Old World might have existed in the Americas. Many people were skeptical; they simply could not believe that Native Americans had achieved anything like the civilizations of the classical world.

Stephens and Catherwood explored, surveyed, and recorded in their drawings and reports a number of ruins lost in the forest and underbrush. These were the ruins like Palenque and Copán whose monuments, pyramids, and temples were described in rich detail by Stephens. Today we know these places were cities of the Maya civilization. The book published by the two young explorers, *Incidents of Travel in Central America*, revealed for the first time to a large public the vanished glories of a forgotten past and it changed forever the way in which the Americas were seen as part of world history. Stephens was convinced: "Savages," he said, "did not build these places." He captured the story and the enigma of American civilization: "Here were the remains of a cultivated, polished, and peculiar people, who had passed through all the stages incident to the rise and fall of nations."

Although there were some parallels with developments in Asia and north Africa, what took place in the Americas seems to have had no connection to the classical world we have examined thus far. American separateness was vital to making the achievements of civilization all the more impressive but also constraining them. Separateness meant that American chronology had only accidental connections with the classical civilizations. It was based instead on regional interchanges and, like Old World civilizations, it encountered similar problems of internal deterioration and outside attack. Civilization in the New World moved to its own rhythm. Crucial developments in American civilization occurred during the classical period of world history, but our exploration of American developments in this chapter also extends before and after the 1000 B.C.E.–500 C.E. span. With few large domesticated animals, the Americas drew on a different resource base than Europe, Asia, or Africa, but the Americas also developed a number of plants that yielded a higher caloric output than those of Asia or Europe. The Americas present an excellent opportunity to examine the range of social patterns leading to the development of civilizations even when certain elements such as writing or metallurgy were not always present.

20,000 B.C.E.	9000 B.C.E.	5000 B.C.E.	1000 B.C.E.	1 C.E.	500 C.E.	1000 C.E.
20,000–8000 Earliest migration from Asia	9000–7000 Clovis and Folsom style weapons and tools in North America	5000 Plant domestication becoming widespread	900 Maya civilization beginnings; classic period in Mesoamerica	1–650 Teotihuacan flourishes in central Mexico	600–1000 Huari state	1200–1400 Chimu state
9500 Earliest evidence of human occupation	7000 Evidence of agriculture; Guitarrero cave in Peru	4000 Maize domesticated in Mexico	850–250 Early Horizon; Chavín culture flourishes	100–600 Mound builders of Adena	800–1300 Mississippian culture in Cahokia flourishes	1350 Rise of the Aztecs
		4000–2000 Archaic cultures	300 B.C.E.–900 C.E. Height of Maya civilization	c. 100–700 Hopewell culture	900–1500 Postclassic era	
		c. 3000–1500 Initial period; evidence of cotton cultivation, metallurgy, ceramics	200 B.C.E.–500 C.E. Nazca culture	200–700 Mochica culture	900–1500 Maya cities under Mexican influence flourish in Yucatan	
		3000 Early pottery of Puerto Hormiga, Colombia		200–1300 Anasazi culture in Southwest	900–1200 Toltec Empire in central Mexico	
		2000 B.C.E.–500 C.E. Early southwestern cultures		300–900 Intermediate Horizon		
		2000 Pottery in use in Mesoamerica		300–900 Tihuanaco		
		1800–1200 Ceremonial centers in the highlands		400–800 Monte Alban flourishes in Oaxaca		
		1500–800 Olmec civilization flourishes				

The history of the Western Hemisphere is part of the greater story of human development, and the cultures and civilizations of the Americas bear marked similarities to those of the Old World. But there were also important differences in the pace of development and the level of technology that ultimately placed the inhabitants of the Americas at a disadvantage. By the time Europeans arrived in the early 16th century, they encountered great empires, such as that of the Aztecs, with a technology similar to those of earlier American civilizations that had preceded them by 1000 years and in some ways similar to the civilizations of the ancient Near East.

Origins of American Societies

 During the last ice age, peoples from Asia entered the Americas. These ancient hunters eventually created diverse societies, and with the development of agriculture in Mesoamerica and Peru, they formed civilizations organized as chiefdoms, states, and sometimes empires.

Peoples from Asia, moving during the period of the last ice age when the level of the oceans fell, were probably the first inhabitants of America. *Homo sapiens* in Europe and Asia had moved onto the northern steppes and tundra by about 20,000 B.C.E. From there, these people moved across the land bridge that formed in the present Bering Strait between Siberia and Alaska. Mammoths, mastodons, and other large game probably crossed this route, and the hunters followed them. A subsequent rise in the world's temperature about 10,000 years ago caused the ice to melt and eventually raised the level of the oceans, and the land migrations from Asia stopped. The last migrations by the ancestors of the Inuits (Eskimos) probably were made across the polar ice or in boats, a method that other earlier migrants to America had also used.

These migrations took place between about 20,000 B.C.E. and 8000 B.C.E. The earliest definite archeological evidence of people in the Americas dates from about 9500 B.C.E., but many scholars believe that occupation is much older than that, as early as 40,000 B.C.E. How long it took for the American continents to be widely occupied is open to question.

The Ancient Hunters

Crude spearheads document the presence of hunting bands in the Americas (Figure 8.1). By about 11,000 years ago, stone tools and simple spear points associated with these early hunters were widely dispersed over North America.

As the climate became dryer and warmer, the ice began to melt. The great mammal herds diminished and some species disappeared. The ancient Americans seem to have been particularly successful hunters, and it has been argued that the disappearance of such animals as the mammoth, the ancient horse, the camel, and the giant anteater was caused, at least in part, by overhunting. After all, the climate changed in Eurasia as well, but nowhere else in the world did the number of mammals that became extinct equal that in the

Americas, especially North America. Still, changes in mean temperatures, especially between seasons, may have been particularly hard on the young of large mammal species and led to their decline.

Little is known about the society of these early ice age hunters. They probably lived in small groups or bands of 20 to 25 people, following the game in a seasonal pattern. Kinship provided the basis of social organization, and there was little specialization or hierarchy in society. Age and gender were the main determinants of an individual's roles and his or her contributions to the group.

American Diversity

The ancestors of the first Americans, sometimes called the Paleo-Indians, included peoples of different physical types and languages. Some migrated before the Mongoloid peoples who predominated in Asia. The remains of a man found in Kennewick, Washington, who died over 9000 years ago, seem similar to the ancient Ainu of Japan. The fact that all Indians of South America are of blood type O, whereas type B

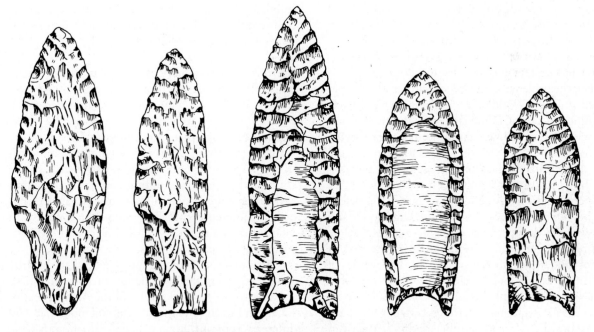

Figure 8.1 *Early spearheads indicating the presence of human populations in the Americas by 10,000 B.C.E. were discovered at Folsom (second from right) and Clovis (center), New Mexico. Folsom points found in 1927 in conjunction with extinct bison species changed scientific thinking about the timing of human occupation in the New World.*

predominates today in Asia, indicates the diversity of physical types involved in the migration and suggests that the migration may have occurred before the present genetic makeup of Asian populations emerged.

Studies of DNA evidence have led some scholars to believe that most Native Americans came from a single, small population group in Asia, but these findings are still in question. Still, all the genetic evidence indicates a large degree of common ancestry and a relative isolation from other human populations. The variations between Indians can be attributed to adaptations and localized natural selection. American Indian languages also indicate growing diversity. These languages seem to have developed from a few parent stocks into a variety of languages.

The Question of Outside Contacts

The possibility of later contacts with the Americas across the Pacific or the Atlantic continues to fascinate archeologists and cause heated debate. Definite mysteries and gaps in the history of pre-Columbian cultures remain unresolved. Artistic motifs and styles in the Americas similar to those of Shang China and southeast Asia seem to indicate contact. Plants such as cotton and bottle gourds seem to be of Old World origin, and their presence in the Americas suggests spread by human agents. Although many scholars admit the possibility of sporadic transoceanic contacts with Chinese, Phoenicians, Africans, Polynesians, and others, the evidence is still mostly circumstantial. No identifiable Old World object has ever been positively identified in a pre-Columbian archeological site, and if Phoenicians or Chinese introduced pottery or writing to the Americas, why they failed to introduce the wheel or bronze at the same time remains a puzzle.

Biological and archeological records indicate that the peopling of the Americas took place long before the beginnings of agriculture in the Old World, and that with the disappearance of the Bering land bridge, this population lived in isolation from the rest of humankind. Most scholars believe that the peoples of the Americas developed their cultures independently of the Old World. Still, occasional contacts were possible, and ideas and material things certainly may have been introduced from elsewhere into American Indian cultures.

Independent development and isolation also had some negative results when Native American populations came into contact with the peoples of Europe, Africa, and Asia. Their lack of the wheel, the plow, and iron put American Indians at a disadvantage. Dogs, turkeys, and guinea pigs were domesticated, but with the exception of llamas in the Andes, the lack of large mammals such as cattle and horses was also a disadvantage in terms of diet, transportation, and power. With the exception of a limited area in the high Andes, pastoralism, so important in the Old World, was not a way of life in the Americas. Most importantly, the isolation of American populations from the disease environment of the larger Old World populations left the inhabitants of the Americas with no immunities to several diseases of Asia, Europe, and Africa. This vulnerability proved disastrous after permanent contact was established.

The Archaic Cultures

By about 9000 B.C.E., small bands of hunters were widely dispersed over the American continents. Changes in climate with the ending of the last ice age may lie behind changes in diet and ways of life. The culture of these early, or **archaic,** populations adapted to the changing environment. People made baskets and used stone grinding tools to prepare the roots and plants they collected for food. As the seacoasts stabilized between 5000 and 4000 B.C.E., populations concentrated around lagoons and river mouths to exploit fish and shellfish.

Agriculture in the Americas   There is evidence from highland Peru of cultivation as early as 7000 B.C.E., and by 5000 B.C.E. plant domestication had taken place in many regions in the Americas. The introduction of agriculture, the American version of the Neolithic revolution, was not as complete and drastic a change as we once thought, and many peoples continued to practice hunting and gathering along with some cultivation. In many places, farmers and hunter-gatherers eventually lived in close contact with each other as a result of social choices and different adaptations to environments.

Eventually, agriculture was practiced all over the Americas, from the woodlands of eastern North America to the tropical forests of the Amazon basin. American Indians eventually cultivated more than 100 different crops, including peppers, squash, tomatoes, and the grains amaranth and quinoa. Some crops, particularly maize, potatoes, and manioc, became essential sources of food for dense populations. As in Asia earlier, agriculture restricted human behavior and the patterns of human action; as American societies depended increasingly on agriculture, a process was set in motion that resulted in the development of complex social, economic, and political systems.

Maize, Manioc, and Potatoes By about 4000 B.C.E., the domestication of **maize** had taken place in central Mexico. Along with it came the cultivation of peppers, squash, and beans. These expanded and more dependable food resources resulted in population growth. Maize cultivation spread far and wide. By 2000 B.C.E. peoples in Peru grew it along with the potato and other crops native to that region. Maize spread northward to the present southern United States, and by about 1000 C.E., it was grown by groups such as the Iroquois in Canada.

In the tropical forests of the Orinoco and Amazon basins, people had developed an agriculture based on varieties of **manioc,** or cassava, a root that could be made into flour. The introduction of maize in areas that had depended on manioc probably resulted in population growth and the rise of more complex societies. Potatoes were the staple in highland South America, and manioc was the principal crop of the lowlands of South America and the islands of the Caribbean, but maize spread in all directions and was often grown in those areas along with other staples. In **Mesoamerica,** the area from north central Mexico to Nicaragua, maize dominated the diet of agricultural peoples.

It seems clear that in most cases, agriculture allowed societies to achieve the surplus production and complexity needed to develop the elements usually associated with civilization. With the adoption of agriculture and a sedentary way of life, the process of civilization was set in motion in the Americas.

Types of American Indian Societies

In the regions of Mesoamerica and the Peruvian orbit, including the coastal areas of Ecuador and Peru and the Andean highlands (Map 8.1), civilizations developed based on intensive agriculture and including most of the features usually associated with Old World civilizations. In both areas, several cycles of cultural advancement and sometimes of empire building took place. Artistic styles flourished and declined, and states rose and fell over thousands of years.

Some scholars suggest that the area between these cultural hearths, including present-day Panama and Colombia, also contained advanced societies with great cultural achievements (especially in metallurgy and goldworking) that differed only in that they did not build large stone buildings. Thus, the whole region from central Mexico to Chile formed a continuous core of American civilizations. On the edges of this core, by influence and imitation, other Indian peoples adopted features of these civilizations, but we should also note that recent archeological findings from the Amazon region suggest that some of the cultural spread may have gone in the other direction and that the lowlands also were areas of great ingenuity and early development.

Many differences and variations existed among American cultures, but there were also similarities in organization, subsistence, technology, and belief that made them more like one another than any one of them was to the civilizations of the Old World. To some extent we can distinguish between ancient American societies on the basis of their economic and political organization. Sedentary agriculture, and with it population density, was a key. Hunters and gatherers continued to occupy large portions of the continents, divided into small bands and moving seasonally to take advantage of the resources. These peoples sometimes were organized in larger tribes and might recognize a chief, but generally their societies were organized around family groups or clans, and there was little hierarchy or specialization of skills. With some exceptions, the material culture of these people tended to be simple.

Peoples who had made a partial transition to agriculture lived in larger and more complex societies. Here the village of 100 or 200 rather than the band of 25 was more common. Men often continued to hunt or make war, but women tilled the fields. Agricultural techniques tended to be simple and often necessitated periodic migration when soils were depleted. The villages of these tribes of semisedentary farmers and hunters have been found on the Brazilian coast and in the woodlands of eastern North America.

It was among peoples who had adopted sedentary agriculture that the complex societies emerged most clearly, for it was here that surplus production was most firmly established. These populations could reach the millions. Men shifted into agriculture, forming a peasant base for a hierarchical society that might have included classes of nobles, merchants, and priests. Strong states and even empires could result, and the extraction of tribute from subject peoples and redistribution by central authority formed the basis of rule.

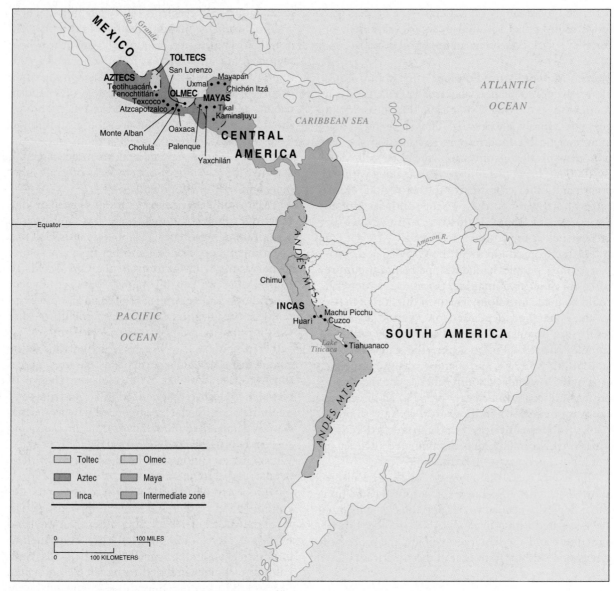

Map 8.1 *Civilizations of Central and South America*

Chiefdoms and States

To some extent, the large imperial states with highly developed religious and political systems and monumental architecture (which we call civilizations) were variants of a common pattern, the **chiefdom.** From the Amazon to the Mississippi valley, hereditary chieftains ruled from central towns over a large territory, including smaller towns and villages that paid tribute to the ruler. The governed populations sometimes numbered in the tens of thousands. The predominant town often had a ceremonial function, with large temples and a priest class. Beautiful pottery and other goods indicate specialization of labor.

Many chiefdoms had a social hierarchy with classes of nobles and commoners. It is sometimes argued that in the state-building societies, ceremonial centers became true cities and social classes replaced clan or family relations. The scale of society differed, but in terms of social organization, ceremonies, and warfare, there were many similarities between the large states and chiefdoms. In South America and

Figure 8.2 *Cahokia near modern St. Louis was a large walled city that may have had 30,000 people. It was inhabited for over 200 years.*

southeastern North America these chiefdoms flourished, but since they often did not build in stone, archaeology has revealed less about them. Cahokia (near modern St. Louis), for example, was an important town of the Mississippian culture (c. 1050–1200 C.E.). It had great earthen mounds covering an area of 5 square miles, and probably supported a population of more than 30,000—as large as the great cities of the Maya civilization (Figure 8.2).

Spread of Civilization in Mesoamerica

The Olmec civilization, which appeared abruptly, spread certain elements of culture over the Mesoamerican region. This led to a classic era of great cultural achievement in art, architecture, and astronomy at Teotihuacan and especially in the Maya city-states, where a complex system of writing and mathematics also developed. These classic civilizations eventually collapsed for partially unknown reasons.

Geographically, the region of Mesoamerica is a complex patchwork of zones that is also divided vertically into cooler highlands, tropical lowlands and coasts, and an intermediate temperate zone (Map 8.2). These climatic variations created different possibilities for human exploitation. They also created a basis for trade as peoples attempted to acquire goods not available locally. Much trade flowed from the tropical lowlands to the cooler central plateau.

Beginning about 5000 B.C.E., gathering and an increasing use of plant foods eventually led to the domestication of certain plants. People grew beans, peppers, avocados, squash, and eventually maize. Later innovations such as pottery took place about 2000 B.C.E. When the Shang dynasty ruled in China, permanent sedentary villages based to some extent on agriculture were first beginning to appear in Mesoamerica. These were small, modest settlements without much hierarchy or social differentiation and an apparent lack of craft specialization. But the number of these archaic villages proliferated, and population densities rose.

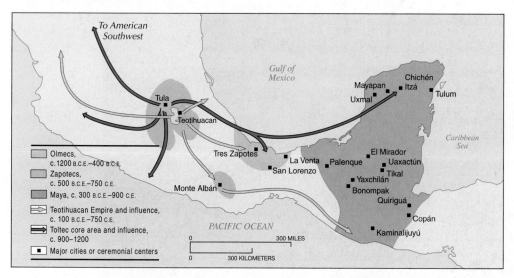

Map 8.2 *Mesoamerican Settlements*

The Olmec Mystery

Quite suddenly, a new phenomenon appeared. On the southeastern coast of Mesoamerica (Veracruz and Tabasco), without much evidence of gradual development in the archeological record, a cultural tradition emerged that included irrigated agriculture, monumental sculpture, urbanism, an elaborate religion, and the beginnings of calendar and writing systems. We call these people **Olmecs** but their origins remain unknown. Their impressive settlements, drainage systems, temple complexes, and ability to move stones weighing tons attest to a high degree of social organization and artistic skill. The major Olmec sites at San Lorenzo (1200–900 B.C.E.) and La Venta (900–500 B.C.E.) are in the wet tropical forests of the Gulf coast of eastern Mexico, but Olmec objects and art style spread to the drier highlands of central Mexico and toward the Pacific coast to the south.

The Olmecs have been called the mother civilization of Mesoamerica. They grew maize, especially along the rivers, and it provided the basis for a state ruled by a hereditary elite in which the ceremonialism of a complex religion dominated life. About the time that Tutankhamen ruled in Egypt, the Olmec civilization flourished in Mesoamerica.

The Olmecs remain an enigma. Some of their monumental sculptures are great stone heads made from basalt rocks weighing tons that were moved many miles without the use of the wheel. Some of these seem to have Negroid features (Figure 8.3); others appear to be representations of humans with feline attributes. The Olmecs were great carvers of jade, and they traded or conquered to obtain it. They developed a vigesimal numerical system (based on 20) and a calendar that combined a 365-day year with a 260-day ritual cycle. This became the basis of all Mesoamerican calendar systems. What language they spoke and what became of their civilization remain unknown. The major cities were eventually abandoned or destroyed, but the reasons for the decline are unclear. Some scholars believe that they were the ancestors of the great Maya civilization that followed.

During this preclassic period (c. 2000–300 B.C.E.), other civilizations were developing elsewhere in Mesoamerica. Olmec objects and, probably, Olmec influence and religious ideas spread into many areas of the highlands and lowlands, such as the Zapotec ceremonial center at **Monte Alban** in Oaxaca, creating the first generalized culture in the region. Farther to the south, some early Maya centers began to appear. In the central valley of Mexico, Olmec artistic influence could be seen in expanding communities.

Much of what we know about these cultures must be interpreted from their architecture and art and the symbols they contain. Art, especially public art, was both decorative and functional. It defined the place of the individual in society and the universe. It had political and religious functions; in the Americas, as in many civilizations, these aspects usually were united. The interpretation of artistic styles and symbols presents a variety of problems in the absence of

Figure 8.3 *The origins of the Olmecs remain shrouded in mystery. Some of the enormous stone sculptures seem to have definite African features that indicate trans-Atlantic contact, but similar features also appear on Khmer art from southeast Asia.*

written sources. The spread of Olmec symbols is a good example of the problem. Did the use of these symbols by other peoples in distant places indicate trade networks, missionary activity, colonies, conquest, or simply aesthetic appreciation? We do not know, but clearly Olmec influence was widely felt throughout the region.

The Classic Era of Mesoamerican Civilization

After the Olmec initiative, the period from about 150 to 900 C.E. was a great age of cultural achievement in Mesoamerica. Archeologists refer to it as the *classic* period, and during it great civilizations flourished in many places. The two main centers of civilization were the high central valley of Mexico and the more

humid tropical lands of southern Mexico, Yucatan, and Guatemala.

The Valley of Mexico: Teotihuacan   In central Mexico, the city of **Teotihuacan,** near modern Mexico City, emerged as an enormous urban center with important religious functions. It was supported by intensive agriculture in the surrounding region and probably by crops planted around the great lakes that dominated the central valley of Mexico. The city developed slowly but by the first centuries C.E. it was flourishing. Teotihuacan's enormous temple pyramids rival those of ancient Egypt and suggest a large state apparatus with the power to mobilize many workers. Population estimates for this city, which covered 9 square miles, are as high as 200,000. This would make it greater than the cities of ancient Egypt or Mesopotamia and probably second only to ancient Rome of the cities of classical antiquity.

Certain trades and ethnic groups had their own residential districts, and there is much evidence of wide social distinctions between the priests, nobles, and common people. The many gods of Mesoamerica, still worshiped when the Europeans arrived in the 16th century, were already honored at Teotihuacan. The god of rain, the feathered serpent, the goddess of corn, and the goddess of waters all appear in the murals and decorations of the palaces and temples. In fact, almost all Teotihuacan art seems to have been religious.

The influence of Teotihuacan extended as far south as the Maya states in Guatemala, and tribute probably was exacted from many regions. Teotihuacan objects, such as pottery and finely worked obsidian, and Teotihuacan artistic styles are found in many other areas. Teotihuacan influence was strong at Monte Alban in Oaxaca. Images of warriors dressed in the style of Teotihuacan can be found far to the south in the Maya region, and their presence their may indicate increasing militarization of Teotihuacan.

Teotihuacan represented a political empire or a dominant cultural and ideological style that spread over much of central Mexico and beyond. The lack of battle scenes on the walls of Teotihuacan has led some scholars to believe that the dominance of Teotihuacan led to a long period of peace maintained by the authority and power of the great city. Internally, the fact that the later buildings tend to be secular palaces rather than temple pyramids may indicate a shift in power from religious to civil authority. By the 8th century C.E. the city was in decline, and it was finally abandoned after attacks probably from nomadic raiders from the north. But for centuries thereafter, the memory of Teotihuacan lived on among the peoples of Mesoamerica as a golden age of cultural achievements.

The Classic Maya   Between about 300 and 900 C.E., at roughly the same time that Teotihuacan dominated the central plateau, the **Maya** peoples were developing Mesoamerican civilization to its highest point in southern Mexico and Central America. While the Tang dynasty ruled China, Charlemagne created his domain in Europe, and Islam spread its influence from Spain to India after the classical period had ended in the Old World, this great civilization flourished in the American tropics. The American classic period, launched as the Old World classical civilizations were coming to an end, lasted well into the next period of world history. We can use the Maya as an example of the classic period in Mesoamerican development: Although their civilization was distinctive, it was based on some principles common to the area.

The Maya culture extended over a broad region that now includes parts of five different countries: Mexico, Guatemala, Belize, Honduras, and El Salvador. It included several related languages, and it had considerable regional variation, as can be seen in its art styles. The whole region shared a common culture that included monumental architecture, a written language, a calendar and mathematical system, a highly developed religion, and concepts of statecraft and social organization. Using only stone tools in an area of dense forests, plagued by insects and poor soils, as many as 50 city-states flourished.

How did the large urban-religious centers, such as Tikal, Copán, Quirigua, and Palenque, with populations between 30,000 and 80,000, support themselves? **Slash and burn agriculture,** practiced today in the region, was not enough. The classic Maya used several agricultural systems. Evidence of irrigation, swamp drainage, and a system of artificially constructed ridged fields at river mouths (where intensive agriculture was practiced) seems to explain the Mayan ability to support large urban centers and a total population of perhaps 5 million. Although some authorities still believe that the Maya centers were ceremonial and were occupied primarily by rulers, artisans, and an elite, it seems clear that populations were concentrated in and around these centers. The

Maya cities vary in size and layout, but almost all include large pyramids surmounted by temples, complexes of masonry buildings that served administrative or religious purposes, elite residences, a ritual ball court, and often a series of altars and memorial pillars. These memorial monuments, or **stelae,** were erected to commemorate triumphs and events in the lives of the Maya rulers or to mark ceremonial occasions. The stelae usually were dated and were inscribed with a hieroglyphic script. A complex calendar and a sophisticated writing system were two of the greatest Maya achievements.

Religion, Writing, and Society   The calendar system and sophisticated astronomical observations were made possible by a vigesimal system of mathematics (that is, based on 20). The Maya knew the concept of zero and used it in conjunction with the concept of place value or position. With elegant simplicity and with signs for only 1, 5, and 0, they could make complex calculations. As among all the Mesoamerican peoples, the Maya calendar was based on a concept of recurring cycles of different length. The Maya had a sacred cycle of 260 days divided into months of 20 days each, within which there was a cycle of 13 numbers. This ritual calendar meshed with a solar calendar of 365 days, or 18 months of 20 days each, with 5 "dead" or inauspicious days at the end of the year. The two calendars operated simultaneously, so any day had two names, but the particular combination of those two days recurred only once every 52 years. Thus, among the Maya and most Mesoamericans, cycles of 52 years were sacred.

The classic Maya differed from their neighbors in that they also kept a **long count,** or a system of dating from a fixed date in the past. This date, 3114 B.C.E. by our Christian calendar, probably marked the beginning of a great cycle of 5200 years since the creation of the world. Like other Mesoamericans and the ancient Peruvians, the Maya believed in great cycles of creation and destruction of the universe. The long count enabled the Maya to date events with precision. The earliest recorded Maya date that survives is the equivalent of 292 C.E., and the last would be 928 C.E.

A second great Maya accomplishment was the creation of a writing system. The Maya wrote on stone monuments, murals, and ceramics and in books of folded bark paper and deerskin, only four of which survive. Scribes were honored and held an important

Document

Deciphering the Maya Glyphs

Of all the peoples of ancient America, the Maya developed the most complex system of writing to record their history, religion, philosophy, and politics. Maya hieroglyphs have baffled and fascinated researchers since the 1820s, when the first steps toward deciphering the rich glyphs and symbols of Maya monuments, ceramics, and the few surviving Maya books were made. This process continues, and although we are not yet able to read all the surviving texts, those that have been deciphered have changed our view of Maya society and its underlying beliefs.

One of the problems of decipherment was a false start. In the 16th century, a Spanish bishop of Yucatan, Diego de Landa, burned many books in an attempt to stamp out Maya religion. Landa's attempt to describe the Maya writing, based on his questioning of Indian informants, was badly flawed. Landa thought the glyphs were letters, not syllables, so his description confused scholars. Despite his deficiencies, however, Landa provided the only guide available for many years. Unlike the decipherment of Egyptian hieroglyphs, no text with Maya and some other known language side by side exists, so the problem of reading the Maya glyphs remains difficult.

The first modern advances were made in reading Maya numbers and identifying glyphs for the months in the calendar cycle. By the 1940s, scholars could read the dates rather well, and because so many inscriptions and the four remaining books seemed to be numerical and related to the calendar, most specialists believed that the Maya writing was primarily about the calendar system and that the Maya were obsessed with time. Many things complicated the reading of the other glyphs, such as the fact that scholars were not sure which of the various Maya languages that survive was the language of the inscriptions. In 1952, a young Russian researcher argued that the Maya glyphs combined signs that stood for whole words with others that represented sounds or syllables. In this, the Maya script was like ancient Egyptian and cuneiform writings. Although the theory was not fully accepted at first, it has proved to be accurate.

A major breakthrough took place in 1960, when art historian Tatiana Proskouriakoff noted that on certain sets of monuments the earliest and last dates were never more than 62 years apart, and that the first date was always accompanied by one certain glyph and the next always by another. She recognized that the images on the monuments were not gods or mythical figures, but kings,

This relief from the Mayan palace complex at Yaxchilan shows a kneeling woman pulling a rope barbed with thorns across her tongue to draw blood. Her husband, a king named Shield-Jaguar, holds a torch above her head. The king's hair is adorned with the shrunken head of a sacrificial victim.

and that the first glyph indicated birth and the second accession. Sixty-two years was consistent with a human lifespan. With this approach, scholars have figured out the names of the rulers and their families and something about the dynastic history of a number of Maya cities.

Scholars now understand that despite regional variations, the texts were written in a language widely understood throughout the Maya region. The glyphs combine syllables, symbols, emblems, and ideas in what is basically a complex phonetic system. Now that we are

(continued)

able to read numbers, dates, place or city emblems, and a few nouns and verbs, a new window has been opened on the ancient Maya.

Questions: What do the elaborate ritual life and sumptuous clothing suggest about the nature of Maya society? Do the complex calendar and writing system indicate widespread literacy or the power of an elite class that controlled this esoteric knowledge? Does the role of writing in Mesoamerican civilization seem similar to that in ancient Egypt, Sumer, and China?

place in society. Although we still cannot fully decipher many inscriptions, recent advances now permit the reading of many texts. The Maya written language, like Chinese and Sumerian, was a logographic system, which combined phonetic and semantic elements. With this system and about 287 symbols, the Maya recorded complex ideas. The few surviving books are religious and astronomical texts, and many inscriptions on ceramics deal with the cult of the dead and the complex Maya cosmology, but hundreds of the inscriptions refer to the reign of kings, their victories, their accomplishments, and their lineages.

The Maya had a complex religious system with many deities, but there was a basic Mesoamerican concept of dualism—male and female, good and bad, day and night. This idea, similar to that found in some Asian religions, emphasized the unity of all things. Each god had a parallel female consort or feminine form and often an underworld equivalent as well. In addition, there were patron deities of various occupations and classes. The number of gods and goddesses in the inscriptions seems overwhelming, but they should be understood as manifestations of a more limited set of supernatural forces, much like the various incarnations of the Hindu gods.

From the historical inscriptions we know that the major Maya centers were the cores of city-states, which controlled outlying territories. There was constant warfare, and rulers such as Pacal of Palenque (who died in 683 C.E.) expanded their territories by conquest. Pacal's victories were recorded on his funerary monuments and in his lavish tomb, discovered inside a pyramid at Palenque.

The rulers exercised civil and probably religious power, and an elite aided their rule and performed administrative functions. A class of scribes, or perhaps priests, tended to the cult of the state and specialized in the complex calendar observations and calculations. The ruler and the scribes organized and participated in rituals of self-mutilation and human sacrifice that among the Maya, as in much of Mesoamerica, were an important aspect of religion. Also, as a form of both worship and sport, the Maya, like other Mesoamerican peoples, wagered on and played a ritual **ball game** on specially constructed courts (Figure 8.4) in which players moved a ball with their hips or elbows. The stakes were high. Losers might forfeit their possessions or their lives.

Builders, potters, scribes, sculptors, and painters worked in the cities for the glory of the gods and the rulers. However, most people were peasant farmers whose labor supported the elaborate ritual and political lives of the elite. Captives were enslaved. Patrilineal families probably formed the basis of social life, as they did among the Maya of later days, but the elite traced their families through both fathers and mothers. Elite women often are represented in dynastic monuments in positions of importance. State marriages were important, and elite women retained many rights. Among the common people, women were responsible for food preparation and domestic duties, including the production of fine cloth on small looms. The division of tasks by gender probably was supported by religious belief and custom.

Classic Collapse

Between about 700 and 900 C.E., the Mesoamerican world was shaken by the rapid decline of the great cultural centers. The reasons for this collapse are not fully understood, but it was widespread. In the central plateau, Teotihuacan was destroyed about 650 C.E. by outside invaders, probably nomadic hunters from the north, perhaps with the help of some of the groups under the dominance of Teotihuacan. The city may have already been in decline because of increasing problems with agriculture.

The most mysterious aspect of the collapse was the abandonment of the Maya cities. During the 8th century C.E., Maya rulers stopped erecting com-

Figure 8.4 *Ball courts such as this one at Copán existed throughout Mesoamerica. The ball game was both a sport and a religious ceremony.*

memorative stelae and large buildings, and population sizes dwindled. By 900 C.E., most of the major Maya centers had been deserted. Scholars do not agree whether this process was the result of ecological problems and climatic change, agricultural exhaustion, internal revolt, or foreign pressure. The collapse took place at different times in different places and seems to have been the result of several processes, of which increasing warfare was either a cause or a symptom. The warfare may be related to the decline of Teotihuacan and the attempt of Maya city-states to control old trade routes.

The primary explanation for the Maya collapse is agricultural exhaustion. The Mayan ability to create a civilization in the dense rain forest of the Peten in Guatemala and in the Chiapas lowlands was based on a highly productive agricultural system. By the 8th century, the limits of that system, given the size and density of population, may have been reached. Tikal had an estimated density of more than 300 people per square mile. Maintaining the great population centers was an increasing burden. Epidemic disease has also been suggested as a cause of the collapse, perhaps indicating some unrecorded contact with the Old World. Others believe that the peasants simply refused to bear the burdens of serving and feeding the political and religious elite and that internal rebellion led to the end of the ruling dynasties and their cities.

The cultural achievements of the classic period were not attained again. Long-count dating ended, the stelae cult ceased, and the quality of ceramics and architectural accomplishments declined. But as the great Maya centers of the southern lowlands and highlands were abandoned or declined, Maya cities in the Yucatan and in the Guatemala highlands expanded and carried on some of the traditions, also receiving much cultural influence from central Mexico. Mexicanized ruling families established themselves at **Chichén Itzá** and other towns in Yucatan. The northern Maya area accommodated these influences and created a new synthesis of Maya and central

Mexican culture. In the great southern Maya cities, such as Tikal and Palenque, the rain forest soon overran the temples and palaces.

After 1000 C.E., the **Nahuatl**-speaking **Toltecs,** one of the new groups that occupied the central plateau after the fall of Teotihuacan, established political control over a large territory and eventually extended their influence into Maya territory. Their genius seems to have been military, and much of their culture was derived from classic traditions. From their capital at Tula in central Mexico, Toltec influence and trade may have spread as far as the American Southwest, where the cliff-dwelling Anasazi people, the ancestors of the Pueblo Indians, produced beautiful ceramics and cultivated maize in the desert valleys. In Yucatan, the ruling families claimed descent from Toltec invaders. Even when the Toltec empire fell, about 1200 C.E., the cultural traditions of Mesoamerica did not die, for imperial states and civilization do not necessarily go together. Eventually, however, a new power, the **Aztecs,** rose in the central plateau of Mexico. The Aztecs initiated yet another cycle of expansion based on the deep-rooted ways of life and thought of Mesoamerica.

The Peoples to the North

 To the north of Mesoamerica, complex cultures developed, often based on agriculture. The extent of their contact with Mesoamerica is not clear, but in the Mississippi basin and the American Southwest, the ancestors of the later Indian peoples formed complex societies with large populations.

Archeologists have distinguished various stages of archaic culture, from Alaska to northern Mexico, among the ancestors of the North American Indians. We cannot deal in detail with the many cultural traditions that evolved from those cultures of the archaic period, but two broad regions in North America merit special attention because of the complex, sedentary agricultural societies that developed there: the eastern woodlands of what is now the southern United States and the arid Southwest.

The Mound Builders

In the valleys of the Mississippi and Ohio rivers, people began to practice agriculture by 2000 B.C.E. By 700 B.C.E., a society that combined hunting and agriculture had begun to emerge. In southern Ohio and neighboring areas, these peoples built large earthen constructions and mounds. Some of the mounds were defensive, and others served as places for burials. These burials contain pottery, pipes (indicating the use of tobacco), jewelry, and copper objects that indicate long-distance trade from as far away as Michigan. This culture may have been spread by migrants or by trade contacts to other places, such as New York State and Maryland, where it lasted as late as 700 C.E. In Ohio and southern Illinois, however, it was already being replaced by a more complex culture.

The **Hopewell culture** (c. 200–500 C.E.) introduced new levels of scale and complexity. Elaborate mounds, some of great size and often organized into groups, were characteristic of this mound-building culture. Some of the mounds, such as Serpent Mound in Ohio, were built as effigies, or representations, of animals. Burials contained jewelry, personal items, weapons, and religious symbols of copper, quartz, galena, and mica. Conch shells and shark teeth indicate long-distance trade with peoples of the Gulf coast, and other materials were brought from as far away as the Rocky Mountains. Hopewell artisans worked in stone and clay and produced beautiful pottery, pipes, and effigies, luxury items seemingly designed for the cult of the dead. By about 400 C.E., large-scale construction of mounds had ceased in the main centers of Hopewell culture, and the trade network had begun to break down.

After about 400 years, the Hopewell culture was succeeded by a new complex that spread throughout the Mississippi valley. Between 800 and 1300 C.E., very large towns and ceremonial centers, such as Moundville (Alabama) and Cahokia (Illinois), flourished throughout the southeastern region. Mound building here was not only for burials or effigies but also for fortification and large pyramid platforms. Cahokia had one temple mound about 100 feet high, containing more than 2 million cubic feet of earth. Large populations and smaller towns lived around these Mississippian centers. For example, at least 50 communities appear to have been under Cahokia's influence. Except for the absence of stone architecture, Cahokia seemed to parallel the urban development of Mesoamerica.

The rich variety and excellent quality of artifacts indicate social divisions within this society, but we know little about its social organization. The best clues come from the 18th-century observations of the Natchez Indians, who carried on the Mississippian tradition. They were organized as a powerful chiefdom under a ruler known as the Great Sun, who ruled a society composed of four distinct social classes, the lowest of which were called the stinkards. The Natchez were the last remnants of a culture that had mostly disappeared by 1400 C.E.

One explanation for the rise of **Mississippian culture** was the introduction of new strains of maize from Mesoamerica and its adoption of maize, bean, and squash cultivation. Mississippians depended more fully on agriculture than their Hopewell and earlier predecessors. Mississippian populations were larger than those of previous cultures, and the search for new agricultural lands seems to have been a motive for political expansion. The large towns and urban centers, temple complexes, pyramid mounds, religious symbols, and crops appear to reflect a strong Mesoamerican influence, but no identifiable Mesoamerican artifacts have been found in Mississippian sites.

The Desert Peoples

Across the American Southwest a different cultural tradition developed with great local variation. By about 300 B.C.E., settled communities developed in this region, living first in pit houses partially beneath the ground and later in stone structures. Irrigation was used to grow maize, beans, and other crops, and ball courts and temple mounds that appeared by 600 C.E. suggest the influence of Mesoamerican cultures. Distinctive pottery developed in each cultural region, and there seems to have been trade between these areas and with Mexico. In southern New Mexico by about 1000 C.E., multiroom stone dwellings were being used.

Perhaps the most famous southwestern regional tradition is that of the **Anasazi** (Navajo for "the ancient ones"), who lived in the Four Corners region of New Mexico, Arizona, Colorado, and Utah. Settled in the region from about 200 B.C.E., they began to live in large, multistory adobe and stone dwellings by 700 C.E. Apparently, pressure from hostile neighbors caused them to build these dwellings in protected canyons or in cliffs, where access is difficult. The existing cliff-dwelling ruins at Mesa Verde and Canyon de Chelly are excellent examples of Anasazi settlements (Figure 8.5).

Figure 8.5 *Anasazi dwelling at Mesa Verde*

In Depth

Different Times for Different Peoples

In this presentation of the indigenous civilizations of the Americas that were often concerned with time, it is appropriate to examine the importance of time and its measurement in world history. The calendar and timekeeping are so much a part of everyday life that we often think of these measures only as aspects of the natural order. We divide the day into 24 hours of 60 minutes each, and the year into 12 months or 365 days, without much reflection on the meaning or origins of these divisions. Our lives are guided by the clock and marked by its division into working hours, doctor's appointments, class periods, and TV time slots, all of which reflect not only a widely accepted system of measurement but also an ideology of time and its value.

The marking and division of time is a complex matter with cultural, political, and even biological aspects. The concept and meaning of time have varied greatly from culture to culture and have changed historically within cultures. The leaders of both the French Revolution of 1789 and the Russian Revolution of 1917 created new calendar systems to represent what they hoped were the beginnings of new historical ages. Calendar systems and time measurement reflect ideas about politics and history as well as perceptions of the natural world.

Observing the cyclical motion of the heavens was the key for constructing a yearly calendar by which agriculture could be regulated and religious cycles could be set. Early peoples observed the recurring patterns of the stars and planets. Clearly observed stages of the moon guided the ancient Babylonians, but because the annual cycle of the moon differed from the **solar cycle,** the lunar calendar was not an accurate guide to the seasons. The **lunar cycle** calendar constantly needed adjustment, or intercalation, which added extra days or months so that the seasons would occur in the same place in the cycle in each calendar year. Despite its difficulties, the lunar calendar was adopted by the Hebrews. It is still in use by Jews and is also the basis of the Muslim calendar.

The ancient Egyptians were the first to use a solar year, and as early as 4000 B.C.E. they had devised a calendar of 12 months of 30 days each, to which they added 5 days of celebration at the start of each year. (The Maya and other peoples of Mesoamerica had a similar solution but added their 5 days at the end of the year.) The Egyptian solar calendar, though not exact and also needing periodic adjustments, was the basis for the Julian calendar of the Roman Empire established by Julius Caesar in 45 B.C.E. This calendar was modified and improved in the Gregorian calendar, instituted by Pope Gregory XIII in the late 16th century and adopted slowly throughout Europe.

Other peoples and civilizations also worked out calendar systems based on observation of the heavens, and these in turn were related to concepts about time and history. The Maya peoples were acute observers of the heavens. They built observatories and wrote treatises on the movement of the stars and planets. Like other Mesoamerican peoples, they used two calendars simultaneously: a 260-day ritual calendar and a 365-day lunar calendar. The days of the two lined up only every 52 years, creating a cyclical view of time divided into 52-year cycles. Thus for the ancient peoples of Mesoamerica, as in India and Sumer, time was cyclical. The events of history fit into recurring patterns that might reveal a divine purpose or plan but did not lead in any particular direction. Both the ancient Hindus and the Maya calculated great cycles of thousands of years as part of a divine plan.

The ancient Chinese were concerned with measuring time, and water clocks were used during the Shang period, about 1500 B.C.E. By the 11th century, Su Sung, a court official, had designed an elaborate clock regulated by the flow of water for the emperor. But Chinese interest in mechanical clocks did not continue, and time did not figure prominently in Chinese philosophical thought or in the lives of most people. A new emperor often introduced a new calendar, for control of the calendar was viewed as an attribute of power. The Chinese concept of history was marked by belief in a divine mandate that was given to each dynasty and then withdrawn when it failed in its duties and obligations. Thus, time and history were redefined as each dynasty attempted to fulfill this Mandate of Heaven.

For the ancient Hebrews, whose ideas on this subject were later taken up by Christians and Muslims, history was not cyclical but linear: It moved toward an end, the revelation of God's will. The present was influenced by the past and the future. It has been suggested that a concept of the future and of progress depends on a linear view of time and history.

Before the 19th century, the vast majority of the world's people, including the peasants of the most technologically advanced societies, measured time by the cycle of work and daily tasks: when the cows had to be milked, how much time until dinner, how many hours of daylight remained. These natural rhythms kept work and life close together, and there was little concern for time as a separate thing that could be precisely measured and counted, lost or gained. The day might be divided by the hours of daily prayer or by the duration of a task, but exact time was of little importance.

Although the Chinese had experimented with clocks, and other cultures had used sundials, candles, and water clocks to measure the passage of time, synchronizing these instruments was difficult. Clocks were curiosities and vehicles for artistic expression, more likely to be found in royal collections than in private homes. In 807 C.E., for example, Europeans marveled at a mechanical water clock sent as a gift by the Muslim leader Haroun al-Rashid to Charlemagne, but despite such wonders, the inaccurate instruments of antiquity were of limited use.

It was in Europe that time measurement was transformed. Perhaps the deficiencies of sundials and water clocks in the cloudy and frosty climates of northern Europe led to the perfection of the mechanical clock. The cause simply could have been Europe's growing interest in machines.

Between the 14th and 17th centuries, the measurement of time experienced a profound but gradual transformation. Church and town clocks appeared in the major urban centers, and clocks began to appear in private homes, especially after the introduction of pendulum clocks in about 1660. By the end of the 17th century, pocket watches based on balance springs made accurate timekeeping a personal matter, and the aristocrats, master artisans, and merchants of Europe began to live their lives by the clock. When Catholic missionaries arrived in China in the 17th century, the Chinese were amazed by the complexity and accuracy of the clocks they brought. Some authors see Europe's fascination with time and perfection of the clock as a symbol of changes in attitudes about labor and nature. Moreover, accurate clocks were precise machines and symbolized the development of technology that accompanied the scientific revolution of the 17th century and then the Industrial Revolution of the 18th century.

The "revolution in time," as historian David Landes calls it, was related to changes in work discipline needed in the new industries, where synchronizing tasks in a factory called for precision and a sense of time different from that of rural labor. Such coordination had already begun to appear in activities such as shipbuilding and on sugar plantations. Time became something that workers sold and employers bought, and the concept of productivity measured by the amount of work done in a specific amount of time became a basic part of the industrial work ethic. The shift was difficult, however. Older working patterns were slow to change, and industrialists complained that workers still honored "Saint Monday" by not showing up for work on that day, or that they preferred to work not by the hour but by the job. Early industrial workers were not eager to become captives of the machine and the clock.

Preindustrial habits and attitudes of work persisted in most of the world outside of Europe in the 19th century. Most people still lived with a rhythm of intense labor at some times of the year and less work at others, and they thought in terms of the job and not by the amount of time it took to do it. European travelers to Asia, Africa, the Pacific, and the Americas commented on the natives' lack of punctuality, the natural or religious rhythms of their life, their inability to measure time, and often their seeming disregard for it. The myth of the lazy native was being born. The clock became a measure of what Europeans and North Americans valued and what set them apart. When an English missionary in southern Africa wrote in his diary, "Today we have unpacked our clock and we seem a little more civilized," he summarized a great deal of modern world history.

Questions: Why did measuring time become important in the early civilizations of Egypt, the Near East, and China? How did concepts of time reflect a view of history? What are the implications of the technological changes in keeping time?

A characteristic feature of these villages and towns is the circular pit, or **kiva,** used for religious meetings by the men of the community. This structure is still used today by the Pueblo Indians of the region.

Kivas are also found in another type of Anasazi settlement. The ruins of about 125 towns in New Mexico's Chaco Canyon and the surrounding areas are remarkable for their planning and the care of their stone and adobe construction. Many of these towns were connected by an extensive system of what seem to be roads or ritual lines, which linked the city to celestial or natural phenomena. The Anasazi produced excellent pottery without the potter's wheel, and they had trading contacts with Mesoamerica, where the turquoise of their region was traded for items such as parrots, valued for their feathers.

A long period of drought in the late 13th century seems to explain the decline of the Anasazi and other southwestern peoples. Perhaps their technology in managing water resources was unable to keep pace with a drought that lasted for hundreds of years. Anasazi decline, followed by pressure from nomads such as the Navajo and Apache, eventually led to the abandonment of the towns, but many scholars believe that the traditions of the Anasazi have continued in the culture of the modern Hopi and other Pueblo Indians of the American Southwest.

The contacts with Mesoamerican civilization are clearer among the ancient peoples of the southwestern United States than in the eastern woodlands. However, both regions demonstrate the spread of many aspects of civilization and the development of settled agricultural societies throughout the Americas.

The Andean World

The rise of civilization in South America paralleled many of the processes in Mesoamerica. Periods of broadly shared culture were followed by periods of regional diversity. The civilization of Chavín spread along the Peruvian coast and created a horizon of widely shared culture. It was followed by vibrant regional cultures such as Nazca and Moche and then by another horizon centered on the highland states of Huari and Tihuanaco. The decline of these states led to new regional developments.

The Andean world presented a peculiar geography of complex microregions with extreme changes in altitude and temperature (Map 8.3). The narrow, arid strip on the western coast, cut by a few rivers that flow to the Pacific, gives way quickly to the high Andes, where some peaks rise to more than 15,000 feet. Between the two major chains of the Andes lie high valleys and steppes, or **puna,** that form the highlands,

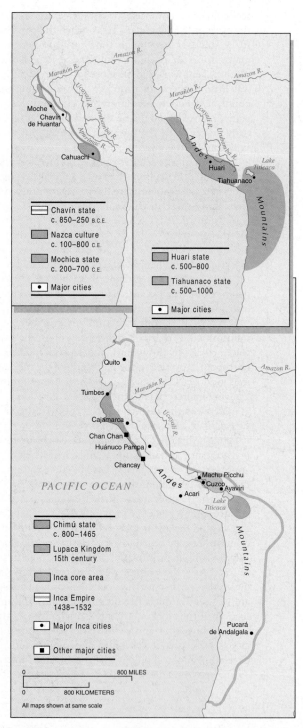

Map 8.3 *Andean Societies. Note the development of civilization centers on the coast and in the highlands.*

or altiplano. On these cool uplands (usually above 10,000 feet), the land is level and there is adequate water. Here potatoes and maize could be grown, and the puna provided good grazing for **llamas** and **alpacas,** the "sheep of the Andes." Andean populations were concentrated here or down on the arid coast in the river valleys that made irrigation possible. On the eastern slopes of the Andes, large rivers run down into the tropical rain forest concentrated at the basins of the Amazon and La Plata rivers. This is the humid **montaña,** where tropical fruits and coca leaf grow.

This rugged topography imposed limitations and created opportunities for civilization to develop. The arid coastal valleys had to be irrigated, and this spurred population growth and social complexity. In the highlands, irrigation and terracing increased the food supply in regions where the amount of arable land was limited. Populations were concentrated in the fertile valleys but were separated from one another by steep mountains. Trade and communication were difficult. It took large, well-organized projects to build roads, bridges, and agricultural terraces. The reasons for state building were good. The warfare, military images, and trophy heads seen in much ancient Peruvian art represent a world of limited resources and competition.

In the Andean world, sharp vertical changes created microclimates within short distances. Peoples and even individual communities or families strove to control the different ecological zones where different kinds of crops could be raised. A community might live in the altiplano, growing potatoes and quinoa (an Andean grain), but could also have fields in the lower valleys to grow maize, pastures miles away at a higher elevation for the llamas, and even an outer colony in the montaña to provide cotton, coca, and other tropical products. In fact, access to a variety of these ecological zones by colonization, occupation, conquest, or trade seems to have been a constant feature in Andean life, which determined pre-Columbian patterns of settlement and influenced the historical development of the Andean world.

Early Developments and the Rise of Chavín

Much of early Andean history alternates between periods of decentralization, in which various local or regional centers developed distinctive cultures, and periods in which one of these centers spread its control over very large areas, establishing a cultural horizon under centralized authority. Between 3000 and 2000 B.C.E., permanent agricultural villages were established in the Andean highlands and on the arid Pacific coast. Maize was introduced from Mesoamerica and was grown along with indigenous crops such as the potato. Pottery appeared by about 2700 B.C.E., first on the north coast in present-day Ecuador and then in the highlands of central Peru. This early pottery, called Valdivia ware, indicates advanced techniques of production. It is remarkably similar to Japanese Jomon-period (3rd millennium B.C.E.) ceramics, and this has led some scholars to suggest trans-Pacific contact by Japanese fishers. Whatever the origins of pottery in the region, the presence of sedentary agriculture, ceramics, weaving, and permanent villages marked a level of productivity that was soon followed by evidence of political organization. Early sites, such as El Paraiso on the Peruvian coast, contain monumental buildings of great size, but we know little of the societies that built them.

Between 1800 and 1200 B.C.E., ceremonial centers with large stone buildings were constructed in the highlands and on the coast. Pottery was now widely distributed, the llama had been domesticated, and agriculture had become more complex, with evidence of simple irrigation at some places. The most important of these centers was Chavín de Huantar (850–250 B.C.E.) in the Peruvian highlands. Chavín contained several large temple platforms and adobe and stone buildings. Its artisans worked in ceramics, textiles, and gold. **Chavín culture** was characterized by artistic motifs that were spread widely through much of the Andean region and seem to represent a cult or a system of religious beliefs. Jaguars, snakes, birds of prey, and humans with feline characteristics were used as decorations, often along with scenes of war and violence.

The Chavín artistic style was so widely diffused that archeologists call this epoch a **horizon,** a period when a broad central authority seems to have integrated a widely dispersed region. In truth, we do not know whether conquest, trade, or missionary activity spread the religion of Chavín, nor do we know the religion's origins. Its artistic style does have some

Visualizing the Past

Ancient Agriculture

The ancient peoples of the Americas devised complex systems of irrigation, combining their knowledge of agriculture and hydrology to produce high yields in areas of drought, frost, or difficult soil that even today present great challenges to agriculture. Some of the projects were enormous, involving miles of canals and ditches. In the lowlands of Bolivia and in arid coastal Peru there is evidence of ridged fields in which irrigation apparently supported dense populations. At Tihuanaco, near the shores of Lake Titicaca in the Andes, canals were dug, and the mud from them was used to fertilize the fields alongside. Estimates are that productivity in such fields was as much as seven times greater than in nonirrigated fields. Similar systems were developed elsewhere in the Americas. The ingenuity and importance of irrigation for many American Indian civilizations seems clear.

Questions: What are the implications of such systems about social and political organization? Are states necessary to create such projects? What are the demographic implications, and their consequences? Does the existence of such systems throughout the Americas indicate diffusion or parallel developments?

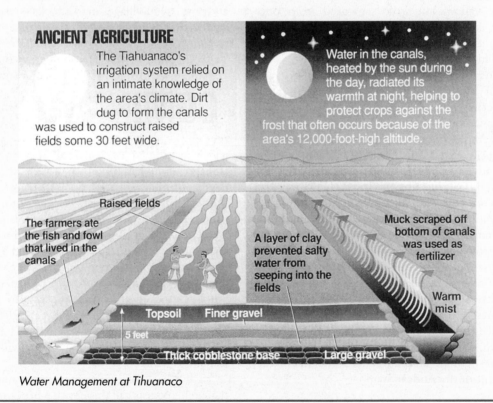

ANCIENT AGRICULTURE

The Tiahuanaco's irrigation system relied on an intimate knowledge of the area's climate. Dirt dug to form the canals was used to construct raised fields some 30 feet wide.

Water in the canals, heated by the sun during the day, radiated its warmth at night, helping to protect crops against the frost that often occurs because of the area's 12,000-foot-high altitude.

Raised fields

The farmers ate the fish and fowl that lived in the canals

A layer of clay prevented salty water from seeping into the fields

Muck scraped off bottom of canals was used as fertilizer

Warm mist

Topsoil   Finer gravel

5 feet

Thick cobblestone base   Large gravel

Water Management at Tihuanaco

remarkable similarities with Olmec art in Mesoamerica. Some archeologists point out certain tropical features in both and suggest the Amazonian lowlands as a possible point of origin for both traditions.

The evidence of warfare in early Peruvian agricultural societies may indicate a general process. With the development of intensive agriculture and a limited amount of arable land, it became necessary to organize irrigation and create political authority and eventually states that could mobilize to protect or expand the available land.

Regional Cultures and a New Horizon

By 300 B.C.E., Chavín was in decline, and whatever unity the widely spread Chavín style indicated was lost. The Andean world became characterized by regional centers, each with its own cultural and artistic traditions. This was a period without political unity, but it produced some of the Andean world's finest art. Irrigated agriculture that produced a wide variety of crops, the domestication of llamas and related animals, dense populations, and hierarchical societies could be found in many places. Some societies, such as those in Nazca on the south coast and Moche to the north, produced remarkable pottery and weaving.

Nazca weaving reached a high point for the Americas. Discovery in the 1920s of a group of richly dressed mummies at Paracas, near Nazca, revealed the artistic accomplishments of these ancient weavers. More than 100 colors were used, and many weaving techniques and cloth types were produced; the designs often were abstract. The plain near Nazca is also the scene of great figures of various animals, which cover many hundreds of feet and can be seen only from the air (Figure 8.6). There are also great straight lines or paths that cut across the plain and seem to be oriented toward distant mountains or celestial points. Why these lines and designs were drawn is unknown.

The **Mochica state** (200–700 C.E.), in the Moche valley and on the coast to the north of Chavín, mobilized workers to construct great clay brick temples, residences, and platforms. Artisans produced gold and silver jewelry and copper tools. The potter's art reached a high point; scenes on Mochica ceramics depict rulers receiving tribute and executing prisoners. Nobles, priests, farmers, soldiers, and slaves are also portrayed in remarkably lifelike ways; many vessels are clearly portraits of individual members of the elite. The Mochica also produced a great number of pottery vessels showing a variety of explicit sexual acts. These scenes are almost always in a domestic setting and indicate descriptions of everyday life rather than ritual unions.

Moche expanded its control by conquest. Mochica art contains many representations of war, prisoners, and the taking of heads as trophies. There is also archeological evidence of hilltop forts and military posts. Politically, Moche and the other regional states seem to have been military states or chiefdoms, supported by extensive irrigated agriculture and often at war.

Some idea of life in Moche society was spectacularly revealed with the discovery in 1988 of the tomb of a warrior-priest. Buried with servants and his dog, this nobleman was covered with gold, silver, and copper ornaments, fine cloth, and jewelry. The scenes on these objects and on the pottery buried with him include depictions of captive prisoners, ritual sacrifice, and warfare.

This pattern of regional development continued until about 300 C.E., when two large centers, **Tihuanaco** on the shores of Lake Titicaca and **Huari** farther to the north in southern Peru, began to emerge as large states. How much centralized political control they exerted is unclear, but as in the earlier case of Chavín, the religious symbols and artistic style associated with these centers spread widely through the Andean world, creating perhaps a second or intermediate horizon (c. 300–900 C.E.) roughly contemporary with the classic Maya and Teotihuacan in Mesoamerica.

Tihuanaco was an urban ceremonial center with a population of perhaps 40,000, supported by extensive irrigated agriculture. Recent archeological work has revealed an extensive system of raised fields, irrigated by canals, that could produce high yields. Tihuanaco's inhabitants probably spoke Aymara, the language of the southern Andes that is spoken today in Bolivia. The art style of Tihuanaco and the representations of its gods, especially the Staff God, spread all over the southern Andean zone.

In typical Andean fashion, Tihuanaco extended its political control through colonies as far away as Chile and the eastern Andean slopes in order to ensure access to fish, coca, and tropical plants, the products of different ecological zones. Huari may have begun as a colony of Tihuanaco, but it eventually exercised wide influence over much of the north Andean zone. The period of its control was short, but the urban area of Huari eventually covered more than 6 square miles, and its influence was spread by a system of roads.

Figure 8.6 *At the plain of Nazca, on the southern Peruvian coast, mysterious geometric designs and the shapes of animals, such as this spider, were traced on the ground. The purpose of these shapes, which can be seen only from the air, remains unknown.*

The intermediate horizon, represented by Tihuanaco and Huari, came to an end in the 9th century C.E., about the same time as the end of the classic period in Mesoamerica. Whether these two processes were connected remains unknown. With the decline of these expansive cultures in Peru, another period of regional development followed as different peoples, especially those along the coast, tried to establish control over their neighbors. The **Chimu state** on the north coast eventually controlled more than 600 miles of the coastal zone.

The Chimu state, founded about 800 C.E., was still expanding when it fell to the Incas in 1465. During this period other small states had formed. In the highlands various ethnic groups were struggling for control of their neighbors. One of these, a group of Quechua-speaking clans, or **ayllus,** took control of the highlands around Cuzco and began to expand, especially after 1400 C.E. These were the **Incas,** who were creating a new horizon of centralized control and cultural influence over the various ethnic and linguistic groups of the Andean world from Ecuador to Chile when the Europeans arrived in 1532.

Andean Lifeways

Although it is difficult to reconstruct much of the social and political organization of early Andean societies on the basis of archeological evidence, by using later observations from Inca times along with archeological materials we can identify some characteristic features. We have already spoken of verticality, or the control of several economic niches at different altitudes, as a principle of Andean life. This control and the related self-sufficiency sometimes were the objective of states, but they were also the goal of families and communities. Kin groups were another constant of the Andean world.

Andean peoples were divided into ethnic groups and spoke several languages, although Aymara came to predominate in the Bolivian highlands, and the Incas later spread Quechua from the central Andes to the coast and north to Ecuador. Despite ethnic and linguistic differences, communities generally were composed of households, which together recognized some form of kinship. Members of a kinship unit, or ayllu, traced their descent from a common, sometimes mythical ancestor, and they referred to other members of the ayllu as brother and sister. People usually married within their ayllu. The ayllu assigned land and access to herds and water to each household. But rights and access were not equal for every household or family within an ayllu. Ayllus often were divided into halves, which might have different functions or roles. The peoples of the highland civilizations shared this form of organization with many tribes of the Amazonian forests.

There were also community leaders who had privileges of dress and access to resources. Groups of ayllus sharing a similar dialect, customs, and dress were bound together into ethnic groups, and sometimes several of these were forged into a state. The ties of kinship were used to mobilize the community for cooperative labor and war. The ayllu was a basic organization, and kinship provided an understanding of cooperation and conflict from the village to the empire. Some authors suggest that even in the large states, conflicts were more often between ayllus or groups of ayllus than between secondary social classes.

The principle of reciprocity that lay beneath the cooperative organization of the ayllu infused Andean social life. Reciprocal obligations existed at many levels: between men and women within the family, between households within the ayllu, and between the leaders or **curacas**, who were expected to represent the interests of the ayllu. Eventually, in theory at least, reciprocity also existed between communities and a large state such as Huari, which in return for labor and tribute was expected to provide access to goods or to mobilize large projects, such as irrigation or terracing, that would benefit the community. Reciprocity also underlay religious belief. Andean peoples lived in a world where sacred spirits and powers, or **huacas**, were apparent in caves, mountains, rocks, rivers, and other natural phenomena. Worship of the huacas and of the mummies of ancestors (which were also considered holy and part of Andean religious life), at least from the Nazca period, was a matter of reciprocal exchange as well.

GLOBAL CONNECTIONS: American Civilizations and the World

There are striking parallels in the cultural development and the chronology of the two major areas of civilization in the Americas. This may be a result of convergence—that is, people in different places often work out similar solutions to the same problems—but there also seems to have been a great deal of contact between these regions over a long period of time. Much of this contact probably was indirect, funneled through the intermediate areas of Colombia and Panama where large-scale chiefdoms based on intensive cultivation flourished. Their societies were hierarchical, and their crafts, especially metallurgy, were highly developed and widely traded. South American gold artifacts turn up in offerings at Mayan shrines in Yucatan. Through such intermediate societies, contact between Mesoamerica and the Andean world may have been made. There are other examples of cultural spread and contact. The ritual ball game that was played for sport and worship on special courts throughout Mesoamerica and the Maya area has been found as far away as the American Southwest and even among the peoples of the Caribbean islands.

American Indian peoples and civilizations shared much, but there were differences as well. The Peruvian cultures developed metallurgy to a greater degree than other cultures in the Americas and eventually produced bronze tools. The puna supported herds of llamas and permitted a form of pastoralism unknown in Mesoamerica. Unlike the Maya, the ancient peoples of the Andes never invented a writing system. Still, in many ways the civilizations of the Americas had more in common with each other than with those of the Old World, and that fact probably indicates their shared origins and their contacts over thousands of years.

It should be clear that there is much we do not know about the history of the Western Hemisphere. The long history of civilization in the New World, the strength of Indian languages, traditions, and beliefs, and the crops of the Americas domesticated by the ancestors of the Indians all affected the history of these continents, but in terms of global connections, the Americas remained relatively isolated from the developments in the rest of the world after the arrival and dispersion of the Paleo-Indians. The long isolation of the Americas from the populations, and therefore from the diseases, of the Old World and the inability of the Americas to share in the technological advances of the Old World proved disastrous after the first contact with Europeans. Ultimately, however, the resilience of Indian cultures shaped the societies of the Americas in many ways.

Further Readings

An excellent, up-to-date survey of the early history of the Americas is Stuart Fiedel's *Prehistory of the Americas* (1987). Also extremely useful for its information and its excellent maps is Michael Coe et al., *Atlas of Ancient America* (1986).

On the early history of Peru, Richard L. Burger, *Chavin and the Origins of Andean Civilization* (1992) is a good starting point while Edward P. Lanning's *Peru before the Incas* (1967), despite its age, is a classic sensitive to the geography and ecology of the Andean region. Nigel Davies' *The Ancient Kingdoms of Mexico* (1983) offers a broad overview that combines archeology, art history, and history.

One of the best books on the Maya is Norman Hammond's *Ancient Maya Civilization* (1982). Well illustrated and well written, this book covers the major aspects of classic Maya culture and is especially good on the calendar system. An excellent short survey is Michael D. Coe's *The Maya*, 4th ed. (1987). Mary Ellen Miller, *Maya Art and Architecture* (1999) provides an excellent survey. On deciphering the Maya glyphs and the new history they are revealing, see Linda Schele and David Freidel, *A Forest of Kings: The Untold Story of the Ancient Maya* (New York, 1990). A popular interpretation of the advances in the field is seen in David Drew, *The Lost Chronicles of the Maya Kings* (1999).

Two good introductions to the ancient cultures of North America are Robert Silverberg, *Mound Builders of Ancient America* (1968), and George G. Gumerman, ed., *The Anasazi in a Changing Environment* (1988). George S. Stuart's *America's Ancient Cities* (1988) uses a good text and excellent photos to emphasize the continuity between the peoples of North America and Mesoamerica.

A fine example of a scholarly monograph that demonstrates that exciting discoveries about the ancient Americas do not all center on great cities and lost civilizations is Anna C. Roosevelt's *Parmana: Prehistoric Maize and Manioc Subsistence Along the Amazon and Orinoco* (1980). This scientific study shows how archeologists are probing questions such as the origins and spread of agriculture. Finally, the *Cambridge History of Native Peoples of the Americas*, 3 vols. in 6 parts (1996-2000) is the best general history available.

On the Web

Web sites offer virtual visits to Teotihuacan (http://www.wsu.edu/~dee/CIVAMRCA/TEO.HTM), Tenochtitlan (http://www.taisei.co.jp/cg_e/ancient_world/azteca/aazteca.html), Monte Alban, (http://www. sfu. ca/archaeology/museum/laarch/tour/monte/monte1.html), the Inca center of Machu Picchu, (http://www.machupicchu.org/library/ http://www.ucalgary.ca/applied_history/tutor/eurvoya/inca.html), the Hopewell Amerindian site (http://www.nps.gov/hocu/museum.htm), and the cliff dwellings of the Anasazi (http://www.co.blm.gov/ahc/index.htm).

The Maya are the subject of several excellent Web sites that offer a virtual visit to their capital at Chichen Itza (http://www.mysteriousplaces.com/mayan/TourEntrance.html), illuminate their solar calendar (http://www.mayacalendar.com/mayacalendar.html), (http://www.civilization.ca/civil/maya/mmc06eng.html), and even offer an animated look at a Mayan ball player and the continuing controversy over the nature and purpose of this Mayan sport (http://www.ballgame.org/main.asp and http://www.maya-art-books.org/html/BALLlec.html).

Virtual visits to mound-builder cultures worldwide (http://www.worldclass.net/TeachingGlobally/AncientWorld/MOUND%20BUILDERS.htm), in North America (http://medicine.wustl.edu/~mckinney/cahokia/cahokia.html and http://www.adena.com/adena/ad/ad01.htm), in Northern Europe (http://www.stonepages.com/Scotland/Scotland.html), and in Japan (http://fischer.jinkan.kyoto-u.ac.jp/soramitsu/kofun.html) reveal both unique and universal elements of early civilizations.

CHAPTER 9

THE SPREAD OF CIVILIZATIONS AND THE MOVEMENT OF PEOPLES

This 18th-century painting shows Kazak nomads bringing tribute horses to the emperor of China. Such tribute payments often were used by nomadic peoples to acknowledge their subordination to or alliances with strong dynasties in the civilized core regions, such as China. But splendid presents also were given by kings and emperors to nomad leaders. These exchanges of gifts also were used, particularly by the Chinese, to establish broader, more regular trading relationships.

The prows of great Polynesian outrigger canoes cutting through the waves of the vast Pacific Ocean to reach uninhabited islands, or hardened central Asian archers, able to guide their mounts only using their knees, sweeping their foes before them as they migrate in search of plunder and new pastures, are images of the great movements of peoples that throughout history have shaped the cultures of the world. Sometimes such movements have been a way of life as nomadic herders or hunters have followed the cycles of the seasons to care for their animals or follow the game. In other cases, the movements have been great migrations over tremendous distances bringing peoples and their cultures to new lands, and as conquerors, transforming the societies that they encountered. The encounter between the centers of civilization and the nomads or the clash between the great migratory waves and the settled societies has been as important in the diffusion of civilization among the world's peoples as was the spread of influence from the centers like Egypt, Rome, or Teotihuacan.

We have concentrated thus far on the centers of civilization and their internal developments in the classical societies of the Old World and the emerging civilizations in the Americas. In this chapter we explore the connections between the established centers and the rest of the world's peoples. The major civilizations have been expansive, and their innovations and cultures have influenced their neighbors and sometimes peoples who lived far away. Although scholars still debate the issue, many believe that important early breakthroughs, such as agriculture, the domestication of animals, pottery, and metallurgy, were not repeatedly reinvented across the globe but rather were spread by contacts and migration. For example, agriculture may have been "invented" more than once, but most people learned about it by contact with those who already practiced it.

How do cultures spread? At times, as with Rome, conquest has been the means of imposing ideas, language, and institutions. Roman culture and law were carried to the far ends of the empire by the conquering Roman legions. In other places, long-distance traders have carried ideas as well as goods. The ship, the caravan, and the sword have thus been instruments of cultural spread.

The history of Rome after the empire was invaded demonstrates another possibility, for it is not always conquerors who spread their culture; sometimes it is the conquered. In late Rome, as in pre-Columbian Mesoamerica and China, the "barbarian" conquerors of a civilization absorbed its culture and adopted its ways. The result was a new fusion of cultural elements. In other places, trade or missionary activity has spread civilization. In this chapter, for example, our discussion of early Japanese society will demonstrate

7000 B.C.E.	1000 B.C.E.	500 B.C.E.	1 C.E.	500 C.E.	1000 C.E.
7000–3000 Desiccation of the Sahara **c. 5000** Early migrations and settlement of Japan **3200** Unification of Upper and Lower Egypt **3000–2000** Jomon culture **3000–1000** Spread of agriculture south of the Sahara **2000 ff.** Germanic peoples settle in Scandinavia (present-day Denmark) **1500–500** Beginnings of Polynesian migrations; Lapita pottery found in Fiji, Tonga, Samoa **1500–300** Horses introduced to Africa by way of Egypt	**1000 ff.** Germans spread through Germany, displacing Celts **800 B.C.E.–1000 C.E.** Migration of Bantu speakers throughout sub-Saharan Africa **7th–3rd centuries** Scythian state in southern Russia **750–666** Kings of Meroë rule Egypt **600 B.C.E.–1000 C.E.** Iron diffused throughout Africa **600** Legendary Emperor Jimmu establishes state in Japan	**100** Germans in southern Germany, on Roman borders	**c. 55–112** Tacitus writes about Germans **100 ff.** Improvements in German political organization, rise of local kings, movement of some Germans into Roman Empire **100 ff.** Increasing movement of Slavs into eastern Europe **100** Rise of kingdom of Axum **100–200** Camels introduced from Asia **300** Meroë declines **300–400** Yamato clan establishes imperial control **300–700** Conversion to Christianity of Nubian kingdoms in Axum **300–1000** Polynesian migrations; settlement of Hawaii and Easter Island **4th century** Germans pressed by Huns **401 ff.** Larger Germanic invasions of Roman Empire **400** Chinese script introduced	**580s** Buddhism adopted **679** Bulgars (Turkic people) migrate to Balkans, become largely Slavicized, set up first Slavic kingdom in Balkans **700–800** Islam sweeps across North Africa **800–1100** Growth of the trans-Sahara trade for gold **900** New Zealand settled **985** Conversion to Islam of king of Gao	**1000** Ghana at height of its power **1076** Ghana conquered by Almoravids **1100–1300** Series of voyages from Hawaii to Tahiti

the peaceful spread of Chinese culture and its transformation in Japan, a process in which Buddhism played a major role.

In this chapter we shall examine five areas of the world—sub-Saharan Africa, central Asia, northern Europe, Japan, and the Pacific islands—which at the time their cultures took shape were not civilization centers. Nevertheless, the peoples of these areas were influenced by developments or innovations in those centers or, in the case of the Pacific islands, by earlier cultural developments on the Asian mainland. Central Asia provides its own special case, as a seedbed for major nomadic societies that interacted with civilizations through trade, migration, and invasion. In each case, we will also see how ideas, techniques, and material objects were adapted to new environments and different social circumstances so that the spread of civilization and the contact of cultures usually was a creative process, not simply a matter of copying.

It may at first seem strange to discuss peoples as different as the Polynesians, the Germanic tribes, the Slavs, the Japanese, and the early sub-Saharan Africans together. But the processes of migration, cultural spread, and cultural development are the basis for our discussion. Moreover, unlike earlier chapters, in which the chronological limits have been fairly precise, our discussion here ranges more broadly over time because the pace and rhythm of cultural spread varied greatly in these widely separated parts of the world.

The story of how these peoples began to develop their distinctive cultures, often in contact with centers of civilization, should be our focus, rather than a limited time frame. Finally, this chapter also introduces some peoples whose role in world history later became particularly important.

The Spread of Civilization in Africa

 Africa, the continent where earliest humans developed and the home of Egypt's remarkable civilization, experienced climatic changes such as the drying of the Sahara between 2500 and 2300 B.C.E., and foreign influences such as the introduction of the horse around 1000 B.C.E. and of iron around 500 B.C.E., which set in motion a series of cultural changes. The migration of Bantu-speaking peoples from west Africa across the continent often was accompanied by the introduction of iron and agriculture. Kingdoms such as Axum in Ethiopia and Ghana in the western Sudan represented the growth of African civilizations.

Africa is a vast continent, almost 12 million square miles, or about three times the size of the United States. Most of it lies in the tropics, and although we often think of Africa in terms of its rain forests, less than 10 percent of the continent is covered by tropical forests. Much of the African surface is covered by savannas, or open grasslands, and by arid plains and deserts. Large rivers—the Congo, the Nile, the Zambezi, and the Niger—begin in the interior of the continent and flow to the sea over great falls and cataracts that mark the passage from plateau to coast. These falls have historically made movement from the coast to the interior difficult, but the great river systems have also provided the African interior with communication routes.

Africa was the scene of human beginnings. Even before the appearance of *Homo sapiens* (the ancestors of modern human beings) about 300,000 years ago, other hominid species, such as *Homo erectus*, had moved outward from Africa to Asia and Europe. In Chapter 2 we discussed the remarkable civilization of Egypt in the Nile valley and its extension to the upper Nile kingdoms of Kush and Ethiopia. In this chapter, we will examine the spread of elements of civilization to other areas of Africa.

Despite the false image of Africa as the dark and isolated continent, it was often in contact with other areas of the world. Technology, crops, ideas, and material goods from Asia and Europe stimulated social and cultural innovations. Moreover, the contacts were not always in one direction; there is much evidence that not only early humans but also certain languages, crops, and political and cultural influences spread outward to Europe and Asia from Africa.

Climatic change altered the appearance of the African continent and seems to have set a whole series of historical processes in motion. That change centers on the **Sahara,** which during the Late Stone Age (6000 B.C.E. to 500 B.C.E.) received 10 to 50 times as much rain as it does today (Map 9.1). Archeological evidence indicates that several peoples inhabited the area of the Sahara during this period, including the ancestors of the modern-day Berbers and Tuaregs of north Africa, who speak languages related to ancient Egyptian, and the ancestors of the Negro peoples of sub-Saharan Africa, some of whom also spoke these Afro-Asiatic languages and others of whom did not. About 9000 years ago, these conditions began to change as temperatures in the Sahara rose and rainfall became erratic. By about 3000 B.C.E., much of the area was desert. This process continues today (Figure 9.1).

As the Sahara became less habitable, the populations moved north toward the Mediterranean coast and south into the area of the dry **sahel,** or fringe, and especially onto the grassy savannas suitable for agriculture and grazing that stretch across Africa from the mouth of the Senegal River on the west coast to Lake Chad and the upper Nile valley. This broad region, the Sudan, became a center of cultural development after about 300 B.C.E. The movement of peoples into the Sudan and toward the Nile valley and the Mediterranean set the stage for major developments in the later history of Africa.

Agriculture, Livestock, and Iron

Agriculture may have developed independently in Africa, but many scholars believe that the spread of

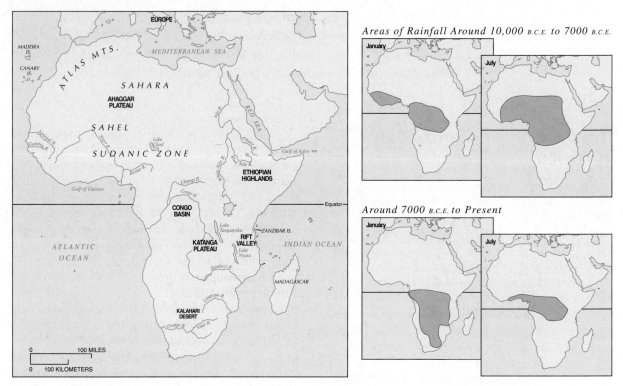

Map 9.1   *Africa: Variations in Climate*

agriculture and iron throughout Africa is evidence of the continent's links to centers of civilization in the Near East and the Mediterranean world. The drying of the Sahara had pushed many peoples to the south into sub-Saharan Africa. These were the ancestors of the Negro peoples. They settled at first in scattered hunting-and-gathering bands, although fishers lived near lakes and rivers. Agriculture seems to have reached these peoples from the Near East because the first domesticated crops were millet and sorghum, whose origins are not African but west Asian. The route of agricultural distribution may have gone through Egypt or Ethiopia, which long had contacts across the Red Sea with the Arabian peninsula. There is evidence of agriculture before 3000 B.C.E. Also, in Africa, unlike other areas, herding may have preceded cultivation. These developments may be the result of climatic change, a long wet period from 12,000 to 7500 years ago when north Africa received much more moisture than before.

Once the idea of planting spread, Africans began to develop their own crops, such as certain varieties of rice, and continued to be receptive to new imports. African crops were domesticated in a band that extends from Ethiopia across the southern Sudan to west Africa. Later, other crops such as bananas were introduced from southeast Asia, and in the 16th century C.E. American crops, such as maize and manioc, spread throughout Africa.

Livestock also came from outside Africa. Cattle, goats, and domestic sheep were introduced from Asia. Horses apparently were introduced to Africa from west Asia by the Hyksos invaders of Egypt (1780–1560 B.C.E.) and then spread across the Sudan to west Africa. Rock paintings in the Sahara show the use of horses and chariots to traverse the desert, and by 300–200 B.C.E. trade routes extended across the desert. Horses became the symbol of kingly authority and a basis of military power in some states that developed large cavalry regiments. One observer claimed that in the 14th century B.C.E. the later west African empire of Mali could field 10,000 riders. The obvious power and utility of the horse might have led to even wider use, but as with other new technolo-

Figure 9.1 *Although an obstacle, the Sahara could be traversed, especially after the camel was introduced, and an active trade developed between black Africa and the Mediterranean world.*

gies and cultural elements, the physical environment was a limiting factor. The horse was widely adopted in the west African grasslands, but in humid tropical forests and brush where the **tsetse fly** thrived, raising livestock became almost impossible. The tsetse fly carried "sleeping sickness," or trypanosomiasis, to which horses, cattle, and humans are susceptible. Cavalry campaigns were impossible in the rainy season, when the range of the flies increased. This tiny but tenacious foe brought African cavalries to a halt.

Environment created both limits and opportunities, but the balance between them was sometimes changed by new elements. The introduction of the camel from Asia about the 1st century C.E. was an important innovation. Its ability to thrive in harsh desert conditions and to carry large loads cheaply made it an effective and efficient means of transportation. The camel transformed the desert from a barrier into a still difficult but more accessible route of trade and communication.

Livestock provided a living to peoples in the arid portions of the savanna belt and the Sahara and allowed a **transhumant,** or seasonally moving, way of life to flourish in certain inhospitable regions. In some areas, it appears that livestock and agriculture arrived about the same time.

Ironworking also came from west Asia, although by routes somewhat different from those of agricul-ture. In most of Africa, societies moved directly from a technology of stone to iron without passing through the intermediate stage of copper or bronze, although some early copperworking sites have been found in west Africa. Iron had been worked in the Near East and Anatolia for at least a thousand years before it began to penetrate into sub-Saharan Africa. The Phoenicians carried the knowledge of iron smelting to their colonies, such as Carthage in north Africa, by the 8th century B.C.E., and from there to their trading ports along the coast of Morocco. By sea down the coast or by land across the Sahara, this knowledge penetrated into the forests and savannas of west Africa during the last millennium B.C.E., or at roughly the same time that ironmaking was reach-ing western Europe. Evidence of ironmaking has been found in Nigeria, Ghana, and Mali, and iron implements seem to have slowly replaced stone ones at several sites.

This technological shift caused profound changes in the complexity of African societies. Iron repre-sented power. In west Africa, the blacksmith who made tools and weapons had an important place in society, often with special religious powers and func-tions. Those who knew the secrets of ironmaking gained ritual and sometimes political power.

Ironmaking seems to have traveled from the Red Sea into Ethiopia and east Africa and down the Nile

Document

Myths of Origin

Legends and myths have long fascinated anthropologists, literary scholars, and folklorists because they offer an opportunity to see how various peoples have explained the universe and themselves within it. Noted French anthropologist Claude Lévi-Strauss believed that all myths were built around certain basic structures of human thought and that those structures could be revealed by the comparative study of myths. He also argued that for some cultures, such as those of South American Indians, myths with their essentially recurring structures were the primary means of explaining life, while in other cultures, such as those of western Europe and China, a sense of change and history came to predominate in these explanations. Recent scholarship has begun to question the separation of myth and history and has begun to look at the possible historical context and content of myths.

In this chapter, we have examined several peoples whose origins are shrouded in mystery and about whom many questions remain unanswered. The following excerpts provide these peoples' explanations of their own origins or those of their world.

A Bantu Myth of Migration

A series of origin epics and tales among the Luba peoples, who lived in central Africa to the east of the Kongo kingdom, were collected in the 20th century. The concept of splitting off from an existing village and settling in new territory is part of many African origin myths.

> In the country of the east, on the right bank of the Lualaba River, there once was a man and a woman. Their names mean respectively "he who builds many houses," and "she who makes much pottery." They lived in ignorance of each other. Guided by the sound of chopping, the man discovered the woman, who was preparing firewood. They lived for a long time under the same roof, sleeping in separate beds. The copulation of a pair of jackals gave them the idea of sleeping together. They brought forth twins of opposite sex, who became inseparable companions. One day the twins found a locality that was exceptionally rich in fish. They finally obtained permission from their parents to leave the village and devote themselves entirely to fishing. In their turn, they brought forth twins, who lived in the same incestuous manner, far from their parents. This new generation took up trapping. So pairs of twins, moving each generation a little farther westward, populated the country.

Source: Luc de Heusch, *The Drunken King or the Origin of the State* (Bloomington: Indiana University Press, 1982), pp. 11–12.

A Germanic Myth: The Birth of the Gods

This tale from the rich Norse mythology deals with the birth of the gods. Drawn from the songs and sagas of the Germanic peoples, these stories were part of an oral literature until about the 12th century, when they were committed to writing.

> In the beginning of the ages there lived a cow, whose breath was sweet and whose milk was bitter. The cow was called Audhumla and she lived by herself in a frosty, misty plain, where there was nothing to be seen but heaps of snow and ice. A giant named Ymir came out of the dark north and lay down on the ice near Audhumla. "You must let me drink of your milk," said the giant to the cow; and though her milk was bitter, he liked it well. The cow saw a few grains of salt sprinkled over the ice, so she licked the salt and breathed with her sweet breath. Then long golden locks rose out of the ice, and the southern day shone on them, making them bright and glittering. The giant frowned but the cow continued to lick the salt, and after three licks an entire man arose—a hero strong and beautiful.
>
> When the giant looked full in the face of that beautiful man, he hated him with all his heart and he took a terrible oath that he would never cease fighting until either he or Bur, the hero, should lie dead on the ground. He kept this vow.
>
> Afterwards when the sons of the hero began to grow up, the giant and his sons fought against them too, and were very near conquering them many times. There was one of the sons of these heroes, called Odin, who after many combats did at last slay the great old giant Ymir, and pierced his body with a keen spear. The blood poured forth in a torrent and drowned all the hideous brood, except for one who fled.
>
> After this, Odin gathered around him his sons, brothers, and cousins and spoke to them thus:
>
> "Heroes, we have won a great victory; our enemies are dead, or have fled. We cannot stay any longer here where there is nothing evil for us to fight against." The heroes looked around them at the words of Odin. They spoke out with one voice, "It is well spoken, Odin; we will follow you."

"Southward," answered Odin, "heat lies, and north-ward night. From the dim east the sun begins his journey westward home."

"Westward home!" they shouted all.

Odin rode in the midst of them, and they all paid to him reverence and homage as to a king and father. On his right hand rode Thor, Odin's strong, warlike, eldest son. On his left hand rode Baldur, the most beautiful of his children. After him came Tyr, the Brave; the silent Vidar; and many more mighty lords and heroes; and then came a shell chariot, in which sat Frigga, the wife of Odin, with all her daughters, friends, and maids.

Source: Adapted from A. and E. Keary, *The Heroes of Asgard: Tales from Scandinavian Mythology* (New York: Macmillan, 1909), pp. 1–4.

The Birth of Japan

According to Japanese legend, the Lord of Heaven sent two young gods, Izanagi and his consort, Izanami, to subdue chaos and create beauty after the earth had been created. Descending on a carriage of clouds, Izanagi took the divine spear given to him by the Lord of Heaven and, stirring the fog, created a beautiful island in the midst of the sea. But the island was too small for goodness to grow. Izanagi and Izanami were married and built a shrine.

When Izanagi and his wife came out of the shrine, they stood transfixed. Before them stretched the long, curving shore of a vast island, and on the far horizon were the shapes of others. In great joy the two set out to view their new domains. From island to island they went, marveling at each new land; and when they had traveled them all, they found that there were eight, and to them they gave these names in the order of their birth; first the island of Shikoku, followed by Kyushu, Oki and Sado which [each] were born as twins, Tsushima, and finally Iki. Together they were called the country of the eight great islands, and as time passed they became known as Japan.

More and more islands appeared, and every day Izanagi traveled the land and sea watching over them. Sometimes Izanami went with him, but serving in the shrine took much of her time and she found the long journeys exhausting.

"My dear husband, there is nothing I wish to do more than to live here with you in peace and contentment. But now that so many islands have been born I pray that we too may bear children for our help and delight."

Her prayers were answered and in the years that fol-lowed many children were born to them. The first was the Sea Spirit, the next a Mountain Spirit, and then in suc-cession, the spirits of fields, trees, rivers, and all natural things. Under their care and guidance the islands grew more and more verdant and beautiful. Soon the seasons were born, and the breaths of the winds and rains brought their changing cycles to the mountains and fields. Every-where the forests grew thick and dense, and in the groves flocks of birds gathered and sang. Crops and harvests multiplied and flowers and bushes bloomed in profusion.

Izanagi and his wife lived in utmost contentment among their family, and when a daughter was born to them, who was the goddess of the Sun, their joy was unbounded. She was the most beautiful and radiant being.... Everywhere she went she filled the darkest air with light and brilliance. Her they named Amaterasu.

Source: Helen and William McAlpine, *Japanese Tales and Legends* (London: Oxford University Press, 1958), pp. 13–14.

A Polynesian Creation Story

In this tale from Tahiti, Tangaroa, the ancestor of all the gods and the creator of Havaiki, the birthplace of the land, the gods, and chiefs, and humanity, creates the world. This version of the story was collected in Tahiti in 1822.

For a long time Tangaroa lived within his shell. It was round like an egg and in the lasting darkness it revolved in the void. There was no sun, there was no moon, there was no land nor mountain, all was moving in the void. There was no man, no fowl, no dog, no living thing; there was no water, salt or fresh.

At the end of a great time Tangaroa flicked his shell, and it cracked and fell apart. Then, Tangaroa stepped forth and stood upon that shell and called:

"Who is above there? Who is below there?"

No voice replied. He called again:

"Who is in front there? Who is behind there?"

Still no voice answered. Only Tangaroa's voice was heard; there was no other.

Then Tangaroa said, "O rock, crawl here!"

But no rock was to crawl to him.

He therefore said, "O sand, crawl here!"

There was no sand to crawl to him. And Tangaroa became angry because he was not obeyed. He therefore overturned his shell and raised it up to form a dome for the sky, and he named it Rumia, that is, Overturned.

After a time great Tangaroa, wearied from confine-ment, stepped out from another shell that covered him; and he took this shell for rock and sand. But his anger was not finished, and so he took his backbone for a mountain range and his ribs for the ridges that ascend. He took his innards for the broad floating clouds and his flesh for the fatness of the earth, and his arms and legs for the strength of the earth....Of his feathers he made trees and shrubs and plants to clothe the land.

And the blood of Tangaroa became hot, and it floated away to make the redness of the sky, and also rainbows. All that is red is made from Tangaroa's blood.

Tangaroa called forth gods. It was only later that he called forth man [people], when Tu was with him.

(continued)

As Tangaroa had shells, so everything has a shell. The sky is a shell, which is endless space, where the gods placed the sun, the moon, the constellations, and the other stars.

The land is a shell to the stones and the water, and to the plants that spring from it. The shell of a man is woman, since it is from her that he comes forth. And a woman's shell is woman, since it is from here that she comes forth.

No one can name the shells of all the things that are in the world.

Source: Anthony Alpers, *Legends of the South Seas* (New York: Thomas Crowell, 1970), pp. 51–54.

Questions: Do myths seem to encode history, or are they an alternative way to explain the past? What are the roles of men and women in the myths recorded here and what do they indicate about these early societies? Do the origin myths of the civilizations, such as China, Greece, and Rome, differ greatly from those recorded here?

from Egypt into the Sudan, where large African states such as Meroë were in close contact with dynastic Egypt. By the 1st century C.E., iron was known in sub-Saharan Africa, and within about a thousand years, it had reached the southern end of the continent. Iron tools and weapons increased the efficiency of both agriculture and war. In the later stages of this story, after about 1200 C.E., the adoption of agriculture and the use of iron tools and weapons were roughly simultaneous.

Unlike the peoples of the Americas, for whom metallurgy was a very late and limited development, Africans had iron from an early date, developing ingenious furnaces to produce the high heat (1100 degrees Fahrenheit) needed for production. The **Nok** culture, which flourished in northern Nigeria from around 800 B.C.E. to 200 C.E., was characterized by the use of iron as well as impressive sculptures. It was probably the cultural tradition on which later artistic traditions in that region drew. Bronzeworking was also known to Africans, and by 1000 C.E. remarkably lifelike bronze sculptures were cast at the city-state of Ife in Nigeria by the **Yoruba** people (see Figure 9.2). Ife became a kind of cultural and ritual capital in the region, a recognition of its historical importance and cultural leadership.

The Bantu Dispersal

The spread of agriculture and later of iron was accompanied by a great movement of people, who may have carried these innovations. These **Bantu** peoples probably originated in eastern Nigeria in west Africa. Their migration may have been set in motion by an increase in population caused by a movement into their homelands of peoples fleeing the drying of the Sahara (Map 9.2). They spoke proto-Bantu (*Bantu* means "the people"), which is the parent

Figure 9.2 *Remarkable bronze figures were cast at Ife (Nigeria) by Yoruba artisans.*

tongue of many related languages still spoken throughout sub-Saharan Africa. In fact, about 90 percent of the languages south of a line from the Bight of Benin on the west coast to Somalia on the east coast are part of the Bantu family.

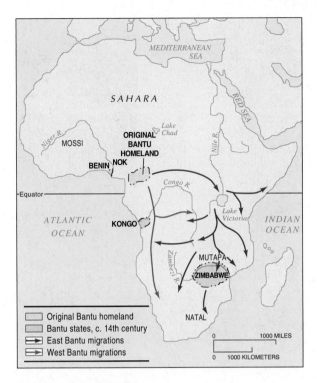

Map 9.2 *Bantu Migrations*

Why and how these peoples spread out into central and southern Africa remains a mystery, but archeologists believe that at some stages their iron weapons allowed them to conquer hunting-and-gathering societies, which still used stone implements. Still, the process is uncertain, and peaceful migration—or simply rapid demographic growth—may have also caused the Bantu expansion.

The migrations moved first to the central Sudan and then into the forests of west and central Africa. The rivers, especially the Congo basin, provided the means of movement; the migration was long, gradual, and intermittent. Moving outward from central Africa, Bantu peoples arrived at the east coast, where they met cattle-raising peoples of a different linguistic tradition. By the 12th century, the Bantu speakers pushed south of the Zambezi River into modern Zimbabwe and eventually into south Africa.

From the study of the related Bantu languages, it is possible to learn something about the original culture of the proto-Bantu speakers. The early Bantu depended on agriculture and fishing. They grew sorghum and raised goats and perhaps cattle. They were village dwellers who organized their societies

around kinship ties. Leadership of the villages probably was in the hands of a council of elders. The spirits of the natural world played a large role in the lives of these peoples. They looked to their ancestors to help deal with those spirits, and they depended on village religious specialists to deal with calamity and to combat witchcraft, which they feared greatly.

People's lives and societies changed during the course of the migrations. Long-distance trade in pottery, metals, canoes, and crafts developed in some regions. In many places ritual forms of kingship reinforced by elaborate ceremonies replaced older systems of authority based on age or kinship. Cultural life flourished in forms as diverse as great oral epics, polyphonic music, and sophisticated wood sculpture. These societies gave birth to wisdom, too. Consider this poem of the Yoruba peoples of Nigeria about children:

> A child is like a rare bird.
>
> A child is like precious coral
>
> A child is precious like brass.
>
> You cannot buy a child on the market.
>
> Not for all the money in the world.
>
> The child you can buy for money is a slave....
>
> A child is the beginning and end of happiness.
>
> One must not rejoice too soon over a child.
>
> Only the one who is buried by his child,
>
> Is the one who has truly born a child.

Source: The Horizon History of Africa (American Heritage Publishers, 1971), p. 206.

In about a thousand years the Bantu-speaking peoples expanded over much of the continent, spreading their languages and cultures among the existing populations, absorbing those original peoples and being absorbed by them. By the 13th century C.E., cattle-raising, iron-using Bantu peoples had approached the southern end of the continent. Winter rains prevented sorghum from growing beyond that point, and their progress stopped. Earlier inhabitants, the Khoisan speakers, remained farther to the south. By that time, Africa's major features were in place. A few purely hunting peoples remained, such as the **Pygmies** of central Africa, but their way of life was different from that of most Africans. Agricultural and herding societies with ironworking knowledge could be found throughout sub-Saharan Africa. Although pockets of peoples still speaking non-Bantu languages existed, such as the Khoi-Khoi and San of southern

Africa, and in east Africa the influence of Ethiopian culture was still strong, Bantu languages predominated in southern and central Africa and marked the trail of one of the world's great migrations.

Africa, Civilization, and the Wider World

The development of Egyptian civilization paralleled developments in the Fertile Crescent, but many aspects of Egyptian life, such as ideas about religion and kingship, strongly resembled those of other African societies. There is much debate on whether the Egyptian idea of the king as a divine being with special powers over natural phenomena (an idea also found in some west African kingdoms) came from the common origins of both or whether these concepts spread from Egypt to other areas of Africa. There are other striking parallels, such as brother-sister marriage among rulers and certain rituals when a ruler takes office, that seem to tie the cultures of sub-Saharan Africa to Egypt. Whatever the African origins of Egyptian civilization, there is no doubt of extensive contact between Egypt and peoples living southward along the Nile valley in the Sudan and northern Ethiopia.

Axum: A Christian Kingdom   We discussed the Egyptian contacts with Kush in Chapter 2 and the fact that the Kushites and their capitals were influenced by Egyptian culture. For a short period, from 751 B.C.E. until the invasion of Egypt by the Assyrians in 666 B.C.E., the kings of Meroë also ruled as pharaohs of Egypt. Meroë had the ores and fuels needed to produce iron on a large scale. That technology, and its extensive trade with Egypt and the Mediterranean, allowed Meroë to flourish. But Meroë was not alone. Other town-based societies also existed in the region of the Sudan and Ethiopia.

The kingdom of Axum in the Ethiopian highlands, which eventually surpassed Meroë in importance around the 1st century C.E., introduces another cultural stream into the history of Africa. Axum seems to have received strong influences and perhaps settlers from the Arabian peninsula (Figure 9.3). Its population probably consisted of a mixture of these immigrants and peoples from Eritrea and the Ethiopian highlands. Axum became a great city with large palaces and monuments. It developed a writing system based on a south Arabian script. Ge'ez, the language of the people of Axum, is a Semitic language, but Axum's rulers also spoke Greek and perhaps used it as a language of trade.

Figure 9.3 *Axum, a large state in the Ethiopian highlands, received cultural influences from Arabia and traded widely in the Indian Ocean. Its capital contained large buildings and monuments such as this 70-foot-high, solid granite obelisk.*

Axum was a powerful state. It controlled several ports, such as Adulis along the Red Sea coast, and it participated in the commerce of the Indian Ocean, where its ivory, salt, and slaves were in great demand. It also traded with Alexandrian Egypt and eventually with Rome, Byzantium, and India. Those contacts led to a fusion of cultural elements. By about 200 C.E., Axum was involved in military and political affairs across the Red Sea on the Arabian peninsula. By the mid-3rd century C.E., Axum had defeated Meroë and emerged as the dominant power in the horn of Africa. The history of Axum underlines the cross-fertilization of cultures across the Red Sea.

About 350 C.E., Ezana, the king of Axum, converted to Christianity, and that religion spread among Axum's peoples over the following centuries. Monasteries and churches were established, the Bible was translated, and a religious literature was developed that linked the Queen of Sheba, wife of the biblical King Solomon, to Axum and demonstrated the area's supposed progression from Judaism to Christianity. All this established a certain religious legitimacy to the negus, or ruler, of Axum. The form of Christianity that spread among the Axumites during the 5th and 6th centuries C.E. increased the kingdom's ties to the Greeks of the eastern Mediterranean, although eventually Ethiopian Christianity became somewhat isolated.

All this indicates considerable influence and contact between this African kingdom and the outside world well before the arrival of Islam. The civilization of Axum became the basis for much of the distinctive culture of Christian Ethiopia in the centuries that followed. Here, as along the Mediterranean coast of Africa, where Phoenician, Greek, and Roman settlements were established, or up the Nile valley, the ideas, techniques, and material goods from the Mediterranean and western Asia mixed with African peoples and practices.

An area of grassy savanna extends across the Sudan into west Africa, and the defeated leaders of Meroë apparently moved westward into the Sudan and reestablished themselves at Darfur and Kordofan in the 4th century C.E. Their influence may have extended even farther west. Several accounts and myths associated with royal families and ancient kingdoms in west Africa point to Egypt, Arabia, and even Persia as the original home of the founders. But in west Africa, there is also evidence of long-term contact with the Mediterranean world directly across the Sahara. These long-distance external influences were paralleled by an extended period of internal development among the peoples of west Africa such as the Yoruba, Mande, and Fulbe.

Golden Ghana: A Trading State   The peoples of the savanna took advantage of their location to serve as intermediaries between the southern gold-producing forest zone in the region of the Niger and Senegal river valleys and the markets of north Africa. Trading salt for gold to the peoples of the forest and then sending the gold north along established caravan routes that crossed the Sahara, several states like Gao and Ghana took form before the 8th century C.E. as intermediaries in the trans-Sahara trade (Map 9.3).

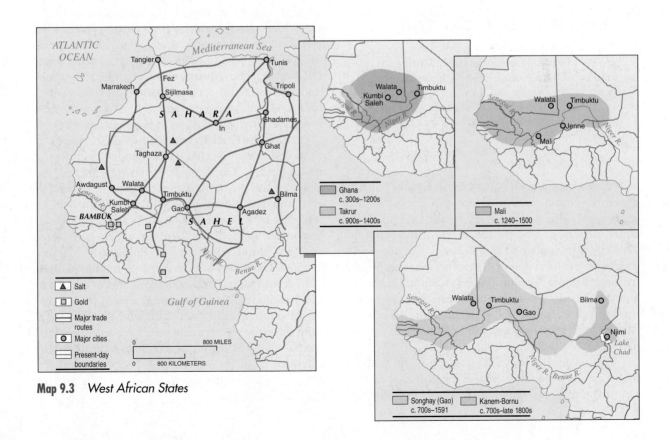

Map 9.3   *West African States*

The trans-Sahara commerce was the basis for the growth of the empire of **Ghana,** which lay squarely on the trade route. This was a trading state created by the west African Soninke peoples. Early Arab chroniclers wrote that in Ghana, 20 kings had ruled before the time of Muhammad, which was a way of saying that the kingdom was an ancient one. When Arab visitors began to write about Ghana and other **Sudanic states** in the 9th century C.E., these states were already well-established kingdoms. Their position was a result of their advantageous geographic position and a joint heritage of internal development and external influences and trade. The external influences increased with the arrival of Islam. In 985 C.E., the king of Gao converted to Islam and set in motion a series of conversions among the elite of the west African states. Conversion of the masses proceeded more slowly.

The ancient kingdom of Ghana (not to be confused with the modern nation of Ghana) lay mostly within the boundaries of the present-day Republic of Mali. It traded for salt, cloth, and manufactured goods from north Africa and the Mediterranean in return for gold. Ghana's power depended on its location and control over subject states and provinces, especially gold-producing regions in the forest zones to the south. In 1067 C.E., al-Bakri, a scholar from Muslim Spain, described Ghana's splendor and power.

> The Court of Appeals is held in a domed pavilion around which stand ten horses covered with gold-embroidered materials. Behind the king stand ten pages holding shields and swords decorated with gold and on his right are the sons of vassal kings of his country wearing splendid garments and their hair plaited with gold.
>
> *Source: The Horizon History of Africa* (American Heritage Publishers, 1971) p. 182.

At that time, the capital of Ghana, **Kumbi Saleh,** appears to have been divided into two cities about 6 miles apart. One was occupied by the king and his court, surrounded by the dwellings of the people. This city also contained buildings for worship and shrines to the local deities. The other was inhabited by long-distance Muslim traders, religious leaders, and scholars. Its mosques and houses were built in the style of the mud-walled architecture of north Africa. Together, the population of these cities may have reached 20,000.

Tax revenues from the gold and salt trades increased the kingdom's wealth. Historian al-Bakri reported that Ghana could field an army of 200,000 men. Even if we allow for exaggeration, it should be noted that the Normans invaded England at about this time with fewer than 5000 men. Al-Bakri's account describes the existence of a powerful and well-organized kingdom dominated by the royal family and a group of elite retainers, whose strength rested on control of the trade and on the tribute collected from neighboring peoples.

The image of Ghana in contemporary Arab sources was one of fabled wealth. The account of al-Bakri stated that the king had a monopoly on all gold nuggets found, but the people could gather as much gold dust as they wanted for trade. His description of a royal audience noted that doors of the chamber were guarded by "dogs of excellent breed, who never leave the king's seat; they wear collars of gold and silver, ornamented with the same metals." The king was known as Kaya-Maghan, or "the king of Gold."

Although a certain amount of fantasy was mixed in these accounts, Ghana obviously was a powerful kingdom. Its influence eventually spread into the Sahara, and major trading towns were brought under its control. The Berber and Tuareg tribes of the Sahara had converted to Islam in the 7th century, and by the 11th century a new movement, whose followers were called the Almoravids, had begun to sweep across the western desert, Morocco, and Spain. One branch of this movement, under Abu Bakr ibn Umar (d. 1087), launched a series of campaigns in the western Sudan. The **Almoravids** controlled the gold trade across the Sahara and began to move toward its sources. Ghana was conquered in 1076, and a new fusion of Sudanic and Saharan peoples took place.

Although Ghana continued to exist, its power was weakened, and other states emerged to challenge its leadership. The growth of Islam weakened the kingdom and may have deepened division between its elite and the common people. Former provinces broke away, and a period of political instability and fragmentation followed, during which new states emerged among the Soninke, Fulbe, and Malinke peoples. The power of Ghana ended, but its tradition of trade and military power and the fusion of African and Islamic traditions continued among the successor states. Eventually, a new kingdom, **Mali**, emerged from this struggle. In many ways Mali was the heir to the power in the region, and it ruled a territory that extended from the bend of the Niger River to the Atlantic coast, which included much of the ancient kingdom of Ghana.

In Depth

Language as a Historical Source

Historians constantly search for new ways to understand the past. For much of the early history of the world we must depend on the archeological record. Cultures leave their traces not only in pottery, weapons, temples, and mummies but also in language, written or not. Language is a guide to the thought patterns of a people and to their society and institutions. Moreover, language is a guide to its speakers' historical relationships to others. The development of historical linguistics has greatly furthered our understanding of the past and has provided a set of theories and techniques that have become indispensable aids to the study of both preliterate and literate societies. The Bantu migration is a case in point.

The early study of languages was motivated by a recognition of the close relationship between thought and language and the relationship between the structure of thought and language and the overall culture of a people. Early students of language, such as the French thinker Condillac, who wrote in the mid-18th century, believed that "each language expresses the character of the people that speak it." However, linguistic insights sometimes were influenced by cultural bias. Some later linguists shared the opinion of the learned Wilhelm von Humboldt, who wrote in his essay "On Language" (1836) that some languages were "more perfect" and better suited to the "mental cultivation of mankind." Not surprisingly, he believed that the Indo-European languages like his own German best fit that definition. By the 20th century the early work of people such as von Humboldt had laid the foundation for the modern study of historical linguistics.

The great migration of the Indo-European peoples from central Asia into India and western Europe, the movement of the Bantu peoples throughout southern Africa, and the spread of the Polynesians across the Pacific are among the world's greatest migrations. Much of what can be said in all three cases—and in the study of the early settlement of the Americas—is based on a study of the vocabulary, structure, and spread of languages.

The study of language as a historical record is based on some fundamental ideas. Languages change over time, as any reading of Chaucer or Shakespeare immediately reveals. As they change they may diverge from related languages. Languages with strong similarities in structure and vocabulary that cannot be explained by borrowing or contacts are considered to be part of the same family, and it is assumed that sometime in the past an original language was the parent of all the languages in that family. As groups of people separated, their language changed and diverged. Further separation resulted in further divergence, so that over time a large number of related languages could result from the original language. The proto-Indo-European language was the parent of Sanskrit, Persian, and Latin, but Latin later split into French, Italian, Rumanian, Portuguese, and other related languages. By looking at structural and vocabulary similarities, we can establish linguistic subgroups and their relationship to each other as well as to the parent language. The study of the 300 to 600 (experts disagree) Bantu languages spoken today by more than 400 million people across much of the African continent is a case in point. From the comparative study of their vocabulary we can tell much about their original cultures, but how can language be used to chart their history?

It can be assumed that the more diversity between languages, the more time has elapsed since their separation from each other. For a while, some linguists thought that if they could establish the rate at which linguistic changes took place, they could calculate the time that had elapsed since one language and its speakers had separated from another. On the basis of 100 or 200 basic words, they attempted to calculate the percentage of change or loss from one language to another. This technique, called glottochronology, is no longer popular because it is clear that languages do not change at a constant rate of speed, and such change depends on many factors. Still, rates of change in written languages can be studied, and when used in conjunction with archeology, language can provide further historical evidence.

It is simple enough to see that the similarity of words in languages (barring random coincidence or words borrowed directly from a foreign language) can indicate a common origin. *Mother* in English, *mater* in Latin, and *mata* in Hindi all point to their common Indo-European origin. The word for *eye* in Tahiti was *mata*, in Hawaii, *maka*, and among the New Zealand Maori, *mata*; these similarities point to their common heritage as Polynesian languages. Despite the similar sounds involved in these two sets, the meanings indicate that we are dealing with two different language families.

(continued)

Although historical linguistics has developed various methods for establishing these relationships, explaining the divergence or the reason for the separation of the peoples that speak the languages is another story. Without the help of archeology, oral traditions, or written records, historical linguistics cannot describe the course of change.

The study of languages can tell us much about the values, social structure, and material life of peoples in the past. A language with 12 adjectives to describe the color of the sea between the speaker and the horizon, or another language that has 20 ways of describing the color of a llama's coat, indicates the importance of those things to the people involved. A language that has no word for private property or nobility probably lacked those concepts. The grammar and pronunciation of a language can be independent of the physical world of its speakers, but the vocabulary cannot. It reflects what people knew and thought about. It can be assumed that if all the languages that split off from a parent tongue have the same word for iron, dog, cattle, or canoe, then the original speakers must have had these things. This kind of reasoning lies behind much of what we can say about the early Polynesians, the Bantu, and the Indo-Europeans. For example, by studying the distribution of words in various Polynesian languages, linguists have argued that even though we do not know the original home of the Polynesians, the original speakers of the parent language were inhabitants of some mountainous tropical island or islands in the western Pacific islands, and they grew taro, yams, bananas, and sugar cane before their expansion and dispersal.

Putting the linguistic evidence together with the historical record is challenging. When that record is available, as in the case of Aztec and Roman expansion, we can see that language change and spread sometimes are the result of intentional policy rather than undirected change.

Historical linguistics also concerns itself with variations and subdivisions within languages, or dialects, and with their geographic distribution. What is the difference between a dialect and a language? Linguists argue on this point, but some unknown skeptic once said, "A language is a dialect with an army behind it." That comment should focus our attention on the social and historical reasons for the predominance of some languages. It also underlines the necessary relationship between linguistics and other methods of knowing the past as tools that should be used together whenever possible.

Questions: In what ways are language and literacy expressions of social or political power? What are some ways in which changes in our own language indicate broad historical changes? Is there a problem in using language as historical evidence because spoken language often differs from written language?

Nomadic Societies and Indo-European Migrations

 As agriculture had developed in several key centers, herding economies, relying on domesticated animals, took shape in other areas including central Asia. Some of these peoples later pushed into Europe. Beyond the boundaries of the Hellenistic kingdoms in the Middle East and southern Europe, and to the north of the expanding Roman Empire, lived a mixture of peoples mostly of Indo-European origin. The major groups included Celts, Germans, and Slavs, all of whom developed some agriculture by the classical period. Political organization in northern Europe developed some significant features but—outside of Rome's boundaries—lagged behind the kingdoms of sub-Saharan Africa.

In the vast expanse of territory that stretched from the steppes of the Ukraine across the center of Asia to the northern borders of China lived a variety of nomadic, herding peoples whose way of life revolved around their animals. These were peoples who practiced pastoralism, moving their herds seasonally, and living in close relation to their animals (Figure 9.4). Whether these **pastoral nomads** tended camels in the Sahara, or reindeer on the tundra of northern Russia, or sheep and horses in central Asia, their way of life had many similarities. They tended to live in small groups of clansmen that could come together as tribes, migrating year after year in regular patterns to feed and water their flocks or herds, influenced by climate, rainfall, and distance. Wealth and status were often directly measured by the size and quality of the herd or by military prowess, for the nomadic way of life was hard and it placed great value on the virtues of courage and strength. These were

Figure 9.4 *The seasonal journey in progress for these horse-riding, cattle-herding nomads fording a small river in present-day Iran was an annual occurrence for peoples who followed a pastoral way of life. As grasses, and often water, for the nomads' herds dried up in the heat of the summer months, they had to pack up all of their possessions and set off with their herds on difficult, and sometimes dangerous, migrations to riverine or hilly areas where food and water could be found. In the early spring, they would return to the plains, where the grasses had recovered and there was ample fodder for the domesticated animals around which they organized their lives.*

societies that jealously guarded their pastures or water holes but made hospitality a virtue, a necessity for travelers in the vast expenses of the deserts or plains where the nomads lived. The loyalties of extended families were essential, and the ability to lead often combined a dynamic or charismatic personality, per-

sonal courage, and the support of kinsmen. Women often had more varied roles than was true in the settled civilizations, including service in marketing goods. The arts of the nomads often made use of the products of their herds or flocks—woolen carpets, leather tents, tools made of horn—and incorporated their animals in their decorative designs.

Nomadic peoples had long lived in a relation of both attraction and rejection with the centers of civilization. They raided the sedentary populations of towns and villages, drawn by their surplus food and richer material culture, but were sometimes also employed by the settled societies that sought to exploit the military prowess of the nomads. Nomads also facilitated long-distance trade, including the traffic along the silk roads from western China to the Middle East. The civilizations of China, Byzantium, Persia, and Rome all lived in a close and ambiguous relation with the nomads on their borders. Sometimes the nomads captured or destroyed empires and civilizations and created their own successor states, as the Hyksos did in Egypt in the 2nd millennium B.C.E. or the Aryans did in India in the 1st millennium B.C.E. But, while the nomads could conquer the centers of civilization as the Mongols, Hittites, and Turks were later to do, they usually had to adopt the institutions, social arrangements, and economic practices of the settled peoples whose accomplishments in technology, science, or the arts usually outstripped what the nomads with their more limited resources and populations could do. Most of history has been lived and made by the sedentary agrarian peoples and the city dwellers they supported, but the dynamic interplay with the nomads has often affected the course of civilized history and sometimes dominated it.

While various peoples like the Turks and Mongols lived this way of life, the first nomadic peoples about whom we know a good deal are the Indo-European tribes of the mid-2nd millennium B.C.E. For more than a thousand years thereafter, these horse nomads threatened the early civilizations of the Middle East and the Indus plains. Some Indo-European peoples, such as the Hittites and Hyksos, also established their own empires and centers of civilization, while others, such as the early Greeks, settled in the lands to which they migrated. As late as the last centuries B.C.E., these settled groups still struggled to fight off the incursions of later Indo-European migrants such as the Scythians, who invaded Europe

Visualizing the Past

Varieties of Human Adaptation and the Potential for Civilization

Perhaps the best way to understand and compare various human adaptations to environmental conditions is to relate them to the two extreme types of adaptation that ecologists call the *niche* and the *holding* patterns. In the first instance, the human group works its way into the environment in which it lives rather than transforming that environment. Like the plants and animals with which they share a particular ecosystem, these peoples simply occupy one of many niches available in the overall ecosystem. Their activities have a minimal impact on the other niches or the life forms that occupy them. In the most extreme manifestations of the niche pattern, exhibited by rainforest peoples of Central and South America, southeast Asia, and Africa, small human groups, *forest farmers*, hunt game and gather fruits and vegetables in the jungle without altering the forest environment. These peoples move continuously through large areas of the forest, ingeniously tapping the many sources of plant and animal food.

Before the Industrial Revolution, *sedentary wet-rice agriculture*, which depended on elaborate irrigation systems, was the most developed form of the holding approach to ecological adaptation. Peoples who practice this approach extensively transform the natural environments in which they live. Wet-rice farmers, for example, clear forests, haul away stones, and plow grasses and weeds to prepare large tracts of land for cultivation. They dig ditches to carry water to the rice fields, which are surrounded by dikes to hold the water in during the growing season. In addition, they clear fields and forests to support domesticated animals. Thus, the original vegetation and animal life are supplanted by domesticated plants and livestock. The domesticated plants are arranged in

patterns determined by human needs rather than natural processes. They are protected from wild animals by fences and shelters, and wild plants are removed. Areas near the rice fields are also transformed by the construction of human dwellings, shrines, and granaries, which are combined to form villages and sometimes grow into cities.

Between the niche pattern and the holding pattern, several intermediate forms of human adaptation have developed. One of the most important of these in terms of the numbers of humans supported by it is *dry farming* of grain crops such as wheat, rye, barley, and millet. Although the environment is not as extensively transformed by dry farming as by wet-rice agriculture, both involve building permanent villages, raising livestock, and building systems of food storage and transportation.

Shifting cultivation (or *slash and burn* farming), concentrated in the rain forests of both the Eastern and Western Hemispheres, is an adaptation that is much closer to the niche pattern than either form of sedentary agriculture. Shifting cultivators burn off the jungle undergrowth but leave the large trees and the cover they provide to protect the fragile tropical soils. Using the ashes created by their fires as a natural fertilizer, shifting farmers cultivate the area cleared on the forest floor. The foods grown in this manner form the staples of their diet, which are supplemented by meat, wild berries, and other forest plants. After working a particular clearing for a year or two, shifting farmers move to another patch in the forest, where they again begin the burning-cultivating sequence.

Pastoral nomadism is a second major alternative between hunting and gathering and sedentary agriculture. Although nomadic groups differ in the kinds of ani-

and Asia Minor, or the Aryans who menaced Harappan civilization in India. Another group that became important in the age of the classic civilizations were the Hsiung-nu (later known in Europe as the Huns). They devastated China beginning in the 4th century B.C.E. and then centuries later toppled the Gupta Empire in India and smashed into the crumbling Roman Empire.

The original homeland of the Indo-Europeans was probably the area of the Dnieper River north of the Black and Caspian seas. Linguistic evidence indicates that they were herders and farmers. Although they first used their horses to pull chariots and carts, eventually they became riders. By about 3000 B.C.E. Indo-European peoples had moved into Anatolia and were moving eastward toward India. From the

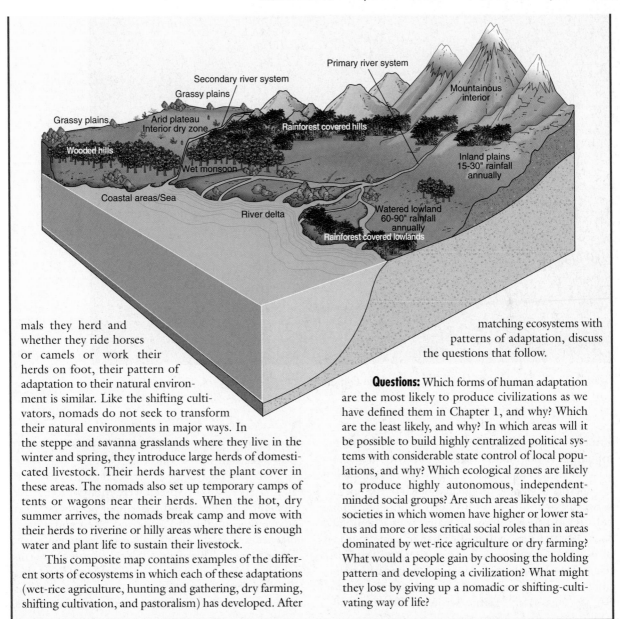

mals they herd and whether they ride horses or camels or work their herds on foot, their pattern of adaptation to their natural environment is similar. Like the shifting cultivators, nomads do not seek to transform their natural environments in major ways. In the steppe and savanna grasslands where they live in the winter and spring, they introduce large herds of domesticated livestock. Their herds harvest the plant cover in these areas. The nomads also set up temporary camps of tents or wagons near their herds. When the hot, dry summer arrives, the nomads break camp and move with their herds to riverine or hilly areas where there is enough water and plant life to sustain their livestock.

This composite map contains examples of the different sorts of ecosystems in which each of these adaptations (wet-rice agriculture, hunting and gathering, dry farming, shifting cultivation, and pastoralism) has developed. After matching ecosystems with patterns of adaptation, discuss the questions that follow.

Questions: Which forms of human adaptation are the most likely to produce civilizations as we have defined them in Chapter 1, and why? Which are the least likely, and why? In which areas will it be possible to build highly centralized political systems with considerable state control of local populations, and why? Which ecological zones are likely to produce highly autonomous, independent-minded social groups? Are such areas likely to shape societies in which women have higher or lower status and more or less critical social roles than in areas dominated by wet-rice agriculture or dry farming? What would a people gain by choosing the holding pattern and developing a civilization? What might they lose by giving up a nomadic or shifting-cultivating way of life?

ancient homeland also came the populations that occupied Europe.

The Celts and the Germans

Celtic peoples spoke an Indo-European language. The **Celts** formed Europe's first culture, which stretched from Spain northward and into the British Isles. They were organized in small regional kingdoms with fierce warrior leaders, and they mixed agricultural and hunting economies. They had no cities and no writing, and their most impressive buildings were crude stone forts and arrays of stone set up to honor the gods of nature (Figure 9.5). The Romans considered the Celtic peoples barbarians, but as Rome expanded its empire into Gaul, Spain, and

Figure 9.5 *Stonehenge, a Neolithic monument in England*

Britain, various Celtic peoples came under Roman influence. A population of Romanized Celts developed in villages and towns across western Europe.

Germanic peoples populated much of the northwestern portion of the European continent. Their culture and institutions in many ways resembled those of the Celts (whom they had in some regions displaced). Certainly, to Roman observers, the Germanic tribes north of the empire's boundaries were undistinguished barbarians, pure and simple. As the Roman historian Tacitus wrote, "Who, indeed, would leave Asia, Africa, or Italy to seek Germany, with its desert scenery, its harsh climate, its sullen manners and aspect?" He might have added "and its warlike people," for by Tacitus' time the Romans had already developed a wary respect for the German warriors.

Tacitus had other comments on the Germans, although at times he emphasized their virtues as a way of criticizing what he considered to be Rome's moral degeneracy. The strength and bravery of the German warriors impressed him. He pointed out that warriors were pledged to support their chiefs and that the chiefs led by example and tried to outdo their men in battle. The size of a chief's retinue was a mea-sure of his power and distinction, and men strove to gain a place in such a following.

Women, the elderly, and slaves did agriculture and all household tasks. Women were thought to have an element of holiness and the gift of prophecy. Their advice was sought and respected. Men and women married rather late, and usually a bride-price was paid to the woman. This included oxen, a horse, and arms, which symbolized the union of the couple and their shared responsibilities. Women were supposed to pass these gifts on to their children. Strong matrilineal ties existed, and the relationship between a man and his sisters' sons was particularly strong. The married state was respected, adultery was rare, and infanticide was not practiced. In a criticism of the Rome of his day, Tacitus said, "Good morality is more effective in Germany than good laws are elsewhere."

But Tacitus also commented on the rude material life of the Germans, their lack of cities, their simple dwellings, their lack of writing, and their constant fighting. Judgments of this sort accurately reflected the fact that the peoples of northwestern Europe had not formulated a civilization. However, they overlooked several important achievements and changes among some groups, such as the Germanic tribes, that accelerated during the final centuries of the classical era. Like the Celts, the Germanic peoples typically mixed agriculture and hunting, and they also herded cattle in a nomadic pattern. They had no cities. Among many Germans, however, agriculture steadily improved in the 1st centuries C.E. There were also marked improvements in iron use and the manufacture of cloth and other items. Some of these improvements resulted from knowledge of Roman skills, which spread beyond the empire's boundaries.

Political cohesion among some German groups improved by the 3rd and 4th centuries C.E. Like many traditionally nomadic peoples, the Germans had long been organized in decentralized tribes of a few thousand members each, and even the tribes were loosely organized, with individual family groups settling most disputes. A tribe might have a king or an assembly of warrior chiefs; in either case, vigorous discussion of any policy issue among all fighting men was essential. Group loyalty and a certain amount of political equality were important parts of this tradition and would

affect European institutions in the centuries after the classical era. After about 200 C.E., some German tribes merged into larger units as they learned to copy Roman military structure somewhat and were forced by Roman pressure to improve their organizational ability. The power of individual kings increased as they ruled large confederations of tribes. Thus, even apart from the Germans who filtered into the Roman Empire or joined its armies, integrating portions of Roman civilization directly, there were important changes in the Germanic lands during the classical era, with improvements in agriculture, trade, manufacture, and politics.

However, Germanic culture seems to have changed little outside Rome's boundaries. The German religion, like that of the Bantu, was animistic, worshiping the spirits of nature. Horses were the most common sacrifice.

The Germans made their first clear mark in world history as growing bands began to move southward into the Roman Empire, ultimately probing into Italy, Spain, and north Africa (Map 9.4). Their movement,

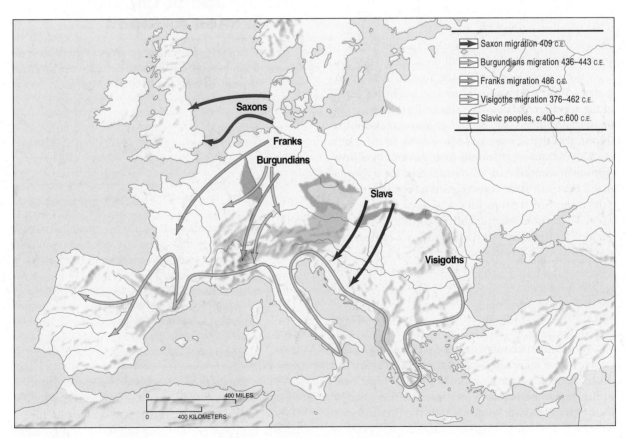

Map 9.4   *Germanic Peoples on the Move, 375–450* C.E.

the *Völkerwanderungen,* resulted from population growth in their own lands, the nomadic tradition, Rome's attractiveness and growing weakness, and invasions by Asian groups on the eastern flanks of the Germanic region. German pressure within the Roman Empire played a major role in toppling it.

Growing cohesion among some Germanic groups had an influence beyond the pressures on Rome. It helped prepare larger areas of Europe for the gradual development of civilization in the centuries after Rome's fall. This new civilization reflected many Roman legacies and a strong Christian influence, but it also built on some Germanic elements. Even as Rome fell, in fact, a new Germanic center was taking shape in Scandinavia that would have wide influence in the following centuries. Far from Roman influence, Scandinavian populations were growing, and political confederations were being formed by the 5th century. This would soon lead to invasions and trade throughout much of the Mediterranean world.

The Slavs in Eastern Europe

While developments among various Germanic peoples held the stage in northwestern Europe, a somewhat similar pattern of precivilizational advance emerged in various parts of eastern Europe, with some influence from the Hellenistic kingdoms and then the eastern portions of the Roman Empire. As early as 3000 B.C.E., agriculture had been established in the southern part of what is now Russia, spreading from the Middle East. Bronze tools were also introduced, and then a wave of Indo-European invasions, about 1000 B.C.E., brought iron. Several new invasions from central Asia followed, and a loosely organized Scythian state controlled the region from the 7th to the 3rd centuries B.C.E. The Scythians were nomadic warriors, but agriculture continued to flourish in the plain north of the Black Sea. Scythian rule was followed by an invasion by a people known as the Sarmatians, some of whose descendants live in the central Caucasus region of Russia today. Under both Scythians and Sarmatians, Greek and Persian trade and cultural influence, including artistic styles, spread into this region.

By the final centuries of the classical era, Slavic peoples were increasingly migrating into Russia and other parts of eastern Europe. Some **Slavs** had been in this region before, and the origin of these people is disputed. What is known is that the Slavic people were an Indo-European group, that they had become

increasingly noticeable in Russia and the Balkans by the time of the early Roman Empire, and that they would ultimately dominate much of eastern Europe from the Balkans northward. Slavic political organization may have been a bit less developed than Germanic, but by the 5th century C.E. some regional kingdoms had been formed, notably in Bulgaria. Agriculture and manufacturing, including skilled ironwork, gained ground steadily, and (in advance of the Germanic northwest) some trading cities had been formed.

As with the Germans to the west, it would be premature to refer to a civilization of eastern Europe beyond the Mediterranean zone at the time of Rome's fall, and the Slavic peoples were severely disrupted by invasions from central Asia as the Huns and others cut across their lands. Nevertheless, an increasingly prosperous agricultural economy and rudiments of political organization beyond the tribal level characterized parts of the Slavic world toward the end of the classical era and presaged more important developments.

The Spread of Chinese Civilization to Japan

 Although its full impact on global history has not been felt until the last century or so, the transmission of key elements in Chinese culture to the offshore islands that came to make up Japan clearly is one of the most important examples of the spread of civilization from a central core area to neighboring or overseas peoples. In the first centuries C.E., the peoples of Japan imported a wide range of ideas, techniques of production, institutional models, and material objects from the Chinese mainland. After adapting these imports to the sophisticated culture they had already developed, the Japanese used what they had borrowed from China to build a civilization of their own. New patterns of rice growing and handicraft production enhanced the economic base of the Yamato clan chieftains, who, beginning in the 3rd century C.E., extended their control over the most populous regions of the main Japanese island of Honshu.

The Japanese developed a unique civilization from a blend of their own culture and a selective importation and conscious refashioning of Chinese influences. Not conquering armies, but merchants and traveling monks—and eventually Japanese students who studied in China—were the most important agents by which elements of Chinese culture were transmitted across the sea. Especially in the early centuries of borrowing, from the 1st to the 5th centuries C.E., interchange between China and Japan was largely indirect. It was mediated by the peoples and kingdoms of Korea, who had adapted key aspects of Chinese civilization to their own cultures somewhat earlier than the Japanese.

In contrast to the Vietnamese, who were ruled by the Chinese for nearly a millennium, and the peoples of south China, who were eventually absorbed by Chinese civilization, the Japanese initiated and controlled the process of cultural borrowing from China. Despite a willingness to acknowledge the cultural superiority of the Chinese Middle Kingdom, the Japanese retained political independence throughout the centuries of intense borrowing. Consequently, they could be more selective in their adoption of Chinese ideas than most of the other peoples influenced by China.

Natural Setting and the Peopling of the Islands

The four main islands that make up the homeland of the Japanese people rise abruptly and dramatically from the Pacific Ocean along the northeast coast of Asia (Map 9.5). Formed by volcanic eruptions that still occur periodically, the islands are dominated by mountains and rugged hills. Only a small portion of their surface area is level and extensive enough for the cultivation of wet rice, which from prehistoric times has been the staple of the Japanese diet. Thus, from the time of the earliest settlements, the Japanese have occupied mainly the coastal plains, especially in the south central portions of the largest island, **Honshu,** which remain the most heavily populated areas of the islands today.

Though poor in natural resources, the islands are difficult to match in their combination of temperate climate and subtle natural beauty that instilled in the Japanese people a refined aesthetic sensibility and sensitivity to the natural world reflected in their religion,

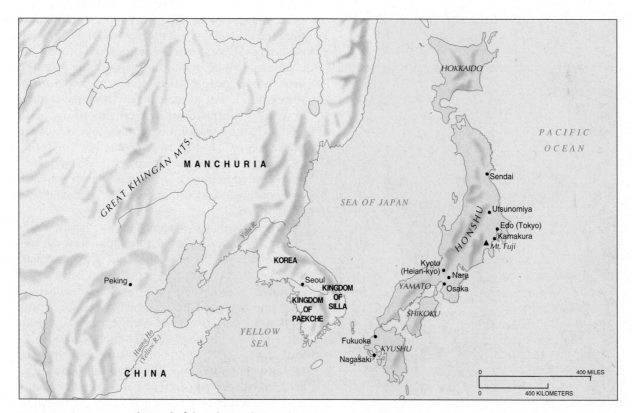

Map 9.5 *East Asia at the End of the Classical Period*

art, and architecture. At the same time, the islands' limited resource base nurtured a disciplined, hard-working population that was regulated by strict legal codes and ruled through much of the islands' history by warrior elites.

Archeological evidence suggests that as early as 5000 B.C.E., the ancestors of the Japanese people had begun to migrate to the islands. Drawn from numerous east Asian ethnic groups, the migrants came in small bands and periodically in larger waves over many centuries. One of these waves of migrants produced the **Jomon culture** in the 3rd millennium B.C.E. The Jomon were a hunting-and-gathering people who lived in pits dug in the ground. They produced a distinctive pottery whose cordlike decoration gave the people their name.

Most of the new settlers crossed to the islands from the Korean peninsula and Manchuria (Map 9.6). Because they were isolated from political upheavals and social transformations occurring on the mainland, by the first centuries C.E. the diverse migrant streams had blended into a homogenous population with a distinctive Japanese language, culture, and physical appearance. By then they had driven the Ainu, who had settled the islands before

them, into northern Honshu and Hokkaido. Over the past two millennia, the Japanese have gradually displaced or absorbed nearly all the remaining Ainu, building a strong sense of cultural and ethnic identity.

Indigenous Culture and Society

Long before Chinese cultural influences began to shape Japanese historical development, the indigenous peoples of the islands had taken significant steps toward creating a civilization of their own. In the last centuries B.C.E., migrants from the mainland introduced wet-rice agriculture and ironworking into Japan. In this period, which is known as the **Yayoi epoch,** the Japanese also produced wheel-turned pottery and very sophisticated bronzeware, including elaborately decorated bells that were sometimes 4 or 5 feet high.

Until the early 5th century C.E., most of the Japanese population was divided into hundreds of clans, each dominated by a small warrior aristocracy. The clan elites drew their support from the peasantry, which made up over 90 percent of the population of the islands. They were also served by slaves, who like their counterparts in China were only a small minority of the Japanese people. Early visitors from the mainland noted the rigid social distinctions, including different sorts of tattoos and other body markings, that separated the warrior elite from the mass of the people. They also remarked on the strong position of women in early Japanese culture, in marked contrast to their clear subordination in China. Early Japanese households appear to have been matriarchal—that is, dominated by childbearing women. Women also played key roles as shamans, who were central to Japanese religious ceremonies and worship, as leaders of some of the clans, and later as empresses.

The importance of women in early Japanese culture is also indicated by their legends about the creation of the world. The sun goddess, **Amaterasu,** played a central role, and her worship became the central element in the **Shinto** religion developed by the island peoples. Shinto devotees worshiped many gods and spirits associated with the natural world. Some of these deities were identified with objects, such as huge trees or mountains such as the famous Mount Fuji. Others were linked to animals that were believed to possess special powers. Gods and spirits were believed to be capable of doing good or evil to humans. To ensure that they brought blessings rather

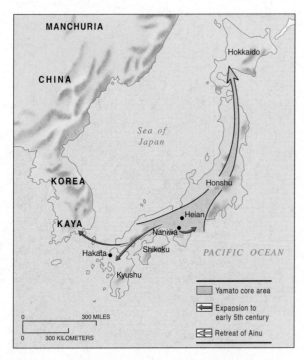

Map 9.6 *The Rise of Japanese Civilization*

CHAPTER 9 The Spread of Civilizations and the Movement of Peoples

than misfortune, the Japanese made offerings of food and prayers to the gods and nature spirits at special shrines that were built of unfinished wood and were notable for their simple lines and lack of ornamentation. They gave rise to a unique Shinto style of Japanese architecture, which persists to the present day and has had a great impact on architecture in the modern world (Figure 9.6).

In the 4th and 5th centuries C.E., when one of the clans, the **Yamato,** gained power over the others, an imperial cult developed around the sun goddess and Shinto worship. A central shrine was established at Ise near the Honshu political heartland of early Japanese history, and the priest-chief heads of the Yamato clan claimed descent from the sun goddess herself. Building on this powerful source of legitimacy, the Yamato brought most of the lowland plains of the southern islands under their control through alliances and conquest. By the late 4th century C.E., their sway also extended to southern Korea. This

overseas extension of the Yamato domains brought intensified contacts with Chinese civilization, then about to enter one of its most illustrious phases. The combination of these contacts and the Yamatos' successful campaigns to unify the Japanese people led to profound transformations in Japanese society and culture in the centuries that followed.

The Chinese Model and the Remaking of Japan

The introduction of the Chinese script in the 4th century C.E. was a major turning point in Japanese cultural development. Writing with the Chinese characters, which were adapted only with great difficulty to the Japanese language, made it possible for the Yamato to begin to build a real bureaucracy and thus more firmly establish their control over vassal clan heads and the peasantry. The use of the Chinese written language also meant that the Japanese could

Figure 9.6 *The most venerated of the Shinto shrines is that dedicated to the sun goddess, Amaterasu, at Ise in central Honshu. The thatched roof, unpainted cypress wood, simplicity of design, and beautiful forest setting in which the shrine is located are characteristics of Shinto architecture.*

learn from Chinese texts on all manner of subjects, from science and philosophy to art and religion. These works, as well as Chinese scribes to make additional copies and interpret them, were imported from the 5th century onward. Later, Japanese students and scholars who were fluent in Chinese were sent to China to acquire new learning firsthand.

From the mid-6th century, the Buddhist religion became a pivotal factor in the transmission of Chinese influence to Japan. In the period of chaos that followed the fall of the Han dynasty in the early 3rd century C.E., Buddhism was widely adopted by the distressed populace of China and the rulers of the warring kingdoms that succeeded the Han. The pervasive influence of the religion in China in this era and the powerful position of Buddhist monks at the courts of Chinese rulers gave great impetus to its spread to Korea and Japan. In the mid-6th century, a Korean ruler sent Buddhist images and scriptures as presents to the Japanese emperor and urged him to adopt the religion and convert his subjects to it. After considerable debate and even open strife among the families serving the imperial household over the advantages and dangers of introducing Buddhism into Japan, it was officially adopted as the religion of the Yamato domains in the late 580s (Figure 9.7).

From that time onward, Japanese rulers tried to propagate the new religion among their subjects. Warrior aristocrats and peasants converted to the new beliefs, but without giving up their long-standing reverence for Shinto spirits and deities. Thus, Shintoism and Buddhism developed side by side as twin pillars of state and society in Japan. The Japanese elite supported the efforts of Buddhist monks to spread their faith, and the monks in turn served as advisors to the emperor and regional lords. In their teachings of Buddhism, the monks stressed scriptural passages and Buddhist ethical prescriptions that supported rule by a strong monarch and a centralized state.

Although converts from aristocratic Japanese families studied the complex beliefs of Buddhist philosophy and practiced its highly developed meditation techniques, to the illiterate mass of the Japanese people Buddhism was little more than a magical cult. Buddhist monks provided colorful rituals that enriched the peasants' monotonous lives and charms to ward off sickness or evil spirits, but the common people knew little of Buddhist teachings beyond highly mythologized versions of the Buddha's life.

Figure 9.7 *The critical role of Buddhism in transmitting key elements of Chinese civilization to Japan is strikingly illustrated by early Buddhist monasteries and temples such as this one at Nara. Comparison with the Shinto shrine at Ise underscores the contrast between the sparse indigenous art and architectural styles and the more ornate Buddhist structures that were modeled on Chinese prototypes.*

Political and Social Change

Beginning in the early 7th century, the Yamato rulers styled themselves the "emperors of the rising sun" in official letters to (one imagines) the somewhat dismayed Chinese "emperors of the setting sun." Inspired by Chinese examples, they established councils and government departments and tried to introduce genuine bureaucratic control at the local level. At **Nara** and later **Heian,** the Japanese emperors laid out courts and capital cities patterned after the ancient imperial centers of China. The Yamato rulers strove to build a peasant conscript army and impose legal codes and a landholding system similar to those in China.

In the centuries after the introduction of Buddhism, Chinese influences were felt in virtually all spheres of Japanese society. Alongside the traditional warrior elite, a class of monks and scholars developed that for several centuries exercised power at the imperial court. Trade with China and Korea and improved communication within Japan enriched existing merchant groups and led to their emergence as a distinct class. New tools and techniques imported from the mainland increased the output of Japanese farmers and made possible a great expansion of the islands' previously marginal mining industry.

The introduction into Japan of the patriarchal and patrilineal family, which had long been dominant in China, presented a major challenge to traditional Japanese approaches to gender roles and relationships. For several centuries, the position of women within the family remained strong, and the ideal of wives and lovers who were accomplished in literature and the arts was preserved by the courtly elites at the imperial capitals of Nara and Heian. But the adoption of Chinese law codes eroded the control that Japanese women had over their own children and eventually reduced their overall social status. These changes were reflected in the spread of polygamy among the Japanese aristocracy. From the early 9th century, the changes were even more evident in the elite's refusal to allow women from the imperial family to rule in their own right, as they had periodically in the early centuries of Japanese history. Japanese women, like those in China and India, were increasingly subordinated to their fathers and husbands. As in China and India, entry into religious orders or successful careers as courtesans were nearly the only alternatives to careers as subordinated wives and mothers.

Chinese Influence and Japanese Resistance

Contacts with China and innovations based on the Chinese model were pushed, from the 4th century C.E. onward, by those at the top of Japanese society. Japanese rulers and their chief advisors were motivated mainly by the desire to increase the power of the state to control the warrior nobles and to extract resources from the peasantry. Buddhist ethics and Confucian legal codes enhanced the rulers' legitimacy, Chinese rituals gave a new dignity and luster to court routines, and the growth of a Chinese-style bureaucracy provided the means for creating the first genuine state in Japanese history. Because the Japanese remained politically independent from China, their rulers could convincingly argue that the adoption of Chinese ways was voluntary and carefully controlled. Only imports that would strengthen the Japanese state or contribute to the well-being of the Japanese populace need be accepted. Chinese ideas and institutions could be reworked to suit conditions in Japan and fit the needs of the Japanese people. Selective borrowing from their ancient and advanced Chinese neighbors, the innovators argued, allowed the Japanese to become fully civilized without destroying their own culture and identity.

Because Japanese rulers lacked the resources of the Chinese emperors and worked with a society that differed greatly in scale and organization, many of their efforts to imitate Chinese patterns failed. The bloated bureaucracies that resulted from the imitation of China were a growing burden for the peasants who had to support them. Efforts to establish local control and reorganize landholding along Chinese lines foundered because of the opposition of regional lords and their retainers. The warrior elite also frustrated the attempt to make soldiers of the peasantry. Conscripts in Japan in this era were little more than forced laborers. Many of the imported Chinese legal injunctions bore little relation to social conditions in Japan and were not enforced. The impressive capital cities laid out by the emperors' architects remained half-built and underpopulated, even at the height of the early dynasties' power.

Japan could not simply be made in China's image. From the outset, the introduction of writing, Buddhism, and other imports from China had given rise to concerns about preserving Japan's own culture. At times, as in the 580s and the mid-7th century, controversy over foreign influences became a central element in violent struggles between the aristocratic families closest to the throne. But until the 8th century each struggle was won by the forces favoring continuing imports from abroad and the further transformation of Japan along Chinese lines.

The Scattered Societies of Polynesia

 Peoples from Asia migrated across the vast expanse of the Pacific, occupying many of the islands. Masters of navigation, they adapted to a variety of environments. On the island groups of Polynesia, such as Hawaii and New Zealand, these peoples created complex societies based on agriculture and maritime resources, mostly in isolation from the rest of humankind.

The peoples of the far Pacific who had left the Asian mainland before the rise of classical China and India were unaffected by the spread of Chinese and Indian civilization. They had brought with them the cultural features of late Neolithic Asia, and in isolation they had developed these features on the islands of the vast Pacific.

Certainly one of the great epics of human achievement for which we have only fragmentary evidence is the peopling of the islands of the Pacific Ocean. The distance across the Pacific from southeast Asia to Central America is some 12,000 miles, and the waters of that ocean are dotted with thousands of islands (Map 9.7). These islands vary in size from tiny atolls formed by coral reefs, to large "high" islands with volcanic peaks and lush valleys, to the great continent of Australia. Most of these islands lie in the tropics, although some, like New Zealand, do not. They are inhabited by a variety of peoples whose physical appearance, language, and culture are quite different but whose origins for the most part seem to be in Asia.

The remarkable story of the Polynesians can serve as a case study of the spread of culture by long-distance maritime migration in the Pacific. Here we are not dealing with the spread from a great center of civilization but with the migration of peoples and their adaptation to new challenges in isolation.

Between roughly 1500 B.C.E. and 1000 C.E., almost all the major islands west of New Guinea were visited, and many were settled, by the ancestors of the peoples we call Polynesians. They left no written records, so we must depend on the evidence of archeology and linguistics, their own oral traditions, and the observations of Europeans who first contacted them to reconstruct the history of their societies (Figure 9.8).

Linguistic evidence is a starting point. The Polynesians speak about 30 related languages from a family of languages called **Austronesian,** which is also found in the Philippines, Indonesia, and southeast Asia. The Austronesians were clearly peoples from Asia, but they were not the first migrants in the Pacific. By the time of their expansion about 4000 years ago, New Guinea and Australia had already long been settled (probably since 38,000 B.C.E.) by dark-skinned peoples who spoke languages unrelated to Austronesian. New DNA analyses may provide other clues. Recent studies indicate that the pre-Chinese peoples of Taiwan are the closest relatives to the Polynesian peoples of New Zealand.

The Great Migration

Groups of these Austronesians, speaking a language ancestral to the Polynesian languages, began to

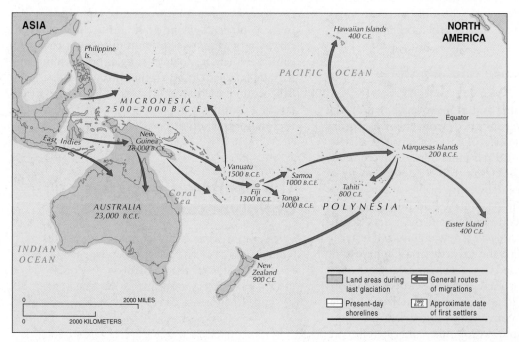

Map 9.7 *The Spread of Polynesian Peoples*

Figure 9.8 *Large double-hulled Polynesian canoes were used for the long voyages of discovery that sometimes covered over a thousand miles. The Polynesian mariners were great navigators who explored the far reaches of the Pacific Ocean.*

expand eastward from Melanesia to Fiji, Tonga, and Samoa. By the time of this expansion, these people practiced agriculture, growing yams, taro (a tuber), and other crops; raised dogs, pigs, and chickens; and had already developed a variety of complex fishing techniques. Archeologists can identify their scattered settlements by a distinctive type of pottery called *Lapita*, with stamped decorations, and by polished stone adzes, fishhooks, and other implements.

From Tonga and Samoa these peoples began to spread eastward to **Polynesia** proper. Polynesia includes the islands contained in a rough imaginary triangle whose points lie at Hawaii to the north, New Zealand to the south, and Easter Island far to the east. Another group of these peoples seems to have moved westward, eventually settling on the island of Madagascar off the African coast.

On the widely dispersed islands of the Pacific, each culture and language began to adapt and evolve differently and thus to diverge from the ancestral Polynesian forms. Some constants in the shared heritage of the ancestral Polynesian culture remained, however. For example, in the 18th century, English explorer Captain James Cook was surprised to find that the words he had learned from the Tahitians were understandable to the Hawaiians, although almost 2500 miles separated those two island groups. Also, a Tahitian named Tupia served Captain Cook effectively as a translator when he contacted the **Maori** of New Zealand.

Basic principles of economy and social organization could also be found throughout Polynesia, especially on the larger islands. From small groups of original colonists, island populations grew in size and density. By the late 18th century, the island populations totaled 700,000. Although potterymaking was abandoned or forgotten, in many places agriculture became increasingly complex and intensive. Stratified societies with powerful chiefdoms based on lineage characterized many Polynesian islands, and in some places, such as Hawaii, they became extremely hierarchical. Chiefs were able to mobilize their followers for ceremonial and public architecture, or for wars and interisland raiding. Ritual and religion oriented many aspects of life and served as the basis of the chiefs' power.

The Voyagers of the Pacific

How did these ancient Polynesians discover and occupy the islands of the vast Pacific? The Polynesians knew how to make a variety of seaworthy vessels, but for long-distance voyaging, they used great double canoes, or **pahi.** These vessels usually carried a platform between the two hulls on which shelter could be given to people, animals, and plants. With large triangular sails, these vessels, some of which were 60 to 100 feet long, were capable of long voyages at sea and could travel more than 120 miles a day in good weather. They could sail windward, against the winds and tides of the Pacific, which tend to move from east to west.

Naturally, navigation was a problem. Some scholars have held that the voyages were accidental—boats were blown off course, which led to the occupation of new islands—but Polynesian traditions and the continuing ability of some Pacific islanders to navigate long distances by observing the stars, wave patterns, and other techniques support the idea that voyages of colonization were planned. Moreover, sometimes they were two-way. For example,

Hawaiian traditions commemorate the arrival of Tahitian chiefs who made voyages to and from Hawaii for about 200 years (1100–1300 C.E.). In 1976, to establish the possibility of such voyaging, the Hokulé, a reconstructed double canoe based on traditional proportions and using only traditional navigational techniques, was sailed from Hawaii to Tahiti in about 35 days. In the main, however, much of the voyaging seems to have been sporadic, as groups pushed by war, population pressure, famine, or a spirit of exploration followed a chief or navigator into the unknown. In the 18th century, when the Europeans arrived, such long-range voyaging was rarely practiced. By that time, however, the Polynesians had explored and colonized almost every habitable island in the vast Pacific.

Ancient Hawaii

We can use the widely separated large islands, New Zealand and Hawaii, as examples of Polynesian societies that developed in isolation in response to particular environmental conditions. Hawaii includes eight major islands in a chain about 300 miles long. The volcanic nature of the islands and the tropical climate created an environment of great beauty and majesty that impressed the early inhabitants. The islands probably were settled in at least two migratory waves beginning about 300 C.E. There, early Polynesian culture was adapted and elaborated in isolation over a long period of time. The islands had good soil, and the population grew large, reaching about 200,000 people by the time of European contact in the 1700s. Towns and cities were absent, and houses, here as elsewhere in Polynesia, were scattered along the coast and in valleys leading to the higher interior. A number of chiefly families competed for control of the islands. It was not until after European contact that **King Kamehameha I** united all the islands under his control in 1810.

Of all the Polynesian societies, Hawaii became the most hierarchical. The high chiefs, or **ali'i,** claimed descent from the gods. In some cases, marriage to their sisters ensured the purity of the chiefly family. Their power, authority, and sacredness, or **mana,** came from their lineages and enabled them to extract labor or tribute from their subjects or even take their land. Feathered capes and helmets as well as tattoos distinguished the chiefs. The ali'i were revered and feared. A Hawaiian proverb held that "The chief is a shark that swims on land." A class of lesser nobility and subchiefs of their relatives supported the rule of the ali'i.

Society rested on the commoners. Hawaiian society was intensely agricultural, and the community's control of land was a central aspect of social and political relations. Within the hierarchy, commoners were viewed almost as a separate people or at least as a people lacking in lineage. Their lives were constrained and limited by a complex set of **kapu** (*tapu* in Tahiti), or taboo, which forbade certain activities and regulated social discourse. It was kapu for women to eat certain foods, to enter the house of a chief, to eat together with men, to view certain ceremonies limited to the chiefs, or even to cast a shadow on a chief. Violations could lead to death. The number of kapu surrounding a chief was a measure of his status and his sanctity, as much a sign of his position in his society as material goods might be in our society.

Many aspects of life were ritualized. The many gods were honored at ceremonial centers whose precincts were sacred. Ritual feasting and hula, or dancing, accompanied many ceremonies. Human and other sacrifices were offered to Ku, the god of war, and to the other deities. Lono, the god of fertility and agricultural rebirth, held special importance to the Hawaiians. The great Makahiki festival of thanksgiving, which lasted for four months and at which the chiefs received their tribute from the commoners, was celebrated in honor of the annual return of Lono. During this time war was kapu, hulas were danced, and sexual activity was engaged in frequently in the hope of stimulating fertility. In fact, lovemaking was an art and a preoccupation of the Hawaiians, with important religious, kinship, and political meanings.

Of the various Polynesian societies, Hawaii can be seen as the most successful in terms of its political and social complexity, economic foundations, art and material culture, and religion. With a Neolithic technology, the Hawaiians created a complex culture on their islands. Although they lacked a written language, their legends and oral histories, which could trace the genealogies of chiefly families back to the original canoes of the first migrants, were remarkable achievements that formed and preserved their culture.

The New Zealand Landfall and the Development of Maori Culture

Perhaps as early as the 8th century C.E., the crews of canoes or rafts from the Society Islands and other parts of eastern Polynesia had sailed thousands of miles to the southwest and by chance discovered the two large islands that today make up New Zealand. Over the centuries additional bands of seafarers reached the islands, where they embarked on a struggle to survive in an environment that was colder and harsher than their home islands in Polynesia. Their success is evidenced by the large numbers of **Maori**—perhaps as many as 200,000 people descended from the Polynesian seafarers—who lived in the islands when the Europeans first came to stay in the late 18th century.

The "land of the long white clouds," as the Polynesians referred to the mist-covered islands of New Zealand, had few edible plants beyond berries and fern roots. There were no native land mammals except bats and various kinds of **moa,** or large, wingless birds, soon overhunted to extinction. Fishing and the introduction by later migrants of many of the staple crops of Polynesia, including the sweet potato, taro, and yam, filled the dietary gap left by the disappearance of the moa.

The moderate climate and rich soils of the north island rendered it more suitable for settlement than the cold and desolate south island, which stretched beneath the 40th parallel toward the South Pole. Consequently, Maori tribes numbering in the thousands warred over control of the forests and croplands on the north island. Long before the arrival of the Europeans, tribal territories with clearly defined boundaries had been established throughout most of the north island.

Maori Culture and Society   Each Maori tribe was divided into subgroups called **hapu,** the primary unit of identity and community. The Maori lived in extended families in large, elaborately carved wooden houses. All the land the Maori farmed for their subsistence was owned by the hapu village and allotted by a communal council to each of the extended families for their support.

Each hapu was led by a male chief, who was not a specialized political leader but rather a particularly skillful warrior. Chieftainships were hereditary, although weak leaders were soon displaced by more able warriors. Despite the magical aura associated with the hapu and tribal chieftains, their actual power was limited by village and tribal councils made up of the free men of a given group. Virtually all hapu communities also included slaves, usually prisoners of war or their descendants.

Although they had a strong voice within the family, women were clearly subordinated to men. Male dominance was evidenced by the monopoly they enjoyed with regard to positions of leadership and to highly prestigious activities such as making war and woodcarving.

Maori society could not support full-time specialists, but many kinds of religious and craft experts were recognized. Priests were of several kinds, varying according to social status and functions. The most esteemed were the chiefs, who were also trained as priests. The chief-priest presided over communal ceremonies and knew the special prayers to protect the tribe or hapu. The Maori world was alive with spirits, gods, and goddesses who intervened constantly in human affairs. At the other end of the social scale were shamans, who specialized in healing and served as the mediums by which gods and spirits made their desires known to humans.

A War-Oriented Society   In addition to priests, Maori society had a wide variety of experts, ranging from those who built canoes, to woodcarvers, and tattoo specialists. The most important experts, however, were those with skills relating to making war. Maori society was obsessed with war. During the appropriate season, tribes and hapus fought regularly with their neighbors or distant confederations. Young men proved their worth as warriors, and leaders could not long maintain their positions without demonstrating their martial prowess. Much of the time and energy of Maori men was devoted to planning campaigns against neighboring tribes or building the intricate hilltop fortresses found throughout the north island. Although the loss of life in Maori wars was low by European standards, their combats were fierce. Hand-to-hand fighting with spears and exquisitely carved war clubs was the preferred mode of combat. Successful ambushes and surprise attacks were highly admired. The priest-leader of a hapu or tribe would cut out the heart of the first enemy killed in battle and offer it to the gods of his people. Enemy casualties sometimes were eaten, and enemy prisoners were enslaved.

On the Threshold of Civilization   Polynesian seafarers had accomplished much in the harsh but beautiful environment of their New Zealand landfall. Mainly on the basis of imported crops, they had developed a fairly steady and productive agricultural system. Although they did not work metals, their material culture was quite impressive. In woodworking and decoration, in particular, they surpassed the Polynesian societies from which their ancestors had come. They had also developed a wonderfully rich oral tradition, which placed a premium on oratorical skills and produced a complex and fascinating collection of myths and legends. Though divided and politically decentralized, the Maori had developed closely knit and well-organized communities within the hapu and the tribe.

Their isolation and limited resources prevented the Maori from achieving the full occupational specialization that, as we have seen, was critical to the advance to true civilization elsewhere. Isolation limited Maori technological advances and their resistance to disease. These limits rendered them vulnerable to peoples such as the Europeans, who had more sophisticated tools and weapons and transmitted diseases that decimated the tribes of New Zealand. Although their skills in war and their adaptability allowed the Maori to survive in the long run, they could do little to prevent the disintegration of their culture and the destruction of much of the world they had known before the coming of the Europeans.

GLOBAL CONNECTIONS: The Emerging Cultures

Two important features were shared by the societies that formed on the fringes of the major core of world civilizations during the classical period and slightly beyond. First, as they adopted or imported agriculture, they were able to form more structured political units and develop a more complex social hierarchy. Second, each of the emerging societies exhibited important characteristics from its own past. These characteristics carried forward into the history of these regions, even as other influences were encountered.

Most of the fringe societies obviously participated in a new range of contacts, either through migration into greater interaction with an established civilization or, as with Japan, through deliberate imitation. Nomadic peoples more generally also enhanced contacts, bringing new influences through trade, migration, or invasion.

The four emerging areas also displayed one vital difference in addition to particular distinctions in art, language, and the like. Three of the areas—northern and eastern Europe, Japan, and sub-Saharan Africa—were in contact with more established civilization centers, at least to some extent. Polynesia stood apart by its early separation from Asia. This resulted in an impressive set of independent achievements as Poly-

nesian society advanced and spread, but also in important constraints, most obviously in technology. In other words, the availability of outside influence can explain important differences between societies.

Further development of contacts with more established centers for the Japanese, the Slavs, Celts, and Germans, and the Sudanic kingdoms of Africa depended on changes in the classical civilizations themselves. The decline of the great classical empires after the 2nd century C.E., then the new influences that helped reestablish vigorous societies in the same areas, had a vital spillover effect in northern Europe and Asia and in sub-Saharan Africa. This fact returns us to the classical centers, as they declined but also brought forth dynamic new forces capable of transforming wide stretches of the Old World.

Further Readings

The general process of cultural migration and the problems of interpreting archeological and linguistic evidence are the subjects of Irving Rouse's *Migrations in Prehistory* (1986), which includes excellent chapters on the Japanese and the Polynesians.

The history, society, and geography of Africa are all treated in an informative way in Paul Bohannan and Philip Curtin's *Africa and the Africans,* (4th ed. 1995). A very useful introduction to and synthesis of Africa's ancient past are provided in David Phillipson's *African Archaeology* (1985); Joseph Harris, *Africans and Their History* (2nd ed., 1998); and James Newman, *The Peopling of Africa: A Geographic Interpretation* (1995). Philip Curtin et al., eds., *African History: from Earliest Times to Independence* (2nd ed., 1995), contains excellent chapters on various regions. Nehemia Levitzion's *Ancient Ghana and Mali* (1973) provides a succinct survey based on the original sources.

New work on the Indo-Europeans is found in J. P. Mallory, *In Search of the Indo-Europeans* (1989) and L. L. Cavalli-Sforza, *The Great Human Diasporas* (1995). Justine Davis Randers-Pehrson's *Barbarians and Romans: The Birth Struggle of Europe, A.D. 400-700* (1983) gives a broad overview of the Germans and Slavs during this period. Tacitus' classic on the Germans is easily available in the translation by H. Mattingly, *The Agricola and the Germania* (1970).

The fullest, but somewhat dated, account of early Japanese cultural development available in English is included in G. B. Sansom's *A History of Japan to 1334* (2nd ed., 1961). Useful introductions to the early period can also be found in Mikiso Hane's *Pre-Modern Japan: An Historical Survey* (1990); E. O. Reischauer and Alfred M. Craig, *Japan: Story of a Nation* (4th ed., 1989); and (especially for political developments) John W. Hall's *Japan from Prehistory to Modern Times* (1970). The best introductions to society and culture in the early period are provided by G. B. Sansom's *Japan: A Short Cultural History* (3rd ed. 1986) and H. Paul Varley's *Japanese Culture: A Short History* (4th ed., 2000).

Peter Bellwood's *The Polynesians: Prehistory of an Island People* (rev. ed., 1978) is an excellent short introduction to the Polynesians. Jesse D. Jennings, ed., *The Prehistory of Polynesia* (1979) contains survey articles on various areas of Polynesia. Patrick Vinton Kirch's *Feathered Gods and Fishhooks* (1985) surveys the archeology of Hawaii. Classic accounts of Maori society and customs include *Te Rangi Hiroa* (Peter Buck), *The Coming of the Maori* (1949) and the works of Elsdon Best, especially *Some Aspects of Maori Myth and Religion* (1923).

On the Web

Overviews created by ongoing studies of nomadic life can be found at http://hsc.csu.edu.au/pta/gtansw/publications/archive/nomads.html and http://www.csen.org/. The latter site and http://www.heritagenet.unesco.kz/kz/content/history/monument/berel/berel_text1.htm offer exceptional coverage of Eurasian nomads. An excellent survey of the inner working of nomadic societies, past and present, that includes portraits of two such societies in the western Sahara and in western Tibet can be found at http://hsc.csu.edu.au/pta/gtansw/publications/archive/nomads.html. Links to the art of nomadic peoples are provided at http://www.utexas.edu/students/husa/origins/nomadart.html.

While horse and camel nomads (http://depts.washington.edu/uwch/silkroad/exhibit/trade/horcamae.html and http://whc.unesco.org/exhibits/afr_rev/africa-c.htm) are familiar factors in the evolution of civilization, the less well-known reindeer nomads also have a place in the history, as http://www.enontekio.fi/english/travel/hist7.html reminds us. Nomads were not always dependant on animal transport, as is suggested by the "sea nomads" of Southeast Asia (http://www.unesco.org/csi/act/thailand/moken_e.htm).

Nomadic and pastoral peoples played a major role in the functioning of major conduits of long distance trade and cultural exchange in the ancient world, such as the Silk Road. A virtual tour of the Silk Road center of Dunhuang is available at http://www.silk-road.com/ and http://www.metmuseum.org/toah/hd/ince/hd_ince.htm. Though designed as a study guide, http://www.isop.ucla.edu/eas/sum-inst/links/silkunit.htm#background is very useful for identifying the factors that led to cultural exchange along the Silk Road. The "Spice Road" across southwest Asia to Petra and beyond can be traveled at http://www.avu.cz/star/maps_txt.html.

The view of the society and culture of early Japan offered at http://www.japan-guide.com/e/e2131.html features a narrative loaded with links that further illuminate virtually all the subjects addressed in this chapter, including Jomon culture, Yamato, and the coming of Buddhism to Japan. One of these links, to Shinto at http://www.religioustolerance.org/shinto.htm, provides clear illustrations of Shinto practice and tradition. A virtual exhibit of Japan's traditional arts is on display at http://www.jinjapan.org/museum/menu.html.

An introduction to the peopling of the Pacific is provided at http://www.hawaii.edu/cpis/region.html. A comprehensive guide to Internet sources on the peoples and peopling of the Pacific is provided at http://www.cwis.org/wwwvl/indig-vl.html#pacific. Insight into the life of one of the best known leaders of a Pacific people, the Hawaiian King Kamehameha, may be found at http://www.ksbe.edu/endowment/hawaiian/history/kk1.html and http://www.americaslibrary.gov/cgi-bin/page.cgi/aa/kamehameh.

Bantu language migration and the multiethnic character of Africa can be explored at http://www.wsu.edu/~dee/CIVAFRCA/IRONAGE.HTM and http://emuseum.mnsu.edu/cultural/oldworld/africa/bantu.html. The Web offers a brief history of Axum (http://www.wsu.edu:8080/~dee/CIVAFRCA/AXUM.HTM), accounts of this and other Nubian kingdoms (http://www.fordham.edu/halsall/ancient/nubia1.html), and images of their cities and monuments (http://www.hp.uab.edu/image_archive/um/umn.html). How the trans-Saharan trade was captured by the state of Ghana and how it flourished before its conquest by the Almoravids is discussed at http://www.mrdowling.com/609-trade.html.

CHAPTER 10

THE END OF THE CLASSICAL ERA: WORLD HISTORY IN TRANSITION, 200–700 C.E.

The conversion of kings, such as Clovis, king of the Franks, helped inspire wider conversions and gave the Christian clergy some symbolic power over the state.

This chapter focuses on several related themes, describing the end of the classical period and the movement toward a new world history framework. Classical civilizations weakened, but in different ways. The causes of this development must be explored. The same time period also saw the spread of major religions in Asia, Africa, and Europe.

Between 200 and 600 C.E., all three of the great classical civilizations collapsed, at least in part. The western portion of the Roman Empire suffered a major setback. The fates of Han China, Gupta India, and the eastern part of the Roman Empire were better, but those places also underwent change. The timing of these developments raises one of the principal issues in world history: What causes civilizations to lose vigor? How can historians figure out the reasons for such major change?

The decline of the great empires also marks the close of one major period in time and the opening of a new, postclassical era in world history. For along with decline and fall, important new developments, including the spread of great religions, set up many of the leading characteristics of the next stage in world history.

This chapter returns to a primary focus on the centers of classical civilization in Eurasia and north Africa. The end of the classical era is defined by changes in Asia and the Mediterranean, not the whole world. Nevertheless, the fading of the great classical empires had consequences beyond their borders. The resulting change in civilization boundaries unleashed new forces that affected sub-Saharan Africa, northern Europe, and other parts of Asia.

Outside invasions accelerated during this period of decline. They created new pressures on all the classical empires, but they also resulted from newly perceived weakness. Various groups of Huns, from central Asia, affected first China, then Rome, then India. They may have been spurred by new population pressure. They provided another example, though not the last, of the importance of nomadic peoples in world history. Skilled horsemen, they also benefited from new equipment, notably the stirrup. But their invasions could have been turned back by the empires at their height. The process of decline invites additional explanation.

Attila the Hun

In Europe, the most famous invader was Attila the Hun, who lived from 406 to 453. Attila led the nomadic Huns, fighting with great fierceness. He organized a loose kingdom that ran from Germany to China. Known by the Christians as the "scourge of God," Attila invaded what is now France in 451. He was resisted by both Romans and Germanic tribes. An end run to Italy brought him to Rome, where the pope pleaded with him to spare the

100 C.E.	200 C.E.	300 C.E.	400 C.E.	500 C.E.	600 C.E.
88 Beginning of Han decline **180 ff.** Beginning of Rome's decline; population decline **184** Daoist Yellow Turban rebellion	**220** Last Han emperor deposed; Time of Troubles begins; nomadic invasions in north **231** Initial Germanic invasion effort **284–305** Diocletian emperor	**300–700** Spread of Buddhism **312–337** Constantine; division of empire administration; toleration of Christianity **330–379** Basil organizes Eastern monasticism **354–430** Augustine	**400–500** Decline of Buddhism; evolution of popular Hinduism **401 ff.** Increased Germanic invasions **410** Rome sacked by Germanic tribe **450** Hun invasions begin **476** Last Roman emperor in West deposed **480–547** Benedict and Western monasticism	**527–565** Justinian, Eastern emperor **c. 540** Collapse of Gupta dynasty **589–618** Sui dynasty	**618** Tang dynasty **606–647** Loose empire under Harsha in India **610** Beginning of Islam **657 ff.** Rajput (regional princes) predominate in India; periodic clashes with Islamic armies in northwest

city—to no avail. Attila highlighted and contributed to Rome's collapse. His own kingdom fell after his death. But his success did call attention to the importance of cavalry in warfare, something the Greeks and Romans, with their preference for infantry, had largely ignored.

Upheavals in Eastern and Southern Asia

 The decline of the Han dynasty in China and, later, the Gupta Empire in India, and pressure from nomadic invaders, mark the key transition in the Asian civilizations away from some of the characteristics of the classical period.

Decline and Fall in Han China

The process of classical decline began first in China. After a brief faltering after the reign of Wudi, the Han dynasty seemed to recover, and by about 80 C.E. the central government was about as effective and the economy about as prosperous as before. The Chinese launched a new expansion campaign in central Asia. After about 88 C.E., however, the quality of the emperors began to decline. Most reigns were short and full of plotting; empresses and officials joined the fray (see Chapter 4). On several occasions, bureaucrats and popular protesters were massacred. At a basic level, conditions among the peasantry began to deteriorate. Large landowners, always powerful under the Han, grew more so, avoiding taxes and forming private armies. Taxes on peasants increased, and many farmers, forced into serfdom, provided labor and turned over much of their own produce as fees to the landlords. Social protest increased, often laced with Daoist beliefs.

Peasant unrest culminated in a great revolutionary effort led by the Daoists in 184 C.E. Leaders called the **Yellow Turbans** promised a golden age to be brought about by divine magic. Han generals suppressed this rebellion but set themselves up as regional rulers, a clear sign of the collapse of the central state. The last Han emperor was deposed in 220 C.E. China was divided into three kingdoms for several decades, but finally even these began to collapse. For several centuries, China was ruled by the landowning class, operating beyond the control of formal government. Southern and northern China also pulled apart, with the south maintaining higher levels of economic growth and continuing to absorb tribal peoples into Chinese culture.

No firm dynasties could be established in this 350-year period, although there were short-lived regimes in the south. Northern China was pressed by invasions from central Asia. Nomadic peoples had been incorporated into Chinese armies, much as later Roman rulers tried to use Germanic troops, but as the government deteriorated the nomads broke loose and began to invade the Middle Kingdom. Several nomad-dominated states were formed, but none lasted long. Internal warfare became endemic in this unusually long breakdown in Chinese stability.

Into this chaos came the new fascination with Buddhism, which offered spiritual solace in response to political uncertainty and economic distress; also, like Christianity in Europe, it provided cultural cohesion at a time when political links had broken down. Imported from India—the only case until modern times when China borrowed a major idea from abroad—and disseminated by silk merchants and missionaries, Buddhism spread among both the Chinese and the nomadic warriors, helping gradually to mold a common culture in which Chinese ingredients predominated. Buddhist influence also brought to China a new impetus for art and sculpture, altering the established styles and themes.

Buddhism came under periodic attack by Daoist regional rulers, but the faith reached throughout China by the 5th century C.E., and it spread rapidly for many decades (Map 10.1). Buddhist monasteries for women as well as men gained ground. Many Chinese monks made pilgrimages to India, and Buddhist literature and philosophy spread widely. Chinese Buddhists blended practices from many Indian Buddhist sects, using meditation, prayers, and devotional exercises. The Document section shows what benefits Chinese converts might expect from their new religion. The Chinese imposed some of their own values on Buddhism as well; for instance, they insisted on the importance of forming families so that the ancestral line could be preserved. Typically, as a result, only second sons became Buddhist monks, and first sons maintained the family responsibilities. Buddhists were also pressed into political loyalty, paying taxes to the government and submitting to government regulations on the formation of monasteries.

Buddhism had a fascinating impact on women in China, among families who converted. On the face of things, Buddhism should have disrupted China's firm belief in patriarchal power, because Buddhists believed that women had souls along with men. Indeed, some individual women in China won great attention because of their spiritual accomplishments. But Chinese culture generated changes in Buddhism within the empire. Buddhist phrases like "husband supports wife" were changed to "husband controls his wife," while "the wife comforts the husband"—another Buddhist phrase from India—became "the wife reveres her husband." Finally, many men valued pious Buddhist wives, because they might benefit the family's salvation and because Buddhist activity could keep their wives busy, calm, and out of mischief. Buddhism could be meaningful to Chinese women, but it did not really challenge patriarchy. A biography of one Buddhist wife put it this way: "At times of crisis she could be tranquil and satisfied with her fate, not letting outside things agitate her mind."

The growing Buddhist influence also had an impact on Daoism, forcing greater formalization of Daoist doctrine and more efforts to reach the common people. Many Chinese found great similarities between the two faiths, although Buddhism continued to have the advantage of offering a clearer doctrine of personal salvation—the chance of holy life after death—and a firmer set of personal ethics. Daoist leaders developed a variety of practices, including meditation and dietary restrictions, that might bring immortality. Popular Daoism, mixing Daoist beliefs with an animistic pantheon of many gods, tended to hold that good or evil done in this life would be compensated by heavens or hells hereafter. Popular Daoism also provided priests and shamans who practiced faith healing to cure disease. These ramifications of Daoism appealed to the Chinese peasantry, lasting in some parts of eastern Asia even today.

Confucianism lost ground during this confused period in Chinese history, eclipsed by the more otherworldly interests. But the legacy of Chinese institutions and secular beliefs did not disappear, and, as nomadic invaders were partly converted to Chinese ways, the opportunity for political revival reemerged

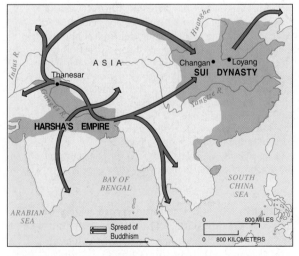

Map 10.1 *Asia, c. 600 C.E. Buddhism spread from India to China and other parts of Asia at the end of the classical era.*

Document

The Popularization of Buddhism

Chinese Buddhism, unlike most Chinese beliefs, spread among all regions and social groups. Although it divided into many sects that disagreed over details of theology and rituals by commenting on earlier Buddhist scriptures (the Sutras), many ordinary Chinese believers cared little for such details and were more concerned with direct spiritual benefits. Often they arranged to have Buddhist sermons copied, as a means of obtaining merit, while adding a note of their own. The following passages come from such notes, written mainly in the 6th century. They suggest the various reasons people might go through the challenging process of converting to a new religion.

Recorded on the 15th day of the fourth month of 531.

The Buddhist lay disciple Yuan Jung—having lived in this degenerate era for many years, fearful for his life, and yearning for home—now makes a donation of a thousand silver coins to the Three Jewels [the Buddha, the Law, and the Monastic Order]. This donation is made in the name of the Celestial King Vaisravana. In addition, he makes a donation of a thousand to ransom himself and his wife and children [from their earthly existence], a thousand more to ransom his servants, and a thousand more to ransom his domestic animals. This money is to be used for copying sutras. It is accompanied by the prayer that the Celestial King may attain Buddhahood; that the disciple's family, servants, and animals may be blessed with long life, may attain enlightenment, and may all be permitted to return to the capital.

Dated the 29th day of the fourth month of 550.

Happiness is not fortuitous: Pray for it and it will respond. Results are not born of thin air: Pay heed to causes and results will follow. This explains how the Buddhist disciple and nun Tao-jung—because her conduct in her previous life was not correct—came to be born in her present form, a woman, vile and unclean.

Now if she does not honor the awesome decree of Buddha, how can future consequences be favorable for her? Therefore, having cut down her expenditures on food and clothing, she reverently has had the Nirvana Sutra copied once. She prays that those who read it carefully will be exalted in mind to the highest realms and that those who communicate its meaning will cause others to be so enlightened.

She also prays that in her present existence she will have no further sickness or suffering, that her parents in seven other incarnations (who have already died or will die in the future) and her present family and close relatives may experience joy in the four realms [earth, water, fire, and air], and that whatever they seek may indeed come to pass. Finally, she prays that all those endowed with knowledge may be included within this prayer.

Recorded on the 28th day of the fifth month of 583.

The Army Superintendent, Sung Shao, having suffered the heavy sorrow of losing both his father and mother, made a vow on their behalf to read one section each of [many] sutras. He prays that the spirits of his parents will someday reach the Pure Land [paradise] and will thus be forever freed from the three unhappy states of existence and the eight calamities and that they may eternally listen to the Buddha's teachings.

He also prays that the members of his family, both great and small, may find happiness at will, that blessings may daily rain down upon them while hardships disperse like clouds. He prays that the imperial highways may be open and free of bandits, that the state may be preserved from pestilence, that wind and rain may obey their proper seasons, and that all suffering creatures may quickly find release. May all these prayers be granted!

The preceding incantation has been translated and circulated.

If this incantation is recited 7, 14, or 21 times daily (after having cleansed the mouth in the morning with a willow twig, having scattered flowers and incense before the image of Buddha, having knelt and joined the palms of the hands), the four grave sins, the five wicked acts, and all other transgressions will be wiped away. The present body will not be afflicted by untimely calamities; one will at last be born into the realm of immeasurably long life; and reincarnation in the female form will be escaped forever.

Now, the Sanskrit text has been reexamined and the Indian Vinaya monk Buddhasangha and other monks have been consulted; thus we know that the awesome power of this incantation is beyond comprehension. If it is recited 100 times in the evening and again at noon, it will destroy the four grave sins and five wicked acts. It will pluck out the very roots of sin and will ensure rebirth in the Western Regions. If, with sincerity of spirit, one is able to complete 200,000 recitations, perfect intelligence will be born and there will be no relapses. If 300,000 recitations are completed, one will see Amita Buddha face to face and will certainly be reborn into the Pure Land of tranquility and bliss.

Copied by the disciple of pure faith Sun Szu-chung on the 8th day of the fourth month of 720.

Questions: Why did Buddhism spread widely in China by the 6th century? How did popular Buddhism compare with original Buddhist teachings (see Chapter 6)? How did Chinese Buddhists define holy life? How do these documents suggest some of the troubles China faced after the collapse of the Han dynasty?

toward the end of the 6th century. A series of strong rulers in the north drove out nomadic bands and then merged, under a general of Chinese–Turkish background, into a new **Sui** dynasty. Under this brief dynasty, northern China was united and south China was reconquered. The government built new canals and repaired the Great Wall. Attempts to expand into Korea and central Asia brought financial collapse, along with new rebellions, and only in 618 C.E. was the more durable **Tang** dynasty established. The time of troubles had ended. New artistic works (Figure 10.1) reflected renewed political integration.

The decline and fall of the Han had thus disrupted Chinese civilization and opened it to new religious influences. But old values survived as well. Even the competing landlords retained some training in Confucianism and with that training the idea of a united empire. With its greater cultural homogeneity established in the classical era, China differed markedly from the Mediterranean, where Christianity and Islam came close to displacing older philosophical concerns while challenging earlier political loyalties. Many nomadic invaders imitated Chinese styles and thus encouraged the revival of older political habits.

The End of the Guptas: Decline in India

The decline of classical civilization in India was in one sense less drastic than the collapse of Han China in that India had not depended so heavily on political structures to hold its civilization together. Yet the Gupta collapse left durable traces in later Indian history, for political unity became more difficult than ever before. The high point of Gupta rule came under Chandragupta II early in the 5th century, but his immediate successors managed to remain prosperous. India about 450 C.E. probably was the most stable and peaceful area in the world. However, in 440 C.E., the nomadic Huns began a series of invasions that gradually reduced the empire's strength. The Gupta pattern of somewhat decentralized rule, whereby vassal princes were treated as partial allies rather than subject to direct central administration, made response to invasion more difficult. The Huns controlled much of northwestern India—the typical invasion route of the subcontinent— by 500 C.E. By this time, the quality of Gupta kings was also diminishing, and this added to the problem (see Chapter 6). It was a regional prince, **Harsha** Vardharna, not the Guptas themselves, who broke the hold of the Huns in the northwest about 530 C.E., and the Guptas were too weak to restore their claims. The dynasty collapsed entirely about 550 C.E.

A few echoes of Gupta splendor were heard during the 7th century. Harsha, a descendant of the Guptas through his grandmother, established a loose empire across northern India between 616 and 657. But he died without heirs, and his empire broke up again. From this point onward, until a better-organized series of outside invasions began, northern India

Figure 10.1 *Stone relief from the tomb of the Tang emperor T'ai Tsung (7th century), showing one of his warhorses attended by a bearded "barbarian" groom. How does this relief suggest the barbarian threat was being handled after China's crisis period had ended?*

was politically divided. Regional dynasties occasionally were powerful, but few lasted very long. A section of northern India was invaded by Tang Chinese–led Tibetan troops, who captured a young Indian prince and took him back to the Chinese capital in 648. This was the first and, until our own era, the only military clash between China and India. The northern regional princes, collectively called the **Rajput**, emphasized military prowess; although there were many local wars, few political events had great significance.

In this localized framework, Indian culture continued to evolve. Buddhism declined steadily in India. The Guptas had preferred Hinduism, and the Hun invaders disliked the other-worldly tone of Buddhism as well. Military-minded princes had little sympathy for the Buddhist principles of calm and contemplation. Hindu beliefs gained ground, converting the Hun leaders, among other groups. Within Hinduism, worship of a mother goddess, **Devi**, spread widely, which encouraged a new popular emotionalism in religious ritual (Figure 10.2). In essence, India partially redefined its core culture by emphasizing the Hindu strain more clearly while relying heavily on cultural cohesion at a time when political life became more difficult. The reassertion of Hinduism also promoted the caste system, now spreading to southern India. The number and complexity of jati, or castes, increased as invaders were assimilated into the system, but the basic principles remained.

India's economic activity also remained strong, although in periods of outright invasion there were new hardships. Here too, Indian civilization did not collapse to the extent of Han China or the western Mediterranean. Indeed, the decades after the fall of the Guptas saw new outreach in trade and even some conquest by southern Tamil kingdoms, which were trying to establish firmer strongholds along the Indian Ocean in southeast Asia.

Although Indian civilization largely maintained its position, albeit with a more diverse political lineup, another threat came after 600 C.E. from the new Middle Eastern religion of Islam (see Chapters 11 and 12). At first, India's contacts with this new force were limited. Arab armies, fighting under the banners of their god Allah, reached India's northwestern frontier during the 7th century, and although there was initially little outright conquest, Islam won some converts in the north. By the 8th century, Islamic competition also began to hit India's international economic position. Arab traders soon took control of the Indian Ocean from Tamil merchants and reduced India's commercial strength.

The Decline and Fall of the Roman Empire

 The decline of the Roman Empire fit chronologically between the collapse of the Han and that of the Gupta dynasty. It was more disruptive than either of these Asian developments. For many educated Westerners, the fall of Rome has had a powerful impact on the imagination.

Figure 10.2 *Hindu statues gave vivid forms to holy figures, many of them female. This scene portrays a goddess subduing a mythological cosmic monster.*

The Causation of Roman Decline

Signs of decay at various levels began to emerge in the Roman Empire in the late 2nd century. Population size declined, as birth rates no longer kept pace with mortality rates, and it became more difficult to recruit effective armies. Political signs included the greater brutality and arbitrariness of many later Roman emperors—victims, according to one commentator at the time, of "lustful and cruel habits." Tax collection became increasingly difficult as residents of the empire fell on hard times. The governor of Egypt complained that "the once numerous inhabitants of the aforesaid villages have now been reduced to a few, because some have fled in poverty and others have died … and for this reason we are in danger owing to impoverishment of having to abandon the tax-collectorship."

Above all there were the human symptoms. Inscriptions on Roman tombstones increasingly ended with the motto "I was not, I was, I am not, I have no more desires," suggesting despair. As the structures of the empire deteriorated, meaning in life became harder to find, and this mood made efforts at structural revival more difficult. The signs of change in the quality of political and economic life began to emerge after about 180 C.E., at which point the empire's geographic expansion had slightly receded from its high point. Unlike Han China or Gupta India, the Roman Empire had depended extensively on expansion, not only to provide prestige but to recruit the necessary slaves. With the empire's boundaries now pushed to the limits it could support, Rome had to restructure its labor policies on the great commercial estates and in the mines. This restructuring reduced economic vitality and market production.

Initially more pressing were the internal issues of politics and population. Government leadership became a problem. Growing political confusion, including disputes over how emperors should be appointed and controlled, produced a series of weak rulers and many battles over succession to the throne. Intervention of the army in the selection of emperors, as the army became an increasingly separate institution, complicated political life and contributed to the worsening of rule. The decline of the Roman state raises the question of human agency: When things go badly in a society, are weak leaders an accident, causing growing disarray, or do larger trends cause the selection of inferior rulers?

Still more important in this decline was a series of plagues that swept over the empire at the end of the 2nd century C.E. These plagues decimated the

population and severely disrupted economic life. Some authorities argue that Rome's urban population also suffered lead poisoning from the pipes leading from the aqueducts, which further weakened people and reduced their numbers. Lower population added to the problems of finding labor. Recruiting troops became more difficult, and the empire had to hire Germanic soldiers to guard its frontiers. The need to pay troops added to the demands on the state's budget, just as declining production cut into tax revenues and the absence of new conquests cut into other rewards for soldiers. Environmental deterioration in north Africa reduced grain supply and hurt the Roman tax base: Overuse had reduced soil fertility and advanced desertification.

This may be the key to the process of decline: a set of general problems, including a cycle of plagues that could not be prevented, resulting in a spiral that steadily worsened, particularly as the selection of emperors deteriorated. But there is another side to Rome's downfall, although whether it was a cause or result of the initial difficulties is hard to say. Rome's upper classes became steadily more pleasure-seeking and individualistic, turning away from the political devotion and economic vigor that had characterized the republic and early empire. Cultural life decayed. Aside from some truly creative Christian writers, the fathers of Western theology, there was very little sparkle to the art or literature of the later empire. The Romans wrote textbooks about rhetoric instead of displaying rhetorical talent in actual political life; they wrote simple compendiums about animals or geometry that barely captured the essentials of what earlier intellectuals had known, and they often added superstitious beliefs that previous generations would have scorned. This cultural decline was not clearly caused by disease or economic collapse; it began in some ways before these larger problems hit. Something was happening to the Roman elite, perhaps because of the deadening hand of authoritarian political rule, perhaps because of a new commitment to luxuries and sensual indulgence. Military service became less attractive to the upper class, which forced the recruitment of paid soldiers from groups such as the Germanic tribes along the northern borders of the empire (Figure 10.3).

The Process of Roman Decline

As the quality of imperial rule declined and as life became more dangerous and economic survival more

Figure 10.3 *This plaque portrays Stilicho, a Vandal by birth, who rose to be Master of Soldiers and Consul of Rome.*

precarious, many farmers clustered around the protection of large landlords, surrendering full control of their plots of land, hoping for military and judicial protection. The decentralization of political and economic authority, which was greatest in the western, or European, portions of the empire, foreshadowed the manorial system of Europe in the Middle Ages. The estate system gave great political power to the landlords and could provide some local stability. But it weakened the emperor's power and tended to drive the economy away from the elaborate trade patterns of Mediterranean civilization in its heyday. Many estates attempted to produce almost everything needed on the spot. Trade and production declined

further, causing tax revenues to drop and cities to shrink. The empire was locked in a vicious circle in which the responses to initial deterioration merely lessened the chances of recovery.

Some later emperors tried to reverse the flow. **Diocletian,** who ruled from 284 to 305 C.E., tightened up the administration of the empire and tried to improve tax collection. Regulation of the dwindling economy increased. Diocletian also tried to monopolize political loyalty, increasing the pressure to worship the emperor as god. This was what prompted him to persecute Christians with particular viciousness, for they would not give Caesar preference over their god. The emperor **Constantine,** who ruled from 312 to 337, tried other experiments. He set up a second capital city, Constantinople, to regulate the eastern half of the empire more efficiently. He tried to use the religious force of Christianity to unify the empire spiritually, extending toleration and adopting it as his own faith. These measures were not without result. The eastern empire, ruled from Constantinople (formerly the Greek colony of Byzantium, now the Turkish city of Istanbul), remained an effective political and economic unit. Christianity spread under official sponsorship, although some new problems were attached to success.

But none of these measures revived the empire as a whole. Human agency could have real impact, setting new forces in motion, but it could not reverse basic trends. Division merely made the weakness of the western half worse. Attempts to regulate the economy reduced economic initiative and lowered production; ultimately, tax revenues declined once again. The army deteriorated further. When the Germanic invasions began in earnest in the 400s, there was little resistance. Many peasants, burdened by the social and economic pressures of the decaying empire, actually welcomed the barbarians. A priest noted, "In all districts taken over by the Germans, there is one desire among all the Romans, that they should never again find it necessary to pass under Roman jurisdiction." German kingdoms were set up in many parts of the empire by 425, and the last Roman emperor in the West was displaced in 476 (Map 10.2). The Germanic invaders numbered, at most, 5 percent of the population of the empire, but so great was the earlier decline that this small, uncoordinated force put an end to one of the world's great political structures.

The fall of Rome echoes some of the same questions that apply to China and India. Do civilizations

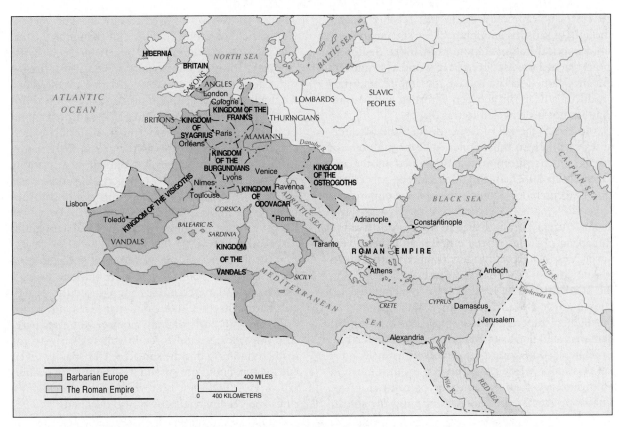

Map 10.2 *Germanic Kingdoms After the Invasions. Nomadic tribes converged mainly on the western part of the Roman Empire, invading Rome itself and its European outposts. Was this the cause or result of greater weakness in the West than in the empire's eastern territory?*

inevitably fall, or at least undergo cycles of decline? When the collapse involves outside invading forces, does one look primarily at internal decay? Germanic or central Asian invaders had a few military advantages. Their reliance on hunting and herding gave them some skills, including excellent equestrian skills in the case of the Huns, that allowed them to overrun more populous peasant settlements where people were unaccustomed to battle. From their contacts on the Roman borders, the Germans had also learned new organizational methods that made them a more formidable force. But there is no question that in their glory days, the professional armies of Rome or Han China could have contained the invaders; it was internal weakness that allowed the invaders to have such disruptive effects. Rome seemed headed for downfall even before the Germanic intruders dealt the final blows. At the same time, the luxurious living of the upper classes and the impressive reputation of the classical empires helped lure the invaders in.

Results of the Fall of Rome

The collapse of Rome echoed through the later history of Europe and the Middle East. Rome's fall split the unity of the Mediterranean lands that had been won through Hellenistic culture and then the Roman Empire itself. This was one sign that the end of the Roman Empire was more serious than the displacement of the last classical dynasties in India and China. Greece and Rome, unlike China, had not produced the shared political culture and bureaucratic traditions that could allow revival after a period of chaos. Nor had Mediterranean civilization, for all its vitality, generated a common religion that reached deeply enough, or satisfied enough needs, to maintain unity amid political fragmentation, as in India. Such religions reached the Mediterranean world as Rome fell, but they came too late to save the empire, and they produced a deep rift between Christian and Muslim that has not been healed to this day.

In effect, the fall of Rome divided the Mediterranean world into three zones, the starting point of three distinct civilizations that developed in later centuries (Map 10.3). In the northeastern part of the empire, centered in Constantinople, the empire in a sense did not fall. Classical civilization was more deeply entrenched there than in some of the western European portions of the empire, and there were fewer pressures from invaders. Emperors continued to rule Greece, other parts of southeast Europe, and the northern Middle East. This eastern empire, later known as the **Byzantine Empire,** was a product of the Hellenistic era and late imperial Rome, and it demonstrated great survival power (see Chapter 14).

The second zone that devolved from Rome's fall was more seriously disrupted, though more in political terms than in economic or cultural terms. This zone consisted of north Africa and the south-eastern shores of the Mediterranean. The eastern empire held its ground briefly, but then pulled back. Several regional kingdoms briefly succeeded the empire. Although Christianity spread in the area—indeed, one of the greatest Christian theologians, Augustine, was a bishop in north Africa—it was not as uniformly triumphant as in the Byzantine Empire or western Europe. Furthermore, differing beliefs and doctrines soon split north African Christianity from the larger branches, producing most notably the Coptic church in Egypt, which still survives as a Christian minority in that country, and another branch in Ethiopia. Soon much of north Africa was filled with the still newer doctrines of Islam and a new Arab Empire.

Finally, there was the western part of the empire: Italy, Spain, and points north. Here is where Rome's fall not only shattered unities but reduced the level of civilization itself. Crude, regional Germanic kingdoms grew in parts of Italy, France, and elsewhere. The only clearly vital force in this region was not Roman tradition but the spread of Christianity. Even Christianity could not sustain sophisticated literature, art, or even theology, however. In Rome's collapse, cities and commercial activity also declined.

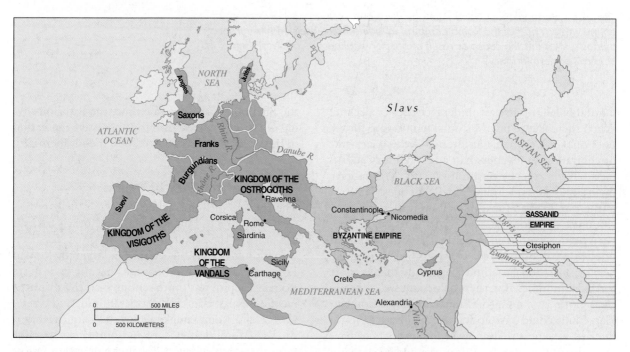

Map 10.3 *The Mediterranean, Middle East, Europe, and North Africa, c. 500 C.E. After the fall of Rome, the former empire split into three zones. Western and eastern Europe divided; much of the eastern Mediterranean and North Africa became more separate still.*

In Depth

The Problem of Decline and Fall

Explaining the decline of civilizations has fascinated observers since civilizations began to decline. As Rome's vitality ebbed, many writers tried to figure out what was going on. Christian theologians such as Augustine wrote massive tomes to prove that Christianity was not to blame, for some non-Christian philosophers argued that the religion's other-worldly emphasis had sapped Rome's strength. Both Christian and pagan writers worried that the cause of Rome's collapse was immorality, a loss of the virtues of self-denial and devotion to the common good that had made Rome great in the first place. Many of these arguments have been taken up by world historians in more recent times. In the 18th century, Edward Gibbon, a British philosopher–historian who was hostile to religion, returned to the attack on Christianity, holding that it contradicted key Roman qualities of military valor and civic devotion and so brought the empire's fall. Several 20th-century historians argued that Rome's moral decline—the growing self-indulgence and pleasure-seeking of the aristocracy and the urban masses—led the people to accept forms of government in which they no longer participated. This argument is interesting because it corresponds to some undeniable changes in the culture of the later Roman Empire. It also has won attention because of anxieties contemporary Westerners have about their own society: too materialistic, too devoted to sexual indulgence, too dominated by the tastes of the masses. Analogy—that is, real or imagined similarities between situations that cause a historical phenomenon to be seen as corresponding to a current one, and vice versa—plays a big role in the concern about moral decline.

Another approach to the problem of decline argues that it is almost inevitable. Civilizations, like individual humans, go through a period of vigor and reach the mature height of their powers but then begin to lose their grip and deteriorate. At the civilization level, this means that government officials focus on protecting their position rather than seeking new ways to do things; that upper classes become soft and selfish; and that territories expand farther than a society can control, leaving supply routes and defenses overextended and vulnerable to attack. An American diplomatic historian, Paul Kennedy, recently argued that this last process of overextension, which reduces internal economic vitality through its sheer costliness, occurred not only in Rome but in 19th-century Britain and most recently in the United States and Russia.

World history certainly lends itself to a search for patterns in the life cycles of civilizations. But it also generates some warnings. Civilization decline does not occur in the same ways in all cases. The result is not necessarily the death of a civilization but rather a period of regrouping, after which the civilization may reemerge with new combinations of tradition and innovation. Rome's fall, after all, was unusual at the end of the classical era and really occurred only in the western portion of the empire. Eastern Rome remained highly civilized and successful. China and India, though not unchanged by the decline of the great classical empires, did not perish as civilizations. So the question of decline must be phrased carefully, with awareness of the diverse examples world history yields.

Questions: How great a role did moral decline play in the collapse of the classical empires? What historical "laws" accurately describe what happened not only in Rome but in Gupta India and Han China? Why can it be argued that the eastern part of the Roman Empire did not decline? Why was Rome more vulnerable than India, and why was western Rome more vulnerable than the eastern Mediterranean?

The Development and Spread of World Religions

The decline of the classical empires contributed to the spread of the great world religions. Buddhism and Christianity, soon to be joined by Islam, spread well beyond the boundaries of a single region. Even religions still regional, such as Daoism in China and Hinduism in India, won new levels of active popular adherence.

Christianity and Buddhism Compared

As with the period of chaos in China, Rome's decline brought vital new religious influences to societies around the Mediterranean. Christianity moved westward from its original center in the Middle East, just as in Asia Buddhism was spreading east from India. Though initially less significant than Buddhism in terms of numbers of converts, Christianity ultimately became one of the two largest world faiths. It played a direct role in forming the postclassical civilizations of eastern and western Europe. Christianity resembled Buddhism in important ways. It could stress the unimportance of things of this world, urging a focus on spiritual destiny and divinity. Not surprisingly, Christianity, like Buddhism, produced an important monastic movement, in which people seeking holiness came together in groups to live a spiritual life and serve their religion. Christianity resembled the version of Buddhism that spread to China (and later Korea and Japan) by stressing the possibility of an afterlife and the role holy leaders could play in helping to attain it.

The Chinese version of Buddhism, called **Mahayana**, or the Greater Vehicle, placed considerable emphasis on Buddha as god or savior. Statues of the Buddha as god violated the earlier Buddhist hostility to religious images, but they emphasized the religion as a channel of salvation (Figure 10.4). Well-organized temples, with priests and rituals, also helped bring religious solace to ordinary people in east Asia. The idea developed also that Buddhist holy men, or **bodhisattvas,** built up such spiritual merit that their prayers, even after death, could aid people and allow them to achieve some holiness. Christianity in many respects moved in similar directions. It also came to emphasize salvation, with well-organized rituals. Religious images, though contrary to Jewish beliefs against idol worship, helped focus popular belief in most versions of Christianity. Holy men and women, sometimes granted the title **saint** after their deaths, were revered because their spiritual attainments could lend merit to the strivings of more ordinary people. The broad similarities between Christianity and the evolving Buddhism of east Asia remind us of the common processes at work as new religions spread amid the ruins of great empires.

Yet Christianity had a flavor of its own. More than any of the forms of Buddhism, it emphasized church organization and structure, copying the

Figure 10.4 *The spread of Buddhism produced major new themes in Chinese art, many of which focused on stylized figures of Buddha himself. Buddha became an object of worship in this process, with statues great and small conveying his majesty.*

example of the Roman Empire. It also placed greater value on missionary activity and widespread conversions, believing that error must be actively opposed in God's name. More perhaps than any other major religion—certainly more than the contemplative and tolerant Buddhism—Christianity stressed its possession of exclusive truth and its intolerance of competing beliefs. Such fierce confidence was not the least of the reasons for the new religion's success.

Early Christianity

Christianity began as part of a Jewish reform movement. Initially, there seems to have been no intent to found a new religion. After Jesus' crucifixion, the disciples expected his imminent return and with it the end of the world. Only gradually, when the Second Coming did not happen, did the disciples begin to fan out and, through preaching, pick up supporters in various parts of the Roman Empire.

The message of Jesus and his disciples seemed clear: There was a single God who loved humankind despite earthly sin. A virtuous life should be dedicated to the worship of God and fellowship with other believers; worldly concerns were secondary, and a life of poverty might be most conducive to holiness. God sent Jesus, called Christ (from the Greek word *Christos*, "God's anointed"), to preach his holy word and, through his sacrifice, to prepare for the possibility of an afterlife of heavenly communion with God. Belief, good works, and discipline of fleshly concerns would lead toward heaven; rituals, such as commemorating Christ's Last Supper with wine and bread, would promote the same goal.

This message spread at an opportune time. The official religion of the Greeks and Romans had long seemed rather sterile, particularly to many of the poor. The Christian emphasis on the beauty of poverty and the spiritual equality of all people, plus the fervor of the early Christians and the satisfying rituals they provided, gained growing attention. The wide reach of the Roman Empire made it easy for Christian missionaries to travel through Europe and the Middle East and spread the new word. Then, when conditions began to deteriorate in the empire, the solace of this other-worldly religion won even more converts.

Paul of Tarsus (c. 10–67 C.E.) was a key Christian leader. Initially a Jewish rabbi, he was hostile to Christians as heretics. But on a journey to try to round up the Christians in Damascus, a vision of Jesus came to him. He became an ardent Christian missionary and contributed to several adjustments in Christian doctrine. He spent his last years in jail, first in Roman-ruled Jerusalem, then in Rome, because of the official opposition to Christianity.

The adjustments made by early Christian leaders drew even more converts. Under the guidance of Paul, Christians began to see themselves as part of a new religion rather than a Jewish reform movement, and they welcomed non-Jewish converts. Paul also encouraged more formal organization in the new church, with local groups selecting elders to govern them; soon, a single leader, or bishop, was appointed for each major city. This structure paralleled the provincial government of the empire. Finally, Christian doctrine became increasingly well organized as the writings of several disciples and others were collected into what became the New Testament of the Christian Bible.

Christianity Gains Ground

During the first three centuries after Christ, the new religion competed with several Eastern mystery religions. It also faced periodic persecution from the normally tolerant imperial government. Even so, by the time Constantine converted to the religion, Christianity had won perhaps 10 percent of the empire's population. One convert was Constantine's mother, who visited the Holy Land and founded many churches there. Constantine's favor brought some new troubles to Christianity as the state began to interfere in matters of doctrine. But it became much easier to spread Christianity with official backing. Christian writers began to claim that both church and empire were works of God. At the same time, continued deterioration of the empire added to the motives to join this successful new church. In the eastern Mediterranean, where imperial rule remained strong, state control of the church became a way of life and an important motive, for certain people, for adopting Christianity in the first place. A pagan prefect of Constantinople, Cyrus of Panopolis, facing the disapproval of an imperial official in the mid-5th century, could save himself only by converting and becoming a Christian bishop. But in the west, where conditions were far more chaotic, bishops had a freer hand.

A centralized church organization under the leadership of the bishop of Rome, called **pope** from the Latin word *papa*, or father, gave the Western church unusual strength and independence. By the time Rome collapsed, Christianity had thus demonstrated immense spiritual power and a solid organization, although it differed from east to west. The new church faced several controversies over doctrine but managed to promote certain standard beliefs. A key tenet was a complex doctrine of the Trinity, which held that the one God had three persons, the Father, the Son (Christ), and the Holy Ghost (God as present in human spiritual experience). In 325 C.E., the church **Council of Nicaea,** under imperial sponsorship, met to debate a doctrine known as Arianism, which argued that Christ was divine but not of the same nature as God the Father. Ruling against Arianism, the resultant Nicene Creed insisted on the shared divinity of all three parts of the Trinity. An important but complex decision, it showed how important unified doctrine was to Christianity, in contrast to the greater toleration of diversity in Hinduism and Buddhism. Experience in fighting heresies promoted the Christian interest in defending a single belief and strengthened its intolerance for any competing doctrine or faith.

In its founding but also in its consolidation, Christianity was aided by strong individual leadership, although it can be debated how much this leadership caused religious success and how much it flowed from the religion's appeal. For example, Pope Leo I (d. 461) most clearly established the papacy as the supreme authority in western Europe (Figure 10.5). Born a Roman aristocrat, he faced the rapid collapse of the empire, negotiating with German rulers to save the city of Rome and using their backing to assert his authority over church leaders in France and elsewhere. Leo competed with the patriarch of Alexandria for spiritual primacy in Christianity, centralizing the Western church and standardizing its rituals, prayers, and doctrine.

Early Christianity also produced an important formal theology through formative writers such as Augustine. This theology blended many elements of classical philosophy with Christian belief and helped the church gain respectability among intellectuals. Theologians such as Augustine grappled with such problems as freedom of the will: If God is all-powerful, can mere human beings have free will? And if not, how can human beings be justly punished for sin? By working out these issues in elaborate doctrine, the early theologians, or church fathers, provided an important role for formal, rational thought in a religion that continued to emphasize the primary importance of faith.

Like all successful religions, Christianity combined several appeals. It offered blind devotion to an all-powerful God. One church father, denying the validity of human thought, simply stated, "I believe because it is absurd." But Christianity also developed its own complex and fascinating intellectual system. Mystical holy men and women flourished under Christian banners, particularly in the Middle East. In the West, soon after the empire's collapse, this impulse

Figure 10.5 *Raffaello (1483–1520), "Encounter of Pope Leo the Great with Attila." This is a later representation from an artist's imagination. What does it suggest about the characteristics that came to be ascribed to popes?*

was partially disciplined through the institution of monasticism, which gained ground in Italy under **Benedict of Nursia** early in the 6th century. Benedict started a monastery to demonstrate the true holy life to Italian peasants in a region still (to Benedict's horror) worshiping the sun-god Apollo. The Benedictine rule, which soon spread to many other monasteries and convents, urged a disciplined life, with prayer and spiritual development alternating with hard work in agriculture and study. Monastic movements also developed in the eastern empire, in Greece and Turkey, and in Egypt. Eastern monasticism was organized by St. Basil in the 4th century.

Thus, Christianity tried to encourage but also to discipline intense piety and to avoid a complete gulf between the lives of saintly men and women and the spiritual concerns of ordinary people. Christianity's success and organizational strength obviously appealed to political leaders. But the new religion never became the creature of the upper classes alone because its message of ritual and salvation continued to draw the poor. Like Hinduism in India, Christianity provided some religious unity among different social groups. It even held special interest for women. Christianity did not preach equality between men and women, but it did preach the equal importance of women's and men's souls, and unlike many other faiths it encouraged men and women to worship together.

Christianity promoted a new culture among its converts. The rituals, the other-worldly emphasis, and the interest in spiritual equality were very different from the central themes of classical Mediterranean civilization. Christianity modified classical beliefs in the central importance of the state and political loyalties. Although Christians accepted the state, they did not put it first. Christianity also worked against other classical institutions, such as slavery, in the name of brotherhood (although later Christians accepted slavery in other contexts). Particularly through the values promoted by Western monasticism, Christianity may have fostered a greater respectability for disciplined work than had been current in the aristocratic ethic of Mediterranean civilization.

Christianity preserved important classical values in addition to the interest in solid organization and some of the themes of classical philosophy. Church buildings in western Europe retained Roman architectural styles, though often with greater simplicity, if only because of the poverty of the later empire and the Germanic states. Latin remained the language of the church in the West, Greek the language of most Christians in the eastern Mediterranean. Monasticism played a very valuable role in preserving classical as well as Christian learning through the patient librarianship of the monks.

The New Religious Map

The centuries after the rise of Christianity, the spread of Buddhism, and the inception of Islam (610 C.E.) saw the conversion of most of the civilized world to one or another of the great faiths, producing a religious map that in Europe, Asia, and parts of Africa did not change greatly until our own time. The spread of the great religions caused many people in many different societies to shift their beliefs away from age-old adherence to the idea of a host of divine spirits in nature to concentration on a single divine force and on new hopes for an afterlife. Hinduism, Christianity, and Islam provided shared beliefs that could transcend divided, bickering political units. The great religions could facilitate international trade because they did not depend on local customs but on an ever-present God as organizer of all nature or at least a coherent divine order; in turn, successful trade could help spread the new religions. A new force was at work in world history.

In the Wake of Decline and Fall

By 600 C.E., the major civilizations looked very different from the classical world at its height, and many of the differences have never been erased. The results of classical decline went beyond the striking shifts in religious allegiance. Some areas, however, changed far more than others. China was unique in its ability to recapture so many classical ingredients. China and India shared an ability to maintain substantial cultural cohesion, based on widespread beliefs as well as restored politics in China's case. Today, Indian and Chinese civilizations are in essentially the same places where they had taken root by late classical times, and until quite recently, they still abundantly reflected the classical heritage: India in the caste system and an other-worldly cultural tone, China in Confucian beliefs and a fascination with a strong, bureaucratic state.

The case was quite different in the Mediterranean zone. The Roman Empire split, in part because it had not been able to spread shared beliefs very widely. Classical Mediterranean civilization left a very real heritage, but in part because geographic

Visualizing the Past

Religious Geography

The distribution of the world's major religions calls for knowledge both of numerical data and geography. This map and table, using contemporary data, also suggest which aspects of the world's religious distribution were beginning to solidify at the end of the late classical period and which aspects depended on developments yet to come.

Questions: Where are the greatest concentrations of the four major religions today? Which religions affect the largest landmasses? Which affect the largest numbers of people? Which aspects of modern religious geography follow from the patterns of religious dissemination under way by the end of the classical period? Which cannot be explained by these late classical developments? If you had been well informed about world religions and classical history in the 5th century, and magically gained knowledge about religions' distrib-

ution in the 21st century, which features would you find most surprising in light of logical 5th-century predictions?

Religions and Their Distribution in the World Today

Religion	Distribution*
Christianity	2 billion
Islam	1.3 billion
Hinduism	900 million
Buddhism	360 million
Shintoism	4 million
Daoism and other Chinese traditional religions	225 million
Judaism	14 million
Non-religious	850 million

*Figures for several religions have been reduced over the past 50 years by the impact of communism in Eastern Europe and parts of Asia.

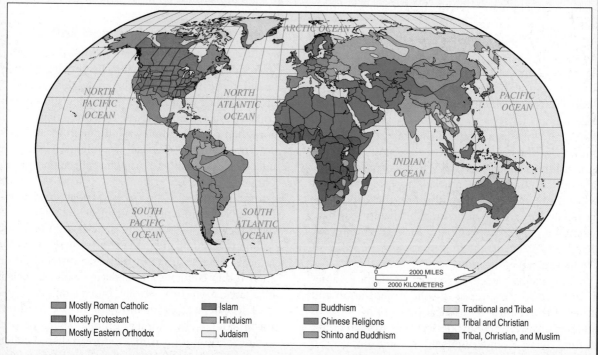

Legend:
- Mostly Roman Catholic
- Mostly Protestant
- Mostly Eastern Orthodox
- Islam
- Hinduism
- Judaism
- Buddhism
- Chinese Religions
- Shinto and Buddhism
- Traditional and Tribal
- Tribal and Christian
- Tribal, Christian, and Muslim

Major Religions of the Modern World

unity was lost, this heritage was used by successor civilizations far more selectively than was true in eastern or southern Asia.

 GLOBAL CONNECTIONS: The Late Classical Period and the World

During most of the classical period, key developments often focused within civilizations. We have seen that there were wider contacts. Each civilization radiated trade and other influences to a larger region; thus India had contacts with other parts of south-southeast Asia, and China with Korea and Vietnam. Trade along the Silk Roads through central Asia, conducted mainly by nomadic merchants, was another key connection.

As the classical civilizations began to fail, contacts in some ways accelerated—but they also encountered new difficulties. Overland travel between China and Rome became more dangerous, because government protection faltered in both empires. This placed a new premium on using shipping connections, particularly in the Indian Ocean. On the other hand, traders, missionaries, and of course nomadic invaders began to reach out in new ways, as borders became more porous. The end of the classical period thus witnessed important new cultural exchanges across regions. These included the spread of Buddhism from India to China and to other parts of east Asia, and the spread of Christianity beyond the Roman empire into parts of northeast Africa and into Armenia. These developments set new bases for connections among various societies in Afro-Eurasia.

Further Readings

The fall of the Roman Empire has generated rich and interesting debate. For interpretation and discussion of earlier views, see A. H. M. Jones' *The Decline of the Ancient World* (1966); J. Vogt's *The Decline of Rome* (1965); and F. W. Walbank's *The Awful Revolution: The Decline of the Roman Empire in the West* (1960). On India and China in decline, worthwhile sources include R. Thaper, *History of India*, vol. 1 (1966); R. C. Majumdar, ed., *The Classical Age* (1966); Raymond Dawson, *Imperial China* (1972); and J. A. Harrison, *The Chinese Empire* (1972). See also J. R. Fairbank and E. O. Reischauer, *China: Tradition and Transformation* (1989), a fine survey with good postclassical coverage.

On the role of disease in imperial decline, W. McNeill's *Plagues and Peoples* (1977) is provocative and useful. Spec-

ulations on the causes of the rise and fall of civilizations, including those of the classical world, are addressed in Jared Diamond, *Guns, Germs and Steel: The Fate of Human Societies* (1997); Christopher Chase-Dunn and Thomas D. Hall, *Rise and Demise: Comparing World Systems* (1997); A. H. M. Jones, *The Decline of the Ancient World* (1966); Joseph A. Tainter, *The Collapse of Complex Societies* (1988); and Norman Yoffee and George L. Cowgill, eds., *The Collapse of Ancient States and Civilizations* (1991).

For the rise and spread of new religions, a good introduction is Geoffrey Parinder, ed., *World Religions* (1971); see also Lewis M. Hopfe, *Religions of the World* (rev. ed., 1997), and Jamail Ragi al Farugi, ed., *Historical Atlas of the Religions of the World* (1974). On Hinduism, see N. C. Chandhuri's *Hinduism, A Religion to Live By* (1979). Two good studies of Buddhism are N. Ross Reat's *Buddhism: A History* (1994) and A. F. Wright's *Buddhism in Chinese History* (1959). Christianity's spread is the subject of S. Renko's *Pagan Rome and the Early Christians* (1986) and M. Hengel's *Acts and the History of Earliest Christianity* (1986). Important special topics are covered in J. Bowker, *Problems of Suffering in Religions of the World* (1975), a fascinating comparative effort; A. Sharma, ed., *Women in World Religions* (1987); and on Christianity, B. Witherington, *Women in the Earliest Churches* (1988). An important study of civilization contacts in this period and later is Jerry Bentley's *Old World Encounters: Cross-Cultural Exchanges and Contacts in Pre-Modern Times* (1993).

On the Web

The Web provides easy access to the lives of the leaders of the early Byzantine world, such as Diocletian (http://latter-rain.com/eccle/diocle.htm), Constantine (http://salve5.salve.edu/~romanemp/Constiv.htm), Justinian (http://www.roman-emperors.org/justinia.htm), Benedict of Nursia (http://www.worth.org.uk/guides/m6.htm), Saint Basil (http://www.orthodox.net/saints/st_basil.html), and Hypatia of Alexandria, an important philosopher and mathematician (http://www.cosmopolis.com/people/hypatia.html). There are useful Web sites devoted to the fall of the Roman West (http://ancienthistory.about.com/library/weekly/aa061599.htm and http://www.fordham.edu/halsall/source/gibbon-fall.html), to the Council of Nicea (http://www.columbia.edu/cu/augustine/arch/sbrandt/nicea.htm), to the Hindu concept of the female aspect of the divine (http://www.asia.si.edu/devi/interpretingdevi.htm), to Mahayana Buddhism (http://www.geocities.com/Athens/8916/index2.html), to Islam (http://islamicity.com/mosque/Intro_Islam.htm) and the Vikings (http://viking.no/ and http://www.pbs.org/wgbh/nova/vikings/who.html), all of which leave little doubt that the world of antiquity was fraught with portent for succeeding eras.

PART III

The Postclassical Era

Introduction

The next 10 chapters concentrate on the time period that runs from the 5th to the 15th century C.E., or from about 450 to about 1450. Most of the chapters deal with specific civilizations; many changes were occurring in old civilization centers (in the aftermath of the decline of the great classical empires) and in newer ones. Before we turn to individual cases, however, it is vital to get a sense of some overall patterns in this 1000-year period. The postclassical period witnessed the emergence of a coherent interregional framework. Instead of the parallelisms and tentative contacts between individual civilizations of the classical period, a genuine world historical dynamic was taking shape. From this point onward, regular, explicit exchange became a standard part of world history.

The Chronology of the Postclassical Period

 As with the classical period, there are two ways to define the postclassical age: in terms of the events that opened and closed it, and in terms of coherent trends that emerged between the beginning and the end.

The stage for the postclassical era was set by the same developments that ended its predecessor: the collapse of the Roman Empire and thus the end of Mediterranean unity, and the decline of classical empires in Asia. The 5th century saw most of these developments draw together, although the fall of the Guptas in India occurred slightly later and China's period of chaos occurred a bit earlier. Capped by invasions of nomadic peoples, the classical decline produced huge changes in the map of the world's civilizations.

The end of the postclassical era was heralded by another set of invasions from central Asia, even more powerful than the surge of the Huns that had helped close the classical period. During the 13th and 14th centuries, nomadic Mongol invaders poured through much of Asia and eastern Europe, ending or changing many governments. By 1400, much of Asia was beginning to recover from the Mongol onslaught, but a series of new changes was taking shape, including the beginning of western Europe's explorations into the wider world. These developments spanned about two centuries, from the early 13th to the mid-15th century; as before, the end of a world history period was not an overnight affair. The postclassical period closes with Mongol invasions and subsequent realignments. The realignments included the collapse of two key political units in the Middle East: the Arab caliphate and the Byzantine Empire.

The Postclassical Millennium and the World Network

 One of the most striking developments in the postclassical period was the formation of more regular connections among major societies in Asia, Africa, and Europe. This world network focused on a series of trade routes. Major routes ran east-west, but a series of north-south routes linked in as well.

Four overarching developments define the postclassical centuries, affecting most individual civilizations in different ways. The expanding influence of the Arabs and Islam, within their Middle Eastern base and well beyond, is one basic feature. The spread of civilization to additional regions of the world is another. A widespread shift in basic belief systems, from polytheism to several great world religions, is a third. The fourth general theme is the development of a world network consisting of increasingly regular and influential relations among most of the individual civilizations.

The Rise of Islam

Soon after the period began, a "leading civilization" emerged in terms of its expansionist capacity and ability to influence other civilizations. Islamic civilization, initially spread by the Arabs, spearheaded the creation of a new empire in the Middle East and north Africa as well as important political initiatives in India, Africa, southern Europe, and central Asia. Its religious outreach brought conversions to Islam in other parts of Africa and Asia. Arab commerce spread across the Indian Ocean to the western Pacific, down the east coast of Africa, and across the Sahara desert. In the classical period, the three major civilization areas had been roughly balanced, although India's outreach was

500 C.E.	600 C.E.	700 C.E.	800 C.E.	900 C.E.
527–565 Justinian, Eastern Roman (Byzantine) emperor	**610–613** Origins of Islam	**711** First Islamic attack in India	**800–814** Charlemagne Empire in western Europe	**960–1127** Song dynasty (China)
570–632 Muhammad	**618–907** Tang dynasty	**718** Byzantines defeat Arab attack on Constantinople	**c. 855** Russian kingdom around Kiev	**968** Tula established by Toltecs (Mesoamerica)
589–618 Sui dynasty (China)	**634–750** Arab invasions in Middle East; spread of Islam in North Africa	**750** Abbasid caliphate	**864** Cyril and Methodius missionaries in eastern Europe	**980–1015** Conversion of Vladimir I of Russia
	661–750 Ummayad Caliphate	**777** Independent Islamic kingdoms begin in North Africa	**878** Last Japanese embassy to China	
	668 Korea becomes independent from China			

particularly impressive. The postclassical era reshuffled the balance of power and created a definite world leader. Correspondingly, the decline of the Islamic imperial system was one of the key features leading to the end of this period and the emergence of a new era in world history.

The Expansion of Civilization

In the postclassical era, civilization began to spread geographically, covering many parts of the world not previously embraced by this kind of human organization. During these centuries the structures of civilization, including great regional trading kingdoms, spread across sub-Saharan Africa, in contrast to the previous concentration in a few centers such as the upper Nile River basin. Civilization also spread widely in northern Europe, both east and west, and became more fully established in Japan. The zones of civilization expanded in the Americas. The civilization map of the world was much larger in 1450 than it had been a thousand years before. At least seven diverse areas command attention in the postclassical era: the Middle East and north Africa, China and east Asia, eastern Europe, western Europe, sub-Saharan Africa, India and southeast Asia (where influences from several other civilizations intermingled), and the Americas.

The rise of new civilization centers meant new opportunities to define key characteristics. But several of the new civilizations shared certain features; for example, both eastern and western Europe, though different in many respects, were predominantly Christian. Many new centers actively imitated other areas, as parts of sub-Saharan Africa did with Islam and western Europe with the eastern Mediterranean. In dealing with the expanded civilization roster, defining separate identities raises some complexities. In addition, civilization areas continued to interact with potent nomadic societies, which took on new importance in the postclassical period.

1000 c.e.	1100 c.e.	1200 c.e.	1300 c.e.	1400 c.e.
1000 Ghana Empire at its height (Africa)	**c. 1100** Invention of explosive powder (China)	**1200** Rise of empire of Mali	**1320s** Europeans first use cannon in war	**1400** End of Polynesian expeditions
1054 Schism between Eastern and Western Christianity	**1150** Disintegration of Toltec Empire	**1206** Delhi sultanate in India	**1320–1340** Bubonic plague breaks out in Gobi desert and spreads to other parts of Asia	**1405–1433** Chinese trading expeditions
1055 Seljuk Turks control Abbasid caliphate	**1150–1350** Spread of Gothic style; scholasticism in western Europe	**1231–1392** Mongols rule Korea	**1325** Rise of Aztec Empire	**1439** Portugal acquires Azores
1066 Norman conquest of England; rise of feudal monarchy in western Europe	**1185–1333** Kamakura Shogunate (Japan)	**1236** Capture of Russia by Mongols	**1338–1453** Hundred Years' War in Europe	**1453** Turks capture Constantinople; end of Byzantine Empire
1096–1099 First Christian Crusade to Palestine		**1258** Capture of Baghdad by Mongols; end of Abbasid caliphate	**1350** Rise of Incas (Andes)	**1471–1493** Peak of Inca Empire
		1260 Death of Sundiata	**1392–1910** Yi dynasty (Korea)	
		1265 First English parliament		
		1279–1368 Mongol Empire in China		
		1290s Islam begins to spread to southeast Asia		

The World Religions

The postclassical era was also defined by the spread of major religions across much of Asia, Europe, and Africa. Although this process had already begun in the late classical era, it defined the new period far more clearly. While Hinduism took fuller shape as the majority religion in India and a few pockets in southeast Asia, Buddhism spread to China and other parts of central and east Asia, including Japan, and also to much of southeast Asia. Islam ran across the Middle East and north Africa and became an important minority religion in India, western China, and parts of sub-Saharan Africa. It also began to make inroads in southeast Asia toward the end of the period. Finally, Christianity spread northward in Europe, both east and west. The major world religions differed widely in many respects, but they did bring a new focus on issues of spirituality and an afterlife. People began to move away from a belief in multiple nature spirits or gods and toward a greater concentration on an overriding divinity or single supernatural force. The world religions shared an ability to extend beyond local cultures and win the adherence of diverse peoples to a core of beliefs and rituals. In this crucial sense, they and their mutual rivalries became part of the new set of international exchanges. In other words, the postclassical era saw widespread and fundamental shifts in religious belief and practices that included elites and ordinary people alike. In many cases, this huge change brought new institutions to the fore, such as the leading Christian churches, Buddhist monasteries, and the religious and legal experts of Islam.

Why did so many people in different areas change their basic beliefs? Pressed by political confusion after the fall of the classical empires, many people looked for new religious meaning. Islam, Christianity, and Buddhism were active propagating faiths. Many groups were converted to one of the new religions by the persuasion of missionaries or other emissaries such as the Muslim Sufis or by the powerful example of political and commercial

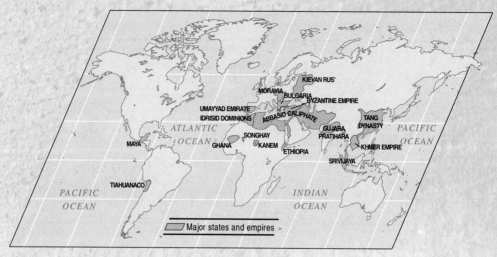

The Postclassical World Takes Shape, c. 900 C.E.

splendor in the seats of the new religious authority. Thus, Russia moved toward Christianity in part because of its leaders' awe at the civilized power of the Byzantine Empire and in part because of missionary influence. A growth in international trade also encouraged religious change, for local gods made less sense to people who exchanged goods with diverse and distant areas. The result was no agreement on belief—several of the new religions competed fiercely, with mutual hatred—but a vital underlying pattern nonetheless.

The World Network

The fourth major characteristic of the postclassical period, emerging with great force by about 1000 C.E., was ultimately the most important of all. An increasing level of interchange developed among the major civilizations of Asia, Europe, and Africa. Interregional trade grew. This particularly followed from the surge of Arab commerce but also resulted from continued activity by Indian merchants, Chinese exchanges with other parts of eastern and southeastern Asia, the development of new north-south trading connections in eastern and western Europe, and the rise of African merchant routes along the eastern coast and through the Sahara. With growing trade and periodic military encounters as civilizations new and old redefined their boundaries, other kinds of exchanges occurred across civilizations: Technology spread. Thus, the knowledge of paper, developed earlier in China, was gained by Muslim troops fighting on China's western border in the 9th century. Paper production in the Middle East resulted. As western Europeans gained new links with this region through trade and religious wars, they learned of the new product. The first European paper manufacture was set up in Italy in the 13th century. Technological spread of this sort was hardly speedy, but it occurred at a more rapid pace than innovations in previous epochs had. Cultural exchange was another vital source of con-

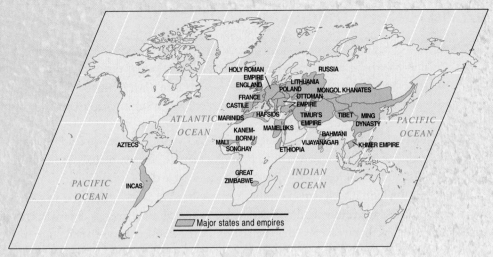

The Postclassical World in Transition, c. 1400 C.E.

tact. In addition to religions, other kinds of ideas spread. Arabs gained knowledge of Indian mathematics, including the number system. Later in the period, western Europeans began to learn Arab mathematics, including the same number system, and they elaborated their philosophy by using and reacting to Arab thought.

In contrast to the very limited interregional trade of the classical period, the great trading system of the Indian Ocean, which stretched from east Africa to south China, expanded dramatically. At the far end of the system, wealthy Europeans in 1300 bought silks and other goods from Asia. World trade continued to involve luxury products, for the most part, but compared to the classical period the volume was higher, the geographic range was farther, and the impact on regional economies was greater. The spread of disease accelerated as well, and in the 14th century a new international epidemic of bubonic plague (the "Black Death") brought home the downside of more fluid international exchange.

The world network was a phenomenon of the Old World, extending an active framework of exchange among the various societies of Asia, Europe, and northern, central, and eastern Africa. However, it was not yet global because the Americas, Polynesia, Australia, and several other regions were not included.

The postclassical era was not a time of fundamental technological innovation, although important advances occurred, particularly in China (such as printing and explosive powder) and at the end of the period in western Europe. But existing technical knowledge spread more widely. Developments such as the compass and lateen sail (vital to expanding Arab commerce) promoted the extension of intensified oceanic trade.

The postclassical era also witnessed a great variety of political forms but no dominant political definition. Empire declined as a common political form, partly because religious ties became more important in holding civilizations together.

World History Themes

 Because of new interregional connections and the spread of world religions, several world history themes took on new features during the postclassical period. Changes in the role of nomadic societies and new opportunities for human agency headed the list. Social inequality changed less, though religions created a more complex cultural context for it.

Basic characteristics of the postclassical period had various effects on leading world history themes. For example, this was not a period of massive environmental change. Agriculture claimed additional territory—there was considerable deforestation in Europe, for example—but the kind of soil depletion that had occurred in Roman days was less common. The spread of agriculture and population growth in central America did cause environmental problems that weakened this civilization by the 15th century. Overall, however, given the fact that few fundamental new technologies were introduced, environmental change reflected mainly population expansion. Nor did basic structures of social and gender inequality shift greatly, although new religious emphases highlighted spiritual equality. Slavery declined in some places but not all, and several societies introduced important new constraints on women. The role of nomads in history peaked with the Mongol invasions. After this, the impact of nomadic groups began to lessen. Even in the postclassical era itself, nomads began to play a lesser role in interregional trade, compared to organized merchants from the Middle East, India, Africa, China, and Europe. Trading companies, with regular representatives in distant ports, became the leading innovators in formal interregional relations.

Expanding civilizations and new religions also provided opportunities for human agency. Ordinary people could attain religious leadership through piety and organizational skill, reshaping religious ideas and practices in the process. Trade also called for creative people whose efforts would accumulate to solidify new trading patterns. Purely political leaders made their mark as well, but with states more loosely organized than in the classical period, few kings really changed the course of history even within a single civilization. Finally, the classic tension between individual civilizations and interregional contacts and forces was redefined in the postclassical centuries, as interregional exchanges grew in range and intensity.

Exchange and Imitation in the Postclassical World

 Three characteristics of the postclassical period highlight the importance of imitating established centers. Growing trade intensified contacts between outlying regions and the most prosperous established civilizations. Missionary activity did the same. Finally, the expansion of civilization as an organized form built on the possibility of explicit imitation.

The best-developed manufacturing centers and largest bureaucracies of the postclassical centuries continued to be located in places where classical civilizations had originally

250

developed. These areas also contained the greatest cities: Constantinople, Baghdad, Zhangan, and Hangzhou. Thus, the Middle East (now dominated by Arabs), China, India, and the Byzantine Empire remained widely influential. Clustered around them were areas where civilization was newer: Japan, northern Europe, much of southeast Asia, and much of sub-Saharan Africa. These areas traded with the major centers but at some disadvantage, sending more raw materials in return for manufactured products. They imitated actively, although there were some features, most notably in centralized government, that they usually did not reproduce successfully. Cultural spread through contact was one of the leading features of the period, although the specific timing varied widely.

The chapters dealing with the postclassical millennium are arranged according to the major themes outlined here. Chapters 11 through 13 explore the emergence of the Arabs as major historical actors, the rise of Islam, and the spread of this new religion to key regions such as India, southeast Asia, and Africa. The parts of the world particularly influenced by Islam illustrate all the overriding themes of the period: the rise of a world-class civilization, the expansion of civilization, changes in belief systems, and the impact of international exchange. Civilization expansion, religious change, and complex links to the world network are the focus of Chapters 14 and 15, on eastern and western Europe. The separate expansion of civilizations in the Americas is covered in Chapter 16. Chapter 17 turns to China, which was linked to larger patterns and the world network, but in distinctive ways. The expansion of east Asian civilization—another example of the spread-of-civilization theme—and the rise of the Mongol Empire (Chapters 18 and 19) lead to a final chapter on the changing world balance at the end of the postclassical period in the 15th century, Chapter 20.

CHAPTER 11

THE FIRST GLOBAL CIVILIZATION: THE RISE AND SPREAD OF ISLAM

The graceful "horseshoe" arches of the Alhambra palace in southern Spain provide a striking example of the sophistication and beauty attained by Islamic art and architecture. Because Spain was on the western fringe of the Islamic world, the superb creations of its Muslim era also remind us of the global reach of a vast civilization.

Although there were important contacts between the civilized centers of the classical world, no single civilization had bound together large portions of the ancient world in either the Western or the Eastern Hemisphere. But in the 7th century C.E., the followers of a new religion, **Islam** (which literally means "submission, the self-surrender of the believer to the will of the one, true God, **Allah**"), spread from the Arabian peninsula and began a sequence of conquest and conversion that would forge the first truly global civilization. Until then, Arabia had been a nomadic backwater on the periphery of the civilizations of the eastern Mediterranean. Within decades, the **Muslims** (as the followers of the new faith and its prophet, **Muhammad,** were called) had conquered an empire extending from Spain in the west to central Asia in the east—an empire that combined the classical civilizations of Greece, Egypt, and Persia.

In succeeding centuries, Islamic civilization was spread by merchants, wandering mystics, and warriors across Africa, Asia, and southern Europe (Map 11.1). It spread throughout the steppes of central Asia (including most of what is today southern Russia) to western China and into south Asia. Islam also spread along the oceanic trade routes to maritime southeast Asia and down the eastern coast of Africa. It followed the overland trade routes across north Africa and down through the Sahara desert to west Africa (see Map 11.1). In addition, Muslim conquerors captured Asia Minor and advanced into the European heartland of Islam's great rival, Christendom.

During most of the millennium after the 7th century C.E., Islamic civilization provided key links and channels for exchange among what had been the main civilized centers of the classical era in the Eastern Hemisphere. Muslim merchants, often in cooperation with Jewish, Armenian, Indian, and other regional commercial groups, became key links in the trade between civilizations from the western Mediterranean to the South China Sea. Muslim traders and conquerors became the prime agents for the transfer of food crops, technology, and ideas among the many centers of civilization in the Eastern Hemisphere. Muslim scholars studied, preserved, and improved on the learning of these ancient civilizations, especially those of Greece, Persia, Egypt, and south Asia.

For several centuries, Muslim works in philosophy, literature, mathematics, and the sciences elevated Arabic (the language of the **Qur'an,** the holy book containing Allah's revelations to Muhammad) to the status of the international language of the educated and informed. Thus, building on the achievements of earlier civilizations, Muslim peoples forged a splendid

600 C.E.	620 C.E.	640 C.E.	660 C.E.	680 C.E.
c. 570–632 Lifetime of the prophet Muhammad	**622** Muhammad's flight *(hijra)* from Mecca to Medina	**644–656** Caliph Uthman	**661–680** Mu'awiya	**680** Karbala, death of Ali's son Husayn
597–626 Wars between the Byzantine and Sasanian (Persian) empires	**624–627** Wars between the followers of Muhammad and the Quraysh of Mecca	**656–661** Caliph Ali; first civil war	**661–750** Umayyad caliphate	**680–692** Second civil war
610 Muhammad's first revelations	**628** Muslim–Meccan truce			**744–750** Third civil war; Abbasid revolt
613 Muhammad begins to preach the new faith	**630** Muhammad enters Mecca in triumph			**750** Abbasid caliphate
	632 Death of Muhammad			
	632–634 Caliph Abu Bakr			
	633–634 Ridda Wars in Arabia			
	634–643 Early Muslim conquests in the Byzantine Empire			
	634–644 Caliph Umar			
	637 Arab invasion and destruction of Sasanian Empire			

new civilization that excelled in most areas of human endeavor, from poetry and architecture to the sciences and urban development.

The rise of the Arabs and of Islam defined much of the Middle East and north Africa from the postclassical period onward. It also defined much of the postclassical period itself, in its larger impact on other regions and on trading patterns throughout Afro-Eurasia. Innovations in the Arab tradition were central to the new developments, but the larger legacy of the classical Mediterranean and of Rome's collapse helped set the stage as well.

Desert and Town: The Arabian World and the Birth of Islam

 In the 7th century C.E., a new religion arose in the Arabian peninsula. Built on the revelations received by the prophet Muhammad, originally a trader from the town of Mecca, the new faith won over many of the camel-herding tribes of the peninsula within decades. Though initially an Arab religion, in both beliefs and practices Islam contained a powerful appeal that eventually made it one of the great world religions.

The Arabian peninsula (see Map 11.2) was a very unlikely birthplace for the first global civilization. Much of the area is covered by some of the most inhospitable desert in the world. An early traveler wrote of the region,

All about us is an iron wilderness; a bare and black shining beach of heated volcanic stones … a vast bed and banks of rusty and basaltic bluish rocks … stubborn as heavy matter, as iron and sounding like bell metal; lying out eternally under the sand-driving desert wind.

In the scrub zones on the edges of the empty quarters, or uninhabitable desert zones, a wide variety of **bedouin,** or nomadic, cultures had developed over the centuries, based on camel and goat herding. In oases like that pictured in Figure 11.1, which dotted the dry landscape, towns and agriculture flourished on a limited scale. Only in the coastal regions of the far south had extensive agriculture, sizeable cities, and regional kingdoms developed in ancient times. Over much of the rest of the peninsula, the camel nomads, organized in tribes and clans, were dominant. Yet in the rocky regions adjacent to the Red Sea, several trading towns had developed that played pivotal roles in the emergence of Islam.

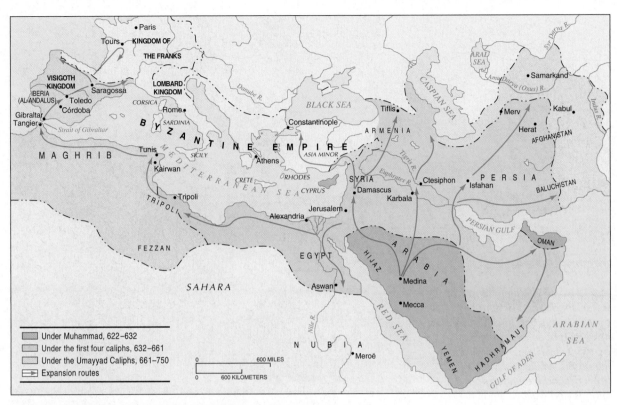

Map 11.1   *The Expansion of Islam in the 7th and 8th Centuries*

Although the urban roots of Islam have often been stressed by writers on Muslim civilization, the bedouin world in which the religion arose shaped the career of its prophet, his teachings, and the spread of the new beliefs. In fact, key towns such as Mecca and Medina were largely extensions of the tribal culture of the camel nomads. Their populations were linked by kinship to bedouin peoples. For example, Mecca had been founded by bedouins and at the time of Muhammad was ruled by former bedouin clans. The safety of the trade routes on which the towns depended was in the hands of the nomadic tribes that lived along the vulnerable caravan routes to the north and south. In addition, the town dwellers' social organization, which focused on clan and family, as well as their culture, including language and religion, were much like those of the nomads.

Clan Identity, Clan Rivalries, and the Cycle of Vengeance

The harsh desert and scrub environment of Arabia gave rise to forms of social organization and a lifestyle that were similar to those of other nomadic peoples. Bedouin herders lived in kin-related clan groups in highly mobile tent encampments. Clans, in turn, were clustered in larger tribal groupings, but these were rarely congregated together and then only in times of war or severe crisis. The struggle for subsistence in the unforgiving Arabian environment resulted in a strong dependence on and loyalty to one's family and clan. Survival depended on cooperation with and support from kin. To be cut off from them or expelled from the clan encampment was in most cases fatal. The use of watering places and grazing lands, which were essential to maintaining the herds on which bedouin life depended, was regulated by clan councils. But there could be wide disparities of wealth and status within clan groups and between clans of the same tribe. Though normally elected by councils of elder advisors, the **shaykhs,** or leaders of the tribes and clans, were almost always men with large herds, several wives, many children, and numerous retainers. The shaykhs' dictates were enforced by bands of free warriors, whose families made up a majority of a given clan group. Beneath the warriors

Figure 11.1 *With their supply of water, shade, and date palms, oases like this one in central Arabia have long been key centers of permanent settlement and trade in the desert. Major towns usually grew around the underground springs and wells or small rivers that fed the oases. Travelers' and traders' caravans stopped at the oases to water their camels and horses and to rest and eat after their arduous treks through the desert. As points of concentration of wealth, food, and precious water, oases were tempting targets for raids by bedouin bands.*

were slave families, often the remnants of rival clans defeated in war, who served the shaykhs or the clan as a whole.

Clan cohesion was reinforced by fierce interclan rivalries and struggles to control vital pasturelands and watering places. If the warriors from one clan found those from another clan drawing water from one of their wells, they were likely to kill them. Wars often broke out as a result of one clan encroaching on the pasture areas of another clan. In a culture in which one's honor depended on respect for one's clan, the flimsiest pretexts could lead to interclan violence. For instance, an insult to a warrior in a market town, the theft of a prize stallion, or one clan's defeat in a horse race by another clan could end in battles

between clan groups. All the men of a given clan joined in these fights, which normally were won by the side that could field several champions who were famed for their strength and skill with spears or bows and arrows.

These battles were fought according to a code of chivalry that was quite common in early cultures. Although battles usually were small in terms of the numbers involved, they were hard-fought and often bloody affairs. Almost invariably the battles either initiated or perpetuated clan feuds, which could continue for hundreds of years. The deaths of the warriors of one clan required that revenge be taken on the clan that had killed them. Their deaths led in turn to reprisals. This constant infighting weakened the bedouins in relation to the neighboring peoples and empires and allowed them to be manipulated and set against each other.

Towns and Long-Distance Trade

Although bedouin herders occupied most of the habitable portions of Arabia, farmers and town dwellers carved out small communities in the western and southern parts of the peninsula in the classical era. Foreign invasions and the inroads of bedouin peoples had all but destroyed these civilizations centuries before the birth of Muhammad. But a number of cities had developed farther north as links in the transcontinental trading system that stretched from the Mediterranean to east Asia. The most important of these cities was **Mecca**, located in the mountainous region along the Red Sea on the western coast of Arabia (see Map 11.2). The town had been founded by the **Umayyad** clan of the **Quraysh** bedouin tribe, and members of the clan dominated its politics and commercial economy.

The wealth and status of Mecca and its merchant elite were enhanced by the fact that the city was the

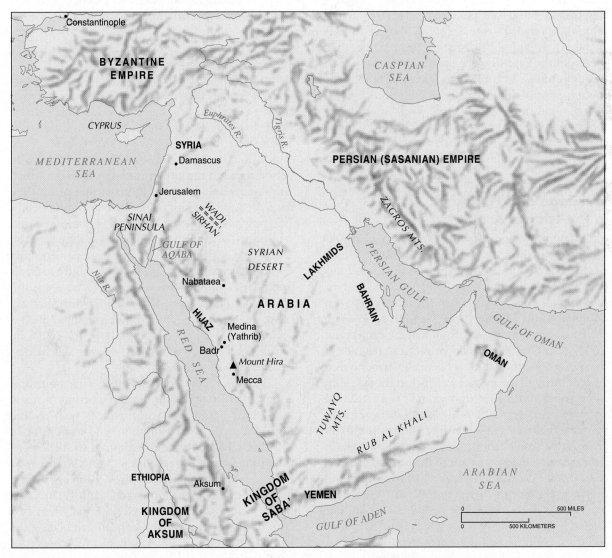

Map 11.2 *Arabia and Surrounding Areas Before and During the Time of Muhammad*

site of the **Ka'ba,** one of the most revered religious shrines in pre-Islamic Arabia. Not only did the shrine attract pilgrims and customers for Mecca's bazaars, but at certain times of the year it was the focus of an obligatory truce in the interclan feuds. Freed from fears of assault by rival groups, merchants and bedouins flocked to the town to trade, exchange gossip, and taste the delights of city life.

Northeast of Mecca was a town named Yathrib (see Map 11.2) that later came to be known as **Medina,** or the city of the prophet (Muhammad). Like most of the other towns in the peninsula, Medina was established in an oasis. Wells and springs made sedentary agriculture possible. In addition to wheat and other staples, Medina's inhabitants grew date palms, whose fruit and seeds (which were fed to camels) they traded to the bedouins. Medina was also engaged, though on a much smaller scale than Mecca, in the long-distance caravan trade that passed through Arabia. In contrast to Umayyad-dominated Mecca, control in Medina was contested by two bedouin and three Jewish clans. Their quarrels left the city a poor second to Mecca as a center of trade, and these divisions proved critical to the survival of the prophet Muhammad and the Islamic faith.

Marriage and Family in Pre-Islamic Arabia

Although the evidence is scant, there are several indications that women in pre-Islamic Arabian bedouin culture enjoyed greater freedom and higher status than those who lived in neighboring civilized centers, such as the Byzantine and Sasanian empires that then dominated the Middle East (Map 11.2). Women played key economic roles, from milking camels and weaving cloth to raising children. Because the men of the clan were often on the move, many tribes traced descent through the mother rather than the father. In some tribes, both men and women were allowed multiple marriage partners. To seal a marriage contract, the man was required to pay a bride-price to his prospective wife's family, rather than the woman's father sending a dowry or gift to the prospective husband. Unlike the women (especially those of elite status) in neighboring Syria and Persia, women in pre-Islamic Arabia were not secluded and did not wear veils. Their advice was highly regarded in clan and tribal councils, and they often wrote poems that were the focus of bedouin cultural life in the pre-Islamic era.

Despite these career outlets, women were not by any means considered equal to men. They could not gain glory as warriors, the most prized occupation of the bedouins, and often they were little more than drudge laborers. Their status depended on the custom of individual clans and tribes rather than on legal codes. As a result, it varied widely from one clan or family to the next. Customary practices of property control, inheritance, and divorce heavily favored men. In the urban environment of trading centers such as Mecca, the rise of a mercantile elite and social stratification appear to have set back the position of women on the whole. The more stable family life of the towns led to the practice of tracing descent through the male line, and while men continued to practice polygamy, women were expected to be monogamous.

Poets and Neglected Gods

Because of the isolation of Arabia in the pre-Islamic age and the harshness and poverty of the natural environment, Arab material culture was not highly developed. Except in the far south, there was little art or architecture of worth. Even Mecca made little impression on the cosmopolitan merchants who passed through the city in caravans from the fabled cities of the ancient civilizations farther north. The main focus of bedouin cultural creativity in the pre-Islamic era was poetry, which was composed and transmitted orally because there was as yet no written language. Clan and tribal bards narrated poems that told of their kinsmen's heroics in war and the clan's great deeds. Some poets were said to have magical powers or to be possessed by demons. More than any other source, their poems provide a vision of life and society in pre-Islamic Arabia. They tell of lovers spurned and passion consummated, war and vendettas, loyalty, and generosity.

Bedouin religion was for most clans a blend of animism and polytheism, or the worship of many gods and goddesses. Some tribes, such as the Quraysh, recognized a supreme god named Allah. But they seldom prayed or sacrificed to Allah, concentrating instead on less abstract spirits who seemed more relevant to their daily lives. Both spirits and gods (for example, the moon god, Hubal) tended to be associated with night, a cool period when dew covered the earth, which had been parched by the blaze of the desert sun. Likewise, the worship of nature spirits focused on sacred caves, pure springs, and groves of trees—places where the bedouins could take shelter from the heat and wind. Religion appears to have had little to do with ethics. Rather, standards of morality and proper behavior were rooted in tribal customs and unwritten codes of honor.

How seriously the bedouins took their gods is also a matter of some doubt. Their lukewarm adherence is illustrated by the famous tale of a bedouin warrior who had set out to avenge his father's death at the hands of a rival clan. He stopped at an oracle along the way to seek advice by drawing arrows that indicated various courses of action he might take. Three times he drew arrows that advised him to abandon his quest for revenge. Infuriated by this counsel, he hurled the arrows at the idol of the oracle and exclaimed, "Accursed one! Had it been thy father who was murdered, thou would not have forbidden my avenging him."

The Life of Muhammad and the Genesis of Islam

 By the 6th century C.E., the camel nomads were dominant throughout much of Arabia. The civilized centers to the south were in ruins, and trading centers such as Mecca and Medina depended on alliances with neighboring bedouin tribes to keep the caravan routes open. The constricted world of clan and kin, nomadic camp, blood feud, and local gods persisted despite the lure of the empires and cosmopolitan urban centers that stretched in a great arc to the north and east of the Arabian peninsula. But pressures for change were mounting. Both the Byzantine and Sasanian empires struggled to assert greater control over the nomadic tribes of the peninsula. In addition, Arab peoples migrated into Mesopotamia and other areas to the north, where they came increasingly under foreign influence. From these regions, the influence of established monotheistic religions, especially Judaism and Christianity, entered Arabia. These new currents gave rise to a number of Arab prophets who urged the bedouin tribes to renounce idol worship and rely on a single, almighty god. The prophet Muhammad and the new religion that his revelations inspired in the early decades of the 7th century responded both to these influences flowing into Arabia and to related social dislocations that were disrupting Arab life.

The hardships of Muhammad's early life underscore the importance of clan ties in the Arabian world. He was born around 570 C.E. into a prominent clan of the Quraysh tribe, the Banu Hashim, in a bedouin encampment where he spent the first six years of his life. Because his father died before he was born, Muhammad was raised by his father's relatives. The loss of his father was compounded by the death of Muhammad's mother shortly after he went to live with her some years later. Despite these early losses, Muhammad had the good fortune to be born into a respected clan and powerful tribe. His paternal uncle, Abu Talib, was particularly fond of the boy and served as his protector and supporter through much of his early life. Muhammad's grandfather, who like other leading members of the clan was engaged in commerce, educated the young man in the ways of the merchant. With Abu Talib, Muhammad made his first caravan journey to Syria, where on this and later trips he met adherents of the Christian and Jewish faiths, whose beliefs and practices had a great impact on his teachings.

In his adolescence, Muhammad took up residence in Mecca. By his early 20s he was working as a trader for **Khadijah** (the widow of a wealthy merchant), whom he married some years later. His life as a merchant in Mecca and on the caravan routes exposed Muhammad to the world beyond Arabia and probably made him acutely aware of the clan rivalries that had divided the peoples of the region for millennia. He would also have become increasingly concerned about new forces undermining solidarity within the clans. The growth of the towns and trade had enriched some clan families and left others behind, often in poverty. It had also introduced a new source of tension between clan and tribal groupings because some clans, such as the Umayyads, grew rich on the profits from commerce, whereas others maintained their herding lifestyle.

As a trader and traveler, Muhammad would almost certainly have been aware of the new religious currents that were sweeping Arabia and surrounding areas in the early 7th century. Particularly notable among these was the spread of monotheistic ideas and a growing dissatisfaction with the old gods that had been venerated by the bedouin peoples. In Muhammad's time, several prophets had arisen, proclaiming a new faith for the Arabs.

Though socially prominent, economically well off, and widely admired for his trading skills and trustworthiness, Muhammad grew increasingly distracted and dissatisfied with a life focused on material gain. He spent increasing amounts of time in meditation in the hills and wilderness that surrounded Mecca. In 610 or earlier, he received the first of many revelations, which his followers believe Allah transmitted to him through the angel Gabriel. These revelations were later written in Arabic and collected in the Qur'an. The teachings and injunctions of the Qur'an formed the basis of the new religion that Muhammad began to preach to his clan and the people of Mecca.

Persecution, Flight, and Victory

At first Muhammad's following was small, consisting mainly of his wife, several clanspeople, and some servants and slaves. As his message was clarified with successive revelations, the circle of the faithful grew so that the Umayyad notables who dominated Meccan life saw him as a threat to their own wealth and power. Above all, the new faith threatened to supplant the gods of the Ka'ba, whose shrines had done so much to establish the city as a center of commerce and bedouin interchange. Although he was protected for a time by his own clan, Muhammad was increasingly threatened by the Umayyads, who plotted with other clans to murder him. It was clear that Muhammad must flee Mecca, but where was he to find refuge? Muhammad's reputation as a skillful and fair negotiator prepared the way for his successful flight from Umayyad persecution. The quarrels between the clans in the nearby city of Medina had set off increasingly violent clashes, and the oasis community was on the verge of civil war. Leaders of the bedouin clans in Medina sent a delegation to invite Muhammad, who was related to them on his mother's side, to mediate their disputes and put an end to the strife that had plagued the town. Clever ruses and the courage of his clansman **Ali,** who at one point took Muhammad's place and thus risked becoming the target of assassins, secured in 622 the safe passage of Muhammad and a small band of followers from Mecca to Medina—the *hijra,* or flight to Medina, which marks the first year of the Islamic calendar. In Medina (where he is depicted in Figure 11.2 working with his followers), he was given a hero's welcome. He soon justified this warm reception by deftly settling the quarrels between the bedouin clans of the town. His wisdom and skill as a political leader won him new followers, who joined those who had accompanied him from Mecca as the core believers of the new faith.

Figure 11.2 *In this miniature painting, Muhammad, surrounded by the flaming halo, joins his disciples in laying the brick foundation for the large house where he lived with his family after his flight to Medina three years after Khadijah's death. The house also served the Muslim faithful as their main mosque until Mecca was captured in 629. After that date, the former pagan shrine called the Ka'ba was gradually transformed into a magnificent mosque. The Ka'ba soon became the central point for Muslims throughout the world, who were enjoined to always face Mecca when they offered their prayers to Allah.*

In the eyes of the Umayyad notables, Muhammad's successes made him a greater threat than ever. Not only was he preaching a faith that rivaled their own, but his leadership was strengthening Mecca's competitor, Medina. Muslim raids on Meccan caravans provided yet another source of danger. Determined to put an end to these threats, the Quraysh launched a series of attacks in the mid-620s on Muhammad and his followers in Medina. These attacks led to several battles. In these clashes, Muhammad proved an able leader and courageous fighter.

The ultimate victory for Muhammad and his followers was signaled by a treaty with the Quraysh in 628, which included a provision granting the Muslims permission to visit the shrine at Ka'ba in Mecca during the season of truce. By then Muhammad's community had won many bedouin allies, and more than 10,000 converts accompanied him on his triumphal return to his hometown in 629. After proving the power of Allah, the single god he proclaimed, by smashing the idols of the shrine, Muhammad gradually won over the Umayyads and most of the other inhabitants of Mecca to the new faith.

Arabs and Islam

Although Islam was soon to become one of the great world religions, the beliefs and practices of the prophet Muhammad were initially adopted only by the Arab town dwellers and bedouins among whom he had grown up. There is a striking parallel here with early Christianity, which focused on Jewish converts. The new religion preached by Muhammad had much to offer the divided peoples of Arabia. It gave them a form of monotheism that belonged to no single tribe and transcended clan and class divisions. It provided a religion that was distinctly Arab in origin and yet the equal of the monotheistic faiths held by the Christians and Jews, who lived in the midst of the bedouin tribes. If anything, the monotheism preached by Muhammad was even more uncompromising than that of the Christians because it allowed no intermediaries between the individual and God. God was one; there were no saints, and angels were nothing more than messengers. In addition, there were no priests in the Christian or Jewish sense of the term.

Islam offered the possibility of an end to the vendettas and feuds that had so long divided the peoples of Arabia and undermined their attempts to throw off the domination of neighboring empires. The **umma,** or community of the faithful, transcended old tribal boundaries, and it made possible a degree of political unity undreamed of before Muhammad's time. The new religion provided a single and supernaturally sanctioned source of authority and discipline. With unity, the skills and energies that the bedouins had once channeled toward warring

with each other were turned outward in a burst of conquest that is perhaps unmatched in human history in its speed and extent. From vassals, march warriors, or contemptible "savages" of the desert waste, the Arab bedouins were transformed into the conquerors and rulers of much of the Middle Eastern world.

The new religion also provided an ethical system that did much to heal the deep social rifts within Arabian society. Islam stressed the dignity of all believers and their equality in the eyes of Allah. It promoted a moral code that stressed the responsibility of the well-to-do and strong for the poor and weak, the aged and infirm. Payment of the **zakat,** a tax for charity, was obligatory in the new faith. In both his revelations and his personal behavior, Muhammad enjoined his followers to be kind and generous to their dependents, including slaves. He forbade the rich to exploit the poor through exorbitant rents or rates of interest for loans.

The prophet's teachings and the revelations of the Qur'an soon were incorporated into an extensive body of law that regulated all aspects of the lives of the Muslim faithful. Held accountable before Islamic law on earth, they lived in a manner that would prepare them for the Last Judgment, which in Islam, as in Christianity, would determine their fate in eternity. A stern but compassionate God and a strict but socially minded body of law set impressive standards for the social interaction between adherents of the new faith.

Universal Elements in Islam

Although only Arabs embraced the religion of Islam in its early years, from the outset it contained beliefs and practices that would give it a strong appeal to peoples at virtually all stages of social development and in widely varying cultural settings. Some of these beliefs—Islam's uncompromising monotheism, highly developed legal codes, egalitarianism, and strong sense of community—were the same as the attributes that had won it support among the peoples of Arabia. Its potential as a world religion was enhanced by the fact that most of the attributes of Islam were to some degree anticipated by the other Semitic religions, particularly Judaism and Christianity, with which Muhammad had contact for much of his life. He accepted the validity of the earlier divine revelations that had given rise to the Jewish and Christian faiths. He taught that the revelations he had received were a refinement of these earlier ones and that they were the last divine instructions for human behavior and worship.

In addition to the beliefs and practices that have given Islam a universal appeal, its **five pillars,** principles that must be accepted and followed by all believers, provided the basis for an underlying religious unity. (1) The confession of faith was simple and powerful: "There is no God but Allah, and Muhammad is his Prophet." The injunctions (2) to pray, facing the holy city of Mecca, five times a day and (3) to fast during the month of **Ramadan,** enhanced community solidarity and allowed the faithful to demonstrate their fervor. (4) The zakat, or tithe for charity, also strengthened community cohesion and won converts from those seeking an ethical code that stressed social responsibility and the unity of all believers. (5) The **hajj,** or pilgrimage to the holy city of Mecca, to worship Allah at the Ka'ba, shown in Figure 11.3, drew together the faithful from Morocco to China. No injunction did more to give Islam a universal character.

The Arab Empire of the Umayyads

Muhammad's victory over the Umayyads and the resulting allegiance of many of the bedouin tribes of Arabia created a new center of power in the Middle Eastern cradle of civilization. A backward, nonagrarian area outside the core zones of Egypt, Mesopotamia, and Persia suddenly emerged as the source of religious and political forces that would eventually affect the history of much of the known world. But when the prophet Muhammad died suddenly in 632, it appeared that his religion might disappear. Despite internal disputes, the Muslim community held together and soon expanded beyond Arabia. Muhammad's old adversaries, the Umayya clan, emerged after several years' struggle as the dominant force in the Islamic community. Under Umayyad rule, the Arabs rapidly built a vast empire, which had established the foundations for an enduring Islamic civilization by the time of its fall in the mid-8th century C.E.

Many of the bedouin tribes that had converted to Islam renounced the new faith in the months after Muhammad's death, and his remaining followers quarreled over who should succeed him. Although these quarrels were never fully resolved,

Figure 11.3 *The Ka'ba in Mecca, with masses of pilgrims. Each year tens of millions of the Muslim faithful make the journey to the holy sites of Arabia from all around the world. The rituals associated with Mecca and Medina are key religious duties for all who can afford to travel to the holy cities.*

the community managed to find new leaders who directed a series of campaigns to force those who had abandoned Islam to return to the fold. Having united most of Arabia under the Islamic banner by 633, Muslim military commanders began to mount serious expeditions beyond the peninsula, where only probing attacks had occurred during the lifetime of the prophet and in the period of tribal warfare after his death. The courage, military prowess, and religious zeal of the warriors of Islam, and the weaknesses of the empires that bordered on Arabia, resulted in stunning conquests in Mesopotamia, north Africa, and Persia, which dominated the next two decades of Islamic history. The empire built from these conquests was Arab rather than Islamic. Most of it was ruled by a small Arab warrior elite, led by the Umayyads and other prominent clans. These groups had little desire to convert the subject populations, either Arab or otherwise, to the new religion.

Consolidation and Division in the Islamic Community

The leadership crisis brought on by Muhammad's death in 632 was compounded by the fact that he had not appointed a successor or even established a procedure by which a new leader would be chosen. Opinion within the Muslim community was deeply divided as to who should succeed him. In this moment of extreme danger, a strong leader who could hold the Islamic community together was urgently needed. On the afternoon Muhammad died, one of the clans that remained committed to the new faith called a meeting to select a leader who would be designated as the **caliph,** the political and religious successor to Muhammad. Several choices were possible, and a deadlock between the clans appeared likely—a deadlock that would almost certainly have been fatal to a community threatened by enemies on all sides. One of the main candidates, Ali, the cousin and son-in-law of Muhammad, was passed over because he was considered too young to assume a position of such great responsibility. This decision later proved to be a major source of division in the Islamic community. But in 632, it appeared that a difficult reconciliation had been won by the choice of one of Muhammad's earliest followers and closest friends, **Abu Bakr** (caliph from 632 to 634). In addition to his courage, warmth, and wisdom, Abu Bakr was well versed in the genealogical histories of the bedouin tribes, which meant that he knew which tribes could be turned against each other and which ones could be enticed into alliances. Initially, at least, his mandate was very limited. He received no financial support from the Muslim community. Thus, he had to continue his previous occupation as a merchant on a part-time basis, and he only loosely controlled the military commanders.

These commanders turned out to be very able. After turning back attacks on Mecca, the Islamic faithful routed one after another of the bedouin tribes. The defeat of rival prophets and some of the larger clans in what were known as the **Ridda Wars** soon brought about the return of the Arabian tribes to the Islamic fold. Emboldened by the proven skills of his generals and the swelling ranks of the Muslim faithful, Abu Bakr oversaw raids to the north of Arabia into the sedentary zones in present-day Iraq and Syria and eastward into Egypt (see Map 11.2).

The unified bedouin forces had originally intended to raid for booty and then retreat back into the desert. But their initial probes revealed the vulnerability of the Byzantine and Persian empires, which dominated or ruled the territories into which the Muslim warriors rode. The invaders were also encouraged by the growing support of the Arab bedouin peoples who had been migrating into the Fertile Crescent for centuries. These peoples had long served as the vassals and frontier guardians of the Byzantine and Persian empires. Now they joined their brethren in a combined assault on the two empires.

Motives for Arab Conquests

The Arab warriors were driven by many forces. The unity provided by the Islamic faith gave them a new sense of common cause and strength. United, they could stand up to the non-Arab rulers who had so long played them against each other and despised them as unwashed and backward barbarians from the desert wastelands. It is also probable that the early leaders of the community saw the wars of conquest as a good way to release the pent-up energies of the martial bedouin tribes they now sought to lead. Above all, the bedouin warriors were drawn to the campaigns of expansion by the promise of a share in the booty to be won in the rich farmlands raided and the tribute that could be exacted from towns that came under Arab rule. As an early Arab writer observed, the bedouins forsook their life as desert nomads not out of a promise of religious rewards, but because of a "yearning after bread and dates."

The chance to glorify their new religion may have been a motive for the Arab conquests, but they were not driven by a desire to win converts to it. In fact, other than fellow bedouin tribes of Arab descent, the invaders had good reason to avoid mass conversions. Not only would Arab warriors have to share the booty of their military expeditions with ever larger numbers if converts were made, but Muslims were exempted from some of the more lucrative taxes levied on Christian, Jewish, and other non-Muslim groups. Thus, the vision of **jihads,** or holy wars launched to forcibly spread the Muslim faith, which has long been associated with Islam in the Christian West, misrepresents the forces behind the early Arab expansion.

Weaknesses of the Adversary Empires

Of the two great empires that had once fought for dominance in the Fertile Crescent transit zone, the Sasanian Empire of Persia proved the more vulnerable. Power in the extensive Sasanian domains was formally concentrated in the hands of an autocratic emperor. By the time of the Arab explosion, the emperor was manipulated by a landed, aristocratic class that harshly exploited the farmers who made up most of the population of the empire. Zoroastrianism, the official religion of the emperor, lacked popular roots. By contrast, the religion of a visionary reformer named Mazdak, which had won considerable support among the peasants, had been brutally suppressed by the Sasanian rulers in the period before the rise of Islam. At first, the Sasanian commanders had contempt for the Arab invaders and set out against them with poorly prepared forces. By the time the seriousness of the Islamic threat was made clear by decisive Arab victories in the Fertile Crescent region and the defection of the Arab tribes on the frontier, Muslim warriors had broken into the Sasanian heartland. Further Muslim victories brought about the rapid collapse of the vast empire. The Sasanian rulers and their forces retreated eastward in the face of the Muslim advance. The capital was taken, armies were destroyed, and generals were slain. When in 651 the last of the Sasanian rulers was assassinated, Muslim victory and the destruction of the empire were ensured.

Despite an equally impressive string of Muslim victories in the provinces of their empire, the Byzantines proved a stronger adversary (see Chapter 14). However, their ability to resist the Muslim onslaught was impeded by both the defection of their own frontier Arabs and the support the Muslim invaders received from the Christians of Syria and Egypt. Members of the Christian sects dominant in these areas, such as the **Copts** and **Nestorians,** had long resented the rule of the Orthodox Byzantines, who taxed them heavily and openly persecuted them as heretics. When it became clear that the Muslims would not only tolerate the Christians but tax them less heavily than the Byzantines did, these Christian groups rallied to the Arabs.

Weakened from within and exhausted by the long wars fought with Persia in the decades before the Arab explosion, the Byzantines reeled from the Arab assaults. Syria, western Iraq, and Palestine were quickly taken by the Arab invaders, and by 640 a series of probes had been made into Egypt, one of the richest provinces of the empire (see Map 11.1). In the early 640s, the ancient center of learning and commerce, Alexandria, was taken, most of Egypt was occupied, and Arab armies extended their conquests into Libya to the west. Perhaps even more astounding from the point of view of the Byzantines, by the mid-640s the desert bedouins were putting together war fleets that increasingly challenged the long-standing Byzantine mastery of the Mediterranean. The rise of Muslim naval supremacy in the eastern end of the Mediterranean sealed the loss of Byzantium's rich provinces in Syria and Egypt. It also opened the way to further Muslim conquests in north Africa, the Mediterranean islands, and even southern Italy (see Map 11.1). For a time the Byzantines managed to rally their forces and stave off further inroads into their Balkan and Asia Minor heartlands. But the early triumphs of the Arab invaders had greatly reduced the strength of the Byzantine Empire. Although it survived for centuries, it was henceforth a kingdom under siege.

The Problem of Succession and the Sunni–Shi'a Split

The stunning successes of Muslim armies and the sudden rise of an Arab empire diverted attention, for a time at least, from continuing divisions within the community. Although these divisions were often generations old and the result of personal animosities, resentments had also begun to build over how the booty from the conquests should be divided among the tribal groups that made up the Islamic community. In 656, just over two decades after the death of the prophet, the growing tensions broke into open violence. The spark that began the conflict was the murder of the third caliph, **Uthman,** by mutinous warriors returning from Egypt. His death was the signal for the supporters of Ali to proclaim him as caliph. Uthman's unpopularity among many of the tribes, particularly those from Medina and the prophet's earliest followers, arose in part from the fact that he was the first caliph to be chosen from Muhammad's early enemies, the Umayyad clan. Already angered by Uthman's murder, the Umayyads rejected Ali's claims and swore revenge when he failed to punish Uthman's assassins. Warfare erupted between the two factions.

Ali was a famous warrior and experienced commander, and his deeply committed supporters soon gained the upper hand. After his victory at the Battle of the Camel in late 656, most of the Arab garrisons shifted to his side against the Umayyads, whose supporters were concentrated in the province of Syria and the holy city of Mecca. Just as Ali was on the verge of defeating the Umayyad forces at the **Battle of Siffin** in 657, he was won over by a plea for mediation. His decision to accept mediation was fatal to his cause. Some of his most fervent supporters renounced his leadership and had to be suppressed violently. While representatives of both parties tried unsuccessfully to work out a compromise, the Umayyads regrouped their forces and added Egypt to the provinces backing their claims. In 660, **Mu'awiya,** the new leader of the Umayyads, was proclaimed caliph in Jerusalem, directly challenging Ali's position. A year later, Ali was assassinated, and his son, Hasan, was pressured by the Umayyads into renouncing his claims to the caliphate.

In the decades after the prophet's death, the question of succession generated deep divisions in the Muslim community. The split between the **Sunnis,** who backed the Umayyads, and the **Shi'a,** or supporters of Ali, remains to this day the most fundamental in the Islamic world. Hostility between these two branches of the Islamic faithful was heightened in the years after Ali's death by the continuing struggle between the Umayyads and Ali's second son, Husayn. After being abandoned by the clans in southern Iraq, who had promised to rise in a revolt supporting his claims against the Umayyads, Husayn and a small party were overwhelmed and killed at **Karbala** in 680. From that point on, the Shi'a mounted sustained resistance to the Umayyad caliphate.

Over the centuries, factional disputes about who had the right to succeed Muhammad, with the Shi'a recognizing none of the early caliphs except Ali, have been compounded by differences in belief, ritual, and law that have steadily widened the gap between Sunnis and Shi'a. These divisions have been further complicated by the formation of splinter sects within the Shi'a community in particular, beginning with those who defected from Ali when he agreed to arbitration.

The Umayyad Imperium

After a pause to settle internal disputes over succession, the remarkable sequence of Arab conquest was renewed in the last half of the 7th century. Muslim armies broke into central Asia, inaugurating a rivalry with Buddhism in the region that continues to the present day (see Map 11.1). By the early 8th century, the southern prong of this advance had reached into northwest India. Far to the west, Arab armies swept across north Africa and crossed the Straits of Gibraltar to conquer Spain and threaten France. Although the Muslim advance into western Europe was blocked by the hard-fought victory of Charles Martel and the Franks at Poitiers in 732, the Arabs did not fully retreat beyond the Pyrenees into Spain until decades later. Muslim warriors and sailors dominated much of the Mediterranean, a position that was solidified by the conquest of key islands such as Crete, Sicily, and Sardinia in the early decades of the 9th century. By the early 700s, the Umayyads ruled an empire that extended from Spain in the west to the steppes of central Asia in the east. Not since the Romans had there been an empire to match it; never had an empire of its size been built so rapidly.

Although Mecca remained the holy city of Islam, under the Umayyads the political center of community shifted to **Damascus** in Syria, where the Umayyads chose to live after the murder of Uthman. From Damascus a succession of Umayyad caliphs strove to build a bureaucracy that would bind together the vast domains they claimed to rule. The empire was very much an Arab conquest state. Except in the Arabian peninsula and in parts of the Fertile Crescent, a small Arab and Muslim aristocracy ruled over peoples who were neither Arab nor Muslim. Only Muslim Arabs were first-class citizens of this great empire. They made up the core of the army and imperial administration, and only they received a share of the booty derived from the ongoing conquests. They could be taxed only for charity. The Umayyads sought to keep the Muslim warrior elite concentrated in garrison towns and separated from the local population. It was hoped that isolation would keep them from assimilating to the subjugated cultures because intermarriage meant conversion and the loss of taxable subjects.

Converts and "People of the Book"

Umayyad attempts to block extensive interaction between the Muslim warrior elite and their non-Muslim subjects had little chance of succeeding. The citified bedouin tribes were soon interacting intensively with the local populations of the conquered areas and intermarrying with them. Equally critical, increasing numbers of these peoples were voluntarily converting to Islam, despite the fact that conversion did little to advance them socially or politically in the Umayyad period. In this era Muslim converts, **mawali,** still had to pay property taxes and in some cases the **jizya,** or head tax, levied on nonbelievers. They received no share of the booty and found it difficult, if not impossible, to get important positions in the army or bureaucracy. They were not even considered full members of the umma but were accepted only as clients of the powerful Arab clans.

As a result, the number of conversions in the Umayyad era was low. By far the greater portion of the population of the empire were the **dhimmi,** or "people of the book." As the name suggests, it was originally applied to Christians and Jews who shared the Bible with the Muslims. As Islamic conquests spread to other peoples, such as the Zoroastrians of Persia and the Hindus of India, the designation dhimmi was necessarily stretched to accommodate the majority groups within these areas of the empire. As the early illustration of Jewish worship in Muslim Spain in Figure 11.4 shows, the Muslim overlords generally tolerated the religions of dhimmi. Although they had to pay the jizya and both commercial and property taxes, their communities and legal systems were left intact, and they were allowed to worship as they pleased. This approach made it a good deal easier for these peoples to accept Arab rule, particularly because many had been oppressed by their pre-Muslim overlords.

Family and Gender Roles in the Umayyad Age

Broader social changes within the Arab and widening Islamic community were accompanied by signif-

Figure 11.4 *Jews worshiping in a synagogue. As dhimmi, or "people of the book," Jews were allowed to build impressive synagogues and worship freely throughout the Muslim world. Jewish merchant families amassed great wealth, often as partners of Muslim counterparts, and Jewish scholars were revered for their many contributions to learning from Spain to Baghdad.*

icant shifts in the position of women, both within the family and in society at large. In the first centuries of Arab expansion, the greatly strengthened position of women under Islam prevailed over the seclusion and subordination that were characteristic features of women's lives through much of the rest of the Middle East. Muhammad's teachings and the dictates of the Qur'an stressed the moral and ethical dimensions of marriage. The kindness and concern the prophet displayed for his own wives and daughters did much to strengthen the bonds between husband and wife and the nuclear family in the Islamic community. Muhammad encouraged marriage as a replacement for the casual and often commercial sexual liaisons that had been widespread in pre-Islamic Arabia. He vehemently denounced adultery on the part of both husbands and wives, and he forbade female infanticide, which apparently had been widely practiced in Arabia in pre-Islamic times. Men were allowed to marry up to four wives. But the Qur'an forbade multiple marriages if the husband could not support more than one wife or treat all of his wives equally. Women could not take more than one husband. But Muhammad gave his own daughters a say as to whom they would marry and greatly strengthened the legal rights of women in inheritance and divorce. He insisted that the bride-price paid by the husband's family be given to his future wife rather than to her father.

The prophet's teachings proclaimed the equality of men and women before God and in Islamic worship. Women, most notably his wife Khadijah, were some of Muhammad's earliest and bravest followers. They accompanied his forces to battle (as did the wives of their adversaries) with the Meccans, and a woman was the first martyr for the new faith. Many of the **hadiths,** or traditions of the prophet, which have played such a critical role in Islamic law and ritual, were recorded by women. In addition, Muhammad's wives and daughters played an important role in compiling the Qur'an.

Although women were not allowed to lead prayers, they played an active role in the politics of the early community. Muhammad's widow, Aisha, actively promoted the claims of the Umayyad party against Ali, while Zainab, Ali's daughter, went into battle with the ill-fated Husayn. Through much of the Umayyad period, little is heard of veiled Arab women, and women appear to have pursued a wide range of occupations, including scholarship, law, and commerce. Perhaps one of Zainab's nieces best epitomizes the independent-mindedness of Muslim women in the early Islamic era. When chided for going about without a veil, she replied that Allah in his wisdom had chosen to give her a beautiful face and that she intended to make sure that it was seen in public so that all might appreciate his grace.

Umayyad Decline and Fall

The ever-increasing size of the royal harem was just one manifestation of the Umayyad caliphs' growing addiction to luxury and soft living. Their legitimacy had been disputed by various Muslim factions since their seizure of the caliphate. But the Umayyads fur-

ther alienated the Muslim faithful as they became more aloof in the early 8th century and retreated from the dirty business of war into their pleasure gardens and marble palaces. Their abandonment of the frugal, simple lifestyle followed by Muhammad and the earliest caliphs—including Abu Bakr, who made a trip to the market the day after he was selected to succeed the prophet—enraged the dissenting sects and sparked revolts throughout the empire. The uprising that proved fatal to the short-lived dynasty began among the frontier warriors who had fought and settled in distant Iran.

By the mid-8th century, more than 50,000 warriors had settled near the oasis town of Merv in the eastern Iranian borderlands of the empire. Many of them had married local women, and over time they had come to identify with the region and to resent the dictates of governors sent from distant Damascus. The warrior settlers were also angered by the fact that they were rarely given the share of the booty, now officially tallied in the account books of the royal treasury, that they had earned by fighting the wars of expansion and defending the frontiers. They were contemptuous of the Umayyads and the Damascus elite, whom they saw as corrupt and decadent. In the early 740s, an attempt by Umayyad palace officials to introduce new troops into the Merv area touched off a revolt that soon spread over much of the eastern portions of the empire (see Map 11.1).

Marching under the black banners of the **Abbasid** party, which traced its descent from Muhammad's uncle, al-Abbas, the frontier warriors openly challenged Umayyad armies by 747. Deftly forging alliances with dissident groups that resisted the Umayyads throughout the empire, their leader, Abu al-Abbas, the great-great-grandson of the prophet's uncle, led his forces from victory to victory. Among his most important allies were the Shi'a, who, as we have seen, had rejected Umayyad authority from the time of Ali. Also critical were the mawali, or non-Arab converts to Islam. The mawali felt that under Umayyad rule they had never been recognized as fully Muslim. In supporting the Abbasids, the mawali hoped to attain full acceptance in the community of believers.

This diverse collection of Muslim rebels made short work of what remained of the Umayyad imperium. Persia and then Iraq fell to the rebels. In

In Depth

Civilization and Gender Relationships

Within a century of Muhammad's death, the strong position women had enjoyed as a result of the teachings and example of the prophet had begun to erode. We do not fully understand all the forces that account for this decline. Ambiguities in the Qur'an provide part of the answer. Muhammad was concerned about good treatment for women and defined certain rights, for example to property. He also, however, stipulated women's inferiority to men in key legal rights (differential punishments for adultery were a case in point). And, like Christianity, Islam argued that women were more likely than men to be sinners. But more critical were the beliefs and practices of the urbanized, sedentary peoples in the areas the Arabs conquered and where many of them settled from the mid-7th century onward. The example of these ancient and long-civilized peoples increasingly influenced the Arab bearers of Islam. They developed a taste for city life and the superior material and artistic culture of the peoples they ruled. In terms of gender roles, most of these influences weakened the position of women. We have seen this apparent connection between increasing political centralization and urbanization and the declining position of women in many of the ancient and classical civilizations treated thus far. In China, India, Greece, and the Middle East, women enjoyed broader occupational options and a stronger voice within the family, and in society as a whole, before the emergence of centralized polities and highly stratified social systems. In each case, the rise of what we have called civilizations strengthened paternal control within the family, inheritance through the male line, and male domination of positions of power and the most lucrative occupations. Women in these societies became more and more subjected to men—their fathers and brothers, husbands and sons—and more and more confined to the roles of homemakers and bearers of children. Women's legal rights were reduced, often sharply. In many civilizations, various ways were devised to shut women off from the world.

As we have seen, women played active and highly valued roles in the bedouin tribes of pre-Islamic Arabia. Particularly in towns such as Mecca, they experienced considerable freedom in terms of sexual and marriage partners, occupational choices (within the limited range available in an isolated pastoral society), and opportunities to influence clan decisions. The position of Muhammad's first wife,

Khadijah, is instructive. Her position as a wealthy widow in charge of a thriving trading enterprise reveals that women were able to remarry and to own and inherit property. They could also pursue careers, even after their husbands died. Khadijah employed Muhammad. After he had successfully worked for her for some time, she asked him to marry her, which apparently neither surprised nor scandalized her family or Meccan society. It is also noteworthy that Khadijah was 10 to 15 years older than the prophet, who was 25 at the time of their betrothal.

The impact of the bedouin pattern of gender roles and relationships is also clear in the teachings and personal behavior of Muhammad. Islam did much to legalize the strong but by no means equal status of women. In addition, it gave greater uniformity to their position from one tribe, town, or region to the next. For a century or two after the prophet's death, women in the Islamic world enjoyed unprecedented opportunities for education, religious expression, and social fulfillment.

Then the influences of the cultures into which the Arabs had expanded began to take hold. The practices of veiling and female seclusion that were long followed by the non-Arab dwellers of Syria and Persia were increasingly adopted by or imposed upon Muslim women. Confined more and more to the home, women saw their occupational options decrease, and men served as their go-betweens in legal and commercial matters.

Ironically, given the earlier status of women such as Khadijah, the erosion of the position of women was especially pronounced among those who lived in the cities that became the focus of Islamic civilization. Upper-class women, in particular, felt growing restrictions on their movement and activities. In the great residences that sprang up in the wealthy administrative centers and trading towns of the Middle East, the women's quarters were separate from the rest of the household and set off by high walls and gardens. In the palaces of Islamic rulers and provincial governors, this separation was marked by the development of the *harem*, or forbidden area. In the harem, the notables' wives and concubines lived in seclusion. They were constantly guarded by the watchful eyes and sharp swords of corps of eunuchs, men castrated specifically to qualify them for the task.

When upper-class women went into the city, they were veiled from head to toe and often were carried in covered sedan chairs by servants who guarded them from the glances of the townsmen and travelers. In their homes, upper-class women were spared the drudgery of domestic chores by large numbers of female slaves. If we are to judge from stories such as those related in the *Arabian Nights* (from which excerpts are included in the Document box), female slaves and servants were largely at the mercy of their male masters. Although veiling, seclusion, and other practices that limited the physical and occupational mobility of women also spread to the lower urban classes and rural areas, they were never as strictly observed there as in urban, upper-class households. Women from poorer families had to work to survive. Thus, they had to go out "veiled but often unchaperoned" to the market or to work as domestic servants. Lower-class women also worked hard at home, not just at housekeeping but at weaving, rugmaking, and other crafts that supplemented the family income. In rural areas and in towns distant from the main urban centers, veiling and confinement were observed less strictly. Peasant women worked the family or local landlord's fields, planted their own gardens, and tended the livestock.

Because of Islamic religion and law, in all locales and at all class levels the position of women in the Middle East never deteriorated to the same extent as in India, China, and many other civilized centers. Because of the need to read the Qur'an, women continued to be educated, family resources permitting, even if they rarely were able to use their learning for scholarship or artistic expression. Islamic law preserved for women property, inheritance, divorce, and remarriage rights that often were denied in other civilized societies. Thus, the strong position women had enjoyed in bedouin cultures, and that in many respects had been built into Islam, was never entirely undone by the customs and practices Muslims encountered as they came to rule the civilized centers in the rest of the Middle East.

The fact that the position of women has also been strong in other cultural areas where authority is decentralized and social organization not highly stratified, such as those in west Africa (see Chapter 13), suggests that at least in certain stages of its development, civilization works against the interests of women. Women in decentralized societies have often been able to own their own property, to engage in key economic activities, and to play important roles in religious ceremonies. The positions and status they have achieved in decentralized societies, such as those in early Arabia or much of sub-Saharan Africa and southeast Asia, suggest factors that may help explain the greater balance in gender roles and power in less centralized societies. The very immediate connection between women and agriculture or stock-raising, which are central to survival in these societies, may also account for the greater respect accorded them and for their often prominent roles in fertility rituals and religious cults. Whatever the explanation, until the present era, higher degrees of centralization and social stratification—both characteristic features of civilized societies—have almost always favored men in the allotment of power and career opportunities.

Questions: Compare the position of upper-class women in classical Indian, Chinese, Greek, and Roman societies with regard to their ability to hold property, opportunity to pursue careers outside the home, rights in marriage and divorce, and level of education. In which of these societies were women better off, and why? Were differences in the position of women at lower-class levels similar between these societies? In what ways were women better off in decentralized pastoral or forest-farming societies? What advantages have they enjoyed in highly urbanized and more centralized civilizations?

750, the Abbasid forces met an army led by the Umayyad caliph himself in a massive **Battle on the River Zab** near the Tigris. The Abbasid victory opened the way for the conquest of Syria and the capture of the Umayyad capital.

Wanting to eliminate the Umayyad family altogether to prevent recurring challenges to his rule, Abu al-Abbas invited many members of the clan to what was styled as a reconciliation banquet. As the Umayyads were enjoying the feast, guards covered them with carpets and they were slaughtered by Abbas's troops. An effort was then made to hunt down and kill all the remaining members of the family throughout the empire. Most were slain, but the grandson of a former caliph fled to Spain and founded there the Caliphate of Córdoba, which lived on for centuries after the rest of the Umayyads' empire had disappeared.

From Arab to Islamic Empire: The Early Abbasid Era

The sudden shift from Umayyad to Abbasid leadership reflected a series of fundamental transformations within an evolving Islamic civilization. The revolts against the Umayyads were a product of growing regional identities and divisions. As Islamic civilization spread even farther under the Abbasids, these regional interests and religious divisions made it increasingly difficult to hold together the vast areas the Arabs had conquered. They also gave rise to new divisions within the Islamic community that have sapped its strength from Abbasid times to the present. In addition, the victory of the Abbasids led to bureaucratic expansion, absolutism, and luxury on a scale beyond the wildest dreams of the Umayyads. The Abbasids also championed a policy of active conversion and the admission of converts as full members of the Islamic community. As a result, Islam was transformed from the religion of a small, Arab warrior elite into a genuinely universal faith with tens of millions of adherents from Spain to the Philippine islands.

The rough treatment the Umayyad clan had received at the hands of the victorious Abbasids should have forewarned their Shi'a and mawali allies of what was to come. But the Shi'a and other dissenting groups continued the support that allowed the Abbasids to level all other centers of political rivalry. Gradually, the Abbasids rejected many of their old allies, becoming more and more righteous in their defense of Sunni Islam and increasingly less tolerant of what they called the heretical views of the various sects of Shi'ism. With the Umayyads all but eliminated and their allies brutally suppressed, the way was clear for the Abbasids to build a centralized, absolutist imperial order.

The fact that they chose to build their new capital, **Baghdad,** in Iraq near the ancient Persian capital of Ctesiphon was a clear sign of things to come. Soon the Abbasid caliphs were perched on jewel-encrusted thrones, reminiscent of those of the ancient Persian emperors, gazing down on the great gatherings of courtiers and petitioners who bowed before them in their gilt and marble audience halls. The caliphs' palaces and harems expanded to keep pace

with their claims to absolute power over the Islamic faithful as well as the non-Muslim subjects of their vast empire.

The ever-expanding corps of bureaucrats, servants, and slaves who strove to translate Abbasid political claims into reality lived and worked within the circular walls of the new capital at Baghdad. The bureaucratization of the Islamic Empire was reflected above all in the growing power of the **wazir,** or chief administrator and head of the caliph's inner councils. It was also embodied in a more sinister way in the fearful guise of the royal executioner, who stood close to the throne in the public audiences of the Abbasid rulers. The wazirs oversaw the building of an administrative infrastructure that allowed the Abbasids to project their demands for tribute to the most distant provinces of the empire. Sheer size, poor communication, and collusion between Abbasid officials and local notables meant that the farther the town or village was from the capital, the less effectively royal commands were carried out. But for more than a century, the Abbasid regime was fairly effective at collecting revenue from its subject peoples and preserving law and order over much of the empire.

Islamic Conversion and Mawali Acceptance

The Abbasid era saw the full integration of new converts, both Arab and non-Arab, into the Islamic community. In the last decades of the Umayyad period, there was a growing acceptance of the mawali, or non-Arab Muslims, as equals. There were also efforts to win new converts to the faith, particularly among Arab peoples outside the Arabian peninsula, such as those at prayer in Figure 11.5. In the Abbasid era, when the practice of dividing booty between the believers had long been discarded, mass conversions to Islam were encouraged for all peoples of the empire, from the Berbers of north Africa to the Persians and Turkic peoples of central Asia. Converts were admitted on an equal footing with the first generations of believers, and over time the distinction between mawali and the earlier converts all but disappeared.

Most converts were won over peacefully through the great appeal of Islamic beliefs and the advantages they enjoyed over non-Muslim peoples in the empire. Not only were converts exempt from paying the head tax, but they had greater opportunities to get advanced schooling and launch careers as administrators, traders, or judges. No group demonstrated the

Figure 11.5 *Massed Muslim worshipers. Whether in a nearby mosque or in their homes and shops, Muslims are required to pray five times a day, facing the holy city of Mecca. Those congregating in the mosque, as in this photo, are oriented to Mecca by the qibla wall, which is marked by a highly ornamented inset built into it, which indicates the direction of the holy city. Men congregate in the open spaces in the center of the mosque, while women pray in areas on the sides or in the back, or sometimes in balconies above, that are usually screened off by pillars or carved panels from the areas where the men worship.*

new opportunities open to converts as dramatically as the Persians, who, in part through their bureaucratic skills, soon came to dominate the upper levels of imperial administration. In fact, as the Abbasid rulers became more dissolute and less interested in affairs of state, several powerful Persian families close to the throne became the real locus of power in the imperial system.

Town and Country: Commercial Boom and Agrarian Expansion

The rise of the mawali was paralleled in the Abbasid era by the growth in wealth and social status of the merchant and landlord classes of the empire. The Abbasid age was a time of great urban expansion that was linked to a revival of the Afro-Eurasian trading network, which had declined with the fall of the Han dynasty in China in the early 3rd century C.E. and the slow collapse of the Roman Empire in the 4th and 5th centuries. The Abbasid domains in the west and the great Tang and Song empires in the east became the pivots of the revived commercial system.

From the western Mediterranean to the South China Sea, Arab **dhows,** or sailing vessels with lateen (triangular) sails, which later influenced European ship design, carried the goods of one civilized core to

be exchanged with those of another. Muslim merchants, often in joint ventures with Christians and Jews (which, because each merchant had a different Sabbath, meant that the firm could do business all week), grew rich by supplying the cities of the empire with provisions. Mercantile concerns also took charge of the long-distance trade that specialized in luxury products for the elite classes. The great profits from trade were reinvested in new commercial enterprises, the purchase of land, and the construction of the great mansions that dominated the central quarters of the political and commercial hubs of the empire. Some wealth also went to charity, as required by the Qur'an. A good deal of the wealth was spent on building and running mosques and religious schools, baths, and rest houses for weary travelers (Figure 11.6). Large donations were also made to hospitals, which in the numbers of their patients and the quality of their medical care surpassed those of any other civilization of that time.

The growth of Abbasid cities was also fed by a great increase in handicraft production. Both government-run and privately owned workshops expanded or were established to produce a wide range of products, from necessities such as furniture and carpets to luxury items such as glassware, jewelry, and tapestries. Although the artisans often were poorly paid and

Figure 11.6 *The rulers and nobility of the Abbasid capital in Baghdad frequented baths like that shown in this Persian miniature painting. Here the caliph, Haroun al-Rashid, receives a haircut while servants prepare the steam rooms. At the baths, the Abbasid elite could relax, exchange gossip, and enjoy expert massages.*

some worked in great workshops, they were not slaves or drudge laborers. They owned their own tools and were often highly valued for their skills. The most skilled of the artisans formed guildlike organizations, which negotiated wages and working conditions with the merchants and supported their members in times of financial difficulty or personal crisis.

In towns and the countryside, much of the unskilled labor was left to slaves, often attached to prominent families as domestic servants. Large numbers of slaves also served the caliphs and their highest advisors. It was possible for the more clever and ambitious slaves to rise to positions of great power, and many eventually were granted their freedom or were able to buy it. Less fortunate were the slaves forced into lives of hard labor under the overseer's whip on rural estates and government projects, such as those devoted to draining marshlands, or into a lifetime of labor in the nightmare conditions of the great salt mines in southern Iraq. Most of these drudge laborers were non-Muslims captured on slaving raids in east Africa.

In the countryside, a wealthy and deeply entrenched landed elite called the **ayan** emerged in

Document

The Thousand and One Nights as a Mirror of Elite Society in the Abbasid Era

The luxurious lifestyle of the Abbasid rulers and their courtiers reflected the new wealth of the political and commercial elites of the Islamic Empire. At the same time, it intensified sectarian and social divisions in the Islamic community. As the compilation of folktales from many parts of the empire titled *The Thousand and One Nights* testifies, life for much of the elite in Baghdad and other major urban centers was luxurious and oriented to the delights of the flesh. Caliphs and wealthy merchants lived in palatial residences of stone and marble, complete with gurgling fountains and elaborate gardens, which served as retreats from the glare and heat of the southern Mediterranean climate. In the Abbasid palaces, luxurious living and ostentation soared to fantastic heights. In the Hall of the Tree, for example, there was a huge artificial tree, made entirely of gold and silver and filled with gold mechanical birds that chirped to keep the caliph in good cheer.

Because the tales were just that—tall tales—there is some exaggeration of the wealth, romantic exploits, and sexual excesses of the world depicted. But for some members of the elite classes, the luxuries, frivolities, and vices of the Abbasid age were very real. The following passages are taken from an English translation of *The Thousand and One Nights*. Each is selected to reveal a different facet of high society in the Abbasid era. The first, which describes the sumptuous interior of a mansion in Baghdad, indicates that conspicuous material consumption existed far beyond the palace:

> They reached a spacious ground-floor hall, built with admirable skill and beautified with all manner of colors and carvings, with upper balconies and groined [sharply curved] arches and galleries and cupboards and recesses whose curtains hung before them. In the midst stood a great basin full of water surrounding a fine fountain, and at the upper end on the raised dais was a couch of juniper wood set with gems and pearls, with a canopy-like mosquito curtain of red satin-silk looped up with pearls as big as filberts [hazelnuts] and bigger.

In another tale, a fallen prince details the proper upbringing and education for a person of substance:

> I am a king, son of a king, and was brought up like a prince. I learned intoning the Koran [Qur'an] according [to] the seven schools and I read all manner [of] books,

and held disputations on their contents with the doctors and men of science. Moreover, I studied star lore and the fair sayings of poets, and I exercised myself in all branches of learning until I surpassed the people of my time. My skill in calligraphy [writing, in this case Arabic and perhaps Persian] exceeded that of all of the scribes, and my fame was bruited abroad over all climes and cities, and all the kings learned to know my name.

In the following passage, a stylishly dressed woman from the elite classes is described in great detail:

> There stood before him an honorable woman in a mantilla [veil] of Mosul silk broidered with gold and bordered with brocade [a rich cloth with a raised design, often of gold or silver]. Her walking shoes were also [bordered] with gold, and her hair floated in long plaits. She raised her face veil … showing two black eyes fringed with jetty lashes, whose glances were soft and languishing and whose perfect beauty was ever blandishing.

The woman leads a porter to a marketplace, which again reflects the opulence accessible to the rich and powerful of Abbasid society:

> She stopped at the fruiter's shop and bought from him Shami apples and Osmani quinces and Omani peaches, and cucumbers of Nile growth, and Egyptian limes and Sultani oranges and citrons, besides Aleppine jasmine, scented myrtle berries, Damascene nenuphars [water lilies], flower of privit and camomile, blood-red anemones, violets, and pomegranate bloom, eglantine [wild rose], and narcissus, and set the whole in the porter's crate.

Questions: What objects are key symbols of wealth in Abbasid society? In what ways do these descriptions convey the cosmopolitan nature of Baghdad elite life? What attainments are highly valued for upper-class men? What do they tell us about occupations and talents that brought high status in Abbasid society, and how do they compare with career aspirations in our own? In comparison, what attributes of women are stressed in these passages? How do they compare with the preoccupations of the "jet-setters" of the late 20th century?

the early decades of Abbasid rule. Many of these land-lords had been long established. Others were new-comers: Arab soldiers who invested their share of the booty in land or merchants and administrators who funneled their profits and kickbacks into sizeable estates. In many regions, most peasants did not own the land they worked. They occupied it as tenants, sharecroppers, or migrant laborers who were required to give the greater portion of the crops they har-vested to the estate owners.

The First Flowering of Islamic Learning

When the Arabs first came out of the desert, they were for the most part illiterate and ignorant of the wider world. Their cultural backwardness was no bet-ter revealed than when the victorious Muslim armies came within sight of the city of Alexandria in Egypt. Chroniclers of the great conquests wrote that the vet-eran Arab warriors halted and sat on their horses, mouths open in wonderment, before the great walls of the city that stretched across the horizon from the Pharos lighthouse in the north to perhaps the great-est library in the ancient world in the south. As this confrontation suggests, the Arab conquerors burst suddenly into some of the most ancient and highly developed centers of civilization in human history. Within the confines of the Islamic domains were located the centers of the Hellenistic, Persian, Indian, Egyptian, and Mesopotamian civilizations as well as the widely dispersed Christian and Jewish traditions of thought and learning. The sparse cultural tradition of the Arabs made them receptive to influences from the subject peoples and remarkably tolerant of the great diversity of their styles and approaches to thought and artistic creativity.

In the first phase of Abbasid rule, the Islamic contribution to human artistic expression focused on the great mosques, such as those featured in the Visu-alizing the Past box, and great palaces. In addition to advances in religious, legal, and philosophical dis-course, the Islamic contribution to learning focused on the sciences and mathematics. In the early Abbasid period, the main tasks were recovering and preserv-ing the learning of the ancient civilizations of the Mediterranean and Middle East. Beyond the works of Plato, for example, much of Greek learning had been lost to the peoples of western Europe. Thanks to Muslim and Jewish scholars, the priceless writings of the Greeks on key subjects such as medicine, alge-bra, geometry, astronomy, anatomy, and ethics were saved, recopied in Arabic, and dispersed throughout the empire. From Spain, Greek writings found their way into Christendom. Among the authors rescued in this manner were Aristotle, Galen, Hippocrates, Ptolemy, and Euclid.

In addition, scholars working in Arabic transmit-ted ideas that paralleled the rise of Arab traders and merchants as the carriers of goods and inventions. For example, Muslim invaders of south Asia soon learned of the Indian system of numbers. From India they were carried by Muslim scholars and merchants to the Middle Eastern centers of Islamic civilization. Eventually the Indian numerical system was trans-mitted across the Mediterranean to Italy and from there to northern Europe. Along with Greek and Arab mathematics, Indian numbers later proved crit-ical to the early modern Scientific Revolution in west-ern Europe.

 GLOBAL CONNECTIONS: Early Islam and the World

The rise of Islamic civilization from the 7th to 9th centuries C.E. was a stunning development without precedent in human history. Not only had the largely nomadic peoples from an Arabian backwater built one of the greatest empires of the preindustrial world, but they had laid the basis for the first truly global civ-ilization if one excludes the Americas, which were unknown to the peoples of the Eastern Hemisphere. Building on earlier religious traditions, especially Christianity and Judaism, Arab culture had nurtured Islam, one of the great universal religions of humankind. The mosques, the prayer rituals and pil-grimages of the faithful, and the influence of Islamic law proclaimed the pervasive effects of this new creed on societies from Spain to eastern Indonesia and from central Asia to the savannas of west Africa.

Islamic and Arab commitment to trade and mer-chant activity was crucial in setting up wider connec-tions among Asia, Africa, and Europe, with the Middle East as hub. The region's earlier functions in commerce, in and between the Indian Ocean and Mediterranean Sea, expanded greatly.

Visualizing the Past

The Mosque as a Symbol of the Islamic Civilization

From one end of the Islamic world to the other, Muslim towns and cities can be readily identified by the domes and minarets of the mosques where the faithful are called to prayer five times daily. The following illustrations trace the development of the mosque and the refinement of mosque architecture, the crowning glory of Islamic material culture, during the early centuries of Muslim expansion. As you look at these pictures and follow the development of the mosque, consider what the functions of the mosque and the evolving style of mosque architecture can tell us about Muslim beliefs and values and the impact of earlier religions, such as Judaism and Christianity, on Islam.

Given the low level of material culture in pre-Islamic Arabia, it is not surprising that the earliest prayer houses were simple in design and construction. In fact, these first mosques were laid out along the lines suggested by Muhammad's own house. They were square enclosures with a shaded porch on one side, a columned shelter on the other, and an open courtyard in between. The outer perimeter of the earliest mosques was made of reed mats,

but soon more permanent stone walls surrounded the courtyard and prayer areas. After Mecca was taken and the Ka'ba became the central shrine of the new faith, each mosque was oriented to the qibla, or Mecca wall, which always faced in the direction of the holy city.

In the last years of the prophet, his chair was located so that the faithful could see and hear him during prayer sessions. During the time of the first caliphs, the raised area became the place from which sermons were delivered. From the mid-8th century, this space evolved into a genuine pulpit. Somewhat earlier, the practice of build-

(continued)

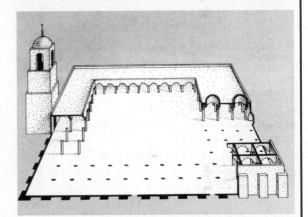

Domes and Minarets of Persian Mosques

Dome of the Rock

Pulpit

mosques, or the ruins of these structures were mined for stone for mosque construction. In the larger cities, the courtyards of the great mosques were surrounded by columns and arches, and eventually they were enclosed by great domes such as that at the Dome of the Rock in Jerusalem.

The first minarets, or towers from which the faithful were called to prayer, were added in the early 8th century and soon became a key feature of the mosque complex. As mosques grew larger and more architecturally refined, elaborate decoration in brightly colored ceramic tiles, semiprecious stones, and gold and silver filigree adorned their sides and domes. Because human and animal images were forbidden, geometric designs, passages from the Qur'an in swirling Arabic, and flower and plant motifs were favored. Nowhere were these decorations more splendid than in the great mosques of Persia. Thus, in the early centuries of Islam, these great houses of worship became the focal points of Islamic cities, key places of community worship and socialization, and, with the schools that were often attached, vital intellectual and educational centers of the Islamic world.

Questions: What do the design and decoration of Muslim mosques tell us about the Islamic view of God and the relationship between God and humans? Discuss the Christian and Jewish influences you detect in mosque design and the pattern of religious worship conducted there. What do you think is the significance of the lavish application of color and the frequent use of floral and plant motifs and Arabic verses from the Qur'an in the decoration of mosques through much of the Muslim world?

ing a special and often elaborately decorated niche in the qibla had developed.

Over time mosques became more elaborate. Very often the remains of Greek or Roman temples or abandoned Christian churches formed the core of major

Qibla Wall with Decorated Section Facing Mecca

In the arts and sciences, the Muslims initially relied heavily on the achievements of the classical civilizations of Greece and Mesopotamia. But the work of preserving and combining the discoveries of earlier peoples soon led to reformulation and innovation. As in religion and politics, Muslim peoples were soon making important contributions to learning, invention, and artistic creativity, which were carried by their armies and religious teachers to other civilizations in Europe, Africa, and Asia.

Never before had a civilization spanned so many different cultures and combined such a patchwork of linguistic groups, religions, and ethnic types. Never before had a single civilization mediated so successfully between the other centers of civilized life. Never had a civilized lifestyle so deeply affected so many of the nomadic cultures that surrounded the pools of sedentary agriculture and urban life. Ironically, the contacts Islamic mediation made possible between the civilized cores of the Eastern Hemisphere contributed much to the transformations in technology and organization that increasingly tilted the balance of power against the Muslim peoples. But those reversals were still far in the future. In the short run, Islamic conversion and contact ushered in an age of unparalleled nomadic intervention in and dominance over global history.

Further Readings

There are many accounts of Muhammad's life and the rise of Islam. The most readable is Karen Armstrong's *Muhammad: A Biography of the Prophet* (1992). A sense of the very different interpretations that have been offered to explain these pivotal developments in global history can be gained by comparing W. Montgomery Watt's *Muhammad: Prophet and Statesman* (1961); Tor Andrae's *Muhammad: The Man and His Faith* (1960); Maxime Rodinson's *Mohammad* (1971); and the more recent revisionist (and somewhat less accessible) writings of Elizabeth Crone and Michael Cook.

H. A. R. Gibb's *Mohammedism* (1962) remains a useful introduction to Islam as a religion. John Esposito's *Islam: The Straight Path* (1991) and Karen Armstrong's *Islam: A Short History* (2000) also provide good and updated overviews of the faith. On early Islamic expansion and civilization through the first centuries of the Abbasid caliphate, see G. E. von Grunebaum's *Classical Islam* (1970); M. A. Shaban's *Islamic History: An Interpretation* (1971); and *The Abbasid Revolution* (1970). On nearly all of these topics, it is difficult to surpass Marshall G. S. Hodgson's brilliant analysis, *The Venture of Islam* (1974, vol. 1), but some grounding in the history

and beliefs of the Muslims is recommended before one attempts this sweeping and provocative work. More accessible but still authoritative and highly interpretive are Ira M. Lapidus' *A History of Islamic Societies* (1988) and Albert Hourani's *A History of the Arab Peoples* (1991).

On early Islamic society generally, see M. M. Ahsan's *Social Life Under the Abbasids* (1979). On women in Islam specifically, there is a superb essay by Guity Nashat, "Women in the Middle East, 8000 B.C.–A.D. 1800," in the collection titled *Restoring Women to History*, published in 1988 by the Organization of American Historians. See also the relevant portions of the essays in Lois Beck and Nikki Keddi, eds., *Women in the Muslim World* (1978), and the early chapters of Leila Ahmed, *Women and Gender in Islam* (1992). For a broad treatment of the roles and position of women in ancient civilizations more generally, see Sarah and Brady Hughes, *Women in Ancient Global History* (1998). For insights into Islamic culture and civilization from a literary perspective, a good place to begin is Eric Schroeder's delightful *Muhammad's People: A Tale by Anthology* (1955) and N. J. Dawood's translation of *Tales from the Thousand and One Nights* (1954). Of the many works on Muslim architecture, John D. Hoag's *Western Islamic Architecture* (1963) gives a good overview, but K. A. Creswell's *Early Muslim Architecture*, 2 vols. (1932–1940) and the more recent Markus Hattstein and Peter Delius, eds., *Islam: Art and Architecture* (2000), provide greater detail and far better illustrations.

On the Web

The religion and society of Islam (http://islamicity.com/mosque/Intro_Islam.htm), Islam's revealed text, the Qur'an (http://www.usc.edu/dept/MSA/quran), and its arts (http://islamicart.com/) set new standards for civilization for much of the world. Islam sought submission to the will of God, Allah (http://www.usc.edu/dept/MSA/fundamentals/tawheed/), through the message vouchsafed to the Prophet Muhammad (http://www.bbc.co.uk/worldservice/people/features/world_religions/islam_life.shtml and http://www.pbs.org/muhammad/timeline_html.shtml), whose immediate successor as leader of the fledgling Muslim community, Abu Bakr (http://i-cias.com/e.o/abubakr.htm), proved equal to the task of ensuring its survival.

The evolution of Islamic art from its Arab roots, its capacity to influence non-Islamic art, and its capacity for synthesis of non-Arab themes can be traced at http://www.islamicart.com/main/architecture/impact.html and http://www.lacma.org/islamic_art/intro.htm. The golden age of Islamic science, literature, and scholarship, as well as religious philosophy, can be studied at http://islamicity.com/mosque/IGC/knowledge.htm. A gorgeous site explicating the Muslim pilgrimage to Mecca can be found at http://www.the-webplaza.com/hajj/index.html.

CHAPTER 12

ABBASID DECLINE AND THE SPREAD OF ISLAMIC CIVILIZATION TO SOUTH AND SOUTHEAST ASIA

The richness and depth attained by Muslim civilizations in the far-flung regions in which they were found is illustrated by this 17-century, miniature painting of a scholar-poet in an imagined nighttime garden in Kashmir in northern India. The meditative figure with book in hand and framed by the flowering tree in the background captures the commitment to learning and refined aesthetic sense that was cultivated by members of the elite classes throughout the Islamic world.

By the mid-9th century C.E., the Abbasid dynasty had begun to lose control over the vast Muslim empire that had been won from the Umayyads a century earlier (Map 12.1). From north Africa to Persia, rebellious governors and new dynasties arose to challenge the Abbasid caliphs' claims to be the rightful overlords of all Islamic peoples. Paradoxically, even as the political power of the Abbasids declined, Islamic civilization reached new heights of creativity and entered a new age of expansion. In architecture and the fine arts, in literature and philosophy, and in mathematics and the sciences, the centuries during which the Abbasid Empire slowly came apart were an era of remarkable achievement.

At the same time, political fragmentation did little to slow the growth of the Islamic world through political conquest and, more importantly, enduring peaceful conversion. From the 10th to the 14th century, Muslim warriors, traders, and wandering mystics carried the faith of Muhammad into the savanna and desert of west Africa, down the coast of east Africa, to the Turks and many other nomadic peoples of central Asia, and into south and southeast Asia. For more than five centuries, the spread of Islam played a central role in the rise, extension, or transformation of civilization in much of the Afro-Asian world. The Islamic world also became a great conduit for the exchange of ideas, plants and medicines, commercial goods, and inventions both between centers of urban and agrarian life and between these core regions of civilization and the areas dominated by nomadic peoples that still encompassed much of the globe.

The Islamic Heartlands in the Middle and Late Abbasid Eras

The vast Abbasid empire gradually disintegrated between the 9th and 13th centuries. Revolts spread among the peasants, slavery increased, and the position of women was further eroded. Divisions within the empire opened the way for Christian crusaders from western Europe to invade and, for a short time, establish warrior kingdoms in the Muslim heartlands. Political decline and social turmoil were offset for many by the urban affluence, inventiveness, and artistic creativity of the Abbasid age.

As early as the reign of the third Abbasid caliph, **al-Mahdi** (775–785), the courtly excesses and political divisions that eventually contributed to the decline of the empire were apparent. Al-Mahdi's efforts to reconcile the moderates among the Shi'a opposition to Abbasid rule ended in failure. This meant that Shi'a revolts and assassination attempts against Abbasid officials would plague the dynasty to the end of its days. Al-Mahdi also abandoned the frugal ways of his predecessor. In the brief span of his reign, he established a taste for luxury and monumental building and surrounded himself

700 C.E.	800 C.E.	900 C.E.	1000 C.E.	1200 C.E.
661–750 Umayyad caliphate (Damascus)	**800** Independent dynasty established in Tunisia	**945** Persian Buyids capture Baghdad; caliphs made into puppet rulers	**c. 1020** Death of Firdawsi, author of the *Shah-Nama*	**1206** Establishment of the Delhi sultanate in India
711–713 First Muslim raids into India	**809** First war of succession between Abbasid princes	**973–1050** Life of al-Biruni, scientist	**1055** Seljuk Turks overthrow Buyids, control caliphate	**1290s** Beginning of the spread of Islam in southeast Asia
750 Establishment of the Abbasid caliphate (Baghdad)	**813–833** Reign of al-Ma'mun; first mercenary forces recruited	**998** Beginning of Ghanzi raids into western India	**1096–1099** First Christian Crusade in Palestine	**1291** Fall of Acre; last Crusader stronghold in Middle East
775–785 Reign of al-Mahdi	**865–925** Life of al-Razi, physician and scientist		**1111** Death of al-Ghazali, philosopher and scientist	**1258** Fall of Baghdad to Mongols; end of Abbasid caliphate
777 Independent dynasty established in Algeria			**1123** Death of Omar Khayyam, scientist and poet	
786–809 Reign of al-Rashid				
788 Independent dynasty established in Morocco				

with a multitude of dependant wives, concubines, and courtiers. These habits would prove to be an ever greater financial drain in the reigns of later caliphs.

Perhaps most critically, al-Mahdi failed to solve the vexing problem of succession. Not only did he waver between which of his older sons would succeed him, but he allowed his wives and concubines, the mothers of different candidates, to become involved in the palace intrigues that became a standard feature of the transfer of power from one caliph to the next. Although a full-scale civil war was avoided after al-Mahdi's death, within a year his eldest son and successor was poisoned. That act cleared the way for one of the most famous and enduring of the Abbasid caliphs, **Harun al-Rashid** (786–809), to ascend the throne.

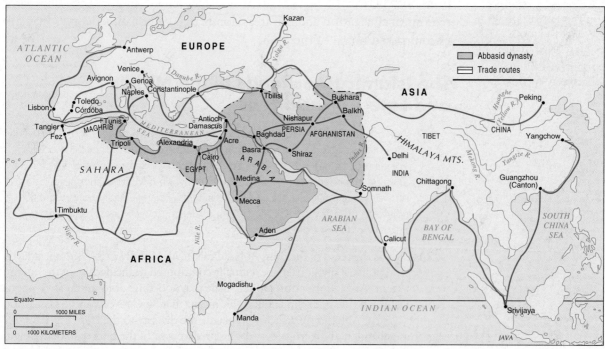

Map 12.1 *The Abbasid Empire at Its Peak*

Figure 12.1 *The richness and vitality of urban life in the Islamic world in the Abbasid age and later eras are wonderfully captured in this 16th-century Persian illustration from the Khamsah (Five Poems) of Nizami. Nizami gives us a bird's-eye view of a rather typical night in one of the great palaces of Baghdad. The multiple scenes vividly capture the bustle and high artistry of the splendidly decorated rooms and gardens, from a group of musicians serenading a man who is presumably the lord of the mansion to kitchen servants buying food and preparing to serve it to the lord and his guests.*

Imperial Extravagance and Succession Disputes

Emissaries sent in the early 9th century to Baghdad from Charlemagne, then the most powerful monarch in Christian Europe, provide ample evidence that Harun al-Rashid shared his father's taste for sumptuous living. Harun al-Rashid dazzled the Christians with the splendor of Baghdad's mosques, palaces, and treasure troves, which is reflected in the painting of nightlife in a palace in Figure 12.1. He also sent them back to Charlemagne with presents, including an intricate water clock and an elephant, that were literally worth a king's ransom.

The luxury and intrigue of Harun's court have also been immortalized by the tales of *The Thousand and One Nights* (see the Document in Chapter 11), set in the Baghdad of his day. The plots and maneuvers of the courtesans, eunuchs, and royal ministers related in the tales suggest yet another source of dynastic weakness. Partly because he was only 23 at the time of his accession to the throne, Harun became heavily dependant, particularly in the early years of his reign, on a family of Persian advisors. Although he eventually resisted their influence, the growth of the power of royal advisors at the expense of the caliphs became a clear trend in succeeding reigns. In fact, from the mid-9th century onward, most caliphs were pawns in the power struggles between different factions at the court.

Harun al-Rashid's death prompted the first of several full-scale civil wars over succession. In itself, the precedent set by the struggle for the throne was deeply damaging. But it had an additional consequence that would all but end the real power of the caliphs. The first civil war convinced the sons of al-Ma'mun (813–833), the winner, that they needed to build personal armies in anticipation of the fight for the throne that would break out when their father died. One of the sons, the victor in the next round of succession struggles, recruited a "bodyguard" of some 4000 slaves, mostly Turkic-speaking nomads from central Asia. On becoming caliph, he increased this mercenary force to more than 70,000.

Not surprisingly, this impressive force soon became a power center in its own right. In 846, slave mercenaries murdered the reigning caliph and placed one of his sons on the throne. In the next decade, four more caliphs were assassinated or poisoned by the mercenary forces. From this time onward, the leaders of the slave mercenary armies were often the real power behind the Abbasid throne and were major players in the struggles for control of the capital and empire. The mercenaries also became a major force for violent social unrest. They were often the catalyst for the food riots that broke out periodically in the capital and other urban centers.

Imperial Breakdown and Agrarian Disorder

In the last decades of the 9th century, the dynasty brought the slave armies under control for a time, but at a great cost. Constant civil violence drained the treasury and alienated the subjects of the Abbasids. A further strain was placed on the empire's dwindling revenues by some caliphs' attempts to escape the turmoil of Baghdad by establishing new capitals near the original one. The construction of palaces, mosques, and public works for each of these new imperial centers added to the already exorbitant costs of maintaining the court and imperial administration. Of course, the expense fell heavily on the already hard-pressed peasantry of the central provinces of the empire, where some imperial control remained. The need to support growing numbers of mercenary troops also increased the revenue demands on the peasantry.

Spiraling taxation and outright pillaging led to the destruction or abandonment of many villages in the richest provinces of the empire. The great irrigation works that had for centuries been essential to agricultural production in the fertile Tigris–Euphrates basin fell into disrepair, and in some areas they collapsed entirely. Some peasants perished through flood, famine, or violent assault; others fled to wilderness areas beyond the reach of the Abbasid tax collectors to neighboring kingdoms. Some formed bandit gangs or joined the crowds of vagabonds that trudged the highways and camped in the towns of the imperial heartland. In many cases, dissident religious groups, such as the various Shi'a sects, instigated peasant uprisings. Shi'a participation meant that these movements sought not only to correct the official abuses that had occurred under the Abbasid regime but to destroy the dynasty itself.

The Declining Position of Women in the Family and Society

The harem and the veil became the twin emblems of women's increasing subjugation to men and confinement to the home in the Abbasid era. Although the seclusion of women had been practiced by some Middle Eastern peoples since ancient times, the harem was a creation of the Abbasid court. The wives and the concubines of the Abbasid caliphs were restricted to the forbidden quarters of the imperial palace. Many of the concubines were slaves, who could win their freedom and gain power by bearing healthy sons for the rulers. The growing wealth of the Abbasid elite created a great demand for female and male slaves, who were found by the tens of thousands in Baghdad and other large cities. Most of these urban slaves continued to perform domestic services in the homes of the wealthy. One of the 10th-century caliphs is said to have had 11,000 eunuchs among his slave corps; another is said to have kept 4000 slave concubines.

Most of the slaves had been captured or purchased in the non-Muslim regions surrounding the empire, including the Balkans, central Asia, and Sudanic Africa. They were purchased in the slave markets found in all of the larger towns of the empire. Female and male slaves were prized for both their beauty and their intelligence. Some of the best-educated men and women in the Abbasid Empire were slaves. Consequently, caliphs and high officials often spent more time with their clever and talented slave concubines than with their less well-educated wives. Slave concubines and servants often had more personal liberty than freeborn wives. Slave women could go to the market, and they did not have to wear the veils and robes that were required for free women in public places.

Although women from the lower classes farmed, wove clothing and rugs, or raised silkworms to help support their families, rich women were allowed almost no career outlets beyond the home. Often married at puberty (legally set at age 9), women were raised to devote their lives to running a household and serving their husbands. But at the highest levels of society, wives and concubines cajoled their husbands and plotted with eunuchs and royal advisors to advance the interests of their sons and win for them the ruler's backing for succession to the throne. Despite these brief incursions into power politics, by the end of the Abbasid era, the freedom and influence—both within the family and in the wider world—that women had enjoyed in the first centuries of Islamic expansion had been severely curtailed.

Nomadic Incursions and the Eclipse of Caliphal Power

Preoccupied by struggles in the capital and central provinces, the caliphs and their advisors were powerless to prevent further losses of territory in the outer reaches of the empire. In addition, areas as close to the capital as Egypt and Syria broke away from Abbasid rule (see Map 12.1). More alarmingly, by the mid-10th century, independent kingdoms that had formed in areas that were once provinces of the empire were moving to supplant the Abbasids as lords of the Islamic world. In 945, the armies of one of these regional splinter dynasties, the **Buyids** of Persia, invaded the heartlands of the Abbasid Empire and captured Baghdad. From this point onward, the caliphs were little more than puppets controlled by families such as the Buyids. Buyid leaders took the title of *sultan* ("victorious" in Arabic), which came to designate Muslim rulers, especially in the West.

The Buyids controlled the caliph and the court, but they could not prevent the further disintegration of the empire. In just over a century, the Buyids' control over the caliphate was broken, and they were supplanted in 1055 by another group of nomadic invaders from central Asia via Persia, the **Seljuk Turks**. For the next two centuries, Turkic military leaders ruled the remaining portions of the Abbasid Empire in the name of caliphs, who were usually of Arab or Persian extraction. The Seljuks were staunch Sunnis, and they moved quickly to purge the Shi'a officials who had risen to power under the Buyids and to rid the caliph's domains of the Shi'a influences the Buyids had tried to promote. For a time, the Seljuk military machine was also able to restore political initiative to the much reduced caliphate. Seljuk victories ended the threat of conquest by a rival Shi'a dynasty centered in Egypt. They also humbled the Byzantines, who had hoped to take advantage of Muslim divisions to regain some of their long-lost lands. The Byzantines' crushing defeat also opened the way to the settlement of Asia Minor, or Anatolia, by nomadic peoples of Turkic origins, some of whom would soon begin to lay the foundations of the **Ottoman Empire**.

The Impact of the Christian Crusades

Soon after seizing power, the Seljuks faced a very different challenge to Islamic civilization. It came from Christian crusaders, knights from western Europe (see Chapter 15) who were determined to capture the portions of the Islamic world that made up the Holy Land of biblical times. Muslim political divisions and the element of surprise made the first of the crusaders' assaults, between 1096 and 1099, by far the most successful. Much of the Holy Land was captured and divided into Christian kingdoms. In June 1099, the main objective of the Crusade, Jerusalem, was taken, and its Muslim and Jewish inhabitants were massacred by the rampaging Christian knights.

For nearly two centuries, the Europeans, who eventually mounted eight **Crusades** that varied widely in strength and success, maintained their precarious hold on the eastern Mediterranean region. But they posed little threat to the more powerful Muslim princes, whose disregard for the Christians was demonstrated by the fact that they continued to quarrel among themselves despite the intruders' aggressions. When united under a strong leader, as they were under Salah-ud-Din (known as **Saladin** in Christian Europe) in the last decades of the 12th century, the Muslims rapidly reconquered most of the crusader outposts. Saladin's death in 1193 and the subsequent breakup of his kingdom gave the remaining Christian citadels some respite. But the last of the crusader kingdoms was lost with the fall of Acre in 1291.

Document

Ibn Khaldun on the Rise and Decline of Empires

Although he lived in the century after the Abbasid Caliphate was destroyed in 1258, **Ibn Khaldun** was very much a product of the far-flung Islamic civilization that the Abbasids had consolidated and expanded. He was also one of the greatest historians and social commentators of all time. After extensive travels in the Islamic world, he served as a political advisor at several of the courts of Muslim rulers in north Africa. With the support of a royal patron, Ibn Khaldun wrote a universal history that began with a very long philosophical preface called *The Muqaddimah*. Among the subjects he treated at length were the causes of the rise and fall of dynasties. The shifting fortunes of the dynasties he knew well in his native north Africa, as well as the fate of the Abbasids and earlier Muslim regimes, informed his attempts to find persistent patterns in the confusing political history of the Islamic world. The following passages are from one of the most celebrated sections of *The Muqaddimah* on the natural life span of political regimes.

We have stated that the duration of the life of a dynasty does not as a rule extend beyond three generations. The first generation retains the desert qualities, desert toughness, and desert savagery. [Its members are used to] privation and to sharing their glory [with each other]; they are brave and rapacious. Therefore, the strength of group feeling continues to be preserved among them. They are sharp and greatly feared. People submit to them.

Under the influence of royal authority and a life of ease, the second generation changes from the desert attitude to sedentary culture, from privation to luxury and plenty, from a state in which everybody shared in the glory to one in which one man claims all the glory for himself while the others are too lazy to strive for [glory], and from proud superiority to humble subservience. Thus, the vigor of group feeling is broken to some extent. People become used to lowliness and obedience. But many of [the old virtues] remain in them, because they had direct personal contact with the first generation and its conditions.

The third generation, then, has [completely] forgotten the period of desert life and toughness, as if it had never existed. They have lost [the taste for] group feeling, because they are dominated by force. Luxury reaches its peak among them, because they are so much given to a life of prosperity and ease. They become dependent on the dynasty and are like women and children who need to be defended [by someone else]. Group feeling disappears completely. People forget to protect and defend themselves and to press their claims. With their emblems, apparel, horseback riding, and [fighting] skill, they deceive people and give them the wrong impression. For the most part, they are more cowardly than women upon their backs. When someone comes and demands something from them, they cannot repel him. The ruler, then, has need of other, brave people for his support. He takes many clients and followers. They help the dynasty to some degree, until God permits it to be destroyed, and it goes with everything it stands for.

Three generations last one hundred and twenty years. As a rule, dynasties do not last longer than that many years, a few more, a few less, save when, by chance, no one appears to attack [the dynasty]. When senility becomes preponderant [in a dynasty], there may be no claimant [for its power, and then nothing will happen] but if there should be one, he will encounter no one capable of repelling him. If the time is up [the end of the dynasty] cannot be postponed for a single hour, no more than it can be accelerated.

Questions: What does this passage reveal about Ibn Khaldun's views of the contrasts between nomads and urban dwellers? Why does he see the former as a source of military power and political strength? What forces undermine dynasties in later generations? How well do these patterns correspond to the history of the Umayyad and Abbasid dynasties we have been studying? How well do they work for other civilizations we have examined? Can elements of Ibn Khaldun's theory be applied to today's political systems? If so, which and how? If not, why not?

Undoubtedly, the impact of the Crusades was much greater on the Christians who launched them than on the Muslim peoples who had to fend them off. Because there had long been so much contact between western Europe and the Islamic world through trade and through the Muslim kingdoms in Spain and southern Italy, it is difficult to be sure which influences to attribute specifically to the Crusades. But the crusaders' firsthand experiences in the eastern Mediterranean certainly intensified European borrowing from the Muslim world that had been going on for centuries. Muslim weapons, such as the famous damascene swords (named after the city of Damascus), were highly prized and sometimes copied by the Europeans, who were always eager to improve on their methods of making war. Muslim techniques of building fortifications were adopted by many Christian rulers, as can be seen in the castles built in Normandy and coastal England by William the Conqueror and his successors in the 11th and 12th centuries. Richard the Lionhearted's legendary preference for Muslim over Christian physicians was but one sign of the Europeans' avid centuries-old interest in the superior scientific learning of Muslim peoples.

From Muslims and Jews in Spain, Sicily, Egypt, and the Middle East, the Europeans recovered much of the Greek learning that had been lost to northern Europe during the waves of nomadic invasions after the fall of Rome. They also mastered Arabic (properly Indian) numerals and the decimal system, and they benefited from the great advances Arab and Persian thinkers had made in mathematics and many of the sciences. The European demand for Middle Eastern rugs and textiles is demonstrated by the Oriental rugs and tapestries that adorned the homes of the European upper classes in Renaissance and early modern paintings. It is also reflected in European (and our own) names for different kinds of cloth, such as *fustian*, *taffeta*, *muslin*, and *damask*, which are derived from Persian terms or the names of Muslim cities where the cloth was produced and sold.

Muslim influences affected both the elite and popular cultures of much of western Europe in this period. These included Persian and Arabic words, games such as chess (like numbers, passed on from India), chivalric ideals and troubadour ballads, as well as foods such as dates, coffee, and yogurt. Some of these imports, namely the songs of the troubadours, can be traced directly to the contacts the crusaders made in the Holy Land. But most were part of a process of exchange that extended over centuries, and was largely a one-way process. Though Arab traders imported some manufactures, such as glass and cloth, and raw materials from Europe, Muslim peoples in this era showed little interest in the learning or institutions of the West. Nevertheless, the Italian merchant communities, which remained after the political and military power of the crusaders had been extinguished in the Middle East, contributed a good deal more to these ongoing interchanges than all the forays of Christian knights.

An Age of Learning and Artistic Refinements

 The avid interest in Muslim ideas and material culture displayed by European knights and merchants in this era cautions us against placing too great an emphasis on the political divisions and struggles that were so prominent in the later Abbasid era. It also invites comparison with neighboring civilizations, such as those of India and western Europe, that were much more fragmented and racked by warfare in late Abbasid times. In the midst of the political turmoil and social tensions of the Abbasid age, Muslim thinkers and artisans living in kingdoms from Spain to Persia created, refined, and made discoveries in a remarkable range of fields. Their collective accomplishments mark one of the great ages of human ingenuity and creativity.

Although town life became more dangerous, the rapid growth and increasing prosperity that characterized the first centuries of Muslim expansion continued until late in the Abbasid era. Despite the declining revenue base of the caliphate and deteriorating conditions in the countryside, there was a great expansion of the professional classes, particularly doctors, scholars, and legal and religious experts. Muslim, Jewish, and in some areas Christian entrepreneurs amassed great fortunes supplying the cities of the empire with staples such as grain and barley, essentials such as cotton and woolen textiles for clothing, and luxury items such as precious gems, citrus fruits, and sugar cane. Long-distance trade between the Middle East and Mediterranean Europe and between coastal India and island southeast Asia, in addition to the overland caravan trade with China, flourished through much of the Abbasid era (see Map 12.1).

Among the chief beneficiaries of the sustained urban prosperity were artists and artisans, who continued the great achievements in architecture and the crafts that had begun in the Umayyad period. Mosques and palaces grew larger and more ornate in most parts of the empire. Even in outlying areas, such as Córdoban Spain, which is pictured in Figure 12.2, Muslim engineers and architects created some of the great architectural treasures of all time. The tapestries and rugs of Muslim peoples, such as the Persians, were in great demand from Europe to China. To this day, Muslim rugs have rarely been matched for their exquisite designs, their vivid colors, and the skill with

Figure 12.2 *A forest of graceful arches fills the interior of the mosque at Córdoba in Spain. This style of architecture (only one of many variants in the Islamic world, as we saw in the Visualizing the Past box in Chapter 11) can be seen over a large area that includes the entire Iberian peninsula and much of north Africa. Such an architectural feat in an area on the furthest fringe of the Islamic world illustrates the depth and expansive power of Muslim civilization. It also dramatically demonstrates the engineering skill and refined aesthetic sensibilities of Muslim architects and their wealthy patrons.*

which they are woven. Muslim artisans also produced fine bronzes and superb ceramics.

The Full Flowering of Persian Literature

As Persian wives, concubines, advisors, bureaucrats, and—after the mid-10th century—Persian caliphs came to play central roles in imperial politics, Persian gradually replaced Arabic as the primary written language at the Abbasid court. Arabic remained the language of religion, law, and the natural sciences. But Persian was favored by Arabs, Turks, and Muslims of Persian descent as the language of literary expression, administration, and scholarship. In Baghdad and major cities throughout the Abbasid Empire and in neighboring kingdoms, Persian was the chief language of "high culture," the language of polite exchanges between courtiers as well as of history, poetic musings, and mystical revelations.

Written in a modified Arabic script and drawing selectively on Arabic vocabulary, the Persian of the Abbasid age was a supple language as beautiful to look at when drafted by a skilled calligrapher as it was to read aloud (see Figure 12.3). Catch phrases ("A jug of wine, a loaf of bread—and Thou") from the *Rubaiyat* of Omar Khayyam are certainly the pieces of Persian literature best known in the West. But other writers from this period surpassed Khayyam in profundity of thought and elegance of style. Perhaps the single most important work was the lengthy epic poem ***Shah-Nama*** (Book of Kings), written by Firdawsi in the late 10th and early 11th centuries. The work relates the history of Persia from the beginnings of time to the Islamic conquests, and it abounds in dramatic details of battles, intrigues, and illicit love affairs. Firdawsi's Persian has been extolled for its grand, musical virtuosity, and portions of the *Shah-Nama* and other Persian works were read aloud to musical accompaniment. Brilliantly illustrated manuscripts of Firdawsi's epic history are among the most exquisite works of Islamic art.

In addition to historical epics, Persian writers in the Abbasid era wrote on many subjects, from doomed love affairs and statecraft to incidents from everyday life and mystical striving for communion with the divine. One of the great poets of the age, Sa'di, fuses an everyday message with a religious one in the following relation of a single moment in his own life:

> Often I am minded, from the days of my
>   childhood,
> How once I went out with my father on
>   a festival;
> In fun I grew preoccupied with all the
>   folk about,
> Losing touch with my father in the popular
>   confusion;
> In terror and bewilderment I raised up a cry,
> Then suddenly my father boxed my ears:
> "You bold-eyed child, how many times, now,

Figure 12.3 *As the intricate details of this vividly illuminated book of tales of the prophet Muhammad illustrates, Muslim scripts, whether Arabic, Persian, or Turkish, were viewed as works of art in themselves. Artists were expected to be masters of writing and pictorial representation, and books such as this were usually produced in workshops, at times employing several master painters and hundreds of artisans. Verses from the Qur'an, exquisitely rendered in porcelain tiles, were frequently used to decorate mosques and other public buildings.*

Have I told you not to lose hold of my skirt?"

A tiny child cannot walk out alone,

For it is difficult to take a way not seen;

You too, poor friend, are but a child upon
    endeavour's way:

Go, seize the skirts of those who know the way!

This blend of the mystical and commonplace was widely adopted in the literature of this period. It is epitomized in the *Rubaiyat*, whose author is much more concerned with finding meaning in life and a path to union with the divine than with extolling the delights of picnics in the garden with beautiful women.

Achievements in the Sciences

From preserving and compiling the learning of the ancient civilizations they had conquered in the early centuries of expansion, Muslim peoples—and the Jewish scholars who lived peacefully in Muslim lands—increasingly became creators and inventors in their own right. For several centuries, which spanned much of the period of Abbasid rule, Islamic civilization outstripped all others in scientific discoveries, new techniques of investigation, and new technologies. The many Muslim accomplishments in these areas include major corrections to the algebraic and geometric theories of the ancient Greeks and great advances in the use of basic concepts of trigonometry: the sine, cosine, and tangent.

Two discoveries in chemistry that were fundamental to all later investigation were the creation of the objective experiment and al-Razi's scheme of classifying all material substances into three categories: animal, vegetable, and mineral. The sophistication of Muslim scientific techniques is indicated by the fact that in the 11th century, al-Biruni was able to calculate the specific weight of 18 major minerals. This sophistication was also manifested in astronomical instruments such as those in Figure 12.4, developed through cooperation between Muslim scholars and skilled artisans. Their astronomical tables and maps of the stars were in great demand among scholars of other civilizations, including those of Europe and China.

As these breakthroughs suggest, much of the Muslims' work in scientific investigation had very practical applications. This practical bent was even greater in other fields. For example, Muslim cities such as Cairo boasted some of the best hospitals in the world. Doctors and pharmacists had to follow a regular course of study and pass a formal examination before they were allowed to practice. Muslim scientists did important work on optics and bladder ailments. Muslim traders introduced into the Islamic world and Europe many basic machines and techniques—namely, papermaking, silk-weaving, and ceramic firing—that had been devised earlier in China. In addition, Muslim scholars made some of

Figure 12.4 *This 15th-century Persian miniature of a group of Arab scientists testing and working with a wide variety of navigational instruments conveys a strong sense of the premium placed on scientific investigation in the Muslim world in the Abbasid age and the centuries thereafter. Muslim prototypes inspired European artisans, cartographers, and scientists to develop instruments and maps, which were essential to European overseas expansion from the 14th century onward.*

the world's best maps, which were copied by geographers from Portugal to Poland.

Religious Trends and the New Push for Expansion

The contradictory trends in Islamic civilization—social strife and political divisions versus expanded trading links and intellectual creativity—were strongly reflected in patterns of religious development in the later centuries of the caliphate. On one hand, a resurgence of mysticism injected Islam with a new vibrancy. On the other, orthodox religious scholars, such as the **ulama,** grew increasingly suspicious of and hostile to non-Islamic ideas and scientific thinking. The Crusades had promoted the latter trend. This was particularly true regarding Muslim borrowing from ancient Greek learning, which the ulama associated with the aggressive civilizations of Christian Europe. Many orthodox scholars suspected that the questioning that characterized the Greek tradition would undermine the absolute authority of the Qur'an. They insisted that the Qur'an was the final, perfect, and complete revelation of an all-knowing divinity. Brilliant thinkers such as **al-Ghazali,** perhaps the greatest Islamic theologian, struggled to fuse the Greek and Qur'anic traditions. Their ideas were often rejected by orthodox scholars.

Much of the religious vitality in Islam in the later Abbasid period was centered on the Sufist movement. Like the Buddhist and Hindu ascetics earlier in India, **Sufis** (whose title was derived from the woolen robes they wore) were wandering mystics who sought a personal union with Allah. In its various guises—including both Sunni and Shi'a manifestations—Sufism was a reaction against the impersonal and abstract divinity that many ulama scholars argued was the true god of the Qur'an. Like the Indian mystics, the Sufis and their followers tried to see beyond what they believed to be the illusory existence of everyday life and to delight in the presence of Allah in the world. True to the strict monotheism of Islam, most Sufis insisted on a clear distinction between Allah and humans. But in some Sufist teachings, Allah permeated the universe in ways that appeared to compromise his transcendent status.

Some Sufis gained reputations as great healers and workers of miracles; others led militant bands that tried to spread Islam to nonbelievers. Some Sufis used asceticism or bodily denial to find Allah; others used meditation, songs, drugs, or (in the case of the famous dervishes) ecstatic dancing. Most Sufis built up a sizeable following, and the movement as a whole was a central factor in the continuing expansion of the Muslim religion and Islamic civilization in the later centuries of the Abbasid caliphate.

Visualizing the Past

The Patterns of Islam's Global Expansions

The table shows the present-day distribution of Muslims in key countries from Africa to Asia. It indicates the total number of Muslims in each of the countries represented, the percentage of Muslims in the total population of that area, and the numbers and percentages of other religious groups. The table also indicates the manner in which Islam was spread to each of these areas and the key agents of that diffusion. After using the table to compare the patterns of Islamization in different areas, answer the questions that follow.

Questions: Which areas have the highest absolute numbers of Muslims in the present day? Is this distribution what you would have expected or is it surprising? What factors might explain these distribution patterns? What were the main ways that Islam was transmitted to most areas? and to the areas with the largest number of Muslims? What does this say about the popular notion that Islam was historically a militant religion spread primarily by forcible conversion? Does Islam appear to be able to coexist with other faiths?

Comparative Statistics of Modern States with a Sizeable Muslim Population

	Total Population (2000 est.)	Total Number of Muslims	Percentage of Muslims	Total Number of Non-Muslims	Percentages of Other Religious Groups	Principle Agents/Modes of Conversion
Nigeria	114 million	57 million	50	57 million	40–Christian; 10–Other (African religions)	Trading Contacts Sufi Missionaries
Egypt	67 million	63 million	94	4 million	4–Christian; 2–Other	Arab Migration Voluntary Mass Conversion
Iraq	22.5 million	21.8 million	97: Shi'a: 60–65; Sunni: 32–37	700,000	3–Other (Zoroastrian, Christian, Jewish)	Arab Migration Voluntary Mass Conversion
Iran	65 million	64.35 million	99: Shi'a: 89; Sunni: 10	650,000	1–Other (Zoroastrian, Bahai, Christian, Jewish)	Arab Migration Voluntary Mass Conversion
Pakistan	138 million	133.85 million	97: Shi'a: 20; Sunni: 77	4.15 million	3–Other (Hindu, Christian, Buddhist)	Sufi Missionaries Voluntary Mass Conversion
India	1.001 billion	140.1 million	14	860.9 million	80–Hindu; 6–Other (Buddhist, Sikh, Christian)	Sufi Missionaries Trading Contacts Voluntary Mass Conversion

(continued)

	Total Population (2000 est.)	Total Number of Muslims	Percentage of Muslims	Total Number of Non-Muslims	Percentages of Other Religious Groups	Principle Agents/Modes of Conversion
Indonesia	216 million	188 million	87	28 million	6–Protestant; 7–Other (Catholic, Buddhist, etc.)	Sufi Missionaries Trading Contacts
The Philippines	79.5 million	4 million	5	75.5 million	83–Catholic; 9–Protestant; 3–Other	Trading Contacts Sufi Missionaries
Morocco	30 million	29.7 million	99	300,000	1–Other	Voluntary Mass Conversion Sufi Missionaries

Note: Numbers based on information from Wiesenfeld and Famighetti et al., eds., *The World Almanac and Book of Facts 2000* (Mahwah, NJ: World Almanac Books, 1999).

New Waves of Nomadic Invasions and the End of the Caliphate

As we have seen, in the 10th and 11th centuries the Abbasid domains were divided by ever growing numbers of rival successor states. In the early 13th century, a new threat arose at the eastern edge of the original Abbasid domains. Another central Asian nomadic people, the **Mongols,** united by their great war commander, **Chinggis Khan,** first raided in the 1220s and then smashed the Turko-Persian kingdoms that had developed in the regions to the east of Baghdad. Chinggis Khan died before the heartlands of the Muslim world were invaded, but his grandson, **Hulegu,** renewed the Mongol assault on the rich centers of Islamic civilization in the 1250s. In 1258, the Abbasid capital at Baghdad was taken by the Mongols, and much of it was sacked. The 37th and last Abbasid caliph was put to death by the Mongols. They then continued westward until they were finally defeated by the **Mamluks,** or Turkic slaves, who then ruled Egypt. Baghdad never recovered from the Mongol attacks. In 1401, it suffered a second capture and another round of pillaging by the even fiercer forces of Tamerlane. Baghdad shrank from the status of one of the great cities of the world to a provincial backwater. It was gradually supplanted by Cairo to the west and then Istanbul to the north.

The Coming of Islam to South Asia

 From the 7th century onward, successive waves of Muslim invaders, traders, and migrants carried the Islamic faith and elements of Islamic civilization to much of the vast south Asian subcontinent. By the 12th and 13th centuries, Muslim dynasties ruled much of north and central India. Muslim conquests and growing numbers of conversions provoked a variety of Hindu responses. They also prompted efforts on the part of some followers of both religions to reconcile their differences. Although these measures resulted only in an uneasy standoff between the two communities, Islamic influences had clearly become a major force in south Asian historical development.

All through the millennia when a succession of civilizations from Harappa to the brahmanic empire of the Guptas developed in south Asia, foreigners had entered India in waves of nomadic invaders or as small bands of displaced peoples seeking refuge. Invariably, those who chose to remain were assimilated into the civilizations they encountered in the lowland areas. They converted to the Hindu or Buddhist religion, found a place in the caste hierarchy, and adopted the dress, foods, and lifestyles of the farming and city-dwelling peoples of the many regions of the subcontinent. This capacity to absorb peoples moving into the area resulted from the strength and flexibility of India's civilizations and from the fact that India's peoples usually enjoyed a higher level of material culture than migrant groups entering the subcontinent. As a result, the persistent failure of Indian rulers to unite against aggressors meant periodic disruptions and localized destruction but not fundamental challenges to the existing order. All of this changed with the arrival of the Muslims in the last years of the 7th century C.E. (see Map 12.2).

With the coming of the Muslims, the peoples of India encountered for the first time a large-scale influx of bearers of a civilization as sophisticated, if not as ancient, as their own. They were also confronted by a religious system that was in many ways the very opposite of the ones they had nurtured. Hinduism, the predominant Indian religion at that time, was open, tolerant, and inclusive of widely varying forms of religious devotion, from idol worship to meditation in search of union with the spiritual source of all creation. Islam was doctrinaire, proselytizing, and committed to the exclusive worship of a single, transcendent god.

Socially, Islam was highly egalitarian, proclaiming all believers equal in the sight of God. In sharp contrast, Hindu beliefs validated the caste hierarchy. The latter rested on the acceptance of inborn differences between individuals and groups and the widely varying levels of material wealth, status, and religious purity these differences were believed to produce. Thus, the faith of the invading Muslims was religiously more rigid than that of the absorptive and adaptive Hindus. But the caste-based social system of India was much more compartmentalized and closed than the society of the Muslim invaders, with their emphasis on mobility and the community of believers.

Because growing numbers of Muslim warriors, traders, Sufi mystics, and ordinary farmers and herders entered south Asia and settled there, extensive interaction between invaders and the indigenous peoples was

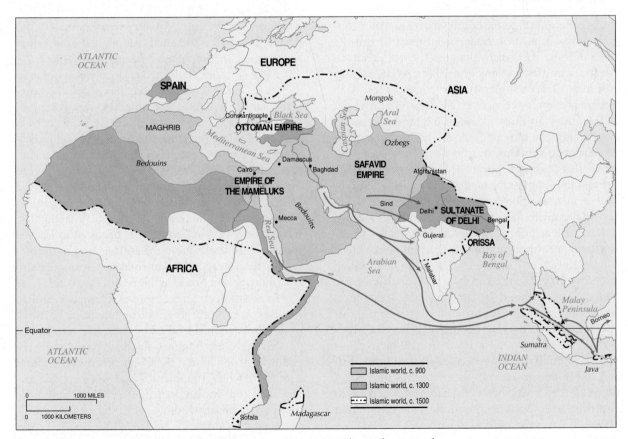

Map 12.2 *The Spread of Islam, 10th–16th Centuries. Arrows indicate the routes by which Islam spread to south and southeast Asia.*

inevitable. In the early centuries of the Muslim influx, conflict, often violent, predominated. But there was also a good deal of trade and even religious interchange between them. As time passed, peaceful (if wary) interaction became the norm. Muslim rulers employed large numbers of Hindus to govern the largely non-Muslim populations they conquered, mosques and temples dominated different quarters within Indian cities, and Hindu and Muslim mystics strove to find areas of agreement between their two faiths. Nonetheless, tensions remained, and periodically they erupted into communal rioting or warfare between Hindu and Muslim lords.

Political Divisions and the First Muslim Invasions

The first and least enduring Muslim intrusion, which came in 711, resulted indirectly from the peaceful trading contacts that had initially brought Muslims into contact with Indian civilization. Since ancient times, Arab seafarers and traders had been major carriers in the vast trading network that stretched from Italy in the Mediterranean to the South China Sea. After converting to Islam, these traders continued to visit the ports of India, particularly those on the western coast. An attack by pirates sailing from Sind in western India (see Map 12.2) on ships owned by some of these Arab traders prompted the viceroy of the eastern provinces of the Umayyad Empire to launch a punitive expedition against the king of Sind. An able Arab general, **Muhammad ibn Qasim,** who was only 17 years old when the campaign began, led more than 10,000 horse- and camel-mounted warriors into Sind to avenge the assault on Arab shipping. After victories in several fiercely fought battles, Muhammad ibn Qasim declared the region, as well as the Indus valley to the northeast, provinces of the Umayyad Empire.

In these early centuries, the coming of Islam brought little change for most inhabitants of the Indian subcontinent. In fact, in many areas, local leaders and the populace surrendered towns and districts willingly to the conquerors because they promised lighter taxation and greater religious tolerance. The Arab overlords decided to treat both Hindus and Buddhists as protected "people of the book," despite the fact that their faiths had no connection to the Bible, the book in question. This meant that although they were obliged to pay special taxes, non-Muslims, like Jews and Christians, enjoyed the freedom to worship as they pleased.

As in other areas conquered by the Arabs, most of the local officials and notables retained their positions, which did much to reconcile them to Muslim rule. The status and privileges of the brahman castes were respected. Nearly all Arabs, who made up only a tiny minority of the population, lived in cities or special garrison towns. Because little effort was expended in converting the peoples of the conquered areas, they remained overwhelmingly Hindu or Buddhist.

Indian Influences on Islamic Civilization

Although the impact of Islam on the Indian subcontinent in this period was limited, the Arab foothold in Sind provided contacts by which Indian learning was transmitted to the Muslim heartlands in the Middle East. As a result, Islamic civilization was enriched by the skills and discoveries of yet another great civilization. Of particular importance was Indian scientific learning, which rivaled that of the Greeks as the most advanced of the ancient world. Hindu mathematicians and astronomers traveled to Baghdad after the Abbasids came to power in the mid-8th century. Their works on algebra and geometry were translated into Arabic, and their instruments for celestial observation were copied and improved by Arab astronomers.

Most critically, Arab thinkers in all fields began to use the numerals that Hindu scholars had devised centuries earlier. Because these numbers were passed on to the Europeans through contacts with the Arabs in the early Middle Ages, we call them Arabic numerals today, but they originated in India. Because of the linkages between civilized centers established by the spread of Islam, this system of numerical notation has proved central to two scientific revolutions. The first in the Middle East was discussed earlier in this chapter. The second, discussed in Chapter 22, occurred in Europe some centuries later. From the 16th century to the present, it has brought fundamental transformations to both Europe and much of the rest of the world.

In addition to science and mathematics, Indian treatises on subjects ranging from medicine to music were translated and studied by Arab scholars. Indian physicians were brought to Baghdad to run the well-endowed hospitals that the Christian crusaders found a source of wonderment and a cause for envy. On several occasions, Indian doctors were able to cure Arab rulers and officials whom Greek physicians had pronounced beyond help. Indian works on statecraft, alchemy, and palmistry were also translated into Arabic, and it is believed that some of the tales in the *Arabian Nights* were based on ancient Indian stories. Indian musical instruments and melodies made their way into the repertoires of Arab performers, and the Indian game of chess became a favorite of both royalty and ordinary townspeople.

Arabs who emigrated to Sind and other Muslim-ruled areas often adopted Indian dress and hairstyles, ate Indian foods, and rode on elephants as the Hindu *rajas* (kings) did. As Figure 12.5 illustrates, the conquerors also adopted Indian building styles and artistic motifs. In this era, additional Arab colonies were established in other coastal areas, such as Malabar to the south and Bengal in the east (see Map 12.2). These trading enclaves later provided the staging areas from which Islam was transmitted to island and mainland southeast Asia.

From Booty to Empire: The Second Wave of Muslim Invasions

After the initial conquests by Muhammad ibn Qasim's armies, little territory was added to the Muslim foothold on the subcontinent. In fact, disputes between the Arabs occupying Sind and their quarrels with first the Umayyad and later the Abbasid caliphs gradually weakened the Muslim hold on the area. This was reflected in the reconquest of parts of the lower Indus valley by Hindu rulers. But the gradual Muslim retreat was dramatically reversed by a new series of military invasions, this time launched by a Turkish slave dynasty that in 962 had seized power in Afghanistan to the north of the Indus valley. The third ruler of this dynasty, **Mahmud of Ghazni,** led a series of expeditions that began nearly two centuries of Muslim raiding and conquest in northern India. Drawn by the legendary wealth of the subcontinent and a zeal to spread the Muslim faith, Mahmud repeatedly raided northwest India in the first decades of the 11th century. He defeated one confederation of Hindu princes after another, and he drove deeper and deeper into the subcontinent in the quest of ever richer temples to loot.

Figure 12.5   *Built in 1626 at Agra, this exquisite tomb of white marble encrusted with semiprecious stones is a superb example of the blending of Islamic and Hindu architectural forms, building materials, and artistic motifs. Although this structure was built centuries after the first Muslims entered India, from the outset this blending of traditions was evident.*

The raids mounted by Mahmud of Ghazni and his successors gave way in the last decades of the 12th century to sustained campaigns aimed at seizing political control in north India. The key figure in this transition was a tenacious military commander of Persian extraction, **Muhammad of Ghur.** After barely surviving several severe defeats at the hands of Hindu rulers, Muhammad put together a string of military victories that brought the Indus valley and much of north central India under his control. In the following years, Muhammad's conquests were extended along the Gangetic plain as far as Bengal, and into west and central India, by several of his most gifted subordinate commanders. After Muhammad was assassinated in 1206, **Qutb-ud-din Aibak,** one of his slave lieutenants, seized power.

Significantly, the capital of the new Muslim empire was at Delhi along the Jumna River on the Gangetic plain. Delhi's location in the very center of northern India graphically proclaimed that a Muslim dynasty rooted in the subcontinent itself, not an extension of a Middle Eastern central Asian empire, had been founded. For the next 300 years, a succession of dynasties ruled much of north and central India. Alternately of Persian, Afghan, Turkic, and mixed descent, the rulers of these imperial houses proclaimed themselves the *sultans of Delhi* (literally, princes of the heartland). They fought each other, Mongol and Turkic invaders, and the indigenous Hindu princes for control of the Indus and Gangetic heartlands of Indian civilization.

Patterns of Conversion

Although the Muslims fought their way into India, their interaction with the indigenous peoples soon came to be dominated by accommodation and peaceful exchanges. Over the centuries when much of the north was ruled by dynasties centered at Delhi, sizeable Muslim communities developed in different areas of the subcontinent. The largest of these were in Bengal to the east and in the northwestern areas of the Indus valley that were the points of entry for most of the Muslim peoples who migrated into India.

Few of these converts were won forcibly. The main carriers of the new faith often were merchants, who played a growing role in both coastal and inland trade, but were most especially Sufi mystics. The lat-

ter shared much with Indian gurus and wandering ascetics in both style and message. Belief in their magical and healing powers enhanced the Sufis' stature and increased their following. Their mosques and schools often became centers of regional political power. Sufis organized their devotees in militias to fend off bandits or rival princes, oversaw the clearing of forests for farming and settlement, and welcomed low-caste and outcaste Hindu groups into Islam. After their deaths, the tombs of Sufi mystics became objects of veneration for Indian Muslims as well as Hindu and Buddhist pilgrims.

Most of the indigenous converts, who came to form a majority of the Muslims living in India, were drawn from specific regions and social groups. Surprisingly small numbers of converts were found in the Indo-Gangetic centers of Muslim political power, a fact that suggests the very limited importance of forced conversions. Most Indians who converted to Islam were from Buddhist or low-caste groups. In areas such as western India and Bengal, where Buddhism had survived as a popular religion until the era of the Muslim invasions, esoteric rituals and corrupt practices had debased Buddhist teachings and undermined the morale of the monastic orders.

This decline was accelerated by Muslim raids on Buddhist temples and monasteries, which provided vulnerable and lucrative targets for the early invaders. Without monastic supervision, local congregations sank further into orgies and experiments with magic. All of these trends opposed the Buddha's social concerns and religious message. Disorganized and misdirected, Indian Buddhism was no match for the confident and vigorous new religion the Muslim invaders carried into the subcontinent. This was particularly true when those who were spreading the new faith had the charisma and organizing skills of the Sufi mystics.

Buddhists probably made up the majority of Indians who converted to Islam. But untouchables and low-caste Hindus, as well as animistic tribal peoples, were also attracted to the more egalitarian social arrangements promoted by the new faith. As was the case with the Buddhists, group conversions were essential because those who remained in the Hindu caste system would have little to do with those who converted. Some conversions resulted from the desire of Hindus or Buddhists to escape the head tax the Muslim rulers levied on unbelievers. It was also prompted by intermarriage between local peoples and

Muslim migrants. In addition, Muslim migrants swelled the size of the Islamic community in the subcontinent. This was particularly true in periods of crisis in central Asia. In the 13th and 14th centuries, for example, Turkic, Persian, and Afghan peoples retreated to the comparative safety of India in the face of the Mongol and Timurid conquests that are examined in detail in Chapter 19.

Patterns of Accommodation

Although Islam won many converts in certain areas and communities, it initially made little impression on the Hindu community as a whole. Despite military reverses and the imposition of Muslim political rule over large areas of the subcontinent, high-caste Hindus in particular saw the invaders as the bearers of an upstart religion and as polluting outcastes. Al-Biruni, one of the chief chroniclers of the Muslim conquests, complained openly about the prevailing Indian disdain for the newcomers:

> The Hindus believe that there is no country but
> theirs, no nation like theirs, no kings like theirs,
> no religion like theirs, no science like theirs.
> They are haughty, foolishly vain, self-conceited
> and stolid.

Many Hindus were willing to take positions as administrators in the bureaucracies of Muslim overlords or as soldiers in their armies and to trade with Muslim merchants. But they remained socially aloof from their conquerors. Separate living quarters were established everywhere Muslim communities developed. Genuine friendships between members of high-caste groups and Muslims were rare, and sexual liaisons between them were severely restricted.

During the early centuries of the Muslim influx, the Hindus were convinced that like so many of the peoples who had entered the subcontinent in the preceding millennia, the Muslims would soon be absorbed by the superior religions and more sophisticated cultures of India. Many signs pointed to that outcome. Hindus staffed the bureaucracies and made up a good portion of the armies of Muslim rulers. In addition, Muslim princes adopted regal styles and practices that were Hindu-inspired and contrary to the Qur'an. Some Muslim rulers proclaimed themselves to be of divine descent, and others minted coins decorated with Hindu images such as Nandi, the bull associated with a major Hindu god, Shiva.

More broadly, Muslim communities became socially divided along caste lines. Recently arrived Muslims generally were on top of the hierarchies that developed, and even they were divided depending on whether they were Arab, Turk, or Persian. High-caste Hindu converts came next, followed by "clean" artisan and merchant groups. Lower-caste and untouchable converts remained at the bottom of the social hierarchy. This may help to explain why conversions in these groups were not as numerous as one would expect given the original egalitarian thrust of Islam. Muslims also adopted Indian foods and styles of dress and took to chewing *pan*, or limestone wrapped with betel leaves.

The Muslim influx had unfortunate consequences for women in both Muslim and Hindu communities. The invaders increasingly adopted the practice of marrying women at the earlier ages favored by the Hindus and the prohibitions against the remarriage of widows found especially at the high-caste levels of Indian society. Some upper "caste" Muslim groups even performed the ritual of **sati,** the burning of widows on the same funeral pyres as their deceased husbands, which was found among some high-caste Hindu groups.

Islamic Challenge and Hindu Revival

Despite a significant degree of acculturation to Hindu lifestyles and social organization, Muslim migrants to the subcontinent held to their own distinctive religious beliefs and rituals. The Hindus found Islam impossible to absorb and soon realized that they were confronted by an actively proselytizing religion with great appeal to large segments of the Indian population. Partly in response to this challenge, the Hindus placed greater emphasis on the devotional cults of gods and goddesses that earlier had proved so effective in neutralizing the challenge of Buddhism.

Membership in these **bhaktic** cults was open to all, including women and untouchables. In fact, some of the most celebrated writers of religious poetry and songs of worship were women, such as **Mira Bai.** Saints from low-caste origins were revered by warriors and brahmans as well as by farmers, merchants, and outcastes. One of the most remarkable of these mystics was a Muslim weaver named **Kabir.** In plain and direct verse, Kabir played down the significance of religious differences and proclaimed that all could provide a path to spiritual fulfillment. He asked,

> O servant, where do thou seek Me?
>
> Lo! I am beside thee.
>
> I am neither in temple nor in mosque:
>
> Neither am I in rites and ceremonies, nor in Yoga and renunciation.

Because many songs and poems, such as those by Mira Bai and Kabir, were composed in regional languages, such as Bengali, Marathi, and Tamil, they were more accessible to the common people and became prominent expressions of popular culture in many areas.

Bhakti mystics and gurus stressed the importance of a strong emotional bond between the devotee and the god or goddess who was the object of veneration. Chants, dances, and in some instances drugs were used to reach the state of spiritual intoxication that was the key to individual salvation. Once one had achieved the state of ecstasy that came through intense emotional attachment to a god or goddess, all past sins were removed and caste distinctions were rendered meaningless. The most widely worshiped deities were the gods Shiva and Vishnu, the latter particularly in the guise of Krishna the goatherder, depicted in the folk painting in Figure 12.6. The goddess Kali was also venerated in a number of different manifestations. By increasing popular involvement in Hindu worship and by enriching and extending the modes of prayer and ritual, the bhakti movement may have done much to stem the flow of converts to Islam, particularly among low-caste groups.

Stand-Off: The Muslim Presence in India at the End of the Sultanate Period

The attempts of mystics such as Kabir to minimize the differences between Hindu and Islamic beliefs and worship won over only small numbers of the followers of either faith. They were also strongly repudiated by the guardians of orthodoxy in each religious community. Sensing the long-term threat to Hinduism posed by Muslim political dominance and conversion efforts, the brahmans denounced the Muslims as infidel destroyers of Hindu temples and polluted meat-eaters. Later Hindu mystics, such as the 15th-century holy man Chaitanya, composed songs that focused on love for Hindu deities and set

Figure 12.6 *This Indian miniature painting of milkmaids serving the Hindu god Krishna reflects the highly personalized devotional worship that was characteristic of the bhakti movement. The eroticism in the milkmaids' songs, in praise of Krishna's great beauty, reveals a blending of sacred and secular, carnal and spiritual that is a recurring motif in Hindu worship and art.*

out to convince Indian Muslims to renounce Islam in favor of Hinduism.

For their part, Muslim ulama, or religious experts, grew increasingly aware of the dangers Hinduism posed for Islam. Attempts to fuse the two faiths were rejected on the grounds that although Hindus might argue that specific rituals and beliefs were not essential, they were fundamental for Islam. If one played down the teachings of the Qur'an, prayer, and the pilgrimage, one was no longer a true Muslim. Thus, contrary to the teachings of Kabir and like-minded mystics, the ulama and even some Sufi saints stressed the teachings of Islam that separated it from Hinduism. They worked to promote unity within the Indian Muslim community and to strengthen its contacts with Muslims in neighboring lands and the Middle Eastern centers of the faith.

After centuries of invasion and migration, a large Muslim community had been established in the Indian subcontinent. Converts had been won, political control had been established throughout much of the area, and strong links had been forged with Muslims in other lands such as Persia and Afghanistan. But non-Muslims, particularly Hindus, remained the overwhelming majority of the population of the vast and diverse lands south of the Himalayas. Unlike the Zoroastrians in Persia or the animistic peoples of the Maghrib and the Sudan, most Indians showed little inclination to convert to the religion of the Muslim conquerors. After centuries of Muslim political dominance and missionary activity, south Asia remained one of the least converted and integrated of all the areas Muhammad's message had reached.

The Spread of Islam to Southeast Asia

 The spread of Islam to various parts of coastal India set the stage for its further expansion to island southeast Asia. Arab traders and sailors regularly visited the ports of southeast Asia long before they converted to Islam. From the 13th century, these traders, and the Sufi mystics they sometimes carried aboard their ships, spread Islam to Java and much of the rest of island southeast Asia. As was the case in India, conversion was generally peaceful, and the new believers combined Islamic teachings and rituals with elements of the animist, Hindu, and Buddhist religions that had spread throughout the area in preceding centuries.

From a world history perspective, island southeast Asia had long been mainly a middle ground. It was the zone where the Chinese segment of the great Euro-Asian trading complex met the Indian Ocean trading zone to the west (see map in the Visualizing the Past section, Chapter 6). At ports on the coast of the Malayan peninsula, east Sumatra, and somewhat later north Java, goods from China were transferred from east Asian vessels to Arab or Indian ships. In these same ports, products from as far west as Rome were loaded into the emptied Chinese ships to be carried to east Asia. By the 7th and 8th centuries c.e., sailors and ships from areas of southeast Asia, particularly Sumatra and Malaya, had become active in the seaborne trade of the region. Southeast Asian products had also become important exports to China, India, and the Mediterranean region. Many of these products were luxury items, such as aromatic woods from the rain forests of Borneo and Sumatra and spices such as cloves, nutmeg, and mace from the far end of the Indonesian archipelago. These trading links were to prove even more critical to the expansion of Islam in southeast Asia than they had earlier been to the spread of Buddhism and Hinduism.

From the 8th century onward, the coastal trade of India came increasingly to be controlled by Muslims from such regions as Gujarat in western India and various parts of south India. As a result, elements of Islamic culture began to filter into island southeast Asia. But only in the 13th century, after the collapse of the far-flung trading empire of **Shrivijaya,** centered on the Strait of Malacca between Malaya and the northeast of Sumatra (see Map 12.2), was the way open for the widespread introduction of Islam. Indian traders, Muslim or otherwise, were welcome to trade in the chain of ports controlled by Shrivijaya. But because the rulers and officials of Shrivijaya were devout Buddhists, there was little incentive for the traders and sailors of southeast Asian ports to convert to Islam, the religion of growing numbers of the merchants and sailors from India. With the fall of Shrivijaya, incentives increased for the establishment of Muslim trading centers and efforts to preach the faith to the coastal peoples.

Trading Contacts and Conversion

As in most of the areas to which Islam spread, peaceful contacts and voluntary conversion were far more important than conquest and force in spreading the faith in southeast Asia. Throughout the islands of the region, trading contacts paved the way for conversion. Muslim merchants and sailors introduced local peoples to the ideas and rituals of the new faith and impressed on them how much of the known world had already been converted. Muslim ships also carried Sufis to various parts of southeast Asia, where they played as vital a role in conversion as they had in India. The first areas to be won to Islam in the late 13th century were several small port centers on the northern coast of Sumatra. From these ports, the religion spread in the centuries that followed across the Strait of Malacca to Malaya.

On the mainland, the key to widespread conversion was the powerful trading city of **Malacca,** whose smaller trading empire had replaced the fallen Shrivijaya. From Malacca, Islam spread along the coasts of Malaya to east Sumatra and to the trading center of **Demak** on the north coast of Java. From Demak, the most powerful of the trading states on north Java,

In Depth

Conversion and Accommodation in the Spread of World Religions

Although not all great civilizations have produced world religions, the two tend to be closely associated throughout human history. World religions are those that spread across many cultures and societies, forge links between civilized centers, and bring civilized lifestyles to nomadic pastoral or shifting-cultivating peoples. Religions with these characteristics appeared before the rise of Islam. As we have seen, India alone produced two of these faiths in ancient times: Hinduism, which spread to parts of southeast and central Asia, and Buddhism, which spread even more widely in the Asian world. At the other end of the Eastern Hemisphere, Christianity spread throughout the Mediterranean region before claiming northern and western Europe as its core area. Judaism spread not because it won converts in non-Jewish cultures but because the Jewish people were driven from their homeland by Roman persecution and scattered throughout the Middle East, north Africa, and Europe.

Because religious conversion affects all aspects of life, from the way one looks at the universe to more mundane decisions about whom to marry or how to treat others, a world religion must be broad and flexible enough to accommodate the existing culture of potential converts. At the same time, its core beliefs and practices must be well enough defined to allow its followers to maintain a clear sense of common identity despite their great differences in culture and society. These beliefs and practices must be sufficiently profound and sophisticated to convince potential converts that their own cultures can be enriched and their lives improved by adopting the new religion.

Until the 16th century, when Christianity spread through the Western Hemisphere, no world religion could match Islam in the extent to which it spread across the globe and in the diversity of peoples and cultures that identified themselves as Muslims. Given its uncompromising monotheism, very definite doctrines, and elaborate rituals and principles of social organization, Islam's success at winning converts from very different cultural backgrounds is surprising at first glance. This is particularly true if it is compared with the much more flexible beliefs and ceremonial patterns of earlier world religions such as Buddhism and Hinduism. However, closer examination reveals that Islamic beliefs and social practices, as written in the Qur'an and interpreted by the ulama, proved quite flexible and adaptable when the religion was introduced into new, non-Islamic cultures.

The fact that Islam won converts overwhelmingly through peaceful contacts between long-distance traders and the preaching and organizational skills of Sufis exemplifies this capacity for accommodation. Those adopting the new religion did not do so because they were pressured or forced to convert but because they saw Islam as a way to enhance their understanding of the supernatural, enrich their ceremonial expression, improve the quality of their social interaction, and establish ongoing links to a transcultural community beyond their local world.

Because Islam was adopted rather than imposed, those who converted had a good deal to say about how much of their own cultures they would change and which aspects of Islam they would emphasize or accept. Certain beliefs and practices were obligatory

the Muslim faith spread to other Javanese ports. After a long struggle with a Hindu-Buddhist kingdom in the interior, the rest of the island was eventually converted. From Demak, Islam was also carried to the Celebes and the spice islands in the eastern archipelago, and from the latter to Mindanao in the southern Philippines.

This progress of Islamic conversion shows that port cities in coastal areas were particularly receptive to the new faith. Here trading links were critical.

Once one of the key cities in a trading cluster converted, it was in the best interest of others to follow suit to enhance personal ties and provide a common basis in Muslim law to regulate business deals. Conversion to Islam also linked these centers, culturally as well as economically, to the merchants and ports of India, the Middle East, and the Mediterranean.

Islam made slow progress in areas such as central Java, where Hindu-Buddhist dynasties contested its spread. But the fact that the earlier conversion to these for all true believers—the worship of a single god, adherence to the prophet Muhammad and the divine revelations he received as recorded in the Qur'an, and the observance of the five pillars of the faith. But even these were subject to reinterpretation. In virtually all cultures to which it spread, Islamic monotheism supplanted but did not eradicate the animistic veneration of nature spirits or person and place deities. Allah was acknowledged as the most powerful supernatural force, but people continued to make offerings to spirits that could heal, bring fertility, protect their homes, or punish their enemies. In such areas as Africa and western China, where the veneration of ancestral spirits was a key aspect of religious life, the spirits were retained not as powers in themselves but as emissaries to Allah. In cultures such as those found in India and southeast Asia, Islamic doctrines were recast in a heavily mystical, even magical mode.

The flexibility of Islam was exhibited in the social as well as the religious sphere. In Islamic southeast Asia and, as we shall see in Chapter 13, in sub-Saharan Africa, the position of women remained a good deal stronger in critical areas, such as occupation and family law, than it had become in the Middle East and India. In both regions, the male-centric features of Islam that had grown more pronounced through centuries of accommodation in ancient Middle Eastern and Persian cultures were played down as Islam adapted to societies where women had traditionally enjoyed more influence, both within the extended family and in occupations such as farming, marketing, and craft production. Even the caste system of India, which in principle is opposed to the strong egalitarian strain in Islam, developed among Muslim groups that migrated into the subcontinent and survived in indigenous south Asian communities that converted to Islam.

Beyond basic forms of social organization and interaction, Islam accommodated diverse aspects of the societies into which it spread. For example, the African solar calendar, which was essential for coordinating the planting cycle, was retained along with the Muslim lunar calendar. In India, Hindu-Buddhist symbols of kingship were appropriated by Muslim rulers and acknowledged by both their Hindu and Muslim subjects. In island southeast Asia, exquisitely forged knives, called *krises*, which were believed to have magical powers, were among the most treasured possessions of local rulers both before and after they converted to Islam.

There was always the danger that accommodation could go too far—that in winning converts, Islamic principles would be so watered down and remolded that they no longer resembled or actually contradicted the teachings of the Qur'an. Sects that came to worship Muhammad or his nephew Ali as godlike, for example, clearly violated fundamental Muslim principles. This danger was a key source of the periodic movements for purification and revival that have been a notable feature of nearly all Islamic societies, particularly those on the fringes of the Islamic world. But even these movements, which were built around the insistence that the Muslim faith had been corrupted by alien ideas and practices and that a return to Islamic fundamentals was needed, were invariably cast in the modes of cultural expression of the peoples who rallied to them.

Questions: Can you think of ways in which world religions, such as Christianity, Hinduism, and Buddhism, changed to accommodate the cultures and societies to which they spread? Do these religions strike you as more or less flexible than Islam? Why?

Indian religions had been confined mainly to the ruling elites in Java and other island areas left openings for mass conversions to Islam that the Sufis eventually exploited. The island of Bali, where Hinduism had taken deep root at the popular level, remained largely impervious to the spread of Islam. The same was true of most of mainland southeast Asia, where centuries before the coming of Islam, Buddhism had spread from India and Ceylon and won the fervent adherence of both the ruling elites and the peasant masses.

Sufi Mystics and the Nature of Southeast Asian Islam

Because Islam came to southeast Asia primarily from India and was spread in many areas by Sufis, it was often infused with mystical strains and tolerated earlier animist, Hindu, and Buddhist beliefs and rituals. Just as they had in the Middle East and India, the Sufis who spread Islam in southeast Asia varied widely in personality and approach. Most were believed by those who followed them to have magical powers, and nearly all Sufis established mosque and school centers from which they traveled in neighboring regions to preach the faith.

In winning converts, the Sufis were willing to allow the inhabitants of island southeast Asia to retain pre-Islamic beliefs and practices that orthodox scholars would have found contrary to Islamic doctrine. Pre-Islamic customary law remained important in regulating social interaction, whereas Islamic law was confined to specific sorts of agreements and exchanges. Women retained a much stronger position, both within the family and in society, than they had in the Middle East and India. For example, trading in local and regional markets continued to be dominated by small-scale female buyers and sellers. In such areas as western Sumatra, lineage and inheritance continued to be traced through the female line after the coming of Islam, despite its tendency to promote male dominance and descent. Perhaps most tellingly, pre-Muslim religious beliefs and rituals were incorporated into Muslim ceremonies. Indigenous cultural staples, such as the brilliant Javanese puppet shadow plays that were based on the Indian epics of the brahmanic age, were refined, and they became even more central to popular and elite beliefs and practices than they had been in the pre-Muslim era.

GLOBAL CONNECTIONS: Islam: A Bridge Between Worlds

Although problems of political control and succession continued to plague the kingdoms and empires that divided the Muslim world, the central position of Islamic civilization in global history was solidified during the centuries of Abbasid rule. Its role as the go-between for the more ancient civilizations of the Eastern Hemisphere grew as Arab trading networks expanded into new areas. More than ever, it enriched the lives of nomadic peoples, from the Turks and Mongols of central Asia to the Berbers of north Africa and the camel herders of the Sudan. Equally critically, Islam's original contributions to the growth and refinement of civilized life greatly increased. From its great cities and universities and the accomplishments they generated in the fine arts, sciences, and literature to its vibrant religious and philosophical life, Islam

pioneered patterns of organization and thinking that would affect the development of human societies in major ways for centuries to come.

In the midst of all this achievement, however, there were tendencies that would put the Muslim peoples at a growing disadvantage, particularly in relation to their long-standing European rivals. Muslim divisions would leave openings for political expansion that the Europeans would eagerly exploit, beginning with the island southeast Asian extremities of the Islamic world and then moving across north India. The growing orthodoxy and intolerance of the ulama, as well as the Muslim belief that the vast Islamic world contained all requirements for civilized life, caused Muslim peoples to grow less receptive to outside influences and innovations. These tendencies became increasingly pronounced at precisely the time when their Christian rivals were entering a period of unprecedented curiosity, experimentation, and exploration of the world beyond their own heartlands.

Further Reading

M. A. Shaban's *Islamic History: An Interpretation*, 2 vols. (1971), contains the most readable and thematic survey of early Islam, concentrating on the Abbasid period. Although Philip Hitti's monumental *History of the Arabs* (1967) and J. J. Saunders' *A History of Medieval Islam* (1965) are now somewhat dated, they contain much valuable information and some fine insights into Arab history. Also useful are the works of G. E. von Gruenebaum, especially *Classical Islam* (1970), which covers the Abbasid era. On changes in Islamic religion and the makeup of the Muslim community, Marshall Hodgson's *Venture of Islam* (1974, vol. 2) is indispensable, but it should not be tackled by the beginner. *The Cambridge History of Islam*, 2 vols. (1970); Ira Lapidus' *A History of Islamic Societies* (1988); and Albert Hourani's *A History of the Islamic Peoples* (1991) are excellent reference works for the political events of the Abbasid era and Muslim achievements in various fields. D. M. Dunlop's *Arab Civilization to A.D. 1500* (1971) also contains detailed essays on Islamic culture as well as an article on the accomplishments of Muslim women in this era.

On social history, B. F. Musallam's *Sex and Society in Islam* (1983) has material on the Abbasid period, and Ira Lapidus' *Muslim Cities in the Later Middle Ages* (1967) remains the standard work on urban life in the premodern era. Two essential works on the spread of Islam to India are S. M. Ikram's *Muslim Civilization in India* (1964) and Aziz Ahmad's *Studies in Islamic Culture in the Indian Environment* (1964). For the role of the Sufis in Islamic conversion, Richard Eaton's *Sufis of Bijapur* (1978) and *The Rise of Islam and the Bengal Frontier* (1993) are particularly revealing. The best introduction to the pattern of Islamic conversion in southeast Asia is H. J. de Graaf's essay in *The Cambridge History of Islam* (1976, vol. 2). Clifford Geertz's *Islam Observed* (1968) provides a sweeping and provocative interpretation of the process of conversion in general and of the varying forms Islam takes in Java and Morocco in particular. Toby Huff's *The Rise of Early Modern Science: Islam, China, and the West* (1993) is a stimulating account of the ways in which science and technology were transmitted between these key centers of the Eastern Hemisphere and the effects of these exchanges on global history.

On the Web

Abbasid Baghdad is examined at http://www.fordham.edu/halsall/source/1000baghdad.html. Oman Khayyam was no mere writer of verses, but a leading scientist (http://www-gap.dcs.st-and.ac.uk/~history/Mathematicians/Khayyam.html), as were many Abbasid intellectuals (http://cyberistan.org/islamic/places1.html).

A Turkic people's homepage (http://www.ee.surrey.ac.uk/Societies/turksoc/intro/r_who.html) provides an introduction to Turkish history, including the empire of the Seljuk Turks. It also contains information about the status of women in Turkey, past and present.

The Seljuk Turks had to confront both the Crusades (http://www.islamset.com/islam/civil/seljuk.html) and the Mongol warriors of Chinggis Khan (http://www.pma.edmonton.ab.ca/vexhibit/genghis/intro.htm), but they succeeded in helping to preserve the Islamic heartland, while Islam spread even further into Africa and south and southeast Asia and China (http://users.erols.com/zenithco/indiamus.htm), a process that owed much to Sufism (http://www.geocities.com/Athens/5738/intro.htm).

Islam could arrive via the sword, but it was more often than not spread by Muslim mystics seeking cultural synthesis, such as the Muslim Indian bhakti poet, Kabir (http://www.upanishad.org/kabir/index.htm, http://www.boloji.com/kabir/, and http://www.cs.colostate.edu/~malaiya/kabir.html), whose message is sufficiently universal that he is claimed by adherents of many religions as one of their own.

CHAPTER 13

AFRICAN CIVILIZATIONS AND THE SPREAD OF ISLAM

In 1324, Mali ruler Mansa Musa made a pilgrimage to Mecca that brought the attention of the Muslim world to the wealth of the Mali kingdom. Cartographer Abraham Cresques depicted the trip more than 50 years later in the map shown below, where Mansa Musa is drawn holding a golden sceptre and nugget.

In 1324, a great caravan of hundreds of camels and slaves crossed the arid Sahara desert and wended its way into Cairo on the banks of the Nile. Mansa Musa, lord of the African empire of Mali, was making the *hajj*, the pilgrimage to Mecca, distributing gold with an open hand. His wealth and prodigality dazzled all who witnessed it and his fame spread throughout the Islamic world and beyond. Mansa Musa's caravan symbolized the wealthy potential of Africa, but even by the time he made his trip, west African gold was already well-known in the world economy and Africa was already involved in contacts of various kinds with other areas of the world.

Africa below the Sahara was never totally isolated from the centers of civilization in Egypt, west Asia, or the Mediterranean, but for long periods the contacts were difficult and intermittent. At the time of the Roman Empire, sub-Saharan Africa, like northern Europe, was on the edge of the major centers of civilization. After the fall of Rome, the civilizations of Byzantium and the Islamic world provided a link between the civilizations of the Middle East and the Mediterranean as well as the areas on their frontiers, such as northern Europe and Africa. In Africa, between roughly 800 and 1500 C.E., contacts with the outside world increased as part of the growing international network. Social, religious, and technological changes took place. Chief among these changes was the arrival of the followers of the prophet Muhammad. The spread of Islam from its heartland in the Middle East and north Africa to India and southeast Asia revealed the power of the religion and its commercial and sometimes military attributes. Civilizations were changed by Islam but retained their individuality. A similar pattern developed in sub-Saharan Africa as Islam provided new influences and contacts without uniting African culture as a whole with the Middle Eastern core. New religious, economic, and political patterns developed in relation to the Islamic surge, but great diversity remained.

The spread of Islam across much of the northern third of Africa produced profound effects on both those who converted and those who resisted the new faith. Islamization also linked Muslim Africa even more closely to the outside world through trade, religion, and politics. Trade and long-distance commerce were carried out in many parts of the continent and linked regions beyond the Muslim world. Until about 1450, however, Islam provided the major external contact between sub-Saharan Africa and the world.

State-building took place in many areas of the continent under a variety of conditions. For example, west Africa experienced both the cultural influence of Islam and its own internal civilization developments that produced great artistic accomplishments in some places. The formation of some powerful states, such as Mali and Songhay, depended more on military power

100 C.E.	600 C.E.	1000 C.E.	1200 C.E.	1400 C.E.
100–200 Camels introduced for trade in the Sahara **300** Origins of the kingdom of Ghana	**600–700** Islam spreads across North Africa	**1000** Ghana at height of its power **1100** Almoravid movement in the Sahara	**1200** Rise of the empire of Mali **1260** Death of Sundiata; earliest stone buildings at Zimbabwe; Lalibela rules in Ethiopia; Yoruba culture flourishes at Ile-Ife **1300** Mali at its height; Kanem Empire as a rival **1324** Pilgrimage of Mansa Musa	**1400** Flourishing of cities of Timbuktu and Jenne; Ethiopian Christian kingdom; Swahili cities flourish on East Africa coast **1417, 1431** Last Chinese trade voyages to East Africa **1500** Songhay Empire flourishes; Benin at height of power

and dynastic alliances than on ethnic or cultural unity. In this aspect and in the process of state formation itself, Africa paralleled the roughly contemporaneous developments of western Europe. The development of city-states, with strong merchant communities in west Africa and on the Indian Ocean coast of east Africa, bore certain similarities to the urban developments of Italy and Germany in this period. However, disparities between the technologies and ideologies of Europeans and Africans by the end of this period also created differences in the ways in which their societies developed. The arrival of western Europeans—the Portuguese—in the 15th century prompted a series of exchanges that drew Africans increasingly into the world economy and created a new set of relationships that characterized African development for centuries to come.

Several features characterize the history of Africa in the postclassical centuries. Northern Africa and the east African coast became increasingly incorporated into the Arab Muslim world, but even other parts of the continent reflected the power of Islamic thought and institutions. New centers of civilization and political power arose in several parts of sub-Saharan Africa, illustrating the geographic diffusion of civilization. African civilizations built somewhat less clearly on prior societies than did other postclassical civilizations. Some earlier themes, such as the Bantu migration and the formation of large states in the western Sudan, persisted. Overall, sub-Saharan Africa remained a varied and distinctive setting; parts of it were drawn into new contacts with the growing world network, but much of it retained a certain isolation.

African Societies: Diversity and Similarities

 African societies developed diverse forms, from large centralized states to stateless societies organized around kinship or age sets rather than central authority. Within this diversity were many shared aspects of language and beliefs. Universalistic faiths penetrated the continent and served as the basis for important cultural developments in Nubia and Ethiopia.

Like most continents, Africa is so vast and its societies so diverse that it is almost impossible to generalize about them. Differences in geography, language, religion, politics, and other aspects of life contributed to Africa's lack of political unity over long periods of time. Unlike in many parts of Asia, Europe, and north Africa, neither universal states nor universal religions characterized the history of sub-Saharan Africa. Yet universal religions, first Christianity and later Islam, did find adherents in Africa and sometimes contributed to the formation of large states and empires.

Stateless Societies

Some African societies had rulers who exercised control through a hierarchy of officials in what can be called states, but others were **stateless societies,** organized around kinship or other forms of obligation and lacking the concentration of political power and authority we normally associate with the state. Sometimes the stateless societies were larger and more extensive than the neighboring states. Stateless societies had forms of government, but the authority and power normally exercised by a ruler and his court in a kingdom could be held instead by a council of families or by the community, with no need to tax the population to support the ruler, the bureaucrats, the army, or the nobles, as was usually the case in state-building societies. Stateless societies had little concentration of authority, and that authority affected only a small part of the peoples' lives. In these societies, government was rarely a full-time occupation.

Other alternatives to formal government were possible. Among peoples of the west African forest, secret societies of men and women controlled customs and beliefs and were able to limit the authority of rulers. Especially among peoples who had sharp rivalries between lineages or family groupings, secret societies developed that cut across the lineage divisions. Members' allegiance to these groups transcended their lineage ties. The secret societies settled village disputes. They acted to maintain stability within the community, and they served as an alternative to the authority of state institutions.

Throughout Africa many stateless societies thrived, perhaps aided by the fact that internal social pressures or disputes often could be resolved by allowing dissidents to leave and establish a new village in the sparsely populated continent. Still, stateless societies found it difficult to resist external pressures, mobilize for warfare, organize large building projects, or create stable conditions for continuous long-distance trade with other peoples. All these needs or goals contributed to the formation of states in sub-Saharan Africa.

Common Elements in African Societies

Even amid the diversity of African cultures, certain similarities in language, thought, and religion provided some underlying unities. As we saw in Chapter 9, the spread of the Bantu-speaking peoples provided a linguistic base across much of Africa, so that even though specific languages differed, structure and vocabulary allowed some mutual understanding between neighboring Bantu speakers.

The same might be said of the animistic religion that characterized much of Africa. The belief in the power of natural forces personified as spirits or gods and the role of ritual and worship—often in the form of dancing, drumming, divination, and sacrifice—in influencing their actions was central to the religion of many African peoples. Africans, like Europeans, believed that some evil, disasters, and illnesses were produced by witchcraft. Specialists were needed to combat the power of evil and eliminate the witches. This led in many societies to the existence of a class of diviners or priests who guided religious practice and helped protect the community. Above all, African religion provided a cosmology—a view of how the universe worked—and a guide to ethics and behavior.

Many African peoples shared an underlying belief in a creator deity whose power and action were expressed through spirits or lesser gods and through the founding ancestors of the group. The ancestors often were viewed as the first settlers and thus the "owners" of the land or the local resources, and through them the fertility of the land, game, people, and herds could be ensured. Among some groups, working the land took on religious significance, so the land itself had a meaning beyond its economic usefulness.

Religion, economics, and history were thus closely intertwined. The family, lineage, or clan around which many African societies were organized also had an important role in dealing with the gods. Deceased ancestors often were a direct link between their living relatives and the spirit world. Veneration of the ancestors and gods was part of the same system of belief. Such a system was strongly linked to specific places and people. It showed remarkable resiliency even in the face of contact with monotheistic religions such as Islam and Christianity.

The economies of Africa are harder to describe in general terms than some basic aspects of politics and culture. North Africa, fully involved in the Mediterranean and Arab economic world, stands clearly apart. Sub-Saharan Africa varied greatly from one region to the next. In many areas, settled agriculture and skilled ironwork had been established before or advanced rapidly during the postclassical period. Specialization encouraged active local and regional trade, the basis for many lively markets and the many large cities that grew in both the structured states and the decentralized areas. The bustle and gaiety of market life were important ingredients of African society, and women as well as men participated actively. Professional merchants, in many cases in hereditary kinship groupings, often controlled trade. Participation in international trade increased in many regions in this period, mainly with the Islamic world and often through Arab traders.

Finally, one of the least known aspects of early African societies is the size and dynamics of their populations. This is true not only of Africa but of much of the world. Archeological evidence, travelers' reports, and educated guesses are used to estimate the population of early African societies, but in truth, our knowledge of how Africa fits into the general trends of the world population is very slight. By 1500, Africa may have had 30 to 60 million inhabitants.

The Arrival of Islam in North Africa

Africa north of the Sahara had long been part of the world of classical antiquity, where Phoenicians, Greeks, Romans, and Vandals traded, settled, built, battled, and destroyed. The Greek city of Cyrene (c. 600 B.C.E.) in modern Libya and the great Phoenician outpost at Carthage (founded c. 814 B.C.E.) in Tunisia attest to the part north Africa played in the classical world. After the age of the pharaohs, Egypt (conquered by Alexander in 331 B.C.E.) had become an important part of the Greek world and then later a key province in the Roman Empire, valued especially for its grain. Toward the end of the Roman Empire, Christianity had taken a firm hold in Mediterranean Africa, but in the warring between the Vandals and the Byzantines in north Africa in the 5th and 6th centuries C.E., great disruption had taken place. During that period, the Berber peoples of the Sahara had raided the coastal cities. As we have seen with Egypt, north Africa was linked across the Sahara to the rest of Africa in many ways. With the rise of Islam, those ties became even closer.

Between 640 and 700 C.E., the followers of Muhammad swept across north Africa from Suez to Morocco's Atlantic shore. By 670 C.E., Muslims ruled Tunisia, or **Ifriqiya**—what the Romans had called Africa. (The Arabs originally used this word as the name for eastern north Africa and **Maghrib** for lands

to the west.) By 711, Arab and Berber armies had crossed into Spain. Only their defeat in France by Charles Martel at Poitiers in 732 brought the Muslim advance in the West to a halt. The message of Islam found fertile ground among the populations of north Africa. Conversion took place rapidly within a certain political unity provided by the Abbasid dynasty. This unity eventually broke down, and north Africa divided into several separate states and competing groups.

In opposition to the states dominated by the Arabic rulers, the peoples of the desert, the Berbers, formed states of their own at places such as Fez in Morocco and at Sijilimasa, the old city of the trans-Saharan caravan trade. By the 11th century, under pressure from new Muslim invaders, a great puritanical reformist movement, whose followers were called the **Almoravids,** grew among the desert Berbers of the western Sahara. Launched on the course of a *jihad*—a holy war waged to purify, spread, or protect the faith—the Almoravids moved south against the African kingdoms of the savanna and west into Spain. In 1130 another reformist group, the **Almohadis,** followed the same pattern. These north African and Spanish developments were an essential background to the penetration of Islam into sub-Saharan Africa.

Islam offered many attractions within Africa. Its fundamental teaching that all Muslims are equal within the community of believers made the acceptance of conquerors and new rulers easier. The Islamic tradition of uniting the powers of the state and religion in the person of the ruler or caliph appealed to some African kings as a way of reinforcing their authority. The concept that all members of the umma, or community of believers, were equal put the newly converted Berbers and later Africans on an equal footing with the Arabs, at least in law. Despite these egalitarian and somewhat utopian ideas within Islam, practices differed considerably at local levels. Social stratification remained important in Islamicized societies, and ethnic distinctions also divided the believers. Despite certain teachings on the equality between men and women, the fine for killing a man was twice that for killing a woman. The disparity between law and practice—between equality before God and inequality within the world—sometimes led to utopian reform movements. Groups such as the Almohadis are characteristic within Islamic history, often developing in peripheral areas and dedicated to purifying society by returning to the original teachings of Muhammad.

The Christian Kingdoms: Nubia and Ethiopia

Islam was not the first universalistic religion to take root in Africa, and the wave of Arab conquests across northern Africa had left behind it islands of Christianity. Christian converts had been made in Egypt and Ethiopia even before the conversion of the Roman Empire in the 4th century C.E. In addition to the Christian kingdom of Axum, Christian communities thrived in Egypt and Nubia, further up the Nile. The Christians of Egypt, the Copts, developed a rich tradition in contact with Byzantium, translating the gospels and other religious literature from Greek to Coptic, their own tongue, which was based on the language of ancient Egypt. On doctrinal and political issues they eventually split from the Byzantine connection. When Egypt was conquered by Arab armies and then converted to Islam, the Copts were able to maintain their faith; Muslim rulers recognized them as followers of a revealed religion and thus entitled to a certain tolerance. The Coptic influence had already spread up the Nile into Nubia, the ancient land of Kush. Muslim attempts to penetrate Nubia were met with such stiff resistance in the 9th century that the Christian descendants of ancient Kush were left as independent Christian kingdoms until the 13th century.

The Ethiopian kingdom that grew from Axum was perhaps the most important African Christian outpost. Cut off from Christian Byzantium by the Muslim conquest of Egypt and the Red Sea coast, surrounded by pagan neighbors, and probably influenced by pagan and Jewish immigrants from Yemen, the Christian kingdom turned inward. Its people occupied the Ethiopian highlands, living in fortified towns and supporting themselves with agriculture on terraced hillsides. Eventually, through a process of warfare, conversion, and compromise with non-Christian neighbors, a new dynasty appeared, which under King Lalibela (d. 1221) sponsored a remarkable building project in which 11 great churches were sculpted from the rock in the town that bore his name (Figure 13.1).

In the 13th and 14th centuries, an Ethiopian Christian state emerged under a dynasty that traced its origins back to the biblical marriage of Solomon and Sheba. Using the Geez language of Axum as a religious language and Amharic as the common speech, this state maintained its brand of Christianity in isolation while facing constant pressure from its increasingly Muslim neighbors.

The struggle between the Christian state in the Ethiopian highlands and the Muslim peoples in Somalia and on the Red Sea coast shaped much of the history of the region and continues to do so today.

Figure 13.1 *The 13th-century churches of Lalibela, some cut from a single rock, represent the power of early Christianity in Ethiopia.*

When one of these Muslim states, with help from the Ottoman Turks, threatened the Ethiopian kingdom, a Portuguese expedition arrived in 1542 at Massawa on the Red Sea and turned the tide in favor of its Christian allies. Portuguese attempts thereafter to bring Ethiopian Christianity into the Roman Catholic church failed, and Ethiopia remained isolated, Christian, and fiercely independent.

Kingdoms of the Grasslands

 In the sahel grasslands, several powerful states emerged that combined Islamic religion and culture with local practices. The kingdoms of Mali and Songhay and the Hausa states were African adaptations of Islam and its fusion with African traditions.

As the Islamic wave spread across north Africa, it sent ripples across the Sahara, not in the form of invading armies but at first in the merchants and travelers who trod the dusty and ancient caravan routes toward the savanna. Africa had three important "coasts" of contact: the Atlantic, the Indian Ocean, and the savanna on the southern edge of the Sahara.

On the edge of the desert, where several resource zones came together, African states such as Ghana had already formed by the 8th century by exchanging gold from the forests of west Africa for salt or dates from the Sahara or for goods from Mediterranean north Africa. Camels, which had been introduced from Asia to the Sahara between the 1st and 5th centuries C.E., had greatly improved the possibilities of trade, but these animals, which thrived in arid and semiarid environments, could not live in the humid forest zones because of disease. Thus, the **sahel,** the extensive grassland belt at the southern edge of the Sahara, became a point of exchange between the forests to the south and north Africa—an active "coast" where ideas, trade, and people from the Sahara and beyond arrived in increasing numbers. Along that coast, several African states developed between the trading cities, taking advantage of their position as intermediaries in the trade. But their location on the open plains of the dry sahel also meant that these states were subject to attack and periodic droughts.

In Chapter 9 we discussed the rise of the kingdom of Ghana among the Soninke peoples of the western Sudan. Founded probably in the 3rd century C.E., Ghana rose to power by taxing the salt and gold exchanged within its borders. By the 10th century, its rulers had converted to Islam, and Ghana was at the height of its power. At a time when William the Conqueror could muster perhaps 5000 troops for his invasion of England, Muslim accounts reported that the king of Ghana could field an army many times that size. Eventually, however, Almoravid armies invaded Ghana from north Africa in 1076, and although the kingdom survived, its power was in decline, so that by the beginning of the 13th century, new states had risen in the savanna to take its place of leadership.

Sudanic States

There were several Sudanic kingdoms, and even during the height of Ghana's power, neighboring and competing states persisted, such as Takrur on the Senegal River to the west and Gao (Kawkaw) on the Niger River to the east. Before we deal with the most important kingdoms that followed Ghana, it is useful to review some of the elements these states had in common.

The **Sudanic states** often had a patriarch or council of elders of a particular family or group of lineages as leaders. Usually these states had a territorial core area in which the people were of the same linguistic or ethnic background, but their power extended over subordinate communities. These were conquest states, which drew on the taxes, tribute, and military support of the subordinate areas, lineages, and villages. The effective control of subordinate societies and the legal or informal control of their sovereignty are the usual definition of empires. The Sudanic states of Ghana, Mali, and Songhay fit that definition (Map 13.1).

The rulers of these states were considered sacred and were surrounded by rituals that separated them from their subjects. With the conversion of the rulers of Ghana and Takrur after the 10th century, Islam was used to reinforce indigenous ideas of kingship, so that Islam became something of a royal cult. Much of the population never converted, and the Islamicized ruling families also drew on their traditional powers to fortify their rule.

Several savanna states rose among the various peoples in the Sudan. We can trace the development and culture of two of the most important, Mali and Songhay, as an example of the fusion of Islamic and

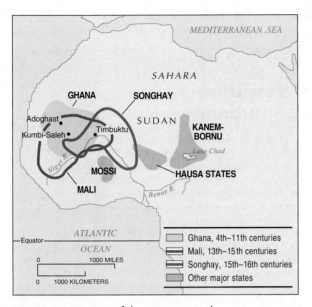

Map 13.1 *Empires of the Western Sudan*

indigenous African cultures within the context of trade and military expansion.

The Empire of Mali and Sundiata, the "Lion Prince"

The empire of **Mali,** centered between the Senegal and Niger rivers, was the creation of the Malinke peoples, who in the 13th century broke away from the control of Ghana, which was by then in steady decline. In Mali the old forms of kingship were reinforced by Islam. As in many of the Sudanic states, the rulers supported Islam by building mosques, attending public prayers, and supporting preachers. In return, sermons to the faithful emphasized obedience and support of the king. Mali became a model of these Islamicized Sudanic kingdoms. The economic basis of society in the Mali Empire was agriculture. This was combined with an active tradition of trade in many products, although like Ghana Mali also depended on its access to gold-producing areas to the south. Malinke merchants, or **juula,** formed small partnerships and groups to carry out trade throughout the area. They spread beyond the borders of the empire and throughout much of west Africa. The beginning of Malinke expansion is attributed to **Sundiata** (sometimes written Sunjata), a brilliant leader whose exploits were celebrated in a great oral tradition. The **griots,** professional oral historians who also served as keepers of traditions and advisors to kings, began their epic histories of Mali with Sundiata, the "Lion Prince."

> Listen then sons of Mali, children of the black people, listen to my word, for I am going to tell you of Sundiata, the father of the Bright Country, of the savanna land, the ancestor of those who draw the bow, the master of a hundred vanquished kings.... He was great among kings, he was peerless among men; he was beloved of God because he was the last of the great conquerors.

After a difficult childhood, Sundiata emerged from a period of interfamily and regional fighting to create a unified state. Oral histories ascribed to him the creation of the basic rules and relationships of Malinke society and the outline of the government of the empire of Mali. He became the mansa, or emperor. It was said that Sundiata "divided up the world," which meant that he was considered the originator of social arrangements. Sixteen clans of free people were entitled to bear arms and carry the bow and quiver of arrows as the symbol of their status, five clans were devoted to religious duties, and four clans were specialists such as blacksmiths and griots. Division and grouping by clans apparently represented traditional patterns among the peoples of the savanna in ancient Ghana as well, but Sundiata as the hero of origins was credited with creating this social arrangement. Although he created the political institutions of rule that allowed for great regional and ethnic differences in the federated provinces, he also stationed garrisons to maintain loyalty and security. Travel was secure and crime was severely punished, as **Ibn Batuta,** the Arab traveler, reported: "Of all peoples," he said, "the Blacks are those who most hate injustice, and their emperor pardons none who is guilty of it." The security of travelers and their goods was an essential element in a state where commerce played so important a role.

Sundiata died about 1260, but his successors expanded the borders of Mali until it controlled most of the Niger valley almost to the Atlantic coast. A sumptuous court was established and hosted a large number of traders. Mali grew wealthy from the trade. Perhaps the most famous of Sundiata's successors was Mansa Kankan Musa (c. 1312–1337), who made a pilgrimage to Mecca in 1324 and brought the attention of the Muslim world to Mali. The trip caused a

Document

The Great Oral Tradition and the Epic of Sundiata

Oral traditions take various forms. Some are simply the shared stories of a family or people, but in many west African societies, the mastery of oral traditions is a skill practiced by *griots*. Although today's griots are professional musicians and bards, historically they held important places at the courts of west African kingdoms. The epic of Sundiata, the great ruler of Mali, has been passed down orally for centuries. In the following excerpts from a version collected among the Mandingo (Malinke) people of Guinea by the African scholar D. T. Niane, the role of the griot and the advantages of oral traditions are outlined.

> We are now coming to the great moments in the life of Sundiata. The exile will end and another sun will rise. It is the sun of Sundiata. Griots know the history of kings and kingdoms and that is why they are the best counsellors of kings. Every king wants to have a singer to perpetuate his memory, for it is the griot who rescues the memories of kings from oblivion, as men have short memories. Kings have prescribed destinies just like men, and seers who probe the future know it. They have knowledge of the future, whereas we griots are depositories of the knowledge of the past. But whoever knows the history of a country can read its future.
>
> Other peoples use writing to record the past, but this invention has killed the faculty of memory among them. They do not feel the past any more, for writing lacks the warmth of the human voice. With them everybody thinks he knows, whereas learning should be a secret. The prophets did not write and their words have been all the more vivid as a result. What paltry learning is that which is concealed in dumb books!

The following excerpt describes the preparation for a major battle fought by Sundiata against the forces of Soumaoro, king of the Sossos, who had taken control of Mali and who is called an evil sorcerer in the epic. Note the interweaving of proverbs, the presence of aspects of Muslim and animist religion, the celebration of Sundiata's prowess, the recurring references to iron, and the high value placed on the cavalry, the key to military power in the savanna. Note how the story of Alexander the Great inspires this "African Alexander."

> Every man to his own land! If it is foretold that your destiny should be fulfilled in such and such a land, men can do nothing against it. Mansa Tounkara could not keep Sundiata back because the destiny of Songolon's son was bound up with that of Mali. Neither the jealousy of a cruel stepmother, nor her wickedness could alter for a moment the course of great destiny.

> The snake, man's enemy, is not long-lived, yet the serpent that lives hidden will surely die old. Djata (Sundiata) was strong enough now to face his enemies. At the age of eighteen he had the stateliness of the lion and the strength of the buffalo. His voice carried authority, his eyes were live coals, his arm was iron, he was the husband of power.
>
> Moussa Tounkara, king of Mema, gave Sundiata half of his army. The most valiant came forward of their own free will to follow Sundiata in the great adventure. The cavalry of Mema, which he had fashioned himself, formed his iron squadron. Sundiata, dressed in the Muslim fashion of Mema, left the town at the head of his small but redoubtable army. The whole population sent their best wishes with him. He was surrounded by five messengers from Mali, and Manding Bory [Sundiata's brother] rode proudly at his side. The horsemen of Mema formed behind Djata a bristling iron squadron. The troop took the direction of Wagadou, for Djata did not have enough troops to confront Soumaoro directly, and so the king of Mema advised him to go to Wagadou and take half the men of the king, Soumaba Cissé. A swift messenger had been sent there and so the king of Wagadou came out in person to meet Sundiata and his troops. He gave Sundiata half of his cavalry and blessed the weapons. Then Manding Bory said to his brother, "Djata, do you think yourself able to face Soumaoro now?"
>
> "No matter how small a forest may be, you can always find there sufficient fibers to tie up a man. Numbers mean nothing; it is worth that counts. With my cavalry I shall clear myself a path to Mali."
>
> Djata gave out his orders. They would head south, skirting Soumaoro's kingdom. The first objective to be reached was Tabon, the iron-gated town in the midst of the mountains, for Sundiata had promised Fran Kamara that he would pass Tabon before returning to Mali. He hoped to find that his childhood companion had become king. It was a forced march and during the halts the divines, Singbin Mara Cissé and Mandjan Bérété, related to Sundiata the history of Alexander the Great and several other heroes, but of all of them Sundiata preferred Alexander, the king of gold and silver, who crossed the world from west to east. He wanted to outdo his prototype both in the extent of his territory and in the wealth of his treasury.

Questions: Can oral traditions be used like other sources? Even if they are not entirely true, do they have historical value? Judging from this epic, how did people of the Sudan define the qualities of a king? What aspects of the epic reveal contacts between this part of Africa and the wider world?

sensation across the Sudan and into Egypt, where it was said that so much gold was distributed by his retinue that a general devaluation of currency took place. The trip and the ruler became almost legendary. In 1375, Abraham Cresques, a Jewish mapmaker in Spain, illustrated a map of Africa with an image of the ruler of Mali holding a golden sceptre (see Chapter 13 opening photo). Mansa Musa's trip had other consequences as well. From Mecca he brought back poet and architect Ishak al-Sahili, who came from Muslim Spain. The architect directed the building of several important mosques, and eventually a distinctive form of Sudanic architecture developed that made use of beaten clay. This can still be seen in the great mosque of Jenne (Figure 13.2). Mali's contact with the outer world brought change and innovation.

City Dwellers and Villagers

The cities of the western Sudan began to resemble those of north Africa, but with a distinctive local architectural style. The towns were commercial and often included craft specialists and a resident foreign merchant community. The military expansion of states such as Ghana, Mali, and later Songhay contributed to their commercial success because the power of the state protected traders. A cosmopolitan court life developed as merchants and scholars were attracted by the power and protection of Mali. Mandinka traders ranged across the Sudan and exploited their position as intermediaries. "Port" cities flourished, such as Jenne and **Timbuktu,** which lay just off the flood plain on the great bend in the Niger River. Timbuktu was reported to have a population of 50,000, and by the 14th century, its great Sankore mosque contained a library and an associated university where scholars, jurists, and Muslim theologians studied. The book was the symbol of civilization in the Islamic world, and it was said that the book trade in Timbuktu was the most lucrative business.

For most people in the empire of Mali and the other Sudanic states, life was not centered on the

Figure 13.2   *The spread of Islam and the importance of trade in Africa are represented by the great mosque at Jenne on the Niger River in the modern Republic of Mali.*

royal court, the great mosque, or long-distance trade but rather on the agricultural cycle and the village. Making a living from the land was the preoccupation of most people, and about 80 percent of the villagers lived by farming. This was a difficult life. The soils of the savanna were sandy and shallow. Plows were rarely used. The villagers were people of the hoe who looked to the skies in the spring for the first rains to start their planting. Rice in the river valleys, millet, sorghums, some wheat, fruits, and vegetables provided the basis of daily life in the village and supplied the caravan trade. Even a large farm rarely exceeded 10 acres, and most were much smaller. Clearing land often was done communally, accompanied by feasts and competition, but the farms belonged to families and were worked by them. A man with two wives and several unmarried sons could work more land than a man with one wife and a smaller family. Polygamy, the practice of having multiple wives, was common in the region, and it remains so today.

Given the difficulties of the soil, the periodic droughts, insect pests, storage problems, and the limitations of technology, the farmers of the Sudanic states—by the methods of careful cultivation, crop rotation, and, in places such as Timbuktu, the use of irrigation—were able to provide for their people the basic foods that supported them and the imperial states on which they were based. The hoe and the bow became symbols of the common people of the savanna states.

The Songhay Kingdom

As the power of Mali began to wane, a successor state from within the old empire was already beginning to emerge. The people of **Songhay** dominated the middle areas of the Niger valley. Traditionally, the society of Songhay was made up of "masters of the soil," that is, farmers, herders, and "masters of the waters," or fishers. Songhay had begun to form in the 7th century as an independent kingdom, perhaps under a Berber dynasty. By 1010, a capital was established at Gao on the Niger River, and the rulers had become Muslims, although the majority of the population remained pagan. Dominated by Mali for a while, by the 1370s Songhay had established its independence again and began to thrive as new sources of gold from the west African forests began to pass through its territory. Gao became a large city with a resident foreign merchant community and several mosques. Under a dynamic leader, Sunni Ali (1464–1492), the empire of Songhay was forged.

Sunni Ali was a great tactical commander and a ruthless leader. His cavalry expanded the borders and seized the traditional trading cities of Timbuktu and Jenne. The middle Niger valley fell under his control, and he developed a system of provincial administration to mobilize recruits for the army and rule the far-flung conquests. Although apparently a Muslim, he met any challenge to his authority even when it came from the Muslim scholars of Timbuktu, whom he persecuted. A line of Muslim rulers who took the military title *askia* succeeded him. These rulers, especially **Muhammad the Great,** extended the boundaries of the empire so that by the mid-16th century Songhay dominated the central Sudan.

Life in the Songhay Empire followed many of the patterns established in the previous savanna states. The fusion of Islamic and pagan populations and traditions continued. Muslim clerics and jurists sometimes were upset by the pagan beliefs and practices that continued among the population, and even more by the local interpretation of Islamic law. They wanted to impose a strict interpretation of the law of Islam and were shocked that men and women mixed freely in the markets and streets, that women went unveiled.

Songhay remained the dominant power in the region until the end of the 16th century. In 1591, a Muslim army from Morocco, equipped with muskets, crossed the Sahara and defeated the vastly larger forces of Songhay. This sign of weakness stimulated internal revolts against the ruling family, and eventually the parts of the old empire broke away.

The demise of the Songhay imperial structure did not mean the end of the political and cultural tradition of the western Sudan. Other states that combined Muslim and pagan traditions rose among the **Hausa** peoples of northern Nigeria, based on cities such as Kano and Katsina. The earliest Muslim ruler of Kano took control in the late 14th century and turned the city into a center of Muslim learning. In Kano and other Hausa cities of the region, an urbanized royal court in a fortified capital ruled over the animistic villages, where the majority of the population lived. With powerful cavalry forces these states extended their rule and protected their active trade in salt, grains, and cloth. Although these later Islamicized African states tended to be small and their goals were local, they reproduced many of the social, political, and religious forms of the great empires of the grasslands.

Beyond the Sudan, Muslim penetration came in various forms. Merchants became established in most of the major trading cities, and religious communities developed in each of these, often associated with particular families. Networks of trade and contact were established widely over the region as merchants and groups of pastoralists established their outposts in the area of Guinea. Muslim traders, herders, warriors, and religious leaders became important minorities in these segmented African societies, composed of elite families, occupational groups, free people, and slaves. Intermarriage often took place, but Muslim influence varied widely from region to region. Nevertheless, families of traders and lineages that became known as specialists in Muslim law spread widely through the region, so that by the 18th century Muslim minorities were scattered widely throughout west Africa, even in areas where no Islamicized state had emerged.

Political and Social Life in the Sudanic States

We can generalize from these brief descriptions of Mali and Songhay about the nature of the Sudanic states. The village communities, clans, and various ethnic groups continued to organize many aspects of life in the savanna. The development of unified states provided an overarching structure that allowed the various groups and communities to coexist. The large states usually represented the political aims and power of a particular group and often of a dominant family. Many states pointed to the immigrant origins of the ruling families, and in reality the movement and fusion of populations were constant features in the Sudan. Islam provided a universalistic faith that served the interests of many groups. Common religion and law provided solidarity and trust to the merchants who lived in the cities and whose caravans brought goods to and from the savanna. The ruling families used Islamic titles, such as *emir* or *caliph*, to reinforce their authority, and they surrounded themselves with literate Muslim advisors and scribes, who aided in government administration. The Muslim concept of a ruler who united civil and religious authority reinforced traditional ideas of kingship. It is also important to note that in Africa, as elsewhere in the world, the formation of states heightened social differences and made these societies more hierarchical.

In all the Sudanic states, Islam was fused with the existing traditions and beliefs. Rulership and author-

ity were still based on the ability to intercede with local spirits, and although Sundiata and Sunni Ali were nominally Muslim, they did not ignore the traditional basis of their rule. For this reason, Islam in these early stages in the Sudan tended to accommodate pagan practice and belief. Large proportions of the populations of Mali and Songhay never converted to Islam, and those who did convert often maintained many of the old beliefs as well.

We can see this fusion of traditions clearly in the position of women. Several Sudanic societies were matrilineal, and some recognized the role of women within the lines of kinship, contrary to the normal patrilineal customs inscribed in the **Sharia,** or Islamic law. As in the case of Songhay, north African visitors to the Sudan were shocked by the easy familiarity between men and women and the freedom enjoyed by women.

Finally, slavery and the slave trade between black Africa and the rest of the Islamic world had a major impact on women and children in these societies. Various forms of slavery and dependant labor had existed in Africa before Islam was introduced. Although we know little about slavery in central Africa in this period, slavery had been a marginal aspect of the Sudanic states. Africans had been enslaved by others before, and Nubian (African) slaves had been known in the classical world, but with the Muslim conquests of north Africa and commercial penetration to the south, slavery became a more widely diffused phenomenon, and a slave trade in Africans developed on a new scale.

In theory, Muslims viewed slavery as a stage in the process of conversion—a way of preparing pagans to become Muslims—but in reality, conversion did not guarantee freedom. Slaves in the Islamic world were used in a variety of occupations, as domestic servants and laborers, but they were also used as soldiers and administrators who, having no local ties and affiliations, were considered to be dependant and thus trustworthy by their masters. Slaves were also used as eunuchs and concubines, hence the emphasis on enslaving women and children. The trade caravans from the sahel across the Sahara often transported slaves as well as gold, and as we shall see, other slave trade routes developed from the African interior to the east African coast. The tendency for the children of slave mothers to be freed and integrated into Muslim society, though positive in one sense, also meant a constant demand for more slaves. Estimates of the volume of this trade vary widely. One scholar places the total in the trans-Saharan trade at 4.8 million, with another 2.4 million sent to the Muslim ports on the Indian Ocean coast. Actual figures may have been considerably lower, but the trade extended over 700 years and affected a large area. In a way, it was one more way in which Islamic civilization changed sub-Saharan Africa.

The Swahili Coast of East Africa

 A string of Islamicized African ports tied to the trade across the Indian Ocean dotted the east African coast. Although these cities were Islamicized, African customs and the Bantu Swahili language remained so strong that they represented a cultural fusion, mostly limited to the coast.

While the kingdoms of west Africa came under the influence of Islam from across the Sahara, another center of Islamic civilization was developing on the seaboard and offshore islands of Africa's Indian Ocean coast (Map 13.2). Along that coast, extending south from the horn of Africa to modern-day Mozambique, a string of Islamicized trading cities developed that reflected their cosmopolitan contacts with trading partners from Arabia, Persia, India, and China. Islam provided the residents of these towns a universal set of ethics and beliefs that made their maritime contacts easier, but in east Africa, as in the savanna kingdoms of west Africa, Islamization was slow to reach the general population. When it did, the result often was a compromise between indigenous ways and the new faith.

The Coastal Trading Ports

A 1st-century Greek account of the Indian Ocean, *The Periplus of the Erythraean Sea*, mentioned some ports in east Africa but was vague about whether the inhabitants were Africans or immigrants from the Arabian peninsula. From that century to the 10th century, the wave of Bantu migration had clearly reached the east African interior. Bantu-speaking herders in the north and farmers in the south mixed with older populations in the region. Other peoples were also moving to the African coast. Contact across the Indian Ocean dated back to at least the 2nd century B.C.E. From Indonesia or Malaya, seaborne immigrants settled on the large island of Madagascar

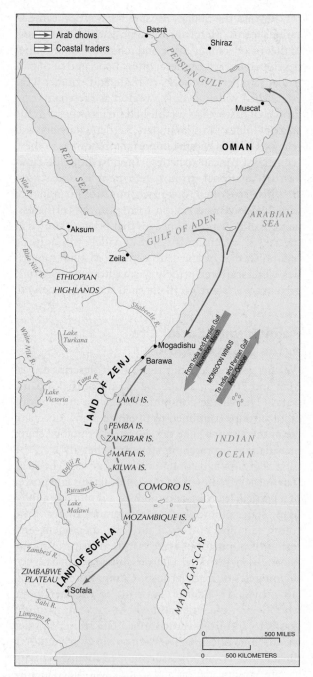

Map 13.2 *The Swahili Coast; African Monsoon Routes and Major Trade Routes*

and from there introduced foods such as bananas and coconuts to the African coast. These were widely adopted and spread rapidly along the coast and into central Africa. Small coastal villages of fishers and farmers, making rough pottery and working iron, dotted this coast. By the 8th and 9th centuries, visitors and refugees from Oman and the Persian Gulf had established themselves at some of these villages, attracted by the possibilities of trade with the land of **Zenj,** the Arabic term for the east African coast.

By the 13th century, a string of urbanized east African trading ports had developed along the coast. These towns shared the common Bantu-based and Arabic-influenced Swahili (which means "coastal") language and other cultural traits, although they were governed by separate Muslim ruling families. Towns such as Mogadishu, Mombasa, Malindi, Kilwa, Pate, and Zanzibar eventually contained mosques, tombs, and palaces of cut stone and coral. Ivory, gold, iron, slaves, and exotic animals were exported from these ports in exchange for silks from Persia and porcelain from China for the ruling Muslim families. The Arab traveler Ibn Batuta was impressed with the beauty and refinement of these towns. He described Kilwa as "one of the most beautiful and well-constructed towns in the world" and was also impressed by the pomp and luxury of its ruler. Kilwa was particularly wealthy because it controlled the southern port of Sofala, which had access to the gold produced in the interior (near Great Zimbabwe), and because of its location as the farthest point south at which ships from India could hope to sail and return in a single monsoon season.

From the 13th to the 15th centuries, Kilwa flourished in the context of international trade, but it was not alone. As many as 30 of these port towns eventually dotted the coast. They were tied to each other by an active coastal commerce and, in a few places, to the interior by a caravan trade, although it was usually Africans who brought the goods to the coast. Some Chinese ports sent goods directly to Africa in the 13th century, and as late as 1417 and 1431, large, state-sponsored expeditions sailing directly from China stopped at the east African coast to load ivory, gold, and rare woods. The Chinese discontinued such contact after 1431, and goods from China came to the coast thereafter in the ships of Arab or Indian traders.

The Mixture of Cultures on the Swahili Coast

The Islamic influence in these towns promoted long-distance commerce. The 13th century was a period of great Islamic expansion, and as that faith spread eastward to India and Indonesia, it provided a religious bond of trust and law that facilitated trade throughout

ports of the Indian Ocean. The ruling families in the east African trading ports built mosques and palaces; the mosque at Mogadishu was begun in 1238. Many of these ruling families claimed to be descendants of immigrants from Shiraz in Persia—a claim intended to legitimize their position and orthodoxy. In fact, some evidence indicates that the original Muslim families had emigrated to the Somali coast and from there to other towns farther south. The institutions and forms of the Muslim world operated in these cities. Whereas the rulers and merchants tended to be Muslim, the majority of the population on the east African coast, and perhaps even in the towns themselves, retained their previous beliefs and culture.

African culture remained strong throughout the area. The Swahili language was essentially a Bantu language containing a large number of Arabic words, although many of these words were not incorporated until the 16th century. The language was written in an Arabic script some time before the 13th century; the ruling families could also converse in Arabic. Islam itself penetrated very little into the interior among the hunters, pastoralists, and farmers. Even the areas of the coast near the trading towns remained largely unaffected. In the towns, the mud and thatch houses of the non-Muslim common peoples surrounded the stone and coral buildings of the Muslim elite. Islamization was to some extent class based. Still, a culture developed that fused Islamic and traditional elements. For example, family lineage was traced both through the maternal line, which controlled property (the traditional African practice), and through the paternal line, as was the Muslim custom. Swahili culture was a dynamic hybrid, and the Swahili people spread their language and culture along the coast of east Africa.

By the time the Portuguese arrived on this coast around 1500, the Swahili culture was widely diffused. Kilwa was no longer the predominant city, and the focus of trade had shifted to Malindi and Mombasa on the Kenya coast, but the commerce across the Indian Ocean continued. Eventually, the Portuguese raided Kilwa and Mombasa in an attempt to take control of trade. Their outpost on Mozambique Island and their control of Sofala put much of the gold trade in their hands. Although the Portuguese built a major outpost at Fort Jesus in Mombasa in 1592, they were never able to control the trade on the northern Swahili coast. The east African patterns, as established by 1500, persisted even more than those of the Sudanic kingdoms.

In Depth

Two Transitions in the History of World Population

Africa and the ancient Americas are two regions that make clear the difficulty of establishing the past size and structure of populations. Estimates based on fragmentary sources, the amount of available resources, and analysis of agricultural or hunting techniques have been used as rough guesses about population size. The results often are inadequate or controversial, but historians believe that the question is important. **Demography,** the study of population, has increasingly become a valued tool of historical inquiry. Clearly, unless we know the size, density, age structure, health, and reproductive capacity of a population, it is difficult to understand many aspects of its society, politics, and economy. In the contemporary world, most nations conduct periodic censuses to assess the present situation of their populations and to plan for the future. Before the mid-18th century, when census-taking became a regular procedure, population estimates and counts were sporadic and usually inaccurate. Estimating populations in the past, especially in nonliterate societies, is a highly speculative exercise in which archeological evidence and estimates of productive capacity of agricultural practices and technology are used. The earliest date for a population estimate with a margin of error less than 20 percent is probably 1750.

The history of human population can be divided into two basic periods: a long era—almost all of human history—of very slow growth and a very short period—about 250 years from 1750 to the present—of very rapid growth. For most of this history, the human population was very small and grew very slowly. Before agriculture was developed, the hunting-and-gathering economies of the world's populations supported 5 to 10 million people, if modern studies of such populations can be used as a guide. After about 8000 B.C.E., when plants and animals were domesticated, population began to increase more rapidly but still at a modest level. Agriculture provided a more secure and larger food supply, but population concentration in villages and towns may have made people more susceptible to disease and thus reduced their numbers. Other historians believe that the settled agricultural life also led to intensified warfare (because of the struggle for land and water) and increasing social stratification within societies. Still, the Neolithic revolution and the development of agriculture stimulated population growth. It was the first major transition in the history of world pop-

ulation. One estimate, based on Roman and Chinese population counts and some informed guesses about the rest of the world, is an annual growth rate of about 0.36 per million. By 1 C.E., the world population may have been about 300 million people. It increased between 1 C.E. and 1750 C.E. to about 500 million people. We should bear in mind that during this period of general increase, there were always areas that suffered decline, sometimes drastic, because of wars, epidemics, or natural catastrophes. The disastrous decline of American Indian populations after contact with Europeans, caused by disease, conquest, and social disruption, is a case in point. The effect of the slave trade on Africa, though still debated, is another. Sharp population changes usually resulted in profound social and cultural adjustments. Some scholars argue that the slave trade had just such an impact on social and political patterns in Africa.

A second and extremely important transition took place between the mid-17th and the mid-18th centuries. Initially based on new food resources, this transition often is associated with the Industrial Revolution, when new sources of energy were harnessed. The growth rate greatly increased during this period in the countries most affected. Between 1750 and 1800, the world population grew at a rate of more than 4 percent a year to more than a billion people. By the mid-20th century, the world growth rate had tripled, and by 1990 world population had risen to more than 5 billion.

This **demographic transition** took place first in Europe and is still more characteristic of the developed world. Most premodern agrarian economies were characterized by a balance between the annual number of births and deaths; both were high. Life expectancy usually was less than 35 years, and the high mortality was compensated by high fertility; that is, women had many children. Improvements in medicine, hygiene, diet, and the general standard of living contributed to a decrease in mortality in the 18th century. This allowed populations to begin to grow at a faster rate. By the 19th century in most of western Europe, the decline in mortality was followed by a decline in fertility brought about by contraception. In some countries such as France, these two transitions took place at about the same time, so population growth was limited. In much of Europe, however, the decline in fertility lagged behind the decrease in mortality, so there was a period of rapid population growth. Until the 1920s, population growth in western Europe and the United States was higher than in the rest of the world, especially in the less industrialized countries. In recent times, that situation has been reversed.

Some demographers believe that demographic transition is part of the process of shifting from a basically agrarian society to an industrial, urbanized one and that the improvements in medicine, technology, and higher standards of living will necessarily result in a change to a modern demographic structure. They believe that a decreasing need for children as part of the family economic unit, laws against child labor, and state intervention in family planning will eventually lower the world birth rate and decrease the pressure of population on economic growth. This assumption remains to be proved, and responses may vary greatly from one region of the world to another because of economic conditions and cultural attitudes about proper family size.

Finally, we should also note that responses to demographic transition can vary greatly according to historical conditions. In the 18th and 19th centuries, Europe resolved the problem of population growth with an enormous wave of emigration to the Americas, Australia, and various colonies around the globe. Present-day political circumstances make this solution less possible, although the new waves of migration in the global economy may indicate that the process is continuing.

Still, it is clear that a demographic transition has begun to take place in the developing world of Latin America, Africa, and Asia. Mortality has dropped very rapidly since 1950 because of modern medical technology, and life expectancy has doubled. To cite a single example, in Sri Lanka the mortality rate was almost cut in half between 1945 and 1952 simply by eliminating malarial mosquitoes. Fertility has declined in many places in Asia and Latin America, but in Africa, where children continue to have an important economic and social role in the extended family, it remains high. It is difficult to project what demographic transitions will take place in these areas of the world. However, all countries are faced with the problem of balancing their population's growth against the ability of the society to feed and provide an adequate standard of living to the people.

At present, the world's population is growing because of a moderate rate of growth in the industrialized nations and a high rate in the developing countries. In the 1970s, demographer Ansley Coale pointed out that the rate of growth, about 2 percent a year, is 100 times greater than it had been for most of human history. At this rate the world's population would be multiplied by 1000 every 350 years. The results of such growth would be disastrous. Coale concluded that the present period of growth is transitory. Some people who are concerned with rapid population growth believe that the solution is to limit population growth in the developing nations by state intervention, through incentives to have smaller families and education about birth control. Others believe that a redistribution of resources from rich nations to poor nations would alleviate the human misery created by population pressure and eventually lead to political and social conditions that would contribute to a gradual lowering of the birth rates. Clearly, demographic questions must always be set in political, economic, and social contexts.

Questions: Why do nations differ in their need to control population growth? Why has the rate of population growth varied in different areas of the world? Is overpopulation essentially a biological, social, or political problem?

Peoples of the Forest and Plains

 Across central Africa, kingdoms developed that were supported by complex agrarian societies capable of great artistic achievements. At Benin, in the Kongo, in the Yoruba city-states, and at Great Zimbabwe, royal authority—often considered divinely inspired—led to the creation of powerful states.

As important as the Islamic impact was on the societies of the savanna and the east African coast, other African peoples in the continent's interior and in the forests of west Africa were following their own trajectories of development. By 1000 C.E., most of these societies were based on a varied agriculture, sometimes combined with herding, and most societies used iron tools and weapons. Many were still organized in small village communities. In various places, however, states had formed. Some of them began to resolve the problems of integrating large territories under a single government and ruling subject peoples. Whereas Egypt, Kush, and Ethiopia had developed writing and other areas borrowed the Arabic script, many sub-Saharan African societies were preliterate and transmitted their knowledge, skills, and traditions by oral methods and direct instruction. The presence or absence of writing has often been used as a measure of civilization by Western observers, but as in pre-Columbian Peru, various African societies made great strides in the arts, building, and statecraft, sometimes in the context of highly urbanized settings, without a system of writing.

Artists and Kings: Yoruba and Benin

In the forests of central Nigeria, terra-cotta objects of a realistic and highly stylized form have been discovered near the village of **Nok.** These objects, most of which date from about 500 B.C.E. to 200 C.E., reveal considerable artistic skill. The inhabitants of ancient Nok and its region practiced agriculture and used iron tools. They remain something of a mystery, but it appears that their artistic traditions spread widely through the forest areas and influenced other peoples. Nevertheless, there is a long gap in the historical and archeological record between the Nok sculptures and the renewed flourishing of artistic traditions in the region after about 1000 C.E.

Among the Yoruba-speaking peoples of Nigeria, at the city of Ile-Ife, remarkable terra-cotta and bronze portrait heads of past rulers were produced in the period after 1200 C.E. The lifelike quality of these portraits and the skill of their execution place them among the greatest achievements of African art (Figure 13.3). The artists of Ile-Ife also worked in wood and ivory. Much of the art seems to be associated with kings and the authority of kingship. Ile-Ife, like other **Yoruba** states, seems to have been an agricultural society supported by a peasantry and dominated by a ruling family and an aristocracy. Ile-Ife was considered by many peoples in the region to be the original cultural center, and many of them traced their own beginnings to it.

Yoruba origins are obscure. Ile-Ife was seen as the holiest city of the Yoruba, their place of birth. Another legend maintained by the royal historians was that Oduduwa, a son of the king of Mecca, migrated from the east and settled in Yoruba. Modern historians have suggested that the real origins were perhaps Meroë and Nubia, or at least in the savanna south of the Sahara. In any case, the Yoruba spoke a non-Bantu language of the west African Kwa

Figure 13.3 *In the 13th and 14th centuries, Ife artists worked in terra-cotta as well as bronze and produced personalized portraits.*

family and recognized a certain affinity between themselves and neighboring peoples, such as the Hausa, who spoke Afro-Asian languages.

The Yoruba were organized in small city-states, each controlling a radius of perhaps 50 miles. The Yoruba were highly urbanized, although many of the town inhabitants farmed in the surrounding countryside. These city-states developed under the strong authority of regional kings, who were considered divine. A vast royal court that included secondary wives, musicians, magicians, and bodyguards of soldier-slaves surrounded the king. His rule was not absolute, however. We can use the example of the Yoruba state of Oyo, which had emerged by the 14th century. Its king, the alafin, controlled subject peoples through "princes" in the provinces, drawn from local lineages, who were allowed to exercise traditional rule as long as they continued to pay tribute to Oyo. In the capital, a council of state, made up of nobles from the seven city districts, advised the ruler and limited his power, and the Ogboni, or secret society of religious and political leaders, reviewed decisions of the king and the council. The union of civil and supernatural powers in the person of the ruler was the basis of power. The highly urbanized nature of Yoruba society and the flourishing of artisan traditions within these towns bear some similarity to those of the city-states of medieval Italy or Germany.

Patterns similar to those in the Yoruba city-states could be found among Edo peoples to the east of Yoruba. A large city-state called **Benin** was formed sometime in the 14th century. Under Ewuare the Great (r. 1440–1473), Benin's control extended from the Niger River to the coast near modern Lagos. Benin City was described by early European visitors in the 16th century as a city of great population and broad avenues. The Oba, or ruler, lived in a large royal compound surrounded by a great entourage, and his authority was buttressed by ritual and ceremony.

That authority was also the theme of the magnificent artistic output in ivory and cast bronze that became characteristic of Benin. Tradition had it that Iguegha, an artisan in bronze casting, was sent from Ile-Ife to introduce the techniques of making bronze sculptures. Benin then developed its own distinctive style, less naturalistic than that of Ile-Ife but no less impressive. Celebration of the powers and majesty of the royal lineage as well as objects for the rituals surrounding kingship were the subjects of much of this art. When the first Europeans, the Portuguese, visited Benin in the 1480s, they were impressed by the power of the ruler and the extent of his territory. Similarly, the artists of Benin were impressed with the Portuguese, and Benin bronzes and ivories began to include representations of Portuguese soldiers and other themes that reflected the contact with outsiders (Figure 13.4).

Figure 13.4 *Copper plaque of Benin ruler and retainers with Portuguese soldiers.*

Central African Kingdoms

South of the rain forest that stretched across Africa almost to Lake Victoria lay a broad expanse of savanna and plain, cut by several large rivers such as the Kwango and the Zambezi. From their original home in Nigeria, the Bantu peoples had spread into the southern reaches of the rain forest along the Congo River, then southward onto the southern savannas, and eventually to the east coast. By the 5th century C.E., Bantu farmers and fishers had reached beyond the Zambezi, and by the 13th century they were approaching the southern end of the continent. Mostly beyond the influence of Islam, many of these central African peoples had begun their own process of state formation by about 1000 C.E., replacing the pattern of kinship-based societies with forms of political authority based on kingship. Whether the idea of kingship developed in one place and was diffused elsewhere or had multiple origins is unknown, but the older system based on seniority within the kinship group was replaced with rule based on the control of territory and the parallel development of rituals that reinforced the ruler's power. Several important kingdoms developed. In Katanga, the Luba peoples modified the older system of village headmen to a form of divine kinship in which the ruler and his relatives were thought to have a special power that ensured fertility of people and crops; thus, only the royal lineage was fit to rule. A sort of bureaucracy grew to administer the state, but it was hereditary, so that brothers or male children succeeded to the position. In a way, this system was a half step toward more modern concepts of bureaucracy, but it provided a way to integrate large numbers of people in a large political unit.

The Kingdoms of Kongo and Mwene Mutapa

Beginning about the 13th century, another kingdom was forming on the lower Congo River. By the late 15th century this kingdom, **Kongo,** was flourishing. On a firm agricultural base, its people also developed the skills of weaving, pottery, blacksmithing, and carving. Individual artisans, skilled in the working of wood, copper, and iron, were highly esteemed. There was a sharp division of labor between men and women. Men took responsibility for clearing the forest and scrub, producing palm oil and palm wine, building houses, hunting, and long-distance trade. Women took charge of cultivation in all its aspects,

the care of domestic animals, and household duties. On the seacoast, women made salt from seawater, and they also collected the seashells that served as currency in the Kongo kingdom. The population was distributed in small family-based villages and in towns. The area around the capital, Mbanza Kongo, had a population of 60,000 to 100,000 by the early 16th century.

The kingship of the Kongo was hereditary but local chieftainships were not, and this gave the central authority power to control subordinates. In a way, the Kongo kingdom was a confederation of smaller states brought under the control of the manikongo, or king, and by the 15th century it was divided into eight major provinces. The word *mani* means "blacksmith," and it demonstrated the importance of iron and the art of working it in its association with political and ritual power.

Farther to the east, another large Bantu confederation developed among the farming and cattle-herding Shona-speaking peoples in the region between the Zambezi and Limpopo rivers. Beginning in the 9th century C.E., migrants from the west began to build royal courts in stone, to which later immigrants added more polished constructions. There were many of these zimbabwe, or stone house, sites (about 200 have been found) that housed local rulers and subchiefs, but the largest site, called **Great Zimbabwe,** was truly impressive (Figure 13.5). It was the center of the kingdom and had a religious importance, associated with the bird of God, an eagle that served as a link between the world and the spirits. The symbol of the bird of God is found at the ruins of Great Zimbabwe and throughout the area of its control. Great Zimbabwe (not to be confused with the modern nation of Zimbabwe) included several structures, some with strong stone walls 15 feet thick and 30 feet high, a large conical tower, and extensive cut-stone architecture made without the use of mortar to join the bricks together. Observers in the 19th century suspected that Phoenicians or Arabs had built these structures, mostly because their prejudices prevented them from believing that Africans were capable of erecting such structures, but archeologists have established that a Bantu kingdom had begun construction in stone by the 11th century C.E. and had done its most sophisticated building in the 14th and 15th centuries.

By the 15th century, a centralized state ruled from Great Zimbabwe had begun to form. It con-

Figure 13.5 *Great Zimbabwe was one of several stone settlement complexes in southeastern Africa. Added to at different times, it served as the royal court of the kingdom.*

trolled a large portion of the interior of southeast Africa all the way to the Indian Ocean. Under a king who took the title *Mwene Mutapa* (which the Portuguese later pronounced "Mono-motapa"), this kingdom experienced a short period of rapid expansion in the late 15th and 16th centuries. Its dominance over the sources of gold in the interior eventually gave it great advantages in commerce, which it developed with the Arab port of Sofala on the coast. Evidence of this trade is found in the glass beads and porcelain unearthed by archeologists at Great Zimbabwe. By the 16th century, internal divisions and rebellion had split the kingdom apart, and perhaps an emphasis on cattle as a symbol of wealth led to soil exhaustion. Control of the gold fields still provided a source of power and trade. Representatives of the Mwene Mutapa called at the east coast ports to buy Indian textiles, and their regal bearing and fine iron weapons impressed the first Europeans

who saw them. As late as the 19th century, a much smaller kingdom of Mwene Mutapa survived in the interior and provided some leadership against European encroachment, but pastoralism had come to play a central role in the lives of the Shona people who descended from the great tradition.

 GLOBAL CONNECTIONS: Internal Development and Global Contacts

This chapter has concentrated on the Sudanic states and the Swahili coast, where the impact of Islam was the most profound and where, because of the existence of written sources, it is somewhat easier to reconstruct the region's history. Sub-Saharan Africa had never been totally isolated from the Mediterranean world or other outside contacts, but the spread of Islam obviously brought large areas of Africa into more intensive contact with the global community, even though Africa remained something of an Islamic frontier. Still, the fusion of Islamic and indigenous African cultures created a synthesis that restructured the life of many Africans. Sudanic kingdoms and the Swahili coast participated in extensive borrowing and interactions with north Africa and the Middle East, similar to imitation efforts by several other societies in the postclassical period. Islamic contacts were also heavily involved in the growing integration of several parts of sub-Saharan Africa with global trade.

Although the arrival of Islam in Africa in the period from 800 to 1500 was clearly a major event, it would be wrong to see Africa's history in this period exclusively in terms of the Islamic impact. Great Zimbabwe and the Kongo kingdom, to cite only two examples, represented the development of Bantu concepts of kingship and state-building independently of trends taking place elsewhere on the continent. Similar processes and accomplishments could also be seen in Benin and among the Yoruba of west Africa. Meanwhile in Ethiopia, east Africa, and the eastern Sudan, the impact of the pre-Islamic Mediterranean world had been long felt. The dynamic relationship between the impact of the civilizations and peoples external to Africa and the processes of development within the continent itself was a major theme in Africa's history.

By the late 15th century, when the first Europeans, the Portuguese, began to arrive on the west and east coasts of Africa, in many places they found well-developed, powerful kingdoms that were able to deal with the Portuguese as equals. This was even truer in the parts of Africa that had come under the influence of Islam and through it had established links with other areas of Muslim civilization. In this period, Africa had increasingly become part of the general cultural trends of the wider world. Moreover, the intensified export trade in ivory, slaves, and especially gold from Africa drew Africans, even those far from the centers of trade, into a widening network of global relations. With the arrival of Europeans in sub-Saharan Africa in the late 15th century, the pace and intensity of the cultural and commercial contacts became even greater, and many African societies faced new and profound challenges.

Further Readings

Several of the books recommended on Africa in Chapter 9 are also useful in relation to this chapter. The period covered in this chapter is summarized in Roland Oliver and Anthony Atmore's *The African Middle Ages, 1400–1800* (1981). Basil Davidson has produced many excellent popular books that provide a sympathetic view of African development. A good example, prepared to accompany a television series, is *The Story of Africa* (1984). A readable book that gives an overview of African history and emphasizes broad common themes and everyday life is Robert W. July's *Precolonial Africa* (1975). Essential reading on central Africa is Jan Vansina, *Paths in the Rainforests* (1990). On the Swahili craft, see A. Mazrui and I. Shariff, *The Swahili: Idiom and Identity of an African People* (1994).

A very good survey of the early history of Africa with interesting comments on the Nok culture is Susan Keech McIntosh and Roderick J. McIntosh's "From Stone to Metal: New Perspectives on the Later Prehistory of West Africa," *Journal of World History*, vol. 2, no. 1 (1988), 89–133. Basil Davidson and F. K. Buah, *A History of West Africa* (1966), is a good introduction for that region. More detailed, however, is J. F. Ade Ajayi and Michael Crowder's *History of West Africa*, 2 vols. (2nd ed., 1987), which contains excellent review chapters by specialists. N. Levtzion's *Ancient Ghana and Mali* (1973) is still the best short introduction to these kingdoms of the sahel. For the east African coast, an excellent survey and introduction are provided by Derek Nurse and Thomas Spear in *The Swahili: Reconstructing the History and Language of an African Society* (1985).

Two good books on the Kongo kingdom are Anne Hilton's *The Kingdom of the Kongo* (1985), which shows how African systems of thought accommodated the arrival of Europeans and their culture, and Georges Balandier's *Daily Life in the Kingdom of the Kongo* (1969), which makes good use of travelers' reports and other documents to give a rounded picture of Kongo society. David Birmingham and Phyllis Martin's *History of Central Africa*, 2 vols. (1983), is an excellent regional history.

Two multivolume general histories of Africa that provide synthetic articles by leading scholars on many of the topics discussed in this chapter are *The Cambridge History of Africa*, 8 vols. (1975–1986) and the UNESCO *General History of Africa*, 7 vols. to date (1981–).

Some important source materials on African history for this period are D. T. Niane, *Sundiata, an Epic of Old Mali* (1986); G. R. Crone, ed., *The Voyages of Cadamosto*, 2nd series, vol. 80 (1937), which deals with Mali, Cape Verde, Senegal, and Benin; and Ross Dunn, *The Adventures of ibn Batuta, A Muslim Traveler of the 14th Century* (1986).

On the Web

Excellent brief descriptions of various African civilizations are provided on the Internet at http://www.bbc.co.uk/worldservice/africa/features/storyofafrica/index.shtml. Virtual visits and overviews of Great Zimbabwe are provided at http://www.mc.maricopa.edu/~reffland/anthropology/lost_tribes/zimbabwe/ and http://www.campus.northpark.edu/history/WebChron/Africa/GreatZimbabwe.html.

Nubia and sub-Saharan Timbuktu are explored at http://i-cias.com/private/abubakr/nubia/ and http://www.pbs.org/wonders/fr_e5.htm. The art of the sub-Saharan empire of Benin can be explored at http://www.nmafa.si.edu/pubaccess/acrobat/benin.pdf and http://www.metmuseum.org/toah.hd/zimb/hd_zim.htm.

Web sites are devoted to the trans-Saharan empires of Mali and Songhay (http://www.learner.org/exhibits/collapse/mali.html and http://www.ucalgary.ca/applied_history/tutor/islam/fractured/westAfrica.html).

The life of the founder of the empire of Mali, Sundiata, is explored at http://www.mrdowling.com/609-sundiata.html and http://ias.berkeley.edu/orias/sundiata.html. The background to the famous epic story of his life is provided at http://courses.wcupa.edu/jones/his311/notes/sundiata.htm. The career of his most famous successor, Mansa Musa, is examined at http://www.mrdowling.com/609-mansamusa.html, a site that also offers both a gateway to the study of North Africa and also a virtual visit to Timbuktu.

CHAPTER 14

CIVILIZATION IN EASTERN EUROPE: BYZANTIUM AND ORTHODOX EUROPE

Just as theologians through the centuries have worked to understand Christ's message, so too have artists struggled to capture his image. This powerful mosaic of Christ at the Church of Chora in Istanbul was created in the first part of the 14th century.

During the postclassical period, in addition to the great civilizations of Asia and Africa, two major Christian civilizations took shape in Europe. One was anchored in the Byzantine Empire, which straddled western Asia and southeastern Europe and sponsored the spread of Orthodox Christianity to eastern Europe. The other was defined above all by the beliefs and institutions of Catholicism in western and central Europe. Both European civilizations were influenced by Islamic dynamism, but they operated according to different principles. The Byzantine Empire maintained particularly high levels of political, economic, and cultural life during much of the period from 500 to 1450 C.E. It controlled an important but fluctuating swath of territory in the Balkans, the northern Middle East, and the eastern Mediterranean. Its leaders saw themselves as Roman emperors, and their government was in many ways a direct continuation of the eastern portion of the late Roman Empire. Byzantium particularly built on traditions of late Roman emperors like Diocletian and Constantine. This was not really Rome moved eastward. The term *Byzantine*, though not used at the time, accurately suggests the distinction from Rome itself: This was a political heir to Rome, but with geography and focus of its own.

The real significance of the Byzantine Empire goes well beyond its ability to keep Rome's memory alive. The empire lasted for almost a thousand years, between Rome's collapse in the West and the final overthrow of the regime by Turkish invaders. The empire's capital, Constantinople, was one of the truly great cities of the world, certainly the most opulent and important city in Europe in this period. From Constantinople radiated one of the two major branches of Christianity: the Orthodox Christian churches that became dominant throughout most of eastern Europe.

Like the other great civilizations of the period, the Byzantine Empire spread its cultural and political influence to parts of the world that had not previously been controlled by any major civilization. Just as Muslim influence helped shape civilization in parts of Africa south of the Sahara, the Byzantines began to create a new civilization area in the Balkans and particularly in western Russia (present-day Ukraine and Belarus as well as western Russia proper). This was a major expansion of the civilization map, contributing to one of the key characteristics of the early centuries of the postclassical millennium.

Ultimately, the empire's most important stepchild was Russia, whose rise as a civilized area relied heavily on influences from the Byzantines to the south. Russia took many initial cultural and political characteristics from the

100 C.E.	600 C.E.	800 C.E.	1000 C.E.	1200 C.E.	1400 C.E.
1st century C.E.–650 Slavic migrations into eastern Europe **330s** Constantinople made capital of Eastern Roman Empire **527–565** Justinian	**718** Defeat of Arab attack on Constantinople	**855** According to legend, Rurik king of Kievan Russia **864** Beginning of missionary work of brothers Cyril and Methodius in Slavic lands **870** First kingdom in what is now Czech and Slovak republics **896** Magyars settle in Hungary **c. 960** Emergence of Polish state **980–1015** Conversion of Vladimir I of Russia to Christianity	**1018** Defeat of first Bulgarian Empire, taken over by Byzantines **1019–1054** Yaroslav king of Rus' **1054** Schism between Eastern and Western Christianity **1100–1453** Byzantine decline; growing Turkish attack	**1203–1204** Capture of Constantinople during the Fourth Crusade **1237–1241** Capture of Russia by Mongols (Tatars)	**1453** Capture of Constantinople by Ottoman Turks; end of Byzantine Empire **1480** Expulsion of Tatars from Russia

Byzantine Empire and ultimately claimed to inherit the mantle of the empire itself. This heritage blended with other developments after the postclassical period, when Russia emerged from its tentative beginnings.

Studying civilization in eastern Europe requires an understanding of the relationship between the two Christian churches in postclassical Europe. There were many commonalities between developments in eastern Europe and those of the Christian West. In both cases, civilization spread northward because of the missionary appeal of the religion itself. In both cases, polytheism gave way to monotheism, although important compromises were made, particularly at the popular level. In both cases, more northerly political units, such as Russia, Poland, Germany, and France, struggled for political definition without being able to rival the political sophistication of the more advanced civilization areas in Asia and north Africa or in Byzantium itself. In both cases, new trading activities brought northern regions into contact with the major centers of world commerce, including Constantinople. In both cases, newly civilized areas looked back to the Greco-Roman past, as well as to Christianity, for cultural inspiration, using some of the same political ideas and artistic styles.

Yet with all these shared ingredients, the civilizations that expanded in the East and developed in the West operated largely on separate tracks. They produced different versions of Christianity, which culturally as well as organizationally were separate, even hostile. The civilizations had little mutual contact, until late in this period; commercial patterns in both cases ran south to north rather than east to west. During most of the postclassical millennium, major portions of eastern Europe were significantly more advanced than the West in political sophistication, cultural range, and economic vitality. When the two civilizations did meet, in this period and later, they met as distant cousins, related but not close kin.

The Byzantine Empire

 The Byzantine Empire unfolded initially as part of the greater Roman Empire. Then, as this framework shattered with Roman decline, it took on a life of its own, particularly from the reign of the Emperor Justinian onward. It centered on a territory different from and smaller than the eastern Mediterranean as Rome had defined it. This was the result of new pressures, particularly the surge of Islam throughout north Africa and the bulk of the Middle East. Despite many attacks, the empire flourished until the 11th century.

Origins of the Empire

The Byzantine Empire in some senses began in the 4th century C.E., when the Romans set up their eastern capital in Constantinople. This city quickly became the most vigorous center of the otherwise fading imperial structure. Emperor Constantine constructed a host of elegant buildings, including Christian churches, in his new city, which was built on the foundations of a previously modest town called Byzantium. Soon, separate eastern emperors ruled from the new metropolis, even before the western portion of the empire fell to the Germanic invaders. They warded off invading Huns and other intruders while enjoying a solid tax base in the peasant agriculture of the eastern Mediterranean. Constantinople was responsible for the Balkan peninsula, the northern Middle East, the Mediterranean coast, and north Africa. Although for several centuries Latin was the court language of the eastern empire, Greek was the common tongue, and after Emperor Justinian in the 6th century, it became the official language as well. Indeed, in the eyes of the easterners, Latin became an inferior, barbaric means of communication. Knowledge of Greek enabled the scholars of the eastern empire to read freely in the ancient Athenian philosophical and literary classics and in the Hellenistic writings and scientific treatises.

The new empire benefited from the high levels of commerce long present in the eastern Mediterranean. New blood was drawn into administration and trade as Hellenized Egyptians and Syrians, long excluded from Roman administration, moved to Constantinople and entered the expanding bureaucracy of the Byzantine rulers. The empire faced many foreign enemies, although the pressure was less severe than that provided by the Germanic tribes in the West. It responded by recruiting armies in the Middle East itself, not by relying on barbarian troops. Complex administration around a remote emperor, who was surrounded by elaborate ceremonies, increasingly defined the empire's political style.

Justinian's Achievements

The early history of the Byzantine Empire was marked by a recurrent threat of invasion. Eastern emperors, relying on their local military base plus able generalship by upper-class Greeks, beat off attacks by the Sassanian Empire in Persia and by Germanic invaders. Then, in 533 C.E., with the empire's borders reasonably secure, a new emperor, Justinian, tried to reconquer western territory in a last futile effort to restore an empire like that of Rome. He was somber, autocratic, and prone to grandiose ideas. A contemporary historian named Procopius described him as "at once villainous and amenable; as people say colloquially, a moron. He was never truthful with anyone, but always guileful in what he said and did, yet easily hoodwinked by any who wanted to deceive him." The emperor was also heavily influenced by his wife Theodora, a courtesan connected with Constantinople's horse-racing world, who was eager for power. Theodora stiffened Justinian's resolve in response to popular unrest and pushed the plans for expansion.

Justinian's positive contributions to the Byzantine Empire lay in rebuilding Constantinople, ravaged by earlier riots against high taxes, and systematizing the Roman legal code. Extending later Roman architecture, with its addition of domes to earlier classical styles, Justinian's builders created many new structures, the most inspiring of which was the huge new church, the **Hagia Sophia,** long one of the wonders of the Christian world. This was an achievement in engineering as well as architecture, for no one had previously been able to build the supports needed for a dome of its size. Justinian's codification of Roman law reached a goal earlier emperors had sought but not achieved, summing up and reconciling many prior edicts and decisions. Unified law not only reduced confusion but also united and organized the new empire, paralleling the state's bureaucracy. Updated by later emperors, the code ultimately helped spread Roman legal principles in various parts of Europe.

Justinian's military exploits had more ambiguous results. The emperor wanted to recapture the old Roman Empire itself. With the aid of a brilliant general, **Belisarius,** new gains were made in north Africa and Italy. The Byzantines hoped to restore north Africa to its role as grain producer for the Mediterranean world, and Italy would be the symbol of past imperial glories. Unable to hold Rome against the Germans, Justinian's forces made their temporary capital, Ravenna, a key artistic center, embellished by some of the most beautiful Christian mosaics known anywhere in the world (Figure 14.1). But the major Italian holdings were short-lived, unable to withstand Germanic pressure, and north African territory was soon besieged as well.

Furthermore, Justinian's westward ambitions had weakened the empire in its own sphere. Persian forces attacked in the northern Middle East, while new Slavic groups, moving into the Balkans, pressed on another front (Map 14.1). Justinian finally managed to create a new line of defense and even pushed Persian forces back again, but some Middle Eastern territory was lost. Furthermore, all these wars, offensive and defensive alike, created new tax pressures on the government and forced Justinian to exertions that contributed to his death in 565 C.E.

Arab Pressure and the Empire's Defenses

After some hesitations and setbacks, Justinian's successors began to concentrate on defending the eastern empire itself. Persian successes in the northern Middle East were reversed in the 7th century, and the

Figure 14.1 *Mosaics in Ravenna, Italy, from the early period of the Byzantine Empire, illustrate some of the highest achievements of Byzantine religious art and provide a dazzling, ornate environment for worship. This mosaic features a rather militant Christ the Redeemer. Notice the characteristic Christian assertion of human dominance over nature.*

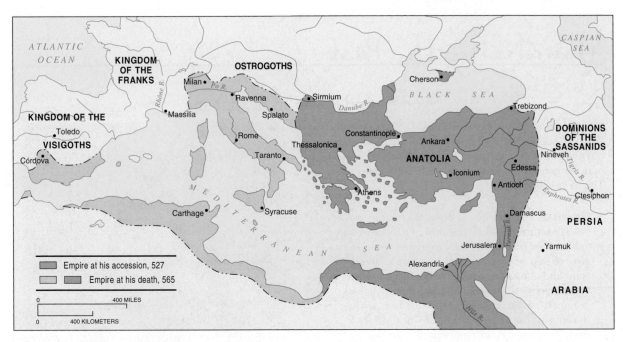

Map 14.1 *The Byzantine Empire Under Justinian. Justinian's expansion exhausted his treasury, and the empire had retreated to the northeastern Mediterranean within 50 years after his death.*

population was forcibly reconverted to Christianity. The resultant empire, centered in the southern Balkans and the western and central portions of present-day Turkey, was a far cry from Rome's greatness. However, it was sufficient to amplify a rich Hellenistic culture and blend it more fully with Christianity while advancing Roman achievements in engineering and military tactics as well as law.

The Byzantine Empire was also strong enough to withstand the great new threat of the 7th century, the surge of the Arab Muslims, though not without massive losses. By the mid-7th century, the Arabs had built a fleet that challenged Byzantine naval supremacy in the eastern Mediterranean while repeatedly attacking Constantinople. They quickly swallowed the empire's remaining provinces along the eastern seaboard of the Mediterranean and soon cut into the northern Middle Eastern heartland as well. Arab cultural and commercial influence also affected patterns of life in Constantinople.

The Byzantine Empire held out nevertheless. A major siege of the capital in 717–718 C.E. was beaten back, partly because of a new weapon, a kind of napalm called **Greek fire** (a petroleum, quicklime, and sulfur mixture) that devastated Arab ships. The

Arab threat was never removed entirely. Furthermore, wars with the Muslims had added new economic burdens to the empire, as invasions and taxation, weakening the position of small farmers, resulted in greater aristocratic estates and new power for aristocratic generals. The free rural population that had served the empire during its early centuries—providing military recruits and paying the bulk of the taxes—was forced into greater dependence. Greater emphasis was given to organizing the army and navy.

After the greatest Arab onslaughts had been faced, the empire was run by a dizzying series of weak and strong emperors. Periods of vigor alternated with seeming decay. Arab pressure continued. Conquest of the island of Crete in the 9th century allowed the Muslims to harass Byzantine shipping in the Mediterranean for several centuries. Slavic kingdoms, especially **Bulgaria,** periodically pressed Byzantine territory in the Balkans, although at times military success and marriage alliances brought Byzantine control over the feisty Bulgarian kingdom. Thus, while a Bulgarian king in the 10th century took the title of *tsar,* a Slavic version of the word *Caesar,* steady Byzantine pressure through war eroded the regional kingdom. In the 11th century, the Byzantine emperor

Visualizing the Past

Women and Power in Byzantium

This mosaic, developed between 1034–1042, portrays the Empress Zoë, her consort, and Christ (in the center). This was a period of unusual power for two women at the head of the empire, as the struggle between Zoë and her sister Theodora suggests.

Questions: What evidence does this mosaic provide about the political relationship between Zoë and her husband? What does it suggest about the relationship between church and state in Byzantium and about ways religion might be used to bolster political power? (Interpreting the haloes is a good start in answering this question.) Why, in terms of the appropriation of Christian tradition, are three figures represented? Can this picture be used to comment on women's conditions in the empire? What sense of history and religion made it reasonable to show Christ between two 11th-century people?

Istanbul, St. Sophia, Mosaic in the South Tribune: Empress Zoë, Her Consort, and Christ, 1034–1042 (Dumbarton Oaks, Center for Byzantine Studies).

Basil II, known as *Bulgaroktonos*, or slayer of the Bulgarians, used the empire's wealth to bribe many Bulgarian nobles and generals. He defeated the Bulgarian army in 1014, blinding as many as 15,000 captive soldiers. The sight of this tragedy brought on the Bulgarian king's death. Bulgaria became part of the empire, its aristocracy settling in Constantinople and merging with the leading Greek families.

Thus, despite all its problems, the imperial core had real strength, governing a territory about half the size of the previous eastern portion of the Roman Empire and withstanding a series of enemies. Briefly, at the end of the 10th century, the Byzantine emperor may have been the most powerful monarch on earth, with a capital city whose rich buildings and abundant popular entertainments awed visitors from western Europe and elsewhere.

Byzantine Society and Politics

The Byzantine political system had remarkable similarities to the earlier patterns in China. The emperor was held to be ordained by God, head of church as well as state. He appointed church bishops and passed religious and secular laws. The elaborate court rituals symbolized the ideals of a divinely inspired, all-powerful ruler, although they often immobilized rulers and inhibited innovative policy.

At key points, women held the imperial throne while maintaining the ceremonial power of the office. The experiences of Empress Theodora (981–1056), namesake of Justinian's powerful wife, illustrate the complex nature of Byzantine politics and the whims of fate that affected women rulers. Daughter of an emperor, Theodora was strong and austere; she refused to marry the imperial heir, who then wed her sister Zoë. Zoë was afraid of Theodora's influence and had her confined to a monastery. A popular rebellion against the new emperor installed Theodora and Zoë jointly (and one assumes uneasily) as empresses. Theodora soon yielded power to Zoë's new husband. When he died, however, Theodora reasserted her rights, at age 70. After brief turmoil, she checked unruly nobles and limited bureaucratic corruption, although her severe retaliation against personal enemies brought criticism. Theodora also had trouble building a reliable staff and was attacked for her reliance on "menials."

Supplementing the centralized imperial authority was one of history's most elaborate bureaucracies. Trained in Greek classics, philosophy, and science in a secular school system that paralleled church education for the priesthood, Byzantine bureaucrats could be recruited from all social classes. As in China, aristocrats predominated, but talent also counted among this elite of highly educated scholars. Bureaucrats were specialized into various offices, and officials close to the emperor were mainly eunuchs. Provincial governors were appointed from the center and were charged with keeping tabs on military authorities. An elaborate system of spies helped preserve loyalty while creating intense distrust even among friends. It is small wonder that the word *Byzantine* came to refer to complex institutional arrangements. At the same time, the system successfully supported the longest-lived single government structure the Mediterranean world has ever known.

Careful military organization arose as well, as Figure 14.2 suggests. Byzantine rulers adapted the later Roman system by recruiting troops locally and rewarding them with grants of land in return for their military service. The land could not be sold, but sons inherited its administration in return for continued military responsibility. Many outsiders, particularly Slavs and Armenian Christians, were recruited for the army in this way. Increasingly, hereditary military leaders assumed regional power, displacing more traditional and better-educated aristocrats. One emperor, Michael II, was a product of this system and was notorious for his hatred of Greek education and his overall personal ignorance. On the other hand, the military system had obvious advantages in protecting a state recurrently under attack from Muslims of various sorts—Persians, Arabs, and later Turks—as well as nomadic intruders from central Asia. Until the 15th century, the Byzantine Empire effectively blocked the path to Europe for most of these groups.

Socially and economically, the empire depended on Constantinople's control over the countryside, with the bureaucracy regulating trade and controlling food prices. The large peasant class was vital in supplying goods and providing the bulk of tax revenues. Food prices were kept artificially low, to content the numerous urban lower classes, in a system supported largely by taxes on the hard-pressed peasantry. Other cities were modest in size—for example, Athens dwindled—

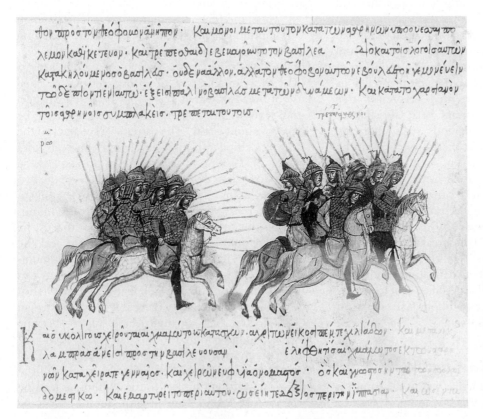

Figure 14.2 *Imperial cavalry, detail from "Chronicle" of John Scylitzes, 14th century. The painting shows the stylized representation characteristic of Byzantine art and suggests the importance of well-organized military activity.*

because the focus was on the capital city and its food needs. The empire developed a far-flung trading network with Asia to the east and Russia and Scandinavia to the north. Silk production expanded in the empire, with silkworms and techniques initially imported from China, and various luxury products, including cloth, carpets, and spices, were sent north. This gave the empire a favorable trading position with less sophisticated lands. Only China produced luxury goods of comparable quality. The empire also traded actively with India, the Arabs, and east Asia while receiving simpler products from western Europe and Africa. At the same time, the large merchant class never gained significant political power, in part because of the elaborate network of government controls. In this, Byzantium again resembled China and differed notably from the looser social and political networks of the West, where merchants were gaining greater voice.

Byzantine cultural life centered on the secular traditions of Hellenism, so important in the education of bureaucrats, and on the evolving traditions of Eastern, or Orthodox, Christianity. Although a host of literary and artistic creations resulted from this mixture, there was little innovation. The Byzantine strength lay in preserving and commenting on past forms more than in developing new ones. Art and architecture were exceptions; a distinct Byzantine style developed fairly early. The adaptation of Roman domed buildings, the elaboration of powerful and richly colored religious mosaics, and a tradition of **icon** painting—paintings of saints and other religious figures, often richly ornamented—expressed this artistic impulse and its marriage with Christianity. The blue and gold backgrounds set with richly dressed religious figures were meant to represent the unchanging brilliance of heaven. An important controversy over religious art arose in the 8th century, when a new emperor attacked the use of religious images in worship (probably responding to Muslim claims that Christians were idol worshipers). This attack, called **iconoclasm** (the breaking of images), roused huge protest from Byzantine monks, which briefly threatened a split between church and state. After a long and complex battle, the use of icons was gradually restored, and the tradition of state control over church affairs also resumed.

The Split Between East and West

Byzantine culture and politics, as well as the empire's economic orientation toward Asia and northeastern

Europe, helped explain the growing break between its Eastern version of Christianity and the Western version headed by the pope in Rome. There were many milestones in this rift. Different rituals developed as the West translated the Greek Bible into Latin in the 4th century. Later, Byzantine emperors deeply resented papal attempts to interfere in the iconoclastic dispute, for the popes, understandably enough, hoped to loosen state control over the Eastern church to make it conform more fully to their own idea of church–state relations. There was also scornful hostility to efforts by a Frankish ruler, Charlemagne, to proclaim himself a Roman emperor in the 9th century. Byzantine officials believed that they were the true heirs of Rome and that Western rulers were crude and unsophisticated. However, they did extend some recognition to the "Emperor of the Franks." Contact between the two branches of Christianity trailed off, though neither East nor West cared to make a definitive break. The Eastern church acknowledged the pope as first among equals, but papal directives had no hold in the Byzantine church, where state control loomed larger. Religious art conveyed different styles and beliefs, as Figures 14.3 and 14.4 suggest. Even monastic movements operated according to different rules.

Then, in 1054, an ambitious church patriarch in Constantinople raised a host of old issues, including a quarrel over what kind of bread to use for the celebration of Christ's last supper in the church liturgy. (The bread quarrel was an old one, relating to ritual use of bread in Christ's day, that Patriarch Michael now revived: Must bread used for communion be baked without yeast?) The patriarch also attacked the Roman Catholic practice, developed some centuries earlier, of insisting on celibacy for its priests; Eastern Orthodox priests could marry. Delegations of the two churches discussed these disputes, but this led only to new bitterness. The Roman pope finally excommunicated the patriarch and his followers; that is, he banished them from Christian fellowship and the sacraments. The patriarch responded by excommunicating all Roman Catholics. Thus, the split between the Roman Catholic church and Eastern Orthodoxy—the Byzantine or Greek, as well as the Russian Orthodox, Serbian Orthodox, and others—became formal and has endured to this day. A late-12th-century church patriarch in Constantinople even argued that Muslim rule would be preferable to that of the pope: "For if I am subject to the Muslim, at least he will not force me to share his faith. But if I have to be

Figure 14.3 *In this mosaic of Christ, dating from about 1100 C.E., notice the difference from the images of Christ common in Western Christianity, which place more emphasis on suffering and less on divine majesty.*

under the Frankish rule and united with the Roman Church, I may have to separate myself from God."

The East-West split fell short of complete divorce. A common Christianity with many shared or revived classical traditions and frequent commercial and cultural contacts continued to enliven the relationship between the two European civilizations. The division did reflect the different patterns of development the two civilizations followed during the postclassical millennium.

The Empire's Decline

Shortly after the split between East and West, the Byzantine Empire entered a long period of decline (Map 14.2). Turkish invaders who had converted to Islam in central Asia began to press on its eastern borders, having already gained increasing influence in the Muslim caliphate. In the late 11th century, Turkish troops, the Seljuks, seized almost all the Asiatic provinces of the empire, thus cutting off the most prosperous sources of tax revenue and the territories that had supplied most of the empire's food. The Byzantine emperor lost the battle of Manzikert in 1071, his larger army was annihilated, and the empire never recovered. It staggered along for another four centuries, but its doom, at least as a significant power, was sealed. The creation of new, independent Slavic kingdoms in the Balkans, such as Serbia, showed the empire's diminished power.

Eastern emperors appealed to Western leaders for help against the Turks, but their requests were largely ignored. The appeal helped motivate Western Crusades to the Holy Land, but this did not help the

Figure 14.4 *The Byzantine Empire developed a distinctively stylized religious art, adapted from earlier Roman painting styles and conveying the solemnity of the holy figures of the faith. This 11th-century miniature features the holy women at the sepulchre of Christ.*

Byzantines. At the same time, Italian cities, blessed with powerful navies, gained increasing advantages in Constantinople, such as special trading privileges—a sign of the shift in power between East and West. One Western Crusade, in 1204, ostensibly set up to conquer the Holy Land from the Muslims, actually turned against Byzantium. Led by greedy Venetian merchants, the Crusade attacked and conquered Constantinople, briefly unseating the emperor and weakening the whole imperial structure. But the West was not yet powerful enough to hold this ground, and a small Byzantine Empire was restored, able through careful diplomacy to survive for another two centuries.

Turkish settlements pressed ever closer to Constantinople in the northern Middle East—in the area that is now Turkey—and finally, in 1453, a Turkish sultan brought a powerful army, equipped with artillery purchased from the West, against the city, which fell after two months. By 1461, the Turks had conquered remaining pockets of Byzantine control, including most of the Balkans, bringing Islamic power farther into eastern Europe than ever before. The great eastern empire was no more.

The fall of Byzantium was one of the great events in world history, and we will deal with its impact in several later chapters. It was a great event because the Byzantine Empire had been so durable and important, anchoring a vital corner of the Mediterranean even amid the rapid surge of Islam. The empire's trading contacts and its ability to preserve and spread classical and Christian learning made it a vital unit throughout the postclassical period. After its demise, its influence affected other societies, including the new Ottoman Empire.

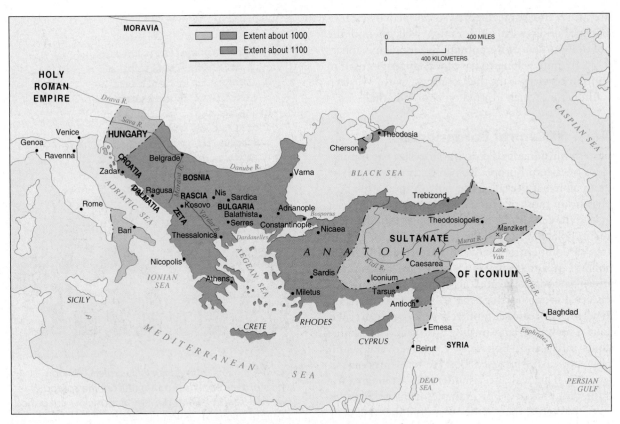

Map 14.2 *The Byzantine Empire, 1000–1100. The Byzantine Empire went from a major to a minor power in the century and a half portrayed on this map. After the Turkish defeat at Manzikert in 1071, the Byzantines maintained effective control of only a small fringe of Anatolia. In the Balkans, the new Serbian, Bulgarian, and Hungarian states grew powerful, even though the Byzantines claimed control over the region.*

The Spread of Civilization in Eastern Europe

Missionary attempts to spread Christianity, new Byzantine conquests in the Balkans (particularly Bulgaria), and trade routes running north and south through western Russia and Ukraine created abundant contacts with key portions of eastern Europe. A number of regional states formed. Kievan Rus', in a territory including present-day Ukraine, Belarus, and western Russia, developed some of the formative features of Russian culture and politics. Mongol invasions ended this period of early Russian history, redividing parts of eastern Europe.

Long before the Byzantine decline after the 11th century, the empire had been the source of a new northward surge of Christianity. Orthodox missionaries sent from Constantinople busily converted most people in the Balkans to their version of Christianity, and some other trappings of Byzantine culture came in their wake. In 864, the Byzantine government sent the missionaries **Cyril** and **Methodius** to the territory that is now the Czech and Slovak republics. Here the venture failed, in that Roman Catholic missionaries were more successful. But Cyril and Methodius continued their efforts in the Balkans and in southern Russia, where their ability to speak the Slavic language greatly aided their efforts. The two missionaries devised a written script for this language, derived from Greek letters; to this day, the Slavic alphabet is known as Cyrillic. Thus, the possibility of literature and some literacy developed in eastern Europe along with Christianity, well beyond the political borders of Byzantium. Byzantine missionaries were quite willing to have local languages used in church services—another contrast with Western Catholicism, which insisted on church Latin.

The East Central Borderlands

Eastern missionaries did not monopolize the borderlands of eastern Europe. Roman Catholicism and the Latin alphabet prevailed not only in the Czech area but also in most of Hungary (which was taken over in the 9th century by a Turkic people, the Magyars) and in Poland. Much of this region would long be an area of competition between Eastern and Western political and intellectual models. During the centuries after the conversion to Christianity, this stretch of eastern Europe north of the Balkans was organized in a series of regional monarchies, loosely governed amid a powerful, land-owning aristocracy. The kingdoms of Poland, Bohemia (Czechoslovakia), and Lithuania easily surpassed most western kingdoms in territory. This was also a moderately active area for trade and industry. For example, ironworking was more developed than in the West until the 12th century. Eastern Europe during these centuries also received an important influx of Jews, who were migrating away from the Middle East but also fleeing intolerance in western Europe. Poland gained the largest single concentration of Jews. Eastern Europe's Jews, largely barred from agriculture and often resented by the Christian majority, gained strength in local commerce while maintaining their own religious and cultural traditions (Figure 14.5). A strong emphasis on extensive education and literacy, though primarily for males, distinguished Jewish culture not only from the rest of eastern Europe but also from most other societies in the world at this time.

The Emergence of Kievan Rus'

Russia shared many features with the rest of northeastern Europe before the 15th century, including hesitant advances in economy and politics. A fullfledged Russian civilization had yet to emerge; this was the beginning of a society that would become more important after 1450. As in much of eastern Europe, the centuries of Byzantine influence were an important formative period that would influence later developments. Slavic peoples had moved into the

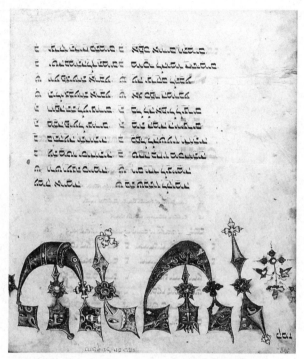

Figure 14.5 *This 14th-century illustrated German Jewish prayer book is a remnant from the spread of Jews and Jewish culture during the postclassical period in central and east-central Europe.*

sweeping plains of Russia and eastern Europe from an Asian homeland during the time of the Roman Empire (Map 14.3). They mixed with and incorporated some earlier inhabitants and some additional invaders, such as the Bulgarians, who adopted Slavic language and customs. The Slavs already used iron, and they extended agriculture in the rich soils of what is now Ukraine and western Russia, where no durable civilization had taken root. Slavic political organization long rested in family tribes and villages. The Slavs maintained an animist religion with gods for the sun, thunder, wind, and fire. The early Russians also had a rich tradition of folk music and oral legends, and they developed some very loose regional kingdoms.

During the 6th and 7th centuries, traders from Scandinavia began to work through the Slavic lands, moving along the great rivers of western Russia, which run south to north, particularly the Dnieper. Through this route the Norse traders were able to reach the Byzantine Empire, and a regular, flourishing trade developed between Scandinavia and Constantinople. Luxury products from Byzantium and the Arab world

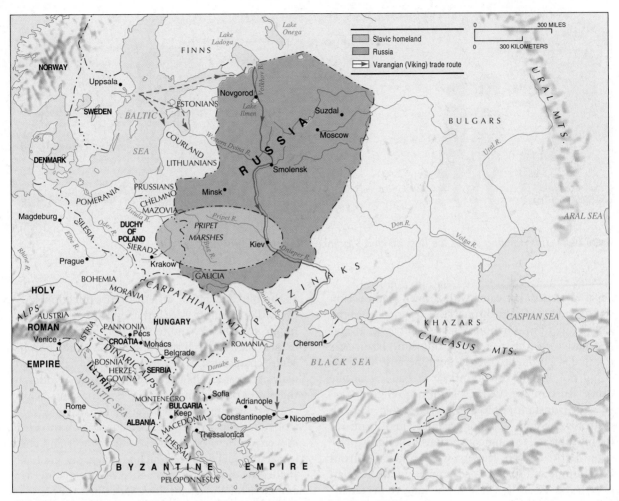

Map 14.3   *East European Kingdoms and Slavic Expansion by c. 1000. Beginning around the 5th century* C.E., *the Slavs moved in all directions from their lands around the Pripet River. Their migrations took them from the Baltic Sea to the Oder River and down to the Adriatic and Aegean seas. The arrival of the Hungarians in the 9th and 10th centuries prevented the Slavs from unifying.*

traveled north in return for furs and other crude products. The Scandinavian traders, militarily superior to the Slavs, gradually set up some governments along their trade route, particularly in the city of **Kiev.** A monarchy emerged, and according to legend a man named **Rurik,** a native of Denmark, became the first prince of what came to be called Kievan Rus' about 855 C.E. This principality, though still loosely organized through alliances with regional, landed aristocrats, flourished until the 12th century. It was from the Scandinavians that the word *Russia* was coined, possibly from a Greek word for "red," for the hair

color of many of the Norse traders. In turn, the Scandinavian minority gradually mingled with the Slavic population, particularly among the aristocracy.

Contacts between Kievan Rus' and Byzantium extended steadily. Kiev, centrally located, became a prosperous trading center, and from there many Russians visited Constantinople. These exchanges led to growing knowledge of Christianity. Prince **Vladimir I,** a Rurik descendant who ruled from 980 to 1015, finally took the step of converting to Christianity, not only in his own name but on behalf of all his people (Figure 14.6). He was eager to avoid the

Figure 14.6   *This painting shows the Russian king Vladimir I accepting Christianity.*

papal influence that came with Roman Catholicism, which he knew about through the experiences of the Polish kingdom. Orthodox Christianity was a valid alternative to the prevailing animism. Islam was rejected, according to one account, because Vladimir could not accept a religion that forbade alcoholic drink. Russian awe at the splendor of religious services in Constantinople also played a role. Having made his decision, Vladimir organized mass baptisms for his subjects, forcing conversions by military pressure. Early church leaders were imported from Byzantium, and they helped train a literate Russian priesthood. As in Byzantium, the king characteristically controlled major appointments, and a separate **Russian Orthodox** church soon developed.

As Kievan Rus' became Christian, it was the largest single state in Europe, though highly decentralized. Rurik's descendants managed for some time to avoid damaging battles over succession to the throne. Following Byzantine example, they issued a formal law code that reduced the severity of traditional punishments and replaced community vendettas with state-run courts, at least in principle. The last of the great Kievan princes, **Yaroslav,** issued the legal codification while building many churches and arranging the translation of religious literature from Greek to Slavic.

Institutions and Culture in Kievan Rus'

Kievan Rus' borrowed much from Byzantium, but it was in no position to replicate major institutions such

as the bureaucracy or an elaborate educational system. Major princes were attracted to Byzantine ceremonials and luxury and to the concept (if not yet the reality) that a central ruler should have wide powers. Many characteristics of Orthodox Christianity gradually penetrated Russian culture. Fervent devotion to the power of God and to many Eastern saints helped organize worship. Churches were ornate, filled with icons and the sweet smell of incense. A monastic movement developed that stressed prayer and charity. Traditional practices, such as polygamy, gradually yielded to the Christian practice of monogamy. The emphasis on almsgiving long described the sense of obligation felt by wealthy Russians toward the poor.

The Russian literature that developed, which used the Cyrillic alphabet, featured chronicles that described a mixture of religious and royal events and showered praises on the saints and the power of God. Disasters were seen as expressions of the just wrath of God against human wickedness, and success in war followed from the aid of God and the saints in the name of Russia and the Orthodox faith. This tone also was common in Western Christian writing during these centuries, but in Kievan Rus' it monopolized formal culture; a distinct philosophical or scientific current did not emerge in the postclassical period.

Russian and Ukrainian art focused on the religious also, with icon painting and illuminated religious manuscripts becoming a Kievan specialty. Orthodox churches, built in the form of a cross surmounted by a dome, similarly aped Byzantine mod-

Document

Russia Turns to Christianity

This document from a monk's chronicle, describing King Vladimir's conversion policy, indicates what was officially believed about the power of Russian princes, Russian social structure, and the relationship between Christianity and earlier animism. These official claims are important, but they may not reflect the whole reality of this important transition in Russia history. Here is a classic case of the need to understand a particular mindset and genre of writing, to understand why particular explanations are offered without accepting their reality.

For at this time the Russes were ignorant pagans. The devil rejoiced thereat, for he did not know that his ruin was approaching. He was so eager to destroy the Christian people, yet he was expelled by the true cross even from these very lands....Vladimir was visited by Bulgars of the Mohammedan faith....[He] listened to them for he was fond of women and indulgence, regarding which he heard with pleasure. But...abstinence from pork and wine were disagreeable to him. "Drinking," said he, "is the joy of the Russes. We cannot exist without that pleasure." [Russian envoys sent to Constantinople were astonished by the beauty of the churches and the chanting], and in their wonder praised the Greek ceremonial....

[Later, Vladimir was suffering from blindness; a Byzantine bishop baptized him] and as the bishop laid his hand upon him, he straightway recovered his sight. Upon experiencing this miraculous cure, Vladimir glorified God, saying, "I have now perceived the one true God." When his followers beheld this miracle, many of them were also baptized....Thereafter Vladimir sent heralds throughout the whole city to proclaim that if any inhabitant, rich or poor, did not betake himself to the river [for mass baptism] he would risk the Prince's displeasure. When the people heard these words, they wept for joy and exclaimed in their enthusiasm, "If this were not good, the Prince and his nobles would not have accepted it."... There was joy in heaven and upon earth to behold so many souls saved. But the devil groaned, lamenting, "Woe is me. How am I driven out hence ... my reign in these regions is at an end."...

He [Vladimir] ordered that wooden churches should be built and established where [pagan] idols have previously stood. He founded the Church of Saint Basil on the hill where the idol of Perun and the other images had been set, and where the prince and the people had offered their sacrifices. He began to found churches, to assign priests throughout the cities and towns, and to bring people in for baptism from all towns and villages. He began to take the children of the best families and send them for instruction from books.

Questions: In what ways might the account be simplistic in describing royal powers and popular response? What explanations does this religious chronicler offer for the conversion of Russians to Christianity? Which of the explanations are most likely, and which are the results of some kind of bias? What kind of church–state relationship did this kind of conversion predict?

els, although the building materials often were wood rather than stone. Domed structures, as Figure 14.7 shows, adapted Byzantine themes to Russian conditions, in what proved to be a durable regional style. Religious art and music were rivaled by popular entertainments in the oral tradition, which combined music, street performances, and some theater. The Russian church unsuccessfully tried to suppress these forms, regarding them as pagan.

Just as Russia's religious culture developed separately from western Europe's, Russian social and economic patterns took distinctive shape. Russian peasants were fairly free farmers, although an aristocratic landlord class existed. Russian aristocrats, called **boyars,** had less political power than their counterparts in western Europe, although the Kievan princes had to negotiate with them.

For all its distinctiveness, Russia was not unaware of other parts of Europe. The greatest ruler of the period, Yaroslav the Wise (1019–1054), used marriages to create ties. He arranged over 30 marriages with central European royalty, including 11 with Germany, pressing six Russian princes to take German wives while inducing five German nobles to accept Russian brides. Even here, however, Yaroslav kept his main focus on Byzantium, promoting Byzantine styles in the great cathedral of Kiev and using Byzantine example as the basis for Russia's first law code.

Figure 14.7 *Cathedral of St. Dimitry, built in the late 12th century in Kiev, at the height of Russia's postclassical prosperity in trade and interactions with Byzantium. The church used a Byzantine classical style but adapted it to Russian conditions, including fewer resources and possibly less architectural experience. Although the towers were topped by characteristic Orthodox domes, there was no major central dome, as in the great churches in Constantinople.*

Kievan Decline

The Kievan principality began to fade in the 12th century. Rival princes set up regional governments, and the royal family often squabbled over succession to the throne. Invaders from Asia whittled at Russian territory. The rapid decline of Byzantium reduced Russian trade and wealth, for the kingdom had always depended heavily on the greater prosperity and sophisticated manufacturing of its southern neighbor. A new kingdom was established briefly around a city

near what is now Moscow, but by 1200 Russia was weak and disunited. The final blow in this first chapter of Russian history came in 1237–1238 and 1240–1241, when two invasions by Mongols from central Asia moved through Russia and into other parts of eastern Europe (see Chapter 19). The initial Mongol intent was to add the whole of Europe to their growing empire. The Mongols easily captured the major Russian cities, but they did not penetrate much farther west because of political difficulties in their Asian homeland. Called **Tatars** in the Russian tradition (from a Turkish word) the invaders were quickly despised but also feared—"the accursed raw-eating Tatars," as one chronicle put it.

For over two centuries much of Russia remained under Tatar control. This control further separated the dynamic of Russian history from that of western Europe. Russian literature languished under Tatar supervision. Trade lapsed in western Russia, and the vigorous north-south commerce of the Kievan period never returned. At the same time, loose Tatar supervision did not destroy Russian Christianity or a native Russian aristocratic class. As long as tribute was paid, Tatar overlords left day-to-day Russian affairs alone. For a time, Tatar control created some new harmony among various Russian social classes: The word *Christian* (*Kirstianin*) was adapted as an accepted term for Russian peasants, which showed their religious commitment but also a common bond with other groups. Thus, when Tatar control was finally forced out in the second half of the 15th century, a Russian cultural and political tradition could reemerge, serving as a partial basis for the further, fuller development of Russian society.

Russian leaders retained an active memory of the glories of Byzantium. When Constantinople fell to the Turks in 1453, just as Russia was beginning to assert its independence from the Tatars, it was logical to claim that the mantle of east European leadership had fallen on Russia. A monk, currying favor, wrote the Russian king in 1511 that whereas heresy had destroyed the first Roman Empire and the Turks had cut down the second, Byzantium—a "third, new Rome"—under the king's "mighty rule" "sends out the Orthodox Christian faith to the ends of the earth and shines more brightly than the sun." "Two Romes have fallen, but the third stands, and there will be no fourth." This sense of an Eastern Christian mission, inspiring a Russian resurgence, was just one result of

In Depth

Eastern and Western Europe: The Problem of Boundaries

Deciding where one civilization ends and another begins is not always easy, particularly when many political units and some internal cultural differences are involved. Defining the territory of the two related civilizations that developed in Europe is particularly difficult. A number of states sat, and still sit, on the borders of the two civilizations, sharing some characteristics of each. Furthermore, political disputes and nationalist attachments, fierce in this border territory of east central Europe during the past two centuries, make territorial definitions an emotional issue. So the question of defining Europe's civilizations is a particularly thorny case of a larger problem.

If a civilization is defined simply by its mainstream culture, then east and west Europe in the postclassical period divide logically according to Orthodox and Catholic territories (and use of the Cyrillic and Greek or of the Latin alphabets). By this reckoning, Poland, the Czech areas, and the Baltic states (these latter did not convert to Catholicism until the 14th century) are western, and Hungary is largely so. South Slavs are mainly but not entirely Orthodox, a regional division that can provoke recurrent violence. Russia and Ukraine are decidedly Orthodox in tradition. Religion matters. Poland and other Catholic regions have long maintained much more active ties with western Europe than Russia has. At the end of the postclassical period, a Czech religious dissenter, named Hus, even foreshadowed the later Protestant Reformation in his attacks on the Catholic church.

Politically, the case is more complicated. Poland, Hungary, and Lithuania formed large regional kingdoms at various times during and after the postclassical period. But these kingdoms were very loosely organized, much more so than the feudal monarchies that were developing in western Europe. Exceptionally large aristocracies in Poland and Hungary (by western or by Russian standards) helped limit these states.

Trade patterns also did not closely unite Poland or Hungary with western Europe until much later, when the two regions were clearly different in economic structure. Also, Polish and Hungarian societies often shared more features with Russia than with western Europe.

Russian expansion later pulled parts of eastern Europe, including Poland, into its orbit, although it never eliminated strong cultural identities. It is also important to remember that borders can change. The Mongol invasions that swept through Russia also conquered Poland and Hungary, but the armies did not stay there. Part of the Ukraine was also free from direct Mongol control, which helped differentiate it from Russia proper. For two centuries, at the end of the postclassical period, the divisions within eastern Europe intensified. Since 1989, many east European countries have again achieved full independence from Russia, and they want to claim their distinctive pasts. Not an easy border area to characterize in terms of a single civilization, east central Europe has also been a victim of many conquests interspersed with periods of proud independence.

Questions: What were the main characteristics of Russian civilization as it first emerged in the postclassical period? In what ways did Poland, Hungary, and the Czech lands differ from these characteristics? Are there other civilization border areas, in the postclassical period or later, that are similarly difficult to define because of their position between two other areas?

this complicated formative period in the emergence of a separate European civilization in the Slavic lands.

The End of an Era in Eastern Europe

With Byzantium and Russia both under siege, east European civilization fell on hard times at the end of the postclassical era. These difficulties confirmed the largely separate trajectories of West and East in Europe, for western Europe remained free from outside control and, despite some new problems, maintained a clearer vigor in politics, economy, and culture. When eastern Europe did reemerge, it was at some disadvantage to the West in terms of power and economic and cultural sophistication—a very different balance from that of the glory days of Byzantium and the vigor of Kievan Russia.

Tatar invasion and Byzantine collapse were profoundly disruptive. Key features of Kievan social structure disappeared in the later development of imperial Russia. Yet continuity was not entirely lost. Not only Christianity but also the east European assumptions about political rulers and church–state relations and the pride in a lively artistic culture served as organizing threads when Russia and other Slavic societies turned to rebuilding.

GLOBAL CONNECTIONS: Eastern Europe and the World

The Byzantine Empire participated actively in interregional trade. Constantinople had become one of the world's great trading cities, a connecting point between Europe and Asia. The Byzantine import of a silk industry from China was a sign of their active awareness of the world beyond their borders. The empire served as an active link in the postclassical global system, between northern Europe and the Mediterranean.

The situation was somewhat different for Russia. Russia's geographical position inevitably encouraged awareness both of Europe and of western Asia. Vladimir I reflected this when he pondered his religious choices, among Western Christianity, Orthodox Christianity, or Islam. But Russia became dependant on Byzantium as its main trading contact with the wider world. When Byzantium declined, and when the Mongols conquered Russia, this led to a period of unusual isolation. Russia was not able to benefit from wider relationships during the Mongol centuries, though the Mongol influence itself left a mark. When, by the 15th century, Russia began to regain independence, it faced decisions about what kind of broader contacts to foster, and how.

Further Readings

J. M. Hussey's *The Byzantine World* (1982) is a useful overview. Byzantine Christianity is studied in G. Every's *The Byzantine Patriarchate, 451–1204* (1978) and S. Runciman's *The Byzantine Theocracy* (1977); see also D. M. Nicol's *Church and Society in the Last Centuries of Byzantium* (1979). On culture, see William Brumfield, ed., *Christianity and the Arts in Russia* (1991); Helen Evans and

William Wixom, *The Glory of Byzantium: Art and Culture of the Middle Byzantine Era A.D. 843–1261* (1997); and E. Kitzinger's *Byzantine Art in the Making* (1977). Byzantine relations with the West are the main topic in H. J. Magoulias' *Byzantine Christianity: Emperor, Church and the West* (1982). On Byzantine influence in eastern Europe, D. Obolensky's *The Byzantine Commonwealth: Eastern Europe, 500–1453* (1971) remains an excellent analysis. See also A. P. Kazhdan and A. W. Epstein, *Changes in Byzantine Culture in the Eleventh and Twelfth Centuries* (1985).

On Russian history, the best survey is Nicholas Riasanovsky's *A History of Russia* (5th ed., 1992), which has a good bibliography. Books dealing with early Russian culture include Mary Charmot, *Russian Painting and Sculpture* (1963); N. P. Kondakov's *The Russian Icon* (1927); J. H. Billington's *The Icon and the Axe: An Interpretive History of Russian Culture* (1966); and Arthur Voyce's *The Art and Architecture of Medieval Russia* (1967). Vladimir Volkoff, *Vladimir the Russian Viking, 960–1015* (1985), offers a unique glimpse of early Russia. Two collections are also very helpful on early Russian history: Thomas Riha, ed., *Readings in Russian Civilization*, vol. 1; *Russia Before Peter the Great, 900–1700* (1970); and especially S. A. Zenkovsky, ed. and trans., *Medieval Russia's Epics, Chronicles and Tales* (1963). The impact of the Mongols on the shaping of Russian history is examined in Robert Marshall, *Storm From the East: From Genghis Khan to Khubilai Khan* (1993), and in an older, but still serviceable work, M. N. Thompson, *The Mongols and Russia* (1966).

On the Web

Useful overviews and assessments of Byzantine Civilization and links to related sites are provided at http://www.adams.edu/academics/art_letters/hgp/civ/110/4easternorthodox.html and http://www.fordham.edu/halsall/byzantium/. It is possible to wander the streets of Byzantine Jerusalem via http://www.american.edu/projects/mandala/TED/hpages/jerusalem/byzantin.htm. A virtual visit to one of the oldest cities of Kievan Rus', Novgorod, is offered by that city at its official Web site, http://www.novgorod.ru/english/city/history, http://emuseum.mnsu.edu/history/russia/kievanrus.html and also at http://www.neva.ru/EXPO96/book/chap1-1.html.

The ruler who converted Kievan Rus' to Orthodox Christianity, Vladimir I (http://elvis.rowan.edu/~kilroy/JEK/07/15.html), and the church leaders who converted the Balkans and southern Russia to that faith, including Cyril and Methodius (http://www.newadvent.org/cathen/04592a.htm), can be studied on the Web. Just as interesting are the lives of the women who rose to positions of power and authority at that time.

The Great Schism that came to separate and define Western Catholicism and Eastern Orthodoxy is examined from the Orthodox perspective at http://orthodoxphotos.com/readings/Orthodox_Church/schism.shtml. The Catholic perspective is offered at http://www.newadvent.org/cathen/13535a.htm.

The Emperor Justinian (http://www.historyguide.org/ancient/justinian.html and http://www.newadvent.org/cathen/08578b.htm) influenced much of the history of the Mediterranean world with Theodora as coruler (http://womenshistory.about.com/library/bio/biblio-theodora.htm and http://campus.northpark.edu/history/Webchron/EastEurope/Theodora.html). Anna Comnena, a politically ambitious daughter of a Byzantine Emperor and also an historian, is revealed at http://womeninworldhistory.com/heroine5.html, http://www.fordham.edu/halsall/source/comnena-cde.html, and http://www.wsu.edu:8080/~wldciv/world_civ_reader/world_civ_reader_1/comnena.html. One of the centerpieces of Byzantine architecture, Hagia Sophia, can be visited at http://www.patriarchate.org/ecumenical_patriarchate/chapter_4/html/hagia_sophia.html.

CHAPTER 15

A NEW CIVILIZATION EMERGES IN WESTERN EUROPE

This scene showing peasants at work in the fields near a grand palace is from an illuminated manuscript that was produced in the early 1400s for the Duc de Berry, an art patron and the brother of the king of France. The manuscript depicts a variety of scenes from the daily life of both peasants and the aristocracy in the 15th century.

The postclassical period in western Europe began with the decline and fall of the Roman Empire and extended until the 15th century. The period is known as the **Middle Ages** in European history (the adjective form is *medieval*). The period featured gradual recovery from the shock of Rome's collapse and growing interaction with other societies, particularly around the Mediterranean. Key characteristics of western European civilization emerged from this dynamic process.

Developments in Western civilization during the Middle Ages reflected many of the larger themes of postclassical world history. The spread of civilization underlay medieval history. Although western Europe had been touched by the Roman Empire at its height, contacts had been superficial outside the Mediterranean zone. Much of the north—most of Germany, northern Britain, and Scandinavia—had been entirely beyond Roman reach. During the Middle Ages, civilization extended gradually to the whole of western Europe.

Western Europe also witnessed the spread of new religious beliefs. The missionary activity of Christianity led most western Europeans to convert from polytheistic faiths in the initial postclassical centuries. Many produced an amalgam in which beliefs in magic and supernatural spirits coexisted with often fervent Christianity.

Finally, medieval western Europe participated in the network of expanding contacts among major societies in Asia, Europe, and parts of Africa. From such contacts medieval Europeans learned new technologies. New tools introduced by invaders from Asia helped spur medieval agriculture from the 10th century onward. New crops from Africa increased food production. Trade in the Mediterranean, bringing contacts with the Arabs, yielded other technological gains, such as the first European paper factory. Medieval culture was at least as powerfully shaped by connections with the wider world. From the Byzantines and the Arabs, Western scholars by the 11th and 12th centuries learned new lessons in mathematics, science, and philosophy. The medieval West unquestionably took more from the emerging world network than it contributed, but it was also challenged by its international position to seek new world roles. The theme of contacts is central to explaining developments in postclassical western Europe.

Two Images

Muslim writers who encountered Europeans, for example during the Crusades in the 12th century, viewed them as tragically backward. One wrote, "Their bodies are large, their manners harsh, their understanding dull and their tongues heavy. Those who are farthest to the north are the most

500 C.E.	800 C.E.	1000 C.E.	1150 C.E.	1300 C.E.	1450 C.E.
500–900 Recovery period after Rome's fall; missionary work in northern Europe **732** Franks defeat Muslims in France	**800–814** Charlemagne's empire **900–1000** Spread of new plows; use of horses in agriculture, transport **962** Germanic kings "revive" Roman Empire	**1018** Beginning of Christian reconquest of Spain **1066** Norman conquest of England, strong feudal monarchy **1070–1141** Peter Abelard **1073–1085** Gregory VII, reform pope **1096–1270** Crusades	**1150–1300** Gothic style spreads **1180** University of Paris **1200–1274** Thomas Aquinas and flowering of scholasticism **1215** Magna Carta **1226–1270** Louis IX of France **1265** First English parliament	**1303** Seizure of papacy by French king **1338–1453** Hundred Years' War **1348** Black Death (bubonic plague)	**1469** Formation of single Spanish monarchy

subject to stupidity, grossness, and brutishness." The comment reflected obvious prejudice. But it also picked up on the fact that Europeans were newer to civilization than many Middle Easterners were, their economy was less advanced, and their manners were less polished.

Thomas Aquinas, an Italian churchman at the University of Paris, was one of the most intelligent thinkers in European history. He dictated his books to secretaries and was so smart that he could juggle three or four sections of a complex argument at the same time, turning first to one secretary, then to another as the first caught up with his words. Working to blend rational knowledge and Christian faith, Aquinas thought he could sum up all essential understanding about man, God, and nature—something that no single individual has thought possible since then.

How, at about the same point in time, could Europe seem backward yet produce such flashes of intellectual brilliance?

Stages of Postclassical Development

 Medieval European development unfolded in two subperiods up to about 1300. Between the 6th and the 10th centuries, chaotic conditions prevailed, despite gains made by the church and Charlemagne's brief empire. Then, improvements in trade and agriculture brought new strength and diversity. Feudal monarchy developed as a stronger political form. During this period, western Europe also developed expansionist tendencies, particularly in the Crusades.

From about 550 C.E. until about 900, western Europe suffered from a number of problems. Rome's decline had left Italy fragmented, its cities and commerce shrinking, and its intellectual life in tatters.

Rome continued to serve as the center of the growing Catholic church, in turn the most powerful institution in the West. But Italy was divided politically. Spain, another key region of the Roman Empire in the West, lay in the hands of the Muslims through much of the Middle Ages. A vibrant intellectual and economic life was focused there, and it would have an important influence on Western developments later on, but it was for the time being out of the Western mainstream. The center of the postclassical West lay in France, the Low Countries, and southern and western Germany, with England increasingly drawn in—areas where civilization, as a form of human organization, was new.

Frequent invasions reflected and prolonged the West's weakness, making it difficult to develop durable government or economic forms. Raids by the seagoing **Vikings** from Scandinavia periodically disrupted life from Ireland to Sicily. With weak rulers and little more than subsistence agriculture, it was small wonder that intellectual activity almost ground to a halt. The few who could read and write were concentrated in the hierarchy and the monasteries of the Catholic church, where they kept learning alive. But they could do little more than copy older manuscripts, including those of the great Christian thinkers of the later Roman Empire. By their own admission, they could not understand much of the philosophy involved, and they often apologized for their inability to write good Latin.

The Manorial System: Obligations and Allegiances

Between Rome's fall and the 10th century, effective political organization was largely local, although Germanic kings ruled some territories, such as a portion of what is France today. **Manorialism** was the system of economic and political relations between landlords and their peasant laborers. Most people were **serfs,** living on self-sufficient agricultural estates called manors. Serfs were agricultural workers who received some protection, including the administration of justice, from the landlords; in return, they were obligated to turn over part of their goods and to remain on the land. The manorial system had originated in the later Roman Empire. It was strengthened by the decline of trade and the lack of larger political structures. Serfs needed the military forces the landlords could muster for their security. Without much market economy to stimulate production and specialization, these same landlords used the serfs' produce and labor to support their own modest establishments.

Life for most serfs was difficult. Agricultural equipment was limited, and production was low. The available plows, copied from Mediterranean models, were too light to work the heavy soils of France and Germany effectively. In the 9th century a better plow, the **moldboard** (a curved iron plate), was introduced that allowed deeper turning of the soil. Most Western peasants early in the postclassical period also left half their land uncultivated each year to restore nutrients. This again limited productivity, although by the 9th century a new **three-field system** improved the situation. Here, only a third of the land was left unplanted each year, to regain fertility.

The obligations of the manorial system bore as heavily on most serfs as did the technological limitations. Serfs had to give their lord part of their crops in return for grazing their animals on his land or milling their grain. They also provided many days of labor repairing the lord's castle or working the lands under his control. Serfs were not slaves: They could not be bought or sold, and they retained essential ownership of their houses and lands as long as they kept up with their obligations; they could also pass their property rights on through inheritance. Nevertheless, life remained hard, particularly in the early postclassical centuries. Some serfs escaped landlord control, creating a host of wanderers who added to the disorder of the early Middle Ages.

The Church: Political and Spiritual Power

During the centuries of recovery after the Roman Empire's collapse in the 6th century, the Catholic church was the only extensive example of solid organization. In theory, and to an extent in fact, the church copied the government of the Roman Empire to administer Christendom. The pope in Rome was the top authority. Regional churches were headed by bishops, who were supposed to owe allegiance to the church's central authority; bishops, in turn, appointed and to some degree supervised local priests. The popes did not always appoint the bishops, for monarchs and local lords often claimed this right, but they did send directives and receive information. The popes also regulated doctrine, beating back several heresies that threatened a unified Christian faith. Moreover, they sponsored extensive missionary activity. Papal missionaries converted the English to Christianity. They brought the religion to northern and eastern Germany, beyond the borders of the previous Roman Empire, and, by the 10th century, to Scandinavia. They were active in the border regions of eastern Europe (see Chapter 14), sometimes competing directly with Orthodox missionaries. The interest of early Germanic kings in Christianity was a sign of the political as well as spiritual power of the church. A warrior chieftain, **Clovis,** converted to Christianity about 496 C.E. to gain greater prestige over local rivals, who were still pagan. This authority, in turn, gave him a vague dominion over the Franks, a Germanic tribe located in much of what is France today. Conversion of this sort also strengthened beliefs by Western religious leaders, particularly the popes, that they had a legitimate authority separate from and superior to the political sphere. As Figure 15.1 suggests, religious commitments continued to expand to many people.

The church also developed an important chain of monasteries during the Dark Ages—the centuries immediately after Rome's fall. Western monasteries helped discipline the intense spirituality felt by some individual Christians, people who wanted to devote themselves to prayer and religious discipline and escape the limits of ordinary material life. The most important set of monastic rules was developed by Benedict of Nursia (in Italy) in the 6th century; the spread of Benedictine monasteries promoted Christian unity in western Europe. Monasteries also served ordinary people as examples of a holy life, adding to the spiritual focus that formed part of the fabric of medieval society. Many monasteries helped improve the cultivation of the land at a time when agricultural techniques were at a low ebb. Monasteries also provided some education and promoted literacy.

Charlemagne and His Successors

One significant development occurred during the early postclassical centuries in the more strictly political sphere. The royal house of the Franks grew in strength during the 8th century. A new family, the **Carolingians,** took over this monarchy, which was based in northern France, Belgium, and western Germany. One founder of the Carolingian line, **Charles Martel,** or "Charles the Hammer," was responsible for defeating the Muslims in the battle of Tours in 732, although his victory had more to do with Arab exhaustion and an overextended invasion force than Carolingian strength. This defeat helped confine the Muslims to Spain and, along with the Byzantine defeat of the Arabs in the same period, preserved Europe for Christianity.

Figure 15.1 Anxiety for Salvation: The Resurrection. *This picture was part of materials to be read in religious services in the 11th century in Germany. The dead are rising from their tombs for the Last Judgment, summoned by angels escorted by the winds. The picture illustrates the goals Christians were urged to make paramount, focusing on life after death.*

A later Carolingian ruler in this same royal line, Charles the Great, or **Charlemagne,** established a substantial empire in France and Germany around the year 800 (see Figure 15.2). Briefly, it looked as if a new Roman Empire might revive in the West; indeed, Charlemagne's successors in Germany continued to use the title of emperor. Charlemagne helped to restore some church-based education in western Europe, and the level of intellectual activity began a slow recovery, in part because of these efforts. When Charlemagne died in 814, however, his empire did not long survive him. Rather, it was split into three portions as inheritance for his three sons: the outlines of modern France, Germany, and a middle strip consisting of the Low Countries, Switzerland, and northern Italy (Map 15.1). Several of Charlemagne's successors, with nicknames such as "the Bald" and "the Fat," were not great leaders even in their regional kingdoms.

From this point onward, the essential political history of western Europe consisted of the gradual emergence of regional monarchies; a durable empire proved impossible, given competing loyalties and the absence of a strong bureaucracy. Western Europe proved to have strong cultural unity, initially centered in Catholic Christianity, but with pronounced political divisions. No single language united this civilization, any more than did a single government. Intellectuals and the church officials used Latin, but during the Middle Ages separate spoken languages evolved, usually merging Germanic and Latin elements. These separate languages, such as French and English, in turn helped form the basis of halting national identities when political and national boundaries roughly

Figure 15.2 *The pope's coronation of the emperor Charlemagne was a vital precedent for the idea that church approval was essential for a legitimate state in western Europe, although in fact Charlemagne's power greatly exceeded the pope's.*

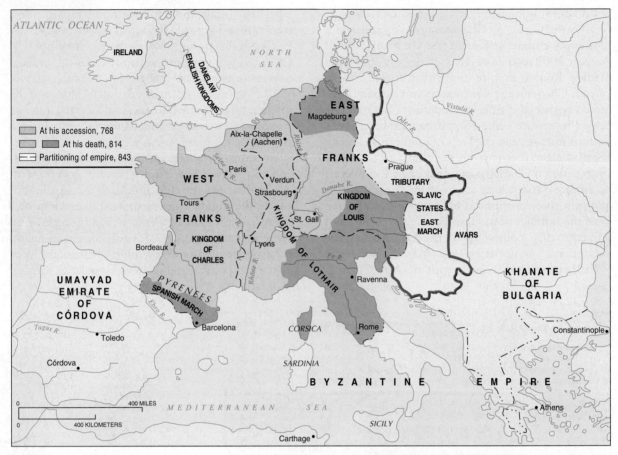

Map 15.1 *Charlemagne's Empire and Successor States. Charlemagne gathered a wide section of western Europe under his sway, but the empire was divided among his three sons after his death.*

coincided, which is what began to happen in key cases after the 9th century.

The royal houses of several lands gained new visibility soon after Charlemagne's empire split. At first, the rulers who reigned over Germany and northern Italy were in the strongest position. It was they who claimed the title *emperor*, beginning around the 10th century. Later they called themselves **Holy Roman emperors,** merging Christian and classical claims. By this time, however, their rule had become increasingly hollow, precisely because they relied too much on their imperial claims and did not build a solid monarchy from regional foundations. Local lords often went their own way in Germany, and city-states showed independence in northern Italy. The future lay elsewhere, with the rise of monarchies in individual states—states that ultimately would become nations.

New Economic and Urban Vigor

By 900, a series of developments began to introduce new sources of strength into Western society that ultimately had clear political and cultural repercussions. New agricultural techniques developed from contacts with eastern Europe and with Asian raiders into central Europe. The new moldboard plow and the three-field system were crucial gains; so was a new horse collar that allowed horses to be yoked without choking. The use of horse collars and stirrups also confirmed the military dominance of the lords, who monopolized fighting on horseback. The European nobility became defined by land ownership and military power. But better plows helped the ordinary people by allowing deeper working of heavy soil and the opening of new land. Monasteries also promoted better agricultural methods (in contrast to the less worldly orientation of monks in eastern Europe). During the 10th century, Viking raids began to taper off, partly because regional governments became stronger (sometimes when the Vikings themselves took over, as in the French province of Normandy) and partly because the Vikings, now Christianized, began to settle down. Greater regional political stability and improved agriculture promoted population growth, an important fact of Western history from the 10th through the 13th centuries.

Population growth encouraged further economic innovation. More people created new markets. There was a wedge here for growing trade, which in turn encouraged towns to expand, another source of demand. Landlords and serfs alike began to look to lands that had not previously been converted to agriculture. Whole regions, such as northeastern Germany, became colonized by eager farmers, and new centers sprang up throughout settled regions such as France. To woo labor to the new farms, landlords typically had to loosen the bonds of serfdom and require less outright labor service, sometimes simply charging a money rent. Harsh serfdom still existed, but most serfs gained greater independence, and some free peasants emerged. Contacts with other countries brought knowledge of new crops, such as durum wheat (from north Africa), the vital ingredient for pasta, and alfalfa (from Persia). The pace of economic life created a less rigid social structure, and more commercial, market-oriented economic motives began to coexist with earlier military and Christian ideals.

The growth of towns reflected the new vigor of western Europe's agriculture. In parts of Italy and the Low Countries, where trade and urban manufacturing were especially brisk, urban populations soared to almost 20 percent of the total by the 13th century. Overall, the townspeople made up about 5 percent of the West's population—a significant figure, though below the often 15 percent levels of the advanced Asian civilizations. Few European cities approached a population level of 100,000 people (in contrast, China had 52 larger cities), but the rise of modest regional centers was an important development. Literacy spread in the urban atmosphere, spurring the popular languages; professional entertainers introduced new songs as well as dazzling tricks such as fire-eating and bear-baiting; urban interests spurred new forms of religious life, including city-based monastic orders dedicated to teaching or hospital work. Merchant activity and craft production expanded.

Europe's economic and urban surge helped feed formal cultural life, which had already gained some-what under Charlemagne's encouragement. By the 9th and 10th centuries, schools began to form around important cathedrals, training children who were destined for church careers. By the 11th century, there was enough demand for educated personnel to sustain the first universities. Italy offered universities to train students in medicine and law; the legal faculties profited from a growing revival in knowledge of Roman law, and medicine benefited from new learning imported from the Arabs and from revived Greek and Hellenistic science. By the 12th century, a more characteristic university was forming in Paris. It specialized in training clergy, with theology as the culminating subject but with faculties in other subjects as well. The Parisian example inspired universities in England (Oxford and Cambridge), Germany, and elsewhere. Solid educational institutions, though destined for only a small minority of Europe's population, supported increasingly diverse and sophisticated efforts in philosophy and theology. At the same time, medieval art and architecture reached a new high point, spurred by the same prosperity.

Feudal Monarchies and Political Advances

Prosperity also promoted political change, influenced by structures established in more unstable times. From the 6th century onward, the key political and military relationships in western Europe had evolved in a system called **feudalism.** Feudal relationships linked military elites, mostly landlords, who could afford the horses and iron weaponry necessary to fight. Greater lords provided protection and aid to lesser lords, called **vassals;** vassals in turn owed their lords military service, some goods or payments, and advice. Early feudalism after Rome's fall was very local; many landlords had armed bands of five or ten local vassals, easily converted into raiding parties. But feudal relationships could be extended to cover larger regions and even whole kingdoms. Charlemagne's empire boosted this more stable version of feudalism. He could not afford to pay his own bureaucracy, so he rewarded most of his military leaders with estates, which they quickly converted into family property in return for pledges of loyalty and service. Many German duchies were created by powerful lords with their own armies of vassals, ostensibly deferring to the Holy Roman emperor. On the whole, European feudalism inhibited the development of strong central states, but it also gradually reduced purely local warfare.

Furthermore, kings could use feudalism to build their own power. Kings of France began to win growing authority, from the 10th century onward, under the Capetian royal family. At first they mainly exploited their position as regional feudal lords in the area around Paris. They controlled many serf-stocked manors directly, and they held most other local landlords as vassals. More attentive administration of this regional base produced better revenues and armies. The kings also formed feudal links with great lords in other parts of France, often through marriage alliances, gradually bringing more territory under their control. They experimented with the beginnings of bureaucratic administration by separating their personal accounts from government accounts, thus developing a small degree of specialization among the officials who served them. Later Capetian kings sent out officials to aid in regional administration.

The growth of a strong feudal monarchy in France took several centuries. By the early 14th century, the process of cautious centralization had gone so far in France that a king could claim rights to make the church pay taxes (an issue that caused great conflict). The king could print money and employ some professional soldiers apart from the feudal armies that still did most of the fighting.

Feudal monarchy in England was introduced more abruptly. The Duke of Normandy, of Viking descent, who had already built a strong feudal domain in his French province, invaded England in 1066. The duke, now known as **William the Conqueror,** extended his tight feudal system to his new kingdom. He tied the great lords of England to his royal court by bonds of loyalty, giving them estates in return for their military service. But he also used some royal officials, called sheriffs, to help supervise the administration of justice throughout the kingdom. In essence, he and his successors merged feudal principles with a slightly more centralized approach, including more standardized national law codes issued by the royal court.

The growth of feudal monarchy unknowingly duplicated measures taken earlier in other centralizing societies, such as China. Developing an explicit bureaucracy, with some specialized functions, and sending emissaries to outlying provinces are examples. In Europe, kings often chose urban business or professional people to staff their fledgling bureaucracies, because unlike the feudal nobles they would be loyal to the ruler who appointed them. Government functions expanded modestly, as kings tried to tax subjects directly and hire a small professional army to supplement feudal forces.

Limited Government

Stronger monarchies did not develop evenly throughout Europe. The West remained politically divided and diverse. Germany and Italy, though nominally controlled by the Holy Roman emperor, were actually split into regional states run by feudal lords and city-states. The pope directly ruled the territory of central Italy. The Low Countries, a vigorous trade and manufacturing region, remained divided into regional units. Equally important were the limitations over the most successful feudal monarchies. The power of the church continued to limit political claims, for the state was not supposed to intrude on matters of faith except in carrying out decisions of the popes or bishops.

Feudalism created a second limitation, for aristocrats still had a powerful independent voice and often their own military forces. The growth of the monarchy cut into aristocratic power, but this led to new statements of the limits of kings. In 1215, the unpopular English King John faced opposition to his taxation measures from an alliance of nobles, townspeople, and church officials. Defeated in his war with France and then forced down by the leading English lords, John was compelled to sign the Great Charter, or **Magna Carta,** which confirmed feudal rights against monarchical claims. John promised to observe restraint in his dealings with the nobles and the church, agreeing, for example, not to institute new taxes without the lords' permission or to appoint bishops without the church's permission.

Late in the 13th century, this same feudal balance led to the creation of **parliaments** as bodies representing not individual voters but privileged groups such as the nobles and the church. (Even earlier, in 1000, the regional kingdom of Catalonia created a parliament.) The first full English parliament convened in 1265, with the House of Lords representing the nobles and the church hierarchy, and the Commons made up of elected representatives from wealthy citizens of the towns. The parliament institutionalized the feudal principle that monarchs should consult with their vassals. In particular, parliaments gained the right to rule on any proposed changes in taxation; through this power, they could also advise the crown on other policy issues. Although the parliamentary tradition became strongest in England, similar institutions arose in France, Spain, Scandinavia, and several of the regional governments in Germany. Here too, parliaments represented the **key three estates:** church, nobles, and urban leaders. They were not widely elected.

Feudal limited government was not modern limited government. People had rights according to the estate into which they were born; nobles transmitted membership in their estate to their children. There was no general concept of citizenship and certainly no democracy. Still, by creating the medieval version of representative institutions, Western feudal monarchy produced the beginnings of a distinctive political tradition. This tradition differed from the political results of Japanese feudalism, which emphasized group loyalty more than checks on central power.

Even with feudal checks, European monarchs did develop more capacity for central administration during the later Middle Ages. The results clearly were uneven and by Asian standards still woefully limited. European rulers also continued to see war as a key purpose. Local battles gave way to larger wars, such as the conflicts between the proud rulers of France and England. In the 14th century, a long battle began— the **Hundred Years' War,** between the national monarchies of France and England—over territories the English king controlled in France and over feudal rights versus the emerging claims of national states.

The West's Expansionist Impulse

During the period of political development and economic advance, western Europe began to show its muscle beyond its initial postclassical borders. Population growth spurred the expansionist impulse, as did the memory of Rome's lost greatness and the righteous zeal provided by Christianity. The most concrete expansion took place in east central Europe from the 11th century onward. Germanic knights and agricultural settlers poured into sparsely settled areas in what is now eastern Germany and Poland, changing the population balance and clearing large areas of forest. A different kind of expansionist surge occurred in Spain. Small Christian states remained in northern Spain by the 10th century, and they gradually began to attack the Muslim government that held most of the peninsula. The "reconquest" escalated by the 11th century, as Christian forces, swelled by feudal warriors from various areas, pushed into central Spain, conquering the great Muslim center of Toledo. Full expulsion of Muslim rulers occurred only at the end of the Middle Ages in 1492, but the trend of the Christian offensive was clear even earlier. During the 15th century regional Spanish monarchies fused through the marriage of Ferdinand and Isabella. At Europe's other extreme, Viking voyagers had pushed out into the northern Atlantic, establishing settlements in Iceland. By the 11th century, other voyages had pushed to Greenland and the Hudson Bay area in what is now Canada, where short-lived outposts were created. By the 13th century, Spanish and Italian seafarers entered the Atlantic from the Mediterranean, though without much initial result except several lost expeditions.

The most dramatic expansionist move involved the great Crusades against the Muslim control of the Holy Land. Pope **Urban II** called for the First Crusade in 1095, appealing to the piety of the West's rulers and common people. Crusaders were promised full forgiveness of sins if they died in battle, ensuring their entry to heaven. The idea of attacking Islam had great appeal, as Figure 15.3 suggests. The attraction of winning spoils from the rich Arab lands added to the inducement, as did the thirst for excitement

Figure 15.3   *This imaginary duel between the noble Christian champion King Richard of England and the Muslim leader Saladin clearly shows the difference between "good guys" and "bad guys."*

among the West's feudal warriors. Internal wars were declining in Europe, and the military values of feudalism sought outlets elsewhere. Three great armies, with tens of thousands of crusaders from various parts of the West, assembled in Constantinople in 1097, much to the distress of the Byzantine government. The Western crusaders moved toward Jerusalem, winning it from the Turkish armies that held the area by that time. For almost a century, Western knights ruled the "kingdom of Jerusalem," losing it to a great Muslim general, Saladin, during the 12th century. Several later Crusades attempted to win back the Holy Land, but many later efforts turned toward other goals or toward pure farce. The Third Crusade at the end of the 12th century led to the death of the German emperor and the imprisonment of the English king, although it did produce a brief truce with Saladin that facilitated Christian pilgrims' visits to Jerusalem. The Fourth Crusade was manipulated by merchants in Venice, who turned it into an attack on their commercial rivals in Constantinople.

The Crusades did not demonstrate a new Western superiority in the wider world, despite brief successes. But in expressing a combination of religious zeal and growing commercial and military vigor on the part of the knights and merchants who organized the largest efforts, the Crusades unquestionably showed the aggressive spirit of the Western Middle Ages at their height. They also helped expose the West to new cultural and economic influences from the Middle East, a major spur to further change and to the West's interaction with the larger world, including a greater thirst for trade. Simply visiting the thriving urban center of Constantinople during the Crusades could open European eyes to new possibilities. One crusader exclaimed, "Oh, what a great and beautiful city is Constantinople! How many churches and palaces it contains, fashioned with wonderful skill! Their tradesmen at all times bring by boat all the necessities of man."

Religious Reform and Evolution

As medieval society developed, the Catholic church went through several periods of decline and renewal. At times, church officials and the leading monastic groups became preoccupied with their land holdings and their political interests. The church was a wealthy institution; it was tempting for many priests and monks to behave like ordinary feudal lords in pursuit

of greater worldly power. Several reform movements fought this secularism, such as the 13th-century flowering that created orders such as the Franciscans, devoted to poverty and service in Europe's bustling cities. St. Clare of Assisi (1194–1253) exemplified this new spirit of purity and dedication to the church (Figure 15.4). She was deeply influenced by St. Francis, also from Assisi, who had converted to a life of piety and preaching in 1205 and who founded a new monastic order around him. Clare refused to marry, as her parents wanted, but rather founded a women's Franciscan order (later known as the Order of St. Clare, or the Poor Clares) with Francis' backing. Like many women in Europe, Clare found in monasticism a vital means of personal expression. She composed rules of severe piety for her order, and many women, including her mother and sister, joined her. People believed that her prayers turned two invading armies away from Assisi, and she was credited with many other miracles in her life and after death. She was can-

Figure 15.4 *St. Clare of Assisi*

In Depth

Western Civilization

For some time, Americans have talked about "Western civilization." The concept of the West was actively used in the cold war with the Soviet Union, yet it is hard to define. We have seen that the classical Mediterranean did not directly identify a "Western" civilization, and this classical heritage was used most selectively by postclassical western Europe. Further, the consistent absence of political unity in western Europe complicates any definition of common structures.

Western Europeans could not have identified Western civilization in the postclassical period, but they would have recognized the concept of Christendom, along with some difference between their version of this religion and that of eastern Europe. The first definition of this civilization was primarily religious, although artistic forms associated with religion also figured in this definition. Regional cultures varied, of course, and there was no linguistic unity, but cultural developments in one area—for example, the creation of universities, which started in Italy—surfaced elsewhere fairly quickly. Supplementing culture were some reasonably common social structures—like manors and guilds—and trade patterns that increasingly joined northern and much of southern Europe. The resulting civilization was by no means as coherent as Chinese civilization; many of its members detested each other, like the English and French, who were often in conflict and sometimes engaged in name-calling (the English were "les goddams," because they swore so much, and the French were "frogs" because of what they ate). Until very recently, Europeans thought in terms of distinctive national histories, not European ones. But it is possible to define some common features that differed from those of neighboring civilizations. Even as the civilization began to change, late in the postclassical period, it preserved some common directions. Debate continues about the balance between the Western and more purely national features.

Defining Western civilization is also complicated in the postclassical period because Western leaders copied so much from other societies. They eagerly learned of new technologies from Asia. They benefited from Arab mathematics and philosophy, and they imitated Muslim commercial law on how to treat tradespeople from outside the locality. But even in imitating, most Europeans were keenly conscious of their distinctiveness as Christians. They sometimes resented the societies they copied from. Toward the end of the Middle Ages, as Europeans began to seek a new role in the world at large, the openness to imitation also began to decline, as part of the further definition of a Western or European identity.

Questions: Was there a Western civilization before the postclassical period? What were the defining features of Western civilization by the end of the postclassical period? Was it separate from eastern Europe, in terms of major features? How does the definition of Western civilization today compare to that of the postclassical period?

---

onized in 1255, and in 1958 Pope Pius XII declared her the patron saint of television, for during her last illness she miraculously heard and saw a Christmas mass being performed on the other side of Assisi.

In addition to monastic leaders, reform-minded popes, such as **Gregory VII** (1073–1085), tried to purify the church and free it from interference by feudal lords. One technique was insistence on the particularly holy character of the priesthood. Reformers stipulated that all priests remain unmarried, to separate the priesthood from the ordinary world of the flesh. Gregory also tried to free the church from any trace of state control. He quarreled vigorously with Holy Roman Emperor Henry IV over the practice of state appointment, or **investiture,** of bishops in Germany. Ultimately, by excommunicating the emperor from the church, Gregory won his point. The emperor appealed to the pope for forgiveness on his knees in the snow of a northern Italian winter, and the investiture controversy ended, apparently in the church's favor. Gregory and several later popes made clear their beliefs that the church not only was to be free from state interference but was superior to the state in its function as a direct channel of God's word. These claims were not entirely accurate because governments still influenced religious affairs, but they were not hollow. Independently of the state, a network of church courts developed to rule on matters of religious law and to bring heretics to trial and occasionally to execution. This was the origin of recurrent Western beliefs in church–state separation.

The High Middle Ages

The postclassical version of Western civilization reached its high mark in the 12th and 13th centuries. Fed by the growing dynamism of western Europe's population, agriculture, and cities, the High Middle Ages were characterized by a series of creative tensions. Feudal political structures, derived from local and personal allegiances, were balanced by emerging central monarchies. The unquestionable authority of the church and the cultural dominance of Christianity jostled with the intellectual vitality and diversity that formed part of university life. A social order and economy, based primarily on agriculture and the labor of serfs, now had to come to terms with important cities, merchants, and some new opportunities even for ordinary farmers.

Western Culture in the Postclassical Era

 Christian culture formed the clearest unifying element in western Europe during the postclassical centuries, although it changed as European society matured. Theologians and artists developed distinctive expressions, although there were other philosophical and artistic currents as Europe's cultural creativity increased.

Theology: Assimilating Faith and Reason

During the centuries before about 1000, a small number of clergy continued the efforts of preserving and interpreting past wisdom, particularly the writings of church fathers such as Augustine, but also the work of some non-Christian Latin authors. During Charlemagne's time, a favorite practice was to gather quotations from ancient writers around key subjects. Efforts of this sort showed little creativity, but they gradually produced a fuller understanding of past thought as well as improvements in Latin writing style. Interest in classical principles of rhetoric, particularly logic, reflected the concern for coherent organization; Aristotle, known to the Middle Ages as *the* philosopher, was valued because of his clear exposition of rational thought.

From 1000 onward, a series of outstanding clerics advanced the logical exposition of philosophy and theology to new levels. They stressed the importance of absolute faith in God's word, but they believed that human reason could move toward an understanding of some aspects of religion and the natural order as well. Thus, according to several theologians, it was possible to prove the existence of God. Fascination with logic led some intellectuals to a certain zeal in pointing out inconsistencies in past wisdom, even in the writings of the church fathers. In the 12th century, **Peter Abelard** in Paris wrote a treatise called *Yes and No* in which he showed several logical contradictions in established interpretations of doctrine. Although Abelard protested his faith, saying, "I would not be an Aristotle if this were to part me from Christ," he clearly took an impish delight in suggesting skepticism. Here was a fascinating case of an individual's role in history. Abelard was clearly working in an established logical tradition, but his personality helped move the tradition to a new critical level. At the same time, his defiant attitudes may have drawn more attack than a softer approach would have done, which had consequences too.

The logical–rationalist current in Western philosophy was hardly unopposed. Apart from the fact that most ordinary Christians knew nothing of these debates, seeing their religion as a matter of received belief and appointed sacraments that would remove sin and promote salvation, many church leaders emphasized the role of faith alone. A powerful monk, **Bernard of Clairvaux,** successfully challenged Abelard. Bernard, an intellectual of a different sort, stressed the importance of mystical union with God, attainable even on this earth in brief blissful glimpses, rather than rationalist endeavor. Bernard believed that reason was dangerous and proud and that God's truth must be received through faith alone.

The debates over how and whether to combine the classical Mediterranean philosophical and scientific tradition with revealed religious faith had much in common with debates among Arab intellectuals during the 10th and 11th centuries. Both Christianity and Islam relied heavily on faith in a revealed word, through the Bible or Qur'an, respectively, but some intellectuals in both cultures strained to include other approaches.

Combining rational philosophy and Christian faith was the dominant intellectual theme in the post-classical West, showing the need to come to terms with both Christian and classical heritages. This combination of rational philosophy and Christian faith also posed formidable and fascinating problems. By the 12th century, the zeal for this kind of knowledge produced several distinctive results. It explained the intellectual vitality of most of the emerging universities, where students flocked to hear the latest debates by leading theologians. Higher education certainly benefited students through resulting job opportunities; for example, trained lawyers could hope for advancement in the growing bureaucracies of church or state. In contrast to China's institutions, however, the new universities were not directly tied into a single bureaucratic system, and the excitement they engendered during the Middle Ages did not follow from opportunism alone. A large number of students, from the whole of western Europe, sought out the mixture of spiritual and rational understanding that leading thinkers were trying to work out. Many early universities had their students pay the teachers directly if they were interested in attending a given set of lectures, and the eagerness for learning could make this system work.

The postclassical intellectual drive also motivated a growing interest in knowledge newly imported from the classical past and from the Arab world, and this knowledge fed the highest achievements of medieval learning. By the 12th century, Western scholars were reading vast amounts of material translated from Greek in centers in the Byzantine Empire, Italy, and Muslim Spain. They gained familiarity with the bulk of ancient Greek and Hellenistic philosophy and science. They also read translations of Arab and Jewish learning, particularly the works in which Middle Eastern scholars had wrestled with the problems of mixing human reasoning with truths gained by faith.

With much fuller knowledge of Aristotelian and Hellenistic science, plus the work of Arab rationalists such as Ibn-Rushd (known in the West as Averroës), Western philosopher–theologians in the 13th century proceeded to the final great synthesis of medieval learning. The leading figure was **Thomas Aquinas,** the Italian-born monk who taught at the University of Paris. Aquinas maintained the basic belief that faith came first, but he greatly expanded the scope given to reason. Through reason alone, humans could know much of the natural order, of moral law, and of the nature of God. Thomas had complete confidence that all essential knowledge could be organized coherently, and he produced a host of *Summas*, or highest works, that used careful logic to eliminate all possible objections to truth as revealed by reason and faith. Essentially, this work restated in Christian terms the Greek efforts to seek a rationality in nature that would correspond to the rational capacities of the human mind. To be sure, a few philosophers carried the interest in logic to absurd degrees. After the 13th century, **scholasticism**—as the dominant medieval philosophical approach was called because of its base in the schools—sometimes degenerated into silly debates such as the one about how many angels could dance on the head of a pin. But at its height, and particularly with Aquinas, scholasticism demonstrated an unusual confidence in the logical orderliness of knowledge and in human ability to know.

Medieval philosophy did not encourage a great deal of new scientific work. The emphasis on mastering past learning and organizing it logically could lead to overemphasis on previous discoveries rather than empirical research. Thus, university-trained doctors stressed memorization of Galen, the Hellenistic authority, rather than systematic practical experience. Toward the end of the 13th century, a current of practical science developed. In Oxford, members of the clergy, such as Roger Bacon, did experimental work with optics, pursuing research done earlier by Muslim scholars. An important by-product of this interest was the invention of eyeglasses. During the 14th and 15th centuries, experimenters also advanced knowledge in chemistry and astronomy. This early work set the stage for the flourishing of Western science.

Popular Religion

Far less is known about popular beliefs than about formal intellectual life in the Middle Ages. Christian devotion undoubtedly ran deep and may well have increased with time among many ordinary people. At least in the early medieval centuries, many people diligently followed Christian rituals yet seemed unaware of how many of their actions might contradict Christian morality. For example, Raoul de Cambrai, hero of a French epic written down in the late 12th century but orally transmitted earlier, sets fire to a convent filled with nuns, then asks a servant to bring him some food. The servant berates him for burning the convent, then reminds him that it is Lent, a time of fasting and repentance before Easter. Raoul denies that his deed was unjust, for the nuns deserved it for insulting his knights, but admits that he had forgotten Lent and goes off to distract himself from his hunger by playing chess.

Whether popular morality improved or not, popular means of expressing religious devotion expanded over time. The rise of cities saw the formation of lay groups to develop spirituality and express their love of God. The content of popular belief evolved as well. Enthusiasm for the veneration of Mary, the mother of Jesus, expanded by the 12th century, showing a desire to stress the merciful side of Christianity, rather than the supposed sternness of God the Father, and new hopes for assistance in gaining salvation. The worship of various saints showed a similar desire for intermediaries between humanity and God. At the same time, ordinary people continued to believe in various magical rituals, and they celebrated essentially pagan festivals, which often involved much dancing and merriment. They blended their version of Christianity with great earthiness and spontaneity, some of which was conveyed by late medieval authors such as English writer Geoffrey Chaucer.

Religious Themes in Art and Literature

Christian art in many ways reflected both the popular outlook and the more formal religion of theologians and church leaders. Religious art was another cultural area in which the medieval West came to excel, as was the case in other societies where religious enthusiasm ran strong, such as the Islamic Middle East or Hindu India. Like philosophy, medieval art and architecture were intended to serve the glory of God. Western painters used religious subjects almost exclusively. Painting mainly on wooden panels, artists in most parts of western Europe depicted Christ's birth and suffering and the lives of the saints, using stiff, stylized figures. By the 14th and 15th centuries, artists improved their ability to render natural scenes realistically and portrayed a host of images of medieval life as backdrops to their religious subjects. Stained glass designs and scenes for churches were another important artistic expression.

Medieval architecture initially followed Roman models, particularly in church building, using a rectangular, or Romanesque, style sometimes surmounted by domes. During the 11th century, however, a new style took hold that was far more original, though it benefited from knowledge of Muslim design plus advances in structural engineering in the West itself. **Gothic** architects built soaring church spires and tall arched windows, as Figure 15.5 illustrates. Although their work focused on creating churches and great cathedrals, some civic buildings and palaces also picked up the Gothic motif. It is not far-fetched to see the Gothic style as representative of Western postclassical culture more generally. Its spiritual orientation showed in the towers cast up to the heavens. It built also on growing technical skills and deep popular devotion, expressed in the money collected to build the huge monuments and the patient labor needed for construction that often lasted many decades. The originality of Gothic styles reflected the growing Western ability to find suitable new means of expression, just as use of Gothic styles in the later Western world showed the ongoing power of medieval models.

Figure 15.5 *Gothic architecture was one of the creative expressions of postclassical western Europe and was used particularly in churches. This major cathedral in Amiens, France, was built over many centuries and dwarfs the surrounding buildings.*

Medieval literature and music reflected strong religious interests. Most Latin writing dealt with points of philosophy, law, or political theory. However, alongside writing in Latin came the development of a growing literature in the spoken languages, or vernaculars, of western Europe. The pattern was not unlike that of India a few centuries earlier after the fall of the Gupta empire, when Sanskrit served as a scholarly language but increasing power was given to popular languages such as Hindi. Vernacular literature helped develop separate European languages and focused largely on secular themes. Several oral sagas, dealing with the deeds of great knights and mythic figures in the past, were written down. From this tradition came the first known writing in early English, *Beowulf*, and in French, *The Song of Roland*. Late in the Middle Ages, a number of writers created adventure stories, comic tales, and poetry in the vernacular tongues, such as Chaucer's *Canterbury Tales*. Much of their work, and also plays written for performance in the growing cities, reflected the tension between Christian values and a desire to portray the richness and coarseness of life on earth. Chaucer's narrative shows a fascination with bawdy behavior, a willingness to poke fun at the hypocrisy of many Christians, and an ability to capture some of the tragedies of human existence. In France, a long poem called *The Romance of the Rose* used vivid sexual imagery, and the poet Villon wrote, in largely secular terms, of the terror and poignancy of death. Finally, again in vernacular language, a series of courtly poets, or troubadours, based particularly in southern France in the 14th century, wrote hymns to the love that could flourish between men and women. Although their verses stressed platonic devotion rather than sexual love and paid homage to courtly ceremonies and polite behavior, their concern with love was the first sign of a new valuation of this emotional experience in the Western tradition.

In sum, medieval intellectual and artistic life created a host of important themes. Religion was the centerpiece, but it did not preclude a growing range of interests, from science to romantic poetry. Medieval culture was a rich intellectual achievement in its own right. It also set in motion a series of developments—in rationalist philosophy, science, artistic representations of nature, and vernacular literature—that would be building blocks for later Western thought and art.

Changing Economic and Social Forms in the Postclassical Centuries

 With the revival of trade and agriculture, commercial ties spread through most of western Europe. Urban merchants gained unusual power, but early capitalism was disputed by the different economic values of the guilds.

Although culture provided the most obvious cement for Western society during the Middle Ages, common features also described economic activity and social structure. Here too, the postclassical West demonstrated impressive powers of innovation, for classical patterns had little hold. As trade revived by the 10th century, the West became a common commercial zone. Most regions produced primarily for local consumption, as was true in agricultural societies generally. But Italian merchants actively sought cloth manufactured in the Low Countries (present-day Belgium and the Netherlands), and merchants in many areas traded for wool grown in England or timber supplies and furs brought from Scandinavia and the Baltic lands. Great ports and trading fairs, particularly in the Low Countries and northern France, served as centers for Western exchange as well as markets for a few exotic products such as spices brought in from other civilizations.

New Strains in Rural Life

The improvements in agriculture after 800 C.E. brought important new ingredients to rural life. Some peasants were able to shake off the most severe constraints of manorialism, becoming almost free farmers with only a few obligations to their landlords, although rigid manorialism remained in place in many areas. Noble landlords still served mainly military functions, for ownership of a horse and armor were prerequisites for fighting until the end of the medieval period. Although most nobles shunned the taint of commerce—like aristocrats in many societies, they found too much money-grubbing demeaning—they did use trade to improve their standard of living and adopt more polished habits. The courtly literature of the late Middle Ages reflected this new style of life.

As many lords sought improved conditions they were often tempted to press their serfs to pay higher

Visualizing the Past

Peasant Labor

This scene, from an illuminated (illustrated) manuscript of the 15th century, shows peasant labor and tools in France, near a stylized great palace.

Questions: What kind of social and gender structure does the picture suggest? What kind of tools were used in farming, and how productive would they be? (The picture clearly indicates what kind of farming activity was being performed.) Interpretation of the picture must also involve the art itself: Is it realistic? What features seem most different from probable rural conditions, and what accounts for the differences? The picture should be compared to earlier medieval representations, such as the representation of Charlemagne's coronation: What were the trends in medieval artistic styles, in terms of dealing with human figures and nature? The manuscript was part of a seasonal book for a French aristocrat. What do the symbols at the top of the picture suggest about developments in medieval science and calendars?

rents and taxes, even as serfs were gaining a new sense of freedom and control over their own land. From the late Middle Ages until the 19th century, this tension produced a recurrent series of peasant–landlord battles in Western society. Peasants sought what they viewed as their natural and traditional right to the land, free and clear. They talked of Christian equality, turning such phrases as "When Adam delved and Eve span, Who was then a gentleman?" A more complex economy clearly brought new social strains, similar to the recurrent wave of popular unrest in China or the rural uprisings in the Middle East, where religion helped prompt egalitarian sentiments as well. The gap between lord and peasant was the crucial social inequality in Europe, but it was open to change and it generated some egalitarian ideas in response.

On the whole, the lives of Western peasants improved during the most dynamic part of the Middle Ages. Landlord controls were less tight than they had become in other societies, such as the Middle East. Western agriculture was not yet particularly advanced technologically (compared with east Asia, for example), but it had improved notably over early medieval levels.

Growth of Trade and Banking

Gains in agriculture promoted larger changes in medieval economic life. Urban growth allowed more specialized manufacturing and commercial activities, which in turn promoted still greater trade. Spearheaded by Italian businesspeople, banking was introduced to the West to facilitate the long-distance exchange of money and goods (Figure 15.6). The use of money spread steadily, to the dismay of many Christian moralists and many ordinary people who preferred the more direct, personal ways of traditional society. The largest trading and banking operations, not only in Italy but in southern Germany, the Low Countries, France, and Britain, were clearly capitalistic. Big merchants invested funds in trading ships and the goods they carried, hoping to make large profits on this capital. Profitmaking was not judged kindly by Christian thinkers such as Thomas Aquinas, who urged that all prices should be "just," reflecting only the labor put into the goods.

Rising trade took several forms. There were exchanges between western Europe and other parts of the known world. Wealthy Europeans developed a taste for some of the luxury goods and spices of Asia. The latter were not used merely to flavor food but were vital in preserving perishable items such as meat. Spice extracts also had great medicinal value. The Crusades played a role in bringing these products to wider attention. A Mediterranean trade redeveloped, mainly in the hands of Italian merchants, in which European cloth and some other products were exchanged for the more polished goods of the East. Commerce within Europe involved exchanges of timber and grain from the north for cloth and metal products manufactured in Italy and the Low Countries. At first an exporter of raw wool, England developed some manufactured goods for exchange by the later Middle Ages. Commercial alliances developed. Cities in northern Germany and southern Scandinavia grouped together in the **Hanseatic League** to encourage trade. With growing banking facilities, it became possible to organize commercial transactions throughout much of western Europe. Bankers, including many Jewish businesspeople, were valued for their service in lending money to monarchs and the papacy.

The growth of trade and banking in the Middle Ages served as the origin of capitalism in Western civilization. The greater Italian and German bankers, the long-distance merchants of the Hanseatic cities, were clearly capitalistic in their willingness to invest in trading ventures with the expectation of profit. Given the dangers of trade by land and sea, the risks in these investments were substantial, but profits of 100 percent or more were possible. In many cities, such as London, groups of powerful merchants banded together to invest in international trade, each buying shares in the venture and profiting or losing accordingly.

Figure 15.6 *This 14th-century miniature shows views of a banking house.*

Individual merchants could amass—and lose—great fortunes. Jacques Coeur (c. 1395–1456), one of Europe's most extraordinary merchants, demonstrated the opportunities and risks of new forms of trade (Figure 15.7). Son of a furrier, he married the daughter of a royal official and served as a tax official until he was caught minting coins with less valuable metals. He then founded a trading company that competed with Italians and Spaniards in dealing with the Middle East. He visited Damascus to buy spices, setting up a regular trade in rugs, Chinese silk, and Indonesian spices and sugar. He also became financial advisor and supplier to the French king and was ennobled. With the largest fleet ever

Figure 15.7   *Jacques Coeur*

owned by a French subject, Coeur surrounded himself with splendor, even arranging with the pope for his 16-year-old son to become an archbishop. But he had enemies, many of them nobles in debt to him, and they turned the king against him. Tortured, he admitted to various crimes, including supplying weapons to Muslims. His property was confiscated, but, adventurer to the last, he died on a Greek island while serving in a papal fleet against the Turks.

By world standards this was not a totally unprecedented merchant spirit. European traders were still less venturesome and less wealthy than some of their Muslim counterparts. Nor was Western society as tolerant of merchants as Muslim or Indian societies were. Yet Western commercial endeavors clearly were growing. Because Western governments were weak, with few economic functions, merchants had a freer hand than in many other civilizations. Many of the growing cities were ruled by commercial leagues. Monarchs liked to encourage the cities as a counterbalance to the power of the landed aristocracy, and in the later Middle Ages and beyond, traders and kings typically were allied. However, aside from taxing merchants and using them as sources of loans, royal governments did not interfere much with trading activities. Merchants even developed their own codes of commercial law, administered by city courts. Thus, the rising merchant class, though not unusual in strength or venturesomeness, was staking out an unusually powerful and independent role in European society.

Capitalism was not yet typical of the Western economy, even aside from the moral qualms fostered by the Christian tradition. Most peasants and landlords had not become enmeshed in the market system. In the cities, the dominant economic ethic stressed group protection, not profitmaking. The characteristic institution was not the international trading firm but the merchant or artisan guild. **Guilds** grouped people in the same business or trade in a single city, sometimes with loose links to similar guilds in other cities. These organizations were new in western Europe, although they resembled guilds in various parts of Asia but with greater independence from the state. They stressed security and mutual control. Merchant guilds thus attempted to give all members a share in any endeavor. If a ship pulled in loaded with wool, the clothiers' guild of the city insisted that all members participate in the purchase so that no one member would monopolize the profits.

Artisan guilds were made up of the people in the cities who actually made cloth, bread, jewelry, or furniture. These guilds tried to limit their membership so that all members would have work. They regulated apprenticeships to guarantee good training but also to ensure that no member would employ too many apprentices and so gain undue wealth. They discouraged new methods because security and a rough equality, not maximum individual profit, were the goals; here was their alternative to the capitalistic approach. Guilds also tried to guarantee quality so that consumers would not have to worry about shoddy quality on the part of some unscrupulous profit-seeker. Guilds played an important political and social role in the cities, giving their members recognized status and often a voice in city government. Their statutes were in turn upheld by municipal law and often backed by the royal government as well.

Despite the traditionalism of the guilds, manufacturing and commercial methods improved in medieval Europe. Western Europe was not yet as advanced as Asia in ironmaking and textile manufacture, but it was beginning to catch up. In a few areas, such as clockmaking—which involved both

Document

Changing Roles for Women

A late-14th-century Parisian manual titled *The Good Wife* revealed the kind of thinking about gender that became more pronounced as medieval society developed in the West. It invites comparison with patriarchal views you have studied in other agricultural civilizations. Is any room left for initiatives by women?

> Wherefore I counsel you to make such cheer to your husband at all his comings and stayings, and to persevere therein; and also be peaceable with him, and remember the rustic proverb, which saith that there be three things which drive the goodman from home, to wit, a leaking roof, a smoky chimney, and a scolding woman. And therefore, fair sister, I beseech you that you keep yourself in the love and good favour of your husband, you be unto him gentle, and amiable, and debonair. Do unto him what the good simple women of our country say hath been done to their sons, when these have set their love elsewhere and their mothers cannot wean them therefrom.
>
> Wherefore, dear sister, I beseech you thus to bewitch and bewitch again your husband that shall be, and beware of roofless house and of smoky fire, and scold him not,

but be unto him gentle and amiable and peaceable. Have a care that in winter he have a good fire and smokeless and let him rest well and be well covered between your breasts, and thus bewitch him....

> And thus shall you preserve and keep your husband from all discomforts and give him all the comforts whereof you can bethink you, and serve him and have him served in your house, and you shall look to him for outside things, for if he be good he will take even more pains and labour therein than you wish, and by doing what I have said, you will cause him ever to miss you and have his heart with you and your loving service and he will shun all other houses, all other women, all other services and households.

Questions: Is this a distinctively Christian view of women? How does it compare with Muslim or Chinese views of women in the postclassical period? Why might postclassical values about women have become more rigorous in the late medieval centuries in the West?

sophisticated technology and a concern for precise time initially linked to the schedule of church services—European artisans led the world. Furthermore, some manufacturing spilled beyond the bounds of guild control. Particularly in the Low Countries and parts of Italy, groups of manufacturing workers were employed by capitalists to produce for a wide market. Their techniques were simple, and they worked in their own homes, often alternating manufacturing labor with agriculture. Their work was guided not by the motives of the guilds but by the inducements of merchant capitalists, who provided them with raw materials and then paid them for their production.

Thus, by the later Middle Ages western Europe's economy and society embraced many contradictory groups and principles. Commercial and capitalist elements jostled against the slower pace of economic life in the countryside and even against the dominant group protectionism of most urban guilds. Most people remained peasants, but a minority had escaped to the cities, where they found more excitement, along

with increased danger and higher rates of disease. Medieval tradition held that a serf who managed to live in the city for a year and a day became a free person. A few prosperous capitalists flourished, but most people operated according to very different economic values, directed toward group welfare rather than individual profit. This was neither a static society nor an early model of a modern commercial society. It had its own flavor and its own tensions—the fruit of several centuries of economic and social change.

Limited Sphere for Women

The increasing complexity of medieval social and economic life may have had one final effect, which is familiar from patterns in other agricultural societies: new limits on the conditions of women. Women's work remained vital in most families. The Christian emphasis on the equality of all souls and the practical importance of women's monastic groups in providing an alternative to marriage continued to have distinctive effects on women's lives in Western society.

The veneration of Mary and other female religious figures gave women real cultural prestige, counterbalancing the biblical emphasis on Eve as the source of human sin. In some respects, women in the West had higher status than their sisters under Islam: They were less segregated in religious services (although they could not lead them) and were less confined to the household. Still, women's voice in the family may have declined in the Middle Ages. Urban women often played important roles in local commerce and even operated some craft guilds, but they found themselves increasingly hemmed in by male-dominated organizations. By the late Middle Ages, a literature arose that stressed women's roles as the assistants and comforters to men, listing supplemental household tasks and docile virtues as women's distinctive sphere. Patriarchal structures seemed to be taking deeper root.

The Decline of the Medieval Synthesis

 Amid new problems of overpopulation and disease, the postclassical version of Western civilization declined after 1300. This decline was evident in the feudal aristocracy, the church, and theology.

After about 1300, some of the characteristics of medieval life at its height began to give way. The international community was affected as strong monarchies consolidated their holdings and adjusted state boundaries (Map 15.2). One problem, both a symptom and a cause of larger issues, was the major war that engulfed France and England during the 14th and 15th centuries. The Hundred Years' War, which sputtered into the mid-15th century, lasted even longer than its name and initially went very badly for France—a sign of new weakness in the French monarchy (Figure 15.8). Not very bloody, the war ultimately demonstrated the futility of some of the military and organizational methods attached to feudalism. As the war dragged on, kings reduced their reliance on the prancing forces of the nobility in favor of paid armies of their own. New military methods challenged the key monopoly of the feudal lords, as ordinary paid archers learned how to unseat armored knights with powerful bows and arrows and

with crossbows. The war ended with a French victory, sparked in part by the heroic leadership of the inspired peasant woman Joan of Arc, but both its devastation and the antifeudal innovations it encouraged suggested a time of change.

Concurrently, from about 1300 onward, key sources of Western vitality threatened to disappear. Medieval agriculture could no longer keep pace with population growth: The readily available new lands had been used up, and there were no major new technological gains to compensate. The result included severe famines and a decline in population levels until the end of the century. A devastating series of plagues that persisted for several centuries, beginning with the **Black Death** in 1348, further challenged Europe's population and social structure (Figure 15.9). New social disputes arose, heightening some of the tensions noted earlier between peasants and landlords, artisans and their employees. Not until the 16th century would the West begin to work out a new social structure. The West's economy did not go into a tailspin; in some respects, as in manufacturing and mining technology, progress may even have accelerated. The 150 to 200 years after 1300 form in Western history a transition period in which the features of the Middle Ages began to blur while new problems and developments began to take center stage. Western civilization was not in a spiral of decline, but the postclassical version of this civilization was.

Signs of Strain

The decline of medieval society involved increasing challenges to several typical medieval institutions. Decline was not absolute but rather a sign of change, as Western society began to shed part of its earlier skin only to emerge, with renewed dynamism, in somewhat different garb by the middle of the 15th century. During the 14th century, the ruling class of medieval society, the land-owning aristocracy, began to show signs of confusion. It had long staked its claim to power on its control of land and its military prowess, but its skill in warfare was now open to question. The growth of professional armies and new weaponry such as cannon and gunpowder made traditional fighting methods, including fortified castles, increasingly irrelevant. The aristocracy did not simply disappear, however. Rather, the nobility chose to emphasize a rich ceremonial style of life, featuring

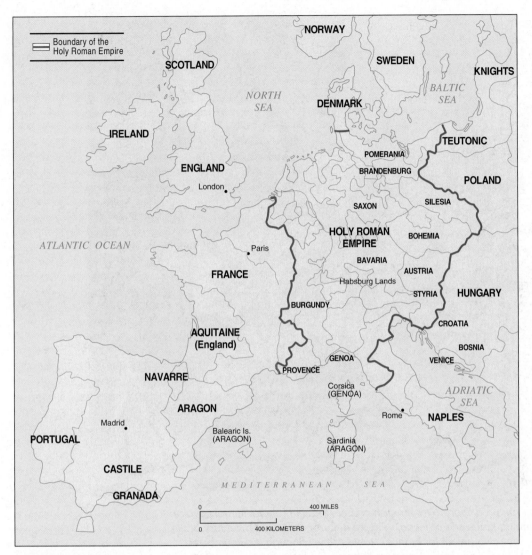

Map 15.2 *Western Europe Toward the End of the Middle Ages, c. 1360 C.E. Near the end of the postclassical period, strong monarchies had consolidated their holdings, and boundaries between states were coming into sharper focus.*

tournaments in which military expertise could be turned into competitive games. The idea of chivalry—carefully controlled, polite behavior, including behavior toward women—gained ground. The upper class became more cultivated. We have seen similar transformations in the earlier Chinese and Muslim aristocracy. Yet at this transitional point in Europe, some of the elaborate ceremonies of chivalry seemed rather hollow, even a bit silly—a sign

that medieval values were losing hold without being replaced by a new set of purposes.

Another key area involved decisive shifts in the balance between church and state that had characterized medieval life. For several decades in the aftermath of the taxation disputes in the early 14th century, French kings wielded great influence on the papacy, which they relocated from Rome to Avignon, a town surrounded by French territory. Then rival

Figure 15.8 *In the Hundred Years' War, English archers fought France's feudal cavalry; this was the beginning of the end of feudal warfare in Europe. This 14th-century battle of Crécy was a resounding defeat for France's noble army, although it outnumbered the English army. Why did this kind of warfare threaten feudalism?*

claimants to the papacy confused the issue further. Ultimately a single pope was returned to Rome, but the church was clearly weakened. Moreover, the church began to lose some of its grip on Western religious life. Church leaders were so preoccupied with their political involvement that they tended to neglect the spiritual side. Religion was not declining; indeed, signs of intense popular piety continued to blossom, and new religious groups formed in the towns. But devotion became partially separated from the institution of the church. One result, again beginning in the

14th century, was a series of popular heresies, with leaders in places such as England and Bohemia (the present-day Czech Republic) preaching against the hierarchical apparatus of the church in favor of direct popular experience of God. Another result was an important new series of mystics, many of them women, who claimed direct, highly emotional contacts with God.

A third area in which medievalism faded was the breakdown of the intellectual and even artistic synthesis. After the work of Aquinas, the sterile philo-

Figure 15.9 *Burying plague victims in coffins at Tournai before mass burial became the only way to keep up with the deaths. The 14th-century Black Death was a massive shock to European society.*

sophical pursuits of the later scholastics seemed petty. Church officials became less tolerant of intellectual daring, and they even declared some of Aquinas's writings heretical. The earlier blend of rationalism and religion no longer seemed feasible. Ultimately, this turned some thinkers away from religion, but this daring development took time. In art, growing interest in realistic portrayals of nature, though fruitful, suggested the beginnings of a shift away from medieval artistic standards. Religious figures became less stylized as painters grew more interested in human features for their own sake. The various constraints on forms of postclassical culture prompted many Western intellectuals to look for different emphases. In Italy most clearly, new kinds of literature and art took shape that differed from the styles and subjects of the postclassical centuries.

The Postclassical West and Its Heritage

Medieval Europe had several faces. The term *Middle Ages* implies a lull, between the glories of Rome and the glitter of more modern Europe. There is some truth to this, for medieval Europe did grapple with backwardness and vulnerability.

But the Middle Ages were also a period of growing dynamism. Particularly after 900 C.E., gains in

population, trade and cities, and intellectual activity created a vigorous period in European history. Key developments set a tone that would last even after the specifically medieval centuries had ended. Universities and Gothic art (often intertwined, as in the many American campuses that revived the Gothic style for their buildings) were an enduring legacy to Western society. Distinctive ideas about government, building on Christian and feudal traditions, constituted another medieval contribution.

The medieval period was also a special moment in the relationship between Europe and the regions around it. Significant change in the relationship occurred during the period, as Europe gained strength. But the opportunities to advance by imitation were particularly striking, from technology to science to trade and consumption. Even the medieval university may have had Arab origins, in the higher schools of the Muslim world. Imitation, indeed, unites the themes of the medieval period: the relative weakness but also the dynamism and the capacity to contribute durable themes to later periods in world history.

Medieval Europe warrants a particular comparison with other areas in which civilization was partially new during the postclassical period and where change and imitation proceeded rapidly. Divided political rule in Europe resembled conditions in west Africa and Japan (the only other feudal society in the period). Imitation targets can be compared among Europe, Africa, Japan, and Russia. But the Crusades suggest a distinctive expansionist spirit in Europe that also warrants attention, in suggesting a more aggressive interest in the wider world than the other emerging societies.

GLOBAL CONNECTIONS: Medieval Europe and the World

Western Europe in the Middle Ages developed something of a love-hate relationship with the world around it. During the early centuries of the Middle Ages, Europe seemed at the mercy of invasions, from the Vikings in the north or various nomadic groups pushing in from central Asia. European leaders were also keenly aware of the power of Islam, which controlled most of the Mediterranean including Spain. Most Europeans saw Islam as a dangerously false religion and an obvious threat.

At the same time, there was much to be learned from this wider world. During the Middle Ages Europeans actively copied a host of features from Islam, from law to science and art. They imported products and technologies from Asia. This process of imitation accelerated during the centuries of Mongol control, when European traders and travelers eagerly pushed into eastern Asia. A key question for Europe at the end of the Middle Ages involved how to gain greater control over the benefits that came from world contacts, while reducing the sense of threat. Partly through weakness, partly because of the advantages that Europeans learned from contact, the new civilization developed an active sense of global awareness.

Further Readings

For the Middle Ages generally, Joseph Strayer's *Western Europe in the Middle Ages* (1982) is a fine survey with an extensive bibliography. Key topics are covered in R. S. Lopez's *The Commercial Revolution of the Middle Ages, 950–1350* (1976) and C. H. Lawrence's *Medieval Monasticism: Forms of Religious Life in Western Europe in the Middle Ages* (1984). National histories are important for the period, particularly on political life; see J. W. Baldwin's *The Government of Philip Augustus: Foundations of French Royal Power in the Middle Ages* (1986); G. Barraclough's *The Origins of Modern Germany* (1984); and M. Chibnall's *Anglo-*

Norman England, 1066–1166 (1986). R. Barlett, *The Making of Medieval Europe* (1992), suggests that Western civilization was the product of cross-cultural fertilization.

Social history has dominated much recent research on the period. See P. Ariès and G. Duby, eds., *A History of Private Life*, vol. 2 (1984), and Barbara Hanawalt, *The Ties That Bound: Peasant Families in Medieval England* (1986), for important orientation in this area. David Herlihy's *Medieval Households* (1985) is a vital contribution, as is J. Chapelot and R. Fossier's *The Village and House in the Middle Ages* (1985). J. Kirshner and S. F. Wemple, eds., *Women of the Medieval World* (1985), is a good collection. On tensions in popular religion, see C. Bynum's *Jesus as Mother: Studies in the Spirituality of the High Middle Ages* (1982) and L. Little's *Religious Poverty and the Profit Economy in Medieval Europe* (1978). A highly readable account of medieval life is E. Leroy Ladurie's *Montaillou: The Promised Land of Error* (1979).

Several excellent studies take up the theme of technological change: J. Gimpel's *The Medieval Machine: The Industrial Revolution of the Middle Ages* (1977); Lynn White Jr.'s *Medieval Technology and Social Change* (1962); and David Landes' *Revolution in Time: Clocks and the Making of the Modern World* (1985). On environmental impact, see Roland Bechmann, *Trees and Man: The Forest in the Middle Ages* (1990).

On intellectual and artistic life, E. Gilson's *History of Christian Philosophy in the Middle Ages* (1954) is a brilliant sketch, and his *Reason and Revelation* (1956) focuses on key intellectual issues of the age. S. C. Ferruolo's *The Origins of the University* (1985) and N. Pevsner's *An Outline of European Architecture* (1963) deal with other important features; see also H. Berman's *Law and Revolution: The Formation of the Western Legal Tradition* (1983). On contacts, see Khalil Semaan, *Islam and the Medieval West: Aspects of Intercultural Relations* (1980). An intriguing classic, focused primarily on culture, is J. Huizinga's *The Waning of the Middle Ages* (1973).

On the Web

The postclassical period of the West witnessed the beginning of a new world order as well as the decline and collapse of the old one. This was visible in the patterns of daily life examined at http://www.learner.org/exhibits/middleages/.

New political systems were emerging to meet new conditions, as exemplified by the career of Charlemagne (http://www.humnet.ucla.edu/santiago/histchrl.html), and by the writing of the later English Magna Carta (http://www.archives.gov/exhibit_hall/featured_documents/magna_carta/ and http://www.yale.edu/lawweb/avalon/medieval/magframe.htm).

Manorial life underwent changes and new economic relations emerged as the monetization of labor (http://www1.enloe.wake.k12.nc.us/enloe/CandC/showme/trading.html) undermined the tradition of serfdom in Western Europe (http://www.fordham.edu/halsall/source/manumission.html and http://courses.washington.edu/balt/SCAND344/celms.htm).

The value, nature, and sources of human knowledge were also being reevaluated in the works of men such as Peter Abelard (http://www.fordham.edu/halsall/source/abelard-ssel.html and http://justus.anglican.org/resources/bio/142.html), Thomas Aquinas (http://www.utm.edu/research/iep/a/aquinas.htm), and those pursuing new avenues in both European and Islamic medicine and science (http://members.aol.com/McNelis/medsci_index.html).

This was not a period that witnessed the advancement of the position of women, but insight into the lives of medieval women, ordinary and extraordinary, can be found at http://www.womeninworldhistory.com/heroine3.html, http://www.umilta.net/, http://library.thinkquest.org/12834/text/distaffside.html, http://www.smu.edu/ijas/ and http://www2.sunysuffolk.edu/westn/essaymedieval.html#Women%20in%20Childbirth.

The Black Death had an impact on all facets of life in the Middle Ages. It can be explored at http://www.iath.virginia.edu/osheim/intro.html, http://www.nytimes.com/books/first/o/oldstone-viruses.html, http://www.brown.edu/Departments/Italian_Studies/dweb/plague/origins/spread.shtml, http://www.byu.edu/ipt/projects/middleages/LifeTimes/Plague.html, and http://www.fidnet.com/~weid/plague.htm.

CHAPTER 16

THE AMERICAS ON THE EVE OF INVASION

The Toltec political and cultural influence spread from its capital at Tula in northern Mexico (shown here as it looks today) to places as far south as Chichén Itzá in Yucatan. The warriors shown here served as columns to support the roof of this large temple.

In central Mexico on the last day of the year and the end of the 52-year cycle of the religious calendar, all the fires in the land, in every temple and in every humble home, were extinguished. At a small temple, not far from today's Mexico City, a prisoner was sacrificed and a new fire kindled on his body. If the gods honored their prayers and the fire took hold, runners would then light their torches in the new flames and carry the fire to every town and village. Life would continue at least for another 52-year cycle, until at some point the gods would create a great cataclysm to destroy the world, as had happened four times in the past.

Some of these concepts and practices of the Aztec peoples of central Mexico were widely shared by many peoples in the Americas. They represent the distinctive cultural processes of the Americas that had continued to develop in the postclassic period after 900 C.E.

By 1500, the Americas were densely populated in many places by Indian peoples long indigenous to the New World. Of course, the term **Indian** is derived from a mistake Columbus made when he thought he had reached the Indies, what Europeans called India and the lands beyond, but the label is also misleading because it implies a common identity among the peoples of the Americas that did not exist until after the arrival of Europeans. *Indian* as a term to describe all the peoples of the Americas could have a meaning only when there were non-Indians from which to distinguish them. Still, the term has been used for so long—and is still in use by many Native Americans today—that we will continue to use it.

As should already be clear, there were many Indian peoples with a vast array of cultural achievements. The variety of cultural patterns and ways of life of pre-Columbian civilizations makes it impossible to discuss each in detail here, but we can focus on a few areas where major civilizations developed, based on earlier achievements. By concentrating on these regions, we can demonstrate the continuity of civilization in the Americas. We shall examine in some detail Mesoamerica, especially central Mexico, and the Andean heartland. In both these areas great imperial states were in place when European expansion brought them into direct contact with the Old World. We shall also discuss in less detail a few areas influenced by the centers of civilization—and some whose development seems to have been independent of them—to provide an overview of the Americas on the eve of invasion.

900 C.E.	1150 C.E.	1300 C.E.	1450 C.E.
900 End of Intermediate Horizon and decline of Tihuanaco and Huari	**1150** Fall of Tula, disintegration of Toltec Empire	**1325** Aztecs established in central Mexico; Tenochtitlan founded	**1471–1493** Inca Topac Yupanqui increases areas under control
900–1465 Chimor Empire based on Chan Chan on north coast	**1200–1500** Mississipian culture flourishes	**1350** Incas established in Cuzco area	**1493–1527** Huayna Capac expands into Ecuador; his death results in civil war
968 Tula established by Toltecs		**1434** Creation of triple alliance	**1502–1520** Moctezuma II
1000 Toltec conquest of Chichén Itzá and influence in Yucatan		**1434–1471** Great expansion under Inca Pachacuti	
		1434–1472 Rule of Nezhualcoyotl at Texcoco	
		1438 Incas dominate Cuzco and southern highlands	
		1440–1469 Moctezuma I	

Postclassic Mesoamerica, 1000–1500 C.E.

 Chief among the civilizations that followed the collapse of Teotihuacan and the abandonment of the classic Maya cities in the 8th century C.E. were the Toltecs and later the Aztecs, who built on the achievements of their predecessors but rarely surpassed them except in political and military organization. The Toltecs created a large empire whose influence extended far beyond central Mexico. In the 15th century, the Aztecs rose from humble beginnings to create an extensive empire organized for war, motivated by religious zeal, and based on a firm agrarian base.

With the collapse of Teotihuacan in central Mexico and the abandonment of the classical Maya cities in the 8th century C.E., Mesoamerica experienced significant political and cultural change. In central Mexico, nomadic peoples from the north took advantage of the political vacuum to move into the richer lands. Among these peoples were the Toltecs, who established a capital at Tula about 968. **Toltec culture** adopted many features from the sedentary peoples and added a strongly militaristic ethic. This included the cult of sacrifice and war that is often portrayed in Toltec art. Later Mesoamerican peoples, such as the Aztecs, had some historical memory of the Toltecs and thought of them as the givers of civilization. However, the archeological record indicates that Toltec accomplishments often were fused or confused with those of Teotihuacan in the memory of the Toltecs' successors.

The Toltec Heritage

Among the legends that survived about the Toltecs were those of **Topiltzin,** a Toltec leader and apparently a priest dedicated to the god **Quetzalcoatl** (the Feathered Serpent) who later became confused with the god himself in the legends. Apparently, Topiltzin, a religious reformer, was involved in a struggle for priestly or political power with another faction. When he lost, Topiltzin and his followers went into exile, promising to return to claim his throne on the same date, according to the cyclical calendar system. Supposedly, Topiltzin and his followers sailed for Yucatan; there is much evidence of Toltec influence in that region. The legend of Topiltzin–Quetzalcoatl was well known to the Aztecs and may have influenced their response when the Europeans arrived.

The Toltecs created an empire that extended over much of central Mexico, and their influence spread from their capital, Tula, to areas as far away as Guatemala. About 1000 C.E., Chichén Itzá in Yucatan was conquered by Toltec warriors, and it and several other cities were ruled for a long time by central Mexican dynasties or by Maya rulers under Toltec influence.

Toltec influence spread northward as well. Obsidian was mined in northern Mexico, and the Toltecs may have traded for turquoise in the American Southwest. It has been suggested that the great Anasazi adobe town at Chaco Canyon in New Mexico was abandoned when the Toltec Empire fell and the trade in local turquoise ended.

How far eastward Toltec influence spread is a matter of dispute. Was there contact between Mesoamerica and the elaborate culture and concentrated towns of the Hopewell peoples of the Ohio and Mississippi valleys, discussed in Chapter 8? Scholars disagree. Eventually, in the lower Mississippi valley from about 700 C.E., elements of Hopewell culture seem to have been enriched by external contact, perhaps with Mexico. This Mississippian culture, which flourished between 1200 and 1500 C.E., was based on maize and bean agriculture. Towns, usually located along rivers, had stepped temples made of earth, and sometimes large burial mounds. Some of the burials include well-produced pottery and other goods and seem to be accompanied by ritual executions or sacrifices of servants or wives. This indicates social stratification in the society. Cahokia, near East St. Louis, Illinois, covered 5 square miles and may have had more than 30,000 people in and around its center. Its largest earthen pyramid, now called Monk's Mound, covers 15 acres and is comparable in size to the largest pyramids of the classic period in Mexico. Many of these cultural features seem to suggest contact with Mesoamerica.

The Aztec Rise to Power

The Toltec Empire lasted until about 1150, when it apparently was destroyed by nomadic invaders from the north, who also seem to have sacked Tula about that time. The center of population and political power in central Mexico shifted to the valley of Mexico and especially to the shores of the large chain of lakes in that basin. These provided a rich aquatic environment. The shores of the lakes were dotted with settlements and towns and supported a dense population. Of the approximately 3000 square miles in the basin of the valley, about 400 square miles were under water. The lakes became the cultural heartland and population center of Mexico in the postclassic period. In the unstable world of post-Toltec Mesoamerica, various peoples and cities jockeyed for control of the lakes. The winners of this struggle, the Aztecs (or, as they called themselves, the *Mexica*), eventually built a great empire, but when they emerged on the historical scene they were the most unlikely candidates for power.

The Aztec rise to power and formation of an imperial state was as spectacular as it was rapid. According to some of their legends, the Mexica had once inhabited the central valley and had known agriculture and the "civilized" life but had lived in exile to the north in a place called Aztlan (from whence we get the name *Aztec*). This may be an exaggeration by people who wanted to lay claim to a distinguished

heritage. Other sources indicate that the Aztecs were simply one of the nomadic tribes that used the political anarchy, after the fall of the Toltecs, to penetrate the area of sedentary agricultural peoples. Like the ancient Egyptians, the Aztecs rewrote history to suit their purposes.

What seems clear is that the Aztecs were a group of about 10,000 people who migrated to the shores of Lake Texcoco (Map 16.1) in the central valley of Mexico around 1325. After the fall of the Toltec Empire, the central valley was inhabited by a mixture of peoples: Chichimec migrants from the northwest and various groups of sedentary farmers. In this period, the area around the lake was dominated by several tribes or peoples organized into city-states. Much like medieval Europe, this was a world of political maneuver and state marriages, competing powers and shifting alliances. These political units claimed authority on the basis of their military power and

Map 16.1 *Central Mexico and Lake Texcoco. An aquatic environment at the heart of the Aztec empire.*

their connections to Toltec culture. Many of these peoples spoke Nahuatl, the language the Toltecs had spoken. The Aztecs also spoke this language, a fact that made their rise to power and their eventual claims to legitimacy more acceptable.

An intrusive and militant group, the Aztecs were distrusted and disliked by the dominant powers of the area, but their fighting skills could be put to use, and this made them attractive as mercenaries or allies. For about a century the Aztecs wandered around the shores of the lake, being allowed to settle for a while and then driven out by more powerful neighbors.

In a period of warfare, the Aztecs had a reputation as tough warriors and fanatical followers of their gods, to whom they offered human sacrifices. This reputation made them both valued and feared. Their own legends held that their wanderings would end when they saw an eagle perched on a cactus with a serpent in its beak. Supposedly, this sign was seen on a marshy island in Lake Texcoco, and there, on that island and one nearby, the Mexica settled. The city of **Tenochtitlan** was founded about 1325.

From this secure base the Aztecs began to take a more active role in regional politics. Serving as mercenaries and then as allies brought prosperity to the Aztecs, especially to their ruler and the warrior nobles, who took lands and tribute from conquered towns. By 1428 Aztecs had emerged as an independent power. In 1434, Tenochtitlan created an alliance with two other city-states that controlled much of the central plateau. In reality, Tenochtitlan and the Aztecs dominated their allies and controlled the major share of the tribute and lands taken.

The Aztec Social Contract

Aztec domination extended from the Tarascan frontier about a hundred miles north of present-day Mexico City southward to the Maya area. Subject peoples were forced to pay tribute, surrender lands, and sometimes do military service for the growing Aztec Empire.

Aztec society had changed in the process of expansion and conquest. From a loose association of clans, the Mexica had become a stratified society under the authority of a supreme ruler. The histories were rewritten and the Mexica were described as a people chosen to serve the gods. Human sacrifice, long a part of Mesoamerican religion, greatly expanded into an enormous cult in which the military class played a central role as suppliers of war cap-

tives to be used as sacrificial victims. A few territories were left unconquered so that periodic "flower wars" could be staged in which both sides could obtain captives for sacrifice. Whatever the religious motivations of this cult, the Aztec rulers manipulated it as an effective means of political terror. By the time of Moctezuma II, the Aztec state was dominated by a king who represented civil power and served as a representative of the gods on earth. The cult of human sacrifice and conquest was united with the political power of the ruler and the nobility.

Religion and the Ideology of Conquest

Aztec religion incorporated many features that had long been part of the Mesoamerican belief system. Religion was a vast, uniting, and sometimes oppressive force in which little distinction was made between the world of the gods and the natural world. The traditional deities of Mesoamerica—the gods of rain, fire, water, corn, the sky, and the sun, many of whom had been worshiped as far back as the time of Teotihuacan—were venerated among the Aztecs. There were at least 128 major deities, but there seemed to be many more: Each deity had a female consort or feminine form because a basic duality was recognized in all things. Moreover, gods might have different forms or manifestations, somewhat like the avatars of the Hindu deities. Each god had at least five aspects, each associated with one of the cardinal directions and the center. Certain gods were thought to be the patrons of specific cities, ethnic groups, or occupations.

This extensive pantheon was supported by a round of yearly festivals and ceremonies that involved feasting and dancing along with penance and sacrifice. This complex array of gods can be organized into three major themes or cults. The first were the gods of fertility and the agricultural cycle, such as **Tlaloc,** the god of rain (called *Chac* by the Maya), and the gods and goddesses of water, maize, and fertility. A second group centered on the creator deities, the great gods and goddesses who had brought the universe into being. The story of their actions played a central role in Aztec cosmography. Much Aztec abstract and philosophical thought was devoted to the theme of creation. Finally, the cult of warfare and sacrifice built on the preexisting Mesoamerican traditions that had been expanding since Toltec times and, under the militaristic Aztec state, became the cult of the state. **Huitzilopochtli,** the Aztec tribal patron, became the central figure of this cult.

The Aztecs revered the great traditional deities—such as Tlaloc and Quetzalcoatl, the ancient god of civilization—so holy to the Toltecs, but their own tribal deity, Huitzilopochtli, was paramount. The Aztecs identified him with the old sun god, and they saw him as a warrior in the daytime sky fighting to give life and warmth to the world against the forces of the night. To carry out that struggle, the sun needed strength, and just as the gods had sacrificed themselves for humankind, the nourishment the gods needed most was that which was most precious: human life in the form of hearts and blood. The great temple of Tenochtitlan was dedicated to both Huitzilopochtli and Tlaloc. The tribal deity of the Aztecs and the ancient agricultural god of the sedentary peoples of Mesoamerica were thus united.

In fact, although human sacrifice had long been a part of Mesoamerican religion, it expanded considerably in the postclassic period of militarism. Warrior cults and the militaristic images of jaguars and eagles devouring human hearts were characteristic of Toltec art. The Aztecs simply took an existing tendency and carried it further. Both the types and frequency of sacrifice increased, and a whole symbolism and ritual, which included ritual cannibalism, developed as part of the cult (Figure 16.1). How much of Aztec sacrifice was the result of religious conviction and how much was a tactic of terror and political control by the rulers and priests is still open to debate.

Beneath the surface of this polytheism, there was also a sense of spiritual unity. **Nezhualcoyotl,** the king of Texcoco, wrote hymns to the "lord of the close vicinity," an invisible creative force that supported all the gods. Yet his conception of a kind of monotheism, much like that of Pharaoh Akhnaten in Egypt, appears to have been too abstract and never gained great popularity.

Although the bloody aspects of Aztec religion have gained much attention, we must also realize that the Aztecs concerned themselves with many of the great religious and spiritual questions that have preoccupied other civilizations: Is there life after death? What is the meaning of life? What does it mean to live a good life? Do the gods really exist?

Nezhualcoyotl, whose poetry survived in oral form and was written down in the 16th century, wondered about life after death:

> Do flowers go to the land of the dead?
>
> In the Beyond, are we dead or do we still live?
>
> Where is the source of light, since that which gives life hides itself?

Figure 16.1 *Human sacrifice was practiced by many Mesoamerican peoples, but the Aztecs apparently expanded its practice for political and religious reasons.*

As in the Vedas of ancient India, he also wondered about the existence of the gods:

> Are you real, are you fixed?
>
> Only You dominate all things
>
> The Giver of Life.
>
> Is this true?
>
> Perhaps, as they say, it is not true.

Aztec religious art and poetry are filled with images of flowers, birds, and song, all of which the Aztecs greatly admired, as well as human hearts and blood, the "precious water" needed to sustain the gods. This mixture of images makes the symbolism of Aztec religion difficult for modern observers to appreciate.

Aztec religion depended on a complex mythology that explained the birth and history of the gods and their relationship to peoples, and on a religious symbolism that infused all aspects of life. As we have seen, the Mesoamerican calendar system was religious, and many ceremonies coincided with particular points in the calendar cycle. Moreover, the Aztecs also believed in a cyclical view of history, and that the world had been destroyed four times before and would be destroyed again. Thus, there was a certain fatalism in Aztec thought and a premonition that eventually the sacrifices would be insufficient and the gods would again bring catastrophe.

Tenochtitlan: The Foundation of Heaven

The Aztecs considered their capital city a sacred space, or as they called it, the "foundation of Heaven." The city-state with its ruler–spokesman was a key central Mexican concept, and it applied to Tenochtitlan. It became a great metropolis, with a central zone of palaces and whitewashed temples, as shown in Figure 16.2. This zone was surrounded by adobe brick residential districts, smaller palaces, and markets. The design and construction were outstanding. Hernán Cortés, the Spanish conqueror who viewed the city, reported, "The stone masonry and the woodwork are equally good; they could not be bettered anywhere." There were gardens, and a zoo was kept for the ruler's enjoyment. The nobility had houses two stories high, sometimes with gardens on the roofs. Tlatelolco also had impressive temples and palaces, and its large market was the most important place of trade and exchange. By 1519, the city covered about 5 square miles. It had a population of 150,000, larger than contemporary European cities such as Seville and Paris.

Its island location gave Tenochtitlan a peculiar character. Set in the midst of a lake, the city was connected to the shores by four broad causeways and was crisscrossed by canals that allowed the constant canoe traffic on the lake access to the city. Each city ward, controlled by a **calpulli,** or kin group, maintained its

Figure 16.2 *The great Aztec capital of Tenochtitlan was dominated by the pyramid and twin temples of Huitzilopochtli, shown here in a modern miniature reconstruction.*

neighborhood temples and civic buildings. The structural achievement was impressive. A Spanish foot soldier who saw it in 1519 wrote,

> Gazing on such wonderful sights, we did not know what to say, or whether what appeared before us was real, for on one side, on the land, there were great cities, and in the lake ever many more, and the lake was crowded with canoes, and in the causeway were many bridges at intervals, and in front of us stood the great city of Mexico.

Tenochtitlan was the heart of an empire and drew tribute and support from its allies and dependents, but in theory it was still just a city-state ruled by a headman, just like the 50 or more other city-states that dotted the central plateau. Present-day Mexico City rises on the site of the former Aztec capital.

Feeding the People: The Economy of the Empire

Feeding the great population of Tenochtitlan and the Aztec confederation in general depended on traditional forms of agriculture and on innovations developed by the Aztecs. Lands of conquered peoples often were appropriated, and food sometimes was demanded as tribute. In and around the lake, however, the Aztecs adopted an ingenious system of irrigated agriculture by building **chinampas** for agriculture. These were beds of aquatic weeds, mud, and earth that had been placed in frames made of cane and rooted to the lake floor. They formed artificial floating islands about 17 feet long and 100 to 330 feet wide. This narrow construction allowed the water to reach all the plants, and willow trees were also planted at intervals to give shade and help fix the roots. Much of the land of Tenochtitlan itself was chinampa in origin, and in the southern end of the lake, more than 20,000 acres of chinampas were constructed. The yield from chinampa agriculture was high: Four corn crops a year were possible. Apparently, this system of irrigated agriculture had been used in preclassic days, but a rise in the level of the lakes had made it impossible to continue. After 1200, however, lowering water levels once again stimulated chinampa construction, which the Aztecs carried out on a grand scale.

Production by the Aztec peasantry, whom we see at work in Figure 16.3, and tribute provided the basic foods. In each Aztec community, the local clan apportioned the lands, some of which were also set

Figure 16.3 *Agriculture was the basis of Aztec society, and a diet centered on maize sustained the dense populations of the Valley of Mexico. The plow was unknown, and planting was done with a digging stick.*

aside for support of the temples and the state. In addition, individual nobles might have private estates, which were worked by servants or slaves from conquered peoples. Each community had periodic markets—according to various cycles in the calendar system, such as every 5 and 13 days—in which a wide variety of goods were exchanged. Cacao beans and gold dust sometimes were used as currency, but much trade was done as barter. The great market at Tlatelolco operated daily and was controlled by the special merchant class, or **pochteca,** which specialized in long-distance trade in luxury items such as plumes of tropical birds and cacao. The markets were highly regulated and under the control of inspectors and special judges. Despite the importance of markets, this was not a market economy as we usually understand it.

The state controlled the use and distribution of many commodities and redistributed the vast amounts of tribute received from subordinate peoples. Tribute levels were assigned according to whether the subject peoples had accepted Aztec rule or had fought against it. Those who surrendered paid less. Tribute payments, such as food, slaves, and sacrificial victims, served political and economic ends. More than 120,000 mantles of cotton cloth alone were collected as tribute each year and sent to Tenochtitlan. The Aztec state redistributed these goods. After the original conquests, it rewarded its nobility richly, and the commoners received far less.

Aztec Society in Transition

Aztec society became more hierarchical as the empire grew and social classes with different functions developed, although the older organization based on the calpulli never disappeared. Tribute was drawn from subject peoples, but Aztec society confronted technological barriers that made it difficult to maintain the large population of central Mexico.

Widening Social Gulf

During their wanderings, the Aztecs had been divided into seven calpulli, or clans, a form of organization that they later expanded and adapted to their imperial position. The calpulli were no longer only kinship groups but also residential groupings, which might include neighbors, allies, and dependants. Much of Aztec local life was based on the calpulli, which performed important functions such as distributing land to heads of households, organizing labor gangs and military units in times of war, and maintaining a temple and school. Calpulli were governed by councils of family heads, but not all families were equal, nor were all calpulli of equal status.

The calpulli obviously had been the ancient and basic building block of Aztec society. In the origins of Aztec society every person, noble and commoner, had belonged to a calpulli, but Aztec power increased and the rule of the empire expanded. The calpulli had been transformed, and other forms of social stratification had emerged. As Aztec power expanded, a class of nobility emerged, based on certain privileged families in the most distinguished calpulli. Originating from the lineages that headed calpulli and from marriages, military achievements, or service to the state, this group of nobles accumulated high offices, private lands, and other advantages. The most prominent families in the calpulli, those who had dominated leadership roles and formed a kind of local nobility, eventually were overshadowed by the military and administrative nobility of the Aztec state.

Although some commoners might be promoted to noble status, most nobles were born into the class. Nobles controlled the priesthood and the military leadership. In fact, the military was organized into various ranks based on experience and success in taking captives (Figure 16.4). Military virtues were linked to the cult of sacrifice and infused the whole society; they became the justification for the nobility's status. The "flowery death," or death while taking prisoners for the sacrificial knife, was the fitting end to a noble life and ensured eternity in the highest heaven—a reward also promised to women who died in childbirth. The military was highly ritualized. There were orders of warriors: The Jaguar and Eagle "Knights" and other groups each had a distinctive uniform and ritual and fought together as units. Banners, cloaks, and other insignia marked off the military ranks.

The social gulf that separated the nobility from the commoners was widening as the empire grew. Egalitarian principles that may have existed in Aztec life disappeared, as happened among the warring German tribes of early medieval Europe. Social distinctions were made apparent by the use of and restrictions on clothing, hairstyles, uniforms, and other symbols of rank. The imperial family became the most distinguished of the pipiltin families.

As the nobility broke free from their old calpulli and acquired private lands, a new class of workers almost like serfs was created to serve as laborers on these lands. Unlike the commoners attached to the land-controlling calpulli, these workers did not control land and worked at the will of others. Their status was low, but it was still above that of the slaves, who might have been war captives, criminals, or peo-

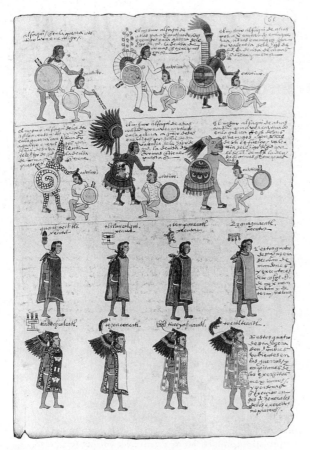

Figure 16.4 *In the militarized society of the Aztec Empire, warriors were organized into regiments and groups distinguished by their uniforms. They gained rank and respect by capturing enemies for sacrifice. Note the symbolic gripping of the defeated captives' hair as a sign of military success.*

ple who had sold themselves into bondage to escape hunger. Finally, there were other social groups. The scribes, artisans, and healers all were part of an inter-mediate group that was especially important in the larger cities. The long-distance merchants formed a sort of calpulli with their own patron gods, privileges, and internal divisions. They sometimes served as spies or agents for the Aztec military, but they were subject to restrictions that hindered their entry into or rivalry with the nobility.

It is possible to see an emerging conflict between the nobility and the commoners and to interpret this as a class struggle, but some specialists emphasize that to interpret Aztec society on that basis is to impose West-ern concepts on a different reality. Corporate bodies such as the calpulli, temple maintenance associations, and occupational groups cut across class and remained important in Aztec life. Competition between corpo-rate groups often was more apparent and more violent than competition between social classes.

Overcoming Technological Constraints

Membership in society was defined by participation in various wider groups, such as the calpulli or a spe-cific social class, and by gender roles and definitions. Aztec women assumed a variety of roles. Peasant women helped in the fields, but their primary domain was the household, where child-rearing and cooking took up much time. Above all, weaving skill was highly regarded. The responsibility for training young girls fell on the older women. Marriages often were arranged between lineages, and virginity at marriage was highly regarded for young women. Polygamy existed among the nobility, but the peasants were monogamous. Aztec women could inherit property and pass it to their heirs. The rights of Aztec women seem to have been fully recognized, but in political and social life their role, though complementary to that of men, remained subordinate.

The technology of the Americas limited social development in a variety of ways. Here we can see a significant difference between the lives of women in Mesoamerica and in the Mediterranean world. In the maize-based economies of Mesoamerica, women spent six hours a day grinding corn by hand on stone boards, or *metates*, to prepare the household's food. Although similar hand techniques were used in ancient Egypt, they were eventually replaced by ani-mal- or water-powered mills that turned wheat into flour. The miller or baker of Rome or medieval Europe could do the work of hundreds of women. Maize was among the simplest and most productive cereals to grow but among the most time-consuming to prepare. Without the wheel or suitable animals for power, the Indian civilizations were unable to free women from the 30 to 40 hours a week that went into preparing the basic food.

Finally, we must consider the size of the popula-tion of the Aztec state. Estimates have varied widely, from as little as 1.5 million to more than 25 million, but there is considerable evidence that population density was high, resulting in a total population that was far greater than previously suspected. Some his-torical demographers estimate that the population of central Mexico under Aztec control reached over 20

Document

Aztec Women and Men

In the mid-16th century, Bernardino de Sahagún, a Spanish missionary, prepared an extraordinary encyclopedia of Aztec culture. His purpose was to gather this information to learn the customs and beliefs of the Indians and their language in order to better convert them. Although Sahagún hated the Indian religion, he came to admire many aspects of their culture. His work, *The General History of the Things of New Spain,* is one of the first ethnographies and a remarkable compendium of Aztec culture. Sahagún used many Indian informants to tell him about the days before the European arrival, and even though this work dates from the postconquest era, it contains much useful information about earlier Aztec life.

In the following excerpts, the proper behavior for people in different roles in Aztec society are described by the Aztecs themselves.

Father

One's father is the source of lineage. He is the sincere one. One's father is diligent, solicitous, compassionate, sympathetic, a careful administrator of his household. He rears, he teaches others, he advises, he admonishes one. He is exemplary; he leads a model life. He stores up for himself; he stores up for others. He cares for his assets; he saves for others. He is thrifty; he saves for the future, teaches thrift. He regulates, distributes with care, establishes order.

The bad father is incompassionate, negligent, unreliable. He is unfeeling … a shirker, a loafer, a sullen worker.

Mother

One's mother has children; she suckles them. Sincere, vigilant, agile, she is an energetic worker—diligent, watchful, solicitous, full of anxiety. She teaches people; she is attentive to them. She caresses, she serves others; she is apprehensive for their welfare; she is careful, thrifty—constantly at work.

The bad mother is evil, dull, stupid, sleepy, lazy. She is a squanderer, a petty thief, a deceiver, a fraud. Unreliable, she is one who loses things through neglect or anger, who heeds no one. She is disrespectful, inconsiderate, disregarding, careless. She shows the way to disobedience; she expounds nonconformity.

The Rulers

The ruler is a shelter—fierce, revered, famous, esteemed, well-reputed, renowned.

The good ruler is a protector: one who carries his subjects in his arms, who unites them, who brings them together. He rules, he takes responsibilities, assumes burdens. He carries his subjects in his cape; he bears them in his arms. He governs; he is obeyed. To him as a shelter, as refuge, there is recourse….

The bad ruler is a wild beast, a demon of the air, an ocelot, a wolf—infamous, avoided, detested as a respecter of nothing. He terrifies with his gaze; he makes the earth rumble; he implants; he spreads fear. He is wished dead.

The Noble

The noble has a mother, a father. He resembles his parents. The good noble is obedient, cooperative, a follower of his parents' ways, a discreet worker; attentive, willing. He follows the ways of his parents; he resembles his father; he becomes his father's successor; he assumes his lot.

One of noble lineage is a follower of the exemplary life, a taker of the good example of others, a seeker, a follower of the exemplary life. He speaks eloquently; he is soft-spoken, virtuous, deserving of gratitude. He is noble of heart, gentle of word, discreet, well-reared, well-taught. He is moderate, energetic, inquiring, inquisitive. He scratches the earth with a thorn. He is one who fasts, who starves his entrails, who parches his lips. He provides nourishment to others. He sustains one, he serves food, he provides comfort. He is a concealer [of himself], a belittler of himself. He magnifies and praises others. He is a mourner for the dead, a doer of penances, a gracious speaker, devout, godly, desirable, wanted, memorable.

The bad noble is ungrateful and forgetful, a debaser, a disparager of things, contemptuous of others, arrogant, bragging. He creates disorder, glories over his lineage, extols his own virtues.

The Mature Common Woman

The good mature woman is candid. She is resolute, firm of heart, constant—not to be dismayed; brave like a man; vigorous, resolute, persevering—not one to falter. She is long-suffering; she accepts reprimands calmly—endures things like a man. She becomes firm—takes courage. She is intent. She gives of herself. She goes in humility. She exerts herself.

The bad woman is thin, tottering, weak—an inconstant companion, unfriendly. She annoys others, chagrins them, shames, oppresses one. She becomes impatient; she loses hope, becomes embarrassed—chagrined. Evil is her life; she lives in shame.

The Weaver of Designs

She concerns herself with using thread, works with thread. The good weaver of designs is skilled—a maker of varicolored capes, an outliner of designs, a blender of colors, a joiner of pieces, a matcher of pieces, a person of good memory. She does things dexterously. She weaves designs. She selects. She weaves tightly. She forms borders. She forms the neck....

The bad weaver of designs is untrained—silly, foolish, unobservant, unskilled of hand, ignorant, stupid. She tangles the thread, she harms her work—she spoils it.

The Physician

The physician is a knower of herbs, of roots, of trees, of stones; she is experienced in these. She is one who conducts examinations; she is a woman of experience, of trust, of professional skill: a counselor.

The good physician is a restorer, a provider of health, a relaxer—one who makes people feel well, who envelops one in ashes. She cures people; she provides them health; she lances them; she bleeds them … pierces them with an obsidian lancet.

Questions: In what ways do the expectations for men and women differ in Aztec society? To what extent do the roles for men and women in Aztec society differ from our own? Did the Aztecs value the same characteristics as our own and other historical societies?

million, excluding the Maya areas. This underlines the extraordinary ability of the Aztec state to intimidate and control such vast numbers of people.

A Tribute Empire

Each city-state was ruled by a speaker chosen from the nobility. The Great Speaker, the ruler of Tenochtitlan, was first among supposed equals. He was in effect the emperor, with great private wealth and public power, and was increasingly considered a living god. His court was magnificent and surrounded with elaborate rituals. Those who approached him could not look him in the eye and were required to throw dirt upon their heads as a sign of humility. In theory he was elected, but his election was really a choice between siblings of the same royal family. The prime minister held a position of tremendous power and usually was a close relative of the ruler. There was a governing council; in theory, the rulers of the other cities in the alliance also had a say in government, but in reality most power was in the hands of the Aztec ruler and his chief advisor.

During a century of Aztec expansion, a social and political transformation had taken place. The position and nature of the old calpulli clans had changed radically, and a newly powerful nobility with a deified and nearly absolute ruler had emerged. The ancient cult of military virtues had been elevated to a supreme position as the religion of the state, and the double purpose of securing tribute for the state and obtaining victims for Huitzilopochtli drove further Aztec conquests.

The empire was never integrated, and local rulers often stayed in place to act as tribute collectors for the Aztec overlords. In many ways the Aztec Empire was simply an expansion of long-existing Mesoamerican concepts and institutions of government, and it was not unlike the subject city-states over which it gained control. These city-states, in turn, were often left unchanged if they recognized Aztec supremacy and met their obligations of labor and tribute. Tribute payments served both an economic and a political function, concentrating power and wealth in the Aztec capital. Archeologists at the recent excavations of the Great Temple beneath the center of Mexico City have been impressed by the large number of offerings and objects that came from the farthest ends of the empire and beyond. At the frontiers, neighboring states such as the Tarascans of Michoacan preserved their freedom, while within the empire independent kingdoms such as Tlaxcala maintained a fierce opposition to the Aztecs. There were many revolts against Aztec rule or a particular tribute burden, which the Aztecs often put down ruthlessly.

In general, the Aztec system was a success because it aimed at exerting political domination and not necessarily direct administrative or territorial control. In the long run, however, the increasing social stresses created by the rise of the nobles and the system of terror and tribute imposed on subject peoples were internal weaknesses that contributed to the Aztec Empire's collapse.

The Aztecs were a continuation of the long process of civilization in Mesoamerica. The civilizations of the classic era did not simply disappear in central Mexico or among the Maya in Yucatan and Central America, but they were reinterpreted and adapted to new political and social realities. When Europeans arrived in Mexico, they assumed that what they found was the culmination of Indian civilization, when in fact it was the militarized afterglow of earlier achievements.

In Depth

The "Troubling" Civilizations of the Americas

From the first encounter with the peoples of the Americas, European concepts and judgments about civilization, barbarism, morality, power, politics, and justice were constantly called into question. The American Indian societies had many religious ideas and practices that shocked Christian observers, and aspects of their social and familial arrangements clashed with European sensibilities. Those sensibilities often were influenced by religious and political considerations. Many of those who most condemned human sacrifice, polygamy, or the despotism of Indian rulers were also those who tried to justify European conquest and control, mass violence, and theft on a continental scale. Other European voices also were heard. Not long after the Spanish conquests in the 16th century, defenders of Indian rights came forward to argue that despite certain "unfortunate" habits, Indian civilization was no less to be admired than that of the ancient (and pagan) Romans and Greeks.

For Western civilization, evaluating and judging non-Western or past societies has always been a complex business that has mixed elements of morality, politics, religion, and self-perception along with the record of what is observed or considered to be reality. That complexity is probably just as true for Chinese, Persian, or any culture trying to understand another. Still, Western society seems to have been particularly troubled by the American civilizations, with their peculiar combination of Neolithic technology and imperial organization. At times this has led to abhorrence and rejection—as of Aztec sacrifice—but at other times it has led to a kind of utopian romanticism in which the accomplishments of the Indian past are used as a critique of the present and a political program for the future.

The existence of **Inca socialism** is a case in point. Some early Spanish authors portrayed Inca rule as despotic, but others saw it as a kind of utopia. Shortly after the conquest of Peru, Garcilaso de la Vega, the son of a Spaniard and an Indian noblewoman, wrote a glowing history of his mother's people in which he presented an image of the Inca Empire as a carefully organized system in which every community contributed to the whole and the state regulated the distribution of resources on the basis of need and reciprocity. There was some truth in this view, but it ignored some aspects of exploitation as well. In the 20th century, Peruvian socialists, faced with underdevelopment and social inequality in their country, used this utopian view of Inca society as a possible model for their own future. Their interpretation and that of historians who later wrote of Inca socialism tended to ignore the hierarchy in the Inca Empire and the fact that the state extracted labor and goods from the subject communities to support the nobles, who held extensive power. The utopian view of the Incas was no less political than the despotic view. Perhaps the lesson here is that what we see in the past often depends on what we think about the present or what we want for the future.

But if Inca socialism and despotism have fascinated students of the past, Aztec religion has caught the imagination of historians and the general public. It causes us to ask how a civilization as advanced as this could engage in a practice so cruel and, to us, so morally reprehensible. Perhaps nothing challenges our appreciation of the American civilizations more than the extensive evidence of ritual torture and human sacrifice, which among the Aztecs reached staggering proportions. On some occasions thousands of people were slain, usually by having their hearts ripped out.

First, we must put these practices in perspective. Cruelty and violence can be found in many cultures, and to a world that has seen genocide, mass killings, and atomic warfare, the Aztec practices are not so different from what our own age has seen. Certain customs in many past civilizations and present cultures seem to us strange, cruel, and immoral. We find Aztec human sacrifice particularly abhorrent, but such practices also were found among the ancient Canaanites and the Celtic peoples, and the Old Testament story of Abraham and Isaac, though its message is against such sacrifice, reflects a known practice. Human sacrifice was practiced in pre-Christian Scandinavia and ancient India. Although by the time of Confucius human sacrifice of wives and retainers at the burial of a ruler was no longer practiced in China, the custom had been known. The issue of sati, the Hindu ritual suicide of the widow on the funeral pyre of her husband, raged in India in the 19th century. The Aztecs certainly were not alone in taking human life as a religious rite. Whatever our moral judgments about such customs, it remains the historian's responsibility to understand them in the context of their own culture and time.

How have historians tried to explain or understand Aztec human sacrifice? Some defenders of

Aztec culture have seen it as a limited phenomenon, greatly exaggerated by the Spanish for political purposes. Many scholars have seen it as a religious act central to the Aztec belief that humans must sacrifice that which was most precious to them—life—to receive the sun, rain, and other blessings of the gods that make life possible. Others have viewed Aztec practice as the intentional manipulation and expansion of a widespread phenomenon that had long existed among many American peoples. In other words, the Aztec rulers, priests, and nobility used the cult of war and large-scale human sacrifice for political purposes, to terrorize their neighbors and subdue the lower classes. Another possible explanation is demographic. If central Mexico was as densely populated as we believe, then the sacrifices may have been a kind of population control.

Other interpretations have been even more startling. Anthropologist Marvin Harris has suggested that Aztec sacrifice, accompanied by ritual cannibalism, was a response to a lack of protein. He argued that in the Old World, human sacrifice was replaced by animal sacrifice, but in Mesoamerica, which lacked cattle and sheep, that transformation never took place. Harris called the Aztec Empire a "cannibal kingdom." Other scholars have strongly objected to Harris' interpretation of the evidence, which gave little attention to the ritual aspects of these acts. Still, human sacrifice shades all assessments of Aztec civilization.

These debates ultimately raise important questions about the role of moral judgments in historical analysis and the way in which our vision of the past is influenced by our own political, moral, ethical, and social programs. We cannot and perhaps should not abandon those programs, but we must always try to understand other times and other peoples in their own terms.

Questions: What special features of Aztec civilization must be explained? Are they really distinctive? What explanations are most persuasive in terms of historical sensitivity and contemporary standards? Are there features of 21st-century society that are similar to those of Aztec civilization and that later generations will need to explain?

Twantinsuyu: World of the Incas

 After about 1300 C.E. in the Andean cultural hearth, a new civilization emerged and eventually spread its control over the whole region. The Inca empire, or **Twantinsuyu,** was a highly centralized system that integrated various ethnic groups into an imperial state. Extensive irrigated agriculture supported a state religion and a royal ancestor cult. With notable achievements in architecture and metallurgy, the Incas, like the Aztecs, incorporated many elements of the civilizations that preceded them.

Almost at the same time that the Aztecs extended their control over much of Mesoamerica, a great imperial state was rising in the Andean highlands, and it eventually became an empire some 3000 miles in extent (Map 16.2). The Inca Empire incorporated many aspects of previous Andean cultures but fused them together in new ways. With a genius for state organization and bureaucratic control over peoples of different cultures and languages, it achieved a level of integration and domination previously unknown in the Americas.

Throughout the Andean cultural hearth, after the breakup of the large "intermediate horizon" states of Tihuanaco and Huari (c. 550–1000 C.E.), several smaller regional states continued to exercise some power. Unlike the breakdown of power that took place in postclassic Mesoamerica, in the Andean zone many large states continued to be important. Some states in the Andean highlands on the broad open areas near Lake Titicaca and the states along rivers on the north coast, such as those in the Moche valley, remained centers of agricultural activity and population density. This was a period of war between rival local chiefdoms and small states and in some ways was an Andean parallel to the post-Toltec militaristic era in Mesoamerica. Of these states, the coastal kingdom of Chimor, centered on its capital of Chan-Chan, emerged as the most powerful. Between 900 and its conquest by the Incas in 1465, it gained control of most of the north coast of Peru.

The Inca Rise to Power

While Chimor spread its control over 600 miles of the coast, in the southern Andean highlands, where there were few large urban areas, ethnic groups and

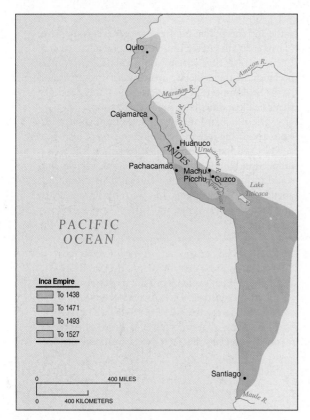

Map 16.2 *Inca Expansion. Each ruler expanded the empire in a series of campaigns to increase wealth and political control.*

politics struggled over the legacy of Tihuanaco. Among these groups were several related Quechua-speaking clans, or ayllus, living near Cuzco, an area that had been under the influence of Huari but had not been particularly important. Their own legends stated that 10 related clans emerged from caves in the region and were taken to Cuzco by a mythical leader. Wherever their origins, by about 1350 C.E. they lived in and around Cuzco, and by 1438 they had defeated their hostile neighbors in the area. At this point under their ruler, or *inca*, **Pachacuti** (r. 1438–1471), they launched a series of military alliances and campaigns that brought them control of the whole area from Cuzco to the shores of Lake Titicaca.

Over the next 60 years, Inca armies were constantly on the march, extending control over a vast territory. Pachacuti's son and successor, Topac Yupanqui, conquered the northern coastal kingdom of Chi-

mor by seizing its irrigation system, and he extended Inca control into the southern area of what is now Ecuador. At the other end of the empire, Inca armies reached the Maule River in Chile against stiff resistance from the Araucanian Indians. The next ruler, Huayna Capac (r. 1493–1527) consolidated these conquests and suppressed rebellions on the frontiers. By the time of his death, the Inca Empire—or, as they called it, Twantinsuyu—stretched from what is now Colombia to Chile and eastward across Lake Titicaca and Bolivia to northern Argentina. Between 9 and 13 million people of different ethnic backgrounds and languages came under Inca rule, a remarkable feat, given the extent of the empire and the technology available for transportation and communication.

Conquest and Religion

What impelled the Inca conquest and expansion? The usual desire for economic gain and political power that we have seen in other empires is one possible explanation, but there may be others more in keeping with Inca culture and ideology. The cult of the ancestors was extremely important in Inca belief. Deceased rulers were mummified and then treated as intermediaries with the gods, paraded in public during festivals, offered food and gifts, and consulted on important matters by special oracles. From the Chimor kingdom the Incas adopted the practice of royal **split inheritance,** whereby all the political power and titles of the ruler went to his successor but all his palaces, wealth, land, and possessions remained in the hands of his male descendants, who used them to support the cult of the dead Inca's mummy for eternity. To ensure his own cult and place for eternity, each new Inca needed to secure land and wealth, and these normally came as part of new conquests. In effect, the greater the number of past Inca rulers, the greater the number of royal courts to support and the greater the demand for labor, lands, and tribute. This system created a self-perpetuating need for expansion, tied directly to ancestor worship and the cult of the royal mummies, as well as tensions between the various royal lineages. The cult of the dead weighed heavily on the living.

Inca political and social life was infused with religious meaning. Like the Aztecs, the Incas held the sun to be the highest deity and considered the Inca to be the sun's representative on earth. The magnif-

Visualizing the Past

Archeological Evidence of Political Practices

The Inca system of split inheritance probably originated in the Chimu kingdom. Chimu king lists recorded 10 rulers' names. Excavations at Chan-Chan, the Chimu capital, have revealed 10 large walled structures. Archeologists believe that each of these palatial compounds was a different king's residence and that each became a mausoleum for his mummy upon his death.

Questions: To what extent does such evidence indicate the composite nature of Inca culture? What are some of the possible problems of archeological interpretation? To what extent can material remains be used to explain or illustrate social phenomena?

City of Chan-Chan

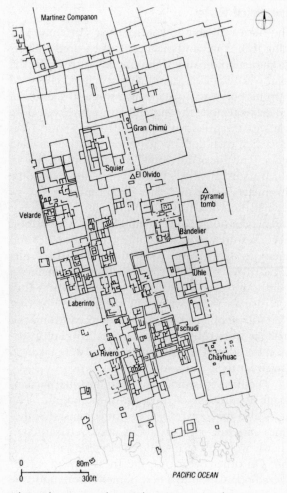

Chan-Chan covered more than 2 square miles. It contained palace compounds, storehouses, residences, markets, and other structures.

icent **Temple of the Sun** in Cuzco was the center of the state religion, and in its confines the mummies of the past Incas were kept. The cult of the sun was spread throughout the empire, but the Inca did not prohibit the worship of local gods.

Other deities were also worshiped as part of the state religion. Viracocha, a creator god, was a favorite of Inca Pachacuti and remained important. Popular belief was based on a profound animism that endowed many natural phenomena with spiritual power. Mountains, stones, rivers, caves, tombs, and temples were considered to be **huacas,** or holy shrines. At these places, prayers were offered and animals, goods, and humans were sacrificed. In the Cuzco area, imaginary lines running from the Temple of the Sun organized the huacas into groups for which certain ayllus took responsibility. The temples were served by many priests and women dedicated to preparing cloth and food for sacrifice. The temple priests were responsible mainly for the great festivals and celebrations and for the divinations on which state actions often depended.

The Techniques of Inca Imperial Rule

The Inca were able to control their vast empire by using techniques and practices that ensured cooperation or subordination. The empire was ruled by the inca, who was considered almost a god. He ruled from his court at Cuzco, which was also the site of the major temple; the high priest usually was a close relative. Twantinsuyu was divided into four great provinces, each under a governor, and then divided again. The Incas developed a state bureaucracy in which almost all nobles played a role. Although some chroniclers spoke of a state organization based on decimal units of 10,000, 1000, 100, and smaller numbers of households to mobilize taxes and labor, recent research reveals that many local practices and variations were allowed to continue under Inca rule. Local rulers, or **curacas,** were allowed to maintain their positions and were given privileges by the Inca in return for their loyalty. The curacas were exempt from tribute obligations and usually received labor or produce from those under their control. For insurance, the sons of conquered chieftains were taken to Cuzco for their education.

The Incas intentionally spread the Quechua language as a means of integrating the empire. The Incas also made extensive use of colonists. Sometimes Quechua-speakers from Cuzco were settled in a newly won area to provide an example and a garrison. On other occasions, the Incas moved a conquered population to a new home. Throughout the empire, a complex system of roads was built, with bridges and causeways when needed (Map 16.3). Along these roads, way stations, or **tambos,** were placed about a day's walk apart to serve as inns, storehouses, and supply centers for Inca armies on the move. Tambos also served as relay points for the system of runners who carried messages throughout the empire. The Inca probably maintained more than 10,000 tambos.

The Inca Empire extracted land and labor from subject populations. Conquered peoples were enlisted in the Inca armies under Inca officers and were rewarded with goods from new conquests. Subject peoples received access to goods not previously available to them, and the Inca state undertook large building and irrigation projects that formerly would have been impossible. In return, the Incas demanded loyalty and tribute. The state claimed all resources and redistributed them. The Incas divided conquered

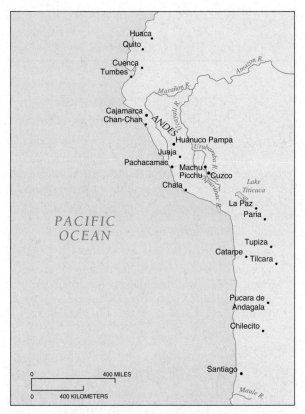

Map 16.3   *The Ancient Cities of Peru. The Inca system of roads, with its series of tambos, linked major towns and cities and allowed rapid communication and troop movement.*

areas into lands for the people, lands for the state, and lands for the sun—that is, for religion and the support of priests. Also, some nobles held private estates.

With few exceptions the Incas, unlike the Aztecs, did not demand tribute in kind but rather exacted labor on the lands assigned to the state and the religion. Communities were expected to take turns working on state and church lands and sometimes on building projects or in mining. These labor turns, or **mita,** were an essential aspect of Inca control. In addition, the Inca required women to weave high-quality cloth for the court and for religious purposes. The Incas provided the wool, but each household was required to produce cloth. Woven cloth, a great Andean art form, had political and religious significance. Some women were taken as concubines for the Inca; others were selected as servants at the temples, the so-called Virgins of the Sun. In all this, the Inca had an overall imperial system but remained sensitive to local variations, so that its application accommodated regional and ethnic differences.

In theory, each community aimed at self-sufficiency and depended on the state for goods it could not acquire easily. The ayllus of each community controlled the land, and the vast majority of the men were peasants and herders. Women worked in the fields, wove cloth, and cared for the household. Roles and obligations were gender specific and theoretically equal and interdependent. Andean peoples recognized parallel descent, so that property rights within the ayllus and among the nobility passed in both the male and female lines. Women passed rights and property to daughters, men to sons. Whether in pre-Inca times women may have served as leaders of ayllus is open to question, but under the Incas this seems to have been uncommon. The Inca emphasis on military virtues reinforced the inequality of men and women.

The concept of close cooperation between men and women was also reflected in the Inca view of the cosmos. Gods and goddesses were worshiped by men and women, but women felt a particular affinity for the moon and the goddesses of the earth and corn: the fertility deities. That special link was recognized in rituals such as that illustrated in Figure 16.5. The inca queen, the inca's senior wife (usually also a sister of the inca), was seen as a link to the moon. Queen and sister of the sun, she represented imperial authority to all women. But despite an ideology of gender equality, Inca practice created a gender hierarchy that paralleled the dominance of the Inca state over subject peoples. This fact is supported, and the power of the empire over local ethnic groups is demonstrated, by the Incas' ability to select the most beautiful young women to serve the temples or be given to the inca.

The integration of imperial policy with regional and ethnic diversity was a political achievement. Ethnic headmen were left in place, but over them were administrators drawn from the Inca nobility in Cuzco. Reciprocity and hierarchy continued to characterize Andean groups as they came under Inca rule; reciprocity between the state and the local community was simply an added level. The Inca state could provide roads, irrigation projects, and hard-to-get goods. For example, maize usually was grown on irrigated land and was particularly important as a ritual crop. State-sponsored irrigation added to its cultivation. The Inca state manipulated the idea of reciprocity to extract labor power, and it dealt harshly

Figure 16.5 *The role of women in Inca agriculture is emphasized in this 17th-century drawing of the symbolic irrigation of the fields. Complex Inca irrigation systems permitted the farming of steep hillsides and marginal lands.*

with resistance and revolt. In addition to the ayllus peasantry, there was also a class of people, the **yanas,** who were removed from their ayllus and served permanently as servants, artisans, or workers for the Inca or the nobility.

Members of the Inca nobility were greatly privileged, and those related to the inca himself held the highest positions. The nobility were all drawn from the 10 royal ayllus. In addition, the residents of Cuzco were given noble status to enable them to serve in high bureaucratic posts. The nobles were distinguished by dress and custom. Only they were entitled to wear the large ear spools that enlarged the ears and caused the Spaniards to later call them *orejones,* or "big ears." Noticeably absent in most of the Inca Empire was a distinct merchant class. Unlike in Mesoamerica, where long-distance trade was so important, the Incas' emphasis on self-sufficiency and state regulation of production and surplus limited trade. Only in the northern areas of the empire, in the chiefdoms of Ecuador, the last region brought under Inca control, did a specialized class of traders exist.

The Inca imperial system, which controlled an area of almost 3000 miles, was a stunning achievement of statecraft, but like all other empires it lasted only as long as it could control its subject populations and its own mechanisms of government. A system of royal multiple marriages as a way of forging alliances created rival claimants for power and the possibility of civil war. That is exactly what happened in the 1520s, just before the Europeans arrived. When the Spanish first arrived in Peru, they saw an empire weakened by civil strife.

Inca Cultural Achievements

The Incas drew on the artistic traditions of their Andean predecessors and the skills of subject peoples. Beautiful pottery and cloth were produced in specialized workshops. Inca metalworking was among the most advanced in the Americas, and Inca artisans worked gold and silver with great skill. The Incas also used copper and some bronze for weapons and tools. Like the Mesoamerican peoples, the Incas made no practical use of the wheel, but unlike them, they had no system of writing. However, the Incas did use a system of knotted strings, or **quipu,** to record numerical and perhaps other information. It worked like an abacus, and with it the Incas took censuses and kept financial records. The Incas had a passion for numerical order, and the population was divided into decimal units from which population, military enlistment, and work details could be calculated. The existence of so many traits associated with civilization in the Old World combined with the absence of a system of writing among the Incas illustrates the variations of human development and the dangers of becoming too attached to certain cultural characteristics or features in defining civilizations.

The Incas' genius was best displayed in their land and water management, extensive road system, statecraft, and architecture and public buildings. They developed ingenious agricultural terraces on the steep slopes of the Andes, using a complex technology of irrigation to water their crops. The empire was linked together by almost 2500 miles of roads, many of which included rope suspension bridges over mountain gorges and rivers. Inca stonecutting was remark-

ably accurate; the best buildings were built of large fitted stones without the use of masonry. Some of these buildings were immense. These structures, the large agricultural terraces and irrigation projects, and the extensive system of roads were among the Incas' greatest achievements, displaying their technical ability as well as their ability to mobilize large amounts of labor.

Comparing Incas and Aztecs

The Inca and the Aztec cultures were based on a long development of civilization that preceded them. Although in some areas of artistic and intellectual achievement earlier peoples had surpassed their accomplishments, both cultures represented the success of imperial and military organization. Both empires were based on intensive agriculture organized by a state that accumulated surplus production and then controlled the circulation of goods and their redistribution to groups or social classes. In both states, older kinship-based institutions, the ayllu and the calpulli, were transformed by the emergence of a social hierarchy in which the nobility was increasingly predominant. In both areas, these nobles also were the personnel of the state, so that the state organization was almost an image of society.

Although the Incas tried to create an overarching political state and to integrate their empire as a unit (the Aztecs did less in this regard), both empires recognized local ethnic groups and political leaders and allowed variation from one group or region to another as long as Inca or Aztec sovereignty was recognized and tribute paid. Both the Aztecs and the Incas, like the Spaniards who followed them, found that their military power was less effective against nomadic peoples who lived on their frontiers. Essentially, the empires were created by the conquest of sedentary agricultural peoples and the extraction of tribute and labor from them.

We cannot overlook the great differences between Mesoamerica and the Andean region in terms of climate and geography or the differences between the Inca and Aztec civilizations. Trade and markets were far more developed in the Aztec Empire and earlier in Mesoamerica in general than in the Andean world. There were differences in metallurgy, writing systems, and social definition and hierarchy. But within the context of world civilizations, it is probably best to view these two empires and the cultural areas they represent as variations of similar patterns and processes, of which sedentary agriculture is the most important. Basic similarities underlying the variations can also be seen in systems of belief and cosmology and in social structure. Whether similar origins, direct or indirect contact between the areas, or parallel development in Mesoamerica and the Andean area explains the similarity is unknown. But the American Indian civilizations shared much with each other; that factor and their isolation from external cultural and biological influences gave them their peculiar character and their vulnerability. At the same time, their ability to survive the shock of conquest and contribute to the formation of societies after conquest demonstrates much of their strength. Long after the Aztec and Inca empires had ceased to exist, the peoples of the Andes and Mexico continued to draw on these cultural traditions.

The Other Indians

 The civilizations of Mesoamerica and the Andes, and the imperial states in place at the moment of contact with the wider world, were high points of an Indian cultural achievement cut short by contact and conquest. However, the Americas continued to be occupied by a wide variety of peoples who lived in different ways, ranging from highly complex sedentary agricultural empires to simple kin-based bands of hunters and gatherers.

Rather than a division between "primitive" and "civilized" Indians, it is more useful to consider gradations of material culture and social complexity. Groups such as the Incas had many things in common with the tribal peoples of the Amazon basin, such as the division into clans or halves—that is, a division of villages or communities into two major groupings with mutually agreed-upon roles and obligations. Moreover, as we have seen, the diversity of ancient America forces us to reconsider ideas of human development based on Old World examples. If social complexity is seen as dependant on an agricultural base for society, that theory is not supported by the existence in the Americas of some groups of fishers and hunters and gatherers, such as the Indians of the northwest coast of the United States and

British Columbia, who developed hierarchical societies. For those who see control of water for agriculture as the starting point for political authority and the state, such societies as the Pimas of Colorado and some of the chiefdoms of South America, who practiced irrigated agriculture but did not develop states, provide exceptions.

How Many Indians?

A major issue that has fascinated students of the Americas for centuries is the question of population size. For many years after the European conquests, many people discounted the early descriptions of large and dense Indian populations as the exaggeration of conquerors and missionaries who wanted to make their own exploits seem more impressive. In the early 20th century, the most repeated estimate of Indian population about 1492 was 8.4 million (4 million in Mexico, 2 million in Peru, and 2.4 million in the rest of the hemisphere). Since that time, new archeological discoveries, a better understanding of the impact of disease on indigenous populations, new historical and demographic studies, and improved estimates of agricultural techniques and productivity have led to major revisions. Estimates still vary widely, and some have gone as high as 112 million at the time of contact. Most scholars agree that Mesoamerica and the Andes supported the largest populations. Table 16.1 summarizes one of the most careful estimates, which places the total figure at more than 67

TABLE 16.1

A Population Estimate for the Western Hemisphere, 1492

Area	Population (thousands)
North America	4,400
Mexico	21,400
Central America	5,650
Caribbean	5,850
Andes	11,500
Lowland South America	18,500
Total	67,300

Sources: William M. Deneven, *The Native Population of the Americas in 1492* (1976), 289–292; John D. Durand, "Historical Estimates of World Population," *Population and Development Review* vol. 3 (1957), 253–296; Russell Thornton, *American Indian Holocaust and Survival* (1987).

million, although an American Indian demographer has increased this figure to 72 million. Other scholars are unconvinced by these estimates.

These figures should be considered in a global context. In 1500, the population of the rest of the world was probably about 500 million, of which China and India each had 75 to 100 million people and Europe had 60 to 70 million, a figure roughly equivalent to the population of the Americas (Table 16.2). If the modern estimates are valid, the peoples of the Americas clearly made up a major segment of humanity.

Differing Cultural Patterns

Although it is impossible to summarize the variety of cultural patterns and lifeways that existed in the Americas on the eve of contact, we can describe the major patterns outside the main civilization areas. In Chapter 8 we noted that northern South America and part of Central America were an intermediate area that shared many features with the Andes and some with Mesoamerica and perhaps served as a point of cultural and material exchange between the two regions. In fact, with the exception of monumental architecture, the intermediate zone chieftainships resembled the sedentary agriculture states in many ways.

TABLE 16.2
World Population, c. 1500

Area	Population (thousands)
China	100,000–150,000
Indian subcontinent	75,000–150,000
Southwest Asia	20,000–30,000
Japan	15,000–20,000
Rest of Asia (except Russia)	15,000–30,000
Europe (except Russia)	60,000–70,000
Russia (USSR)	10,000–18,000
Northern Africa	6,000–12,000
Rest of Africa	30,000–60,000
Oceania	1,000–2,000
Americas	57,000–72,000
Total	389,000–614,000

Sources: William M. Deneven, *The Native Population of the Americas in 1492* (1976), 289–292; John D. Durand, "Historical Estimates of World Population," *Population and Development Review* vol. 3 (1957), 253–296; Russell Thornton, *American Indian Holocaust and Survival* (1987).

Similar kinds of chieftainships based on sedentary agriculture were found elsewhere in the Americas. There is strong evidence of large chieftainships along the Amazon, where the rich aquatic environment supported complex and perhaps hierarchical societies. The island Arawaks, encountered by Columbus on the Caribbean island of Hispaniola, were farmers organized in a hierarchical society and divided into chiefdoms. These Indian chiefdom-level societies strongly resemble the societies of Polynesia. On the bigger Caribbean islands, such as Hispaniola and Puerto Rico, chieftainships ruled over dense populations, which lived primarily on manioc.

Agriculture was spread widely throughout the Americas by 1500. Some peoples, such as those of the eastern North American woodlands and the coast of Brazil, combined agriculture with hunting and fishing. Techniques such as slash and burn farming led to the periodic movement of villages when production declined. Social organization in these societies often remained without strong class divisions, craft specializations, or the demographic density of people who practiced permanent, intensive agriculture. Unlike Europe, Asia, and Africa, the Americas lacked nomadic herders. However, throughout the Americas, from Tierra del Fuego to the Canadian forests, some people lived in small, mobile, kin-based groups of hunters and gatherers. Their material culture was simple and their societies were more egalitarian.

Nowhere is American Indian diversity more apparent than in North America. In that vast continent, by 1500, perhaps as many as 200 languages were spoken, and a variety of cultures reflected Indian adaptation to different ecological situations. By that time, most concentrated towns of the Mississippian mound-builder cultures had been abandoned, and only a few groups in southeastern North America still maintained the social hierarchy and religious ideas of those earlier cultures. In the Southwest, descendants of the Anasazi and other cliff dwellers had taken up residence in the adobe pueblos along the Rio Grande (Figure 16.6), where they practiced terracing and irrigation to support their agriculture. Their rich religious life, their artistic ceramic and weaving traditions, and their agricultural base reflected their own historical traditions.

Elsewhere in North America, most groups were hunters and gatherers or combined those activities with some agriculture. Sometimes an environment

Figure 16.6 *The pueblos of the Rio Grande valley like Taos or Acoma seen here reflected a number of the cultural traditions of the older Native American cultures of the southwestern United States.*

was so rich that complex social organization and artistic specialization could develop without an agricultural base. This was the case among the Indians of the northwest coast, who depended on the rich resources of the sea. In other cases, technology was a limiting factor. The tough prairie grasses could not be farmed easily without metal plows, nor could the buffalo be hunted effectively before Europeans introduced the horse. Thus, the Great Plains were only sparsely occupied.

Finally, we should note that although there was great variation among the Indian cultures, some aspects stood in contrast to contemporary societies in Europe and Asia. With the exception of the state systems of Mesoamerica and the Andes, most Indian societies were strongly kin based. Communal action and ownership of resources, such as land and hunting grounds, were emphasized, and material wealth often was disregarded or placed in a ritual or religious context. It was not that these societies were necessarily egalitarian but rather that ranking usu-

ally was not based on wealth. Although often subordinate, women in some societies held important political and social roles and usually played a central role in crop production. Indians tended to view themselves as part of the ecological system and not in control of it. These attitudes stood in marked contrast to those of many contemporary European and Asian civilizations.

American Indian Diversity in World Context

By the end of the 15th century, two great imperial systems had risen to dominate the two major centers of civilization in Mesoamerica and the Andes. Both empires were built on the achievements of their predecessors, and both reflected a militaristic phase in their area's development. These empires proved to be fragile, weakened by internal strains and the conflicts that any imperial system creates but also limited by their technological inferiority.

The Aztec and Inca empires were one end of a continuum of cultures that went from the most simple to the most complex. The Americas contained a broad range of societies, from great civilizations with millions of people to small bands of hunters. In many of these societies, religion played a dominant role in defining the relationship between people and their environment and between the individual and society. How these societies would have developed and what course the American civilizations might have taken in continued isolation remain interesting and unanswerable questions. The first European observers were simultaneously shocked by the "primitive" tribespeople and astounded by the wealth and accomplishments of civilizations such as that of the Aztecs. Europeans generally saw the Indians as curiously backward. In comparison with Europe and Asia, the Americas did seem strange—more like ancient Babylon or Egypt than contemporary China or Europe—except that without the wheel, large domesticated animals, the plow, and to a large extent metal tools and written languages, even that comparison is misleading. The isolation of the Americas had remained important in physical and cultural terms, but that isolation came to an end in 1492, with disastrous results.

 ## GLOBAL CONNECTIONS: The Americas and the World

Conditions in the Americas before 1492 reveal the importance of global connections in Afro-Eurasia and of their absence in the Americas. American isolation from effective global connections shows in the absence of key technologies, like ironworking and the wheel, that would have been easily transmitted had contacts been available. It shows in the absence of the standard range of domesticated animals. It shows in the absence of any trace of any of the great world religions. It would show, tragically, in the absence of any immunity to some of the standard contagious diseases of Afro-Eurasia.

The absence of several features that had become normal in Afro-Eurasia must be stated carefully. It should not detract from the impressive economic, cultural, and political achievements of the key American Indian civilizations, including their ability (particularly in Mesoamerica) to sustain dense populations. It should not obscure the heritage of these societies to later patterns in the Americas. The comparative distinctions that resulted from lack of wider contact would count only when the Americas were forced into new global connections after 1492—but then they mattered greatly.

Further Readings

Alvin M. Josephy, Jr.'s *The Indian Heritage of America* (2nd revised ed., 1991) is a broad, comprehensive history that deals with North and South America and provides much detail without being tedious. It is a logical starting point for further study. Freiderich Katz's *The Ancient Civilizations of the Americas* (2nd revised ed., 1997) provides the best overall survey that compares Mesoamerica and Peru. It traces the rise of civilization in both areas. Michael Coe et al., *Atlas of Ancient America* (1986), includes excellent maps, illustrations, and an intelligent and comprehensive text.

The literature on the Aztecs is growing rapidly. Sahagún's *Florentine Codex: The General History of the Things of New Spain*, Charles Dibble and Arthur J. O. Anderson, eds. and trans., 2 vols. (1950–1968) is a fundamental source. A good overview is Jacques Soustelle's *Daily Life of the Aztecs* (1961), but more recent is Frances Berdan's *The Aztecs of Central Mexico: An Imperial Society* (1982) and Inga Clendinnin, *Aztecs: An Interpretation* (1995). Miguel Leon-Portilla's *Aztec Thought and Culture* (1963) and *Fifteen Aztec Poets* (1992) deal with religion and philosophy in a sympathetic way. Burr Cartwright Brundage has traced the history of the Aztec rise in several books such as *A Rain of Darts* (1972); his *The Jade Steps* (1985) provides a good analysis of religion. Nigel Davies' *The Aztec Empire* (1987) is a political and social analysis. Susan D. Gillespie's *The Aztec Kings* (1989) views Aztec history in terms of myth.

On Peru, a good overview through solid scholarly articles is provided in Richard W. Keatinge, ed., *Peruvian Prehistory* (1988). The article on Inca archeology by Craig Morris is especially useful. Alfred Metraux's *The History of the Incas* (1970) is an older but still useful and very readable book. John Murra's *The Economic Organization of the Inca State* (1980) is a classic that has influenced much thinking about the Incas. J. Hyslop's *The Inca Road System* (1984) examines the building and function of the road network. The series of essays in John V. Murra, Nathan Wachtel, and Jacques Revel, eds., *Anthropological History of Andean Polities* (1986), shows how new approaches in ethnohistory are deepening our understanding of Inca society. Interesting social history is now being done. Irene Silverblatt's *Moon,*

Sun, and Witches: Gender Ideologies and Class in Inca and Colonial Peru (1987) is a controversial book on the position of women before, during, and after the Inca rise to power.

In Geoffrey W. Conrad and Arthur A. Demerest's *Religion and Empire: The Dynamics of Aztec and Inca Expansionism* (1984), two archeologists compare the political systems of the two empires and the motivations for expansion. The authors find more similarities than differences. Excellent studies on specific themes on Mexico and Peru are found in George A. Collier et al., eds., *The Inca and Aztec States, 1400–1800* (1982).

On the Web

The still vibrant, but soon to perish, worlds of the Aztecs (http://www.taisei.co.jp/cg_e/ancient_world/azteca/aazteca.html), Toltecs (http://emuseum.mnsu.edu/prehistory/latinamerica/meso/cultures/toltec.html), Inca (http://loki.stockton.edu/~gilmorew/consorti/1fcenso.htm), and Maya (http://mayaruins.com/, http://mysteriousplaces.com/mayan/TourEntrance.html, and http://emuseum.mnsu.edu/prehistory/latinamerica/meso/cultures/maya.html) are well represented on the Internet. One of the last Mayan cities, Tulum, can be visited at http://www.geocities.com/RainForest/Vines/4273/index1.htm and http://www.d.umn.edu/cla/faculty/troufs/anth3618/matulum.html. Recent discoveries in ancient MesoAmerican culture are offered at http://www.archaeolink.com/central_american_archaeology.htm.

Child marriage and the complex family structure of the ancient Aztecs (Nahua) can be explored at http://www.hist.umn.edu/~rmccaa/index.html (scroll down to "Nahua Calli" and to "child marriage").

CHAPTER 17

REUNIFICATION AND RENAISSANCE IN CHINESE CIVILIZATION: THE ERA OF THE TANG AND SONG DYNASTIES

Manufacturing silk was a laborious process that involved several steps. Here a woman and a small girl are at work on a roll of embroidered cloth. Textile weaving, sewing, and finishing were often done in the household in family workshops. In this way, women and young girls were income-earning members of the family.

The postclassical period saw a vital consolidation of Chinese civilization. Although less fundamental changes occurred in China than those experienced in eastern and western Europe, the Americas, and certainly the Middle East, Chinese civilization developed in important new ways. Some of these innovations, especially the technological ones, soon affected the wider world.

Attention to postclassical China means returning to one of the core civilization areas of Asia and to the network of relationships that had been developing for millennia among societies from Iberia in the west to Japan in the east. China also established its own orbit of influence in eastern Asia through ongoing exchanges with Japan, Korea, Vietnam, and other parts of southeast Asia. More isolated than the Islamic world and India, China nevertheless contributed vitally to other areas as it flourished under two vigorous dynasties, the Tang and Song, in the postclassical era.

In the era of political division and civil strife after the breakdown of the Han dynasty in the late 2nd century C.E., most of the advances of the Qin–Han era (221 B.C.E. to 220 C.E.) appeared to have been lost. Writers in the Era of Division that followed (220–589 C.E.) feared that the basis for maintaining civilization in China had been swept away by a new series of nomadic invasions and the seemingly endless wars fought by the regional kingdoms that vied for the imperial throne of the fallen Han. The bureaucratic apparatus of the empire collapsed, although many of the successor states aspired to the Qin–Han ideal of state centralization. In most kingdoms the position of the scholar-gentry declined sharply as landed families with aristocratic pretensions dominated regional rulers.

The reemergence of bickering and self-serving aristocratic elites reminded the scholars who recorded China's history of the chaos and suffering of the Warring States period before the rise of the Qin. In the centuries after the fall of the Han, non-Chinese nomads ruled much of China, and a foreign religion, Buddhism, eclipsed Confucian teachings as the prime force in Chinese political and cultural life. The Great Wall was divided between kingdoms and usually poorly defended as nomadic peoples raided and conquered across the north China plain. Trade and city life declined, technology stagnated, and with mainly Buddhist exceptions, thought degenerated into the quest for magical cures and immortality.

Given the magnitude of these reverses and the fact that Chinese civilization was battered for nearly four centuries, its revival at the very end of the 6th century C.E. appears abrupt at first glance. But the reestablishment of a centralized empire under the short-lived Sui dynasty, and then the restoration and growth of Chinese civilization during the 300-year Tang

200 C.E.	*600 C.E.*	*800 C.E.*	*950 C.E.*	*1100 C.E.*	*1250 C.E.*
220 End of the Han dynasty **220–589** Era of Division; political division in China; time of greatest Buddhist influence **589–618** Sui dynasty; building of the Grand Canal	**618–626** Gaozu emperor **618–907** Tang dynasty **627–649** Tang Taizong emperor **688** Korean conquest; vassal state of Silla **690–705** Empress Wu; Buddhist influence in China peaks **712–756** Xuanzong emperor	**840s** Period of Buddhist persecution **907** End of the Tang dynasty	**960–1279** Song dynasty; Neo-Confucian revival **c. 1050** Invention of block printing with movable type **1067–1085** Shenzong emperor; reforms of Wang Anshi	**c. 1100** Invention of gunpowder **1115** Jurchen (Qin) kingdom in North China **1119** First reference to use of compass for sea navigation **1127–1279** Southern Song dynasty	**1279–1368** Mongol (Yuan) dynasty rules all China

reign (618–907) that followed, demonstrated the great strength of the patterns of civilized life that had coalesced in the Qin–Han era. The rapid revival under the Tang was also made possible by the preservation, in the kingdoms that carved up the Han Empire, of the Confucian institutions and ideas that had been so central to the development of civilization in China. Particularly in thought and the arts, the revival begun in the Tang was continued and in some ways brought to full fruition under the Song dynasty (960–1279) that followed.

Rebuilding the Imperial Edifice in the Sui–Tang Eras

 The emergence at the end of the 6th century C.E. of the Sui dynasty from the patchwork of warring states that had dominated Chinese history for nearly four centuries signaled a return to strong dynastic control. In the Tang era that followed the Sui interlude, the bureaucratic institutions begun under the Han were restored, improved, and greatly expanded. A Confucian revival enhanced the position of the scholar-gentry administrators and provided the ideological basis for a return to highly centralized rule under an imperial dynasty.

The initial rise of the Sui dynasty in the early 580s appeared to be just another factional struggle of the sort that had occurred repeatedly in the splinter states fighting for control of China in the centuries after the fall of the Han. **Wendi,** a member of a prominent north Chinese noble family that had long been active in these contests, struck a marriage alliance between his daughter and the ruler of the northern Zhou empire. The Zhou monarch had recently defeated several rival rulers and united much

of the north China plain. After much intrigue, Wendi seized the throne of his son-in-law and proclaimed himself emperor. Although Wendi was Chinese, he secured his power base by winning the support of neighboring nomadic military commanders. He did this by reconfirming their titles and showing little desire to favor the Confucian scholar-gentry class at their expense. With their support, Wendi extended his empire across north China. In 589, Wendi's armies attacked and conquered the weak and divided Chen kingdom, which had long ruled much of the south. With his victory over the Chen, Wendi reunited the traditional core areas of Chinese civilization for the first time in three and a half centuries.

Wendi won widespread support by lowering taxes and establishing granaries throughout his domains. These bins for storing grain were built in all of the large cities and in each village of the empire to ensure that there would be a reserve food supply in case floods or drought destroyed the peasants' crops and threatened the people with famine. Large landholders and poor peasants alike were taxed a portion of their crop to keep the granaries filled. Beyond warding off famine, the surplus grain was brought to market in times of food shortages to hold down the price of the people's staple food.

Sui Excesses and Collapse

The foundations Wendi laid for political unification and economic prosperity were at first strengthened even further by his son **Yangdi,** who murdered his father to reach the throne. Yangdi extended his father's conquests and drove back the nomadic intruders who threatened the northern frontiers of the empire. He established a milder legal code and devoted resources to upgrading Confucian education. Yangdi also sought to restore the examination system for regulating entry into the bureaucracy. These legal and educational reforms were part of a broader policy of promoting the scholar-gentry in the imperial administration. But their advancement often worked to the detriment of the great aristocratic families and nomadic military commanders.

Yangdi was overly fond of luxury and extravagant construction projects. He forcibly conscripted hundreds of thousands of peasants to build palaces, a new capital city at Loyang (see Map 17.1), and a series of great canals to link the various parts of his empire. His demands on the people seemed limitless. In his new capital, Yangdi had an extensive game park laid out. Because there was not enough forest on the site chosen, tens of thousands of laborers were forced to dig up huge trees in the nearby hills and cart them miles to be replanted in the artificial mounds that tens of thousands of other laborers had built.

Even before work on his many construction projects had been completed, Yangdi led his exhausted and angry subjects into a series of unsuccessful wars to bring Korea back under Chinese rule. His failures in the Korean campaigns between 611 and 614 and the near-fatal reverse he suffered in central Asia at the hands of Turkic nomads in 615 set in motion widespread revolts throughout the empire. Provincial governors declared themselves independent rulers, bandit gangs raided at will, and nomadic peoples again seized large sections of the north China plain. Faced with a crumbling empire, the increasingly deranged emperor retreated to his pleasure palaces in the city of Hangzhou on the Yangtze River to the south. When Yangdi was assassinated by his own ministers in 618, it looked as if China would return to the

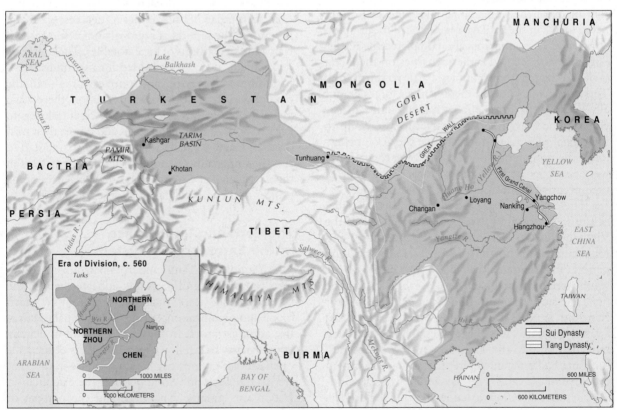

Map 17.1 *China During the Era of Division, the Sui Dynasty, and the Tang Dynasty*

state of political division and social turmoil it had endured in the preceding centuries.

The Emergence of the Tang and the Restoration of the Empire

The dissolution of the imperial order was averted by the military skills and political savvy of one of Yangdi's officials, **Li Yuan,** the Duke of Tang. Of noble and mixed Chinese-nomadic origins, Li Yuan was for many years a loyal supporter of the Sui ruler. In fact, on one occasion Li Yuan rescued Yangdi, whose forces had been trapped by a far larger force of Turkic cavalry in a small fort that was part of the Great Wall defenses. But as Yangdi grew more and more irrational and unrest spread from one end of the empire to another, Li Yuan was convinced by his sons and allies that only rebellion could save his family and the empire. From the many-sided struggle for the throne that followed Yangdi's death and continued until 623, Li Yuan emerged the victor. Together with his second son, Tang Taizong, in whose favor he abdicated in 626, Li Yuan laid the basis for the golden age of the Tang.

Tang armies conquered deep into central Asia as far as present-day Afghanistan. These victories meant that many of the nomadic peoples who had dominated China in the Six Dynasties era had to submit to Tang rule. Tang emperors also completed the repairs begun by the Sui and earlier dynasties on the Great Wall and created frontier armies. Partly recruited from Turkic nomadic peoples, these frontier forces gradually became the most potent military units in the empire. The sons of Turkic tribal leaders were sent to the capital as hostages to guarantee the good behavior of the tribe in question. At the Tang capital, they were also educated in Chinese ways in the hope of their eventual assimilation into Chinese culture.

The empire was also extended to parts of Tibet in the west, the Red River valley homeland of the Vietnamese in the south (see Chapter 18), and Manchuria in the north (see Map 17.1). In the Tang period, the Yangtze River basin and much of the south were fully integrated with north China for the first time since the Han. In 668, under the emperor Kaozong, Korea was overrun by Chinese armies, and a vassal kingdom called Silla was established that long remained loyal to the Tang. In a matter of decades, the Tang had built an empire that was far larger than even that of the early Han—an empire whose boundaries in many directions extended beyond the borders of present-day China.

Rebuilding the Bureaucracy

Crucial for the restoration of Chinese unity were the efforts of the early Tang monarchs to rebuild and expand the imperial bureaucracy. A revived scholar-gentry elite and reworked Confucian ideology played central roles in the process. From the time of the second Sui emperor, Yangdi, the fortunes of the scholar-gentry had begun to improve. This trend continued under the early Tang emperors, who desperately needed loyal and well-educated officials to govern the vast empire they had put together in a matter of decades. The Tang rulers also used the scholar-gentry bureaucrats to offset the power of the aristocracy. As the aristocratic families' control over court life and administration declined, their role in Chinese history was reduced. From the Tang era onward, political power in China was shared by a succession of imperial families and the bureaucrats of the civil service system. Members of the hereditary aristocracy continued to occupy administrative positions, but the scholar-gentry class staffed most of the posts in the secretariats and executive department that oversaw a huge bureaucracy.

This bureaucracy reached from the imperial palace down to the subprefecture, or district level, which was roughly equivalent to an American county. One secretariat drafted imperial decrees; a second monitored the reports of regional and provincial officials and the petitions of local notables. The executive department, which was divided into six ministries—including war, justice, and public works—ran the empire on a day-to-day basis. In addition, there was a powerful Bureau of Censors whose chief task was to keep track of officials at all levels and report their misdeeds or failings. Finally, there was a very large staff to run the imperial household, including the palaces in the new capital at **Changan** and the residences of the princes of the imperial line and other dignitaries.

The Growing Importance of the Examination System

Like Yangdi, the Tang emperors patronized academies to train state officials and educate them in the Confucian classics, which were thought to teach moral and organizational principles essential to effective administrators. In the Tang era, and under the Song dynasty that followed, the numbers of the educated scholar-gentry rose far above those in the Han era. In the Tang and Song periods, the examination system was greatly expanded, and the pattern of advancement in the civil service was much more regularized. Several different kinds of examinations were administered by the **Ministry of Rites** to students from government schools or to those recommended by distinguished scholars.

The highest offices could be gained only by those who were able to pass exams on the philosophical or legal classics and the even more difficult exams on Chinese literature. Those who passed the latter earned the title of **jinshi**. Their names were announced throughout the empire, and their families' positions were secured by the prospect of high office that was opened up by their success. Overnight they were transformed into dignitaries whom even their former friends and fellow students addressed formally and treated with deference. Success in exams at all levels won candidates special social status. This meant that they gained the right to wear certain types of clothing and were exempt from corporal punishment. They gained access to the higher level of material comfort and the refined pleasures that were enjoyed by members of this elite, some of whom are shown at play in Figure 17.1.

Even though a much higher proportion of Tang bureaucrats won their positions through success in civil service examinations than had been the case in the Han era, birth and family connections continued to be important in securing high office. Some of these relationships are clearly illustrated by the peti-tioner's letter printed in the Document section. Established bureaucrats not only ensured that their sons and cousins got into the imperial academies but could pull strings to see that even failed candidates from their families received government posts. Ethnic and regional ties also played a role in staffing bureaucratic departments. This meant that although bright commoners could rise to upper-level positions in the bureaucracy, the central administration was overwhelmingly dominated by a small number of established families. Sons followed fathers in positions of power and influence, and prominent households bought a disproportionate share of the places available in the imperial academies. Many positions were reserved for members of the old aristocracy and the low-ranking sons and grandsons of lesser wives and concubines belonging to the imperial household. Merit and ambition counted for something, but birth and family influence often counted for a good deal more.

State and Religion in the Tang–Song Era

Increasing state patronage for Confucian learning threatened not only the old aristocratic families but also the Buddhists monastic orders, which had become a major force in Chinese life in the Six

Figure 17.1   *As shown in this ink drawing of Chinese philosophers of the Song dynasty, board games and musical recitals were highly esteemed leisure activities for the scholar-gentry class. Members of the scholar-gentry elite might also attend poetry reading or writing parties, travel to mountains to meditate amid scenic splendors, or paint the blossoming plum trees in their gardens. As in their work, members of this highly educated elite admired those who at leisure pursued a diverse array of activities.*

Document

Ties That Bind: Paths to Powers

The following letter was included in a short story by Tang author Niu Su. It was sent by a local functionary named Wu Bao to a high official to whom Wu hoped to attach himself and thus win advancement in the imperial bureaucracy. What can this letter tell us about the ways in which the Chinese bureaucracy worked in the Tang and Song eras?

To my great good fortune, we share the same native place, and your renown for wise counsel is well known to me. Although, through gross neglect, I have omitted to prostrate myself before you, my heart has always been filled with admiration and respect. You are the nephew of the Prime Minister, and have made use of your outstanding talents in his service. In consequence of this, your high ability has been rewarded with a commission. General Li is highly qualified both as a civil and a military official, and he has been put in full command of the expedition [to put down "barbarian" rebellions in the southern parts of the empire]. In his hands he unites mighty forces, and he cannot fail to bring these petty brigands to order. By the alliance of the General's heroic valor and your own talent and ability, your armies' task of subjugation will be the work of a day. I, in my youth, devoted myself to study.

Reaching manhood, I paid close attention to the [Confucian] classics. But in talent I do not compare with other men, and so far I have held office only as an officer of the guard. I languish in this out-of-the-way corner beyond the Chien [mountains], close to the haunts of the barbarians. My native place is thousands of miles away, and many passes and rivers lie between. What is more, my term of office here is completed, and I cannot tell when I shall receive my next appointment. So lacking in talent, I fear I am but poorly fitted to be selected for an official post; far less can I entertain the hope of some meager salary. I can only retire, when old age comes, to some rustic retreat, and "turn aside to die in a ditch." I have heard by devious ways of your readiness to help those in distress. If you will not overlook a man from your native place, be quick to bestow your special favour on me, so that I may render you service "as a humble groom." Grant me some small salary, and a share however slight in your deeds of merit. If by your boundless favor I could take part in this triumphal progress, even as a member of the rear-most company, the day would live engraved on my memory.

Questions: What techniques does Wu use to win the high official's favor? How does Wu expect the official to help him? What does he promise in return? Does birth or merit appear to be more important in his appeals? What does this suggest about the place of the examinations in the political system? What dangers to the imperial system are contained in the sorts of ties that Wu argues bind him to the high official?

Dynasties era. Many of the rulers in the pre-Tang era, particularly those from nomadic origins, were devout Buddhists and strong patrons of the Buddhist establishment. In the centuries after the fall of the Han, Buddhist sects proliferated in China. The most popular were those founded by Chinese monks, in part because they soon took on distinctively Chinese qualities. Among the masses, the salvationist **pure land** strain of Mahayana Buddhism won widespread conversions because it seemed to provide a refuge from an age of war and turmoil. Members of the elite classes, on the other hand, were more attracted to the **Chan** variant of Buddhism, or **Zen** as it is known in Japan and the West. With its stress on meditation and the appreciation of natural and artistic beauty, Zen had great appeal for the educated classes of China.

The goal of those who followed Zen was to come to know the ultimate wisdom, and thus find release from the cycle of rebirth, through introspective meditation. The nature of this level of consciousness often was expressed in poetic metaphors and riddles, such as those in the following lines from an 8th century C.E. treatise called the *Hymn to Wisdom*:

The power of wisdom is infinite.

It is like moonlight reflected in a thousand waves; it can see, hear, understand, and know.

It can do all these and yet is always empty and tranquil.

Being empty means having no appearance.

Being tranquil means not having been created.

One will then not be bound by good and evil,
or be seized by quietness or disturbance.

One will not be wearied by birth and death or
rejoice in Nirvana.

The combination of royal patronage and widespread conversion at both the elite and mass levels made Buddhism a strong social, economic, and political force by the time of the Tang unification. The early Tang rulers continued to patronize Buddhism while trying to promote education in the Confucian classics. Emperors such as Taizong endowed monasteries, built in the style of those pictured in Figure 17.2. They also sent emissaries to India to collect texts and relics and commissioned Buddhist paintings and statuary. However, no Tang ruler matched **Empress Wu** (r. 690–705) in supporting the Buddhist establishment. At one point she tried to elevate Buddhism to the status of a state religion.

Empress Wu also commissioned many Buddhist paintings and sculptures. The sculptures are noteworthy for their colossal size. She had statues of the Buddha, which were as much as two and three stories high, carved from stone or cast in bronze. Some of these statues, such as those pictured in Figure 17.3, were carved out of the rock in the great caves near her capital at Loyang; for cast figures at other locations, Wu had huge pagodas built. With this sort of support, it is not surprising that Buddhism flourished in the early centuries of Tang rule. By the mid-9th century, there were nearly 50,000 monasteries and hundreds of thousands of Buddhist monks and nuns in China.

The Anti-Buddhist Backlash

Buddhist successes aroused the envy of Confucian and Daoist rivals. Some of these attacked the religion as alien, even though the faith followed by most of the Chinese was very different from that originally preached by the Buddha or that practiced in India or southeast Asia. Daoist monks tried to counter Buddhism's appeals to the masses by stressing their own magical and predictive powers. Most damaging to the fortunes of Buddhism was the growing campaign of Confucian scholar-administrators to convince the Tang

Figure 17.2 *Because many of the great Buddhist temples and monasteries in China were destroyed in various waves of persecution, some of the best surviving examples of east Asian Buddhist architecture, such as this monastery in present-day Kyoto, are found in Japan. Some of the most characteristic features of this splendid style of construction are its steeply sloping tiled roofs with upturned corners, the extensive use of fine wood in floors, walls, and ceilings, and the sliding panels that covered doors and windows in inclement weather and opened up the temples or monasteries to the natural world on pleasant days.*

Figure 17.3 *At sites such as Lungmen near the Tang capital of Loyang on the Yellow River and Yunkang far to the north, massive statues of the Buddha were carved out of rocky cliffsides beginning in the 6th century C.E. Before the age of Buddhist predominance, sculpture had not been highly developed in China, and the art at these centers was strongly influenced by that of central and even west Asia. Known more for their sheer size than for artistic refinement, the huge Buddhas of sites such as Lungmen attest to the high level of skill the Chinese had attained in stone- and metalworking.*

rulers that the large Buddhist monastic establishment posed a fundamental economic challenge to the imperial order. Because monastic lands and resources were not taxed, the Tang regime lost huge amounts of revenue as a result of imperial grants or the gifts of wealthy families to Buddhist monasteries. The state was also denied labor power because it could neither tax nor conscript peasants who worked on monastic estates.

By the mid-8th century, state fears of Buddhist wealth and power led to measures to limit the flow of land and resources to the monastic orders. Under Emperor **Wuzong** (r. 841–847), these restrictions grew into open persecution of Buddhism. Thousands of monasteries and Buddhist shrines were destroyed, and hundreds of thousands of monks and nuns were forced to abandon their monastic orders and return to civilian lives. They and the slaves and peasants who worked their lands were again subject to taxation, and monastery lands were parceled out to taxpaying landlords and peasant smallholders.

Although Chinese Buddhism survived this and other bouts of repression, it was weakened. Never again would the Buddhist monastic orders have the political influence and wealth they had enjoyed in the first centuries of Tang rule. The great age of Buddhist painting and cave sculptures gave way to art dominated by Daoist and Confucian subjects and styles in the late Tang and the Song dynastic era that followed. The Zen and pure land sects of Buddhism continued to attract adherents, with those of the latter numbering in the millions. But Confucianism emerged as the central ideology of Chinese civilization for most of the period from the 9th to the early 20th century. Buddhism left its mark on the arts, the Chinese language, and Chinese thinking about things such as heaven, charity, and law, but it ceased to be a dominant influence. Buddhism's fate in China contrasts sharply with its ongoing and pivotal impact on the civilizations of mainland southeast Asia, Tibet, and parts of central Asia.

Tang Decline and the Rise of the Song

After several centuries of strong rule, the Tang dynasty fell on hard times. Beset by internal rebellions and nomadic incursions, the Tang gave way to the Song in the early 10th century. Although the Song domains were smaller than the Tang, the Confucian revival flourished under the successor dynasty. Following new waves of nomadic invasions, in the mid-12th century the Song lost control of north China. A century and a half later, their empire in south China fell, after a prolonged struggle, to the Mongols under Kubilai Khan.

The motives behind the mid-9th-century Tang assault on the Buddhist monastic order were symptomatic of a general weakening of imperial control that had begun almost a century earlier. After the controversial but strong rule between 690 and 705 by Empress Wu, who actually tried to establish a new dynasty, a second attempt to control the throne was made by a high-born woman who had married into the imperial family. Backed by her powerful relatives and a group of prominent courtiers, Empress Wei poisoned her husband, the son of Empress Wu, and placed her own small child on the throne. But Empress Wei's attempt to seize power was thwarted by another prince, who led a palace revolt that ended with the destruction of Wei and her supporters. The early decades of the long reign of this prince, who became the emperor **Xuanzong** (r. 713–756), marked the peak of Tang power and the high point of Chinese civilization under the dynasty.

Initially, Xuanzong took a strong interest in political and economic reforms, which were pushed by the very capable officials he appointed to high positions. Increasingly, his interest in running the vast empire waned. More and more he devoted himself to patronizing the arts and enjoying the pleasures available within the confines of the imperial city. These diversions included music, which he played himself and also had performed by the many musicians he patronized. Thousands of concubines vied in the imperial apartments for the attention of the monarch. After the death of his second wife, the aged and lonely emperor became infatuated with **Yang Guifei,** a beautiful young woman from the harem of one of the imperial princes (Figure 17.4).

Figure 17.4 *This painting of Yang Guifei gives a vivid impression of the opulence and refinement of Chinese court life in the late Tang era. Here a very well-dressed Yang Guifei is helped by some of her servants onto a well-fed horse, presumably for a trot through the palace grounds. Two fan-bearers stand ready to accompany the now powerful concubine on her sedate ride while other attendants prepare to lead the horse through the confined space of the royal enclosure.*

Their relationship was one of the most famous and ill-fated romances in all of Chinese history. Xuanzong promenaded in the imperial gardens and gave flute lessons to Yang. Soon she was raised to the status of royal concubine, and she used her new power to pack the upper levels of the government with her greedy relatives. They and Yang assumed an ever greater role in court politics. The arrogance and excessive ambition of Yang Guifei and her family angered members of the rival cliques at court, who took every opportunity to turn Yang's excesses into a cause for popular unrest. Xuanzong's long neglect of state affairs resulted in economic distress, which fed this discontent. It also led to chronic military weaknesses, which left the government unable to deal with the disorders effectively. The deepening crisis came to a head in 755 when one of the emperor's main military leaders, a general of nomadic origins named An Lushan, led a widely supported revolt with the aim of founding a new dynasty to supplant the Tang.

Although the revolt was crushed and the Tang dynasty preserved, victory was won at a very high cost. Early in the rebellion, Xuanzong's retreating and demoralized troops mutinied, first killing several members of the Yang family and then forcing the emperor to have Yang Guifei executed. Xuanzong lived on for a time, but his grief and disillusionment rendered him incapable of continuing as emperor. None of the Tang monarchs who followed him could compare with the able leaders that the dynasty had consistently produced in the first century and a half of its rule.

Equally critical, to defeat the rebels the Tang had sought alliances with nomadic peoples living on the northern borders of the empire. They had also delegated resources and political power to regional commanders who remained loyal to the dynasty. As had happened so often in the past, in the late 8th and 9th centuries the nomads used political divisions within China to gain entry into and eventually assert control over large areas of the north China plain. At the same time, many of the allied provincial governors became in effect independent rulers. They collected their own taxes, passing little or none on to the imperial treasury. These regional lords raised their own armies and bequeathed their titles to their sons without asking for permission from the Tang court. Worsening economic conditions led to a succession of revolts in the 9th century, some of which were popular uprisings led by peasants.

The Founding of the Song Dynasty

By the end of the 9th century, little remained of the once-glorious Tang Empire. By 907, when the last emperor of the Tang dynasty was forced to resign, China appeared to be entering another phase of nomadic dominance, political division, and social strife. In 960, however, a military commander emerged to reunite China under a single dynasty. **Zhao Kuangyin** had established a far-flung reputation as one of the most honest and able of the generals of the last of the Five Dynasties that had struggled to control north China after the fall of the Tang. Though a fearless warrior, Zhao was a scholarly man who collected books rather than booty while out campaigning. Amid the continuing struggles for control in the north, Zhao's subordinates and regular troops insisted that he proclaim himself emperor. In the next few years, Zhao, renamed Emperor Taizu, routed all his rivals except one, thus founding the Song dynasty that was to rule most of China for the next three centuries.

The one rival Taizu could not overcome was the northern **Liao dynasty,** which had been founded in 907 by the nomadic **Khitan** peoples from Manchuria. This failure set a precedent for weakness on the part of the Song rulers in dealing with the nomadic peoples of the north. This shortcoming plagued the dynasty from its earliest years to its eventual destruction by the Mongols in the late 13th century. Beginning in 1004, the Song were forced by military defeats at the hands of the Khitans to sign a series of humiliating treaties with their smaller but more militarily adept northern neighbors. These treaties committed the Song to paying a very heavy tribute to the Liao dynasty to keep it from raiding and possibly conquering the Song domains. The Khitans, who had been highly *Sinified*, or influenced by Chinese culture, during a century of rule in north China, seemed content with this arrangement. They clearly saw the Song Empire as culturally superior—an area from which they could learn much in statecraft, the arts, and economic organization.

Song Politics: Settling for Partial Restoration

A comparison of the boundaries of the early Song Empire (see Map 17.2) with that of the Tang domains (see Map 17.1) reveals that the Song never matched its predecessor in political or military strength. The weakness of the Song resulted in part

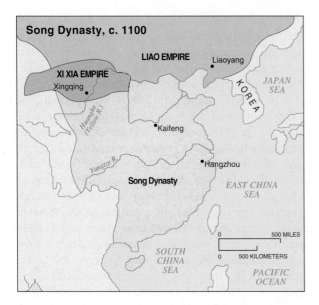

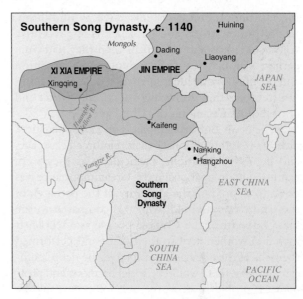

Map 17.2 *China in the Song and Southern Song Dynastic Periods*

from imperial policies that were designed to ward off the conditions that had destroyed the Tang Empire. From the outset, the military was subordinated to the civilian administrators of the scholar-gentry class. Only civil officials were allowed to be governors, thereby removing the temptation of regional military commanders to seize power. In addition, military commanders were rotated to prevent them from building up a power base in the areas where they were stationed.

At the same time, the early Song rulers strongly promoted the interests of the Confucian scholar-gentry, who touted themselves as the key bulwark against the revival of warlordism. Officials' salaries were increased, and many perks—including additional servants and payments of luxury goods such as silk and wine—made government posts more lucrative. The civil service exams were fully routinized. They were given every three years at three levels: district, provincial, and imperial. Song examiners passed a far higher percentage of those taking the exams than the Tang examiners had, and these successful candidates were much more likely to receive an official post than their counterparts in the Tang era. As a result, the bureaucracy soon became bloated with well-paid officials who often had little to do. In this way, the ascendancy of the scholar-gentry class over its aristocratic and Buddhist rivals was fully secured in the Song era.

The Revival of Confucian Thought

The great influence of the scholar-gentry in the Song era was mirrored in the revival of Confucian ideas and values that dominated intellectual life. Many scholars tried to recover long-neglected texts and decipher ancient inscriptions. New academies devoted to the study of the classical texts were founded, and impressive libraries were established. The new schools of philosophy propounded rival interpretations of the teachings of Confucius and other ancient thinkers. They also sought to prove the superiority of indigenous thought systems, such as Confucianism and Daoism, over imported ones, especially Buddhism.

The most prominent thinkers of the era, such as **Zhu Xi,** stressed the importance of applying philosophical principles to everyday life and action. These **neo-Confucians,** or revivers of ancient Confucian teachings, believed that cultivating personal morality was the highest goal for humans. They argued that virtue could be attained through knowledge gained by book learning and personal observation as well as through contact with men of wisdom and high morality. In these ways, the basically good nature of humans could be cultivated, and superior men, fit to govern and teach others, could be developed. Neo-Confucian thinking had a great impact on Chinese intellectual life during the eras of all the dynasties that followed the Song. Its hostility to foreign philosophical systems, such as Buddhism, made Chinese rulers and bureaucrats less receptive to outside ideas and influences than they had been earlier. The neo-Confucian emphasis on tradition and hostility to outside influences was one of a number of forces that eventually stifled innovation and critical thinking among the Chinese elite.

The neo-Confucian emphasis on rank, obligation, deference, and traditional rituals reinforced class, age, and gender distinctions, particularly as they were expressed in occupational roles. Great importance was given to upholding the authority of the patriarch of the Chinese household, who was compared to the male emperor of the Chinese people as a whole. If men and women kept to their place and performed the tasks of their age and social rank, the neo-Confucians argued, there would be social harmony and prosperity. If problems arose, the best solutions could be found in examples drawn from the past. They believed that historical experience was the best guide for navigating the uncertain terrain of the future.

Roots of Decline: Attempts at Reform

The means by which the Song emperors had secured their control over China undermined their empire in the long run. The weakness they showed in the face of the Khitan challenge encouraged other nomadic peoples to carve out kingdoms on the northern borders of the Song domains. By the mid-11th century, **Tangut** tribes, originally from Tibet, had established a kingdom named **Xi Xia** to the southwest of the Khitan kingdom of Liao (see Map 17.2). The tribute that the Song had to pay these peoples for "protection" of their northern borders was a great drain on the resources of the empire and a growing burden for the Chinese peasantry. Equally burdensome was the cost of the army—numbering nearly 1 million soldiers by the mid-11th century—that the Song had to maintain to guard against invasion from the north. But the very size of the army was a striking measure of the productivity and organizational ability of Chinese civilization. It dwarfed its counterparts in other civilizations from Japan to western Europe. The emphasis on civil administration and the scholar-gentry and the growing disdain among the Song elite for the military also took their toll. Although Song armies were large, their commanders rarely were the most able men available. In addition, funds needed to upgrade weapons or repair fortifications often were diverted to the schol-

arly pursuits and entertainments of the court and gentry. At the court and among the ruling classes, painting and poetry were cultivated, while the horseback riding and hunting that had preoccupied earlier rulers and their courtiers went out of fashion.

In the 1070s and early 1080s, **Wang Anshi,** the chief minister of the Song Shenzong emperor, tried to ward off the impending collapse of the dynasty by introducing sweeping reforms. A celebrated Confucian scholar, Wang ran the government on the basis of the Legalist (see Chapter 4) assumption that an energetic and interventionist state could greatly increase the resources and strength of the dynasty. For 20 years, in the face of strong opposition from the conservative ministers who controlled most of the administration, Wang tried to correct the grave defects in the imperial order. He introduced cheap loans and government-assisted irrigation projects to encourage agricultural expansion. He taxed the landlord and scholarly classes, who had regularly exempted themselves from military service. Wang used the increased revenue to establish well-trained mercenary forces to replace armies that had formerly been conscripted from the untrained and unwilling peasantry. Wang even tried to reorganize university education and reorient the examination system. His reforms stressed analytical thinking rather than the rote memorization of the classics that had long been key to success among the scholar-gentry.

Reaction and Disaster: The Flight to the South

Unfortunately, Wang's ability to propose and enact reforms depended on continuing support from the Shenzong emperor. In 1085 that emperor died, and his successor favored the conservative cliques that had long opposed Wang's changes. The neo-Confucians came to power, ended reform, and reversed many of Wang's initiatives. As a result, economic conditions continued to deteriorate, and peasant unrest grew throughout the empire. Faced by banditry and rebellion from within, an unprepared military proved no match for the increasing threat from beyond the northern borders of the empire. In 1115, a new nomadic contender, the **Jurchens,** overthrew the Liao dynasty of the Khitans and established the **Jin** kingdom north of the Song Empire (see Map 17.2). After successful invasions of Song territory, the Jurchens annexed most of the Yellow River basin to what had become the Qin Empire. These conquests forced the Song to flee to the south. With the Yangtze River basin as their anchor and their capital transferred to Hangzhou, the Song dynasty survived for another century and a half. Politically the **Southern Song** dynasty (1127–1279) was little more than a rump state carved out of the much larger domains ruled by the Tang and northern-based Song. Culturally, its brief reign was to be one of the most glorious in Chinese history—perhaps in the history of humankind.

Tang and Song Prosperity: The Basis of a Golden Age

 The Tang and Song period was a time of major transitions in Chinese history. Shifts in the population balance within China, new patterns of trade and commerce, renewed urban expansion, novel forms of artistic and literary expression, and a series of technological breakthroughs contributed to new directions in the development of Chinese civilization.

The attention given to canal building by the Sui emperors and the Tang rulers who followed them was driven by a major shift in the population balance within Chinese civilization. The **Grand Canal,** which Yangdi risked his throne to have built, was designed to link the original centers of Chinese civilization on the north China plain with the Yangtze river basin more than 500 miles to the south (see Maps 17.1 and 17.2). Because the great river systems that were essential to China's agrarian base ran from west to east—from the mountains of central Asia to the sea—the movement of people and goods in that direction was much easier than from north to south. Although no major geographic barriers separated the millet-growing areas of northern China from the rice-producing Yangtze basin, overland travel was slow and difficult. The transport of bulk goods such as millet and rice was prohibitively expensive. The great increase of the Chinese population in the southern regions in the later Han and Six Dynasties periods made it necessary to improve communications between north and south once the two regions were joined by the Sui conquests. Not only did more and more of the emperor's subjects live in the southern regions, but the Yangtze basin and other rice-growing areas in the south were fast becoming the major food-producing areas of the empire. By late Tang and early Song times, the south had surpassed the north in both crop production and total population.

Yangdi's Grand Canal was intended to facilitate control over the southern regions by courts, bureaucracies, and armies centered in ancient imperial centers such as Changan and Loyang in the north. The canal made it possible to transport to the capital revenue collected in the form of grain from the fertile southern regions and to transfer food from the south to districts threatened by drought and famine in the north. No wonder that Yangdi was obsessed with canal construction. By the time the Grand Canal was finished, more than a million forced laborers had worked, and many had died, on its locks and embankments. The completed canal system was an engineering achievement every bit as impressive as the Great Wall. Most stretches of the canal, which was nearly 1200 miles long, were 40 paces wide, and imperial highways lined with willow trees ran along the banks on both sides.

A New Phase of Commercial Expansion

Tang conquests in central Asia and the building of the canal system did much to promote commercial expansion in the Tang and Song eras. The extension of Tang control deep into central Asia meant that the overland silk routes between China and Persia were reopened and protected. This intensified international contacts in the postclassical period. Tang control promoted exchanges between China and Buddhist centers in the nomadic lands of central Asia as well as with the Islamic world farther west. Horses, Persian rugs, and tapestries passed to China along these routes, while fine silk textiles, porcelain, and paper were exported to the centers of Islamic civilization. As in the Han era, China exported mainly manufactured goods to overseas areas, such as southeast Asia, while importing mainly luxury products such as aromatic woods and spices. Trading ships for ocean, canal, and river transport improved dramatically, and their numbers multiplied many times in the Tang and Song eras. In late Tang and Song times, Chinese merchants and sailors increasingly carried Chinese trade overseas instead of being content to let foreign seafarers come to them. Along with the dhows of the Arabs, Chinese **junks** were the best ships in the world in this period. They were equipped with watertight bulkheads, sternpost rudders, oars, sails, compasses, bamboo fenders, and gunpowder-propelled rockets for self-defense. With such vessels, Chinese sailors and merchants became the dominant force in the Asian seas east of the Malayan peninsula.

The heightened role of commerce and the money economy in Chinese life was readily apparent in the market quarters found in all cities and major towns (Figure 17.5). These were filled with shops and stalls that sold products drawn from local farms, regional centers of artisan production, and trade centers as distant as the Mediterranean. The Tang and Song governments supervised the hours and marketing methods in these centers, and merchants specializing in products of the same kind banded together in guilds to promote their interests with local officials and to regulate competition.

This expansion in scale was accompanied by a growing sophistication in commercial organization and forms of credit available in China. The proportion of exchanges involved in the money economy expanded greatly, and deposit shops, an early form of the bank, were found in many parts of the empire. The first use of paper money also occurred in the Tang era. Merchants deposited their profits in their hometowns before setting out on trading caravans to distant cities. They were given credit vouchers, or what the Chinese called **flying money,** which they could then present for reimbursement at the appropriate office in the city of destination. This arrangement greatly reduced the danger of robbery on the often perilous journeys merchants made from one market center to another. In the early 11th century, the government began to issue paper money when an economic crisis made it clear that the private merchant banks could no longer handle the demand for the new currency.

The World's Most Splendid Cities

The expansion of commerce and artisan production was complemented by a surge in urban growth in the Tang and Song eras. At nearly 2 million, the population of the Tang capital and its suburbs at Changan was far larger than that of any other city in the world at the time. The imperial city, an inner citadel within the walls of Changan, was divided into a highly restricted zone dominated by the palace and audience halls and a section crowded with the offices of the ministries and secretariats of the imperial government. Near the imperial city but outside Changan's walls, elaborate gardens and a hunting park were laid out for the amusement of the emperors and favored courtiers. The spread of commerce and the increasing population also fed urban growth in the rest of China. In the north and especially the south, old cities mushroomed as suburbs spread in all directions from the original city walls. Towns grew rapidly into cities, and the proportion of the empire's population living in urban centers grew steadily. The number of people living in large cities in China, which may have been as high as 10 percent, was also far greater than that found in any civilization until after the Industrial Revolution.

Of all China's remarkable urban centers in this era, perhaps none surpassed the late Song capital of **Hangzhou** in size, beauty, and sophistication. Located between a large lake and a river in the Yangtze delta, Hangzhou was crisscrossed by canals and bridges. The city's location near the Yangtze and the coast of the East China Sea allowed its traders and artisans to prosper through the sale of goods or the manufacture of products from materials drawn from both north and south China as well as overseas. By late Song times, Hangzhou had more than a million and a half residents and was famed for its wealth, cleanliness, and the number and variety of diversions it offered.

A visitor to Hangzhou could wander through its 10 great marketplaces, each stocked with products from much of the known world. The less consumption-minded visitor could enjoy the city's many parks and delightful gardens, or go boating on the great Western Lake. There the pleasure craft of the rich mingled with special barges for gaming, dining, or listening to Hangzhou's famous "singing-girls." By late afternoon, one could visit the bath houses that were found throughout the city. At these establishments, one could also get a massage and sip a cup of tea or rice wine. In the evening, one might dine at one of the city's many fine restaurants, which specialized in the varied and delicious cuisines of the different regions of China. After dinner, there was a variety of entertainments from which to choose. One could take in the pleasure parks, where acrobats, jugglers, and actors performed for the passing crowds. Other options included one of the city's ornate tea houses, an opera performance by the lake, or a viewing of landscape paintings by artists from the city's famed academy. Having spent such a day, it would be hard for a visitor to disagree with Marco Polo—who himself hailed from another beautiful city of canals, Venice—that Hangzhou was "the most noble city and the best that is in the world."

Figure 17.5 *One of the many urban scenes painted in the Song era provides a panoramic view of the bustling city of Kaifeng (once an imperial capital) on the Grand Canal. The broad-hulled riverboats pictured here were ideal for transporting bulk goods, such as rice or cloth, between north and south China. But they were no match for the great junks that ventured into the seas to trade with Japan and southeast Asia. The riverfront is dominated by markets and open-air restaurants that spread throughout China in this era of prosperity.*

Expanding Agrarian Production and Life in the Country

The movement of the population southward to the fertile valleys of the Yangtze and other river systems was part of a larger process of agrarian expansion in the Tang and Song period. The expansion of Chinese settlement and agricultural production was promoted by the rulers of both dynasties. Their officials actively encouraged peasant groups to migrate to uncultivated areas or those occupied by shifting cultivators or peoples of non-Chinese descent. The state also supported military garrisons in these areas to protect the new settlements and to complete the task of subduing non-Chinese peoples. State-regulated irrigation and embankment systems advanced agrarian expansion. For example, the great canals made it possible for peasants who grew specialized crops, such as tea, or those who cultivated silkworms to market their produce over much of the empire. The introduction of new seeds, such as the famed Champa rice from Vietnam; better use of human, animal, and silt manures; more thorough soil preparation and weeding; and multiple cropping and improved water control techniques increased the yields of peasant holdings. Inventions such as the wheelbarrow eased the plowing, planting, weeding, and harvesting tasks that occupied much of the time of most Chinese people. The engraving shown in Figure 17.6 gives us a glimpse of rural scenes that were reproduced hundreds of thousands of times across China all through the Tang and Song centuries and much of the millennium that followed.

The rulers of both the Sui and Tang dynasties had adopted policies aimed at breaking up the great estates of the old aristocracy and distributing land more equitably among the free peasant households of the empire. These policies were designed in part to reduce or eliminate the threat that the powerful aristocracy posed for the new dynasties. They were also intended to bolster the position of the ordinary peasants, whose labors and well-being had long been viewed by Confucian scholars as essential to a prosperous and stable social order. To a point, these agrarian measures succeeded. For a time the numbers of the free peasantry increased, and the average holding size in many areas rose. The fortunes of many of the old aristocratic families also declined, thus removing many of them as independent centers of power. They were supplanted gradually in the rural areas by the gentry side of the scholar-gentry combination that dominated the imperial bureaucracy.

The extended-family households of the gentry that were found in rural settlements in the Han era increased in size and elegance in the Tang and Song. The widespread use of the graceful curved roofs with upturned corners that one associates with Chinese civilization dates from the Tang period. By imperial

Figure 17.6 *The farming methods developed in the Song era are illustrated by this 17th-century engraving. Note the overseer, protected by an umbrella from the hot sun. Improved productivity, particularly of staple crops such as irrigated rice, meant that China's long-held advantages over other civilizations in terms of the population it could support increased in this era. By the early 14th century, as much as a quarter of humanity may have lived in the Chinese empire.*

decree, curved roofs were reserved for people of high rank, including the gentry families. With intricately carved and painted roof timbers topped with glazed tiles of yellow or green, the great dwellings of the gentry left no doubt about the status and power of the families who lived in them. At the same time, their muted colors, wood and bamboo construction, and simple lines blended beautifully with nearby gardens and groves of trees.

Family and Society in the Tang–Song Era

Chinese family organization at various class levels in the Tang and Song centuries closely resembled that found in earlier periods. Nonetheless, the position of women showed signs of improving under the Tang and early Song eras, and then deteriorated steadily in the late Song. As in the classical age, extended-family households were preferred, but normally they could be afforded only by the upper classes. The male-dominated hierarchy promoted by Confucius and other early thinkers held sway at all class levels. In the Tang period, the authority of elders and males within the family was buttressed by laws that prescribed beheading as a punishment for children who struck their parents or grandparents in anger, and two and one-half years of hard labor for younger brothers or sisters who hit their older siblings. Over the centuries, a very elaborate process of forging marriage alliances developed. Professional go-betweens, almost always women, helped both families to negotiate such prickly issues as matching young men and women and the amount of the dowry to be paid to the husband's family. Brides and grooms in China, in contrast to those in India, generally were about the same age, probably because of the Confucian reluctance to mix generations.

Both within the family and in society at large, women remained clearly subordinate to men. But some evidence suggests that at least for women of the upper classes in urban areas, the opportunities for personal expression increased in the Tang and early Song. As the example of the empresses Wu and Wei and the concubine Yang Guifei make clear, Tang women could wield considerable power at the highest levels of Chinese society. That they also enjoyed access to a broad range of activities, if not career possibilities, is indicated by a surviving pottery figure from the early Tang period of a young woman playing polo.

Tang and Song law allowed divorce by mutual consent of both husband and wife. There were also laws prohibiting a husband from setting aside his wife if her parents were dead or if he had been poor when they were married and later became rich. These suggest that Chinese wives had more defenses against capricious behavior by their husbands than was the case in India at this time. A remarkable degree of independence is also indicated by the practice, reported in late Song times, of wealthy women in large cities such as Hangzhou taking lovers (or what were politely called "complementary husbands") with the knowledge of their husbands.

The Neo-Confucian Assertion of Male Dominance

Evidence of the independence and legal rights enjoyed by a small minority of women in the Tang–Song era is all but overwhelmed by the worsening condition of Chinese women in general. The assertion of male dominance was especially pronounced in the thinking of the neo-Confucian philosophers, who, as we have seen, became a major force in the later Song period. The neo-Confucians stressed the woman's role as homemaker and mother, particularly as the bearer of sons to continue the patrilineal family line. They advocated confining women and emphasized the importance of virginity for young brides, fidelity for wives, and chastity for widows. Like their counterparts in India, widows were discouraged from remarrying.

At the same time, men were permitted to have premarital sex without scandal, to take concubines if they could afford them, and to remarry if one or more of their wives died. The neo-Confucians attacked the Buddhists for promoting career alternatives for women, such as scholarship and the monastic life, at the expense of marriage and raising a family. They drafted laws that favored men in inheritance, divorce, and familial interaction. They also excluded women from the sort of education that would allow them to enter the civil service and rise to positions of political power.

No practice exemplifies the degree to which women in Chinese civilization were constricted and subordinated as dramatically as **footbinding.** This counterpart of the veil and seclusion in Islam may have had its origins in the delight one of the Tang emperors took in the tiny feet of his favorite dancing girl. Whatever its origins, by the later Song era, upper-class men had developed a preference for small feet for women. This preference later spread to lower-class groups, including the peasantry. In response to male demands, on which the successful negotiation of a young woman's marriage contract might hinge, mothers began to bind the feet of their daughters as early as age five or six. The young girl's toes were turned under and bound with silk, as shown by the illustration in Figure 17.7, which was wound more tightly as she grew. By the time she reached marriageable age, her foot had been transformed into the "lotus petal" or "golden lily" shapes that were presumably preferred by prospective husbands.

Bound feet were a constant source of pain for the rest of a woman's life, and they greatly limited her mobility by making it very difficult to walk even short distances. Limited mobility made it easier for husbands to confine their wives to the family compound. It also meant that women could not engage in occupations except ones that could be pursued within the family compound, such as textile production (see chapter opening illustration). For this reason, the

lower classes, whose households often depended on women's labor in the fields, markets, or homes of the wealthy to make ends meet, were slow to adopt the practice. But once it was in fashion among the scholar-gentry and other elite classes, footbinding became vital to winning a husband. Because a good marriage for their daughters was the primary goal of Chinese mothers, the practice was unquestioningly passed from one generation of women to the next. Footbinding epitomized the extent to which elite women's possibilities for self-fulfillment had been constricted by the later Song period.

A Glorious Age: Invention and Artistic Creativity

Perhaps even more than for political and economic transformations, the Tang and Song eras are remembered as a time of remarkable Chinese accomplishments in science, technology, literature, and the fine arts. Major technological breakthroughs and scientific discoveries were made under each dynasty. Some of them, particularly those involving the invention of new tools, production techniques, and weapons, gradually spread to other civilizations and fundamentally changed the course of human development. Until recent centuries, the arts and literature of China were not well known beyond its borders. Their impact was confined mainly to areas such as central Asia, Japan, and Vietnam, where Chinese imports had long been a major impetus for cultural change. But the poetry and short stories of the Tang and the landscape paintings of the Song are some of the most splendid artistic creations of all human history.

As we have seen, new agricultural tools and innovations such as banks and paper money contributed a great deal to economic growth and social prosperity in the Tang–Song era. In this respect, the engineering feats of the period are particularly noteworthy. In addition to building the Grand Canal, Tang and Song engineers made great advances in building dikes and dams and regulating the flow of water in complex irrigation systems. They also devised ingenious new ways to build bridges, long a major focus of engineering efforts in a land dominated by mountains and waterways. From arched and segmented to suspension and trussed, most of the basic bridge types known to humans were pioneered in China.

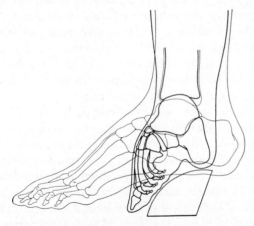

Figure 17.7 *The contrast between the bone structure of a normal foot and that of a Chinese woman whose foot has been bound since she was a young girl is illustrated in this diagram. Young girls with bound feet needed special footwear as they matured. As the diagram shows, most of the foot rested on a thick heel. Little or no sole was needed, and the outer covering came to a point in front where the toes would have been had the foot been allowed to grow normally.*

In Depth

Artistic Expression and Social Values

Studying artistic creativity is one of the most effective ways of probing the beliefs and values of a civilization. In some cases in which the civilization in question did not develop writing, or at least writing that we can now decipher, art and architecture provide much of the evidence by which we can learn about the attitudes and lifestyles of vanished peoples. Some of the most notable examples include the ancient Indus civilization of south Asia and many of the high civilizations of the Americas and sub-Saharan Africa. Even in civilizations for which written records have survived, we can learn a good deal about social structure by discovering who produced the art and for whom it was created, about technology by studying artistic techniques and materials, and about worldviews by exploring the messages the art was intended to convey. In comparing some of the major forms of artistic expression of the great civilizations, we can also identify underlying similarities and differences in the values by which the peoples who developed them organized their societies and responded to the natural and supernatural worlds.

The fact that members of the ruling political elite produced many of the landscape paintings of the Song era is unusual in the history of civilization. The sculptures that adorned the temples of India and the statues, paintings, and stained glass that graced the cathedrals of medieval Europe were created mainly by specialized and highly trained artisans whose skills were passed down over many generations. By contrast, the Song artists were often amateurs who painted in their leisure time. Even the most talented, who won enough patronage to devote themselves to painting full time, began as Confucian scholars and very often administrators. It is not just the amateur and "master of all fields" ideals that are remarkable here but the fact that so much art was produced by the men who also ran the country. In most of the other civilizations we have studied, political life has been dominated by warrior and priestly classes, not artistic scholar-bureaucrats like those who governed China.

Even in civilizations such as those of medieval Europe and Islam, where priests and religious teachers produced fine art in the form of manuscript illu-

minations, the people involved seldom had political responsibilities or power. Thus, the artistic creativity of China's political elite underscores the importance of the preference for civil over military leaders in Chinese society. It also tells us a good deal about the qualities the Chinese associated with a truly civilized and superior person—a person who was deemed worthy to rule the Middle Kingdom.

Song landscapes expressed the reactions and ideals of individual people, whom we can identify by the distinctive seals with which they stamped their paintings. The paintings clearly were intended for the pleasure and edification of the Chinese educated classes, not for museum viewing or mass consumption. Landscape painting reinforced the identity and values of this scholarly elite across the vast spaces of the Chinese empire as well as across time. In a famous incident, the Confucian philosopher Ju Xi remarked on the nobility and loyalty that he saw so clearly in the calligraphy of scholars from the Warring States era.

This individualism and elitism in Chinese art can be contrasted with the anonymous creation of sculptures and religious paintings in Hindu and Buddhist civilizations and medieval Europe or the mosaic decorations of the mosques of Islam. In each of these other civilizations, artistic works that adorned temples, cathedrals, and mosques were intended for a mass audience. The moral instruction for the scholarly few that was contained in the Song landscapes had a very different purpose than the religious sculptures or mosaics of other civilizations. The sculptures and mosaics were created to convey a religious message, to remind the viewers of a key event in the life of Christ or the Buddha, or to impress upon them the horrors of hell or the delights of heaven.

Thus, the highest art forms, linked to a common religion, bridged the gulf between elites and the masses in Hindu, Buddhist, Christian, and Muslim civilizations. Imported Buddhist art forms performed this function in some periods in Chinese history. But the more enduring Confucian-Daoist artistic creativity, best exemplified by landscape painting, accentuated the differences that separated the educated scholar-gentry and the common people.

(continued)

One of the most important of the many technological advances made in the Tang era, the invention of explosive powder, at first had little impact on warfare. For centuries, the Chinese used these potent chemical mixtures mainly for fireworks, which delighted emperors and the masses alike. By the late Song, however, explosive powder was widely used by the imperial armies in a variety of grenades and bombs that were hurled at the enemy by catapults. Song armies and warships also were equipped with naphtha flamethrowers, poisonous gases, and rocket launchers. These projectiles were perhaps the most effective weapons the dynasty used in its losing struggle to check nomadic incursions. On the domestic scene, chairs—modeled on those found in India—were introduced into the household, the habit of drinking tea swept the empire, coal was used for fuel for the first time, and the first kite soared into the heavens.

Although the number of major inventions in the Song era was lower than in the Tang, several were pivotal for the future of all civilizations. Compasses, which had been used since the last centuries B.C.E. by Chinese military commanders and magicians, were applied to sea navigation for the first time in the Song period. The abacus, the ancestor of the modern calculator, was introduced to help merchants count their profits and tax collectors keep track of revenues. In the mid-11th century, a remarkable artisan named Bi Sheng devised the technique of printing with movable type. Although block printing had been perfected in China in the preceding centuries, the use of movable type was a great advance in the production of written records and scholarly books. Combined with paper, which the Chinese had invented in the Han period, printing made it possible for them to attain a level of literacy that excelled that of any preindustrial civilization.

Scholarly Refinement and Artistic Accomplishment

The reinvigorated scholar-gentry elite was responsible for much of the artistic and literary creativity of the Tang–Song era. Buddhist art and architecture had been heavily patronized by the court, prosperous merchants, and wealthy monasteries in the Tang period. But scholar-administrators and Confucian teachers wrote much of the literature for which the Tang is best remembered, and they painted the landscapes that were the most sublime cultural productions of the Song. Confucian thinkers valued skillful writing and painting, and educated people were expected to practice these arts. The Chinese educational establishment was geared to turning out generalists rather than the specialists who are so revered in our own society. A well-educated man dabbled with varying degrees of success in many fields. Thus, after a hard day at the Ministry of Public Works, a truly accomplished official was expected to spend the evening composing songs on his lute, admiring a new painting or creating his own, or sipping rice wine while composing a poem to the harvest moon. Thus, talented and often well-trained amateurs wrote most of the poems, composed much of the music, and painted the landscapes for which the Tang–Song era is renowned (Figure 17.8).

As the Confucian scholar-gentry supplanted the Buddhists as the major producers of art and literature, devotional objects and religious homilies gave way to a growing fixation on everyday life and the delights of the natural world. Much of the short story literature was focused on the lives of the common people, popular beliefs in witchcraft and demons, ill-fated romances, and even detective stories about brutal murders. Tang poetry moved from early verses that dwelt on the "pleasant breezes that envelope[d]

Figure 17.8 *The simplicity of composition, the use of empty space, and the emphasis on nature are all characteristic of Chinese landscape painting at its height in the Song era. The colors used tended to be muted; often only brown or black ink was used. Most artists stamped their work with signature seals, and poems describing scenes related to those in the painting floated in the empty space at the top or sides.*

the emperor's chair" to a seemingly endless variety of ways of celebrating the natural world. No one was better at the latter than the most famous poet of the Tang era, **Li Bo.** His poems, like those of the great Persian authors, blend images of the everyday world with philosophical musings:

The rain was over, green covered the land.

One last cloudlet melted away in the clear sky.

The east wind came home with the spring

Bearing blossoms to sprout on the branches.

Flowers are fading now and time will end.

All mortal men perceive it and their sighs are deep.

But I will turn to the sacred hills

And learn from Tao [Dao] and from magic how to fly.

This intense interest in nature came to full artistic fruition in the landscape paintings of the Song era. Most of them were produced by the cultivated men of the scholar-gentry class, and they pulled together diverse aspects of Chinese civilization. The brushes and techniques used were similar to those used in writing the Chinese language, which itself was regarded as a high art form. The paintings were symbolic, intended to teach moral lessons or explore philosophical ideas. The objects depicted were not only beautiful in themselves but stood for larger concepts: A crane and a pine tree, for example, represented longevity; bamboo shoots were associated with the scholar-gentry class; and a dragon could call to mind any number of things, including the emperor, the cosmos, or life-giving rain.

There was an abstract quality to the paintings that gives them a special appeal in the present day.

The artists were not concerned with depicting nature accurately but rather with creating a highly personal vision of natural beauty. A premium was placed on subtlety and suggestion. For example, the winner of an imperial contest painted a lone monk drawing water from an icy stream to depict the subject announced by the emperor: a monastery hidden deep in the mountains during the winter. Song landscapes often were painted on scrolls that could be read as the viewer unfolded them bit by bit. Most were accompanied by a poem, sometimes composed by the painter, that complemented the subject matter and was aimed at explaining the artist's ideas.

GLOBAL CONNECTIONS: China's World Role

By retreating to the south, the Song rulers managed to survive the assaults of the nomads from the north. But as the dynasty weakened, enduring patterns of nomadic incursions resurfaced and built to the apex of pastoral military and political expansion under the Mongols. The Song emperors could not retreat far enough to escape the onslaught of the most brilliant nomadic commander of them all, Chinggis Khan, who directed perhaps the most powerful military machine the world had seen up to that time. The Song rulers bought time by paying tribute to the Mongol Khan and making alliances with him against their common enemies. But another Mongol leader, Kubilai Khan, who was ready to launch a sustained effort to conquer the southern refuge of the Song dynasty, later emerged as the paramount Mongol lord. He was soon ready to launch a sustained effort to conquer the southern refuge of the Song dynasty, which was completed by 1279.

The long Tang–Song era was truly pivotal in Chinese and world history. Centralized administration and the great Chinese bureaucracy were not only restored but strengthened. The scholar-gentry elite, which had for so long been the critical binding force for Chinese civilization, triumphed over its aristocratic, nomadic, and Buddhist monastic rivals. Under nomadic and indigenous dynasties, the scholar-gentry continued to define and direct Chinese civilization for the next six and a half centuries. During the nearly seven centuries of Tang and Song rule, the area of Chinese civilization had grown dramatically as the south was fully integrated with the north.

From the Tang era until the 18th century, the Chinese economy was one of the world's most advanced in terms of market orientation, volume of overseas trade, productivity per acre, and sophistication of its tools and techniques of craft production. Production of luxury craft goods drew attention from merchants and upper-class consumers in many other regions, feeding expanding Afro-Eurasian trade. Chinese inventions such as paper, printing, and gunpowder, also spreading widely, fundamentally changed the course of development in all other human civilizations. Until the 18th century, the imperial dynasties of China had political power and economic resources unmatched by those of any other civilization.

Further Readings

In addition to the general histories of China suggested in Chapter 5, several important works cover the Tang and Song eras. The volume, edited by Denis Twitchett, devoted to the Tang and Song in the *Cambridge History of China* is an essential reference work. There are detailed works on the founding of the Tang dynasty by C. P. Fitzgerald (1970) and Woodbridge Bingham (1940), but these should be read in conjunction with the more recent *Mirror to the Son of Heaven* (1974), which provides valuable correctives to the interpretations of these earlier authors. Useful insights into political and cultural life in the Tang era can be gleaned from the specialized essays in the volume *Perspectives on the Tang* (1973), edited by Arthur Wright and Denis Twitchett. On social patterns in the Tang era, see Charles Benn, *Daily Life in Traditional China: The Tang Dynasty* (2002). Until recently, the most accessible work on society and politics in the Song era was Jacques Gernet's *Daily Life in China on the Eve of the Mongol Invasion, 1250–1276* (1962), which is highly entertaining and informative. On the great social and economic transitions of the Song era, Mark Elvin's *The Pattern of the Chinese Past* (1973) is insightful, provocative, and controversial. These standard accounts can now be supplemented by P. B. Ebry, *The Aristocratic Families of Early Imperial China* (1978); Heng Chye Kiang, *Cities of Aristocrats and Bureaucrats: The Development of Medieval Chinese Cities* (1999); and D. McMullen, *State and Scholars in T'ang China* (1988). Bret Hinsch's *Women in Early Imperial China* (2002) provides a useful introduction to this subject, which is closely examined in Kathryn Bernhardt, *Women and Property in China, 960-1949* (1999) and Bettine Birge, *Women, Property and Confucian Reaction in Sung and Yüan China, 960-1368* (2002).

Of the numerous works on Chinese art and painting, perhaps the best place to start is with the standard work by Mai-mai Sze, *The Way of Chinese Painting* (1956), which quotes extensively from Chinese manuals. Of more recent works, the general survey by Laurence Sickman and Alexander Soper, as well as James Cahill's study of landscape painting, stand out. And they can be supplemented by Alfreda Murch's recent study of *Poetry and Painting in Song China* (2000). A wonderful sampler of Li Bo's poetry can be found in a volume titled *Bright Moon, Perching Bird* (1987), edited by J. P. Seaton and James Cryer.

On the Web

The art of Six Dynasties, including calligraphy, is the subject of a virtual exhibit at http://www.artsmia.org/arts-of-asia/china/dynasties/six.cfm, http://cla.calpoly.edu/~jwetzel/Study/SECULA~1.HTM and http://depts.washington.edu/chinaciv/callig/7calsixd.htm. Changan, the capital of the most culturally brilliant of these dynasties, the Tang, is presented visually at http://suntzu.larc.calpoly.edu/mrc/320-2002/China%20Tang%20Changan/Home.html and set in the context of Chinese urban history at http://www.owlnet.rice.edu/~arch343/lecture8.html. The remarkable technological achievements of this period of Chinese history, which included the development of explosives and paper, are presented at http://www.silkroadcn.com/chinainfo/fourinvention.htm, and http://geocities.com/Athens/oracle/2793/china.html. Mahayana and Chan Buddhism (http://www.ciolek.com/WWWVL-Buddhism.html) survived the nativist revival that also characterized this era. The prosperity of the times stimulated the spread of the practice of the foot binding of women, the results of which are graphically shown and http://academic.brooklyn.cuny.edu/core9/phalsall/studpages/vento.html, http://www-ec.njit.edu/~jkc1763/fb.htm, and http://www.amonline.net.au/bodyart/shaping/footbinding.htm.

CHAPTER 18

THE SPREAD OF CHINESE CIVILIZATION: JAPAN, KOREA, AND VIETNAM

Buddhist temples and gardens provided havens for peace in the turbulent centuries of warlord domination in Japanese history. Although Chinese motifs and architectural styles were employed by the Japanese, the Vietnamese, and the Koreans, each people evolved its own distinctive style. The Japanese in particular excelled in garden design, producing one of the most emulated traditions of landscape design in human history.

The splendid achievements of the Chinese in nearly all areas of human endeavor were readily apparent to neighboring peoples in east and central Asia. It was perhaps inevitable that surrounding peoples would try to emulate China as a model of civilized development. As we have seen in Chapter 9, Japan, the most important of these neighbors in terms of its impact on global history, began to borrow heavily from China in the critical 5th and 6th centuries C.E., when its own pattern of civilization started to coalesce. China's influence on the nomadic peoples to the north and west and on areas such as Tibet has been noted in earlier chapters. By the last centuries B.C.E., Vietnam and Korea were also drawn into the orbit of Chinese civilization.

This chapter focuses on the interaction and exchanges between China and the three agrarian neighbors it so strongly influenced: Japan, Korea, and Vietnam. In each of these societies, Chinese influences blended with local conditions, preferences, and creativity to produce related but distinctive patterns of civilized development. In the case of the Japanese, we examine the strategies they adopted to build on the foundations laid in the first centuries C.E., which were discussed in Chapter 9. For Korea and Vietnam, we begin with the first contacts between the Chinese and the peoples of these areas and then examine the different paths to civilization each followed.

In each of these areas, Buddhism played key roles in the transmission of Chinese civilization and the development of the indigenous cultures. Because Buddhism originated in India, the layers of cross-cultural interaction in these processes are all the more complex and profound. In each case, ideas and rituals originating in India were filtered through Chinese society and culture before being passed on to Japan, Korea, and Vietnam. Buddhism also provided a critical link between the civilizations developing in Korea and Japan.

Japan: The Imperial Age

 Chinese influence on Japan peaked in the 7th and 8th centuries as Japanese rulers and their courtiers tried to build a Chinese-style bureaucracy and army and to emulate Chinese etiquette and art. But the isolated and ultracivilized court centers at Nara and later Heian lost political control to powerful aristocratic families and local warlords. Intensifying rivalries between these regional military leaders eventually plunged Japan into a long series of civil wars from the 12th to the 17th century.

By the 7th and 8th centuries C.E., the Japanese court at Nara (see Map 18.1) was awash in Chinese imports. Indigenous cultural influences, particularly those linked to Shinto views of the natural and supernatural world, remained central to Japanese cultural development. But in the Taika (645–710), Nara (710–784), and

419

200 B.C.E.	600 C.E.	800 C.E.	1000 C.E.	1200 C.E.	1400 C.E.
206 B.C.E.–220 C.E. Reign of Han dynasty in China	**618–907** Tang dynasty in China	**838** Last Japanese embassy to China	**1160–1185** Taira clan dominant in Japan	**1231–1392** Mongol rule in Korea	**1467–1477** Onin War in Japan
111 Vietnam conquered by Chinese	**646** Taika reforms in Japan	**857–1160** Period of Fujiwara dominance in Japan	**1180–1185** Gempei Wars in Japan	**1279–1368** Mongol rule in China	**1500** Nguyen dynasty in central/south Vietnam founded
109 Choson (Korea) conquered by Chinese	**668** Korea wins independence from Tang conquerors	**918–1392** Koryo dynasty in Korea	**1185–1333** Kamakura Shogunate in Japan	**1392–1910** Yi dynasty in Korea	**1539–1787** Trinh dynasty in Vietnam/Red River area
39 C.E. Trung sisters revolt in Vietnam	**668–918** Silla kingdom in Korea	**939** Vietnam wins its independence from China			**1600** Founding of the Tokugawa Shogunate in Japan
222–589 Era of Division in China	**710–784** Imperial Japanese capital at Nara	**960–1279** Song dynasty in China			
589–618 Sui dynasty in China	**794** Japanese capital shifts to Heian (Kyoto)	**980–1009** Le dynasty in Vietnam			

Heian (794–857) periods, Japanese borrowing from China—though selective—peaked. This borrowing touched nearly all aspects of Japanese life, particularly at the level of the elites and among the people of the court towns.

In 646, the emperor and his advisors introduced the far-reaching **Taika reforms,** aimed at completely revamping the imperial administration along Chinese lines. Japanese court scholars struggled to master thousands of Chinese characters, which bore little relationship to the language they spoke. They wrote dynastic histories patterned after those commissioned by the emperors of China, and followed an elaborate court etiquette that somewhat uneasily combined Chinese protocol with ancient Japanese ideas about politeness and decorum. The Japanese aristocracy struggled to master Confucian ways, worshiped in Chinese-style temples, and admired Buddhist art that was Chinese in subject matter and technique.

Even the common people were affected by the steady flow of influence from the mainland. In the towns they stared in awe at the great Buddhist temples and bowed to passing aristocrats trying to present themselves as Confucian scholars. The peasants turned to Buddhist monks for cures when they were sick or to Buddhist magic when they needed a change of luck. They had begun to mesh the worship of Buddhist deities with that of the ancient *kami*, or nature spirits, of Japan.

Crisis at Nara and the Shift to Heian (Kyoto)

If they had succeeded, the Taika reforms of 646 would have represented the culmination of cen-

turies of Japanese borrowing from China. The central objectives of the proposed changes were to remake the Japanese monarch into an absolutist Chinese-style emperor (even to the point of adding "Son of Heaven" to the Japanese ruler's many titles). The reforms also were intended to create a genuine professional bureaucracy and peasant conscript army in Japan to match those of Han and Tang China. But the changes necessary for these goals to be achieved were frustrated by the resistance of the aristocratic families and the Buddhist monastic orders, who dominated both the emperor and the capital as a whole.

A century after the reforms were introduced, the Buddhist monks in particular had grown so bold and powerful that the court and aristocracy lived in fear of street demonstrations by "rowdy monks" and of the escalating demands of the heads of the monastic orders. Their influence even threatened to engulf the throne in the 760s, when a clever Buddhist prelate worked his way into the inner circle of the empress Koken. His schemes to marry her and become emperor were uncovered and foiled. But it was clear to the emperor's advisors that measures had to be taken to ensure that women could never rule Japan and to check the growing influence of the monastic orders at court.

The emperor, Koken's husband, fled and established a new capital city at Heian (see Map 18.1), or what was later called Kyoto, about 28 miles away. The Buddhists were forbidden to build monasteries in the new capital. But to get around this restriction, the monks established monasteries in the hills surrounding Heian, and they soon reemerged as a potent force at court as royal advisors.

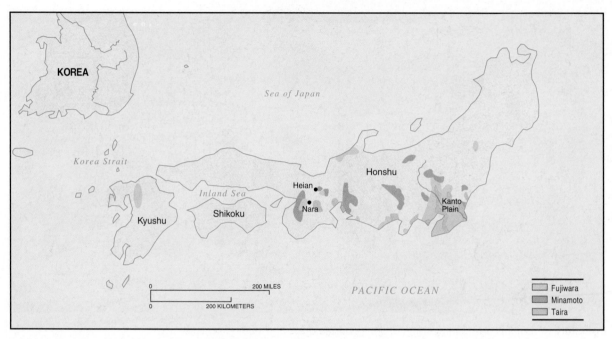

Map 18.1 *Japan in the Imperial and Warlord Periods*

In addition to trying to control the Buddhist monks, the emperor abandoned all pretense of continuing the Taika reforms, which had long been stalled by aristocratic and popular opposition. He fully restored the great aristocratic families, whose power the reforms had been intended to curb. The elaborate system of ranks into which the aristocrats were divided (patterned after that in China) was maintained. But like the Koreans, the Japanese broke with Chinese precedent in determining rank by birth and by allowing little mobility between the various orders. The aristocrats had already taken over most of the positions in the central government. Now, their formal right to build up rural estates was restored as well. The emperor also gave up an ambitious scheme to build a peasant conscript army. In its place, local leaders were ordered to organize militia forces, which would soon play a critical role in further eroding the control of the imperial household.

Ultracivilized: Court Life in the Heian Era

Although the basis of imperial political power had been severely eroded within decades of the shift to Heian, court culture soared to new levels of refine-
ment. For several centuries more, the Japanese emperors and their courtiers continued to inhabit a closed world of luxury and aesthetic delights. Men and women of the aristocratic classes lived their lives in accordance with strict codes of polite behavior, under the constant scrutiny of their peers and superiors. In this hothouse atmosphere, social status was everything, love affairs were a major preoccupation, and gossip was rampant. By our standards, life in this constricted and very artificial world was false and suffocating. Yet rarely in human history has so much energy been so focused on the pursuit of beauty or has social interaction—on the surface at least—been so gracious and well mannered.

At the Heian court, members of the imperial household and the leading aristocratic families lived in a complex of palaces and gardens, a section of which is depicted in the painting in Figure 18.1. The buildings were of unpainted wood, which the Japanese found the most appealing, with sliding panels, matted floors, and wooden walkways running between the separate residences where the many dignitaries lived. Fish ponds, artificial lakes with waterfalls, and fine gardens were scattered among the courtiers' living quarters. Writing verse was perhaps the most valued art at the court. The poems were

Figure 18.1 *From this artist's impression of the elaborate dress and studied poses of Heian courtiers, as well as the carefully cultivated trees and the tasteful decor, one gains a vivid sense of the formality and attention to aesthetic pleasures that dominated the lives of the Japanese elite in this era. As the prominence of women in the painting suggests, the hothouse world of the Heian court provided a tiny minority of Japanese women with outlets for expressing emotion and creativity that have been denied to most women through much of civilized history.*

often written on painted fans or scented paper, and sometimes they were sent in little boats down the streams that ran through the palace grounds. The verse was brief and full of allusions to Chinese and Japanese classical writings. In the following couplet, a young courtier expresses his disappointment at being denied access to a pretty young girl:

> Having come upon an evening blossom
> The mist is loath to go with the morning sun.

Partly to accommodate the need for literary expression of this type, the written script the Japanese had borrowed from the Chinese was simplified, making it more compatible with spoken Japanese. One result of these changes was an outpouring of poetic and literary works that were more and more distinctively Japanese. The most celebrated of these was Lady Murasaki's *The Tale of Genji*. None of the works on court life captured its charm and its underlying tensions and sadness as wonderfully as Lady Murasaki's,

which was the first novel in any language (Figure 18.2). In the story, she relates the life history of a prominent and amorous son of the emperor and the fate of his descendants. As the story makes clear, Genji's life is almost wholly devoted to the pursuit of aesthetic enjoyment, whether in affairs with beautiful women or in musical entertainments in a garden scented with blooming flowers. Uncouth commoners and distasteful things, such as dirt, cheap pottery, and rough popular entertainments, are to be avoided at all costs. When her rivals at the court want to insult Genji's mother, for example, they leave spoiled fruit in the passages where she or her maidservants must pass. An encounter with a shriveled piece of fruit contributes to the illness that leads to her premature death.

Everyone who matters in Genji's world is obsessed with the social conventions that govern everything, from which gown is proper for a given ceremony to the composition of a suitable poem to woo a potential lover or win the emperor's favor. Although women rivaled men as poets, artists, and

In addition to novels such as Lady Murasaki's, some of the most elegant poetry in the Japanese language was written in this era. Again, it is sparing in words but rich in imagery and allusions to the natural world:

> This perfectly still
>
> Spring Day bathed in the soft light
>
> From the spread-out sky,
>
> Why do the cherry blossoms so restlessly scatter down?
>
> Although I am sure
>
> That he will not be coming
>
> In the evening light
>
> When the locusts shrilly call
>
> I go to the door and wait.

As the female authorship of this poem and *The Tale of Genji* clearly illustrate, women at the Heian court were expected to be as poised and cultured as men. Because they were less involved, however, with Chinese cultural imports (presumed to be a superior male preserve) they actually, for a time, played an unusually creative role in Japanese productions. They wrote poems, played flutes or stringed instruments in informal concerts, and participated in elaborate schemes to snub or disgrace rivals. Like their counterparts in China and the Islamic world, they also became involved in palace intrigues and power struggles.

The Decline of Imperial Power

While the emperor and his courtiers admired the plum blossoms and the newest fashions in court dress, some of the aristocratic families at court were busy running the rapidly shrinking imperial bureaucracy. By the mid-9th century, one of these families, the **Fujiwara,** exercised exceptional influence over imperial affairs. Not only did they pack the upper administration with family members and shape imperial policy, but they also increasingly married Fujiwaras into the imperial family. By the middle of the 10th century, one aged Fujiwara chief minister had seen four of his daughters married to emperors.

Families such as the Fujiwara used the wealth and influence of their high office to build up large estates that provided a stable financial base for their growing power. Especially in the vicinity of the capital, they had to compete in these purchases with the Buddhist

Figure 18.2 *The prominent roles played by women at the Japanese imperial court centers are evident in this painting illustrating one of the episodes in Lady Murasaki's* The Tale of Genji. *The painting also captures the intensely inward-looking character of court life that gradually cut the emperor and his entourage off from the warriors, townspeople, and peasants they ruled. The growing isolation of the court provided opportunities for regional lords with a more military orientation and more effective links to the population as a whole to eventually seize effective control of Japan.*

musicians and in their pervasive cultivation of aesthetic pleasure, it was unseemly for them to openly pursue lovers. Nonetheless, as Lady Murasaki's poignant novel makes clear, some women did court prospective lovers with great guile and passion. It was not uncommon for a high-born woman to spurn a suitor and humiliate him in front of her maidservants.

monasteries. But both could work together in the steady campaign to whittle down imperial control and increase their own. As the lands under their control expanded, both the monks and the court nobility greatly increased the number of peasants and artisans they in effect ruled. Cooperation between monastic orders and court aristocrats was promoted by the introduction of the secret texts and ceremonies of esoteric Buddhism in this period. These teachings and techniques to achieve salvation through prayers and meditation, which were focused by mystical diagrams and special hand positions, were the rage among the Heian elite. As aristocrats and monks steadily built up their own power in the capital, however, they failed to reckon with the growing power of the local lords.

The Rise of the Provincial Warrior Elites

The pursuit of landed estates that increasingly preoccupied the court aristocracy was also taken up by elite families in the provinces. Some of these families had aristocratic origins, but most had risen to power as landowners, estate managers, or local state officials. These families came to control land and labor and to deny these resources to the court. They gradually carved out little kingdoms, ruled by "house" governments, in various parts of the islands. They dominated their mini-states within the larger Japanese realm from small fortresses surrounded by wooden or earthen walls and moatlike ditches. The local lord and his retainers were housed within the fortress, constantly on the alert for an attack by a neighboring lord or the forces of one of the powerful families at court. Granaries for storing the rice provided by local peasants, blacksmith forges and stables, wells for water, and even armories made the fortresses self-contained worlds.

Within the mini-states ruled from the forts, the warrior leaders, or **bushi,** administered law, supervised public works projects, and collected revenue—mainly for themselves, not the court. The failure of the court's plans to build conscript armies also allowed the bushi to build up their own armies. These soon became the most effective military forces in the land. Although these mounted troops, or **samurai,** were loyal to the local lords, not to the court or high aristocratic officials, they were increasingly called in to protect the emperor and his retainers and to keep

the peace in the capital. As the imperial government's control over the country weakened in the 11th and 12th centuries, bandits freely roamed the countryside and the streets of the capital. Buddhist monasteries employed armed toughs to protect them and attack rival sects. In this atmosphere of rampant crime and civil strife, the court and high officials hired provincial lords and their samurai retainers to serve as bodyguards and to protect their palaces and mansions from robbery and arson.

These trends proved critical to the emergence of a warrior class, a characteristically fierce member of which is depicted in Figure 18.3. Counting on peasant dependants to supply them with food and other necessities, the bushi and samurai devoted their lives to hunting, riding, archery practice, and other activities that sharpened their martial skills. Until the 12th century, the main weapons of the mounted warriors

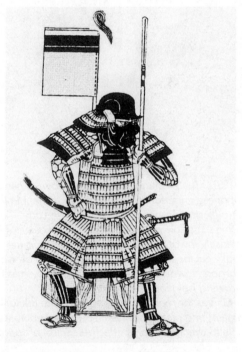

Figure 18.3 *The imposing presence of a fully armed samurai warrior is captured in this pen-and-ink drawing. The slats that make up the warrior's armor were crafted of fine steel braided together with leather, giving him protection against enemy arrows and sword thrusts and some freedom of movement. Note the two finely forged swords, his major weapons, and the flag attached to his armor, which identifies both the lord he serves and the unit to which he is attached.*

were powerful longbows, although they also carried straight swords. From the 12th century on, they increasingly relied on the superbly forged, curved steel swords that we commonly associate with the Japanese samurai. The bushi and the samurai warriors who served them rode into battles that increasingly hinged on the duels of great champions. These combats represented heroic warfare in the extreme. The time and location of battles were elaborately negotiated beforehand, and each side tried to demonstrate the justice of its cause and the treachery of its enemies. Before charging into battle, Japanese warriors proudly proclaimed their family lineage and its notable military exploits to their adversaries, who often missed the details because they were shouting back their own.

A warrior code developed that stressed family honor and death rather than retreat or defeat. Beaten or disgraced warriors turned to ritual suicide to prove their courage and restore their family's honor. They called this practice **seppuku,** which meant disembowelment. But it has come to be known in the West by the more vulgar expression *hara-kiri,* or belly splitting. Battles were chaotic—lots of shouting and clashing but few fatalities—that were won or lost depending on the performance of the champions on each side. Although a full chivalric code did not develop until some centuries later, Japan was steadily moving toward a feudal order that was remarkably similar to that developing in western Europe in this same postclassical period.

The rise of the samurai frustrated all hopes of creating a free peasantry. In fact, Japanese peasants were reduced in the next centuries to the status of serfs, bound to the land they worked and treated as the property of the local lord. They were also separated by rigid class barriers from the warrior elite, which was physically set off by its different ways of dressing and by prohibitions against the peasants carrying swords or riding horses. In their growing poverty and powerlessness, the peasants turned to popular Buddhism in the form of the salvationist pure land sect. The teachings of the pure land offered the promise of bliss in heaven for those who lived upright lives on earth. Colorful figures, such as the dancing monk Kuya, were intended to make Buddhist teachings comprehensible and appealing to both the peasantry and the artisans, who were concentrated in the fortress towns. Buddhist shrines and images became popular destinations for pilgrimages and objects of veneration.

The Era of Warrior Dominance

 From the 12th century onward, Japanese history was increasingly dominated by civil wars between shifting factions of the court aristocracy and local warlords. Chinese influence declined steadily in the centuries that followed. But in the midst of strife and social dislocation, the warrior elite and the artisan classes that served them managed to produce sublime creations in fields as diverse as ceramics, landscape architecture, and religious poetry. However, this creativity was obscured by continuing civil strife, which peaked in the late 15th and 16th centuries and ended only with the rise of the Tokugawa warlord family in the early 1600s.

As the power of the provincial lords grew, that of the imperial household and court aristocracy declined. Powerful families at the court, such as the Fujiwara, increasingly depended on alliances with regional lords to support them in disputes with their rivals. By the 11th and 12th centuries, the provincial families had begun to pack the court bureaucracy and compete for power. By the mid-12th century, competition turned to open feuding between the most powerful of these families, the **Taira** and the **Minamoto.** For a time, the Taira gained the upper hand by controlling the emperor and dominating at court. But when rivalry turned to open warfare in the early 1180s, the Minamoto commanders and their powerful network of alliances with provincial lords in various parts of the country proved superior to the leaders or allies the Taira could muster. More importantly, the Tairas' concentration of their power-grabbing efforts in the capital led to the breakdown of critical links with rural notables, who often sided with the Minamoto in the factional struggles.

The Declining Influence of China

As the power of the imperial house weakened, the relevance of Chinese precedents and institutions diminished for the Japanese. Pretensions to a heavenly mandate and centralized power became ludicrous; the emergence of a scholar-gentry elite was stifled by the reassertion of aristocratic power and prerogatives. Grand designs for an imperial bureaucracy never materialized. Buddhism was increasingly transformed by both aristocrats and peasants into a distinctively Japanese religion. With the decline of the Tang and a return to decades of political uncertainty and social turmoil in China, the Chinese model seemed even less relevant to the Japanese. As early as 838, the Japanese court decided to discontinue its embassies to the much-reduced Tang court. Japanese monks and traders still made the dangerous sea crossing to China, but the emperor's advisors no longer deemed official visits and groveling before the Son of Heaven to be worth all the bother.

For five years, the **Gempei Wars** raged in the heartland of the main island of Honshu (see Map 18.1). This conflict brought great suffering to the peasantry, whose farmlands were ravaged. At the same time, they were compelled to fight against each other. Often large numbers of poorly trained peasants were cut down by the better-armed, professional samurai warriors, who met these hapless rivals in the course of their seemingly endless ritual combats. By 1185, the Taira house faction had been destroyed. The Minamoto then established the **bakufu** (which literally means "tent"), or military government. The Minamoto capital was located at Kamakura in their base area on the Kanto plain, far to the east of the old court center at Heian (see Map 18.1). The emperor and his court were preserved, but real power now rested with the Minamoto and their samurai retainers. The feudal age in Japan had begun.

The Breakdown of Bakufu Dominance and the Age of the Warlords

Yoritomo, the leader of the victorious Minamoto, gravely weakened the Kamakura regime because of his obsessive fear of being overthrown by members of his own family. Close relatives, including his brother Yoshitsune, whose courage and military genius had much to do with the Minamoto triumph over the Taira, were murdered or driven into exile. Fear of spies lent an element of paranoia to elite life under the first of the Kamakura **shoguns,** or the military leaders of the bakufu. Although Yoritomo's rule went unchallenged, the measures he adopted to protect his throne left him without an able heir. His death and the weakness of those who succeeded him led to a scramble on the part of the bushi lords to build up their own power and enlarge their domains. The **Hojo,** one of the warrior families that had long been

closely allied to the Minamoto, soon dominated the Kamakura regime, although they were content to leave the Minamoto as the formal rulers. Thus, a curious and confusing three-tiered system arose. Real power rested in the Hojo family, who manipulated the Minamoto shoguns, who in turn claimed to rule in the name of the emperor who lived at Kyoto.

In the early 14th century, the situation became even murkier when the head of one of the branches of the Minamoto family, **Ashikaga Takuaji,** led a revolt of the bushi that overthrew the Kamakura regime and established the **Ashikaga Shogunate** (1336–1573) in its place. Because the emperor at the time of Ashikaga's seizure of power refused to recognize the usurper and tried to revive imperial power, he was driven from Kyoto to the mountain town of Yoshino. There, with the support of several warlords, the exiled emperor and his heirs fought against the Ashikaga faction and the puppet emperors they placed on the throne at Kyoto for much of the rest of the 14th century.

Although the Ashikaga were finally successful in destroying the rival Yoshino center of imperial authority, the long period of civil strife seriously undermined whatever authority the emperor had left as well as that of the shogunate. The bushi vassals of the warring factions were free to crush local rivals and to seize the lands of the peasantry, the old aristocracy, and competing warlords. As the power of the bushi warlords grew, the court aristocracy, which was impoverished by its inability to defend its estates, was nearly wiped out. The lands the warlords acquired were parceled out to their samurai retainers, who in turn pledged their loyalty and were expected to provide military support whenever their lord called on them.

The collapse of centralized authority was sharply accelerated by the outbreak of full-scale civil war, which raged from 1467 to 1477. Rival heirs to the Ashikaga Shogunate called on the warlord chiefs to support their claims. Samurai flocked to rival headquarters in different sections of Kyoto, where feuding soon broke into all-out warfare. Within a matter of years, the old imperial capital had been reduced to rubble and weed-choked fields. While the shogunate self-destructed in the capital, the provincial lords continued to amass power and plot new coalitions to destroy their enemies. Japan was divided into nearly 300 little kingdoms, whose warlord rulers were called **daimyos** rather than bushi.

In Depth

Comparing Feudalisms

In one sense, the existence of feudalism is easily explained. Many societies generated only weak central government structures simply because they lacked the resources, shared political values, and bureaucratic experience to develop alternatives. China under the Zhou dynasty is sometimes called feudal. The Russian kings from Rurik onward exercised only loose control over powerful landlords. Kings in the divine monarchy systems of sub-Saharan Africa, which flourished from about the 9th to the 19th century in various parts of the continent, similarly relied on deals and compromises with local and regional leaders. Indeed, African historians have often noted that kingdoms such as Ghana and Mali were ruled about as effectively as were Western monarchies during the Middle Ages.

A comparison of this sort reminds us that feudal systems were in many ways early, less sophisticated versions of political societies that were gradually moving from purely local toward more centralized organization. Indeed, almost all civilizations have experienced long periods of semicentralized rule. In all such cases, including feudal ones, the claims of central authorities are not matched by effective power. Regional leaders have armies of their own and do much of the effective administration of their localities. Kings have to make deals with such leaders, relying on personal negotiation and pledges of mutual respect, marriage alliances, negotiation, and a willingness to give the local princes free rein in practice.

The feudal systems that arose in the West and Japan differed in some respects from the many other decentralized systems they resemble. These differences make it desirable not to call all such systems feudal, thus diluting an extremely useful term beyond recognition. For example, Russia was often decentralized and often saw its rulers, whatever their grandiose claims, make concessions to regional nobles because the tsars depended on the loyalty and service of these subordinate lords. But Russia never developed a genuinely feudal political hierarchy, which is one of the features that distinguished it from the West. The same holds true for Zhou China or even the Sudanic empires of Africa.

Japan and the medieval West developed feudal systems grounded in a set of political values that embraced, however imperfectly, most of the participants in the system. The most important of these participants were the aristocratic lords, who effectively controlled the mass of the peasants. The idea of mutual ties and obligations, and the rituals and institutions that expressed them, went beyond the more casual local deals and compromises characteristic of ancient China or medieval and early modern Russia.

In both western Europe and Japan, feudalism was highly militaristic. Both the medieval West and Japan went through long centuries of unusually frequent and bitter internal warfare, based in large part on feudal loyalties and rivalries. Although this warfare was more confined to the warrior-landlord class in Europe than in Japan, in both instances feudalism summed up a host of elite military virtues that long impeded the development of more stable, centralized government. These values included physical courage, personal or family alliances, loyalty, ritualized combat, and often contempt for nonwarrior groups such as peasants and merchants.

The military aura of feudalism survived the feudal era in both cases. It left Japan with serious problems in controlling its samurai class after the worst periods of internal conflict had passed the early 17th century. In the West, the warrior ethic of feudalism persisted in the prominent belief that a central purpose of the state was to make war, thereby providing opportunities for military leaders to demonstrate their prowess. But the legacy of feudalism was not simply military. For example, the idea of personal ties between leaders or among elite groups as a foundation for political activity continued to affect political life and institutions in both the West and Japan, long after the feudal period ended.

The characteristics of feudalism in Japan and in the West were not identical. Western feudalism emphasized contractual ideas more strongly than did Japanese. Although mutual ties were acknowledged by members of the European warrior elite, feudal loyalties were sealed by negotiated contracts, in which the parties involved obtained explicit assurances of the advantages each would receive from the alliance. Japanese feudalism relied more heavily on group and individual loyalties, which were not confirmed by contractual agreements. Probably for this reason, the clearest ongoing legacy of feudalism in the West proved to be parliamentary institutions, where individual aristocrats (as well as townsmen and clergy)

(continued)

could join to defend their explicitly defined legal interests against the central monarch. (Western feudalism also helped encourage the emergence of lawyers, who have never played a comparable role in Japan.) In Japan, the legacy of feudalism involved a less institutionalized group consciousness. This approach encouraged individuals to function as part of collective decision-making teams that ultimately could be linked to the state.

Can the common fact of a feudal heritage be used to explain another similarity between the West and Japan that emerged clearly in the 20th century? Both societies have been unusually successful in industrial development. Both have also proven adept at running capitalist economies. It is certainly tempting to point to feudalism, the medieval feature the two societies uniquely shared, as a partial explanation for these otherwise unexpected 19th- and 20th-century resemblances. The feudal legacy may also help to account for less positive aspects of western European and Japanese development in these centuries, especially their propensity for imperialist expansion and the fact that they frequently resorted to war to solve conflicts with foreign powers. In the case of Japan and Germany, recent historians have established intriguing connections between the persistence of

feudalism late into the early modern era and the rise of right-wing militarist regimes in the 1930s.

When the Japanese talent for group cohesion is identified so strikingly as an ingredient in 20th-century economic success, or when Western nations win political stability through use of parliamentary forms, it surely seems legitimate to point to some persistent threads that run through the experience of the two societies. Whether the common experience of feudalism is a basis for later economic dynamism is a matter for speculation. However, it need not be excluded from a list of provocative uses of comparative analysis simply because the links are challenging.

Questions: Do you think the characteristics of feudalism help explain the later success of Western and Japanese societies? If so, in what ways? If not, why not? Which aspects of feudalism do you think had the greatest effect on these outcomes? If feudalism had persisted in each area, would the outcomes have been as positive as they have been? What other factors should be taken into account if we want to fully analyze these trends? Why might Arab or Chinese historians be skeptical about any claims for feudalism's special importance in world history?

Toward Barbarism? Military Division and Social Change

Although the rituals became more elaborate, the armor heavier, and the swords more superbly forged, the chivalrous qualities of the bushi era deteriorated noticeably in the 15th and 16th centuries. In the place of mud-walled forts, there arose the massive wood and stone castles, such as that at Himeji pictured in Figure 18.4. These imposing structures dominated the Japanese landscape in the centuries that followed. Spying, sneak attacks, ruses, and timely betrayals became the order of the day. The pattern of warfare was fundamentally transformed as large numbers of peasants armed with pikes became a critical component of daimyo armies. Battles hinged less and less on the outcome of samurai combat. Victory depended on the size and organization of a warlord's forces and on how effectively his commanders used them in the field. The badly trained and poorly fed peasant forces became a major source of the growing misery of the common people. As they marched

about the countryside to fight the incessant wars of their overlords, they looted and pillaged. The peasantry in different areas sporadically rose up in hopeless but often ferocious revolts, which fed the trend toward brutality and destruction. It is no wonder that contemporary accounts of the era, as well as those written in later centuries, are dominated by a sense of pessimism and foreboding, a conviction that Japan was reverting from civilized life to barbarism.

Despite the chaos and suffering of the warlord period, there was much economic and cultural growth. Most of the daimyos clearly recognized the need to build up their petty states if they were to survive in the long run. The more able daimyos tried to stabilize village life within their domains by introducing regular tax collection, supporting the construction of irrigation systems and other public works, and building strong rural communities. Incentives were offered to encourage the settlement of unoccupied areas. New tools, the greater use of draft animals, and new crops—especially soybeans—contributed to the well-being of the peasantry in the bet-

Figure 18.4 *Himeji Castle was one of the most formidable of the many fortresses that dominated the Japanese landscape in the age of the warlords. Although the inner buildings were often made of wood, these more vulnerable structures were defended by walls and long, fortified passageways made of stone. Like those of medieval Europe, each castle had wells and granaries for the storage of food that allowed its defenders to withstand long sieges by the forces of rival warlords.*

ter-run domains. Peasants were also encouraged to produce items such as silk, hemp, paper, dyes, and vegetable oils, which were highly marketable and thus potential sources of household income. Daimyos vied with each other to attract merchants to their growing castle towns. Soon a new and wealthy commercial class emerged as purveyors of goods for the military elite and intermediaries in trade between Japan and overseas areas, especially China. As in medieval Europe, guild organizations for artisans and merchants were strong in this era. They helped provide social solidarity and group protection in a time of political breakdown and insecurity.

Evidence reveals that the growth of commerce and the handicraft industries gave some Japanese women opportunities to avoid the sharp drop in status that most experienced in the age of the warring daimyos. Women in merchant and artisan families apparently exercised a fair degree of independence. This was reflected in their participation in guild organizations and business management and by the fact that their positions were sometimes inherited by their daughters. But the status of women in the emerging commercial classes contrasted sharply with that of women in the warrior elites. In earlier centuries, the wives and daughters of the provincial bushi households learned to ride and to use a bow

and arrow, and they often joined in the hunt. By the 14th and 15th centuries, however, the trend among the daimyo families toward primogeniture, or limiting inheritance to the eldest son, dealt a heavy blow to women of the elite classes. The wives and daughters of warrior households, who had hitherto shared in the division of the family estate, now received little or no land or income.

Disinheritance was part of a larger pattern that saw women increasingly treated as defenseless appendages of their warrior fathers or husbands. They were given in marriage to cement alliances between warrior households and reared to anticipate their warrior husband's every desire. They were also taught to slay themselves rather than dishonor the family line by being raped by illicit suitors or enemy soldiers. Japanese women of all classes lost the role of the celebrant in village religious ceremonies and were replaced in Japanese theatrical performances by men specially trained to impersonate women.

Artistic Solace for a Troubled Age

Fears that the constant wars between the swaggering samurai might drag Japan back to barbarism were somewhat mollified by continuing cultivation of the arts. Zen Buddhism, which because of its stress on simplicity and discipline had a special appeal to the warrior elite, played a critical role in securing the place of the arts in an era of strife and destruction. Zen monasteries provided key points of renewed diplomatic and trade contacts with China, which in turn led to a revival of Chinese influence in Japan, at least at the cultural level. Although much painting of the era imitated earlier Chinese work of the Song period, the monochrome ink sketches of Japanese artists were both brilliant and original. Also notable were screen and scroll paintings, such as the one in Figure 18.5, that capture the natural beauty of Japan; others provide us with invaluable glimpses into Japanese life in this period. Zen sensibilities are also prominent in some of the splendid architectural works of this period, including the Golden and Silver Pavilions that Ashikaga shoguns had built in Kyoto (Figure 18.6). Each pavilion was designed to blend into the natural setting in which it was placed to create a pleasing shelter that would foster contemplation and meditation.

This contemplative mood is also evident in the design of some of the more famous gardens of this era. One of these, at the Ryoanji Temple, consisted entirely of islands of volcanic rock set amid white pebbles, which were periodically raked into varying patterns. The influence of Shintoism and Zen Buddhism on such gardens, and the related Japanese ability to find great beauty in the rough and simple, were also present in the tea ceremony that developed in the era of warrior dominance. The graceful gestures, elaborate rituals, and subtly shaped and glazed pots and cups associated with the service of tea on special occasions all lent themselves to composure and introspection.

Figure 18.6 *The Golden Pavilion, also called the Kinkaku-ji Pavilion, is one of the great architectural treasures of the age of the warring houses in Japan. Built on a small lake near Kyoto in the 15th century, the wooden, tile-roofed structure reflects the Zen and Shinto stress on simplicity typical of almost all Japanese artistic production in the centuries of the warring states. Interestingly, its gold-painted exterior and the reflecting pond enhance these sensibilities.*

Figure 18.5 *Patronage of landscape painting and the other fine arts in Japan allowed artistic expression to survive in the long centuries of political division and civil war. In paintings such as the one pictured here, Chinese aesthetic preferences and techniques were strong. In fact, Japanese artists consciously imitated the monochrome (one-colored) paintings of Song China, which they regarded as the apex of the genre. Japanese artists not only concentrated on the same themes, such as landscapes with tiny human figures, but imitated the brushstrokes that they believed had been used by the Song masters.*

Korea: Between China and Japan

◈ Of all the areas to which the Chinese formula for civilized development spread, Korea was the most profoundly influenced for the longest period of time. Because the Korean peninsula is an extension of the Chinese mainland, and because historically Korean kingdoms were dwarfed by their giant neighbor to the west, most observers have treated Korea as little more than an appendage of China. But lumping Korea together with China overlooks the fact that the peninsula was ruled by indigenous dynasties through most of its history, even though these dynasties often paid tribute to the reigning Chinese emperor. Equally important, the Korean people, like the Vietnamese and Japanese, developed a separate identity that was expressed in distinctive forms of dress, cuisine, and a class system that differed significantly from China's.

The peoples who occupied the Korean peninsula represented quite a different ethnic blend from those who, centuries earlier, had come to identify themselves as Chinese. The Koreans descended from the hunting and herding peoples of eastern Siberia and Manchuria rather than the Mongolian- and Turkic-speaking tribes to the west. By the 4th century B.C.E., the peoples who moved into the Korean peninsula had begun to acquire sedentary farming and metalworking techniques from the Chinese. From this point onward, the Koreans played a role in the dynastic struggles that preoccupied the peoples of the north China plain. In 109 B.C.E., the earliest Korean kingdom, **Choson,** was conquered by the Han emperor Wudi. Thereafter, parts of Korea were colonized by Chinese settlers, who remained for nearly four centuries. These colonies soon became a channel by which Chinese influences began to filter into Korean culture in the critical centuries of its early development. A small Japanese enclave in the southeast of the peninsula provided contact with the islands as well, although cultural influences in this era ran overwhelmingly eastward, from China to Korea and then on to Japan.

Despite conquest and colonization under the Han, the tribal peoples of the peninsula, particularly the **Koguryo** in the north, soon resisted Chinese

rule. As Chinese control weakened, the Koguryo established an independent state in the northern half of the peninsula that was soon at war with two southern rivals, **Silla** and **Paekche** (see Map 18.2). Contacts between the splinter kingdoms that ruled north China after the fall of the Han and the Koguryo kingdom resulted in the first wave of **Sinification**—that is, the extensive adoption of Chinese culture—in Korea. As was the case in Japan, Buddhism supplied the key links between Korea and the successors of the Han dynasty in northeast China. Korean rulers patronized Buddhist artists and financed the building of monasteries and pagodas. Korean scholars traveled to China, and a select few went to the source of the Buddhist faith, India.

In addition to Sinified variants of Buddhism, Chinese writing was introduced, even though the spoken Korean language was as ill suited for adaptation to the Chinese characters as the Japanese language had been. The Koguryo monarch imposed a unified law code patterned after that of Han China. He established universities, where Korean youths struggled to master the Confucian classics and their teachers wrote histories of China rather than their

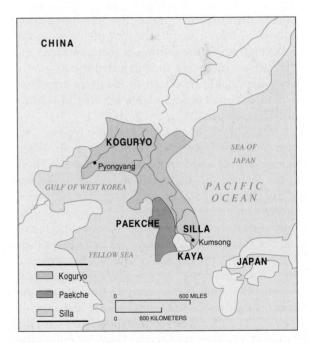

Map 18.2 *The Korean Peninsula During the Three Kingdoms Era*

own land. To expand his power and improve revenue collection, the Koguryo ruler also tried to put together a Chinese-style bureaucracy. But the noble families who supported him had little use for a project that posed such an obvious threat to their own power. Without their support, the monarch did not have the resources for such an ambitious undertaking. Thus, full implementation of these policies had to wait for a more powerful dynasty to emerge some centuries later.

Tang Alliances and the Conquest of Korea

Centuries of warfare between the three Korean kingdoms weakened each without giving paramount power in the peninsula to any. Internal strife also left Korea vulnerable to further attacks from the outside. In addition to the unsuccessful campaigns of the Sui (see Chapter 17), the founders of the more lasting Tang dynasty included Korea in the territories they staked out for their empire. But it was several decades before one of them could finally mount a successful invasion. The stubborn warriors of the Koguryo kingdom bore the brunt of the Tang assaults, just as they had borne those of the Sui rulers. Finally, Tang strategists hit on the idea of taking advantage of Korean divisions to bring the troublesome region into line. Striking an alliance with the rulers of the Silla kingdom to the southeast, they destroyed the Paekche kingdom and then defeated the Koguryo. Thus, the Chinese finally put an end to the long-lived dynasty that had played such a key role in Korea's early development.

The Chinese conquerors began to quarrel with their Silla allies over how to divide the spoils. When the Silla proved able to fight the larger Chinese forces in the peninsula to a standstill and revolts broke out in the former Paekche and Koguryo territories already conquered, the Tang decided it was time to strike a deal. In return for regular tribute payments and the Silla monarch's submission as a vassal of the Tang emperor, the Chinese withdrew their armies in 668. In so doing, they left the Silla the independent rulers of a united Korea. Despite brief lapses, the Koreans maintained this independence and roughly the same boundaries established by the Silla until the occupation of their land by the Japanese in the early 20th century.

Sinification: The Tributary Link

Under the Silla monarchs, who ruled from 668 until the late 9th century, and the Koryo dynasty (918–1392) that followed, Chinese influences peaked and Korean culture achieved its first full flowering. The Silla rulers consciously strove to turn their kingdom into a miniature of the Tang Empire. They regularly sent embassies and tribute to the Tang court, where Korean scholars collected Chinese texts and noted the latest fashions in court dress and etiquette. The Koreans' regular attendance on the Chinese emperors was a key sign of their prominent and enduring participation in the Chinese *tribute system*. At various times, the participants in the system included nomads from central and north Asia, the Tibetans, many of the kingdoms of southeast Asia, and the emperors of Japan. None of these participants were more committed to the tributary arrangements than the Koreans. Rather than try to conquer the Koreans and other surrounding peoples, most Chinese emperors were content to receive their embassies. These emissaries offered tribute in the form of splendid gifts and acknowledged the superiority of the Son of Heaven by their willingness to kowtow to him (kowtowing involved a series of ritual bows in which the supplicant prostrated himself before the throne).

To most of the peoples involved, this seemed a small price to pay for the benefits they received from the Middle Kingdom. Not only did submission and tribute guarantee continuing peace with the Chinese, but it brought far richer gifts than the tribute bearers offered to the Chinese ruler. In addition, the tributary system provided privileged access to Chinese learning, art, and manufactured goods. Tribute missions normally included merchants, whose ability to buy up Chinese manufactures and sell their own goods in the lucrative Chinese market hinged on their country's participation in the Chinese system. Missions from heavily Sinified areas, such as Japan, Korea, and Vietnam, also included contingents of scholars. They studied at Chinese academies or Buddhist monasteries and busily purchased Chinese scrolls and works of art to fill the libraries and embellish the palaces back home. Thus, the tribute system became the major channel of trade and intercultural exchange between China and its neighbors.

The Sinification of Korean Elite Culture

The Silla rulers rebuilt their capital at Kumsong on the Kyongju plain to look like its Tang counterpart. The streets were laid out on a regular grid; there were central markets, parks, lakes, and a separate district to house the imperial family. Fleeing the tedium of the backward rural areas and provincial capitals, the aristocratic families who surrounded the throne and dominated imperial government crowded their mansions into the areas around the imperial palace. With their large extended families and hundreds of slaves and hangers-on, they made up a large portion of the capital's population. Some aristocrats studied in Chinese schools, and a minority even submitted to the rigors of the Confucian examination system introduced under the Silla rulers. Most of the aristocracy opted for the artistic pursuits and entertainments available in the capital. They could do so because most positions in the government continued to be occupied by members of the aristocratic families by virtue of their birth and family connections rather than their knowledge of the Confucian classics.

Partly out of self-interest, the Korean elite continued to favor Buddhism over Confucianism. They and the Korean royal family lavishly endowed monasteries and patronized works of religious art, which became major forms of Korean cultural creativity. The capital at Kumsong soon became crowded with Buddhist temples, which usually were made of wood. Buddhist monks were constantly in attendance on the ruler as well as on members of the royal family and the more powerful aristocratic households. But the schools of Buddhism that caught on among the elite were Chinese. Korean artwork and monastic design reproduced, sometimes splendidly, Chinese prototypes. Even the location of monasteries and pagodas in high places followed Chinese ideas about the need to mollify local spirits and balance supernatural forces.

Sometimes the Koreans borrowed from the Chinese and then outdid their teachers. Most notable in this regard was the pottery produced in the Silla and Koryo eras. The Koreans first learned the techniques of porcelain manufacture from the Chinese. But in the pale green-glazed celadon bowls and vases of the late Silla and Koryo, they created masterworks that even Chinese connoisseurs admired and collected.

They also pioneered in making oxide glazes that were used to make the black- and rust-colored stoneware of this era, which is pictured in Figure 18.7. Both the celadon porcelains and the black stoneware are still recognized as some of the finest pottery ever crafted.

Civilization for the Few

With the exception of Buddhist sects such as the pure land that had strong appeal for the ordinary people, imports from China in this and later eras were all but monopolized by the tiny elite. The aristocratic families were divided into several ranks that neither intermarried nor socialized with each other, much less the rest of the population. They not only filled most of the posts in the Korean bureaucracy but also dominated the social and economic life of

Figure 18.7 *Although all of the major civilized centers of east Asia produced refined ceramics, perhaps nowhere was this art as highly developed as in Korea. As the simple, yet elegant, pitcher in this photo illustrates, Korean pottery was initially crafted for household use. That which has survived from earlier periods of Korean history has become the object of collectors of fine arts and is prominently displayed in major museums.*

the entire kingdom. Much of Korea's trade with the Chinese and Japanese was devoted to providing these aristocrats with the fancy clothing, special teas, scrolls, and artwork that occupied such an important place in their idle lives. In return, Korea exported mainly raw materials, such as forest products and metals such as copper, which was mined by near-slaves who lived in horrendous conditions.

Members of the royal family and the aristocratic households often financed artisan production for export or to supply the court. In addition, some backed mercantile expeditions and even engaged extensively in moneylending. All of this limited the activities of artisans and traders. The former were usually considered low in status and were poorly paid for their talents and labor. The latter were so weak that they did not really form a distinct class.

The aristocrats were the only people who really counted for anything in Korean society. The classes beneath them were oriented to their service. These included government functionaries, who were recognized as a separate social category; commoners, who were mainly peasants; and near-slaves, who were known as the "low born" and ranged from miners and artisans to servants and entertainers. Buddhist festivals periodically relieved the drudgery and monotony of the lives of the common people, and Buddhist salvationist teachings gave them hope for bliss in the afterlife.

Koryo Collapse, Dynastic Renewal

Periodically, the common people and the low born found their lot too much to bear and rose up against a ruling class that was obviously much more devoted to pursuing its own pleasures than to their well-being. Most of these uprisings were local affairs and were ruthlessly repressed by armies of the ruling class. But collectively they weakened both the Silla and Koryo regimes, and in combination with quarrels between the aristocratic households and outside invasions, they contributed to the fall of both dynasties. In the absence of real alternatives, the aristocratic families managed to survive these crises and elevated one of their number to the royal throne. After nearly a century and a half of conflict and turmoil triggered by the Mongol invasion in 1231, the **Yi** dynasty was established in 1392. Remarkably, it ruled Korea until 1910. Although there were some modifications, the Yi quickly restored the aristocratic dominance and links to China that had predominated under their prede-

cessors. Of all of the peoples who received higher civilization from China, none were as content to live in the shadow of the Middle Kingdom as the Koreans.

Between China and Southeast Asia: The Making of Vietnam

 From the Chinese point of view, the Red River valley, which became the heartland of the Vietnamese people in the 1st millennium C.E., was just another rice-growing area to be annexed to their ever-expanding civilization. So much territory and so many peoples had already been absorbed in the fertile southern regions that it was natural to anticipate the same fate for the Red River area and its inhabitants. But the Viets, who lived there, differed in critical ways from the other "southern barbarians" the Chinese had encountered. For one thing, their homeland was farther away from the main centers of Chinese political power on the northern plains than that of any people whom the Chinese had sought to absorb up to that point. For another, the Viets had already developed a sophisticated and, as it turned out, resilient culture of their own—a culture that shared much with the other peoples of southeast Asia.

The preconquest culture of the Vietnamese gave them a strong sense of themselves as a distinct people with a common heritage that they did not want to see overwhelmed by an expanding China. The Viets were well aware of the benefits they derived from the superior technology, modes of political organization, and ideas they received from China. But their gratitude was tempered by their fear of losing their own identity and becoming just another part of China's massive civilization.

Ironically, the Viets first appear in recorded history as a group of "southern barbarians" mentioned by Chinese scholars in accounts of Qin raids in south China in the 220s B.C.E. At that time, their kingdom, which the Chinese called Nam Viet, meaning "people in the south," extended along the southern coastal area of what is now China (see Map 18.3). The initial raids by Qin forces left little lasting Chinese presence. But they probably gave a boost to the lively trade that had been conducted between the

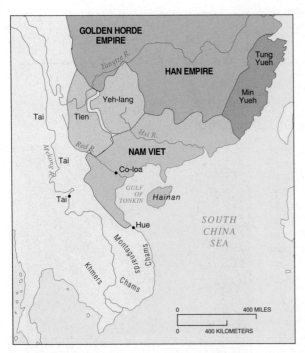

Map 18.3 *South China and Vietnam on the Eve of the Han Conquest*

Viets and the peoples of south China for centuries. In exchange for silk manufactured by the Chinese, the Viets traded ivory, tortoise shells, pearls, peacock feathers, aromatic woods, and other exotic products drawn from the sea and tropical forests. Some decades after the Qin raids, the Viet rulers defeated the feudal lords who controlled the Red River valley and brought their lands under the control of the Viet kingdom. In the centuries that followed, the Viets intermarried and blended with the Mon-Khmer- and Tai-speaking peoples who occupied the Red River area. This proved to be a crucial step in the formation of the Vietnamese as a distinct ethnic group.

As the Viets' willingness to intermarry with ethnic groups such as the **Khmers** (today's Cambodians) and the Tais suggests (see Map 18.3), before their conquest by the Han their culture had many features characteristic of southeast Asia. Their spoken language was not related to Chinese. They enjoyed a strong tradition of village autonomy, physically symbolized by the bamboo hedges that surround northern Vietnamese villages to the present day. The Vietnamese favored the nuclear family to the extended household preferred by the Chinese, and they never developed the clan networks that have been such a prominent

feature of south Chinese society. Vietnamese women have historically had greater freedom and more influence, both within the family and in society at large, than their Chinese counterparts.

Vietnamese customs and cultural forms also differed very significantly from Chinese. The Vietnamese dressed very differently. For example, women preferred long skirts to the black pants that nonelite women wore in China. The Vietnamese delighted in the cockfight, a typical southeast Asian pastime; they chewed betel nut, which the Chinese found disgusting; and they blackened their teeth, which the Chinese also considered repulsive. In the centuries when they were dominated by the Chinese politically, the Vietnamese managed to preserve most of these features of their society. They also became much more fervently attached at the grassroots level to Buddhism, and they developed art and literature, especially poetry, that was refined and distinct from that of the Chinese.

Conquest and Sinification

As the Han rulers who succeeded the Qin tried to incorporate south China into their empire, they came into conflict with the Viets. The Han emperor initially settled for the Viet ruler's admission of his vassal status and periodic payments of tribute. But by 111 B.C.E., the Han thought it best to conquer the feisty Viets outright and to govern them directly using Chinese officials. The Red River area was garrisoned by Chinese troops, and Chinese administrators set to work co-opting the local lords and encouraging them to adopt Chinese culture. Because the Viet elite realized that they had a great deal to learn from their powerful neighbors to the north, they cooperated with the agents of the new regime. Sensing that they had found another barbarian people ripe for assimilation, the Chinese eagerly introduced essential elements of their own culture into the southern lands.

In the centuries after the Chinese conquest, the Vietnamese elite was drawn into the bureaucratic machine that the Han emperors and the shi had developed to hold together the empire won by the Qin. They attended Chinese-style schools, where they wrote in the Chinese script and read and memorized the classical Chinese texts of Confucius and Mencius. They took exams to qualify for administrative posts, whose responsibilities and privileges were defined by Chinese precedents. They introduced Chinese cropping techniques and irrigation technology,

Visualizing the Past

What Their Portraits Tell Us: Gatekeeper Elites and the Persistence of Civilizations

Some decades ago, a distinguished historian of ancient China called the scholar-gentry elite the gatekeepers of Chinese civilization. In his usage, gatekeepers are pivotal elite groups that have emerged in all civilizations and proved critical to their persistence over time. Although they usually shared power with other social groups and often did not rule in their own right, gatekeepers played vital roles in shaping the dominant social values and worldviews of the cultures in which they appeared. In everything from the positions they occupied

A Samurai Warrior

Warrior Ranks from the Aztec Empire

Bankers and Merchants from Western Europe

which soon made Vietnamese agriculture the most productive in southeast Asia. This meant that Vietnamese society, like that of China, could support larger numbers of people. The result was the high population density characteristic of the Red River valley and the lowland coastal areas to the south.

The Vietnamese also found that Chinese political and military organization gave them a decisive edge over the peoples to the west and south, who had adopted Indian patterns of kingship and warfare, and with whom they increasingly clashed over the control of lands to settle and cultivate. Over time, the Vietnamese elite also adopted the extended family model

and took to venerating their ancestors in the Confucian manner. Their Chinese overlords had every reason to assume that the Vietnamese "barbarians" were well on their way to becoming civilized—that is, like the Chinese themselves.

Roots of Resistance

Sporadic revolts led by members of the Vietnamese aristocracy, and the failure of Chinese cultural imports to make much of an impression on the Vietnamese peasantry, ultimately frustrated Chinese hopes for assimilating the Viets. Although they had learned to their manners and fashions in dress, gatekeepers defined the norms and served as role models for much of the rest of society. Some gatekeeper elites, such as the scholar-gentry in China and the brahmans in India, promoted norms and ideals in written treatises on good government or the proper social order. Other gatekeepers, such the samurai of Japan and the Aztec warriors of Tenochtitlan, embodied these ideals in their public personas and military enterprises, which at times were immortalized in songs, legends, and epics.

The illustrations shown here provide portraits of people belonging to gatekeeper elites from four of the civilizations we have considered in depth thus far. Because each of these portraits was produced by artists from the same society as the gatekeeper elite depicted here, we can assume that the portraits capture the values, symbols of legitimacy, and demeanor that these people intended to project to the viewer. Carefully examine each of these portraits, paying special attention to clothing, poses adopted, objects included in the portraits, backgrounds selected, and activities depicted.

For historical background of the civilizations that each exemplifies, see the relevant sections of Chapters 15, 16, 17, and 18. Compare each of the portraits to the others, and then answer the questions that follow.

Questions: What do the dress, poses, and settings of each of these portraits tell you about the values, ideals, and worldviews that each gatekeeper elite group is intended to represent? To what extent were these elite groups politically and socially dominant in the societies to which they belonged? With which elite groups did they share power? How did they legitimize their power and privileges and to what degree is this reflected in the portraits? What occupational roles and ideals bolstered the efforts of each group to perpetuate the civilizations for which they served as gatekeepers? Which elite exercised the greatest control or influence, and why? Are there comparable gatekeeper elite groups in the contemporary United States? If so, which group or groups play this role? If not, why not?

Chinese Scholars Enjoying Their Leisure Time

much from the Chinese, the Vietnamese lords chafed under their rule, in part because the Chinese often found it difficult to conceal their disdain for local customs in what they considered a backward and unhealthy outpost of the empire. Vietnamese literature attests to the less than reverent attitudes felt by Vietnamese collaborators toward Chinese learning and culture. In the following poem, a teacher mocks himself and doubts his usefulness to the people he serves:

I bear the title "Disciple of Confucius."

Why bother with blockheads, wearing such a label?

I dress like a museum piece:

I speak only in learned quotations (poetry and prose); Long since dried out, I still strut like a peacock; Failed in my exams, I've been dropped like a shrivelled root.

Doctorate, M.A.: all out of reach,

So why not teach school, and beat the devil out of my students.

Elsewhere in Vietnamese writings, self-doubt and mockery turn to rage and a fierce determination to resist Chinese dominance, whatever the cost. The following sentiments of a Vietnamese caught up in resistance to the reimposition of rule from China by the Mongols in the 13th century provide a dramatic case in point:

> I myself often forget to eat at mealtime, and in the middle of the night I wake up and caress my pillow. My intestines hurt me incessantly, as if they had been cut off, and tears flow abundantly from my eyes. My only grief is that I have not yet succeeded in hacking apart the enemy's body, peeling off his skin, swallowing his liver, drinking his blood.

The intensity and ferocity of this passage give some sense of why the Chinese failed to assimilate the Vietnamese. They also failed because the peasantry rallied again and again to the call of their own lords to rise up and drive off the alien rulers. The fact that the most famous of these uprisings was led in 39 C.E. by the **Trung sisters,** who were children of a deposed local leader, points to the importance of the more favored position of women in Vietnamese society, in contrast to the Chinese, as a source of resistance.

Vietnamese women were understandably hostile to the Confucian codes and family system that would have confined them to the household and subjected them to male authority figures. We do not know whether this resentment figured in the Trung sisters' decision to revolt. But poetry written in later centuries by female authors leaves little doubt about the reactions of Vietnamese women to Confucian norms or male dominance. One of the most famous of these writers, Ho Xuan Huong, flouts Confucian decorum in the following ribald verse and mocks her male suitors:

> Careful, careful where are you going:
>
> You group of know-nothings!
>
> Come here and let your older sister teach you to write poems.
>
> Young bees whose stingers itch rub them in wilted flowers.
>
> Young goats who have nothing to do with their horns butt them against sparse shrubbery.

In another poem, "Sharing a Husband," Huong ridicules those who advocate polygamy, a practice favored by any self-respecting Confucian:

> One wife is covered by a quilted blanket, while one wife is left in the cold.

> Cursed be this fate of sharing a common husband. Seldom do you have an occasion to possess your husband,
>
> Not even twice in one month.
>
> You toil and endure hardships in order to earn your steamed rice, and then the rice is cold and tasteless. It is like renting your services for hire, and then receiving no wages.
>
> How is it that I have turned out this way,
>
> I would rather suffer the fate of remaining unmarried and living alone by myself.

Winning Independence and Continuing Chinese Influences

In addition to a strong sense of identity and motives for resistance that crossed class and gender barriers, the Vietnamese struggle for independence was assisted by the fragility of the links that bound them to China. Great distances and mountain barriers created nightmare conditions for Chinese administrators responsible for supplying military expeditions to the far south. Only small numbers of Chinese—mostly bureaucrats, soldiers, and merchants—lived in the Red River area, and few of them did so permanently. Most critically, Chinese control over the distant Vietnamese depended on the strength of the ruling dynasties in China itself. The Vietnamese were quick to take advantage of political turmoil and nomadic incursions in northern China to assert their independence. After failing to completely free themselves on several occasions, they mounted a massive rebellion during the period of chaos in China after the fall of the Tang dynasty in 907. By 939, they had won political independence from their northern neighbors. Although both the Mongol and Ming rulers of China later tried to reassert control over the Vietnamese, both efforts ended in humiliating retreats. From 939 until the conquests by the French in the 19th century, the Vietnamese were masters of their own land.

Although the Chinese political hold was broken, Chinese cultural exports continued to play central roles in Vietnamese society. A succession of Vietnamese dynasties beginning with the Le (980–1009), which became the source of legitimacy for the rest, built Chinese-style palaces as in Figure 18.8, in the midst of forbidden cities patterned after those in Changan and Beijing. They ruled through a bureau-

Figure 18.8 *As this view of the moat and part of the palace of the Vietnamese emperors at Hue illustrates, Chinese taste and architectural styles strongly influenced the construction and decoration of Vietnamese court centers. Not only were the upturned, tiled roofs and long galleries built in conscious imitation of prototypes in Changan or Beijing, but they were set amid moats, ponds, and gardens patterned after those Vietnamese envoys had seen in China. Despite this imitation, however, Vietnamese rulers were more accessible to their subjects, and their palaces and capital city made little impression on Chinese visitors, who disparaged the informality and lack of grandeur at the Hue court.*

cracy that was a much smaller copy of the Chinese administrative system, with secretariats, six main ministries, and a bureau of censors to keep graft and corruption in check. Civil service exams were reintroduced, and an administrative elite schooled in the Confucian classics sought the emperor's favor and commanded deference from the common people.

But the Vietnamese equivalent of the Chinese scholar-gentry never enjoyed as much power. For one thing, their control at the village level was much less secure than that of their Chinese counterparts. Much more than those in China, local Vietnamese officials tended to identify with the peasantry rather than with the court and higher administrators. To a much greater degree, they looked out for local interests and served as leaders in village uprisings against the ruling dynasty when its demands on the common people became too oppressive.

The power of the scholar-bureaucrats in Vietnam was also limited in the reign of many dynasties by competition from well-educated Buddhist monks. The fact that the Buddhists had much stronger links with the Vietnamese peasantry than the monastic orders had in China strengthened them in their struggles with the Confucian scholars. The high esteem in which women were held in Buddhist teachings and institutions also enhanced the popularity of the monks in Vietnam. Thus, competing centers of power and influence prevented most Vietnamese dynasties from enjoying the authority of their Chinese counterparts.

The Vietnamese Drive to the South

However watered down, the Chinese legacy gave the Vietnamese great advantages in the struggles within

Document

Literature as a Mirror of the Exchanges Between Civilized Centers

The following passages from Lady Murasaki's classic Japanese account of court life, *The Tale of Genji* (Vintage Press, 1985 edition), and from perhaps the most popular and beloved work of Vietnamese literature, Nguyen Du's *The Tale of Kieu* (Vintage Press, 1973 edition), are superb examples of the important and far-reaching exchanges between the civilizations of south and east Asia. Not surprisingly, Chinese influences, including many allusions to Chinese writings and historical events, are paramount, but Buddhist (hence originally Indian) themes are pervasive in both works. There is also evidence in one of these passages of significant exchanges between the satellite civilizations of China.

[Kieu] dreamed a girl appeared hard by her side and murmured: "Kieu! Your Karma's still undone. How can you shirk your debt of grief to fate? You yet have to play out your woman's role."

The moderator was a man of considerable learning. There was much of interest in his exchanges with the Korean. There were also exchanges of Chinese poetry, and in one of his poems the Korean succeeded most skillfully in conveying his joy at having been able to observe such a countenance on this the eve of his return to his own land.... Summoning an astrologer of the Indian school, the emperor was pleased to learn that the Indian view coincided with the Japanese and the Korean; and so he concluded that the boy should become a commoner with the name of Minamoto or Genji.

Looking at the keepsakes Myobu had brought back, [Genji] thought what a comfort it would be if some wizard were to bring him, like that Chinese emperor, a comb from the world where his lost love was dwelling....There are limits to the powers of the most gifted artist. The Chinese lady in the paintings did not have the luster of life. Yang Kuei-fei was said to have resembled the lotus of the Sublime Pond, the willows of

the Timeless Hall. No doubt she was very beautiful in her Chinese finery.

"You are well-famed as a lute-player," he said. "Like Chung Tzu-ch'i I've longed to hear you play."... Now [Kieu] began to play. A battle scene—oh how they clashed and clanged, Han and Chu swords! The Ssu-ma tune, A Phoenix Seeks His Mate—it sounded like an outburst of pure grief. Then Hsi K'ang's masterpiece, Kuang-ling, was heard: it rushed on like a stream or flew like clouds. Next came what Chao-chin played—she mourned her Prince and all her kinsfolk she must leave behind as she crossed the Great Wall to wed a Hun.

The [abbot] talked of this ephemeral world and of the world to come. His own burden of sin was heavy, thought Genji, that he had been lured into an illicit and profitless affair. He would regret it all his life and suffer even more terribly in the life to come. What a joy to withdraw to such a place [a mountain monastery] as this!

When one must weigh and choose between one's love and filial duty, which will turn the scale? Kieu brushed aside her solemn vows to [the young student] Kim—she'd pay a daughter's debt before all else. Resolved on what to do, she spoke her mind: "Hands off my father, please! I'll sell myself and ransom him."

Questions: From these passages can you identify Chinese precedents in terms of place names and historical personages, allusions to Chinese literary works, and attitudes toward gender or social organization that can be traced to Chinese models? Can you detect passages that convey Buddhist ideas about the nature of the world and human existence? Are additional Indian influences suggested? Are there ideas that are distinctively Japanese or Vietnamese, or are the authors totally caught up in Chinese precedents?

Indochina that became a major preoccupation of independent Vietnamese rulers. Because the Vietnamese refused to settle in the malarial highlands that fringed the Red River area and rose abruptly from the coastal plains farther south, their main adversaries were the **Chams** and Khmers, who occupied the low-

land areas to the south that the Vietnamese sought to settle themselves (see Map 18.3). The Vietnamese launched periodic expeditions to retaliate for raids on their villages by the hill peoples. They also regularly traded with the hill dwellers for forest products. But the Vietnamese tried to minimize cultural exchange with these hunters and shifting cultivators, whom they saw as "nude savages."

As they moved out in the only direction left to them—south along the narrow plain between the mountains and the sea—the Vietnamese made good use of the larger population and superior bureaucratic and military organization that the Chinese connection had fostered. From the 11th to the 18th century, they fought a long series of generally successful wars against the Chams, an Indianized people living in the lowland areas along the coast. Eventually most of the Chams were driven into the highlands, where their descendants, in much smaller numbers, live to the present day. Having beaten the Chams and settled on their former croplands, the Vietnamese next clashed with the Khmers, who had begun to move into the Mekong delta region during the centuries of the Vietnamese drive south. Again, Indianized armies proved no match for the Chinese-inspired military forces and weapons of the Vietnamese. By the time the French arrived in force in the Mekong area in the late 18th century, the Vietnamese had occupied much of the upper delta and were beginning to push into territory that today belongs to Cambodia.

Expansion and Division

As Vietnamese armies and peasant colonists moved farther and farther from the capital at Hanoi, the dynasties centered there found it increasingly difficult to control the commanders and peasants fighting and living in the frontier areas. As the southerners intermarried with and adopted some of the customs of the Chams and Khmers, differences in culture and attitude developed between them and the northerners. Although both continued to identify themselves as Vietnamese, the northerners (much like their counterparts in the United States) came to see the Vietnamese who settled in the frontier south as less energetic and slower in speech and movement. As the hold of the Hanoi-based dynasties over the southern regions weakened, regional military commanders grew less and less responsive to orders from the north and slower in sending taxes to the court. Bickering turned to violent clashes, and by the end of the 16th century a rival, the **Nguyen,** had emerged to challenge the claims of legitimacy of the **Trinh** family that ruled the north.

The territories of the Nguyen at this time were centered on the narrow plains that connected the two great rice bowls of present-day Vietnam along the Red and Mekong rivers. Their capital was at Hue (see Map 18.3), far north of the Mekong delta region that in this period had scarcely been settled by the Vietnamese. For the next two centuries, these rival houses fought for the right to rule Vietnam. Neither accepted the division of Vietnam as permanent; each sought to unite all of the Vietnamese people under a single monarch. This long struggle not only absorbed much of the Vietnamese energies but also prevented them from recognizing the growing external threat to their homeland. For the first time in history, the danger came not from the Chinese giant to the north but from a distant land and religion about which the Vietnamese knew and cared nothing—France and the conversion-minded Roman Catholic church.

GLOBAL CONNECTIONS: In the Orbit of China: The East Asian Corner of the Global System

The first millennium C.E. was a pivotal epoch in the history of the peoples of east Asia. The spread of ideas, organizational models, and material culture from a common Chinese center spawned the rise of three distinct patterns of civilized development in Japan, Korea, and Vietnam. In contrast to the lands of the nomadic peoples who had long been in contact with China from the north and west, each of these regions contained fertile and well-watered lowland areas that were suited to sedentary cultivation, which was essential to the spread of the Chinese pattern of civilized development. In fact, each provided an ideal environment for the cultivation of wet rice, which was increasingly replacing millet and other grains as the staple of China.

Common elements of Chinese culture, from modes of writing and bureaucratic organization to religious teachings and art, were transmitted to each of these three areas. In all three cases, Chinese imports, with the important exception of popular Buddhism, were all but monopolized by court and provincial elite groups, the former prominent in Japan and Korea, the latter in Vietnam. In all three cases, Chinese thought patterns and modes of social organization were actively and willingly cultivated by these local elites, who knew that they were the key to a higher level of development.

Thus, for a time at least, all three areas shared prominent aspects of political organization, social development, and intellectual creativity. But the differing ways in which Chinese influences were transmitted to each of these peoples resulted in very different outcomes. The various combinations of Chinese-derived and indigenous elements produced distinctive variations on a common pattern of civilized life. In Korea, the period of direct Chinese rule was brief, but China's physical presence and military power were all too apparent. Thus, the need for symbolic political submission was obvious and the desire for long-term cultural dependence firmly implanted. In Vietnam, where Chinese conquest and control lasted more than a thousand years, a hard-fought struggle for political independence gave way to a growing attachment to Chinese culture as a counterbalance to the Indian influences that had brought civilization to the southeast Asian rivals of the Vietnamese.

In Japan, where all attempts by Chinese dynasties to assert direct control had failed, Chinese culture was emulated by the courtly elite that first brought civilization to the islands. But the rise of a rival aristocratic class, which was based in the provinces and championed military values that were fundamentally opposed to Chinese Confucianism, led to the gradual limitation of Chinese influence in Japan and the reassertion of Japanese traditional ways. Japanese political patterns, in particular, formed a marked contrast with the predominance of rule by a centralized bureaucracy in China. Nonetheless, in Japan as in the rest of east Asia, China remained the epitome of civilized development; Chinese ways were the standard by which all peoples in this far-flung region were judged.

Despite different patterns, the power of the Chinese model had one other important result for Korea, Japan, and to a large extent Vietnam. Contacts with other parts of the world were slight to nonexistent, because there was no sense that any other place had examples worth emulating. The intensity of interactions within the east Asian region generated a degree of isolation from the world beyond.

Further Readings

There are many good secondary works on early Japanese and Vietnamese history. Some older but accessible works on Korea are William Heathorn's *History of Korea* (1971), which gives some attention to the arts, and

Hatada Takashi's *A History of Korea* (1969). The best new short introduction to the history owf Korea is C. J. Eckert, *Korea Old and New: A History* (1980). K. B. Lee, (trans. by E. Wagner et. al.) *A New History of Korea* (1984) is quite comprehensive, while L. Kendall, *Shamans, Housewives and Other Restless Spirits: Women in Korean Ritual Life* (1985) offers a fresh perspective on Korean social history. The best introductory works on Japanese history and culture are the writings of Reischauer, J. W. Hall's *Japan from Prehistory to Modern Times* (1970), and Mikisio Hane's superb overview, *Japan: A Historical Survey* (1972). H. Paul Varley's *Japanese Culture: A Short History* (1973) has fine sections on the arts, religion, and literature of the warlord era. Also good on this period are Peter Duus' *Japanese Feudalism* (1969); Varley's *Samurai* (1970), which was coauthored with Ivan Morris and Nobuko Morris; and the first and second volumes of George Sansom's *A History of Japan* (1958, 1960).

For an understanding of the Chinese impact on Vietnam, there is no better place to begin than Alexander Woodsides' *Vietnam and the Chinese Model* (1971). The best works on the earliest period in Vietnamese history are translations of the writings of French scholar Georges Coedes and the superspecialized *Birth of Vietnam* (1983) by Keith Taylor. Thomas Hodgkin's survey of Vietnamese history is highly readable and makes extensive use of Vietnamese literature. Troung Buu Lam's edited volume, *Patterns of Vietnamese Response to Foreign Intervention* (1967), along with the Genji and Kieu tales cited in the Document of this chapter, provide wonderful ways for the student to get inside Japanese and Vietnamese culture.

On the Web

The history of Japan during what for Europe was the Middle Ages is traced at http://www.wsu.edu:8080/~dee/FEUJAPAN/CONTENTS.HTM. A brief history of successive Japanese Shogunates, the art and literature of the period, and the lore, weapons, and code of the samurai (Bushido) can be examined at http://victorian.fortunecity.com/duchamp/410/main.html and http://www.samurai-archives.com/. The women warriors and leaders of Japan are discussed at http://www.koryubooks.com/Library/wwj1.html, http://www.samurai-archives.com/women.html, and http://www.womeninworldhistory.com/sample-08.html. The life of Lady Murasaki and her world is illuminated at http://www.reconstructinghistory.com/Japanese/fujiwara.htm and http://mcel.pacificu.edu/as/students/genji/culture.html. *The Tale of Genji* is analyzed at http://www.taleofgenji.org/, http://mcel.pacificu.edu/as/students/genji/homepage.html, and http://webworld.unesco.org/genji/en/index.shtml.

The myths and legends of the people of Korea helped sustain their identity over the centuries of interaction with Chinese civilization and successive independent Korean kingdoms of Koguryo, Packche, and Silla (http://www. asd.k12.ak.us/Schools/West/Countries/Korea/ KoreaHistory.html and http://www.asianinfo.org/ asianinfo/korea/history.htm) retained their identity while adapting facets of Chinese culture. The Queens of Silla receive treatment at http://www. womeninworldhistory.com/heroine7.html. Chinese-influenced Korean court music can be sampled at http:// www.asiasound.com/pages/learn/time/korea.htm. The Korean family structure is explored at http://www. askasia.org/Korea/soc6.html. Korean art in its historical context is displayed at http://asiasocietymuseum.org/ default/asp (scroll to bottom of page and click on "Korea"). Korean technology as expressed via its mechanical toy production is at http://www.askasia.org/Korea/ math1.html

The origin myths of the Vietnamese also performed a sustaining function during their long encounter with Chinese civilization (http://www.askasia.org/frclasrm/ readings/r000061.htm). The lands of present day Vietnam had a long history prior to the coming of the Chinese. An imperial kingdom, Champa, whose society had absorbed ancient Indian, rather than Chinese tradition (http://www.viettouch.com/champa/), had long ruled the southern portion of the country.

In the North, the Vietnamese development of and trade in bronze drums linked it to the wider world prior to the Chinese efforts to conquer them (http://www.viettouch. com/pre-hist/dongson_drums.html).

Vietnam absorbed much Chinese culture, but also sought to retain its own values even within the Chinese model government they adopted, such as by politically constructing a relatively un-Chinese tradition of heroic women warriors like the Trung sisters (http://www. womeninworldhistory.com/heroine10.html, http:// www.fortunecity.com/victorian/postmodern/428/ goddessheart1a4.html, and http://www.richmond.edu/ ~ebolt/history398/TrungSisters.html) and by incorporating nativist ideals in uprisings against the Chinese model Vietnamese state, such as the Tayson Rebellion (http://www.humnet.ucla.edu/humnet/ealc/ faculty/dutton/TSHome.html) during which women also took to the field of battle. The latter, together with profiles of Vietnam's most prominent precolonial rulers, is discussed at http://greenfield.fortunecity.com/ crawdad/204/nguyenhue.html. The Vietnamese admiration for Chinese culture and hostility to Chinese political domination and their equally ambivalent approach to other external forces is examined at http://www.cseas. kyoto-u.ac.jp/seas/40/4/nguyen.pdf. This process can also be seen in images of traditional Vietnam provided at http://www2.centenary.edu/vietnam/lairson/images. html and http://www.sweb.uky.edu/~mnguy2/ histofVN.htm.

CHAPTER 19

THE LAST GREAT NOMADIC CHALLENGES: FROM CHINGGIS KHAN TO TIMUR

A 14th-century miniature painting from Rashid al-Din's History of the World depicts Mongol cavalry charging into battle against retreating Persians. The speed and endurance of Mongol cavalry made it difficult for routed foes to retreat and live to fight another day. As the painting suggests, surrender or death were often the only options for those overrun by Mongol units.

From the first explosion of Mongol military might from the steppes of central Asia in the early 13th century to the death of Timur in 1405, the nomads of central Asia made a stunning return to center stage in world history. Mongol invasions ended or interrupted many of the great empires of the postclassical period and also extended the world network that had increasingly defined the period. Under Chinggis Khan, the Mongols and their many nomadic neighbors were forged into the mightiest war machine the world had seen to that time. With stunning rapidity his Mongol forces conquered central Asia, northern China, and eastern Persia (see Map 19.1). Under Chinggis Khan's sons and grandsons, the rest of China, Tibet, Persia, Iraq, much of Asia Minor, and all of southern Russia were added to the vast Mongol imperium.

Although the empire was divided between Chinggis Khan's sons after his death in 1227, the four **khanates** or kingdoms, which emerged in the struggles for succession, dominated most of Asia for the next one and a half centuries. The Mongol conquests and the empires they produced were the most formidable nomadic challenge to the growing global dominance of the sedentary peoples of the civilized cores since the great nomadic migrations in the first centuries C.E. Except for Timur's devastating but short-lived grab for power at the end of the 14th century, nomadic peoples would never again mount a challenge as massive and sweeping as that of the Mongols.

In most histories until quite recently, the Mongol conquests have been depicted as a savage assault by backward and barbaric peoples on many of the most ancient and developed centers of human civilization. Depending on the civilization from whose city walls a historian recorded the coming of the Mongol "hordes," they were depicted as the scourge of Islam, devils bent on destroying Christianity, persecutors of the Buddhists, or defilers of the Confucian traditions of China. They were indeed fierce fighters and capable of terrible acts of retribution against those who dared to defy them, but the Mongols' conquests brought much more than death and devastation. At the peak of their power, the domains of the Mongol *khans*, or rulers, made up a vast realm in which once-hostile peoples lived together in peace and most religions were tolerated. From the Khanate of Persia in the west to the empire of the fabled Kubilai Khan in the east, the law code first promulgated by Chinggis Khan gave order to human interaction. Like the Islamic expansion that preceded it, the Mongol explosion laid the foundations for more human interaction on a global scale, extending and intensifying the world network that had been building since the classical age.

900 C.E.	1100 C.E.	1200 C.E.	1250 C.E.	1300 C.E.
907–1118 Khitan conquest of North China **1037–1194** Seljuk Turks dominant in the Middle East	**1115–1234** Jurchens (Qin dynasty) rule north China **1126** Song dynasty flees to south China **1130–c. 1250** Almohads rule North Africa and Spain	**1206** Temujin takes the name of Chinggis Khan; Mongol state is founded **1215** First Mongol attacks on north China; Beijing captured **1219–1223** First Mongol invasions of Russia and the Islamic world **1227** Death of Chinggis Khan; Ogedei named successor **1234** Mongols take all of north China; end of Qin dynasty **1235–1279** Mongol conquest of south China; end of southern Song dynasty **1236–1240** Mongol conquest of Russia **1240–1241** Mongol invasion of western Europe	**1253** Mongol victory over Seljuk Turks; rise of Ottoman Turks in Middle East **1258** Mongol destruction of Baghdad **1260** Mamluk (slave) rulers of Egypt defeat Mongols at Ain Jalut; end of drive west **1260–1294** Reign of Kubilai Khan in China **1271–1295** Journey of Marco Polo to central Asia, China, and southeast Asia **1271–1368** Reign of the Yuan (Mongol) dynasty in China **1274–1280** Failed Mongol invasions of Japan **1290s** First true guns used in China	**1336–1405** Life of Timur **mid-14th century** Spread of Black Death in Eurasia

The Mongol Empire of Chinggis Khan

 The Mongols had long been one of the nomadic peoples that intervened periodically in Chinese history. But tribal divisions and rivalries with neighboring ethnic groups, particularly Turkic peoples, had long blunted the expansive poten-

tial of Mongol warrior culture. In the early 13th century, these and other obstacles to Mongol expansion were overcome, primarily because of the leadership of an astute political strategist and brilliant military commander who took the title Chinggis Khan. Within decades, the Mongols and allied nomadic groups built an empire that stretched from the Middle Eastern heartlands of the Islamic world to the China Sea.

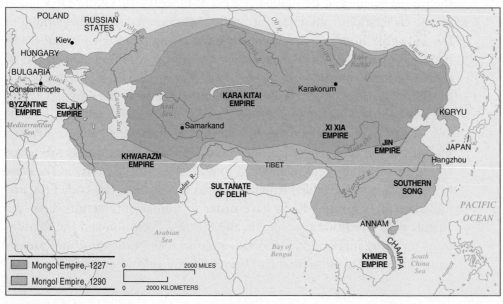

Map 19.1   *The Mongol Empire of Chinggis Khan*

In most ways, the Mongols epitomized nomadic society and culture, whose features were discussed in Chapter 9. Their survival depended on the well-being of the herds of goats and sheep they drove from one pasture area to another according to the cycle of the seasons. Their staple foods were the meat and milk products provided by their herds, supplemented in most cases by grain and vegetables gained through trade with sedentary farming peoples. They also traded hides and dairy products for jewelry, weapons, and cloth made in urban centers. They dressed in sheepskins, made boots from tanned sheep hides, and lived in round felt tents made of wool sheared from their animals (Figure 19.1). The tough little ponies they rode to round up their herds, hunt wild animals, and make war were equally essential to their way of life. Mongol boys and girls could ride as soon as they were able to walk. Mongol warriors could ride for days on end, sleeping and eating in the saddle.

Like the early Arabs and other nomadic peoples we have encountered, the basic unit of Mongol society was the tribe, which was divided into kin-related clans whose members camped and herded together on a regular basis. When threatened by external enemies or preparing for raids on other nomads or invasions of sedentary areas, clans and tribes could be combined in great confederations. Depending on the skills of their leaders, these confederations could be held together for months or even years. But when the threat had passed or the raiding was done, clans and tribes drifted back to their own pasturelands and campsites. At all organizational levels, leaders were elected by the free men of the group. Although women exercised influence within the family and had the right to be heard in tribal councils, men dominated leadership positions.

Courage in battle, usually evidenced by bravery in the hunt, and the ability to forge alliances and attract

Figure 19.1 *This sketch of a Mongol household on the move illustrates the diversity and mobility of one of the nomadic societies that has shaped global history. The Mongols depended on sheep for food, clothing, and shelter, and they rode both horses and camels. As the drawing shows, they also used oxen when they needed animal power for key tasks such as transporting their housing for seasonal or longer-term migrations. This obviously was a cumbersome process, but the Mongols mounted the tents on huge wagons, which were pulled by large teams of oxen. This combination of animal transport and comfortable but movable shelters made the Mongols one of the most mobile preindustrial societies.*

dependants were vital leadership skills. A strong leader could quickly build up a large following of chiefs from other clans and tribal groups. If the leader grew old and feeble or suffered severe reverses, his subordinates would quickly abandon him. He expected this to happen, and the subordinates felt no remorse. Their survival and that of their dependants hinged on attaching themselves to a strong tribal leader.

The Making of a Great Warrior: The Early Career of Chinggis Khan

Since the early millennia of recorded history, nomadic peoples speaking Mongolian languages had enjoyed moments of power and had actually carved out regional kingdoms in north China in the 4th and 10th centuries C.E. In the early 12th century, Chinggis Khan's great-grandfather, Kabul Khan, led a Mongol alliance that had won glory by defeating an army sent against them by the Qin kingdom of north China. Soon after this victory, Kabul Khan became ill and died. His successors could neither defeat their nomadic enemies nor hold the Mongol alliance together. Divided and beaten, the Mongols fell on hard times.

Chinggis Khan, who as a youth was named Temujin, was born in the 1170s into one of the splinter clans that fought for survival in the decades after the death of Kabul Khan (see Figure 19.2). Temujin's father was an able leader who built up a decent following and negotiated a promise of marriage between

Figure 19.2 *In this miniature from a Persian history, Chinggis Khan is shown acknowledging the submission of a rival prince. Though he conquered a vast empire, Chinggis Khan did not live long enough to build a regular bureaucracy to govern it. His rule was dependant on vassal chieftains such as the one shown in the painting, whose loyalty in turn depended on the maintenance of Mongol military might. When the military strength of the Mongol Empire began to decline, subject princes soon rose up to establish the independence of their domains.*

Document

A European Assessment of the Virtues and Vices of the Mongols

As we have seen, much of what we know about the history of nomadic peoples is based on the records and reactions of observers from sedentary cultures that were their mortal enemies. Some of the most famous observers were those, including Marco Polo, who visited the vast Mongol domains at the height of the khans' power in the 12th and 13th centuries. Many tried to assess the strengths and weaknesses of these people, who were suddenly having such a great impact on the history of much of the known world. One of the most insightful of these observers was a Franciscan friar named Giovanni de Piano Carpini. In 1245, Pope Innocent IV sent Piano Carpini as an envoy to the "Great Khan" to protest the recent assaults by his Mongol forces on Christian Europe. The pope's protest had little effect on the Mongol decision to strike elsewhere in the following years. But Piano Carpini's extensive travels produced one of the most detailed accounts of Mongol society and culture to be written in the mid-13th century. As the following passages suggest, like other visitors from sedentary areas, he gave the Mongols a very mixed review:

> In the whole world there are to be found no more obedient subjects than the Tartars [Mongols]....They pay their lords more respect than any other people, and would hardly dare lie to them. Rarely do they revile each other, but if they should, the dispute hardly ever leads to blows. Wars, quarrels, the infliction of bodily harm, and manslaughter do not occur among them, and there are no large-scale thieves or robbers among them....
>
> They treat one another with due respect; they regard each other almost as members of one family, and, although they do not have a lot of food, they like to share it with one another....When riding they can endure extreme cold and at times also fierce heat; they are neither soft, nor sensitive [to the weather]. They do not seem to feel in any way envious of one another, and no public trials occur among them. No one holds his fellow in contempt, but each helps and supports the other to the limits of his abilities.

They are extremely arrogant toward other people and look down on all others with disdain. In fact, they regard them, both noble and humble people alike, as little better than nothing....Toward other people the Tartars tend to anger and are easily roused....They are the greatest liars in the world in dealing with other people [than the Tartars], and hardly a true word escapes from their mouths. Initially they flatter but in the end they sting like scorpions. They are crafty and sly, and wherever possible they try to get the better of everybody else by false pretenses....

They are messy in their eating and drinking and in their whole way of life. Drunkenness is honorable among them....At the same time they are mean and greedy, and if they want something, they will not stop begging and asking for it, until they have got it. They cling fiercely to what they have, and in making gifts they are extremely miserly. They have no conscience about killing other people. In short, if one tried to enumerate all their bad characteristics there would be too many to put on paper.

Questions: What might the qualities of the Mongols that Piano Carpini emphasizes tell us about his own society and its values or shortcomings? How are the Mongol virtues he extols linked to the achievements of Chinggis Khan and the stunning Mongol wars of conquest? To what extent would they be typical of nomadic societies more generally? In what ways might his account of Mongol vices be simply dismissed as "sour grapes" resulting from European defeats? In what ways might these vices be linked to the hardships of Mongol life? How useful do you think this stereotyping is? Why have observers from nearly all cultures resorted to these sorts of generalizations when describing other peoples and societies?

his eldest son and the daughter of a stronger Mongol chief. According to Mongol accounts, just when the family fortunes seemed to be on the upswing, Temujin's father was poisoned by the agents of a rival nomadic group. Suddenly, Temujin, who was still a teenager, was thrust into a position of leadership. But most of the chiefs who had attached themselves to his father refused to follow a mere boy, whose prospects of survival appeared to be slim.

In the months that followed, Temujin's much-reduced encampment was threatened and finally attacked by a rival tribe. He was taken prisoner in 1182, locked into a wooden collar, and led in humiliation to the camp of his enemies. After a daring midnight escape, Temujin rejoined his mother and brothers and found refuge for his tiny band of followers deep in the mountains. Facing extermination, Temujin did what any sensible nomad leader would have done: He and his people joined the camp of a more powerful Mongol chieftain who had once been aided by Temujin's father. With the support of this powerful leader, Temujin avenged the insults of the clan that had enslaved him and another that had taken advantage of his weakness to raid his camp for horses and women.

These successes and Temujin's growing reputation as a warrior and military commander soon won him allies and clan chiefs eager to attach themselves to a leader with a promising future. Within a decade, the youthful Temujin had defeated his Mongol rivals and routed the forces sent to crush him by other nomadic peoples. In 1206, at a **kuriltai,** or meeting of all of the Mongol chieftains, Temujin—renamed Chinggis Khan—was elected the **khagan,** or supreme ruler, of the Mongol tribes. United under a strong leader, the Mongols prepared to launch a massive assault on an unsuspecting world.

Building the Mongol War Machine

The men of the Mongol tribes that had elevated Chinggis Khan to leadership were natural warriors. Trained from youth not only to ride but also to hunt and fight, they were physically tough, mobile, and accustomed to killing and death. They wielded a variety of weapons, including lances, hatchets, and iron maces. None of their weapons was as devastating as their powerful short bows. A Mongol warrior could fire a quiver of arrows with stunning accuracy without breaking the stride of his horse. He could hit enemy soldiers as distant as 400 yards (the range for the roughly contemporary English longbow was 250 yards) while ducking under the belly of his pony, or leaning over the horse's rump. The fact that the Mongol armies were entirely cavalry meant that they moved so rapidly that their advances alone could be demoralizing to enemy forces.

To a people whose very lifestyle bred mobility, physical courage, and a love of combat, Chinggis Khan and his many able subordinate commanders brought organization, discipline, and unity of command. The old quarrels and vendettas between clans and tribes were overridden by loyalty to the khagan. Thus, energies once devoted to infighting were now

directed toward conquest and the forcible exaction of tribute, both in areas controlled by other nomadic groups and in the civilized centers that fringed the steppes on all sides. The Mongol forces were divided into armies made up of basic fighting units called **tumens,** each consisting of 10,000 warriors. Each tumen was further divided into units of 1000, 100, and 10 warriors. Commanders at each level were responsible for training, arming, and disciplining the cavalrymen under their charge. The tumens were also divided into heavy cavalry, which carried lances and wore some metal armor, and light cavalry, which relied primarily on the bow and arrow and leather helmets and body covering. Even more lightly armed were the scouting parties that rode ahead of Mongol armies and, using flags and special signal fires, kept the main force informed of the enemy's movements.

Chinggis Khan also created a separate messenger force whose bodies were tightly bandaged to allow them to remain in the saddle for days, switching from horse to horse to carry urgent messages between the khagan and his commanders. Military discipline had long been secured by personal ties between commanders and ordinary soldiers. Mongol values, which made courage in battle a prerequisite for male self-esteem, were buttressed by a formal code that dictated the immediate execution of a warrior who deserted his unit. Chinggis Khan's swift executions left little doubt about the fate of traitors to his own cause or turncoats who abandoned enemy commanders in his favor. His generosity to brave foes was also legendary. The most famous of the latter, a man named Jebe, nicknamed "The Arrow," won the khagan's affection and high posts in the Mongol armies by standing his ground after his troops had been routed and fearlessly shooting Chinggis Khan's horse out from under him.

A special unit supplied Mongol armies with excellent maps of the areas they were to invade. These were drawn largely according to the information supplied by Chinggis Khan's extensive network of spies and informers. New weapons, including a variety of flaming and exploding arrows, gunpowder projectiles, and later bronze cannons, were also devised for the Mongol forces. By the time Chinggis Khan's armies rode east and west in search of plunder and conquest in the second decade of the 13th century, they were among the best armed and trained and the most experienced, disciplined, and mobile soldiers in the world.

Conquest: The Mongol Empire Under Chinggis Khan

When he was proclaimed the khagan in 1206, Temujin probably was not yet 40 years old. At that point, he was the supreme ruler of nearly one-half million Mongols and the overlord of 1 to 2 million more nomads who had been defeated by his armies or had allied themselves with this promising young commander. But Chinggis Khan had much greater ambitions. He once said that his greatest pleasure in life was making war, defeating enemies, forcing "their beloved [to] weep, riding on their horses, embracing their wives and daughters." He came to see himself and his sons as men marked for a special destiny: warriors born to conquer the known world. In 1207, he set out to fulfill this ambition. His first campaigns humbled the Tangut kingdom of Xi Xia in northwest China (see Map 19.1), whose ruler was forced to declare himself a vassal of the khagan and pay a hefty tribute. Next, the Mongol armies attacked the much more powerful Qin Empire, which the Manchu-related Jurchens had established a century earlier in north China.

In these campaigns, the Mongol armies were confronted for the first time with large, fortified cities whose inhabitants assumed that they could easily withstand the assaults of these uncouth nomads from the steppes. Indeed, the Mongol invaders were thwarted at first by the intricate defensive works that the Chinese had perfected over the centuries to deter nomadic incursions. But the adaptive Mongols, with the help of captured Chinese artisans and military commanders, soon devised a whole arsenal of siege weapons. These included battering rams, catapults that hurled rocks and explosive balls, and bamboo rockets that spread fire and fear in besieged towns.

Chinggis Khan and the early Mongol commanders had little regard for these towns, whose inhabitants they saw as soft. Therefore, when they met resistance, the Mongols adopted a policy of terrifying retribution. Although the Mongols often spared the lives of famous scholars—whom they employed as advisors—and artisans with particularly useful skills, towns that fought back were usually sacked once they had been taken. The townspeople were slaughtered or sold into slavery; their homes, palaces, mosques, and temples were reduced to rubble. Towns that surrendered without a fight were usually spared this fate, although they were required to pay tribute to their Mongol conquerors as the price of their deliverance.

First Assault on the Islamic World: Conquest in China

Once they had established a foothold in north China and solidified their empire in the steppes, the Mongol armies moved westward against the Kara Khitai Empire, which had been established by a Mongolian-speaking people a century earlier (see Map 19.1). Having overwhelmed and annexed the Kara Khitai by 1219, Chinggis Khan dispatched envoys to demand the submission of **Muhammad Shah II,** the Turkic ruler of the Khwarazm Empire to the west. Outraged by the audacity of the still little-known Mongol commander, one of Muhammad's subordinates had some of Chinggis Khan's later envoys killed and sent the rest with shaved heads back to the khagan. These insults meant war—a war in which the Khwarazm were overwhelmed. Their great cities fell to the new siege weapons and tactics the Mongols had perfected in their north China campaigns.

Again and again, the Mongols used their favorite battle tactic in these encounters. Cavalry were sent to attack the enemy's main force. Feigning defeat, the cavalry retreated, drawing the opposing forces out of formation in the hope of a chance to slaughter the fleeing Mongols. Once the enemy's pursuing horsemen had spread themselves over the countryside, the main force of Mongol heavy cavalry, until then concealed, attacked them in a devastating pincer formation.

Within two years, his once-flourishing cities in ruin and his kingdom in Mongol hands, Muhammad Shah II, having retreated across his empire, died on a desolate island in the Caspian Sea. In addition to greatly enlarging his domains, Chinggis Khan's victories meant that he could bring tens of thousands of Turkic horsemen into his armies. By 1227, the year of his death, the Mongols ruled an empire that stretched from eastern Persia to the North China Sea.

Life Under the Mongol Imperium

Despite their aggressiveness as warriors and the destruction they could unleash on those who resisted their demands for submission and tribute, the Mongols were remarkably astute and tolerant rulers. Chinggis Khan himself set the standard. He was a complex man, capable of gloating over the ruin of his enemies but also open to new ideas and committed to building a world where the diverse peoples of his empire could live together in peace. Though illiterate, Chinggis Khan was neither the ignorant savage nor the cultureless vandal often depicted in the accounts of civilized writers—usually those who had never met him. Once the conquered peoples had been subdued, he took a keen interest in their arts and learning, although he refused to live in their cities. Instead, he established a new capital at **Karakorum** on the steppes and summoned the wise and clever from all parts of the empire to the lavish palace of tents with gilded pillars where he lived with his wives and closest advisors.

At Karakorum, Chinggis Khan consulted with Confucian scholars about how to rule China, with Muslim engineers about how to build siege weapons and improve trade with the lands farther west, and with Daoist holy men, whom he hoped could give him an elixir that would make him immortal. Although he himself followed the *shamanistic* (focused on nature spirits) beliefs of his ancestors, all religions were tolerated in his empire. An administrative framework that drew on the advice and talents of both Muslim and Chinese bureaucrats was created. A script was devised for the Mongolian language to facilitate recordkeeping and the standardization of laws.

The Mongol conquests brought a peace to much of Asia that in some areas persisted for generations. In the towns of the empire, handicraft production and scholarship flourished and artistic creativity was allowed free expression. Secure trade routes made for prosperous merchants and wealthy, cosmopolitan cities. One Muslim historian wrote of the peoples within the Mongol Empire that they "enjoyed such a peace that a man might have journeyed from the land of sunrise to the land of sunset with a golden platter upon his head without suffering the least violence from anyone." Paradoxically, Mongol expansion, which sedentary chroniclers condemned as a "barbarian" orgy of violence and destruction, also became a major force for economic and social development and the enhancement of civilized life.

The Death of Chinggis Khan and the Division of the Empire

In 1226, his wars to the west won, Chinggis Khan turned east with an army of 180,000 warriors to complete the conquest of China that he regretted having left unfinished more than a decade earlier. After routing a much larger Tangut army in a battle fought on the frozen waters of the Yellow River, the Mongol armies overran the kingdom of Xi Xia, plundering, burning, and mercilessly hunting down Tangut sur-

vivors. As his forces closed in on the Tangut capital and last refuge, Chinggis Khan, who had been injured in a skirmish some months earlier, fell grievously ill. After lecturing his sons on the dangers of quarreling among themselves for the spoils of the empire, the khagan died in August 1227.

With one last outburst of wrath, this time directed against death itself, the Mongols carried his body back to Mongolia for burial. The Mongol forces escorting the funeral procession hunted down and killed every human and animal in its path. The vast pasturelands the Mongols now controlled were divided between Chinggis Khan's three remaining sons and **Batu,** a grandson and heir of the khagan's recently deceased son, Jochi. Towns and cultivated areas such as those in north China and parts of Persia were considered the common property of the Mongol ruling family. A kuriltai was convened at Karakorum, the Mongol capital, to select a successor to the great conqueror. In accordance with Chinggis Khan's preference, **Ogedei,** his third son, was elected grand khan. Though not as capable a military leader as his brothers or nephews, Ogedei was a crafty diplomat and deft manipulator. As it turned out, these skills were much needed to keep the ambitious heads of the vast provinces of the empire from each other's throats.

For nearly a decade, Ogedei directed Mongol energies into further campaigns and conquests. The areas targeted by this new round of Mongol expansion paid the price for peace within the Mongol Empire. The fate of the most important victims—Russia and eastern Europe, the Islamic heartlands, and China—will be the focus of much of the rest of this chapter.

The Mongol Drive to the West

 While pursuing the Khwarazm ruler, Muhammad Shah II, the Mongols had made their first contacts with the rich kingdoms to the west of the steppe heartlands of Chinggis Khan's empire. Raids into Georgia and across the Russian steppe convinced the Mongol commanders that the Christian lands to the west were theirs for the taking.

Russia and Europe were added to the Mongols' agenda for world conquest. Subjugating these regions became the project of the armies of the **Golden Horde,** named after the golden tent of the early

Visualizing the Past

The Mongol Empire as a Bridge Between Civilizations

Chinggis Khan and his successors actively promoted the growth of trade and travelers by protecting the caravans that made their way across the ancient Asian silk routes. The Mongols also established rest stations for weary merchants and fortified outposts for those harassed by bandits. These measures transformed the Mongol imperium into a massive conduit between the civilizations of Europe, the Middle East, and the rest of Asia. The map below illustrates a wide variety of marketable goods and inventions, as well as the agents and objects of several religions, between areas within the empire and along its lengthy borders. Study these patterns and then answer the questions that follow.

Questions: Discuss some of the major ways in which the Mongol Empire facilitated exchanges and interaction between civilizations and culture areas. What were the main centers of different kinds of products? What were the main directions in which ideas, goods, and new inventions flowed? Based on the discussions in the preceding chapters, who were some of the key agents of these exchanges? Why were the networks of exchange established by the Mongols so short-lived?

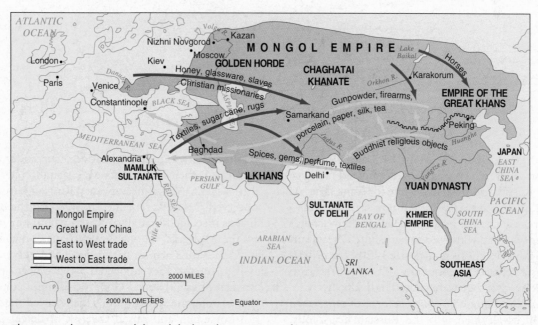

The Mongol Empire and the Global Exchange Network

khans of the western sector of the Mongol Empire. The territories of the Golden Horde made up one of the four great khanates into which the Mongol Empire was divided at the time of Chinggis Khan's death (Map 19.2). Under the rule of Chinggis Khan's grandson Batu, they began an invasion of Russia in 1236. In a very real sense, the Mongol assault on Russia was a side campaign, a chance to fine-tune the war machine and win a little booty on the way to the real prize: western Europe.

As we saw in Chapter 14, in the first half of the 13th century when the Mongol warriors first descended, Russia had been divided into numerous petty kingdoms, centered on trading cities such as

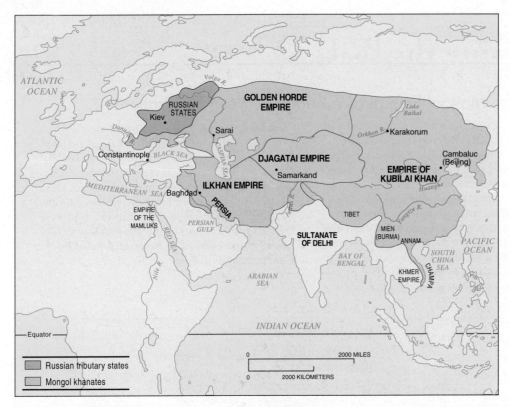

Map 19.2 *The Four Khanates of the Divided Mongol Empire*

Novgorod and Kiev (see Maps 14.3 and 19.2). By this time, Kiev, which originally dominated much of central Russia, had been in decline for some time. As a result, there was no paramount power to rally Russian forces against the invaders. Despite the warnings of those who had witnessed the crushing defeats suffered by the Georgians in the early 1220s, the princes of Russia refused to cooperate. They preferred to fight alone, and they were routed individually.

In 1236, Batu led a Mongol force of more than 120,000 cavalrymen into the Russian heartlands. From 1237 to 1238 and later in 1240, these Tatars, or Tartars (meaning people from hell), as the Russians called them, carried out the only successful winter invasions in Russian history. In fact, the Mongols preferred to fight in the winter. The frozen earth provided good footing for their horses, and frozen rivers gave them access to their enemies. One after another, the Mongol armies defeated the often much larger forces of local nomadic groups and Russian princes. Cities such as Ryazan, Moscow, and Vladimir, which

resisted the Mongol command to surrender, were destroyed; their inhabitants were slaughtered or led into slavery. As a contemporary Russian chronicler observed, "No eye remained to weep for the dead." Just as it seemed that all of Russia would be ravaged by the Mongols, whom the Russians compared to locusts, Batu's armies withdrew. The largest cities, Novgorod and Kiev, appeared to have been spared. Russian priests thanked God; the Mongol commanders blamed the spring thaw, which slowed the Mongol horsemen and raised the risk of defeat in the treacherous mud.

The Mongols returned in force in the winter of 1240. In this second campaign, even the great walled city of Kiev, which had reached a population of more than 100,000 by the end of the 12th century, fell. Enraged by Kievan resistance—its ruler had ordered the Mongol envoys thrown from the city walls—the Mongols reduced the greatest city in Russia to a smoldering ruin. The cathedral of Saint Sophia was spared, but the rest of the city was looted and destroyed, and its inhabitants were smoked out and slaughtered. Novgorod braced itself for the Mongol onslaught. Again, according to the Russian chroniclers, it was "miraculously" spared. In fact, it was saved largely because of the willingness of its prince, Alexander Nevskii, to submit, at least temporarily, to Mongol demands. In addition, the Mongol armies were eager to move on to the main event: the invasion of western Europe, which they perceived as a far richer but equally vulnerable region.

Russia in Bondage

The crushing victories of Batu's armies initiated nearly two and a half centuries of Mongol dominance in Russia. Russian princes were forced to submit as vassals of the khan of the Golden Horde and to pay tribute. Mongol demands fell particularly heavily on the Russian peasantry, who had to give their crops and labor to both their own princes and the Mongol overlords. Impoverished and ever fearful of the lightning raids of Mongol marauders, the peasants fled to remote areas or became, in effect, the serfs (see Chapter 14) of the Russian ruling class in return for protection. Some Russian towns made profits on the increased trade made possible by the Mongol links. Sometimes the gains exceeded the tribute they paid to the Golden Horde. No town benefited from the Mongol presence more than Moscow. Badly plundered and partially burned in the early Mongol assaults, the city was gradually rebuilt, and its ruling princes steadily swallowed up nearby towns and surrounding villages. After 1328, Moscow also profited from its status as the tribute collector for the Mongol khans. Its princes not only used their position to fill their own coffers but also annexed other towns as punishment for falling behind on tribute payments.

As Moscow grew in strength, the power of the Golden Horde declined. Mongol religious toleration benefited both the Orthodox church and Moscow. The choice of Moscow as the seat of the Orthodox leaders brought new sources of wealth to its princes and buttressed its claims to be Russia's leading city. In 1380, those claims got an additional boost when the princes of Moscow shifted from being tribute collectors to being the defenders of Russia. In alliance with other Russian vassals, they raised an army that defeated the forces of the Golden Horde at the **Battle of Kulikova.** Their victory and the devastating blows

Timur's attacks dealt the Golden Horde two decades later effectively broke the Mongol hold over Russia.

Although much of the Mongols' impact was negative, their conquest was a turning point in Russian history in several ways. In addition to their importance to Moscow and the Orthodox church, Mongol contacts led to changes in Russian military organization and tactics and in the political style of Russian rulers. Claims that the Tatars were responsible for Russian despotism, either tsarist or Stalinist, are clearly overstated. Still, the Mongol example may have influenced the desire of Russian princes to centralize their control and reduce the limitations placed on their power by the landed nobility, clergy, and wealthy merchants. By far the greatest effects of Mongol rule were those resulting from Russia's isolation from Christian lands farther west. On one hand, the Mongols protected a divided and weak Russia from the attacks of much more powerful kingdoms such as Poland, Lithuania, and Hungary (see Map 19.2). On the other hand, in the period of Mongol rule, Russia was cut off from key transformations in western Europe that were inspired by the Renaissance and led ultimately to the Reformation.

Mongol Incursions and the Retreat from Europe

Until news of the Mongol campaigns in Russia reached European peoples such as the Germans and Hungarians farther west (see Map 19.2), Christian leaders had been quite pleased by the rise of a new military power in central Asia. Rumors and reports from Christians living in the area, chafing under what they saw as persecution by their Muslim overlords, convinced many in western Europe that the Mongol khan was none other than **Prester John.** Prester John was the name given to a mythical rich and powerful Christian monarch whose kingdom had supposedly been cut off from Europe by the Muslim conquests of the 7th and 8th centuries. Sometimes located in Africa, sometimes in central Asia, Prester John loomed large in the European imagination as a potential ally who could strike the Muslim enemy from the rear and join up with European Christians to destroy their common adversary. The Mongol assault on the Muslim Khwarazm Empire appeared to confirm the speculation that Chinggis Khan was indeed Prester John.

The assault on Christian, though Orthodox, Russia made it clear that the Mongol armies were neither the legions of Prester John nor more partial to Christians than to any other people who stood in their way. The rulers of Europe were nevertheless slow to realize the magnitude of the threat the Mongols posed to western Christendom. When Mongol envoys, one of whom was an Englishman, arrived at the court of King Bela of Hungary demanding that he surrender a group of nomads who had fled to his domains after being beaten by the Mongols in Russia, the king contemptuously dismissed them. King Bela also rebuffed Batu's demand that he submit to Mongol rule. The Hungarian monarch reasoned that he was the ruler of a powerful kingdom, whereas the Mongols were just another ragtag band of nomads in search of easy plunder. His refusal to negotiate provided the Mongols with a pretext to invade. Their ambition remained the conquest and pillage of all western Europe. That this goal was clearly attainable was demonstrated by the sound drubbing they gave to the Hungarians in 1240 and later to a mixed force of Christian knights led by the German ruler, King Henry of Silesia.

These victories left the Mongols free to raid and pillage from the Adriatic Sea region in the south to Poland and the German states of the north. It also left the rest of Europe open to Mongol conquest. Just as the kings and clergy of the western portions of Christendom were beginning to fear the worst, the Mongol forces disappeared. The death of the khagan Ogedei, in the distant Mongol capital at Karakorum, forced Batu to withdraw in preparation for the struggle for succession. The campaign for the conquest of Europe was never resumed. Perhaps Batu was satisfied with the huge empire of the Golden Horde that he ruled from his splendid new capital at Sarai on the Volga river in what is southern Russia today (see Map 19.2). Most certainly the Mongols had found richer lands to plunder in the following decades in the Muslim empires of the Middle East. Whatever the reason, Europe was spared the full fury of the Mongol assault. Of the civilizations that fringed the steppe homelands of the Mongols, only India was as fortunate.

The Mongol Assault on the Islamic Heartland

After the Mongol conquest of the Khwarazm Empire, it was only a matter of time before they struck westward against the far wealthier Muslim empires of Mesopotamia and north Africa (see Maps 12.2 and 19.2). The conquest of these areas became the main project of Hulegu, another grandson of Chinggis Khan and the ruler of the Ilkhan portions of the Mongol Empire. As we saw in Chapter 12, one of the key results of Hulegu's assaults on the Muslim heartlands was the capture and destruction of Baghdad in 1258 (Figure 19.3). The murder of the Abbasid caliph, one of some 800,000 people who were reported to have been killed in Mongol retribution for the city's resistance, ended the dynasty that had

Figure 19.3 *The Abbasid capital at Baghdad had long been in decline when the Mongols besieged it in 1258. The Mongols' sack of the city put an end to all pretense that Baghdad was still the center of the Muslim world. The Mongol assault on Baghdad also revealed how vulnerable even cities with high and extensive walls were to the artillery and other siege weapons that the Mongols and Chinese had pioneered. In the centuries that followed, major innovations in fortifications, many introduced first in Europe, were made to counter the introduction of gunpowder and the new siege cannon.*

ruled the core regions of the Islamic world since the mid-8th century.

Given the fate of Baghdad, it is understandable that Muslim historians treated the coming of the Mongols as one of the great catastrophes in the history of Islam. The murder of the caliph and his family left the faithful without a central authority. The sack of Baghdad and many other cities from central Asia to the shores of the Mediterranean devastated the focal points of Islamic civilization. One contemporary Muslim chronicler, Ibn al-Athir, found the violence the Mongols had done to his people so horrific that he apologized to his readers for recounting it and wished that he had not been born to see it. He lamented,

> In just one year they seized the most populous, the most beautiful, and the best cultivated part of the earth whose inhabitants excelled in character and urbanity. In the countries that have not yet been overrun by them, everyone spends the night afraid that they may yet appear there, too....Thus, Islam and the Muslims were struck, at that time by a disaster such as no people had experienced before.

Given these reverses, one can imagine the relief the peoples of the Muslim world felt when the Mongols were finally defeated in 1260 by the armies of the Mamluk, or slave, dynasty of Egypt. Ironically, **Baibars,** the commander of the Egyptian forces, and many of his lieutenants had been enslaved by the Mongols some years earlier and sold in Egypt, where they rose to power through military service. The Muslim victory was won with the rare cooperation of the Christians, who allowed Baibars' forces to cross unopposed through their much-diminished crusader territories in Palestine. Christian support demonstrated how far the former crusader states had gone in accommodating their more powerful Muslim neighbors.

Hulegu was in central Asia, engaged in yet another succession struggle, when the battle occurred. Upon his return, he was forced to reconsider his plans for conquest of the entire Muslim world. The Mamluks were deeply entrenched and growing stronger; Hulegu was threatened by his cousin **Berke,** the new khan of the Golden Horde to the north, who had converted to Islam. After openly clashing with Berke and learning of Baibars' overtures for an alliance with the Golden Horde, Hulegu decided to settle for the kingdom he already ruled, which stretched from the frontiers of Byzantium to the Oxus River in central Asia (see Map 19.2).

The Mongol Interlude in Chinese History

 Of all the areas the Mongols conquered, perhaps none was administered as closely as China. After decades of hard campaigning in the mid-13th century, the Mongol interlude in Chinese history lasted only about a century. Although the age-old capacity of the Chinese to assimilate their nomadic conquerors was evident from the outset, the Mongols managed to retain a distinct culture and social separateness until they were driven back beyond the Great Wall in the late 1360s. They also opened China to influences from Arab and Persian lands, and even to contacts with Europe, which came to full fruition in the centuries of indigenous Chinese revival that followed under the Ming dynasty.

Soon after Ogedei was elected as the great khan, the Mongol advance into China was resumed. Having conquered the Xi Xia and Qin empires, the Mongol commanders turned to what remained of the Song empire in south China (see Maps 19.1 and 19.2). In the campaigns against the Song, the Mongol forces were directed by **Kubilai Khan** (Figure 19.4). Kubilai was one of the grandsons of Chinggis Khan, and he would play a pivotal role in Chinese history for the next half century. Even under a decadent dynasty that had long neglected its defenses, south China was one of the toughest areas for the Mongols to conquer. From 1235 to 1279, the Mongols were constantly on the march; they fought battle after battle and besieged seemingly innumerable, well-fortified Chinese cities. In 1260, Kubilai assumed the title of the great khan, much to the chagrin of his cousins who ruled other parts of the empire. A decade later, in 1271, on the recommendation of Chinese advisors, he changed the name of his Mongol regime to a Chinese-language dynastic title, the Yuan. Although he was still nearly a decade away from fully defeating the last-ditch efforts of Confucian bureaucrats and Chinese generals to save the Song dynasty, Kubilai ruled most of China. He now set about the task of establishing more permanent Mongol control.

As the different regions of China came under Mongol rule, Kubilai passed many laws to preserve the distinction between Mongol and Chinese. He

Figure 19.4 *This portrait of Kubilai Khan, by far the most important Mongol ruler of China, emphasizes his Mongol physical features, beard and hair styles, and dress. But Kubilai was determined to "civilize" his Mongol followers according to Chinese standards. Not only did he himself adopt a Chinese lifestyle, but he had his son educated by the best Confucian scholars to be a proper Chinese emperor. Kubilai also became a major patron of the Chinese arts and a promoter of Chinese culture.*

forbade Chinese scholars to learn the Mongol script, which was used for records and correspondence at the upper levels of the imperial government. Mongols were forbidden to marry ethnic Chinese, and only women from nomadic families were selected for the imperial harem. Even friendships between the two peoples were discouraged, and Mongol military forces remained separate from the Chinese. Mongol religious ceremonies and customs were retained, and a tent encampment in the traditional Mongol style was set up in the imperial city even though Kubilai usually lived in a Chinese-style palace.

Despite his measures to ensure that the conquering Mongol minority was not completely absorbed by the culture of the defeated, Kubilai Khan had long been fascinated by Chinese civilization. Even before beginning the conquest of the Song Empire, he had surrounded himself with Chinese advisors, some Buddhist, others Daoist or Confucian. His capital at **Tatu** in the north (present-day Beijing) was built on the site occupied by earlier dynasties, and he introduced Chinese rituals and classical music into his own court. Kubilai also put the empire on the Chinese calendar and offered sacrifices to his ancestors at a special temple in the imperial city. But he rebuffed the pleas of his Confucian advisors to reestablish the civil service exams, which had been discontinued by the Qin rulers.

In the Yuan era, a new social structure was established in China, with the Mongols on top and their central Asian nomadic and Muslim allies right below them in the hierarchy. These two groups occupied most offices at the highest levels of the bureaucracy. Beneath them came the north Chinese; below them, the ethnic Chinese and the minority peoples of the south. Thus, ethnic Chinese from both north and south ran the Yuan bureaucracy at the regional and local levels, but they could exercise power at the top only as advisors to the Mongols or other nomadic officials. At all levels, their activities were scrutinized by Mongol functionaries from an enlarged and much-strengthened censors' bureau.

Gender Roles and the Convergence of Mongol and Chinese Culture

Mongol women remained aloof from Chinese culture—at least Chinese culture in its Confucian guise. They refused to adopt the practice of footbinding, which so limited the activities of Chinese women. They retained their rights to property and control within the household as well as the freedom to move about the town and countryside. No more striking evidence of their independence can be found than contemporary accounts of Mongol women riding to the hunt, both with their husbands and at the head of their own hunting parties. The daughter of one of Kubilai's cousins went to war, and she refused to marry until one of her many suitors was able to throw her in a wrestling match.

The persisting influence of Mongol women after the Mongols settled down in China is exemplified by **Chabi,** the wife of Kubilai Khan (Figure 19.5). She was one of Kubilai's most important confidants on

Figure 19.5 *A portrait of Chabi, the energetic and influential wife of Kubilai Khan. Kubilai's determination to adopt Chinese culture without being overwhelmed by it was bolstered by the advice and example of Chabi. Displaying the independent-mindedness and political savvy of many Mongol women, Chabi gave Kubilai critical advice on how to counter the schemes of his ambitious brother and how to handle the potentially hostile scholar-gentry elite and peasantry that came to be ruled by Mongol overlords.*

political and diplomatic matters, and she promoted Buddhist interests in the highest circles of government. Chabi played a critical role in fostering policies aimed at reconciling the majority ethnic Chinese population of the empire to Mongol rule. She convinced Kubilai that the harsh treatment of the survivors of the defeated Song imperial family would only anger the peoples of north China and make them more dif-

ficult to rule. On another occasion, she demonstrated that she shared Kubilai's respect for Chinese culture by frustrating a plan to turn cultivated lands near the capital into pasturelands for the Mongols' ponies. Thus, the imperial couple were a good match of astute political skills and cosmopolitanism, tempered by respect for their own traditions and a determination to preserve those they found the most valuable.

Mongol Tolerance and Foreign Cultural Influence

Like Chinggis Khan and other Mongol overlords, Kubilai and Chabi had unbounded curiosity and very cosmopolitan tastes. Their generous patronage drew scholars, artists, artisans, and office-seekers from many lands to the splendid Yuan court. Some of the most favored came from Muslim kingdoms to the east that had come under Mongol rule. Muslims were included in the second highest social grouping, just beneath the Mongols themselves. Persians and Turks were admitted to the inner circle of Kubilai's administrators and advisors. Muslims designed and supervised the building of his Chinese-style imperial city and proposed new systems for more efficient tax collection. Persian astronomers imported more advanced Middle Eastern instruments for celestial observations, corrected the Chinese calendar, and made some of the most accurate maps the Chinese had ever seen. Muslim doctors ran the imperial hospitals and added translations of 36 volumes on Muslim medicine to the imperial library.

In addition to the Muslims, Kubilai welcomed travelers and emissaries from many foreign lands to his court. Like his grandfather, Kubilai had a strong interest in all religions and insisted on toleration in his domains. Buddhists, Nestorian Christians, Daoists, and Latin Christians made their way to his court. The most renowned of the latter were members of the Polo family from Venice in northern Italy, who traveled extensively in the Mongol Empire in the middle of the 13th century. Marco Polo's account of Kubilai Khan's court and empire, where he lived and served as an administrator for 17 years, is perhaps the most famous travel account written by a European (Figure 19.6). Marco accepted fantastic tales of grotesque and strange customs, and he may have taken parts of his account from other sources. Still, his descriptions of the palaces, cities, and wealth of Kubilai's empire enhanced European interest in Asia

Figure 19.6 *This 15th-century manuscript illumination depicts Marco Polo and his uncle offering homage to the Great Khan. The Polos were Venetian merchants, and Marco's elders had already traveled extensively in Asia in the decade before they set off with Marco. Marco had a great facility with languages, which served him well in his journeys through Asia by land and sea. On his way home in the mid-1290s, he related his many adventures to a writer of romances while both were prisoners of the Genoese, who were fierce rivals of the Venetians. Eventually published under the title* Description of the World, *Polo's account became one of a handful of definitive sources on the world beyond Europe for the explorers of the coming age of overseas expansion.*

and helped to inspire efforts by navigators such as Columbus to find a water route to these fabled lands.

Social Policies and Scholar-Gentry Resistance

Kubilai's efforts to promote Mongol adaptation to Chinese culture were overshadowed in the long run by measures to preserve Mongol separateness. The ethnic Chinese who made up the vast majority of his subjects, particularly in the south, were never really reconciled to Mongol rule. Despite Kubilai's cultivation of Confucian rituals and his extensive employment of Chinese bureaucrats, most of the scholar-gentry saw the Mongol overlord and his successors as uncouth barbarians whose policies endangered Chinese traditions. As it was intended to do, Kubilai's refusal to reinstate the examination route to administrative office prevented Confucian scholars from dominating politics. The favoritism he showed Mongol and other foreign officials further alienated the scholar-gentry.

To add insult to injury, Kubilai went to great lengths to bolster the position of the artisan classes, who had never enjoyed high standing, and the merchants, whom the Confucian thinkers had long dismissed as parasites. From the outset the Mongols had shown great regard for artisans and because of their useful skills had often spared them while killing their fellow city dwellers. During the Yuan period in China, merchants also prospered and commerce boomed, partly because of Mongol efforts to improve transportation and expand the supply of paper money. With amazing speed for a people who had no prior experience with seafaring, the Mongols developed a substantial navy, which played a major role in the conquest of the Song Empire. After the conquest of China was completed, the great Mongol war fleets were used to put down pirates, who threatened river and overseas commerce. Toward the end of Kubilai's reign, the navy also launched a number of overseas expeditions of exploration and conquest, which led to attacks on Japan and a brief reoccupation of Vietnam.

Ironically, despite the Mongols' suspicion of cities and sedentary lifestyles, both flourished in the Yuan era. The urban expansion begun under the Tang and Song dynasties continued, and the Mongol elite soon became addicted to the diversions of urban life. Traditional Chinese artistic endeavors, such as poetry and essay writing, languished under the Mongols in comparison with their flowering in the Tang and Song eras. But popular entertainments, particularly musical dramas, flourished. Perhaps the most famous Chinese dramatic work, *The Romance of the West Chamber,* was written in the Yuan period. Dozens of major playwrights wrote for the court, the rising merchant classes, and the Mongol elite. Actors and actresses, who had long been relegated by the Confucian scholars to the despised status of "mean people," achieved celebrity and social esteem. All of this rankled the scholar-gentry, who waited for the chance to restore Confucian decorum and what they believed to be the proper social hierarchy for a civilized people.

Initially, at least, Kubilai Khan pursued policies toward one social group, the peasants, that the scholarly class would have heartily approved. He forbade Mongol cavalrymen from turning croplands into pasture and restored the granary system for famine relief that had been badly neglected in the late Song. Kubilai also sought to reduce peasant tax and forced-labor burdens, partly by redirecting peasant payments from local nonofficial tax farmers directly to government officials. He and his advisors also developed a revolutionary plan to establish elementary education in the villages. Although the level of learning they envisioned was rudimentary, such a project, if it had been

enacted, would have been a major challenge to the educational system centered on the elite that long had dominated Chinese civilization.

The Fall of the House of Yuan

Historians often remark on the seeming contradiction between the military prowess of the Mongol conquerors and the short life of the dynasty they established in China. Kubilai Khan's long reign encompassed a good portion of the nine decades in which the Mongols ruled all of China. Already by the end of his reign, the dynasty was showing signs of weakening. Song loyalists raised revolts in the south, and popular hostility toward the foreign overlords was expressed more and more openly. The Mongol aura of military invincibility was badly tarnished by Kubilai's rebuffs at the hands of the military lords of Japan and the failure of the expeditions that he sent to punish them, first in 1274 and again in a much larger effort in 1280. The defeats suffered by Mongol forces engaged in similar expeditions to Vietnam and Java during this same period further undermined the Mongols' standing.

Kubilai's dissolute lifestyle in his later years, partly brought on by the death of his most beloved wife, Chabi, and five years later the death of his favorite son, led to a general softening of the Mongol ruling class as a whole. Kubilai's successors lacked his capacity for leadership and cared little for the tedium of day-to-day administrative tasks. Many of the Muslim and Chinese functionaries to whom they entrusted the imperial finances enriched themselves through graft and corruption. This greatly angered the hard-pressed peasantry, who bore the burden of rising taxes and demands for forced labor. The scholar-gentry played on this discontent by calling on the people to rise up and overthrow the "barbarian" usurpers.

By the 1350s, the signs of dynastic decline were apparent. Banditry and piracy were widespread, and the government's forces were too weak to curb them. Famine hit many regions and spawned local uprisings, which engulfed large portions of the empire. Secret religious sects, such as the **White Lotus Society,** were dedicated to overthrowing the dynasty. Their leaders' claims that they had magical powers to heal their followers and confound their enemies helped encourage further peasant resistance against the Mongols. As in the past, rebel leaders quarreled and fought with each other. For a time, chaos reigned as

In Depth

The Eclipse of the Nomadic War Machine

As the shock waves of the Mongol and Timurid explosions amply demonstrate, nomadic incursions into the civilized cores have had an impact on global history that far exceeds what one would expect, given the small numbers of nomadic peoples and the limited resources of the regions they inhabited. From the time of the great Indo-European migrations in the formative epoch of civilized development in the 3rd and 2nd millennia B.C.E. (see Chapters 2 and 3) through the classical and postclassical eras, nomadic peoples periodically emerged from their steppe, prairie, and desert fringe homelands to invade, often build empires, and settle in the sedentary zones of Eurasia, Africa, and the Americas. Their intrusions have significantly changed political history by destroying existing polities and even—as in the case of Assyria and Harappa—whole civilizations. They have also generated major population movements, sparked social upheavals, and facilitated critical cultural and economic exchanges across civilizations. As the Mongols' stunning successes in the 13th century illustrate, the ability of nomadic peoples to break through the defenses of the much more populous civilized zones and to establish control over much richer and more sophisticated peoples arose primarily from the nomads' advantages in waging war.

A reservoir of battle-ready warriors and mobility have proved to be the keys to success for expansion-minded nomads. Harsh environments and ongoing intertribal and interclan conflicts for survival within them produced tough, resourceful fighters who could live off the land on the march and who saw combat as an integral part of their lives. The horses and camels on which pastoral peoples in Eurasia and Sudanic Africa relied gave them a degree of mobility that confounded the sedentary peoples who tried to ward off their incursions. The mounted warriors of nomadic armies had the advantages of speed, surprise, and superior intelligence, gathered by mounted patrols. The most successful nomadic invaders, such as the Mongols, also were willing to experiment with and adapt to technological innovations. Some of these, such as the stirrup and various sorts of harnesses, were devised by the nomads themselves. Others, such as gunpowder and the siege engines—both Muslim and Chinese—that the Mongols used to smash the defenses of walled towns were borrowed from sedentary peoples and adapted to the nomads' fighting styles.

Aside from the military advantages of the nomads' lifestyles and social organization, their successes in war owed much to the weaknesses of their adversaries in the sedentary, civilized zones. Even in the best circumstances, the great empires that provided the main defense for agricultural peoples against nomadic incursions were diverse and overextended polities. Imperial control and protection diminished steadily as one moved away from the capital and core provinces. Imperial boundaries were usually fluid, and the outer provinces were vulnerable to nomadic raids and conquest.

Classical and postclassical empires, such as the Egyptian and Han and the Abbasid, Byzantine, and Song, enjoyed great advantages over the nomads in terms of the populations and resources they controlled. But their armies, almost without exception, were too slow, too low on firepower, and too poorly trained to resist large and well-organized forces of nomadic intruders. In times of dynastic strength in the sedentary zones, well-defended fortress systems and ingenious weapons—such as the crossbow, which the peasant conscripts could master fairly easily—were quite effective against nomadic incursions. Nonetheless, even the strongest dynasties depended heavily on protection payments to nomad leaders and the divisions between the nomadic peoples on their borders for their security. Even the strongest sedentary empires were shaken periodically by nomadic raids into the outer provinces. When the empires weakened or when large numbers of nomads were united under able leaders, such as Muhammad and his successors or Chinggis Khan, nomadic assaults made a shambles of sedentary armies and fortifications.

In many ways, the Mongol and Timurid explosions represented the apex of nomadic power and influence on world history. After these remarkable interludes, age-old patterns of interaction between nomads and town-dwelling peoples were transformed. These transformations resulted in the growing ability of sedentary peoples to first resist and then dominate nomadic peoples, and they mark a watershed in the history of the human community. Some of the causes of the shift were immediate and specific. The most critical of these was the devastation wrought by the Black Death on the nomads of central Asia in the 14th century. Although the epidemic was catastrophic for large portions of the civilized zones as well, it dealt the sparse nomadic populations a blow from which they took centuries to recover.

In the centuries after the Mongol conquests, the rulers of sedentary states found increasingly effective ways to centralize their political power and mobilize the labor and resources of their domains for war. The rulers of China and the empires of the Islamic belt made some improvements, but the sovereigns of the emerging states of western Europe surpassed all others in this regard. Stronger control and better organization allowed a growing share of steadily increasing national wealth to be channeled toward military ends. The competing rulers of Europe also invested heavily in technological innovations with military applications, from improved metalworking techniques to more potent gunpowder and firearms. From the 15th and 16th centuries, the discipline and training of European armies also improved. With pikes, muskets, fire drill, and trained commanders, European armies were more than a match for the massed nomad cavalry that had so long terrorized sedentary peoples.

With the introduction early in the 17th century of light, mobile field artillery into the armies of the warring states of central and western Europe, the nomads' retreat began. States such as Russia, which had centralized power on the western European model, as well as the Ottoman Empire in the eastern Mediterranean and the Qing in China, which had shared many of the armament advances of the Europeans, moved steadily into the steppe and desert heartlands of the horse and camel nomads. Each followed a conscious policy of settling part of its rapidly growing peasant population in the areas taken from the nomads. Thus, nomadic populations not only were brought under the direct rule of sedentary empires but saw their pasturelands plowed and planted wherever the soil and water supply permitted.

These trends suggest that the nomadic war machine had been in decline long before the new wave of innovation that ushered in the Industrial Revolution in the 18th century. But that process sealed its fate. Railways and repeating rifles allowed sedentary peoples to penetrate even the most wild and remote nomadic refuges and subdue even the most determined and fierce nomadic warriors, from the Plains Indians of North America to the bedouin of the Sahara and Arabia. The periodic nomadic incursions into the sedentary zones, which had recurred for millennia, had come to an end.

Questions: What are some of the major ways in which nomadic peoples and their periodic expansions have affected global history? Which of their movements and conquests do you think were the most important? Why were the Mongols able to build a much greater empire than any previous nomadic contender? Why did the Mongol Empire collapse so rapidly, and what does its fall tell us about the underlying weaknesses of the nomadic war machine?

the Yuan regime dissolved, and the Mongols who could escape the fury of the mob retreated into central Asia. The restoration of peace and order came from an unexpected quarter. Rather than a regional military commander or an aristocratic lord, a man from a poor peasant family, **Ju Yuanzhang,** emerged to found the **Ming dynasty,** which ruled China for most of the next three centuries.

Aftershock: The Brief Ride of Timur

Just as the peoples of Europe and Asia had begun to recover from the upheavals caused by Mongol expansion, a second nomadic outburst from central Asia plunged them again into fear and despair. This time the nomads in question were Turks, not Mongols, and their leader, **Timur-i Lang,** or Timur the Lame, was from a noble land-owning clan, not a tribal, herding background (Figure 19.7). Timur's personality was complex. On one hand, he was a highly cultured person who delighted in the fine arts, lush gardens, and splendid architecture and who could spend days conversing with great scholars such as Muslim historian Ibn Khaldun (see the Document in Chapter 12). On the other, he was a ruthless conqueror, apparently indifferent to human suffering and capable of commanding his troops to commit atrocities on a scale that would not be matched in the human experience until the 20th century. Beginning in the 1360s, his armies moved out from his base at Samarkand to conquests in Persia, the Fertile Crescent, India, and southern Russia.

Although his empire did not begin to compare with that of the Mongols in size, he outdid them in the ferocity of his campaigns. In fact, Timur is remembered for little more than barbaric destruction:

Figure 19.7 *In 1398, Timur-i Lang's central Asian armies left Delhi completely destroyed and India politically fragmented. Most of the rest of Timur's conquests were in central Asia, so they had much less of an effect on the Islamic heartlands, Europe, or China than Mongol expansion, which extended to these areas but ironically did not include India. Perhaps Timur's most lasting legacy was through his distant descendant Babur, who founded the last and most splendid Muslim dynasty in south Asia, the Mughals, who ruled much of India from the early 16th until the late 18th century.*

the pyramids of skulls he built with the heads of the tens of thousands of people slaughtered after the city of Aleppo in Asia Minor was taken or the thousands of prisoners he had massacred as a warning to the citizens of Delhi, in north India, not to resist his armies. In the face of this wanton slaughter, the fact that he

spared artisans and scientists to embellish his capital city at Samarkand counts for little. Unlike that of the Mongols, his rule brought neither increased trade and cross-cultural exchanges nor internal peace. Fortunately, his reign was as brief as it was violent. After his death in 1405, his empire was pulled apart by his warring commanders and old enemies anxious for revenge. With his passing, the last great challenge of the steppe nomads to the civilizations of Eurasia came to an end.

 GLOBAL CONNECTIONS: The Mongol Linkages

Although much of what the Mongols did was destructive, their forays into Europe, China, and the Muslim heartlands brought some lasting changes that were often beneficial. They taught new ways of making war and impressed on their Turkic and European enemies the effectiveness of gunpowder. Mongol conquests facilitated trade between the civilizations at each end of Eurasia, making possible the exchange of foods, tools, and ideas on an unprecedented scale. The revived routes brought great wealth to traders, such as those from north Italy, who set up outposts in the eastern Mediterranean, along the Black Sea coast, and as far east as the Caspian Sea. Because the establishment of these trading empires by the Venetians and Genoese provided precedents for the later drives for overseas expansion by peoples such as the Portuguese and English, they are of special significance in global history.

Perhaps the greatest long-term impact of the Mongol drive to the west was indirect and unintended. In recent years, a growing number of historians have become convinced that the Mongol conquests played a key role in transmitting the fleas that carried bubonic plague from south China and central Asia to Europe and the Middle East. The fleas may have hitched a ride on the livestock the Mongols drove into the new pasturelands won by their conquests or on the rats that nibbled the grain transported by merchants along the trading routes the Mongol rulers fostered between east and west. Whatever the exact connection, the Mongol armies unknowingly paved the way for the spread of the dreaded Black Death across the steppes to much of China, to the Islamic heartlands, and from there to most of Europe in the mid-14th century. In so doing, they unleashed possibly the most fatal epidemic in all human history. From mortality rates higher than 50 percent in some areas of Europe and the Middle East to the economic and social adjustments that the plague forced wherever it spread, this accidental but devastating side effect of the Mongol conquests influenced the course of civilized development in Europe, Asia, and north Africa for centuries.

The Mongol framework for Asian-European interactions, though brief, also facilitated other exchanges. Europeans, particularly, gained new knowledge of Chinese products and technologies that they would quickly adapt back home. Explosive powder and printing were the most important examples. Regions more remote from the Mongols, such as Africa, lacked this kind of stimulus. Even the collapse of the Mongol network had an impact. Many societies had an interest in maintaining contacts, though China grew more wary of outsiders. But the Mongol decline made land-based travel more dangerous, which quickly turned attention toward sea routes. Again, the legacy of the Mongol period was both complex and durable.

Further Readings

A substantial literature has developed on the Mongol interlude in global history. The most readable and reliable biography of Chinggis Khan is René Grousset's *Conqueror of the World* (1966). Grousset has also written a broader history of central Asia, *The Empire of the Steppes* (1970). Peter Brent's more recent *The Mongol Empire* (1976) provides an updated overview and wonderful illustrations. Berthold Spuler's *The Mongols in History* (1971) attempts to gauge their impact on world history, and his *History of the Mongols* (1968) supplies a wide variety of firsthand accounts of the Mongols from the founding of the empire to life in its successor states. Robert S. Marshall's *Storm From the East: from Genghis Khan to Khubilai Khan* (1993) and Charles J. Halperin, *Russia and the Golden Horde: The Mongol Impact on Medieval Russian History, 1581-1990* (1996) examine the Mongol impact on Russia. While George Vernadsky's *The Mongols in Russia* (1953) remains the standard work on that subject, some of its views are now contested. Morris Rossabi's *Kubilai Khan: His Life and Times* (1988) is by far the best work on the Mongols in China. George James Chambers' *The Devil's Horsemen* (1979) and Denis Sinor's *History of Hungary* (1957) contain good accounts of the Mongol incursions into eastern and central Europe. T. Allsen's *Mongol Imperialism* (1987) is the best account of the rise and structure of the empires built by Chinggis Khan and his successors. The fullest and most accessible summary of the links between Mongol expansion and the spread of the Black Death can be found in William H. McNeill's *Plagues and Peoples* (1976).

On the Web

The last great empire of the steppe, the Mongol Empire, can be virtually toured at http://www.kiku.com/electric_samurai/virtual_mongol/history.html. Its founder, Chinggis Khan, receives close attention at http://www.fsmitha.com/h3/h11mon.htm and http://www.angelfire.com/mo/QBranch/. An excellent summary of the strategic and tactical elements of Mongol warfare can be found at http://www.humanities.ualberta.ca/history111/jan15/jan15/sld003.htm. The life of Chinggis Khan's grandson, Kubilai Khan, who continued his grandfather's unbroken string of victories with his conquest of China, is described at http://www.1upinfo.com/country-guide-study/mongolia/mongolia27.html.

Two other virtual exhibits (http://www.pma.edmonton.ab.ca/vexhibit/intro.htm and http://www.nationalgeographic.com/features/97/genghis/index.html illuminate the world of inner Asia under Mongol control.

CHAPTER 20

THE WEST AND THE CHANGING WORLD BALANCE

This Persian-style painting depicts the Ottoman Turks as they attack the Hungarians with troops and cannons in a battle in 1526.

The world in 1400 was in fundamental transition. This chapter highlights the main features of this transition. The principal focus is on shifts in the balance of power between civilizations in Asia, Africa, and Europe and related changes in the nature of international contact.

This period of transition began with the decline of Arab strength—symbolized by the fall of the last Arab caliphate in 1258—and the disruptions that Mongol incursions caused elsewhere in Asia and eastern Europe. These developments created new opportunities in the international network that had been established in the postclassical centuries, initially under Arab sponsorship. Various candidates emerged to take a new international role, including for a short time China in its new Ming dynasty.

The most dynamic new contender for international power ultimately proved to be western Europe, and the conditions that propelled Western civilization toward a new position around 1400 are the second key theme of this chapter. The West was not yet the world's major power; it did not replace the Arabs as international leaders quickly or easily. The first stages of the rise of the West were accompanied by important changes in Western civilization itself, also taking shape by about 1400. At this point, Italy, Spain, and Portugal took a new leadership role in western European outreach, which they would hold for about two centuries.

It is also vital to note changes in the societies outside the international network, in the Americas and Polynesia. New difficulties in the great American empires, in particular, inadvertently reduced the ability to respond to a European challenge that was about to arrive.

Focusing on new frameworks for international contacts, this chapter inevitably deals with the question of why individual civilizations reacted differently to key forces. This was a vital period of redefinition, comparable to the centuries that led from the classical to postclassical periods but with developments that had even wider sweep.

The Decline of the Old Order

The first steps in the new world order that was beginning to emerge by 1400 involved major reshuffling in the Middle East and north Africa.

In 1200, the Middle East was still dominated by two powerful empires, the Byzantine in the northwest and the Islamic caliphate through much of the Middle Eastern heartland. By 1400, this structure was in disarray. The Byzantine Empire still existed, but it was in decline, pressed by invading Ottoman Turks. The imperial capital, Constantinople, fell to the Turks in 1453, effectively ending the empire. Two centuries earlier, the caliphate, long sapped by increasing reliance on foreign

1250 C.E.	1300 C.E.	1350 C.E.	1400 C.E.	1450 C.E.
1258 Mongol conquest of Baghdad; fall of Abbasid caliphate **c. 1266–1337** Giotto **1275–1292** Marco Polo in China **1290–1317** New famines in Europe **1291** First Italian expedition seeks route to Indies	**1304–1374** Petrarch; development of Italian Renaissance **1320s** Spread of bubonic plague in Gobi desert **1320s** First European use of cannon in warfare **1330s** Black Death reaches China **1347** Plague reaches Sicily **1348** Peak of Black Death in Middle East **1348–1375** Plague spreads in Europe, including Russia	**1368** Mongols expelled from China; Ming dynasty	**1400** End of Polynesian migrations **1405** Chinese trading expeditions begin **1433** End of Chinese expeditions **1439** Portugal takes over Azores; increasing expeditions into Atlantic, along northwest African coast	**1453** Ottomans capture Constantinople, fall of Byzantine Empire **1469** Union of Aragon and Castile; rise of Spanish monarchy

troops and advisors, including the Turks, had fallen to Mongol invasion. Arabs have never since been able to unite all of their region under their own rule.

Social and Cultural Change in the Middle East

By about 1300, religious leaders in the Islamic Middle East gained the upper hand over poets, philosophers, and scientists. An earlier tension between diverse cultural elements yielded to the predominance of the faith. The new piety associated with the rising Sufi movement, discussed in Chapter 12, was both the cause and the result of this development. In literature, emphasis on secular themes, such as the joys of feasting and hunting, gave way to more strictly religious ideas. Persian poets, writing in their own language instead of Arabic, led the way, and religious poetry—not poetry in general—became part of the education of upper-class children. In philosophy, the rationalistic current encountered new attack. In Muslim Spain, philosopher Ibn Rushd (Averroës) espoused Greek rationalism, but his efforts were largely ignored in the Middle East. In fact, European scholars were more heavily influenced by his work. In the Middle East proper, a more typical philosopher now claimed to use Aristotle's logic to show that it was impossible to discover religious truth by human reason, in a book revealingly titled *The Destruction of Philosophy.* Many Sufi scholars wrote excitedly of their mystical contacts with God and the stages of their religious passion, which led to dramatic new statements of Islam. Islamic science continued, but its role diminished.

Changes in society and the economy were as telling as the shifts in politics and intellectual life. As the authority of the caliphate declined, landlords seized power over the peasantry. As a result, from about 1100 onward, Middle Eastern peasants increasingly lost their freedom, becoming serfs on large estates, providing the labor and produce landlords now sought. This loss was not the peasants' alone, for agricultural productivity suffered as a result. Landlords turned to sucking what they could from their estates rather than trying to develop a more vital agriculture. Tax revenues declined, and Arab and other Middle Eastern traders began to lose ground. Few Arab coins have been found in Europe dating from later than 1100. European merchants began to control their own turf and challenge the Arabs in other parts of the Mediterranean; initiative in this vital trading area was passing to their hands. Arab and Persian commerce remained active in the Indian Ocean, but the time was not too distant when it would face new competition there as well.

The decline of the Islamic caliphate and its economy was gradual and incomplete. It cannot be compared with the dramatic fall of the Roman Empire in the West many centuries before. A more subtle model is needed. The reduced dynamism in trade did not take the Arabs out of major world markets, for example. Indeed, Middle Eastern commerce rebounded somewhat by 1400.

Finally, the political fragmentation of the Arab world did not produce prolonged confusion in the Middle East. The emerging Ottoman Turkish state soon mastered most of the lands of the old caliphate as well as the Byzantine corner, expanding into southeastern Europe. (See Chapter 26 for the development of the new Ottoman Empire.) It is important to realize that the empire was far more powerful, politically and militarily, than the caliphate had been for many centuries. It was thus more frightening to observers in neighboring civilizations such as western Europe.

A Power Vacuum in International Leadership

Even the rise of the Ottoman Empire did not restore the full international vigor that the Islamic caliphate had at the height of its powers. The empire was not the sole hub of an international network, as the Arab caliphate had been a few centuries before.

The Mongols developed the first alternative global framework, with their interlocking holdings that included central Asia, China, and Russia, with thrusts into the Middle East and south Asia. Here was a system that actively encouraged interregional travelers and provided unprecedented opportunities for exchanges of technology and ideas—exchanges that particularly benefited western Europe through contacts with Asia. The Mongol decline, first in China, then gradually elsewhere, raised again the question of domination of international contacts and trade. The end of the Mongol empires also turned attention to seaborne trade, as the overland Asian trade routes were disrupted. Two societies, successively, stepped up to the challenge.

Chinese Thrust and Withdrawal

For a brief time China took full advantage of the new opportunities in international trade. Rebellions in China drove out the deeply resented Mongol overlords in 1368. A rebel leader from a peasant family seized the Mongol capital of Beijing and proclaimed a new Ming—meaning "brilliant"—dynasty that was to last until 1644. This dynasty began with a burst of unusual expansionism. The initial Ming rulers pressed to secure the borders of the Middle Kingdom. This meant pushing the Mongols far to the north, to the plains of what is now Mongolia. It meant reestablishing influence over neighboring governments and winning tribute payments from states in Korea, Vietnam, and Tibet, reviving much of the east Asian regional structure set up by the Tang dynasty. Far more unusual was a new policy, adopted soon after 1400, of mounting huge, state-sponsored trading expeditions to southern Asia and beyond.

A first fleet sailed in 1405 to India, with 62 ships carrying 28,000 men. Later voyages reached the Middle East and the eastern coast of Africa, bringing chinaware and copper coinage in exchange for local goods. Chinese shipping at its height consisted of 2700 coastal vessels, 400 armed naval ships, and at least as many long-distance ships. Nine great treasure ships, the most sophisticated in the world at the time, explored the Indian Ocean, the Persian Gulf, and the Red Sea, establishing regular trade all along the way.

Between 1405 and their termination in 1433, these expeditions were commanded by the admiral **Zhenghe.** A Muslim from western China, Zhenghe was well suited to deal with Muslims in southeast Asia on his trade route. Zhenghe was also a eunuch, castrated for service at the royal court. China's Ming emperors retained a large harem of wives to ensure succession, and eunuchs were needed to guard them without threat of sexual rivalry; many gained bureaucratic powers well beyond this service. Zhenghe's expeditions usually hugged the coastline, but he had an improved compass and excellent maps as well as huge vessels that contained ample supplies—even gardens—as well as goods for trade. His fleets must have impressed, even terrified, the local rulers around the Indian Ocean, many of whom paid tribute to the emperor. For while Zhenghe brought gifts, he also had 28,000 well-armed troops on his expeditions. Several missions visited China from the Middle East and Africa. From Africa also came ostriches, zebras, and giraffes for the imperial zoo; the latter became the unicorns of Chinese fable. But Zhenghe was resented by the Confucian bureaucrats, who refused even to write much about him in their chronicles.

There is no question that the course of world history might have been changed dramatically had the Chinese thrust continued, for the tiny European expeditions that began to creep down the western coast of Africa at about the same time would have been no match for this combination of merchant and military organization. Indeed, historians wonder if one expedition might have rounded Africa to at least glimpse the Atlantic. But China's emperors called the expeditions to a halt in 1433. The bureaucrats had long opposed the new trade policy, out of rivalry with other officials such as Zhenghe, but there were deeper reasons as well. The costs seemed unacceptable, given the continuing expenses of the campaigns against the Mongols and establishing a luxurious new capital city in Beijing.

This assessment was not inevitable and it must be explained. It reflected a preference for traditional expenditures rather than distant foreign involvements.

Chinese merchant activity continued to be extensive in southeast Asia. Chinese trading groups established permanent settlements in the Philippines, Malaysia, and Indonesia, where they added to the cultural diversity of the area and maintained a disproportionate role in local and regional trading activities into the 20th century. Nonetheless, China's chance to become a dominant world trading power was lost, at least for several centuries.

To Western eyes, accustomed to judging a society's dynamism by its ability to reach out and gain new territories or trade positions, China's decision may seem hard to understand—the precursor to decline. But to the Chinese, it was the brief trading flurry that was unusual, not its end. China had long emphasized internal development, amid considerable international isolation and concern over protection against invasion from central Asia. Its leaders were suspicious of any policy that would unduly elevate commercial activity. Ming emperors consolidated their rule over the empire's vast territory. Internal economic development continued as well, with no need for foreign products. Chinese goods continued to be highly valued in the world market. Industry expanded, with growth in the production of textiles and porcelain; ongoing trade with southeast Asia enriched the port cities; agricultural production and population increased.

The shift in Chinese policy unintentionally cleared the way for another, in most ways less organized civilization to work toward a new international position. With the Arabs in partial eclipse and with China briefly moving into the resulting trade vacuum but then retreating, hesitant Western expansionism, ventured before 1400, began to take on new significance. Within a century, Western explorers and traders had launched an attempt to seize international trading dominance and had expanded the international network to include parts of the Americas for the first time.

The Rise of the West

Western Europe began to undergo important changes in the 14th and 15th centuries. Some involved new problems; others created new opportunities. Examining the various strengths and weaknesses of this once backward region sets the stage for Europe's new ventures in world trade.

The West's gradual emergence into larger world contacts during the 15th century was surprising in many respects. Westerners remained awed by the powerful bureaucracies and opulent treasuries of empires in the traditional civilization centers such as Constantinople. Furthermore, the West was changing in some painful ways. The staples of medieval culture at its height were under new question by 1400. The church, which had long been one of the organizing institutions of Western civilization, was under new attack. Medieval philosophy had passed its creative phase. Warrior aristocrats, long a key leadership group in feudal society, softened their style of life, preferring court rituals and jousting tournaments and adopting military armor so cumbersome that real fighting was difficult.

Even more strikingly, the lives and economic activities of ordinary Europeans were in disarray. This was a time of crisis, and Europe's expanding world role could not reverse the fundamental challenges to its internal economic and demographic structure. Europeans began to suffer from recurrent famine after 1300 because population outstripped the food supply and no new food production techniques were discovered. Famine reduced disease resistance, making Europe more vulnerable to the bubonic plagues that spread from Asia.

Bubonic plague, or Black Death, surfaced in various parts of Asia in the 14th century. In China it reduced the population by nearly 30 percent by 1400. Following trade routes, it then spread into India and the Middle East, causing thousands of deaths per day in the larger cities. The plague's worst European impact occurred between 1348 and 1375, by which time 30 million people, one-third of Europe's population, died. The resulting economic dislocation produced bitter strikes and peasant uprisings.

Sources of Dynamism: Medieval Vitality

How could the West be poised for a new international role? The answer to that question is complex. First, several key advances of medieval society were not really reversed by the troubles of the decades around 1400. For example, the strengthening of feudal monarchy provided more effective national or regional governments for much of the West. The Hundred Years' War between Britain and France stimulated innovations in military organization,

Visualizing the Past

Population Trends

Questions: What do these population charts show about relationships in population size, and comparative trends in population size, among the major inhabited regions of the world? Population pressure did not drive European expansion in the 15th century, because population was falling temporarily, but were there longer-term trends, from the year 1000, that might have encouraged the expansionist effort? What societies show the greatest changes

in population levels between 1000 and 1800? What might have caused these changes? Finally, what do the charts suggest about the demographic position of Europe in the 20th century compared to the world as a whole?

Reading population statistics provides vital information, but it also raises questions, including ones about causation, which numbers alone cannot answer. What other data would be most helpful to put these figures in appropriate world history contexts? Which figures are more revealing: absolute numbers or percentages? Why?

Population Levels (Millions)

Continents	1000	1700	1800	1900	1975
Europe	36	120	180	390	635
Asia (includes Middle East)	185	415	625	970	2300
Africa	33	61	70	110	385
Americas	39	13	24	145	545
Oceania (includes Australia)	1.5	2.25	2.5	6.75	23
Totals	294.5	611.25	901.5	1621.75	3888

Note: Earlier figures are only estimates; they are fairly accurate indicators of relative size.

Source: Adapted from Dennis H. Wrong, ed., *Population and Society* (1977).

Percentages or Proportions of Total World Population

Continents	1000	1700	1800	1900	1975
Europe	12.2	19.6	19.7	24	16.3
Asia	62.9	67.6	69.3	59.8	59.2
Africa	11.2	10.0	7.8	6.8	9.9
Americas	13.4	2.1	2.7	8.9	14.0
Oceania	0.4	0.4	0.3	0.3	0.6

Source: Adapted from Dennis H. Wrong, ed., *Population and Society* (1977).

including nonaristocratic soldiers recruited and paid directly by the royal government, that enhanced central political power. Strong regional monarchies took hold in parts of Spain and in Portugal as Christian leaders drove back the Muslim rulers of this region. The growth of cities and urban economies continued to spur the commercial side of Western society. Even the church had made its peace with such key principles of capitalism as profit-seeking. Technology continued to advance, particularly in ironwork—used for bells and weapons—and timekeeping.

In short, explaining the new Western vigor involves an understanding that some of the gains the

West achieved during the Middle Ages continued even as certain characteristic medieval forms wavered.

Imitation and International Problems

Two additional causes involved western Europe's international position. New opportunities for imitation were an obvious advantage. The Mongol Empire established in Asia and eastern Europe in the late 13th and early 14th centuries provided new access to Asian knowledge and technology. Political stability and an openness to foreign visitors by the great khans helped

Westerners learn of Asian technologies, ranging from printing to the compass and explosive powder. Western Europe had ideal access in the Mongol period. It was not disrupted by the Mongols, as eastern Europe and so many parts of Asia were, but it was in active contact, unlike sub-Saharan Africa. Internal European warfare and merchant zeal made western Europe an eager learner, for the Asian technologies promised to meet existing military and commercial needs.

The second international factor was the intensification of European problems in the existing world market and international arena. From the Crusades onward, Western elites had become used to increasing consumption of Asian luxury products, including spices such as cinnamon and nutmeg, silks, sugar, perfumes, and jewels. In exchange for the luxury items, Europeans mainly had cruder goods to offer: wool, tin, copper, honey, and salt. The value of European exports almost never equaled the value of what was imported from Asia. The resulting unfavorable balance of trade had to be made up in gold, but western Europe had only a limited gold supply. By 1400, the constant drain to Asia was creating a gold famine that threatened the whole European economy with collapse.

Furthermore, there were legitimate fears of a new Muslim threat. The Ottoman Empire was taking shape, and Europeans began to fear a new Muslim surge. Even before this, the Muslim capture of the last crusader stronghold (the city of Acre in the Middle East) in 1291 gave Muslim traders, particularly Egyptians, new opportunities to act as intermediaries in the Asian trade, for there were no Western-controlled ports left in the eastern Mediterranean. One response to this was a series of conquests by the city-state of Venice along the eastern coast of the Adriatic. A more important response was to begin exploring alternative routes to Asia that would bypass the Middle East and the feared and hated Muslim realms altogether.

Secular Directions in the Italian Renaissance

The final major ingredient of the West's surge involved changes within the West itself, starting with Italy, where medieval forms had never fully taken hold. In 1400, Italy was in the midst of a vital cultural and political movement known as the **Renaissance,** or rebirth. The early phases of the Renaissance stressed more secular subjects in litera-

ture and art. Religious art remained dominant but used more realistic portrayals of people and nature, and some nonreligious themes surfaced outright (Figure 20.1). The doings of human beings deserved attention for their own sake, in the Renaissance view, not as they reflected a divine plan. Artists and writers became more openly ambitious for personal reputation and glory.

Italy was the center of initial Renaissance culture because it had more contact with Roman tradition than did the rest of Europe and because by the 14th century it led the West in banking and trade. Active commerce and urban manufacturing gave Italian cities the wealth to sponsor new cultural activities, and contacts with some foreign scholars, particularly in Byzantium, helped revive Greco-Roman styles. Finally, the attention to government and diplomacy by the competitive governments of Italy's city-states led intellectuals and political leaders to emphasize worldly culture.

Human Values and Renaissance Culture

Despite its political and commercial roots, the Renaissance was first and foremost a cultural movement, launched in Florence and manifesting itself in literature and various arts. The Renaissance focused on a new interest in stylistic grace and a concern for practical ethics and codes of behavior for urban gentlemen. One leading 14th-century writer, **Francesco Petrarch,** not only took pride in his city and his age but explored the glories of personal achievement with new confidence.

Innovation flourished in the visual arts and music as well. The subject matter of art moved toward nature and people, including cityscapes and portraits of the rich and powerful, whether the themes were religious or secular. Florentine painter Giotto led the way, departing from medieval formalism and stiffness. While still a young apprentice to the painter Cimabue, Giotto painted a fly on the nose of one of Cimabue's portrait subjects, and it was so realistic that Cimabue repeatedly tried to swat it off before going back to work on the canvas. Other painters, beginning later in the 14th century, started to introduce perspective while using new colors and other materials. In architecture, favor shifted away from the Gothic to a classicism derived from the styles of

Figure 20.1   *Europe's new spirit amid old values. Dante, Italian writer of the 14th century, holds a copy of his great work, the* Divine Comedy, *with both religious (souls tormented in hell) and Renaissance (the solid, classical-style urban buildings of the city of Florence) symbolism greeting him. The painting was designed by Domenico di Michelina for the cathedral of Florence in 1465.*

Greece and Rome. Vivid, realistic statues complemented the new palaces and public buildings.

The impact of the early Renaissance must not be exaggerated. It had little influence outside of Italy. Even in Italy, it focused on high culture, not popular culture, and on the arts; there was little initial interest in science. And although it built on distinctive political and economic forms, it was not a full break from medieval tendencies.

Nevertheless, these new cultural currents were an important innovation in Western history. The full ramifications of the Renaissance feed into the next period of both world and Western history (see Chapter 22). The movement was only getting started by 1400. The wide range of Italian commerce and shipping proved to be one of the building blocks of European outreach. By the 14th century, ships, particularly from the western Italian city of Genoa, which was less well placed than Venice for eastern Mediterranean trade and the resultant links to Asia, were ready for new roles. Ambitious city-state governments encouraged new ventures, eager to collect more tax money

Document

Italian Renaissance Culture

Writers in the first phase of the Italian Renaissance were aware that they were defining a culture quite different from that of medieval theologians and philosophers. In the passages that follow, Petrarch (1304–1374) writes about his priorities in literature, including the kind of classical examples he revered, first in a letter to another major writer, Boccaccio, and then in a poem. Petrarch's cultural interests and his definition of personal goals form part of a movement called humanism (see Chapter 22). Judging by the following documents, what defined a Renaissance humanist?

From Petrarch, Letter to Boccaccio (1362)

Neither exhortations to virtue nor the argument of approaching death should divert us from literature; for in a good mind it excites the love of virtue, and dissipates, or at least diminishes, the fear of death. To desert our studies shows want of self-confidence rather than wisdom, for letters do not hinder but aid the properly constituted mind which possesses them; they facilitate our life, they do not retard it…. If it were otherwise, surely the zeal of certain persons who persevered to the end could not have roused such admiration. Cato, I never forget, acquainted himself with Latin literature as he was growing old, and Greek when he had really become an old man. Varro, who reached his hundredth year still reading and writing, parted from life sooner than from his love of study. Livius Drusus, although weakened by age and afflicted with blindness, did not give up his interpretation of the civil law, which he carried on to the great advantage of the state….

Besides these and innumerable others like them, have not all those of our own religion whom we should wish most to imitate devoted their whole lives to literature, and grown old and died in the same pursuit? Some, indeed, were overtaken by death while still at work reading or writing. To none of them, so far as I know, did it prove a disadvantage to be noted for secular learning….

While I know that many have become famous for piety without learning, at the same time I know of no one who has been prevented by literature from following the path of holiness. The apostle Paul was, to be sure, accused of having his head turned by study, but the world has long ago passed its verdict upon this accusation. If I may be allowed to speak for myself, it seems to me that, although the path to virtue by the way of ignorance may be plain, it fosters sloth. The goal of all good people is the same, but the ways of reaching it are many and various. Some advance slowly, others with more spirit; some obscurely, others again conspicuously. One takes a lower path, another takes a higher path. Although all alike are on the road to happiness, certainly the more elevated path is the more glorious. Hence ignorance, however devout, is by no means to be put on a plane with the enlightened devoutness of one familiar with literature. Nor can you pick me out from the whole array of unlettered saints, an example so holy that I cannot match it with a still holier one from the other group.

From Petrarch, the Sonnets (c. 1535)

To a Friend, Encouraging Him to Pursue Poetry

Torn is each virtue from its earthy throne
By sloth, intemperance, and voluptuous ease;
Far hence is every light celestial gone,
That guides mankind through life's perplexing maze….
Who now would laurel, myrtle-wreaths obtain?
Let want, let shame, Philosophy attend!
Cries the base world, intent on sordid gain.
What though thy favourite path be trod by few;
Let it but urge thee more, dear gentle friend,
Thy great design of glory to pursue.

Questions: What are the key purposes of intellectual activity, according to Petrarch? How can these purposes be reconciled with Christianity? How do Petrarch's arguments compare with Cicero's defense of Greek culture (Chapter 7)? To what extent does Petrarch's humanism suggest a more modern outlook than that of medieval Western culture? Does this Renaissance spirit suggest factors that might explain Europe's new expansion? Did the Renaissance encourage human agency? How important were individuals in this major development, compared to the larger causes?

and promote commerce as one of their explicit functions. A general "Renaissance spirit" could also spur innovation. Whereas people such as Petrarch defined human ambition mainly in cultural terms, other urban and commercial leaders, including seafaring men such as Genoa's Christopher Columbus, might apply some of the same confidence and desire for personal glory to different areas, such as exploration or conquest.

The Iberian Spirit of Religious Mission

Along with Italy, a key center for change by the 14th century was the Iberian peninsula, where Christian military leaders had for several centuries been pressing back the boundaries of the Muslim state in Spain. Soon after 1400, major regional monarchies had been established in the provinces of **Castile** and **Aragon,** which would be united through royal marriage in 1469.

Even before the marriage between Ferdinand and Isabella, Spanish and Portuguese rulers had developed a vigorous military and religious agenda. They supported effective armies, including infantry and feudal cavalry. And they believed that government had a mission to promote Christianity by converting or expelling Arabs and Jews and by maintaining doctrinal purity within the church. Close links between church and state, portrayed in art, provided revenues and officials for the royal government. In return, the government supported church courts in their efforts to enforce moral and doctrinal purity. Later in the 15th century, this interaction led to the reestablishment of the church-run courts of the Inquisition in Spain, designed to enforce religious orthodoxy. In other words, Spain and Portugal were developing effective new governments with a special sense of religious mission and religious support. These changes promoted the West's expansion into wider world contacts.

Western Expansion: The Experimental Phase

Specific European attempts to explore the Atlantic (beyond the earlier Viking voyages in the North Atlantic) began in the later 13th century. Early discoveries increased Europeans' interest in setting up a new colonial system.

Early Explorations

As early as 1291, two Italian brothers, the **Vivaldis** from Genoa, sailed with two galleys through the Straits of Gibraltar, seeking a Western route to the "Indies," the spice-producing areas of south and southeast Asia. They were never heard from again. Although they were precursors of a major Western thrust into the southern Atlantic, it is not even entirely clear what they meant by the "Indies." Early

in the 14th century, other explorers from Genoa rediscovered the Canary Islands, in the Atlantic, populated by a hunting-and-gathering people. These islands had been known vaguely since classical times but had never been explored by Europeans. Genoese sailors also visited the Madeiras and probably reached the more distant Azores by 1351. Soon after this, ships from northeastern Spain, based in the port of Barcelona, sailed along the African coast as far south as present-day Sierra Leone.

Until 1430, technological barriers prevented further exploration for alternative routes. Without adequate navigation instruments, Europeans could not risk wider ventures into the Atlantic. They also needed better ships than the shallow-drafted, oar-propelled Mediterranean galleys. However, efforts were under way to develop an oceangoing sailing vessel. At the same time, the crucial navigational problems were met by the compass and the astrolabe, used to determine latitude at sea by reckoning from the stars. Contacts with Arab merchants (who had learned from the Chinese) provided knowledge of these devices. European mapmaking, improving steadily during the 14th century, was also a key innovation. Because of these advances, as well as mistaken geographic assumptions shown on the map in Figure 20.2, Europeans were ready in the decades after 1400 to undertake voyages impossible just a century before. In 1498, the Portuguese explorer **Vasco da Gama** was the first European to reach India by sea, preparing Portuguese entry into the Indian Ocean (Figure 20.3).

Colonial Patterns

Even as these wider-ranging voyages began, Westerners led by the Spanish and Portuguese had begun to take advantage of the new lands they had already discovered. A driving force behind both the further expeditions and the efforts to make already-discovered areas economically profitable was Prince Henry of Portugal, known as **Henry the Navigator.** A student of astronomy and nautical science, Henry sponsored about a third of Portuguese voyages of exploration before his death in 1460. His mixture of motivation—scientific and intellectual curiosity, desire to spread the name of Christ to unfamiliar lands, and financial interest—reflected some of the key forces in late postclassical Europe.

Portugal by 1439 had taken control of the Azores and had granted land to colonists. Soon Spaniards and Portuguese had conquered and colonized the

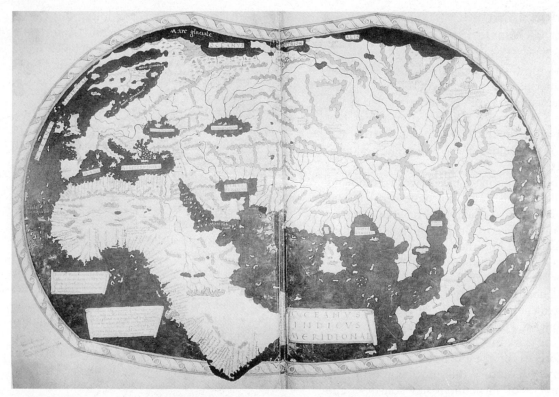

Figure 20.2   *Columbus is supposed to have had a copy of this world map in Spain. The map, dating from about 1489, shows the Old World as Europeans were increasingly coming to know it. Note how reachable India looked to Europeans using this map.*

Madeiras and Canaries, bringing in Western plants, animals, weapons, and diseases. The result was something of a laboratory for the larger European colonialism that would soon take shape, particularly in the Americas. European colonists quickly set up large agricultural estates designed to produce cash crops that could be sold on the European market. First they introduced sugar, an item once imported from Asia but now available in growing quantities from Western-controlled sources. Ultimately, other crops such as cotton and tobacco were also introduced to the Atlantic islands. To produce these market crops the new colonists brought in slaves from northwestern Africa, mainly in Portuguese ships—the first examples of a new, commercial version of slavery and the first sign that Western expansion could have serious impact on other societies as well.

These developments about 1400 remained modest, even in their consequences for Africa. They illustrate mainly how quickly Western conquerors decided what to do with lands and peoples newly in their grasp. The ventures were successful enough to motivate more extensive probes into the southern Atlantic as soon as technology permitted. Indeed, voyages of exploration down the coast of Africa and across the Atlantic began to occur as the island colonies were being fully settled. The ventures summed up the swirl of forces that were beginning to reshape the West's role in the world: inferiorities and fears, particularly with regard to the Muslims; new energies of Renaissance merchants and Iberian rulers; economic pressures; and a long-standing population surge.

Outside the World Network

 The international framework that had developed during the postclassical period embraced most of Asia, Europe, and Africa. This network left out important groups and regions that had their own vigorous histories.

Figure 20.3 *This 18th-century engraving portrays Vasco da Gama's audience with the Indian ruler of Calicut in 1498.*

Developments in the Americas and Polynesia were not affected by the new international exchange. During the next period of world history, these regions all were pulled into a new level of international contact, but a world balance sheet in 1400 must emphasize their separateness.

At the same time, several of the societies outside the international network were experiencing some new problems during the 15th century that would leave them vulnerable to outside interference thereafter. Such problems included new political strains in the leading American civilizations and a fragmentation of the principal island groups in Polynesian culture.

Political Issues in the Americas

As we discussed in Chapter 16, the Aztec and Inca empires ran into increasing difficulties not long after

1400. Aztec exploitation of subject peoples for gold, slaves, and religious sacrifices roused great resentment. What would have happened to the Aztec Empire if the Spaniards had not intervened after 1500 is not clear, but it is obvious that disunity created opportunities for outside intervention that might not have existed otherwise. The Inca system, though far less brutal than that of the Aztecs, provided ongoing tension between central leadership and local initiative. This complicated effective control of the vast expanse of the Inca domains. Here too, overextension made change likely by the 1500s—indeed, the empire was already receding somewhat—even without European intervention. At the same time, other cultures were developing in parts of the Americas that might well have been candidates for new political leadership, if American history had proceeded in isolation.

Expansion, Migration, and Conquest in Polynesia

A second culture that was later pulled into the expanding world network was that of Polynesia. Here, as in the Americas, important changes took place during the postclassical era but with no relationship to developments in societies elsewhere in the world. The key Polynesian theme from the 7th century to 1400 was expansion, spurts of migration, and conquest that implanted Polynesian culture well beyond the initial base in the Society Islands, as Tahiti, Samoa, and Fiji are called collectively (Map 20.1; also see Chapter 9).

One channel of migration pointed northward to the islands of Hawaii. The first Polynesians reached these previously uninhabited islands before the 7th century, traveling in great war canoes. From the 7th century until about 1300 or 1400, recurrent contacts remained between the Hawaiian islands and the larger Society Islands group, allowing periodic new migration. From about 1400 until the arrival of European explorers in 1778, Hawaiian society was cut off even from Polynesia.

Polynesians in Hawaii spread widely across the islands in agricultural clusters and fishing villages amid the volcanic mountains. Hawaiians were inventive in using local vegetation, weaving fabrics as well as making materials and fishing nets from grass. They also imported pigs from the Society Islands—a vital source of meat but a source of devastation to many plant species unique to Hawaii. Politically, Hawaii

In Depth

The Problem of Ethnocentrism

Many cultures encourage an ethnocentric outlook, and the culture of the West is certainly one of them. Ethnocentrism creates problems in interpreting world history. The dictionary definition of *ethnocentrism* is "a habitual disposition to judge foreign peoples or groups by the standards and practices of one's own culture or ethnic group"—and often finding them inferior. Most of us take pride in many of our own institutions and values, and it is tempting to move from this pride to a disapproval of other peoples when they clearly do not share our behaviors and beliefs. Many Americans have a difficult time understanding how other peoples have failed to establish the stable democratic political structure of our own country. Even liberals who pride themselves on a sophisticated appreciation of different habits in some areas may adopt an ethnocentric shock at the oppression (by current American standards) of women that is visible in certain societies today or in the past. Indeed, unless a person is almost totally alienated from his or her own society, some ethnocentric reactions are hard to avoid.

Nevertheless, unexamined ethnocentrism can be a barrier in dealing with world history. We will grasp other times and places better, and perhaps use our own values more intelligently, if we do not too readily dismiss cultures in which "objectionable" practices occur.

Ethnocentrism is not just an issue for modern Westerners. Civilized peoples in the past routinely accused outsiders of barbaric ways, as in the Islamic characterizations of the Mongols described in Chapter 19. But the current power of Western standards makes our own ethnocentric potential a real issue today in dealing with world history, as in the tendency to dismiss any people who did not exploit the latest available military technology as somehow inferior.

Controlling ethnocentrism does not mean abandoning all standards, as if any social behavior were as good as any other. It does involve a certain open-mindedness and sophistication. Reducing distracting levels of ethnocentrism can be aided by some specific procedures. It is important to realize that few cultures behave irrationally over long periods of time. They may differ from our taste, but their patterns respond to valid causes and problems. Our own values are not without complexity. We sometimes believe things about our own society that are not as true as we want, or, in judging other societies, we forget about drawbacks in our own surroundings. Perspective on our own habits, including awareness of how other cultures might judge us, helps us restrain our ethnocentrism.

However, ethnocentrism may become a particularly strong impulse in dealing with some of the changes in world history taking shape about 1400. The West was gaining strength. Because many Americans identify with Western civilization, it is tempting to downplay some of the subtleties and disadvantages of this process or to exaggerate the extent to which the West began to organize world history more generally.

The balance of power among civilizations was beginning to shift about 1400, and it is legitimate—not simply ethnocentric—to note that the West's rise was one of the leading forces of this change. It is unnecessary to ignore the many other patterns continuing or emerging—including new vigor in several other societies—or to gloss over the motives and results that the West's rise entailed. The rise of the West was not just "good." It did not result simply from a triumph of progressive values. At the same time, avoiding ethnocentric impulses in evaluating this crucial transition period in world history does not require an anti-Western approach. Balance and perspective are essential—easy to say, not always easy to achieve.

Questions: Why can ethnocentrism complicate interpretations of world history? How can one balance disapproval and understanding in dealing with practices such as female infanticide? What are some nonethnocentric ways to interpret initial European expansion?

was organized into regional kingdoms, which were highly warlike. Society was structured into a caste system with priests and nobles at the top, who reserved many lands for their exclusive use. Commoners were viewed almost as a separate people, barred from certain activities.

Thus, with a Neolithic technology and no use of metals, the Hawaiians created a complex culture on their islands. Without a written language, their legends and oral histories, tracing the genealogies of chiefly families back to the original war canoes, provided a shared set of stories and values.

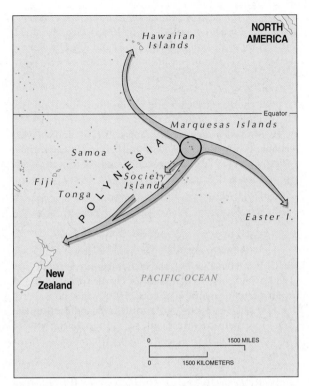

Map 20.1 *Polynesian Expansion. Starting in the 7th century, the Polynesians expanded north and south of their starting point in the Society Islands.*

Isolated Achievements by the Maori

Another group of Polynesians migrated thousands of miles to the southwest of the Society Islands, perhaps as early as the 8th century, when canoe or raft crews discovered the two large islands that today make up New Zealand. The original numbers of people were small but were supplemented over the centuries that followed by additional migrations from the Polynesian home islands. The Polynesians in New Zealand, called the Maori, successfully adapted to an environment considerably colder and harsher than that of the home islands. They developed the most elaborate of all Polynesian art and produced an expanding population that may have reached 200,000 people by the 18th century, primarily on the northern of the two islands. As in Hawaii, tribal military leaders and priests held great power in Maori society; each tribe also included a group of slaves drawn from prisoners of war and their descendants.

All these achievements were accomplished in total isolation from the rest of the world and, par-

ticularly after 1400, substantial isolation of each major island grouping from the rest of the Polynesian complex. Polynesians would be the last of the major isolated cultures to encounter the larger world currents brought forcefully by European explorers in the 18th century. When this encounter did come, it produced the same effects that it had in the Americas: vulnerability to disease, weakness in the face of superior weaponry and technology, and cultural disintegration.

Adding Up the Changes

It is tempting to see some sort of master plan in the various changes that began to occur around 1400. People who emphasize an ethnocentric approach to world history, stressing some inherent superiorities in Western values, might be tempted to simplify the factors involved. However, a series of complex coincidences provides a more accurate explanation, as in other cases in which the framework of world history changed substantially.

Independent developments in the Americas and elsewhere figured in, as did crucial policy decisions in places such as China. Each of the separate steps can be explained, but their combination was partly accidental.

Several elements of the world history transition deserve particular attention. Technology played a role, as opportunities to copy Asian developments were supplemented by European initiative, particularly in gunnery and ship design. The role of individuals, such as Prince Henry, must be compared with the impact of more general forces such as Europe's international trade woes.

The overall result of change affected even societies where existing patterns persisted. Sub-Saharan Africa, for example, was not experiencing great political or cultural shifts around 1400. Regional kingdoms fell and rose: The empire of Mali fell to regional rivals, but another Muslim kingdom, Songhay, soon arose in its stead, flourishing between 1464 and 1591. African political and religious themes persisted for several centuries, but the context for African history was shifting. The decline of the Arabs reduced the vitality of Africa's key traditional contact with the international network. In contrast to the Europeans, Africans had no exchange with the Mongols. Even as Africa enjoyed substantial continuity, its power relationship with western Europe was beginning to change, and this became a source of further change.

GLOBAL CONNECTIONS: 1450 and the World

The end of the postclassical period saw both change and continuity in the contacts that affected so many societies in Asia, Africa, and Europe. Change came in the procession of societies that served as active agents for contacts. Muslim traders and missionaries from the Middle East continued to be active, particularly in the Indian Ocean and in dealing with Africa. But the period of Mongol consolidation had introduced a new set of contacts, many of them land-based and involving Asia and Europe. Mongol overlords turned out to be delighted to encounter different ideas and to use officials from many different places and cultures. Mongol decline returned attention to sea-based contacts, particularly in the Indian Ocean. For a time, China took an unusually active role. The question of leadership in global contacts was a vital one, and by 1450 it was in flux.

The key continuity involved the interest and dependence of many societies on interregional trade and other contacts. African merchants and leaders continued to rely heavily on interactions with the Middle East. Western Europe's involvement in contacts was intensifying. Southeast Asia was increasingly drawn in, not only to trade but also to Muslim missionary efforts. The Middle East, India, and China continued to assume the availability of goods and merchant activities beyond their own borders. The diverse advantages of Afro-Eurasian contacts were widely realized, even amid changes in trade routes and regional initiatives.

Further Readings

On the world network, see Jerry Bentley, *Old World Encounters: Cross Cultural Contacts and Exchanges in Pre-Modern Times* (1993). Crucial changes in the Middle East are covered in F. Babinger's *Mehmed the Conqueror and His Times* (1978) on the Ottoman leader who captured Constantinople, and Bernard Lewis' *The Arabs in History* (4th ed., 1958), which offers a brisk interpretation of Arab decline. See also H. Islamoglu-Inan, ed., *The Ottoman Empire and the World Economy* (1987). On China under the early Ming dynasty, see Charles O. Hucker's *The Ming Dynasty: Its Origins and Evolving Institutions* (1978).

An important, highly readable interpretation of the West's rise in a world context is C. Cipolla's *Guns, Sails and Empires: Technological Innovation and the Early Phases of European Expansion, 1400–1700* (1985). See also J. H. Parry's *Age of Reconnaissance* (1963) and *The Discovery of the Sea* (1981). An important interpretation of new Western interests is S. W. Mintz's *Sweetness and Power: The Place of Sugar in Modern History* (1985).

On the Black Death and economic dislocation, see M. W. Dols' *The Black Death in the Middle East* (1977); W. H. McNeill's *Plagues and Peoples* (1976); and the very readable B. Tuchman's *A Distant Mirror: The Calamitous 14th Century* (1979). A provocative study of relevant Western outlook is P. Ariès's *The Hour of Our Death* (1981).

J. Huizinga's *The Waning of the Middle Ages* (1973) deals with the decline of medieval forms in Europe. The early Renaissance is treated in D. Hay's *The Italian Renaissance* (1977); see also C. Hibbert, *Florence: The Biography of a City* (1993). For more cultural emphasis, see C. Trinkhaus' *The Scope of Renaissance Humanism* (1983). On Spain, see F. Braudel's *The Mediterranean and the Mediterranean World* (2 vols., 1978), and see E. Paris' *The End of Days* (1995) on Spanish Jews and the Inquisition. On expansion in general, see Robert Bartlett's *The Making of Europe: Conquest, Colonization and Cultural Change* (1993).

An excellent overview of the period is Janet L. Abu-Lughod's *Before European Hegemony: The World System A.D. 1250–1350* (1989).

On the Web

This transitional age in human history saw the rise of two great state systems, China's Ming Dynasty (http://www.wsu.edu:8080/~dee/MING/MING1.HTM) and the Ottoman Empire (http://www.friesian.com/turkia.htm and http://www.naqshbandi.org/ottomans/). It witnessed the rise of new navigational technologies that led up to European explorations, (http://www.ucalgary.ca/applied_history/tutor/eurvoya/ship.html and http://www.chenowith.k12.or.us/tech/subject/social/explore.html). It also witnessed the voyages of two of the world's greatest explorers, Cheng Ho (http://chinapage.com/zhenghe.html) and Christopher Columbus (http://www1.minn.net/~keithp/), and the publication of the fabled travel literature of Marco Polo (http://www.korcula.net/mpolo/index.html). It marked the climax of Muslim philosophy and science (http://www.muslimphilosophy.com/) as evidenced by the work of Ibn Rushd (http://users.erols.com/zenithco/rushd.html, http://www.aljadid.com/classics/0320raslan.html and http://www.fordham.edu/halsall/source/1190averroes.html). That Ibn Rushd's work and those of other Muslim scientists helped stimulate the Renaissance in Europe is an issue addressed at http://www.isesco.org.ma/pub/Eng/Arabiculture/page

4.htm, http://www.xmission.com/~dderhak/index/ moors.htm, and http://cyberistan.org/islamic/.

The art and daily life of the period (http://history. evansville.net/renaissa.html) is reflected in the life and work of painters such as Giotto (http://www.kfki.hu/ ~arthp/tours/giotto/, http://www.ibiblio.org/wm/ paint/auth/giotto/, and http://www.artchive.com/ artchive/G/giotto.html), da Vinci, Raphael and Michelangelo (http://www.artcyclopedia.com/ artists/leonardo_da_vinci.html, http://www.kausal. com/leonardo/, http://www.kfki.hu/~arthp/bio/r/ raphael/biograph.html, and http://www.michelangelo. com/buonarroti.html), and in the work of writers such as

Francesco Petrarch (http://latter-rain.com/eccle/ petrarch.htm). However, it also witnessed the Hundred Years War (http://www.ku.edu/kansas/medieval/108/ lectures/hundred_years_war.html), the Inquisition (http://es.rice.edu/ES/humsoc/Galileo/Things/ inquisition.html), and the persistence of the Black Death (http://history.boisestate.edu/westciv/plague/ and http://www.iath.virginia.edu/osheim/intro.html). War and disease, however, could not dim the civic pride, commercial zeal, and artistic achievements of the residents of Renaissance Florence, whose city can be virtually visited at the height of its glory at http://es.rice.edu/ES/ humsoc/Galileo/Student_Work/Florence96/FlorTour. html, http://mega.it/eng/egui/epo/refio.htm and http://www.english.firenze.net/groups/6/29/87/.

PART IV

The World Shrinks, 1450–1750

Introduction

Many developments highlighted world history between 1450 and 1750, which marked a major new period—the early modern—in the global experience. As in most new world history periods, the balance of power among major civilizations shifted; western Europe became the most dynamic force worldwide. Contacts among many civilizations intensified. The world became smaller as international trade affected diverse societies and the speed and range of sailing ships increased. This growth of commerce affected western Europe and areas under its economic influence, such as Africa and the Americas, but commerce grew in China and Japan as well. Partly on the basis of innovations in weaponry, particularly gunpowder, new or revamped empires formed important regional political units in many parts of the world. These developments were especially significant in Asia. In addition to European colonial empires in various parts of the world, land-based empires formed in Russia, Persia, the Middle East and the Mediterranean, and India.

The early modern period was launched during the 15th century when European countries, headed by Portugal and Spain, began new explorations and soon new colonization efforts in Africa, Asia, and the Americas. It was launched also by the formation of the powerful Ottoman Empire in the Middle East, the Mughal and Ming empires in Asia, and the emergence of Russia from two centuries of Mongol control.

On the Eve of the Early Modern Period: The World Around 1450

 A number of societies had expanded during the postclassical period. Russia was one, as a Russian monarchy formed. Western Europe failed to gain political unity but slowly recovered from the 5th-century collapse of the Roman Empire. Western Europeans built important regional kingdoms while expanding the role of urban commerce and establishing an elaborate culture around Catholic Christianity. In sub-Saharan Africa, another set of regional kingdoms formed, although vital areas there were organized more loosely. African trade and artistic expression gained ground steadily. Finally, areas in contact with China built increasingly elaborate societies. Japan, like western Europe, emphasized a decentralized feudal system in politics. But it copied many aspects of Chinese culture and some social forms, including a more patriarchal approach to the status of women.

Other areas of the world featured civilizations or elaborate cultures developing in isolation from any global contacts. This was true of the expanding Polynesian zone in the Pacific Islands and of the populous civilizations of the Americas, focused in Mesoamerica, under the Aztecs, and in the Andes, which by the 15th century were under the vast Inca realm.

The structure of the postclassical world began to shift between the 13th and 15th centuries, setting the stage for a new period in world history. The great Aztec and Inca empires were showing signs of strain and overextension by the later 15th century. In Asia, Africa, and Europe, the key development was the decline of Arab political power and cultural dynamism. Islam continued to expand, but its political and commercial units fragmented. At the same time, there was a new round of invasions from central Asia, launched by the Mongols. In the 13th century, they attacked China, the Middle East, and eastern Europe, toppling established kingdoms and allowing new contacts between Asia and Europe.

By 1400 the Mongol surge was receding, though only slowly in Russia. A new empire emerged in China. The Arab caliphate had perished. But a new Islamic political force, under the Ottoman Turks, was taking shape. The Ottomans unified much of the Middle East and positioned themselves to destroy the venerable Byzantine Empire. Using their growing commercial vigor but also terrified by the emergence of a new Islamic power, western Europeans looked for ways to gain greater control over international trade. The Chinese briefly experimented with a series of mighty trading expeditions across the Indian Ocean. But a shift in emperors led to a retreat, with a decision to concentrate on traditions of internal political, cultural, and commercial development. As it turned out, this left the way open for the western European overseas expeditions. Western explorers and merchants benefited from technologies newly learned from China and the Islamic world, such as the compass and triangular sail, while adding important innovations such as guns and faster oceangoing ships.

The Rise of the West

 Between 1450 and 1750, western Europe, headed initially by Spain and Portugal and then by Holland, Britain, and France, gained control of the key international trade routes. It established colonies in the Americas and, on a much more limited basis, in Africa and parts of Asia.

At the same time, partly because of its new international position, the West itself changed rapidly, becoming an unusual kind of agricultural civilization. Commerce began to change the social structure and also affected basic attitudes toward family life and the

1300 C.E.	1400 C.E.	1500 C.E.	1550 C.E.
1281 Founding of Ottoman dynasty	**1405–1433** Chinese expedition period	**1500–1600** Europe's commercial revolution	**1552** Russia begins expansion in central Asia and western Siberia
1350s Ottoman invasion of south-eastern Europe	**1434–1498** Portuguese expeditions down west African coast	**1501–1510** Safavid conquest of Iran	**1570** Portuguese colony of Angola (Africa)
1368 Ming dynasty in China	**1441** Beginning of European slave trade in Africa	**1509** Spanish colonies on American mainland	**1571** Ottoman naval defeat at Lepanto
1390 Ming restrictions on overseas trade	**1453** Ottoman conquest of Constantinople	**1510–1511** Portugal conquers Goa (India), Malacca (Malaysia)	**1590** Hideyoshi unifies Japan
	1480 Moscow region free of Mongol control	**1517–1541** Protestant Reformation (Europe)	**1591** Fall of Songhay (Africa)
	1492 Columbus expeditions	**1519–1521** Magellan circumnavigates globe	
	1498–1499 Vasco da Gama expedition opens seas to Asia	**1519–1524** Cortés conquers Mexico	
		1520–1566 Suleiman the Magnificent (Ottoman)	
		1526 Babur conquest in northern India (Mughal)	
		1533 Pizarro wins Peru	
		1548 Portuguese government in Brazil	

natural environment. A host of new ideas, some of them springing from religious reformers, created a novel cultural climate in which scientific principles were increasingly valued. The Scientific Revolution gradually reshaped Western culture as a whole. More effective political structures emerged by the 17th century, as Western monarchs began to introduce bureaucratic principles similar to those pioneered long before in China.

A vital facet of the early modern period, then, was the West's expansion as an international force and its internal transformation. Like the previous global civilization, Arab Islam, the West developed a diverse and dynamic culture and society, which was both a result and a cause of its rising international prominence.

The World Economy and Global Contacts

 Fed by new naval technologies, the world network intensified and took on new dimensions. The change involved more than the fact that the Europeans, not the Muslims, dominated international trade. It featured an expansion of the world network to global proportions, well beyond previous international linkages. The Americas were brought into contact with other cultures and included in global exchanges for the first time. At the end of the period, in the 18th century, Polynesian and Australian societies began to undergo the same painful integrating experience.

By 1750 there were no fully isolated societies of any great size. The new globalism of human contacts had a host of consequences that ran through early modern centuries. The human disease pool became fully international for the first time, and peoples who had previously been isolated from the rest of the world suffered greatly from exposure to diseases for which they had developed no immunities. The global network also permitted a massive exchange of plants and animals. Cows and horses were introduced to the Americas,

1600 C.E.	1650 C.E.	1700 C.E.	1750 C.E.
1600 Dutch and British merchants begin activity in India	**1652** Dutch colony South Africa	**1713** New Bourbon dynasty, Spain	**1756–1763** Seven Years' War
1600–1690 Scientific Revolution (Europe)	**1658–1707** Aurangzeb reign, beginning of Mughal decline	**1722** Fall of Safavid dynasty (Iran)	**1763** Britain acquires "New France"
1603 Tokugawa shogunate	**1682–1699** Turks driven from Hungary	**1759–1788** Reforms of Latin American colonial administration	**1764** British East India Company controls Bengal (India)
1607 First British colonies in North America	**1689–1725** Peter the Great (Russia)		**1770s** European–Bantu conflicts in southern Africa
1608 First French North American colonies			**1772–1795** Partition of Poland
1637 Russian pioneers to Pacific			**1775–1783** American Revolution
1640s Japan moves into isolation			**1781** Indian revolts in New Grenada and Peru (Latin America)
1641 Dutch colonies in Indonesia			**1792** Slave uprising in Haiti
1642–1727 Isaac Newton			
1644 Qing dynasty, China			

prompting significant changes in Native American societies and economies. American food crops were spread around the world, bringing sweet potatoes, corn, and manioc to China, corn to Africa, and potatoes and tobacco to Europe. One result through most of the world, beginning in Asia as well as western Europe, was rapid population expansion.

As part of this new globalization, highly unequal relationships were established among many civilizations. During the postclassical millennium, 450–1450 C.E., a few areas had contributed inexpensive raw materials (including labor power in the form of slaves) to more advanced societies, notably China and the Islamic world. These supply areas included western Europe and parts of Africa and southeast Asia. Although economic relationships in these instances were unequal, they did not affect the societies that produced raw materials too severely because international trade was not sufficient to do so. After 1450 or 1500, as Western commerce expanded internationally, the West began to set up unequal relationships with a number of areas. Areas such as Latin America depended heavily on exports of cheap raw materials, on imports of processed goods, and on Western ships and merchants to handle international trade. Dependence of this sort skewed labor relations by encouraging commercial exploitation of slaves and serfs. It is vital to stress that much of the world, particularly in the great Asian civilizations, was not developed by this set of relationships, as they benefited from global trade on their own terms. But the global network spread: Western overseas expansion began to engulf India and parts of Indonesia by the 18th century.

World Boundaries

 The period of 1450–1750 saw an unusual number of boundary changes in world history. The spread of Western colonies was the most obvious development, but the establishment or extension of a number of large land-based empires was almost as significant.

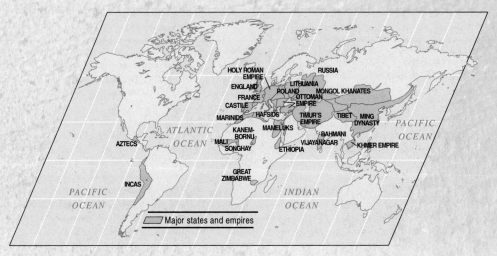

World Boundaries, c. 1453

World Boundaries, c. 1700. Compare with the 1453 map. What were the main changes? What areas were most stable? Why did Western colonies spread in some parts of the world and not in others?

Compare the two maps by tracing the areas of Western penetration. You will see the different forms this penetration took in different parts of the world. Note also what parts of the world offered particular opportunities for rivalries among the leading Western colonial powers and what parts were immune to Western expansion.

The Gunpowder Empires

The rise of western Europe and its growing dominance of world trade was not the only major theme of early modern world history. The centuries after 1450 could also be called the age of the gunpowder empires. The development of cannons and muskets in

486

The power of gunpowder. The gun was introduced into Japan in 1542 by the Portuguese. By 1562, 10,000 Japanese soldiers carried muskets. The scenes depicted here are from a military manual written by one of the greatest generals of the period, Nobunaga.

the 15th and 16th centuries, through the combination of Western technology and previous Chinese invention, spurred the West's expansion. Ship-based artillery was fundamental to the West's mastery of international sea lanes and many ports and islands. But gunnery was picked up by other societies as well. The Ottoman Turks used huge cannons in their successful siege of Constantinople in 1453. The subsequent Ottoman Empire relied heavily on field guns to supplement trained cavalry. The rise of a new Russian Empire after 1480 was also built on the growing use of guns, and the Russian economy was later reshaped to ensure the manufacture of the new military hardware. Three other key empires—the Mughal in India, the Safavid in Persia, and the 17th-century Qing dynasty in China—relied on the new strength of land armies armed with guns. Guns also played a role in Japanese and African history during the period.

Guns supported the forging of new land empires throughout much of Asia and eastern Europe and, to some extent, in Africa. These developments were largely independent of Western influence, and they counterbalanced the growth of Western power. The rise of the Russian Empire ran through the whole period, and though not as important as the expansion of the West, it was certainly a vital theme. The rise of the Ottomans, Safavids, and Mughals was a bit shorter-lived but echoed through the first two centuries of the period and, in the case of the Ottomans, created one of the most durable empires in world history.

Themes

Many of the key themes of world history changed during the early modern centuries. Most strikingly, the impact of nomadic societies—once vital to world history dynamics—declined dramatically after the Mongol incursions. The new gunpowder empires, particularly Russia and China, conquered many of the old nomad strongholds. In many areas nomadic intermediaries were replaced by more direct relations among states or merchant groups. For example, European governments began regular diplomatic contacts, recognizing the importance of consistent interchange. China had received foreign representatives for centuries. In Europe, the practice started among Italian city-states in the Renaissance and then spread more widely. Representation to governments in Africa and Asia was a bit more haphazard, but formal emissaries were sent out to negotiate on trade and other matters.

Developments in the changing world economy had major effects on patterns of inequality. Gender relations did not change greatly in most areas, but labor systems were transformed throughout much of the world. The massive expansion of slavery and harsh serfdom in key parts of the world created new social hierarchies. The same developments also reduced human agency for millions of people who were captured or otherwise forced into slavery or serfdom. Growing wealth and new cultural currents, including the rise of science, created new opportunities for a small number of Europeans, and individual genius in art, trade, science, or military organization ultimately had global effects. Conquests created opportunities for human agency elsewhere as well, as with the imaginative leaders who first established the Mughal Empire in India.

Finally, the early modern centuries saw drastic environmental change, though more because of the exchanges of foods, animals, and diseases with the Americas than because of new technology. Imported horses, sheep, and cattle, reproducing rapidly, had great effects on American grasslands and densely settled Native American farmlands. Imported diseases such as measles and smallpox had even more devastating results. Soil conditions were changed in some places by the introduction of new crops such as sugar, which often replaced native vegetation. From North America to China, settlers in search of land to farm began clearing temperate forests. In a number of regions, the clearing of the world's great rain forests began.

Civilizations and Larger Trends

As in earlier times, many developments during these early modern centuries occurred within individual civilizations, with little or no relationship to more general world trends. Only the Americas came close to being overwhelmed by outside influences. Nevertheless, the impact of the three international trends—Western expansion, intensification and globalization of the world commercial network, and the military and political results of gunpowder—affected patterns in the separate societies in many ways. Each civilization had to respond to these trends. Reactions were diverse, ranging from the eager embrace of new international currents to forced compliance or deliberate isolation.

International pressures increased with time. By 1700 western Europe's activities were looming larger, not just in key areas such as the Americas, the Asian island groups, and the coast of west Africa, but in mainland Asia and eastern Europe as well. A new Russian urge to selectively copy aspects of the West, and the establishment of growing British control in parts of India, were two facets of this shift. Even Japan, which initially responded to the new world economy by effective isolation, began to show a new but modest openness, exemplified by the end of a long-standing ban on translating Western books.

The first two chapters in this section focus on the emergence of Western colonies and Western-dominated world trade and on changes within the West. Then, two chapters deal with two societies that had particular links with the West: Russia, whose expansion was an important theme in its own right, and a new kind of emerging civilization in Latin America. The last three chapters deal with major societies in Asia and Africa, where contacts with the West and the new world economy were significant, particularly as the early modern period wore on, but where separate patterns of activity remained vital.

CHAPTER 21

THE WORLD ECONOMY

In this 16th-century Japanese painting, the artist depicted the Europeans and their African slaves as exotic and unfamiliar.

This chapter deals with the consequences of some key developments long celebrated in American school texts: the voyages of Columbus and the explorers and the empires built by European conquerors and missionaries. The result was a power shift in world affairs, but another set of crucial developments in world history also resulted: the redefinition of interchanges among major societies in the world.

Previous periods had seen important steps toward greater diffusion of goods and ideas. During the classical era, most attention was given to developing larger regional economies and cultural zones, such as the Chinese Middle Kingdom and the Mediterranean basin. Wider international contacts existed, but they were not of fundamental importance to the societies involved. The level and significance of contacts increased in the postclassical era. Missionary religions spilled across civilization boundaries, as with Buddhism in eastern and southeast Asia and above all with Islam. For the Middle East, parts of Africa and Europe, and much of India, interregional trade became an important feature of the basic economic structure, with some regions dominating trade in particular goods.

Despite these important precedents, the global relationships that developed after 1450, mainly but not exclusively sponsored by western Europe, spelled a new period in world history. New areas of the world were for the first time brought into the global complex, particularly the Americas. The rate of global trade also increased in some portions of the Old World, such as the islands of southeast Asia. Furthermore, global trade became so significant that it forged different relationships between key societies, based on the kind of goods and amount of control contributed to the surging **world economy**. The emergence of this new kind of global economy was the most important development in world history during the early modern centuries.

Various nations in western Europe were the key agents in the world economy. As profits flowed in, other changes within western Europe accelerated. Close connections developed between Western changes, discussed in the next chapter, and the world economy. Several parts of the world became increasingly dependent on Western economic control.

But the world economy remained complex, and many Asian societies continued their own strong economic performance. Europe was now able to use New World goods, particularly silver, to help pay for the luxury products still sought in China and India. China, particularly, accumulated more American silver than any other society as a result. Europeans were still trying to improve their role in trading with the big Asian powers at the end of the 18th century.

1400 C.E.	1500 C.E.	1600 C.E.	1700 C.E.
1394–1460 Prince Henry the Navigator	**1509** First Spanish colonies on Latin American mainland	**1607** First British colony in Virginia	**1744** French–British wars in India
1433 China ends great expeditions	**1514** Expedition to Indonesia	**1608** First French colonies in Canada; first trading concession in India to England	**1756–1763** Seven Years' War in Europe, India, and North America
1434 Portugal extends expeditions down west African coast	**1519–1521** Magellan circumnavigates globe	**1641** Dutch begin conquests on Java, in Indonesia	**1763** British acquire New France
1488 Portuguese round Cape of Good Hope	**1534** First French explorations in Canada	**1652** Dutch launch colony in southern Africa	**1775–1783** American Revolution
1492 Columbus' first expedition	**1542** Portuguese reach Japan		**1756** "Black hole" of Calcutta
1497–1498 Vasco da Gama to India	**1562** Britain begins its slave trade		**1764** East India Company control of Bengal
	1571 Ottoman fleet defeated in Battle of Lepanto		
	1588 British defeat Spanish Armada		
	1597 Japan begins isolation policy		

This chapter begins with a discussion of the West's emergence as the world's leading commercial and colonial power. We then turn to the larger world system that the West helped create, which turned out to have a life of its own. New exchanges of goods, ideas, and diseases followed the emergence of the new system. Finally, we sort out the different kinds of reactions that the world economy generated, from substantial isolation to outright subjugation.

Foods

About 30 percent of the foods consumed in the world today come from plants of American origin. These plants—corn and the potato are the most important among them—began to be spread after 1500. China and Africa, encountering American foods through contacts with European traders, adopted them eagerly. Corn became a staple in the African diet. Europeans, ironically, were more conservative. Rumors spread that American foods spread the plague. The foods were not mentioned in the Bible. Only later did the potato begin to gain ground, with fried potatoes (French fries) sold on Paris streets in the 1680s.

The West's First Outreach: Maritime Power

 Between 1450 and 1650, various western European nations gained unprecedented mastery of the world's oceans. Trading patterns and colonial expansion focused on Europe's maritime power. Pioneering efforts by Spain and Portugal were followed by the surge of Britain, Holland, and France.

Various European leaders, particularly merchants but also some princes and clergy, had become increasingly aware of the larger world around them since 1100. The Crusades brought knowledge of the Islamic world's superior economy and the goods that could be imported from Asia. The Mongol Empire, which sped up exchanges between the civilizations of Asia, also spurred European interest. The fall of the khans in China disrupted this interchange, as China became once again a land of mystery to Europeans. Europe's upper classes had by this time become accustomed to imported products from southeast Asia and India, particularly spices. These goods were transported to the Middle East in Arab ships, then brought overland, where they were loaded again onto vessels (mainly from Genoa and Venice, in Italy) for the Mediterranean trade.

Europeans entered into this era of growing contacts with several disadvantages. They remained ignorant of the wider world. Viking adventurers from Scandinavia had crossed the Atlantic in the 10th century, reaching Greenland and then North America, which they named Vinland. However, they quickly lost interest beyond establishing settlements on Greenland and Iceland, in part because they encountered indigenous warriors whose weaponry was good enough to cause them serious problems. And many Europeans continued to believe that the earth was flat, although scientists elsewhere knew otherwise; this belief made them fearful of distant voyages lest they fall off the world's edge.

As Europeans launched a more consistent effort at expansion from 1291 onward, they were pressed by new problems: fear of the strength of the emerging Ottoman Empire and the lack of gold to pay for Asian imports. Initial settlements in island groups in the south Atlantic fed their hopes for further gains. However, the first expeditions were limited by the small, oar-propelled ships used in the Mediterranean trade, which could not travel far into the oceans.

New Technology: A Key to Power

During the 15th century, a series of technological improvements began to change the equation. Europeans developed deep-draft, round-hulled sailing ships for the Atlantic, capable of carrying heavy armaments. They also began to use the compass for navigation (an instrument they copied from the Arabs, who had learned it from the Chinese). Mapmaking and other navigational devices improved as well. Finally, European knowledge of explosives, another Chinese invention, was adapted into gunnery. European metalwork, steadily advancing in sophistication, allowed Western metalsmiths to devise the first guns and cannons. Though not very accurate, these weapons were awesome by the standards of the time (and terrifying to many Europeans, who had reason to fear the new destructive power of their own armies and navies). The West began to forge a military advantage over all other civilizations of the world, at

first primarily on the seas—an advantage it would retain into the 20th century. With an unprecedented ability to kill and intimidate from a distance, western Europe was ready for its big push.

Portugal and Spain Lead the Pack

The specific initiative came from the small kingdom of Portugal, whose Atlantic location made it well-suited for new initiatives. Portugal's rulers were drawn by the excitement of discovery, the harm they might cause to the Muslim world, and a thirst for wealth—a potent mix. A Portuguese prince, Henry the Navigator (Figure 21.1), organized a series of expeditions along the African coast and also outward to islands such as the Azores. Beginning in 1434 the Portuguese began to press down the African coast, each expedition going a little farther than its predecessor. They brought back slaves, spices such as pepper, and many stories of gold hoards they had not yet been able to find.

Later in the 15th century, Portuguese sailors ventured around the **Cape of Good Hope** in an attempt to find India, where direct contact would give Europeans easier access to luxury cloths and spices. They rounded the cape in 1488, but weary sailors forced the expedition back before it could reach India.

Figure 21.1 *Prince Henry the Navigator, of Portugal, sent annual expeditions down the western coast of Africa. He was not a sailor, but his sponsorship was essential.*

Then, after news of Columbus's discovery of America for Spain in 1492, Portugal redoubled its efforts, hoping to stave off the new Spanish competition. Vasco da Gama's fleet of four ships reached India in 1498, with the aid of a Hindu pilot picked up in east Africa. The Portuguese mistakenly believed that the Indians were Christians, for they thought the Hindu temples were churches. They faced the hostility of Muslim merchants, who had long dominated trade in this part of the world, and they brought only crude goods for sale, like iron pots. But fortunately they had a lot of gold as well. They managed to return with a small load of spices. A later trip involved more violence. Da Gama used ships' guns to intimidate, and his forces killed or tortured many Indian merchants to set an example.

Da Gama's success set in motion an annual series of Portuguese voyages to the Indian Ocean, outlined in Map 21.1. One expedition, blown off course, reached Brazil, where it proclaimed Portuguese sovereignty (Figure 21.2). Portugal began to set up forts

on the African coast and also in India—the forerunners of such Portuguese colonies as Mozambique, in east Africa, and Goa, in India. By 1514 the Portuguese had reached the islands of Indonesia, the center of spice production, and China. In 1542 one Portuguese expedition arrived in Japan, where a missionary effort was launched that met with some success for several decades.

Meanwhile, only a short time after the Portuguese quest began, the Spanish reached out with even greater force. Here also was a country only recently freed from Muslim rule, full of missionary zeal and a desire for riches. The Spanish had traveled into the Atlantic during the 14th century. Then in 1492, the same year that the final Muslim fortress was captured in Spain, the Italian navigator **Christopher Columbus,** operating in the name of the newly united Spanish monarchy, set sail for a westward route to India, convinced that the round earth would make his quest possible. As is well known he failed, reaching the Americas instead and mistakenly nam-

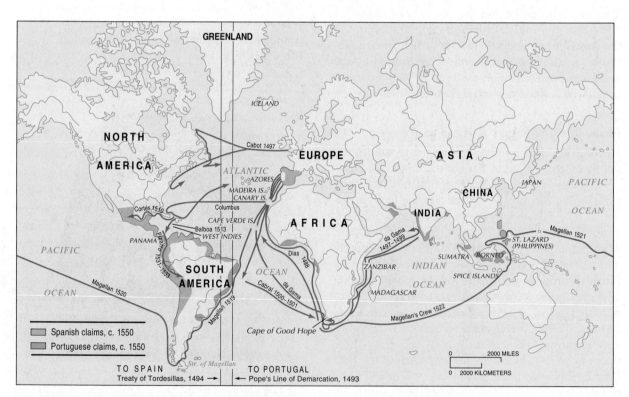

Map 21.1 *Spain and Portugal: Explorations and Colonies, c. 1600. In the early years of new exploration, Spanish and Portuguese voyages surveyed much of the coast of South America and some choice ports in Africa and Asia.*

Figure 21.2 *This is the earliest European sketch of Native Americans at the time of a Portuguese expedition to northern South America about 1500. "The people are thus naked, handsome, brown....They also eat each other...and hang the flesh of them in the smoke. They become a hundred and fifty years of age, and have no government."*

ing their inhabitants "Indians." Although Columbus believed to his death that he had sailed to India, later Spanish explorers realized that they had voyaged to a region where Europeans, Africans, and Asians had not traveled previously. One expedition, headed by Amerigo Vespucci, gave the New World its name. Spain, eager to claim this new land, won papal approval for Spanish dominion over most of what is now Latin America, although a later treaty awarded Brazil to Portugal.

Finally, a Spanish expedition under **Ferdinand Magellan** set sail westward in 1519, passing the southern tip of South America and sailing across the Pacific, reaching the Indonesian islands in 1521 after incredible hardships. It was on the basis of this voyage, the first trip around the world, that Spain claimed the Philippines, which it held until 1898.

Portugal emerged from this first round of exploration with coastal holdings in parts of Africa and in the Indian port of Goa, a lease on the Chinese port of Macao, short-lived interests in trade with Japan, and, finally, the claim on Brazil. Spain asserted its hold on the Philippines, various Pacific islands, and the bulk of the Americas. During the 16th century, the Spanish backed up these claims by military expeditions to Mexico and South America. The Spanish also held Florida and sent expeditions northward from Mexico into California and other parts of what later became the southwestern United States.

Northern European Expeditions

Later in the 16th century, the lead in exploration passed to northern Europe, as newly strong monarchies, such as France and England, got into the act and zealous Protestants in Britain and Holland strove to rival Catholic gains (Map 21.2). In part this shift in dynamism occurred because Spain and Portugal were busy digesting the gains they had already made; in part it was because northern Europeans, particularly the Dutch and the British, improved the design of oceanic vessels, producing lighter, faster ships than those of their Catholic adversaries. Britain won a historic sea battle with Spain in 1588, routing a massive Spanish Armada. From this point onward, the British, the Dutch, and to some extent the French vied for dominance on the seas, although in the Americas they aimed mainly northward because they could not challenge the Spanish and Portuguese colonies. Only in the sugar-rich West Indies did northern Europe seize islands initially claimed by Spain.

The new adventurers, like their Spanish and Portuguese predecessors, appreciated the economic potential of such voyages. Two 16th-century English explorers, trying to find an Arctic route to China, were told to keep an eye out for any native populations en route, for such people would provide a perfect market for warm English woolens. And if the territory was unpopulated, it might be put to use as

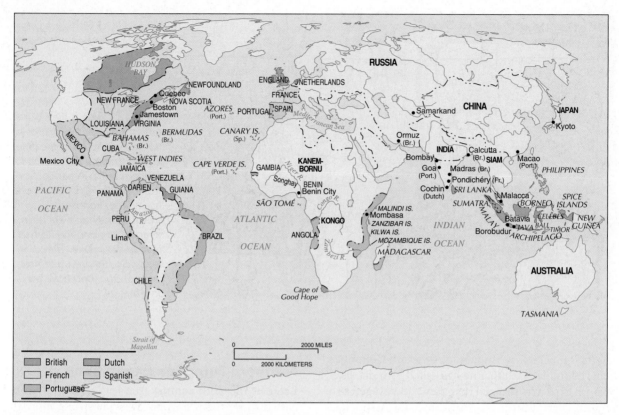

Map 21.2   *French, British, and Dutch Holdings, c. 1700. During the 17th century, northwestern Europe took the initiative in explorations, venturing into North America and seeking convenient trading stations elsewhere.*

a source of fish for Britain. A quest for profit had become a dominant policy motive.

French explorers crossed the Atlantic first in 1534, reaching Canada, which they claimed. In the 17th century, various expeditions pressed down from Canada into the Great Lakes region and the Mississippi valley.

The British also turned their attention to North America, starting with a brief expedition as early as 1497. The English hoped to discover a northwest passage to spice-rich India, but accomplished little beyond exploration of the Hudson Bay area of Canada during the 16th century. England's serious work began in the 17th century, with the colonization of the east coast of North America. Holland also had holdings in North America and, for a time, in Brazil.

The Dutch entered the picture after winning independence from Spain, and Holland quickly became a major competitor with Portugal in southeast Asia. The Dutch sent many sailors and ships to the region, oust-

ing the Portuguese from the Indonesian islands by the early 17th century. Voyagers from the Netherlands explored the coast of Australia, though without much immediate result. Finally, toward the mid-17th century, Holland established a settlement on the southern tip of Africa, mainly to provide a relay station for its ships bound for the East Indies.

The Netherlands, Britain, and France all chartered great trading companies, such as the **Dutch East India Company** and the British firm of similar name. These companies were given government monopolies of trade in the regions designated, but they were not rigorously supervised by their own states. They had rights to raise armies and coin money on their own. Thus, semiprivate companies, amassing great commercial fortunes, long acted almost like independent governments in the regions they claimed. For some time, a Dutch trading company effectively ruled the island of Taiwan off the coast of China; the **British East India Company** played a

In Depth

Causation and the West's Expansion

Because of their interest in social change, historians inevitably deal with causation. What prompted the fall of Rome? Why did Islam spread so widely? What factors explain why most agricultural civilizations developed patriarchal family structures?

Historical causation differs from the kinds of causation many scientists test. When experiments or observations can be repeated, scientists can gain a fairly precise understanding of the factors that produce a phenomenon: Remove an ingredient and the product changes. Historical causation is more complex. Major developments may resemble each other, but they never happen the same way twice. Definitive proof that factor X explains 40 percent of the spread of Buddhism in east Asia is impossible. This is why historians often disagree about causation. But if precision is impossible, high probability is not. We can get a fairly good sense of why things happen, and sloppy causation claims can be disproved. Furthermore, probing causation helps us explore the phenomenon itself. We know more about the nature of Western expansion in the 15th and 16th centuries if we discuss what caused it.

Some historians and other social scientists look to a single kind of cause as the explanation of a variety of circumstances. Some anthropologists are cultural determinists. They judge that a basic set of cultural factors, usually assumed to be very durable, causes the ongoing differences between societies: Chinese and Greeks, on average, respond differently to emotional stimuli because of their different cultural conditioning. More common is a technological or economic determinism. Some historians see technological change as setting other changes in motion. Others, including Marxists, argue that economic arrangements—how the economy is structured and what groups control it—produce at least the basic framework for innovations. At another pole, some historians used to claim "great men" as the prime movers in history. The causes of change thus became Chinggis Khan or Ashoka, with no need to look much farther.

Various approaches to causation have been applied to the West's explorations and colonial conquests in the early modern period. There is room for a "great man" analysis. Many descriptive accounts that dwell on explorers and conquerors (Vasco da Gama and Cortés, for example) and on leaders who sponsored them (such as Henry the Navigator) suggest that the key cause of the West's new role stemmed from the daring and vision of exceptional individuals.

Cultural causation can also be invoked. Somehow, Europe's expansion must relate to the wonders of innovation introduced by the Renaissance. The link with Christian culture is even easier to prove, for a missionary spirit quickly supplemented the efforts of early explorers, leading to more voyages and settlements in Asia and the Americas.

Political causation enters in, if not in causing the initial surge, at least in confirming it. Starting in the 16th century, rivalries between the nation-states motivated a continuing quest for new trade routes and colonies.

There is also room for a simpler, technologically determinist approach. In this view, Europe's gains came from a handful of new inventions. Benefiting from knowledge of advances in China and the Middle East, Europeans introduced naval cannons. Along with steady improvements in navigation and ship design, new techniques explain why Europe gained as it did. Except in the Americas, where they had larger technical and organizational advantages, Europeans advanced in areas they could reach by sea and dominate by ships' guns—port cities, islands, and trade routes—and not elsewhere. Put simply, Europe gained because of these few technological edges.

Like all determinisms, however, this technological approach raises as many questions as it answers. Why were Europeans so ready to adopt new inventions? (What caused the cause?) Why did other societies that were aware of Europe's innovations, such as China, deliberately scorn any adoption of Western naval techniques? Here a different culture determined a reaction different from that of the West. Technology and culture went hand in hand. Clearly, some combined causal framework is needed in this case.

We cannot expect uniform agreement on a precise ordering of causation. However, we can expect fruitful debate—the kind of debate that has already moved our understanding beyond surface causes, such as the powerful personalities of a few people, to a grasp of more underlying contexts.

Questions: If you had to choose a single determinism (cultural, technological, or economic) as basic to social change, which one would you pick? Why? In what ways might the professed motives of Western explorers and colonists have differed from their real motives? Would they necessarily have been aware of the discrepancy?

similar role in parts of India during much of the 18th century. The companies in North America traded actively in furs.

No matter where in Europe they came from, explorers and their crews faced many hardships at sea. The work was tiring and uncertain, with voyages lasting many months or years, and diseases such as scurvy were rampant. One expedition accepted only bachelors for its crew because married men would miss their families too much. A sailor on another trip complained that "he was tired of being always tired, that he would rather die once than many times, and that they might as well shut their eyes and let the ship go to the bottom."

Toward a World Economy

 Europe's maritime dominance and the opening of the Atlantic and Pacific oceans had three major consequences in world history. They created a new international pool for basic exchanges of foods, diseases, and a few manufactured products. They created a new world economy, involving the first embrace of the Americas in international trade but setting a different framework even for Europe and Asia. And they created the conditions for direct Western penetration of some parts of the world through colony formation.

The "Columbian Exchange" of Disease and Food

The impact of wider exchange became visible quickly. The extension of international contacts spread disease (see Chapter 24). The victims were millions of Native Americans who had not previously been exposed to Afro-Eurasian diseases such as smallpox and measles and who therefore had no natural immunities (Figure 21.3). During the 16th and 17th centuries, they died in huge numbers. Overall, in North and South America, more than half the native population would die; some estimates run as high as 80 percent. Whole island populations in the West Indies were wiped out. This was a major blow to earlier civilizations in the Americas as well as an opportunity for Europeans to forge a partially new population of their own citizens and slaves imported from Africa. The devastation occurred over a 150-year period, although in some

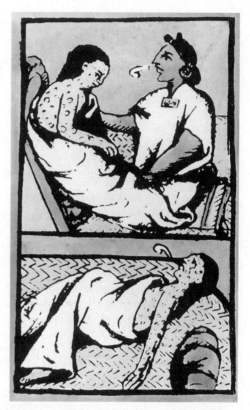

Figure 21.3 *A 16th-century print of Aztecs suffering from smallpox during the Cortés invasion (1518–1519).*

areas it was more rapid. When Europeans made contact with Polynesians and Pacific Coast peoples in the 18th century, the same dreadful pattern played out, again devastating vibrant cultures.

Other exchanges were less dire. New World crops were spread rapidly via Western merchants. American corn and sweet potatoes were taken up widely in China (where merchants learned of them from Spaniards in the Philippines), the Mediterranean, and parts of Africa. In some cases these productive new crops, along with local agricultural improvements, triggered large population increases. For example, China began to experience long-term population pressure in the 17th century, and new crops played a key role. When Europeans introduced the potato around 1700, major population upheaval occurred there as well.

Animal husbandry became more similar across the world as European and Asian animals, such as horses and cattle, were introduced to the New World. The spread of basic products and diseases formed an important backdrop to world history from the 16th century on, with varying effects on population structures in diverse regions.

The West's Commercial Outreach

Europeans did not displace all Asian shipping from the coastal waters of China and Japan, nor did they completely monopolize the Indian Ocean (see Chapter 27). Along the east African coast, while a few European bases were established, Muslim traders remained active, and commerce continued to move toward the Middle East. Generally, however, western Europe dominated a great deal of oceanic shipping, even muscling in on trade between other societies, as between India and southeast Asia. This greatly increased Europe's overall profits, and disproportionate control by the great merchant companies increased the European ability to determine the framework for international trade. In the eastern Mediterranean, for example, a Spanish-directed fleet defeated the navy of the Ottoman Empire in the battle of **Lepanto** in 1571. With this setback, any hope of successful Muslim rivalry against European naval power ended. The Turks rebuilt their fleet and continued their activity in the eastern Mediterranean, but they could not challenge the Europeans on the larger international routes.

Although western Europe did not conquer much inland territory in Africa or Asia, it did seek a limited network of secure harbors. Led by Spain and Portugal, then followed by the various northern powers, European ports spread along the west coast of Africa, several parts of the Indian subcontinent, and the islands of southeast Asia by the 17th century. Even in China, where unusually strong governments limited the Europeans' ability to seize harbors outright, the Portuguese won effective control over the island port of Macao. European-controlled ports served as areas for contact with overland traders (usually local merchants) and provided access to inland goods not directly within the reach of the West.

Where direct control was not feasible, European influence led to the formation of special Western enclaves in existing cities, where Western traders won special legal rights. This was the pattern in the Ottoman Empire, where Western merchants set up colonies within Constantinople, and in Russia, where Western factors (shipping agents) set up first in Moscow and then in St. Petersburg. Elements of this system even emerged in Japan after a firm isolationist policy was launched about 1600, as Dutch traders had some special access to the port of Nagasaki. The point was obvious: International trade gained growing importance in supplementing regional economies. Because western Europe now ran this trade, it won special rights of access.

Imbalances in World Trade

The most active competition in world trade emerged between European nations themselves. Spain briefly dominated, thanks to its imports of silver from the Americas. But it lacked a good banking system and could not support a full commercial surge. England, France, and Holland, where merchants had firmer status, soon pulled in the lion's share of profits from world trade.

Western Europe quickly expanded its manufacturing operations, so that it could export expensive finished goods, such as guns and cloth, in return for unprocessed goods, such as silver and sugar, traded by other societies. Here was another margin for profit.

The dominant **core nations** in the new world system supplemented their growing economic prowess by self-serving political policies. The doctrines of **mercantilism,** which urged that a nation-state not import goods from outside its own empire but sell exports as widely as possible in its own ships, both reflected and encouraged the new world system. Tariff policies discouraged manufacturing in colonial areas and stimulated home-based manufacturing.

Beyond western Europe lay areas that were increasingly enmeshed in the world economy but on a strictly dependant basis. These areas produced low-cost goods: precious metals and cash crops such as sugar, spice, tobacco, and later cotton. Human labor was a vital item of exchange. Parts of sub-Saharan Africa entered the new world economy mainly as suppliers of slaves. The earlier west African patterns of trade across the Sahara yielded to a dominant focus on the Atlantic and therefore to activities organized by Western shippers. In return for slaves and unprocessed goods, Europeans traded their manufactured items, including guns, while profiting from their control of commercial and shipping services.

Visualizing the Past

West Indian Slaveholding

The following table describes the rise of the plantation system, and attendant slaveholding, on the British West Indian island of Antigua, where sugar growing for export gained increasing hold. Trends of the sort indicated in this table raise further analytical issues about cause and effect. What might have caused the main changes in Antigua's estate system? How might the changes have related to the larger framework of the world economy? What do the trends suggest about the European demand for sugar and about production methods used to meet this demand?

What impact would the trends have had on slaves themselves? Laws in the British Caribbean soon began to enforce the estate system, exempting masters from murder charges when slaves died from beatings administered as punishment and fining groups such as the Quakers for daring to bring slaves to religious meetings. How do the statistical trends help explain the imposition of new laws of this sort?

Questions: What main trends in the social and economic structure of this part of Antigua during the

	1688	1706	1767
Taxables	53	36	65
Slaveholders	16	30	65
Planters with 20+ slaves	6	16	46
Planters with 100+ slaves	0	4	22
Slaves	332	1,150	5,610
Acreage	5,811	5,660	12,350

18th century do these figures suggest? What were the main changes in the relationship of slaveholding to property ownership? In the size of estates? In the comparative growth rates of owner and slave populations? Did the estate economy become more or less labor intensive, given the acreage involved? What do the trends suggest about the nature of the European-born or European-derived elite of Antigua?

A System of International Inequality

The new world economic relationships proved highly durable. Most of the areas established as dependant by the 17th century still carry some special burdens in world trade today. The core–dependant system should not be exaggerated, in part because most of the world, including most of Asia and much of Africa, was not yet fully embraced by it. In dependant areas such as Latin America and the slave-supplying parts of Africa, not all people were mired in poverty. African slave traders and princes who taxed the trade might grow rich. In Latin America the silver mines and commercial estates required regional merchants and farmers to supply food. Furthermore, many peasants in Latin America and even more in Africa were not yet involved in a market economy at all—whether regional or international—but rather produced for local subsistence with traditional motives and meth-

ods. However, significant minorities were involved in production for the world market. Also, most African and Latin American merchants and landlords did not fully control their own terms of trade. They might prosper, but their wealth did not stimulate much local manufacturing or general economic advance. Rather, they tended to import European-made goods, including (in the case of American planters) art objects and luxury items.

Coercive labor systems spread. Because dependent economies relied on cheap production of unprocessed goods, there was a tendency to build a system of forced labor that would cost little even when the overall labor supply was precarious. In the Americas, given the population loss from disease, this led to the massive importation of African slaves. Also, for many Native Americans and **mestizos** (people of mixed European and Native American blood), systems of estate management developed that demanded large amounts of labor. More limited examples of estate agriculture, in which peasants were forced into labor without the legal freedom to leave, arose for spice production in the Dutch East Indies and, by the 18th century, in British-dominated agricultural operations in India.

How Much World in the World Economy?

Huge areas of the world were not yet caught up in contact with the world economy. The societies that remained outside the world system did not gain ground as rapidly as the core areas of Europe because they did not have the profit opportunities in international trade. Their technologies changed less rapidly. But until the 18th century or beyond, they did not face great international problems.

China clearly benefited from the world economy, while participating less actively than Europe did. The Chinese government, having renounced large-scale international trade of its own early in the 15th century, deliberately avoided involvement with international trade on someone else's terms. It did copy some firearms manufacturing from the Europeans, but at a fairly low level. Beyond this it depended on extensive government regulation, backed up by a coastal navy, to keep European activities in check. Most of the limited trade that existed was channeled through Macao. European visitors wrote scornfully of China's disdain for military advances. A Jesuit wrote that "the military… is considered mean among them." The Chinese were also disparaged for adhering to tradition. One Western missionary in the 17th century described how, in his opinion, the Chinese could not be persuaded "to make use of new instruments and leave their old ones without an especial order from the Emperor to that effect. They are more fond of the most defective piece of antiquity than of the most perfect of the modern, differing much in that from us who are in love with nothing but what is new."

So China managed to avoid trying to keep up with European developments but also avoided subservience to European merchants. The world economy played only a subordinate role in Chinese history through the 18th century. Chinese manufacturing gains led to a strong export position, which is why Europeans sent a great deal of American silver to China to pay for the goods they wanted. But official isolation persisted. Indeed, at the end of the 18th century, a famous British mission, appealing to the government to open the country to greater trade, was rebuffed. The imperial court, after insisting on extreme deference from the British envoy, haughtily informed him that the Chinese had no need for outside goods. European eagerness for Chinese goods—attested to by the habit adopted in the 17th century of calling fine porcelain "china"—was simply not matched by Chinese enthusiasm, but a trickle of trade continued. Westerners compensated in part by developing their own porcelain industry by the 18th century, which contributed to the early Industrial Revolution, particularly in Britain. Still, there were hopes for commercial entry to China that remained unfulfilled.

Japan, though initially attracted by Western expeditions in the 16th century, also more fully pulled back. So did Korea. The Japanese showed some openness to Christian missions, and they were fascinated by Western advances in gunnery and shipping. Artists captured the interest in exotic foreigners. Guns had particular relevance to Japan's ongoing feudal wars, for there was no disdain here for military life. Yet Japanese leaders soon worried about undue Western influence and the impact this could have on internal divisions among warring lords, as well as the threat guns posed to samurai military dominance. They encouraged a local gunmaking industry that matched existing European muskets and small cannon fairly readily, but having achieved this they cut off most contact with any world trade. Most Japanese were forbidden to travel or trade abroad, the small Christian minority was suppressed, and from the 17th until the 19th centuries Japan entered a period of almost complete isolation except for some Chinese contact and trading concessions to the small Dutch enclave near Nagasaki.

Several other societies were not deeply affected by new world trade, participating at levels too low to have significant impact. The rulers of India's new Mughal Empire in the 16th century were interested in Western traders and even encouraged the establishment of small port colonies. India also sold goods in return for New World silver. Most attention, however, was riveted on internal development and land-based expansion and commerce; world trade was a sideline. The same held true for the Ottoman and Safavid empires in the Middle East through the 17th century, despite the presence of small European enclaves in key cities. Russia also lay outside the world economic orbit until the 18th century. A largely agricultural society, Russia conducted much of its trade with nomadic peoples in central Asia, which further insulated it from west European demands. Finally, much of Africa, outside the slave-trading orbit in western regions, was untouched by world trade patterns.

The Expansionist Trend

The world economy was not stationary; it tended to gain ground over time. South America, the West Indies, a part of North America, and some regions in west Africa were first staked out as dependencies beginning in the 16th century, and the list later expanded. Portions of southeast Asia that produced for world markets, under the dominance of the great Western trading companies, were brought into the orbit by the 17th century.

By the late 17th century, Western traders were advancing in India as the Mughal Empire began to fall apart. The British and French East India Companies staked out increasing roles in internal trade and administration. Early in the 18th century, Britain passed tariffs against the import of cotton cloth made in India as a means of protecting Britain's own cotton industry. The intent was to use India as a market for British-processed goods and a source of outright payments of gold, which the British were requiring by the late 18th century. Indian observers were aware of the shifting balance. An 18th century account noted,

> But such is the little regard which they [the British] show to the people of this kingdom, and such their apathy and indifference for their welfare, that the people under their dominion groan everywhere, and are reduced to poverty and distress.

India maintained a complex regional economy still, with much internal manufacturing and trade; it was not forced into such complete dependency as Latin America, for example. However, what had initially been a position outside the world economy was changing, to India's disadvantage. Manufacturing began to decline.

Eastern Europe also was brought into a growing relationship with the world economy and the west European core. The growth of cities in the West created a growing market for imported grains by the 18th century. Much of this demand was met by east European growers, particularly in Prussia and Poland but also in Russia. Export grains, in turn, were pro-

duced mainly on large estates by serfs, who were subjected to prolonged periods of labor service. This relationship was similar to that which prevailed in Latin America, with one exception: Outside of Poland, east European governments were much stronger than their Latin American counterparts.

Colonial Expansion

 Along with the larger world economic system, a new wave of colonialism took shape after the early Spanish and Portuguese explorations. Key European nations developed direct overseas empires. Two sets of American colonies developed, one in Latin America and the Caribbean, one in parts of North America. The Americas hosted the largest colonies, but colonialism also spread to Africa and Asia.

The Americas: Loosely Controlled Colonies

Opportunities to establish colonies were particularly inviting in the Americas, where European guns, horses, and iron weapons offered special advantages and where political disarray and the population losses provided openings in many cases (see Chapter 24). Spain moved first. The Spanish colonized several West Indian islands soon after Columbus's first voyage, starting with Hispaniola and then moving into Cuba, Jamaica, and Puerto Rico. Only in 1509 did they begin settlement on the mainland, in search of gold; the first colony was established in what is now Panama, under an able but unscrupulous adventurer, **Vasco de Balboa.** Several expeditions fanned out in Central America, and then a separate expedition from Cuba launched the Spanish conquest of the Aztecs in Mexico. Another expedition headed toward the Inca realm in the Andes in 1531, where hard fighting was needed before ultimate victory. From this base several colonial expeditions spread to Colombia, other parts of the Andes, and portions of Argentina.

Expansion resulted from the efforts of a motley crew of adventurers, many of them violent and treacherous, like **Francisco Pizarro** (1478?–1541), admittedly one of the more successful examples (Figure 21.4). Pizarro first came to the Americas in 1502 and settled on the island of Hispaniola. Later, he joined Balboa's colony in Panama, where he received a cattle ranch. Learning of wealth in Peru, he joined

Figure 21.4 *Francisco Pizarro*

with an illiterate soldier and a priest, mounting two expeditions that failed. In 1528 he returned to Spain to gain the king's support and also his agreement that he would be governor of the new province. With these pledges and a force of about 180 men, he attacked the divided Inca empire. Capturing Emperor Atahuallpa, he accepted a large ransom and then strangled him. Several revolts followed during Pizarro's rule from Lima, a coastal city he founded. But the Spanish king ennobled Pizarro for his success. At a dinner in 1541, Pizarro was assassinated by a group of Inca rebels.

Early colonies in the Americas typically were developed by small bands of gold-hungry Europeans, often loosely controlled by colonial administrations back home. Colonial rulers often established only loose controls over native populations at first, content to exact tribute without imposing detailed administration and sometimes leaving existing leaders in place. Gradually, more formal administration spread as agricultural settlements were established and official colonial systems took shape under control of bureaucrats sent from Spain and Portugal. Active missionary efforts, designed to Christianize the native peoples, added another layer of detailed administration throughout the Spanish holdings in North and South America.

France, Britain, and Holland, though latecomers to the Americas, also staked out colonial settlements. French explorations along the St. Lawrence River in Canada led to small colonies around Quebec, from 1608 onward, and explorations in the Mississippi river basin. Dutch and English settlers moved into portions of the Atlantic coastal regions early in the 17th century. Also in the 17th century, all three countries seized and colonized several West Indian islands, which they soon involved in the growing slave trade.

British and French North America: Backwater Colonies

Colonies of European settlers developed in North America, where patterns differed in many respects from those in Latin America and the Caribbean. English colonies along the Atlantic received religious refugees, such as the Calvinists who fled religious tensions in Britain to settle in New England. Government grants of land to major proprietors such as William Penn led to explicit efforts to recruit settlers. New York began as a Dutch settlement but was taken over easily by an English expedition in 1664.

In Canada, the first substantial European settlements were launched by the French government under Louis XIV. The initial plan involved setting up manorial estates under great lords whose rights were carefully restricted by the state. French peasants were urged to emigrate, although it proved difficult to develop an adequate labor force. However, birth rates were high, and by 1755 **New France** had about 55,000 settlers in a peasant society that proved extremely durable as it fanned out around the fortress of Quebec. Strong organization by the Catholic church completed this partial replica of French provincial society. Britain attacked the French strongholds (Figure 21.5) as part of a worldwide colonial struggle

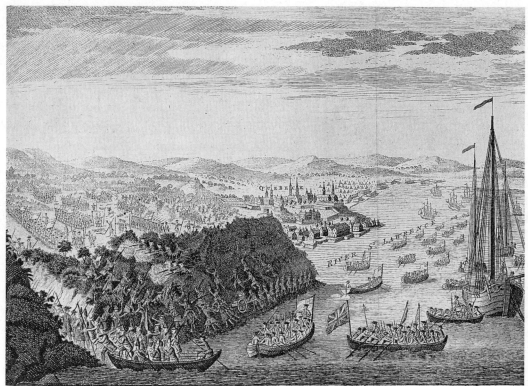

View of the Taking of Quebeck by the English Forces Commanded by Gen.ˡ Wolfe Sep: 13.ᵗʰ 1759

Figure 21.5   *British naval power allowed the light infantry to scale the French fort from the St. Lawrence River and capture Quebec in 1759. The attack nullified the cannon in the French fort in what turned out to be a crucial event in Canada's history.*

between the two powers, the **Seven Years' War.** France lost its colony under the terms of the **Treaty of Paris,** which in 1763 settled the war. France eagerly regained its West Indian sugar islands, along with trading posts in Africa, and Britain took control of Canada and the Mississippi basin. Relations between British officials and the French Canadian community remained strained as British settlements developed in eastern Canada and in Ontario. The flight of many American loyalists after the 1776 revolution added to the English-speaking contingent in Canada.

Colonial holdings along the Atlantic and in Canada were generally of modest interest to Western colonial powers in the 17th and even the 18th centuries. The Dutch were more attached to their Asian colonies. British and French leaders valued their West Indian holdings much more than their North American colonies. The value of North American products, such as timber and furs, was not nearly as great as

profits from the Caribbean or Latin America, so much less attention was given to economic regulation. As a result, some merchant and manufacturing activities emerged among new Americans themselves.

However, the American colonies that would become the United States had a population of a mere 3 million, far smaller than the powerful colonies in Latin America. Southern colonies that produced tobacco and sugar, and then cotton, became important. Patterns there were similar to those of Latin America, with large estates based on imported slave labor, a wealthy planter class bent on importing luxury products from western Europe, and weak formal governments. Still, in world historical terms the Atlantic colonies in North America were a backwater amid the larger colonial holdings staked out in the early modern centuries.

Yet European settlers did arrive. Driven by religious dissent, ambition, and other motives, Euro-

Document

Western Conquerors: Tactics and Motives

In the first passage quoted here, Columbus writes to the Spanish monarchy on his way home from his 1492 expedition. In the second passage, the brother of Francisco Pizarro, the Spanish conqueror of Peru, describes in 1533 how the Inca ruler, Atahuallpa, was defeated.

Columbus's 1492 Expedition

Sir, believing that you will take pleasure in hearing of the great success which our Lord has granted me in my voyage, I write you this letter, whereby you will learn how in thirty-three days' time I reached the Indies with the fleet which the most illustrious King and Queen, our Sovereigns, gave to me, where I found very many islands thickly peopled, of all which I took possession without resistance for their Highnesses by proclamation made and with the royal standard unfurled. To the first island that I found I gave the name of *San Salvador*, in remembrance of His High Majesty, who hath marvelously brought all these things to pass; the Indians call it *Guanaham*....

Espanola is a wonder. Its mountains and plains, and meadows, and fields, are so beautiful and rich for planting and sowing, and rearing cattle of all kinds, and for building towns and villages. The harbours on the coast, and the number and size and wholesomeness of the rivers, most of them bearing gold, surpass anything that would be believed by one who had not seen them. There is a great difference between the trees, fruits, and plants of this island and those of *Juana*. In this island there are many spices and extensive mines of gold and other metals. The inhabitants of this and of all the other islands I have found or gained intelligence of, both men and women, go as naked as they were born, with the exception that some of the women cover one part only with a single leaf of grass or with a piece of cotton, made for that purpose. They have neither iron, nor steel, nor arms, nor are they competent to use them, not that they are not well-formed and of handsome stature, but because they are timid to a surprising degree....

Although I have taken possession of all these islands in the name of their Highnesses, and they are all more abundant in wealth than I am able to express...yet there was one large town in *Espanola* of which especially I took possession, situated in a locality well adapted for the working of the gold mines, and for all kinds of commerce, either with the main land on this side, or with that beyond which is the land of the great Khan, with which there is great profit....

I have also established the greatest friendship with the king of that country, so much so that he took pride in calling me his brother, and treating me as such. Even should these people change their intentions towards us and

become hostile, they do not know what arms are, but, as I have said, go naked, and are the most timid people in the world; so that the men I have left could, alone, destroy the whole country, and this island has no danger for them, if they only know how to conduct themselves.... Finally, and speaking only of what has taken place in this voyage, which has been so hasty, their Highnesses may see that I shall give them all the gold they require, if they will give me but a very little assistance; spices also, and cotton, as much as their Highnesses shall command to be shipped; and mastic, hitherto found only in Greece...slaves, as many of these idolators as their Highnesses shall command to be shipped....

But our Redeemer hath granted this victory our illustrious King and Queen and their kingdoms, which have acquired great fame by an event of such high importance, in which all Christendom ought to rejoice, and which it ought to celebrate with great festivals and the offering of solemn thanks to the Holy Trinity with many solemn prayers, both for the great exaltation which may accrue to them in turning so many nations to our holy faith, and also for the temporal benefits which will bring great refreshment and gain, not only to Spain, but to all Christians.

Why and How Atahuallpa Was Defeated

The messengers came back to ask the Governor to send a Christian to Atahuallpa, that he intended to come at once, and that he would come unarmed. The Governor sent a Christian, and presently Atahuallpa moved, leaving the armed men behind him. He took with him about five or six thousand Indians without arms, except that under their shirts they had small darts and slings with stones.

He came in a litter, and before went three or four hundred Indians in liveries, cleaning straws from the road and singing. Then came Atahuallpa in the midst of his chiefs and principal men, the greatest among them being also borne on men's shoulders.... A Dominican Friar, who was with the Governor, came forward to tell him, on the part of the Governor, that he waited for him in his lodgings, and that he was sent to speak with him. The Friar then told Atahuallpa that he was a Priest, and that he was sent there to teach the things of the Faith, if they should desire to be Christians. He showed Atahuallpa a book ... and told him that book contained the things of God. Atahuallpa asked for the book, and threw it on the ground, saying: "I will not leave this place until you have restored all that you have taken in my land. I know well who you are, and what you have come for."...The Friar went to the Governor and reported what was being done, and that no time was to be lost. The Governor sent to me; and I had arranged with the Captain of the artillery that, when a sign was given, he

(continued)

should discharge his pieces, and that, on hearing the reports, all the troops should come forth at once. This was done, and as the Indians were unarmed, they were defeated without danger to any Christian. Those who carried the litter, and the chiefs who surrounded Atahuallpa, were all killed, falling around him. The Governor came out and seized Atahuallpa, and in protecting him, he received a knife cut from a Christian in the hand. The troops continued the pursuit as far as the place where the armed Indians were stationed, who made no resistance whatever, because it was night. All were brought into town, where the Governor was quartered.

Next morning the Governor ordered us to go to the camp of Atahuallpa, where we found forty thousand pesos worth of gold and two or three pounds of silver....The Governor said that he had not come to make war on the Indians, but that our Lord the Emperor, who was Lord of the whole world, had ordered him to come that he might see the land, and let Atahuallpa know the things of our Faith....The Governor also told him that that land, and all other lands, belonged to the Emperor, and that he must acknowledge him as his Lord. He replied that he was content, and, observing that the Christians had collected some gold, Atahuallpa said to the Governor that

they need not take such care of it, as if there was so little; for that he could give them ten thousand plates, and that he could fill the room in which he was up to a white line, which was the height of a man and a half from the floor.

Questions: What were the main bases for initial European judgments about the characteristics of Native American? How might the native peoples have judged the Europeans? What motives does Columbus appeal to in trying to interest Spanish rulers in the new land?

These documents raise obvious problems of interpretation. They interpret interactions with another, very foreign culture from the European standpoint only. They also attribute motives to the adventurers that may or may not have been predominant. Figuring out how to gain useful, valid information from documents of this sort, which are undeniably revealing of key passages in world history, is a major challenge. What parts of the accounts seem most reliable, and what criteria can be used to sort out degrees of accuracy?

peans, many from the British Isles, colonized the Atlantic coastal region, where native populations were quickly reduced by disease and war. The society that developed in the British colonies was far closer to west European forms than was that of Latin America. The colonies operated their own assemblies, which provided the people with political experience. Calvinist and Quaker church assemblies gave governing power to groups of elders or wider congregations. Many colonists thus had reason to share with some west Europeans a sense of the importance of representative institutions and self-government.

Colonists were also avid consumers of political theories written in Europe, such as the parliamentary ideas of John Locke. There was also wide reading and discussion of Enlightenment materials. Institutions such as the 18th-century American Philosophical Society deliberately imitated European scientific institutes, and hundreds of North Americans contributed scientific findings to the British Royal Society. The colonies remained modest in certain cultural attainments. Art was rather primitive, although many stylistic cues came from Europe. There was no question that in formal culture, North American leaders saw themselves as part of a larger Western world.

By the late 18th century, some American merchants were trading with China, their ships picking up medicinal herbs along the Pacific coast and exchanging them for Chinese artifacts and tea. Great Britain tried to impose firmer limits on this modestly thriving local economy after the Seven Years' War. It hoped to win greater tax revenues and to guarantee markets for British goods and traders, but the effort came too late and helped encourage rebellion in key colonies. Unusual among the colonies, North America developed a merchant class and some stake in manufacturing in a pattern similar to that taking shape in western Europe itself.

The spread of Western values in the Atlantic colonies and in British and French settlements in Canada was facilitated by the modest impact of Native Americans in these settled areas (Figure 21.6). The native population of this part of North America had always been less dense than in Central America or the Andes region. Because few Native American groups in these regions practiced settled agriculture, instead combining hunting with slash and burn corn growing, European colonists found it easy to displace them from large stretches of territory. The ravages of European-imported disease reduced the indigenous population greatly. Many forest peoples were pushed

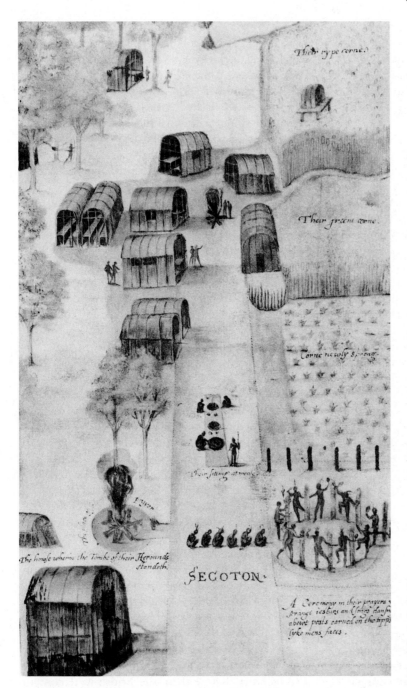

Some of the labels on the watercolor read: *Their rype corne.*, *Their greene corne.*, *Corne newly sprong.*, *Their sitting at meate.*, *The house wherin the Tombe of their Herounds standeth.*, *SECOTON*, *A Ceremony in their prayers with strange testures and (songs) dansing abowt posts carued on the topp lyke mens faces.*

Figure 21.6 *Watercolor by John White (c. 1590) of the Native American settlement of Secoton, Virginia. White was one of the pioneer settlers on Roanoke Island, North Carolina, and was also a pioneer of straightforward observation.*

westward. Some abandoned agriculture, turning to a new horse-based hunting economy on the plains (the horse was brought to Mexico by the Spaniards). Many territorial wars further distracted the Native American groups. The net result of these factors was that although European colonists interacted with Native Americans, learned from them, and feared and mistreated them, the colonists did not combine with them to forge new cultural groups like those emerging in much of Latin America.

By 1700, the importation of African slaves proved to be a more important addition to the

North American experience, particularly in the southern colonies. The practice of slaveholding and interactions with African culture distinguished North American life from its European counterpart. By the 18th century, 23 percent of the population of the English colonies was of African origin.

North America and Western Civilization

On balance, most white settlers intended to transplant key Western habits into their new setting. For example, family patterns were similar. American colonists were able to marry slightly earlier than ordinary western Europeans because of the greater abundance of land, and they had larger families. Still, they reproduced most features of the European-style family, including the primary emphasis on the nuclear unit. The new Americans did have unusual concern for children, if only because they depended so heavily on their work in a labor-scarce environment. European visitors commented on the child-centeredness of American families and the freedom of children to speak up. These variations, though significant, played on trends also becoming visible in Europe, such as the new emphasis on family affection.

Even when key colonies rebelled against European control, as they did in 1776, they moved in the name of Western political ideas and economic goals against the dependency the British tried to impose. They established a government that responded to the new Western political theories, implementing some key ideas for the first time.

Africa and Asia: Coastal Trading Stations

Europeans for the most part contented themselves with small coastal fortresses in Africa, negotiating with African kings and merchants but not trying to claim large territories on their own. Generally, Europeans were deterred by climate, disease, and nonnavigable rivers from trying to reach into the interior. There were two important exceptions. From initial coastal settlements, Portugal sent expeditions into Angola in search of slaves. These expeditions had a more direct and more disruptive impact in this part of southwestern Africa than elsewhere along the Atlantic coast. More important still was the **Cape Colony** planted by the Dutch on the Cape of Good

Hope in 1652. The intent was to form another coastal station to supply Dutch ships bound for Asia. But some Dutch farmers were sent, and these **Boers** (the Dutch word for farmers) began to fan out on large farms in a region still lightly populated by Africans. They clashed with local hunting groups, enslaving some of them. Only after 1770 did the expanding Boer settlements directly conflict with Bantu farmers, opening a long battle for control of southern Africa that raged until the late 20th century in the nation of South Africa.

European colonies in Asia were also exceptional. Spain set up an administration for the Philippines and sent active Catholic missionaries. The Dutch East India company administered portions of the main islands of present-day Indonesia and also (for a time) Taiwan, off the China coast.

Colonization in Asia entered a new phase as the British and French began to struggle for control of India, beginning in the late 17th century when the Mughal Empire weakened. Even before the Mughals faltered after the death in 1707 of their last great emperor, Aurangzeb, French and British forts dotted the east and west coasts, along with Portuguese Goa. As Mughal inefficiency increased, with a resultant surge of regional states ruled by Indians, portions of the subcontinent became an arena for the growing international rivalry between Britain and France.

The British East India Company had two advantages in this competition. Through negotiation with local princes, it had gained a station at **Calcutta,** which gave it some access to the great wealth of the Ganges valley. Furthermore, the company had enormous influence over the British government and, through Britain's superior navy, excellent communication on the ocean routes. Its French rivals, in contrast, had less political clout at home, where the government often was distracted by European land wars. The French also were more interested in missionary work than the British, for Protestants became deeply committed to colonial missions only in the 19th century. Before then, the British were content to leave Hindu customs alone and devote themselves to commercial profits.

French–British rivalry raged bitterly through the mid-18th century. Both sides recruited Indian princes and troops as allies. Outright warfare erupted in 1744 and then again during the Seven Years' War. In 1756, an Indian ruler in Bengal attacked and captured the British base at Calcutta. In the aftermath of the battle, English prisoners were placed in their own jail, where humidity and overcrowding led to perhaps as many as 120 deaths before Indian officials became aware of their plight and released them. The English used this incident, which they dubbed the "black hole" of Calcutta, to rally their forces. The East India Company's army recaptured Calcutta and then seized additional Indian and French territory, aided by abundant bribes to many regional princes. French power in India was destroyed, and the East India Company took over administration of the Bengal region, which stretched inland from Calcutta. Soon after this, the British also gained the island of Ceylon (Sri Lanka) from the Dutch.

The full history of British India did not begin until late in the 18th century, when the British government took a more active hand in Indian administration, supplementing the unofficial government of the East India Company (Figure 21.7). Indeed, British control of the subcontinent was incomplete. The Mughal Empire remained, although it was increasingly weak and it controlled scant territory, as did other regional kingdoms, including the Sikh state. Britain gained some new territories by force but was also content to form alliances with local princes without disturbing their internal administration.

In most colonies, European administration long remained fairly loose. Few settlers arrived, except in South Africa and the Americas. Outside the Americas, cultural impositions were slight. Missionary activity won many converts in the Philippines but not elsewhere in Asia or in Africa at this point. The main impact of colonies supplemented the more general development of the world economy: Colonial administrations pressed for economic advantage for the home country by opening markets and prompting commercial production of cheap foods and raw materials. Here, of course, the consequences to colonial peoples were very real.

Figure 21.7 *This Indian portrait of two women in European dress illustrates the English influence in 18th-century India.*

Impact on Western Europe

Western Europe was hugely affected by its own colonial success, not only economically but also diplomatically. Colonial rivalries and wars added to the existing hostilities between key nation-states. England and Holland early turned against Spanish success, with great effect. The Dutch and the English competed, engaging in many skirmishes in the 17th century. Then attention turned to the growing competition between the British and the French. This contest had extensive geographic scope: The Seven Years' War (1756–1763), fought in Europe, India, and North America, has been called the first world war.

There were also lesser effects on European society. For example, from the mid-17th century onward, the use of colonially produced sugar spread widely. Previously, sugar had been a costly, upper-class item. Now for the first time, except for salt, a basic product available to ordinary people was being traded over long distances. The spread of sugar had cultural as well as social and economic significance in giving ordinary Europeans the ability to obtain pleasurable sensations in quick doses—an interesting foreshadowing of later features of Western consumer behavior. It also promoted a growing role for dentists by the 18th century.

More broadly, the profits Europeans brought in from world trade, including the African slave trade, added wealth and capital. Many Europeans turned to manufacturing operations, as owners and workers, partly because of opportunities for export in world trade. These developments enhanced Europe's commercial character, while reducing dependence on agriculture alone. They provided additional tax revenues for growing governments and their military ambitions.

The Impact of a New World Order

The development of the world economy and European colonialism had immense impact. The imposition of unfree labor systems, to supply goods for world trade, was increasingly widespread. Slavery and serfdom deeply affected Latin America and eastern Europe, while the slave trade disrupted west Africa, and millions of individual lives as well.

Yet the world economy brought benefits as well as hardships, quite apart from the profits to Europe. New foods and wider trade patterns helped some societies deal with scarcity. Individual merchants and landowners gained new wealth virtually everywhere. China prospered from the imports of silver, though rapid population growth checked gains overall. The mixture of profits and compulsion brought more and more people and regions into the world economy network.

GLOBAL CONNECTIONS: The World Economy—And the World

Buoyed by its growing role in the world, western Europe unquestionably saw its economy and military power increase more rapidly than those of any other society during the early modern period. As the next chapter shows, Europe changed internally as well, often in dramatic ways. Because of these facts, it is tempting to see the early modern centuries as a European drama in which other regions either played supporting roles or watched in awe.

Yet the relationships to the world economy were in fact quite complex. They ranged from conscious isolation to controlled participation to undeniable dependency. Many societies retained vibrant political systems and internal economies. Some, although attracted to certain Western features, wanted to stand apart from the values and institutions that world economic success seemed to involve.

Even societies that had changes thrust upon them, like Latin America, were hardly passive. Pressed by missionaries, Latin Americans did not simply adopt European-style Christianity, but rather blended in traditional beliefs and practices and many distinctive artistic forms. The world was growing closer, but it was not necessarily becoming simpler.

Further Readings

Excellent discussions of Western exploration and expansion are Carlo Cipolla's *Guns, Sails and Empires: Technological Innovation and the Early Phases of European Expansion 1400–1700* (1997); J. H. Parry's *The Age of Reconnaissance* (1982); Richard S. Dunn's *Sugar and Slaves: The Rise of the Planter Class in the English West Indies, 1624–1713* (1972); and D. Boorstin's *The Discoverers* (1991). Recent works include Alan K. Smith's *Creating a World Economy: Merchant Capital, Colonialism and World Trade 1460–1825* (1991) and James Tracy, ed., *The Rise of Merchant Empires* (1986) and *The Political Economy of Merchant Empires* (1991). Somewhat more specific facets are treated in D. K. Fieldhouse's *The Colonial Empires* (1971); J. H. Parry's *The Discovery of South America* (1979); and S. Subrahmanyam's *The Portuguese Empire in Asia, 1500–1700* (1993). A vital treatment of the international results of new trading patterns of foods and disease is Alfred Crosby's *The Columbian Exchange: Biological and Cultural Consequences of 1492* (1972); see also Elinor G. Melville's *A Plague of Sheep: Environmental Consequences of the Conquest of Mexico* (1994). For a stimulating reemphasis on Asia, see Andre Geuder Frank's *ReOrient: Global Economy in the Asian Age* (1998).

On slavery and its trade, see Eric Williams' *Capitalism and Slavery* (1964); Orlando Patterson's *Slavery and Social Death: A Comparative Study* (1982); and D. B. Davis' *Slavery and Human Progress* (1984); the last two are important comparative and analytical statements in a major field of recent historical study. See also Philip D. Curtin's *Atlantic Slave Trade* (1972) and his edited volume, *Africa Remembered: Narratives by West Africans from the Era of the Slave Trade* (1967). A good recent survey of developments in Africa and in the period is Paul Bohannan and Philip Curtin's *Africa and Africans* (3rd ed., 1988).

New world trading patterns, including Asia's role in them, are discussed in K. N. N. Shanduri, *Trade and Civilization in the Indian Ocean* (1985); Stephan Frederic Dale, *Indian Merchants and Eurasia Trade: 1600–1750* (1994); and Philip Curtin, *Cross-Cultural Trade in World History* (1984). A controversial theoretical statement about new trade relationships and their impact on politics and social structure is Immanuel Wallerstein's *The Modern World System: Capitalist Agriculture and the Origins of the European World Economy in the Sixteenth Century* (1974) and *The Modern World System: Mercantilism and the Consolidation of the European World Economy 1600–1750* (1980); see also his *Politics of the World Economy: The States, the Movements and the Civilizations* (1984).

For discussions on where colonial North America fits in this period of world history, see Jack Greene and J. R. Pole, eds., *Colonial British America: Essays on the New History of the Early Modern Era* (1984); William J. Eccles, *France in America* (rev. ed., 1990); and Gary Nash, *Red, White and Black: The Peoples of Early America* (rev. ed., 1982).

On the Web

Biographies of leaders of the European age of discovery, from Henry the Navigator to Vasco De Gama, are offered at http://www.win.tue.nl/cs/fm/engels/discovery/. This site also traces the lives of the world's great explorers of every region and era.

Links to the most valuable sites examining the contact between conquistadors and Indians in North America and its aftermath can be found at http://www.nhc.rtp.nc.us:8080/tserve/nattrans/ntecoindian/ecolinksce.htm/. Though seemingly a lesson plan, http://www.yale.edu/ynhti/curriculum/units/1992/2/92.02.01.x.html#a offers excellent overviews of Euro-American contacts and a superb bibliography.

A virtual version of an exhibit mounted by the Library of Congress and other materials that look at the multicultural dimensions of the events of 1492, the life of Christopher Columbus, and the Colombian exchange his voyages initiated can be found at http://www.loc.gov/exhibits/1492/. Other such exhibits and analyses of his career can be found at http://www.ibiblio.org/expo/1492.exhibit/c-Columbus/columbus.html and http://xroads.virginia.edu/~CAP/COLUMBUS/col3.html.

Most discussions on the nature of that exchange rightly focus on the material outcomes of the Atlantic slave trade, such as the development of plantation economies and the exchange of crops, animals, and diseases. However, one site, http://daphne.palomar.edu/scrout/colexc.htm, also examines what it admits to be the controversial notion that the indigenous peoples of the Americas may have contributed toward the evolution of important modern ideas, including Western conceptions of liberty, ecology, and even corporate structure. At the very least, such speculation reminds us that the relationship between the indigenous people of the Americas and their European conquerors was complex.

The relationship between conquistador Hernando Cortez and Donna Maria/La Malinche, his female Nahuatl-speaking translator, certainly was as complicated as Cortez's relations with his Aztec-hating Mesoamerica allies. Both relationships are discussed at http://thedagger.com/conquest.html. Another site, http://www.fordham.edu/halsall/mod/aztecs1.html, offers a text of the discussions between Cortez and Montezuma, that Malinche facilitated as a translator, that foreshadowed the end of the Aztec empire. Malinche's role in the Columbian exchange is examined at http://www.mexconnect.com/mex_/history/malinche.html and http://thedagger.com/archive/conquest/malinche.html.

Francisco Pizarro's encounter with Inca leaders and the imposition of Spanish rule over their empire is presented at http://www.ucalgary.ca/applied_history/tutor/eurvoya/inca.html.

The controversy over the demographic catastrophe that accompanied the conquest of Mexico is analyzed from the perspective of contemporary Spanish and Nahuatl records at http://www.hist.umn.edu/~rmccaa/vircatas/vir6.htm (or scroll down to this subject in 1998 files at http://www.hist.umn.edu/~rmccaa/).

Dutch and British traders soon outstripped their Iberian competitors in the new global economy, a process described at http://www.theeastindiacompany.com/, http://65.107.211.206/post/india/hohenthal/3.1.html, and http://www.fordham.edu/halsall/mod/modsbook03.html. The latter site also contains the chief primary documentation for the early modern world system and includes a summary of Immanuel Wallerstein's World System Theory (http://www.fordham.edu/halsall/mod/wallerstein.html). The pattern of the then emerging new world order can be glimpsed through a visit to the Dutch factory at Batavia at http://batavia.rug.ac.be/index.html.

CHAPTER 22

THE TRANSFORMATION OF THE WEST, 1450–1750

Anatomy as science and as art: The anatomical sketches and notes by Leonardo da Vinci demonstrate his study of the human form. In keeping with the scientific spirit of the age, artists of the late Renaissance sometimes turned to science in order to portray the human body as realistically as possible.

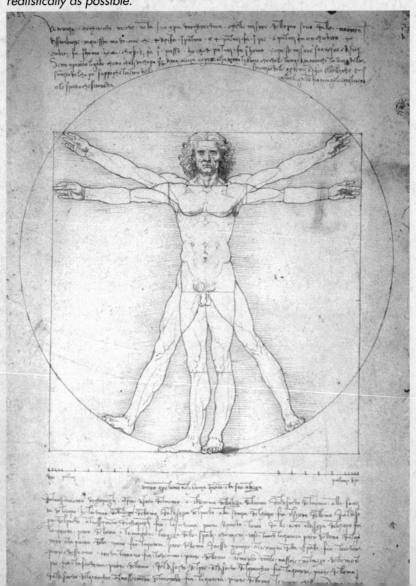

During the three centuries after 1450, Western civilization changed in dramatic ways. Still a largely agricultural society in 1750, the West had become unusually commercially active and had laid out a growing manufacturing sector. Government powers had expanded, and new political ideas complicated the picture. Beliefs had changed. Science came to form the center of Western intellectual life for the first time in the history of any society. Popular beliefs, including ideas about family and nature, also had shifted. In some respects, the West in this period was following a path that other civilizations had already laid out, such as increased bureaucratization in government. But in other areas, such as popular belief and family structure, the West was striking out in new directions.

Changes within western Europe resulted in part from overseas expansion and growing dominance in international trade. In turn, Europe's evolution furthered this international role.

Europe's internal changes unfolded amid much internal conflict. A host of terms, such as *Renaissance* and *Enlightenment*, describe key phases of change. Although there was no master plan, there were focal points: Europe's transformation centered on commerce, the state, and culture, with some support from technology. Between 1450 and 1650, a series of cultural shifts held center stage along with the rise in trade. Thereafter, the scientific revolution and the advent of new political forms introduced additional changes, which were amplified in the 18th-century Enlightenment.

A New Spirit

The Italian writer Francesco Petrarch (1304–1374) once climbed a mountain, Ventoux, in southern France. He wrote of his ascent, proud of his own skill and using the climb as a symbol of what he could achieve. There was a new spirit in this work, intended to be published, compared to the more religious Middle Ages. But Petrarch did not abandon religion, and in later life he talked about how he had given up poetry in favor of reading Christian texts, finding "hidden sweetness which I had once esteemed but lightly."

1300 C.E.	1450 C.E.	1500 C.E.	1550 C.E.	1650 C.E.	1750 C.E.
1300–1450 Italian Renaissance	**1450–1519** Leonardo da Vinci	**1500–1600** "Commercial revolution"	**1550–1649** Religious wars in France, Germany, and Britain	**1670–1692** Decline of witchcraft trials	**1756–1763** Seven Years' War; France, Britain, Prussia, and Austria
	1450–1600 Northern Renaissance	**1515–1547** Francis I of France	**1555–1603** Elizabeth I, England	**1682–1699** Hapsburgs drive Turks from Hungary	**1776** Adam Smith's *Wealth of Nations*
	1455 First European printing press in Mainz, Germany	**1517** Luther's 95 theses; beginning of Protestant Reformation	**1564–1642** Galileo	**1688–1690** Glorious Revolution in Britain; parliamentary monarchy; some religious toleration; political writing of John Locke	**1780–1790** Joseph II, Austria and Hungary
	1469–1527 Machiavelli	**1534** Beginning of Church of England	**1588** Defeat of Spanish Armada by English		**1792** Mary Wollstonecraft's *Vindication of the Rights of Women*
	1475–1514 Michelangelo	**1541–1564** Calvin in Geneva	**17th century** Scientific Revolution	**18th century** Enlightenment	
	1490s France and Spain invade Italian city-states; beginning of Italian decline	**1543** "Copernican revolution"; Copernicus' work on astronomy	**1609** Independence of Netherlands	**1712–1786** Frederick the Great of Prussia; enlightened despotism	
			1618–1648 Thirty Years' War	**1730–1850** European population boom	
			1642–1649 English civil wars	**1733** James Kay invents flying shuttle loom	
			1642–1727 Isaac Newton	**1736** Beginnings of Methodism	
			1643–1715 Louis XIV in France; absolute monarchy		
			1647–1648 Culmination of popular rebellion		

The First Big Changes: Culture and Commerce

 During the 15th century the Renaissance emphasized new styles and beliefs. This was followed by even more sweeping cultural and political change in the 16th century, with the Protestant Reformation and the Catholic response to it. A new commercial and social structure grew up as well, creating new opportunities and intense new grievances.

The Italian Renaissance

The move away from earlier patterns began with the Renaissance, which first developed in Italy during the 14th and 15th centuries. Largely an artistic movement, the Renaissance challenged medieval intellectual values and styles. It also sketched a new, brasher spirit that may have encouraged a new Western interest in exploring strange waters or urging that old truths be reexamined.

Italy was already well launched in the development of Renaissance culture by the 15th century, based on its unusually extensive urban, commercial economy and its competitive city-state politics. Writers such as Petrarch and Boccaccio had promoted classical literary canons against medieval logic and theology, writing in Italian as well as the traditional Latin and emphasizing secular subjects such as love and pride. Painting turned to new realism and classical and human-centered themes. Religion declined as a central focus. The Italian Renaissance blossomed further in the 15th and early 16th centuries. This was a great age of Western art, as Leonardo da Vinci advanced the realistic portrayal of the human body and Michelangelo applied classical styles in painting and sculpture. In political theory, **Niccolo Machiavelli** emphasized realistic discussions of how to seize and maintain power. Like the artists, Machiavelli bolstered his realism with Greek and Roman examples.

Overall, Italian Renaissance culture stressed themes of **humanism:** a focus on humankind as the center of intellectual and artistic endeavor. Religion was not attacked, but its principles were no longer predominant. Historians have debated the reasons for this change. Italy's more urban, commercial environment was one factor, but so was the new imitation of classical Greek and Roman literature and art.

These Renaissance themes had some bearing on politics and commerce. Renaissance merchants improved their banking techniques and became more openly profit-seeking than their medieval counterparts had been. City-state leaders experimented with new political forms and functions. They justified their rule not on the basis of heredity or divine guidance but more on the basis of what they could do to advance general well-being and their city's glory. Thus, they sponsored cultural activities and tried to improve the administration of the economy. They also developed more professional armies, for wars among the city-states were common, and gave new attention to military tactics and training. They also rethought the practice of diplomacy, introducing the regular exchange of ambassadors for the first time in the West. Clearly, the Renaissance encouraged innovation, although it also produced some dependence on classical models.

The Renaissance Moves Northward

Italy began to decline as a Renaissance center by Isaac about 1500. French and Spanish monarchs invaded the peninsula, reducing political independence. At the same time, new Atlantic trade routes reduced the importance of Mediterranean ports, a huge blow to the Italian economy.

As Renaissance creativity faded in its Italian birthplace, it passed northward. The **Northern Renaissance**—focused in France, the Low Countries, Germany, and England—began after 1450. Renaissance styles also affected Hungary and Poland in east central Europe. Classical styles in art and architecture became the rage. Knowledge of Greek and Latin literature gained ground, although many northern humanists wrote in their own languages (English, French, and so on). Northern humanists were more religious than their Italian counterparts, trying to blend secular interests with continued Christian devotion. Renaissance writers such as Shakespeare in England and Rabelais in France also mixed classical themes with an earthiness—a joy in bodily functions and human passions—that maintained elements of medieval popular culture. Renaissance literature established a new set of classics for literary traditions in the major Western languages, such as the writings of Shakespeare in England and Cervantes in Spain.

The Northern Renaissance produced some political change, providing another move toward greater state powers. As their revenues and operations expanded, Renaissance kings increased their pomp and ceremony. Kings such as **Francis I** in France became patrons of the arts, importing Italian sculp-

tors and architects to create their classical-style palaces. By the late 16th century, many monarchs were sponsoring trading companies and colonial enterprises. Interest in military conquest was greater than in the Middle Ages. Francis I was even willing to ally with the Ottoman sultan, the key Muslim leader. His goal was to distract his main enemy, the Habsburg ruler of Austria and Spain. In fact, it was an alliance in name only, but it illustrated how power politics was beginning to abandon the feudal or religious justifications that had previously clothed it in the West.

Yet the impact of the Renaissance should not be overstated, particularly outside Italy. Renaissance kings were still confined by the political powers of feudal landlords. Ordinary people were little touched by Renaissance values; the life of most peasants and artisans went on much as before. Economic life also changed little, particularly outside the Italian commercial centers. Even in the upper classes, women sometimes encountered new limits as Renaissance leaders touted men's public bravado over women's domestic roles.

Changes in Technology and Family

More fundamental changes were brewing in Western society by 1500, beneath the glittering surface of the Renaissance. Spurred by trading contacts with Asia, workers in the West improved the quality of pulleys and pumps in mines and learned how to forge stronger iron products. Printing was introduced in the 15th century when the German **Johannes Gutenberg** introduced movable type, building on Chinese printing technology. Soon books were distributed in greater quantities in the West, which helped expand the audience for Renaissance writers and disseminated religious ideas. Literacy began to gain ground and became a fertile source of new kinds of thinking.

Family structure was also changing. A **European-style family** pattern came into being by the 15th century. This pattern involved a late marriage age and a primary emphasis on nuclear families of parents and children rather than the extended families characteristic of most agricultural civilizations. The goal was to limit family birth rates. By the 16th century, ordinary people usually did not marry until their late 20s—a marked contrast to most agricultural societies. These changes emphasized the importance of husband–wife relations. They also closely linked the family to individual property holdings, for most people could not marry until they had access to property.

The Protestant and Catholic Reformations

In the 16th century, religious upheaval and a new commercial surge began to define the directions of change more fully. In 1517, a German monk named **Martin Luther** nailed a document containing 95 *theses*, or propositions, to the door of the castle church in Wittenberg. He was protesting claims made by a papal representative in selling *indulgences*, or grants of salvation, for money, but in fact his protest went deeper. Luther's reading of the Bible convinced him that only faith could gain salvation. Church sacraments were not the path, for God could not be manipulated. Luther's protest, which was rebuffed by the papacy, soon led him to challenge many Catholic beliefs, including the authority of the pope himself. Luther would soon argue that monasticism was wrong, that priests should marry (as he did), and that the Bible should be translated from Latin so ordinary people could have direct access to its teachings. Luther did not want to break Christian unity, but the church he wanted should be on his terms (or, as he would have argued, the terms of the true faith).

Luther picked up wide support for his views during the mid-16th century and beyond. Many Germans, in a somewhat nationalist reaction, resented the authority and taxes of the Roman pope. German princes saw an opportunity to gain more power because their nominal leader, the Holy Roman emperor, remained Catholic. Princes who turned Protestant could increase their independence and seize church lands. The Lutheran version of **Protestantism** (as the general wave of religious dissent was called) urged state control of the church as an alternative to papal authority, and this had obvious political appeal.

There were reasons for ordinary people to shift their allegiance as well. Some German peasants saw Luther's attack on authority as a sanction for their own social rebellion against landlords, although Luther specifically renounced this reading. Some townspeople were drawn to Luther's approval of work in the world. Because faith alone gained salva-

tion, Lutheranism could sanction moneymaking and other earthly pursuits more wholeheartedly than did traditional Catholicism. Unlike Catholicism, Lutherans did not see special vocations as particularly holy; monasteries were abolished, along with some of the Christian bias against moneymaking.

Once Christian unity was breached, other Protestant groups sprang forward. In England, Henry VIII began to set up an **Anglican church,** initially to challenge papal attempts to enforce his first marriage, which had failed to produce a male heir. (Henry ultimately had six wives in sequence, executing two of them, a particularly graphic example of the treatment of women in power politics.) Henry was also attracted to some of the new doctrines, and his most durable successor, his daughter Elizabeth I, was Protestant outright. Still more important were the churches inspired by **Jean Calvin,** a Frenchman who established his base in the Swiss city of Geneva. Calvinism insisted on God's *predestination*, or prior determination, of those who would be saved. Calvinist ministers became moral guardians and preachers of God's word. Calvinists sought the participation of all believers in local church administration, which promoted the idea of a wider access to government. They also promoted broader popular education so that more people could read the Bible. Calvinism was accepted not only in part of Switzerland but also in portions of Germany, in France (where it produced strong minority groups), in the Netherlands, in Hungary, and in England and Scotland. By the early 17th century, Puritan exiles brought it to North America.

The Catholic church did not sit still under Protestant attack. It did not restore religious unity, but it defended southern Europe, Austria, Poland, much of Hungary, and key parts of Germany for the Catholic faith. Under a **Catholic Reformation,** a major church council revived Catholic doctrine and refuted key Protestant tenets such as the idea that priests had no special sacramental power and could marry. They also attacked popular superstitions and remnants of magical belief, which meant that Catholics and Protestants alike were trying to find new ways to shape the outlook of ordinary folk. A new religious order, the **Jesuits,** became active in politics, education, and missionary work, regaining some parts of Europe for the church. Jesuit fervor also sponsored Catholic missionary activity in Asia and the Americas.

The End of Christian Unity in the West

The Protestant and Catholic Reformations had several results in Europe during the late 16th and early 17th centuries. Most obvious was an important series of religious wars. France was a scene of bitter battles between Calvinist and Catholic forces. These disputes ended only with the granting of tolerance to Protestants through the **edict of Nantes** in 1598, although in the next century French kings progressively cut back on Protestant rights. In Germany, the **Thirty Years' War** broke out in 1618, pitting German Protestants and allies such as Lutheran Sweden against the Holy Roman emperor, backed by Spain. The war was so devastating that it reduced German power and prosperity for a full century, cutting population by as much as 60 percent in some regions (Figure 22.1). It was ended only by the 1648 **Treaty of Westphalia,** which agreed to the territorial toler-

ance concept: Some princely states and cities chose one religion, some another. This treaty also finally settled a rebellion of the Protestant Netherlands against Spain, giving the former its full independence.

Religious fighting punctuated British history, first before the reign of Elizabeth in the 16th century, then in the **English Civil War** in the 1640s. Here too, religious issues combined with other problems, particularly in a battle between the claims of parliament to rights of control over royal actions and some rather tactless assertions of authority by a new line of English kings. The civil war ended in 1660 (well after King Charles I had been beheaded; Figure 22.2), but full resolution came only in 1688–1689, when limited religious toleration was granted to most Protestant (but not Catholic) faiths.

Religious issues thus dominated European politics for almost a century. The religious wars led to a grudging and limited acceptance of the idea of religious pluralism: Christian unity could not be restored, although in most individual countries the idea of full religious liberty was still in the future. The religious wars persuaded some people that religion itself was suspect; if there was no dominant single truth, why all the cruelty and carnage? Finally, the wars affected the political balance of Europe, as Map 22.1 shows. After a period of weakness during its internal strife, France was on the upswing. The Netherlands and Britain were galvanized toward a growing international role. Spain, briefly ascendant, fell back. Internally, some kings and princes benefited from the decline of papal authority by taking a stronger role in religious affairs. This was true in many Catholic and Protestant domains. In some cases, however, Protestant dissent encouraged popular political movements and enhanced parliamentary power.

The impact of religious change went well beyond politics. Popular beliefs changed most in Protestant areas, but Catholic reform produced new impulses as well. Western people gradually became less likely to see an intimate connection between God and nature. Protestants resisted the idea of miracles or other interventions in nature's course. Religious change also promoted greater concentration on family life. Religious writers encouraged love between husband and wife. As one English Protestant put it, "When love is absent between husband and wife, it is like a bone out of joint: there is no ease, no order." This promotion of the family had ambiguous implications

Figure 22.1 *Hans Holbein's* The Dance of Death *illustrated social upheaval encouraged by the continuing plague as well as religious conflict.*

Figure 22.2   *Civil war resulted in the execution of Charles I in London, England, in 1649.*

for women. Protestantism, abolishing religious convents, made marriage more necessary for women than before; there were fewer alternatives for women who could not marry. Fathers were also responsible for the religious training of the children. On the other hand, women's emotional role in the family improved with the new emphasis on affection.

Religious change accompanied and promoted growing literacy along with the spread of the printing press. In the town of Durham, England, around 1570, only 20 percent of all people were literate, but by 1630 the figure had climbed to 47 percent. Growing literacy opened people to additional new ideas and ways of thinking.

The Commercial Revolution

Along with religious upheaval during the 16th century, the economic structure of the West was fundamentally redefined. The level of European trade rose sharply, and many Europeans had new goods available to them. Involvement with markets and merchants increased. Here was the clearest impact of the new world economy in western Europe.

A basic spur to greater commercialization was the price inflation that occurred throughout western Europe during the 16th century. The massive import of gold and silver from Spain's new colonies in Latin America forced prices up. The availability of more money, based on silver supply, generated this price rise. New wealth heightened demand for products to sell, both in the colonies and in Europe, but Western production could not keep pace, hence the price inflation. Inflation encouraged merchants to take new risks, for borrowing was cheap when money was losing value. A sum borrowed one year would be worth less, in real terms, five years later, so it made sense to take loans for new investments.

Inflation and the new colonial opportunities led to the formation of the great trading companies, often with government backing, in Spain, England, the Netherlands, and France. Governments granted regional monopolies to these giant concerns; thus, the Dutch East Indies Company long dominated trade with the islands of Indonesia. European merchants brought new profits back to Europe and developed new managerial skills and banking arrangements.

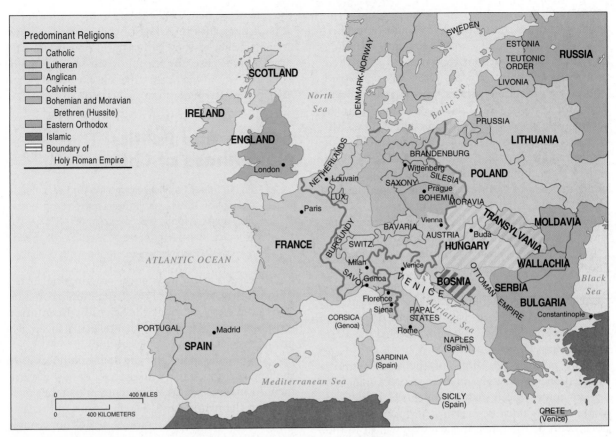

Map 22.1 *Western Europe During the Renaissance and Reformation. Different Protestant denominations made inroads in much of northwestern Europe with the Reformation, but Catholicism maintained its hold on significant portions of the continent.*

Colonial markets stimulated manufacturing. Most peasants continued to produce mainly for their own needs, but agricultural specialty areas developed in the production of wines, cheeses, wool, and the like. Some of these industries favored commercial farming and the use of paid laborers on the land. Shoemaking, pottery, metalworking, and other manufacturing specializations arose in both rural villages and the cities. Technical improvements followed in many branches of manufacture, particularly in metals and mining.

Prosperity increased for many ordinary people as well as for the great merchants. One historian has estimated that by about 1600 the average Western peasant or artisan owned five times as many "things" as his or her counterpart in southeastern Europe. A 16th-century Englishman noted that whereas in the past a peasant and his family slept on the floor and had only a pan or two as kitchenware, by the final decades of the century a farmer might have "a fair garnish of pewter in his cupboard, three or four feather beds, so many coverlets and carpets of tapestry, a silver salt, a bowl for wine ... and a dozen spoons." It was about this time that French peasants began to enjoy wine fairly regularly rather than simply at special occasions—the result of higher productivity and better trade and transport facilities.

Social Protest

There were victims of change as well, however. Growing commercialization created the beginnings of a new **proletariat** in the West—people without access to wealth-producing property. Population growth and rising food prices hit hard at the poor, and many people had to sell their small plots of land. Some proletarians became manufacturing workers, depending on orders from merchant capitalists to keep their tools busy in their cottages. Others became paid laborers on agricultural estates, where landlords were eager for a more manipulable workforce to take advantage of business opportunities in the cities. Others pressed into the cities, and a growing problem of beggars and wandering poor began to affect Western society. By blaming the poor for moral failings, a new, tough attitude toward poverty took shape that has lasted to some extent to the present day.

Not surprisingly, the shifts in popular economic and cultural traditions provoked important outcries. A huge wave of popular protest in western Europe developed at the end of the 16th century and extended until about 1650. Peasants and townspeople alike rose for greater protection from poverty and loss of property. The uprisings did not deflect the basic currents of change, but they revealed the massive insecurity of many workers.

The popular rebellions of the 17th century revealed social tension and new ideas of equality. Peasant songs voiced such sentiments as this: "The whole country must be overturned, for we peasants are now to be the lords, it is we who will sit in the shade." Uprisings in 1648 produced demands for a popular political voice; an English group called the Levelers gained 100,000 signatures on a petition for political rights. Elsewhere, common people praised the kings while attacking their "bad advisors" and high taxes. One English agitator said that "we should cut off all the gentlemen's heads....We shall have a merrier world shortly." In France, Protestant and Catholic peasants rose together against landlords and taxes: "They seek only the ruin of the poor people for our ruin is their wealth."

An unprecedented outburst against suspected witches arose in the same decades in various parts of western Europe and also in New England. Although attacks on witches had developed before, the new scale reflected intense social and cultural upheaval. Between 60,000 and 100,000 suspected witches were accused and killed. The **witchcraft persecution** reflected new resentments against the poor, who were often accused of witchcraft by communities unwilling to accept responsibility for their poverty. The hysteria also revealed new tensions about family life and

the role of women, who were the most common targets of persecution. A few of the accused witches actually believed they had magical powers, but far more were accused by fearful or self-serving neighbors. The whole witchcraft experience revealed a society faced with forces of unusual complexity.

Science and Politics: The Next Phase of Change

 As the impact of the Reformation and commercialization continued, new scientific discoveries and political forms took shape from 1600 onward. These two forces shaped a new round of change that continued into the 18th century.

The revolution in science, culminating in the 17th century, set the seal on the cultural reorientation of the West. Although the **Scientific Revolution** most obviously affected formal intellectual life, it also promoted changes in popular outlook.

At the same time, after the political upheavals of the Reformation, a more decisive set of new government forms arose in the West, centering on the emergence of the nation-state. The functions of the state expanded. The Western nation-state was not a single form, because key variants such as absolute monarchies and parliamentary regimes emerged, but there were some common patterns beneath the surface.

Did Copernicus Copy?

This is a chapter about big changes in western Europe during the early modern period. Big changes are always complex. One key development was the rise of science in intellectual life. A key first step here was the discovery by the Polish monk **Copernicus,** in the 16th century, that the planets moved around the sun rather than the earth, as the Greeks had thought. This discovery set other scientific advances in motion, and more generally showed that new thinking could improve on tradition. Copernicus is usually taken as a quiet hero of Western science and rationalism.

Copernicus based his findings on mathematics, understanding that the Greek view of earth as central raised key problems in calculating planetary motion. Historians have recently uncovered similar geometrical findings by two Arabs, al-Urdi and al-Tusi, from the 13th and 14th centuries. Did Copernicus copy, as Westerners had previously done from the Arabs, while keeping quiet because learning from Muslims was now unpopular? Or did he discover independently? It's also worth noting that scientists in other traditions, such as Chinese, Indian, and Mayan, had already realized the central position of the sun. Change, again, is complicated.

What is certain is that based on discoveries like that of Copernicus, science began to take on more importance in Western intellectual life than had ever been the case in the intellectual history of other societies, including classical Greece. Change may be complicated but it does occur.

Science: The New Authority

During the 16th century, scientific research quietly built on the traditions of the later Middle Ages. After Copernicus, Johannes Kepler (1571–1630; Figure 22.3) was another important early figure in the study of planetary motion. Unusual for a major researcher, Kepler was from a poor family; his father abandoned the family outright, and his mother, once tried for

witchcraft, was unpleasant. But Kepler made his way to university on scholarship, aiming for the Lutheran ministry but drawn to astronomy and mathematics. Using the work of Copernicus and his own observations, he resolved basic issues of planetary motion. He also worked on optics and, with the mixed interests so common in real intellectual life, also practiced astrology, casting horoscopes for wealthy patrons. Also around 1600, anatomical work by the Belgian Vesalius gained greater precision. These key discoveries not only advanced knowledge but also implied a new power for scientific research in its ability to test and often overrule accepted ideas.

A series of empirical advances and wider theoretical generalizations extended the possibilities of science from the 1600s onward. New instruments such as the microscope and improved telescopes allowed gains in biology and astronomy. The Italian **Galileo** publicized Copernicus' discoveries while adding his own basic findings about the laws of gravity and planetary motion. Condemned by the Catholic church for his innovations, Galileo proved the inadequacy of traditional ideas about the universe. He also showed the new pride in scientific achievement, writing modestly how he, "by marvelous discoveries and clear demonstrations, had enlarged a thousand times" the knowledge produced by "the wise men of bygone ages." Chemical research advanced understanding of the behavior of gasses. English physician **John Harvey** demonstrated the circular movement of the blood in animals, with the heart as the "central pumping station."

These advances in knowledge were accompanied by important statements about science and its impact. Francis Bacon urged the value of careful empirical research and predicted that scientific knowledge could advance steadily, producing improvements in technology as well. **René Descartes** established the importance of a skeptical review of all received wisdom, arguing that human reason could develop laws that would explain the fundamental workings of nature.

The capstone to the 17th-century scientific revolution came in 1687, when **Isaac Newton** published his *Principia Mathematica*. This work drew the various astronomical and physical observations and wider theories together in a neat framework of natural laws. Newton set forth the basic principles of all motion (for example, that a body in motion maintains uniform momentum unless affected by outside

Figure 22.3   *Johannes Kepler*

forces such as friction). Newton defined the forces of gravity in great mathematical detail and showed that the whole universe responded to these forces, which among other things explained the planetary orbits described by Kepler. Finally, Newton stated the basic scientific method in terms of a mixture of rational hypothesis and generalization and careful empirical observation and experiment. Here was a vision of a natural universe that could be captured in simple laws (although increasingly complex mathematics accompanied the findings). Here was a vision of a method of knowing that might do away with blind reliance on tradition or religious faith.

The scientific revolution was quickly popularized among educated Westerners. Here was a key step in the cultural transformation of western Europe in the early modern period. New scientific institutes were set up, often with government aid, to advance research and disseminate the findings. Lectures and easy-to-read manuals publicized the latest advances and communicated the excitement that researchers shared in almost all parts of Europe. Attacks on beliefs in witchcraft became more common, and magistrates grew increasingly reluctant to entertain witchcraft accusations in court. Public hysteria began to die down after about 1670. There were growing signs of a new belief that people could control and calculate their environment. Insurance companies sprang up to help guard against risk. Doctors increased their attacks on popular healers, promoting a more scientific diagnosis of illness. Newsletters, an innovation by the late 17th century, began to advertise "lost and found" items, for there was no point leaving this kind of problem to customary magicians, called cunning men, who had poked around with presumably enchanted sticks.

By the 1680s writers affected by the new science, though not themselves scientists, began to attack traditional religious ideas such as miracles, for in the universe of the Scientific Revolution there was no room for disruption of nature's laws. Some intellectuals held out a new conception of God, called **Deism,** arguing that although there might be a divinity, its role was simply to set natural laws in motion. In England, **John Locke** argued that people could learn everything they needed to know through their senses and reason; faith was irrelevant. Christian beliefs in human sinfulness crumbled in the view of these intellectuals, for they saw human nature as basically good.

Finally, scientific advances created wider assumptions about the possibility of human progress. If knowledge could advance through concerted human effort, why not progress in other domains? Even literary authorities joined this parade, and the idea that past styles set timeless standards of perfection came under growing criticism.

Science had never before been central to intellectual life. Science had played important roles in other civilizations, as in China, classical Greece, central America, and Islam. Generally, however, wider religious or philosophical interests predominated. In China most notably, despite some real interest in generalizations about the physical universe derived from Daoism, science continued to be construed mainly in terms of practical, empirical advances. The Western passion for combining empiricism with more sweeping rational formulations—the idea of general laws of nature—clearly built on traditions that had come from Greek thought as mediated by Christian theology and Islamic philosophy during the postclassical period. In sum, the West was not alone in developing crucial scientific data, but it now became the leading center for scientific advance, and its key thinkers stood alone for some time in seeing science as the key to gaining and defining knowledge.

Absolute and Parliamentary Monarchies

The feudal monarchy—the balance between king and nobles—that had defined Western politics since the late postclassical period finally came undone in the 17th century. In most countries, after the passions of religious wars finally cooled, monarchs gained new powers, curtailing the tradition of noble pressure or revolt. At the same time, more ambitious military organization, in states that defined war as a central purpose, required more careful administration and improved tax collection.

The model for this new pattern was France, now the West's most important nation. French kings steadily built up their power in the 17th century. They stopped convening the medieval parliament and passed laws as they saw fit, although some provincial councils remained strong. They blew up the castles of dissident nobles, another sign that gunpowder was undercutting the military basis of feudalism. They appointed a growing bureaucracy drawn from the

Visualizing the Past

Versailles

This picture shows Louis XIV's grand 17th-century palace at Versailles. It displays the sheer opulence of this absolute monarchy, in what was Europe's richest and most populous and influential nation. It also shows the renewed hold of a classical style, seen to be most prestigious for public buildings. What else does it suggest?

Architecture is sometimes thought to be the most socially and historically revealing of all the arts because it depends most heavily on public support; it is harder for architects, particularly dealing with public buildings, to be as idiosyncratic as painters or poets may be.

Questions: What kinds of intentions on the part of Louis and his advisors does this building represent? How can Versailles be interpreted as a statement of absolute monarchy in addition to its obvious showiness? What are the relationships to nature and to spatial arrangement? What would the palace represent to an ordinary French person? To an aristocrat?

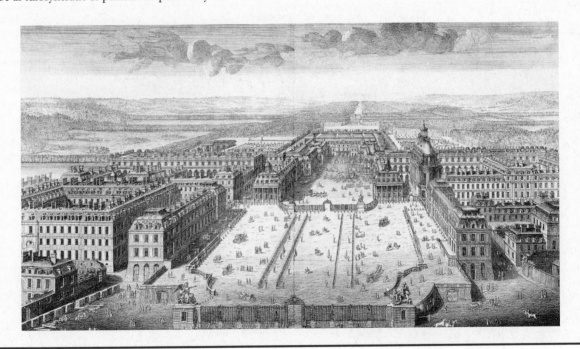

merchants and lawyers. They sent direct representatives to the outlying provinces. They professionalized the army, giving more formal training to officers, providing uniforms and support, and creating military hospitals and pensions.

So great was the power of the monarch, in fact, that the French system became known as **absolute monarchy.** Its most glorious royal proponent, King **Louis XIV,** summed up its principles succinctly: "I am the state." Louis became a major patron of the arts, giving government a cultural role beyond any previous levels in the West. His academies not only encouraged science but also worked to standardize the French language. A sumptuous palace at Versailles was used to keep nobles busy with social functions so that they could not interfere with affairs of state.

Using the new bureaucratic structure, Louis and his ministers developed additional functions for the state. They reduced internal tariffs, which acted as barriers to trade, and created new, state-run manufacturing. The reigning economic theory, mercantilism, held that governments should promote the internal economy to improve tax revenues and to limit imports from other nations, lest money be lost to enemy states. Therefore, absolute monarchs such as Louis XIV set tariffs on imported goods, tried to encourage their merchant fleets, and sought colonies to provide raw materials and a guaranteed market for manufactured goods produced at home.

The basic structure of absolute monarchy developed in other states besides France (see Map 22.2). Spain tried to imitate French principles in the 18th century, which resulted in efforts to tighten control over its Latin American colonies. However, the most important spread of absolute monarchy occurred in the central European states that were gaining in importance. A series of kings in Prussia, in eastern Germany, built a strong army and bureaucracy. They promoted economic activity and began to develop a state-sponsored school system. Habsburg kings in Austria-Hungary, though still officially rulers of the Holy Roman Empire, concentrated increasingly on developing a stronger monarchy in the lands under

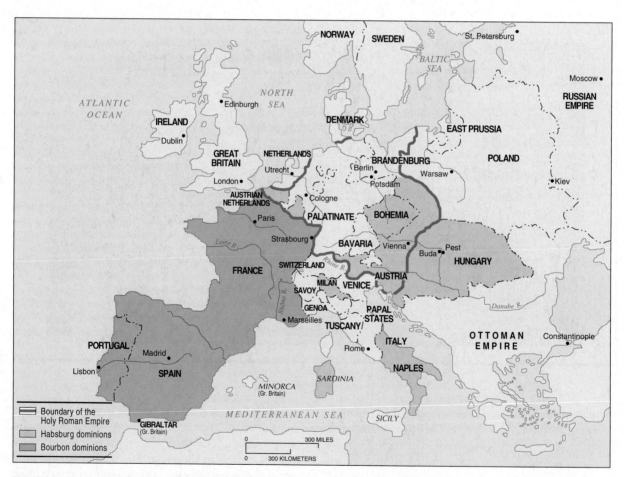

Map 22.2 *Europe Under Absolute Monarchy, 1715. The rise of absolute monarchies led to consolidation of national borders as states asserted full control of areas within their boundaries. For example, a recent study shows that villages that straddled the French–Spanish border were undifferentiated before 1600, but by 1700 they showed marked national differences because of different state policies and the greater impact of belonging to one state or another.*

In Depth

Elites and Masses

What caused the end of witchcraft hysteria in the West by the later 17th century? Did wise rulers calm a frenzied populace or did ordinary people themselves change their minds? One explanation focuses on new efforts by elites, such as local magistrates, to discipline mass impulses. Authorities stopped believing in demonic disruptions of natural processes, and so forced an end to persecutions. But many ordinary people were also thinking in new ways. Without converting fully to a scientific outlook, they became open to new ideas about how to handle health problems, reducing their belief in magical remedies; they needed witches less. Potential "witches" may have become more cautious. Older women, threatened by growing community suspicion, learned to maintain a lower profile and to emphasize benign, grandmotherly qualities rather than seeking a more independent role. Without question, there was a decline both in witchcraft beliefs, once a key element in the Western mentality, and in the hysteria specifically characteristic of the 16th and 17th centuries. This decline reflected new ways of thinking about strangeness and disruption. It involved complex interactions between various segments of Western society: magistrates and villagers, scientists and priests, husbands and widows.

The transformation of Western society after 1450 raises fascinating questions about the role of elites—particularly powerful groups and creative individuals—versus the ordinary people in causing change. The growing importance of social history has called attention to ordinary people, as we have seen, but it has not answered all the questions about their actual role. This role varies by place and time, of course. Some social historians tend to see ordinary people as victims of change, pushed around by the power groups. Others tend to stress the positive historical role of ordinary people in partly shaping the context of their own lives and affecting the larger course of history.

It is easy to read the early modern transformation of western Europe as an operation created by elites, with the masses as passively watching or futilely protesting. Not only the Renaissance and Reformation, but also the commercial revolution, required decisive action by key leadership groups. Leading merchants spurred economic change, and they ultimately began to farm out manufacturing jobs. The resultant rise of dependant wage labor, which tore a growing minority of western Europeans away from property and so from economic control of their lives, illustrates the power disparities in Western society. Ordinary people knuckled under or protested, but they were reacting, not initiating.

The rise of science rivets our attention on the activities of extraordinarily creative individuals, such as Newton, and elite institutions, such as the scientific academies. Some historians have suggested that the rise of science opened a new gap between the ways educated upper classes and masses thought.

Yet the ordinary people of western Europe were not passive, nor did they simply protest change in the name of tradition. Widespread shifts came from repeated decisions by peasants and artisans, not just from those at the top. The steady technological improvements in manufacturing thus flowed upward from practicing artisans, not downward from formal scientists. The European-style family that had taken shape by the 16th century was an innovation by ordinary people long ignored by the elite. It encouraged new parent–child relations and new tensions between young adults and the old that might spur other innovations, including a willingness to settle distant colonies in search of property. The fact that young people often had to wait to marry until their property-owning fathers died could induce many to seek new lands or new economic methods. In other words, ordinary people changed their habits too, and these changes had wide impact.

Questions: Did elites gain new power over the masses in early modern Western society? Are ordinary people more conservative by nature, more suspicious of change, than groups at the top? Can you describe at least two other historical cases in which it is important to determine whether change was imposed on ordinary people from above or whether ordinary people themselves produced important innovations?

their direct control. The power of these Habsburg rulers increased after they pushed back the last Turkish invasion threat late in the 17th century and then added the kingdom of Hungary to their domains.

Most absolute monarchs saw a strong military as a key political goal, and many hoped for territorial expansion. Louis XIV used his strong state as the basis for a series of wars from the 1680s onward. The wars yielded some new territory for France but finally attracted an opposing alliance system that blocked further advance. Prussian kings, though long cautious in exposing their proud military to the risk of major war, turned in the 18th century to a series of conflicts that won new territory.

Britain and the Netherlands, both growing commercial and colonial powers, stood apart from the trend toward absolute monarchy in the 17th century. They emphasized the role of the central state, but they also built parliamentary regimes in which the kings shared power with representatives selected by the nobility and upper urban classes. The English civil wars produced a final political settlement in 1688 and 1689 (the so-called **Glorious Revolution**) in which parliament won basic sovereignty over the king. The English parliament no longer depended on the king to convene, for regular sessions were scheduled. Its rights to approve taxation allowed it to monitor or initiate most major policies.

Furthermore, a growing body of political theory arose in the 17th century that built on these parliamentary ideas. John Locke and others argued that power came from the people, not from a divine right to royal rule. Kings should therefore be restrained by institutions that protected the public interest, including certain general rights to freedom and property. A right of revolution could legitimately oppose unjust rule.

Overall, western Europe developed important diversity in political forms, between absolute monarchy and a new kind of **parliamentary monarchy.** It maintained a characteristic tension between government growth and the idea that there should be some limits to state authority. This tension was expressed in new forms, but it recalled some principles that had originated in the Middle Ages.

The Nation-State

The absolute monarchies and the parliamentary monarchies shared important characteristics as nation-states. Unlike the great empires of many other civilizations, they ruled peoples who shared a common culture and language, some important minorities apart. They could appeal to a certain loyalty that linked cultural and political bonds. This was as true of England, where the idea of special rights of Englishmen helped feed the parliamentary movement, as it was of France. Not surprisingly, ordinary people in many nation-states, even though not directly represented in government, increasingly believed that government should act for their interests. Thus, Louis XIV faced recurrent popular riots based on the assumption that when bad harvests drove up food prices, the government was obligated to help people out.

In sum, nation-states developed a growing list of functions, particularly under the banner of mercantilism, whose principles were shared by monarchists and parliamentary leaders alike. They also promoted new political values and loyalties that were very different from the political traditions of other civilizations. They kept the West politically divided and often at war.

The West by 1750

 The three great currents of change—commercialization, cultural reorientation, and the rise of the nation-state—continued to operate in the West after 1700, along with the growing international influence of the West. Each current produced new changes that furthered the overall transformation of the West.

Political Patterns

Many of the key changes in modern Europe drew together by the mid-18th century. Political changes were least significant. During much of the century, English politics settled into a bloated parliamentary routine in which key political groups competed for influence without major policy differences. Absolute monarchy in France changed little institutionally, but it became less effective. It could not force changes in the tax structure that would give it more solid financial footing because aristocrats refused to surrender their traditional exemptions.

Political developments were far livelier in central Europe. In Prussia, **Frederick the Great,** building on the military and bureaucratic organization of his predecessors, introduced greater freedom of religion while expanding the economic functions of the state.

His government actively encouraged better agricultural methods; for example, it promoted use of the American potato as a staple crop. It also enacted laws promoting greater commercial coordination and greater equity; harsh traditional punishments were cut back. Rulers of this sort claimed to be enlightened despots, wielding great authority but for the good of society at large.

Enlightened or not, the policies of the major Western nation-states produced recurrent warfare. France and Britain squared off in the 1740s and again in the Seven Years' War (1756–1763); their conflicts focused on battles for colonial empire. Austria and Prussia also fought, with Prussia gaining new land. Wars in the 18th century were carefully modulated, without devastating effects, but they demonstrated the continued linkage between statecraft and war that was characteristic of the West.

Enlightenment Thought and Popular Culture

In culture, the aftermath of the Scientific Revolution spilled over into a new movement known as the **Enlightenment,** centered particularly in France but with adherents throughout the Western world. Enlightenment thinkers continued to support scientific advance. Although there were no Newton-like breakthroughs, chemists gained new understanding of major elements, and biologists developed a vital new classification system for the natural species.

The Enlightenment also pioneered in applying scientific methods to the study of human society, sketching the modern social sciences. The basic idea was that rational laws could describe social as well as physical behavior and that knowledge could be used to improve policy. Thus, criminologists wrote that brutal punishments failed to deter crime, whereas a decent society would be able to rehabilitate criminals through education. Political theorists wrote about the importance of carefully planned constitutions and controls over privilege, although they disagreed about what political form was best. A new school of economists developed. In his classic book *Wealth of Nations*, Scottish philosopher **Adam Smith** set forth a number of principles of economic behavior. He argued that people act according to their self-interest but, through competition, promote general economic advance. Government should avoid regulation in favor of the operation of individual initiative and market forces. This was an important statement of economic policy and an illustration of the growing belief that general models of human behavior could be derived from rational thought.

Single individuals could sum up part of the Enlightenment's impressive range. Denis Diderot (1713–1784; Figure 22.4) was a multifaceted leader of the French Enlightenment, best known for his editorial work on the *Encyclopédie* that compiled scientific and social scientific knowledge. Trained initially by the Jesuits, Diderot also wrote widely on philosophy, mathematics, and the psychology of deaf-mutes and also tried his hand at literature. An active friend

Figure 22.4 *Denis Diderot*

Document

Controversies About Women

Changes in family structure and some shifts in the economic roles of women, as well as ambivalent Protestant ideas about women that emphasized the family context but urged affection and respect between wives and husbands, touched off new gender tensions in Western society by the 17th century. Some of these tensions showed in witchcraft trials, so disproportionately directed against women. Other tensions showed in open debate about women's relationships to men; women not content with a docile wifeliness vied with new claims of virtue and prowess by some women. Although the debate was centered in the upper class of Protestant nations such as England, it may have had wider ramifications. Some of these ramifications, though quieter during the 18th century, burst forth again in arguments about inequality and family confinement in the 19th century, when a more durable feminist movement took shape in the West. In the selections here, the antiwoman position is set forth in a 1615 pamphlet by Joseph Swetham; the favorable view implicitly urging new rights is in a 1640 pamphlet pseudonymously authored by "Mary Tattle-Well and Ioane Hit-Him-Home, spinsters."

Swetham's "Arraignment of Women"

Men, I say, may live without women, but women cannot live without men: for Venus, whose beauty was excellent fair, yet when she needed man's help, She took Vulcan, a clubfooted Smith....

For women have a thousand ways to entice thee and ten thousand ways to deceive thee and all such fools as are suitors unto them: some they keep in hand with promises, and some they feed with flattery, and some they delay with dalliances, and some they please with kisses. They lay out the folds of their hair to entangle men into their love; betwixt their breasts in the vale of destruction; and in their beds there is hell, sorrow and repentance. Eagles eat not men till they are dead, but women devour them alive....

It is said of men that they have that one fault, but of women it is said that they have two faults: that is to say, they can neither say well nor do well. There is a saying that goeth thus: that things far fetched and dear bought are of us most dearly beloved. The like may be said of women; although many of them are not far fetched, yet they are dear bought, yea and so dear that many a man curseth his hard pennyworths and bans his own heart. For the pleasure of the fairest woman in the world lasteth but a honeymoon; that is, while a man hath glutted his affections and reaped the first fruit, his pleasure being past, sorrow and repentance remaineth still with him.

Tattle-Well and Hit-Him-Home's "Women's Sharp Revenge"

But it hath been the policy of all parents, even from the beginning, to curb us of that benefit by striving to keep us under and to make us men's mere Vassals even unto all posterity. How else comes it to pass that when a Father hath a numerous issue of Sons and Daughters, the sons forsooth they must be first put to the Grammar school, and after perchance sent to the University, and trained up in the Liberal Arts and Sciences, and there (if they prove not Blockheads) they may in time be book-learned?...

When we, whom they style by the name of weaker Vessels, though of a more delicate, fine, soft, and more pliant flesh therefore of a temper most capable of the best Impression, have not that generous and liberal Education, lest we should be made able to vindicate our own injuries, we are set only to the Needle, to prick our fingers, or else to the Wheel to spin a fair thread for our own undoing, or perchance to some more dirty and debased drudgery. If we be taught to read, they then confine us within the compass of our Mother Tongue, and that limit we are not suffered to pass; or if (which sometimes happeneth) we be brought up to Music, to singing, and to dancing, it is not for any benefit that thereby we can engross unto ourselves, but for their own particular ends, the better to please and content their licentious appetites when we come to our maturity and ripeness. And thus if we be weak by Nature, they strive to make us more weak by our Nurture; and if in degree of place low, they strive by their policy to keep us more under.

Now to show we are no such despised matter as you would seem to make us, come to our first Creation, when man was made of the mere dust of the earth. The woman had her being from the best part of his body, the Rib next to his heart, which difference even in our complexions may be easily decided. Man is of a dull, earthy, and melancholy aspect, having shallows in his face and a very forest upon his Chin, when our soft and smooth Cheeks are a true representation of a delectable garden of intermixed Roses and Lilies.... Man might consider that women were not created to be their slaves or vassals; for as they had not their Original out of his head (thereby to command him), so it was not out of his foot to be trod upon, but in a medium out of his side to be his fellow feeler, his equal, and companion....

Thus have I truly and impartially proved that for Chastity, Charity, Constancy, Magnanimity, Valor, Wisdom, Piety, or any Grace or Virtue whatsoever, women have always been more than equal with men, and that for Luxury, Surquidant obscenity, profanity, Ebriety, Impiety, and all that may be called bad we do come far short of them.

Questions: What are the main disagreements in these 17th-century texts? What kind of approach was more novel, judging by the Western gender tradition to that point? What conditions prompted a more vigorous public debate about gender in the 17th century? How does it connect to religious, commercial, and political change? How does the favorable argument compare with more modern views about women? What kinds of change does it advocate? Did the new arguments about women's conditions suggest that these conditions were improving?

of other philosophers, Diderot also traveled to foreign courts as advisor and visiting intellectual. A visit to Catherine the Great of Russia in 1773–1774, to thank her for generous patronage, harmed his health, but he maintained his relationship with his mistress, Sophie Volland.

More generally still, the Enlightenment produced a set of basic principles about human affairs: Human beings are good, at least improvable, and they can be educated to be better; reason is the key to truth, and religions that rely on blind faith or refuse to tolerate diversity are wrong. Enlightenment thinkers attacked the Catholic church with particular vigor. Progress was possible, even inevitable, if people could be set free. Society's goals should center on improving material and social life.

Although it was not typical of the Enlightenment's main thrust, a few thinkers applied these general principles to other areas. A handful of socialists argued that economic equality and the abolition of private property must become important goals. A few feminist thinkers, such as **Mary Wollstonecraft** in England, argued—against the general male-centered views of most Enlightenment thinkers—that new political rights and freedoms should extend to women. Several journals written by women for women made their first appearance during this extraordinary cultural period. Madame de Beaumere took over the direction of the French *Journal des Dames* from a man, and in Germany, Marianne Ehrmann used her journal to suggest that men might be partly to blame for women's lowly position.

The popularization of new ideas encouraged further changes in the habits and beliefs of many ordinary people. Reading clubs and coffeehouses allowed many urban artisans and businessmen to discuss the latest reform ideas. Leading writers and compilations of scientific and philosophical findings, such as the *Encyclopaedia Britannica*, won a wide audience and, for a few people, a substantial fortune from the sale of books.

Other changes in popular outlook paralleled the new intellectual currents, although they had deeper sources than philosophy alone. Attitudes toward children began to shift in many social groups. Older methods of physical discipline were criticized in favor of more restrained behavior that would respect the goodness and innocence of children. Swaddling—wrapping infants in cloth so they could not move or harm themselves—began to decline as parents became interested in freer movement and greater interaction for young children. Among wealthy families, educational toys and books for children reflected the idea that childhood should be a stage for learning and growth.

Family life generally was changed by a growing sense that old hierarchies should be rethought and revised toward greater equality in the treatment of women and children in the home. Love between family members gained new respect, and an emotional bond in marriage became more widely sought. Parents grew more reluctant to force a match on a son or daughter if the emotional vibrations were not right. Here was a link not only with Enlightenment ideas of proper family relations but with the novels such as Richardson's *Pamela* that poured out a sentimental view of life.

Ongoing Change in Commerce and Manufacturing

Ongoing economic change paralleled changes in popular culture and intellectual life. Commerce continued to spread. Ordinary Westerners began to buy processed products, such as refined sugar and coffee or tea obtained from Indonesia and the West Indies, for daily use. This was a sign of the growing importance of Europe's new colonies for ordinary life and of the beginnings of mass consumerism in Western society. Another sign of change was the growing use of paid professional entertainment as part of popular leisure, even in rural festivals. Circuses, first introduced in France in the 1670s, began to redefine leisure to include spectatorship and a taste for the bizarre.

Agriculture began to change. Until the late 17th century, western Europe had continued to rely largely on the methods and techniques characteristic of the Middle Ages—a severe economic constraint in an agricultural society. The three-field system still meant that a full third of all farmland was left unplanted each year to restore fertility. First in the Netherlands and then elsewhere, new procedures for draining swamps added available land. Reformers touted nitrogen-fixing crops to reduce the need to leave land idle. Stockbreeding improved, and new techniques such as seed-drills and the use of scythes instead of sickles for harvesting increased productivity. Some changes spread particularly fast on large estates, but other changes affected ordinary peasants as well. Particularly vital in this category was the spread of the potato from the late 17th century onward.

A New World crop, the potato had long been shunned because it was not mentioned in the Bible and was held to be the cause of plagues. Enlightened government leaders, and the peasants' desire to win greater economic security and better nutrition, led to widespread use of this crop. In sum, the West improved its food supply and agricultural efficiency, leaving more labor available for other pursuits.

These changes, along with the steady growth of colonial trade and internal commerce, spurred increased manufacturing. Capitalism—the investment of funds in hopes of larger profits—also spread from big trading ventures to the production of goods. The 18th century witnessed a rapid spread of household production of textiles and metal products, mostly by rural workers who alternated manufacturing with some agriculture. Here was a key use of labor that was no longer needed for food. Hundreds of thousands of people were drawn into this domestic system, in which capitalist merchants distributed supplies and orders and workers ran the production process for pay (Figure 22.5). Although manufacturing tools were still operated by hand, the spread of domestic manufacturing spurred important technological innovations designed to improve efficiency. In 1733, James Kay in England introduced the flying shuttle, which permitted automatic crossing of threads on looms; with this, an individual weaver could do the work of two. Improvements in spinning soon followed as the Western economy began to move toward a full-fledged Industrial Revolution (see Chapter 28).

Human changes accompanied and sometimes preceded technology. Around 1700, most manufacturers who made wool cloth in northern England were artisans, doing part of the work themselves. By 1720, a group of loom owners were becoming outright manufacturers with new ideas and behaviors. How were manufacturers different? They spent their time organizing production and sales rather than doing their own work. They moved work out of their homes. They stopped drinking beer with their workers. And they saw their workers as market commodities, to be treated as the conditions of trade demanded. In 1736, one such manufacturer coolly wrote that because of slumping sales, "I have turned off [dismissed] a great many of my makers, and keep turning more off weekly."

Finally, agricultural changes, commercialism, and manufacturing combined, particularly after about 1730, to produce a rapidly growing population in the West. With better food supplies, more people survived, particularly with the aid of the potato. Furthermore, new manufacturing jobs helped landless people support themselves, promoting earlier marriage and sexual relationships. Population growth, in turn, promoted further economic change, heightening competition and producing a more manipulable labor force. The West's great population revolution, which continued into the 19th century, both caused and reflected the civilization's dynamism, although it also produced great strain and confusion.

Innovation and Instability

By the 18th century, the various strands of change were increasingly intertwined in Western civiliza-

Figure 22.5 *A family of woolmakers at home.*

tion. Stronger governments promoted agricultural improvements, which helped prod population growth. Changes in popular beliefs were fed by new economic structures; both encouraged a reevaluation of the family and the roles of children. New beliefs also raised new political challenges. Enlightenment ideas about liberty and fundamental human equality could be directed against existing regimes. New family practices might have political implications as well. Children, raised with less adult restraint and encouraged to value their individual worth through parental love and careful education, might see traditional political limitations in new ways.

There was no perfect fit, no inevitable match, in the three strands of change that had been transforming the West for two centuries or more: the commercial, the cultural, and the political. However, by 1750 all were in place. The combination had

already produced an unusual version of an agricultural civilization, and it promised more upheaval in the future.

 GLOBAL CONNECTIONS: Europe and the World

In 1450, Europeans were convinced that their Christianity made them superior to other people. But they also understood that many societies were impressive in terms of cities and wealth and the strength of their governments.

As Europe changed and prospered, its outlook toward the world changed as well. We saw in the previous chapter how Europeans began to use technology as a measure of society, arguing that other societies that were less interested in technological change were inferior. By the 18th century, criticisms of the superstitions of other people began to surface among Europeans proud of their science and rationalism.

The wider world could still provide a sense of wonder, but increasingly this was focused on natural phenomena and the strange animals being imported to European zoos. The Enlightenment generated the idea of a "noble savage"—a person uncorrupted by advanced civilization and urban ways. But this was largely a fiction designed to comment on Europe itself, not a source of real admiration for other peoples. Increasingly, European power and the rapid changes within Western civilization led to a sense that most other societies were backward, perhaps not even civilized. The idea had powerful impact, not only on European attitudes but also on the ways other societies perceived themselves and reacted.

Further Readings

For an overview of developments in Western society during this period, with extensive bibliographies, see Sheldon Watts' *A Social History of Western Europe, 1450–1720* (1984); Michael Anderson's *Approaches to the West European Family* (1980); and Peter N. Stearns' *Life and Society in the West: The Modern Centuries* (1988). Charles Tilly's *Big Structures, Large Processes, Huge Comparisons* (1985) offers an analytical framework based on major change; see also Tilly's edited volume, *The Formation of National States in Western Europe* (1975).

On more specific developments and periods, J. R. Hale's *The Civilization of Europe in the Renaissance* (1994); J. H. Plumb's *The Italian Renaissance* (1986); F. H. New's *The Renaissance and Reformation: A Short History* (1977); O. Chadwick's *The Reformation* (1983); and Steven Ozment's *The Age of Reform, 1520–1550* (1980) and his *Protestants: The Birth of a Revolution* (1992) are fine introductions to early changes. See also Hubert Jedin and John Dolan, eds., *Reformation and Counter Reformation* (1980). H. Baron, *The Crisis of the Early Italian Renaissance* (1996), examines the place of civic life in Italian humanism. E. Amt, ed., *Women's Lives in the Medieval Europe: A Source-Book* (1992), and A. Vickery, *The Gentleman's Daughter: Women's Lives in Georgian England* (1998), survey the growth or retreat of opportunities for women over time.

Later changes are sketched in Thomas Munck's *Seventeenth Century Europe: 1598–1700* (1990) and Jeremy Black's *Eighteenth Century Europe: 1700–1789* (1990). On England in the civil war period, see Christopher Hill, *A Nation of Change and Novelty* (1990).

Key aspects of social change in this period can be approached through Peter Burke's *Popular Culture in Early Modern Europe* (1978); Robin Biggs' *Communities of Belief: Cultural and Social Tensions in Early Modern France* (1989); Keith Thomas' *Religion and the Decline of Magic* (1971); Lawrence Stone's *The Family, Sex and Marriage in England 1500–1800* (1977); and James Sharpe's *Instruments of Darkness: Witchcraft in Early Modern England* (1997). On popular protest, see Charles Tilly's *The Contentious French* (1986) and H. A. F. Kamen's *The Iron Century: Social Change in Europe 1550–1660* (1971).

On science, A. R. Hall's *From Galileo to Newton, 1630–1720* (1982) is a fine introduction. Relations between science and technology are covered in C. Cipolla's *Before the Industrial Revolution* (1976).

On the Web

Daily life in Renaissance Italy is examined at http://history.evansville.net/renaissa.html. The lives and art of Leonardo da Vinci (http://www.mos.org/leonardo/), Michelangelo (http://www.michelangelo.com/buonarroti.html), and Raphael (http://www.theartgallery.com.au/ArtEducation/greatartists/Raphael/about/) were closely intertwined with the city of Florence, whose history is addressed at http://www.mega.it/eng/egui/epo/secrepu.htm.

Martin Luther's life (http://www.iclnet.org/pub/resources/text/wittenberg/wittenberg-luther.html and http://www.wittenberg.de/e/seiten/personen/luther.html) and the course of the Protestant Reformation/Catholic Reformation are discussed at http://mars.acnet.wnec.edu/~grempel/courses/wc2/lectures/catholicreform.html, http://old.jccc.net/~jjackson/refo.html, and http://www.fordham.edu/halsall/sbook1y.html. The art and literature of the Northern Renaissance is examined at http://www.urtonart.com/history/Renaissance/northrenaiss.htm, http://www.msu.edu/~cloudsar/nrweb.htm, while http://communication.ucsd.edu/bjones/Books/luther.html illustrates the role of the printing press in the Reformation.

The Web provides insight into the role of two of the leading absolute monarchs of Europe, Frederick the Great (http://members.tripod.com/~Nevermore/king7.html) and Louis XIV (http://www.louis-xiv.de/, http://history.hanover.edu./texts/louisxiv.htm, and http://www.chateauversailles.fr/).

Isaac Newton's life and letters can be examined at http://www.cannylink.com/historyissacnewton.htm, while other leading figures of the Scientific Revolution can be explored at http://www.fordham.edu/halsall/mod/SCIREV.html.

The development of modern political and economic theory can be traced through the lives of Niccolo Machiavelli (http://sol.brunel.ac.uk/~jarvis/bola/ethics/mach.html), the Medici family (http://es.rice.edu/ES/humsoc/Galileo/People/medici.html), Adam Smith (http://www.socserv.mcmaster.ca/econ/ugcm/3ll3/smith/index.html), and through the study of the Glorious Revolution of 1688 (http://65.107.211.206/history/Glorious_Revolution.html and http://www.thegloriousrevolution.com). Sites addressing Renaissance women and their texts can be found at http://www.yesnet.yk.ca/schools/projects/renaissance/renaissancewomen.html, http://www.allsands.com/History/People/womanoftheren_vzp_gn.htm, http://womenshistory.miningco.com/cs/medieval/, and http://www.wwp.brown.edu/texts/rwoentry.html.

GLOSSARY

Pronunciation guidance is supplied in square brackets, [], after difficult words. The symbols used for pronunciation are found in the table below. Syllables for primary stress are *italicized*.

a	act, bat, marry	I	bite, ice	u	sum, up
AY	age, rate	j	just, tragic	U	sue, blew, through
âr	air, dare	k	keep, cop	ûr	turn, urge, cur
ä	ah, part, calm	ng	sing	zh	vision, pleasure
ch	chief, beach	o	ox, hot	uh	*a*lone, syst*e*m, eas*i*ly, gall*o*p, circ*u*s
e	edge, set	O	hope, over	A	as in French *a*mi
EE	equal, seat, bee	ô	order, ball	KH	as in German a*ch*, i*ch*
EER	here, ear	oi	oil, joint	N	as in French bo*n*
g	give, trigger	oo	book, tour	OE	as in French d*eux*
h	here	ou	plow, out	R	as in French *r*ouge
hw	which, when	sh	she, fashion	Y	as in German f*ü*hlen
i	if, big	th	thin, ether		

Abbasid [uh bas *id,* ab *uh* sid] Dynasty that succeeded the Umayyads as caliphs within Islam; came to power in 750 C.E. (p. 267)

Abelard, Peter Author of *Yes and No*; university scholar who applied logic to problems of theology; demonstrated logical contradictions within established doctrine. (p. 356)

absolute monarchy Concept of government developed during rise of nation-states in western Europe during the 17th century; featured monarchs who passed laws without parliaments, appointed professionalized armies and bureaucracies, established state churches, imposed state economic policies. (p. 523)

Aeschylus Greek writer of tragedies. (p. 115)

agrarian revolution Occurred between 8000 and 5000 B.C.E.; transition from hunting and gathering to sedentary agriculture. (p. 11)

Akhenaton [äk *nät* n, ä kuh-] Egyptian pharaoh of the New Kingdom; attempted to establish a one-god religion, replacing the traditional Egyptian pantheon of gods. (p. 37)

al-Ghazali Brilliant Islamic theologian; struggled to fuse Greek and Qur'anic traditions; not entirely accepted by ulama. (p. 288)

al-Mahdi [al-*mä* dEE] Third of the Abbasid caliphs; attempted but failed to reconcile moderates among Shi'a to Abbasid dynasty; failed to resolve problem of succession. (p. 279)

al-Rashid, Harun [al-rä *shEEd*] Most famous of Abbasid caliphs; renowned for sumptuous and costly living; dependant on Persian advisors early in reign; death led to civil wars over succession. (p. 281)

Alexander the Great Successor of Philip II; successfully conquered Persian Empire prior to his death in 323 B.C.E.; attempted to combine Greek and Persian cultures. (p. 111)

Alexandria, Egypt One of many cities of that name founded by Alexander the Great; site of ancient Mediterranean's greatest library; center of literary studies. (p. 111)

Ali Cousin and son-in-law of Muhammad; one of orthodox caliphs; focus for Shi'a. (p. 260)

ali'i   [*ä* lEE, *ä* luh EE] High chiefs of Hawaiian society who claimed descent from the gods and rested their claims on their ability to recite in great detail their lineages. (p. 222)

Allah   Supreme God in strictly monotheistic Islam. (p. 253)

Almohadis   [*äl* mO häd EEz] A reformist movement among the Islamic Berbers of northern Africa; later than the Almoravids; penetrated into sub-Sahara Africa. (p. 306)

Almoravids   [al muh *räv* udz] A puritanical reformist movement among the Islamic Berber tribes of northern Africa; controlled gold trade across Sahara; conquered Ghana in 1076; moved southward against African kingdoms of the savanna and westward into Spain. (pp. 206, 306)

alpacas   Along with llamas, domesticated animals of the Americas; basis for only form of nomadic pastoralism in the New World until European importation of larger animals in 15th century C.E. (p. 187)

Amaterasu   [*ä* mä te *Rä* sU] Sun goddess of the Shinto religion. (p. 216)

Anasazi   "The ancient ones"; culture located in southwestern United States; flourished from 200 to 1200 C.E.; featured large multistory adobe and stone buildings built in protected canyons or cliffs. (p. 183)

Anglican church   Form of Protestantism set up in England after 1534; established by Henry VIII with himself as head, at least in part to obtain a divorce from his first wife; became increasingly Protestant following Henry's death. (p. 516)

animism   A religious outlook that sees gods in many aspects of nature and propitiates them to help control and explain nature; typical of Mesopotamian religions. (p. 31)

Antigonids   One of the regional dynasties that followed the death of Alexander the Great; founded in Macedonia and Greece. (p. 111)

Aquinas, Thomas   Creator of one of the great syntheses of medieval learning; taught at University of Paris; author of several *Summas;* believed that through reason it was possible to know much about natural order, moral law, and nature of God. (p. 357)

Aragon   Along with Castile, a regional kingdom of the Iberian peninsula; pressed reconquest of peninsula from Muslims; developed a vigorous military and religious agenda. (p. 475)

archaic cultures   Hunting-and-gathering groups dispersed over the American continents by 9000 B.C.E. (p. 172)

Aristophanes   [ar uh *stof* uh nEEz] Greek writer of the comedies; author of *The Frogs.* (p. 114)

Aristotle   Greek philosopher; teacher of Alexander the Great; knowledge based on observation of phenomena in material world. (p. 113)

Arthashastra   [är thä *shäs* trä] Political treatise written during reign of Chandragupta Maurya; advocated use of spies and assassins, bribery, and scientific forms of warfare. (p. 136)

Aryans   Indo-European nomadic pastoralists who replaced Harappan civilization; militarized society. (p. 54)

Ashikaga Shogunate   Replaced the Kamakura regime in Japan; ruled from 1336 to 1573; destroyed rival Yoshino center of imperial authority. (p. 426)

Ashikaga Takuaji   [ä shEE kä gä tä kwä ji] Member of the Minamoto family; overthrew the Kamakura regime and established the Ashikaga Shogunate from 1336–1573; drove emperor from Kyoto to Yoshino. (p. 426)

Ashoka   [uh *sO* kuh] Grandson of Chandragupta Maurya; completed conquests of Indian subcontinent; converted to Buddhism and sponsored spread of new religion throughout his empire. (p. 137)

Augustine (Saint)   Influential church father and theologian (354–430 C.E.); born in Africa and ultimately Bishop of Hippo in Africa; champion of Christian doctrine against various heresies and very important in the long-term development of Christian thought on such issues as predestination. (p. 165)

Augustus Caesar   Name given to Octavian following his defeat of Mark Anthony and Cleopatra; first emperor of Rome. (p. 154)

Austronesian   Family of 30 related languages found in the Philippines, Indonesia, and southeast Asia; people of this linguistic group migrated throughout the Pacific. (p. 220)

Axum   Kingdom located in Ethiopian highlands; replaced Meroë in first century C.E.; received strong influence from Arabian peninsula; eventually converted to Christianity. (p. 43)

ayan [ä yän] The wealthy landed elite that emerged in the early decades of Abbasid rule. (p. 272)

ayllus [äy zhoos] Households in Andean societies that recognized some form of kinship; traced descent from some common, sometimes mythical ancestor. (p. 190)

Aztecs The Mexica; one of the nomadic tribes that used political anarchy after fall of Toltecs to penetrate into the sedentary agricultural zone of Mesoamerican plateau; established empire after 1325 around shores of Lake Texcoco. (p. 182)

Babylonian empire Unified all of Mesopotamia c. 1800 B.C.E.; collapsed due to foreign invasion c. 1600 B.C.E. (p. 34)

Baghdad Capital of Abbasid dynasty located in Iraq near ancient Persian capital of Ctesiphon. (p. 270)

Baibars [bI *bars*] Commander of Mamluk forces at Ain Jalut; originally enslaved by Mongols and sold to Egyptians. (p. 457)

Bakr, Abu [*bak* uhr, uh bU] One of Muhammad's earliest converts; succeeded Muhammad as first caliph of Islamic community. (p. 263)

bakufu Military government established by the Minamoto following the Gempei Wars; centered at Kamakura; retained emperor, but real power resided in military government and samurai. (p. 426)

Balboa, Vasco de First Spanish captain to begin settlement on the mainland of Mesoamerica in 1509; initial settlement eventually led to conquest of Aztec and

Inca empires by other captains. (p. 502)

ball games Ritual elements of many American cultures; played on formal courts; religious significance required that losing teams pay penalty of forfeiture of goods or their lives. (p. 180)

band A level of social organization normally consisting of 20 to 30 people; nomadic hunters and gatherers; labor divided on a gender basis. (p. 10)

Bantu Originated in eastern Nigeria in west Africa; migrated into central and southern Africa using rivers—particularly the Congo Basin; village dwellers who depended on agriculture and fishing. (p. 202)

Battle of Kulikova Russian army victory over the forces of the Golden Horde; helped break Mongol hold over Russia. (p. 455)

Battle of River Zab Victory of Abbasids over Umayyads; resulted in conquest of Syria and capture of Umayyad capital. (p. 269)

Battle of Siffin Fought in 657 between forces of Ali and Umayyads; settled by negotiation that led to fragmentation of Ali's party. (p. 265)

Batu Ruler of Golden Horde; one of Chinggis Khan's grandsons; responsible for invasion of Russia beginning in 1236. (p. 452)

bedouin Nomadic pastoralists of the Arabian peninsula; culture based on camel and goat nomadism; early converts to Islam. (p. 254)

Belisarius One of Justinian's most important military com-

manders during period of reconquest of western Europe; commanded in north Africa and Italy. (p. 328)

Benedict of Nursia Founder of monasticism in what had been the western half of the Roman Empire; established Benedictine Rule in the 6th century; paralleled development of Basil's rules in Byzantine Empire. (p. 241)

Benin Powerful city-state (in present-day Nigeria) which came into contact with the Portuguese in 1485 but remained relatively free of European influence; important commercial and political entity until the 19th century. (p. 319)

Berke [*ber* kuh] A ruler of the Golden Horde; converted to Islam; his threat to Hulegu combined with the growing power of Mamluks in Egypt forestalled further Mongol conquests in the Middle East. (p. 457)

Bernard of Clairvaux [bûr *närd* uhv klâr *vO*] Emphasized role of faith in preference to logic; stressed importance of mystical union with God; successfully challenged Abelard and had him driven from the universities. (p. 356)

bhaktic cults [*buk* tEEk] Hindu groups dedicated to gods and goddesses; stressed the importance of strong emotional bonds between devotees and the god or goddess who was the object of their veneration; most widely worshipped gods were Shiva and Vishnu. (p. 295)

bishops Headed Christian churches and regional centers and supervised the activities of other churches within the jurisdictional area. (p. 165)

Black Death Plague that struck Europe in 14th century; significantly reduced Europe's population; affected social structure. (p. 364)

bodhisattvas [bO duh *sut* vuhs] Buddhist holy men; built up spiritual merits during their lifetime; prayers even after death could aid people to achieve reflected holiness. (p. 238)

Boers Dutch settlers in Cape Colony, in southern Africa. (p. 508)

boyars Russian aristocrats; possessed less political power than did their counterparts in western Europe. (p. 339)

British East India Company Joint stock company that obtained government monopoly over trade in India; acted as virtually independent government in regions it claimed. (p. 496)

Bronze Age From about 4000 B.C.E., when bronze tools were first introduced in the Middle East, to about 1500 B.C.E., when iron began to replace it. (p. 28)

Buddha Creator of a major Indian and Asian religion; born in 6th century B.C.E. as son of local ruler among Aryan tribes located near Himalayas; became an ascetic; found enlightenment under bo tree; taught that enlightenment could be achieved only by abandoning desires for all earthly things. (p. 125)

Bulgaria Slavic kingdom established in northern portions of Balkan peninsula; constant source of pressure on Byzantine Empire; defeated by Emperor Basil II in 1014. (p. 329)

bushi Regional warrior leaders in Japan; ruled small kingdoms from fortresses; administered the law, supervised public works projects, and collected revenues; built up private armies. (p. 424)

Buyids Regional splinter dynasty of the mid-10th century; invaded and captured Baghdad; ruled Abbasid Empire under title of sultan; retained Abbasids as figureheads. (p. 283)

Byzantine Empire Eastern half of Roman Empire following collapse of western half of old empire; retained Mediterranean culture, particularly Greek; later lost Palestine, Syria, and Egypt to Islam; capital at Constantinople. (p. 236)

Caesar, Julius Roman general responsible for conquest of Gaul; brought army back to Rome and overthrew republic; assassinated in 44 B.C.E. by conservative senators. (p. 154)

Calcutta Headquarters of British East India Company in Bengal in Indian subcontinent; located on Ganges; captured in 1756 during early part of Seven Years' War; later became administrative center for all of Bengal. (p. 508)

caliph The political and religious successor to Muhammad. (p. 263)

calpulli Clans in Aztec society, later expanded to include residential groups that distributed land and provided labor and warriors. (p. 376)

Calvin, Jean French Protestant (16th century) who stressed doctrine of predestination; established center of his group at Swiss canton of Geneva; encouraged ideas of wider access to government, wider public education; Calvinism spread from Switzer- land to northern Europe and North America. (p. 516)

Cape Colony Dutch colony established at Cape of Good Hope in 1652 initially to provide a coastal station for the Dutch seaborne empire; by 1770 settlements had expanded sufficiently to come into conflict with Bantus. (p. 508)

Cape of Good Hope Southern tip of Africa; first circumnavigated in 1488 by Portuguese in search of direct route to India. (p. 493)

Carolingians Royal house of Franks after 8th century until their replacement in 10th century. (p. 348)

Carthage Originally a Phoenician colony in northern Africa; became a major port and commercial power in the western Mediterranean; fought the Punic Wars with Rome for dominance of the western Mediterranean. (p. 152)

caste system Rigid system of social classification first introduced into Indian subcontinent by Aryans. (p. 126)

Castile Along with Aragon, a regional kingdom of the Iberian peninsula; pressed reconquest of peninsula from Muslims; developed a vigorous military and religious agenda. (p. 475)

Çatal Hüyük [*chät* 1 hU *yook*] Early urban culture based on sedentary agriculture; located in modern southern Turkey; was larger in population than Jericho, had greater degree of social stratification. (p. 22)

Catholic Reformation Restatement of traditional Catholic beliefs in response to

Protestant Reformation (16th century); established councils that revived Catholic doctrine and refuted Protestant beliefs. (p. 516)

Celts   Inhabited most of Britain and Ireland; organized in small regional kingdoms; featured mixed agricultural and hunting economies; replaced in most places by Germans. (p. 211)

Chabi   Influential wife of Kubilai Khan; promoted interests of Buddhists in China; indicative of refusal of Mongol women to adopt restrictive social conventions of Chinese. (p. 459)

Chams   Indianized rivals of the Vietnamese; driven into the highlands by the successful Vietnamese drive to the south. (p. 440)

Chan Buddhism   Known as Zen in Japan; stressed meditation and appreciation of natural and artistic beauty; popular with members of elite Chinese society. (p. 400)

Chandragupta Maurya   [chun druh *gUp* tuh *mour* EE uh] Founder of Maurya dynasty; established first empire in Indian subcontinent; first centralized government since Harappan civilization. (p. 136)

Changan   Capital of Tang dynasty; population of 2 million, larger than any other city in the world at that time. (p. 398)

Charlemagne   [*shär* luh mAYn] Charles the Great; Carolingian monarch who established substantial empire in France and Germany c. 800. (p. 349)

Chavín culture   Appeared in highlands of Andes between 1800 and 1200 B.C.E.; typified by

ceremonial centers with large stone buildings; greatest ceremonial center was Chavín de Huantar; characterized by artistic motifs. (p. 187)

Chichén Itzá   Originally a Mayan city; conquered by Toltecs c. 1000 and ruled by Toltec dynasties; architecture featured pyramid of Feathered Serpent (Quetzalcoatl). (p. 181)

Chichimecs   American hunting-and-gathering groups; largely responsible for the disruption of early civilizations in Mesoamerica. (p. 20)

chiefdom   Widely diffused pattern of social organization in the Americas; featured chieftains who ruled from central towns over a large territory including smaller towns or villages that paid tribute; predominant town often featured temples and priest class. (p. 174)

Chimu state   Regional Andean chiefdom that flourished from 800 to 1465 C.E.; fell to Incas. (p. 190)

chinampas   Beds of aquatic weeds, mud, and earth placed in frames made of cane and rooted in lakes to create "floating islands"; system of irrigated agriculture utilized by Aztecs. (p. 377)

Chinggis Khan   [*jeng* guhs *kän*] Born in 1170s in decades following death of Kabul Khan; elected khagan of all Mongol tribes in 1206; responsible for conquest of northern kingdoms of China, territories as far west as the Abbasid regions; died in 1227, prior to conquest of most of Islamic world. (p. 290)

Choson   Earliest Korean kingdom; conquered by Han emperor in 109 B.C.E. (p. 431)

Cicero   Conservative Roman senator; Stoic philosopher; one of great orators of his day; killed in reaction to assassination of Julius Caesar. (p. 154)

city-state   A form of political organization typical of Mesopotamian civilizations; consisted of agricultural hinterlands ruled by an urban-based king. (p. 29)

civilization   Societies distinguished by reliance on sedentary agriculture, ability to produce food surpluses, and existence of nonfarming elites, as well as merchant and manufacturing groups. (p. 32)

Cleisthenes   [*klis* thuh nEEz] Athenian reformer of late 6th century B.C.E.; established democratic Council of 500 in Athens. (p. 105)

clientage   The social relationship whereby wealthy Roman landholders offered protection and financial aid to lesser citizens in return for political support and labor. (p. 151)

Clovis   Early Frankish king; converted Franks to Christianity c 496; allowed establishment of Frankish kingdom. (p. 347)

Columbus, Christopher   Genoese captain in service of king and queen of Castile and Aragon; successfully sailed to New World and returned in 1492; initiated European discoveries in Americas. (p. 494)

Confucius   Also known as Kung Fuzi; major Chinese philosopher; born in 6th century B.C.E.; author of *Analects;* philosophy based on need for restoration of order through advice of superior men to be found among the shi. (p. 78)

Constantine Roman emperor from 312 to 337 C.E.; established second capital at Constantinople; attempted to use religious force of Christianity to unify empire spiritually. (p. 234)

consuls Two chief executives or magistrates of the Roman republic; elected by an annual assembly dominated by aristocracy. (p. 151)

Copernicus Polish monk and astronomer (16th century); disproved Hellenistic belief that the earth was at the center of the universe. (p. 520)

Copts Christian sect of Egypt; tended to support Islamic invasions of this area in preference to Byzantine rule. (p. 264)

core nations Nations, usually European, that enjoyed profit from world economy; controlled international banking and commercial services such as shipping; exported manufactured goods for raw materials. (p. 499)

Corinthian Along with Doric and Ionian, distinct style of Hellenistic architecture; the most ornate of the three styles. (p. 116)

Council of Nicaea Christian council that met in 325 C.E. to determine orthodoxy with respect to the Trinity; insisted on divinity of all persons of the Trinity. (p. 239)

Crusades Series of military adventures initially launched by western Christians to free Holy Land from Muslims; temporarily succeeded in capturing Jerusalem and establishing Christian kingdoms; later used for other purposes such as commercial wars and extermination of heresy. (p. 283)

culture Combinations of the ideas, objects, and patterns of behavior that result from human social interaction. (p. 8)

cuneiform [kyU *nEE* uh fôrm, *kyU* nEE uh-] A form of writing developed by the Sumerians using a wedge-shaped stylus and clay tablets. (p. 29)

curacas Ayllu chiefs with privileges of dress and access to resources; community leaders among Andean societies. (p. 386)

Cyril Along with Methodius, missionary sent by Byzantine government to eastern Europe and the Balkans; converted southern Russia and Balkans to Orthodox Christianity; responsible for creation of written script for Slavic known as Cyrillic. (p. 335)

Cyrus the Great Established massive Persian Empire by 550 B.C.E.; successor state to Mesopotamian empires. (p. 102)

da Gama, Vasco Portuguese captain who sailed for India in 1497; established early Portuguese dominance in Indian Ocean. (p. 475)

daimyos Warlord rulers of 300 small states following Onin War and disruption of Ashikaga Shogunate; holdings consolidated into unified and bounded ministates. (p. 426)

Damascus Syrian city that was capital of Umayyad caliphate. (p. 265)

Daoism Philosophy associated with Laozi; stressed need for alignment with Dao or cosmic force. (p. 81)

Dasas Aryan name for indigenous people of Indus valley

region; regarded as socially inferior to Aryans. (p. 56)

Deism Concept of God current during the Scientific Revolution; role of divinity was to set natural laws in motion, not to regulate once process was begun. (p. 522)

Delian league Alliance formed by Athens after the Persian wars; cities contributed to unified treasury on island of Delos to support alliance fleet; later taken over by Athens and became Athenian Empire. (p. 108)

Demak Most powerful of the trading states on north coast of Java; converted to Islam and served as point of dissemination to other ports. (p. 297)

demographic transition Shift to low birth rate, low infant death rate, stable population; first emerged in western Europe and United States in late 19th century. (p. 316)

demography The study of population. (p. 316)

Descartes, René [dAY *kärt*] Established importance of skeptical review of all received wisdom (17th century); argued that human reason could then develop laws that would explain the fundamental workings of nature. (p. 521)

Devi Mother goddess within Hinduism; widely spread following collapse of Guptas; encouraged new emotionalism in religious ritual. (p. 232)

dharma [*där* muh, *dur*-] The caste position and career determined by a person's birth; Hindu culture required that one accept one's social position and perform occupation to the best of one's ability in order to have a better situation in the next life. (p. 130)

dhimmi   Literally "people of the book"; applied as inclusive term to Jews and Christians in Islamic territories; later extended to Zoroastrians and even Hindus. (p. 266)

dhows   Arab sailing vessels with triangular or lateen sails; strongly influenced European ship design. (p. 271)

Diocletian   Roman emperor from 284 to 305 C.E.; restored later empire by improved administration and tax collection. (p. 234)

Doric   Along with Ionian and Corinthian, distinct style of Hellenistic architecture; the least ornate of the three styles. (p. 116)

Dutch East India Company Joint stock company that obtained government monopoly over trade in Asia; acted as virtually independent government in regions it claimed. (p. 496)

edict of Nantes   Grant of tolerance to Protestants in France in 1598; granted only after lengthy civil war between Catholic and Protestant factions. (p. 517)

Empress Wu   Tang ruler 690–705 C.E. in China; supported Buddhist establishment; tried to elevate Buddhism to state religion; had multistory statues of Buddha created. (p. 401)

English Civil War   Conflict from 1640 to 1660; featured religious disputes mixed with constitutional issues concerning the powers of the monarchy; ended with restoration of the monarchy in 1660 following execution of previous king. (p. 517)

Enlightenment   Intellectual movement centered in France during the 18th century; featured scientific advance, application of scientific methods to study of human society; belief that rational laws could describe social behavior. (p. 527)

Epic of Gilgamesh   The first literary epic in Western civilization; written down c. 2000 B.C.E.; included story of Great Flood. (p. 29)

Ethiopia   A Christian kingdom that developed in the highlands of eastern Africa under the dynasty of King Lalaibela; retained Christianity in the face of Muslim expansion elsewhere in Africa. (p. 164)

Etruscans   Culture that ruled Rome prior to republic; ruled through powerful kings and well-organized armies; expelled by Romans c. 510 B.C.E. (p. 150)

eunuchs   Castrated males used within the households of Chinese emperors, usually to guard the emperors' concubines; became political counterbalance to powerful marital relatives during Later Han. (p. 97)

European-style family Originated in 15th century among peasants and artisans of western Europe, featuring late marriage age, emphasis on the nuclear family, and a large minority who never married. (p. 515)

extended families   Consisted of several generations, including the family patriarch's sons and grandsons with their wives and children; typical of Shang China elites. (p. 60)

feudalism   The social organization created by exchanging grants of land or fiefs in return for formal oaths of allegiance and promises of loyal service; typical of Zhou dynasty and European Middle Ages; greater lords provided protection and aid to lesser lords in return for military service. (pp. 63, 351)

five pillars   The obligatory religious duties of all Muslims; confession of faith, prayer, fasting during Ramadan, zakat, and hajj. (p. 262)

flying money   Chinese credit instrument that provided credit vouchers to merchants to be redeemed at the end of the voyage; reduced danger of robbery; early form of currency. (p. 408)

footbinding   Practice in Chinese society to mutilate women's feet in order to make them smaller; produced pain and restricted women's movement; made it easier to confine women to the household. (p. 411)

forbidden city   Imperial precinct within the capital cities of China; only imperial family, advisors, and household were permitted to enter. (p. 92)

Francis I   King of France in the 16th century; regarded as Renaissance monarch; patron of arts; imposed new controls on Catholic church; ally of Ottoman sultan against Holy Roman emperor. (p. 515)

Frederick the Great   Prussian king of the 18th century; attempted to introduce Enlightenment reforms into Germany; built on military and bureaucratic foundations of his predecessors; introduced freedom of religion; increased state control of economy. (p. 526)

Fujiwara   Japanese aristocratic family in mid-9th century; exercised exceptional influence over imperial affairs; aided in decline of imperial power. (p. 423)

Galileo Published Copernicus' findings (17th century); added own discoveries concerning laws of gravity and planetary motion; condemned by the Catholic church for his work. (p. 521)

Gempei Wars [gem pe] Waged for five years from 1180, on Honshu between Taira and Minamoto families; resulted in destruction of Taira. (p. 426)

Ghana First great sub-Saharan state; created by Soninke people; by 9th century C.E. a major source of gold in the Mediterranean world. (p. 206)

Glorious Revolution English overthrow of James II in 1688; resulted in affirmation of parliament as having basic sovereignty over the king. (p. 526)

Golden Horde One of the four subdivisions of the Mongol Empire after Chinggis Khan's death, originally ruled by his grandson Batu; territory covered much of what is today south central Russia. (p. 452)

Gothic An architectural style developed during the Middle Ages in western Europe; featured pointed arches and flying buttresses as external supports on main walls. (p. 359)

Gracchus, Gaius Along with Tiberius, tribune who attempted to introduce land and citizenship reform within the Roman republic; killed on the command of the Senate. (p. 154)

Gracchus, Tiberius Along with Gaius Gracchus, tribune who attempted to introduce land and citizenship reform within the Roman republic; killed on the command of the Senate. (p. 154)

Grand Canal Built in 7th century during reign of Yangdi during Sui dynasty; designed to link the original centers of Chinese civilization on the north China plain with the Yangtze river basin to the south; nearly 1200 miles long. (p. 407)

Great Wall Chinese defensive fortification intended to keep out the nomadic invaders from the north; initiated during Qin dynasty and reign of Shi Huangdi. (p. 84)

Great Zimbabwe Bantu confederation of Shona-speaking peoples located between Zambezi and Limpopo rivers; developed after 9th century; featured royal courts built of stone; created centralized state by 15th century; king took title of Mwene Mutapa. (p. 320)

Greek fire Byzantine weapon consisting of mixture of chemicals that ignited when exposed to water; utilized to drive back the Arab fleets that attacked Constantinople. (p. 329)

Gregory VII Pope during the 11th century who attempted to free church from interference of feudal lords; quarreled with Holy Roman Emperor Henry IV over practice of lay investiture. (p. 355)

griots [grEE O, grEE O, grEE ot] Professional oral historians who served as keepers of traditions and advisors to kings within the Mali Empire. (p. 309)

guilds Sworn associations of people in the same business or trade in a single city; stressed security and mutual control; limited membership, regulated apprenticeship, guaranteed good workmanship; often established franchise within cities. (p. 362)

Guptas Dynasty that succeeded the Kushans in the 3rd century C.E.; built empire that extended to all but the southern regions of Indian subcontinent; less centralized than Mauryan Empire. (p. 141)

gurus Originally referred to as Brahmans who served as teachers for the princes of the imperial court of the Guptas. (p. 134)

Gutenberg, Johannes Introduced movable type to western Europe in 15th century; credited with greatly expanded availability of printed books and pamphlets. (p. 515)

hadiths Traditions of the prophet Muhammad. (p. 267)

Hagia Sophia [hä juh sä fEE uh] New church constructed in Constantinople during reign of Justinian. (p. 327)

Hammurabi The most important ruler of the Babylonian empire; responsible for codification of law. (p. 34)

Han dynasty Chinese dynasty that succeeded the Qin in 202 B.C.E.; ruled for next 400 years. (p. 77)

Hangzhou [häng jO] Capital of later Song dynasty; located near East China Sea; permitted overseas trading; population exceeded 1 million. (p. 408)

Hannibal Great Carthaginian general during Second Punic War; successfully invaded Italy but failed to conquer Rome; finally defeated at Battle of Zama. (p. 152)

Hanseatic League   An organization of cities in northern Germany and southern Scandinavia for the purpose of establishing a commercial alliance. (p. 361)

hapu   Primary social unit of Maori society in New Zealand; divisions of tribes consisting of extended families; land allotted to extended families in common. (p. 223)

Harappa   Along with Mohenjo-daro, major urban complex of the Harappan civilization; laid out on planned grid pattern. (p. 50)

Harappan civilization   First civilization of Indian subcontinent; emerged in Indus River valley c. 2500 B.C.E. (p. 49)

Harsha   Ruler who followed Guptas in India; briefly constructed a loose empire in northern India between 616 and 657 C.E. (p. 231)

Harvey, John   English physician (17th century) who demonstrated circular movement of blood in animals, function of heart as pump. (p. 521)

Hausa   Peoples of northern Nigeria; formed states following the demise of Songhay Empire that combined Muslim and pagan traditions. (p. 312)

Heian   [*hAϒ*än] Capital city of Japan under the Yamato emperors, later called Kyoto; built in order to escape influence of Buddhist monks; patterned after ancient imperial centers of China; never fully populated. (p. 218)

Hellenism   Culture derived from the Greek civilization that flourished between 800 and 400 B.C.E. (p. 101)

Hellenistic period   That culture associated with the spread of Greek influence as a result of Macedonian conquests; often seen as the combination of Greek culture with eastern political forms. (p. 101)

helots   Conquered indigenous population of Spartan city-state; provided agricultural labor for Spartan landowners; only semifree; largest population of Spartan city-state. (p. 121)

Henry the Navigator
Portuguese prince responsible for direction of series of expeditions along the African coast in the 15th century; marked beginning of western European expansion. (p. 475)

hieroglyphs   The form of writing developed in ancient Egypt; more pictorial than Mesopotamian cuneiform. (p. 38)

Himalayas   Mountain region marking the northern border of the Indian subcontinent; site of the Aryan settlements that formed small kingdoms or warrior republics. (p. 50)

Hittites   An Indo-European people who entered Mesopotamia c. 1750 B.C.E.; destroyed the Babylonian empire; swept away c. 1200 B.C.E. (p. 34)

Hojo   Warrior family closely allied with Minamoto; dominated Kamakura regime and manipulated Minamoto rulers; claimed to rule in name of Japanese emperor at Kyoto. (p. 426)

Holy Roman emperors
Emperors in northern Italy and Germany following split of Charlemagne's empire; claimed title of emperor c. 10th century; failed to develop centralized monarchy in Germany. (p. 350)

Homo sapiens   The humanoid species that emerged as most successful at the end of the Paleolithic period. (p. 7)

Honshu   Largest of the Japanese islands; most heavily populated. (p. 215)

Hopewell culture   A North American mound-building culture; lasted from c. 200 to 500 C.E. (p. 182)

Horace   Poet who adapted Greek poetic meters to the Latin language; author of lyrical poetry laudatory of the empire; patronized by Augustus. (p. 157)

horizon   Archeological term for a period when a broad central authority seems to have integrated a widely dispersed region. (p. 187)

Hsiung-nu   [shEE *oong* nU] Also known as the Huns; horse nomads responsible for the disruption of Chinese, Gupta, and Roman civilizations. (p. 88)

huacas   Sacred spirits and powers that resided or appeared in caves, mountains, rocks, rivers, and other natural phenomena; typical of Andean societies. (p. 385)

Huari   Along with Tihuanaco, large center for regional chiefdoms between 300 and 900 C.E.; located in southern Peru; featured large ceremonial center supported by extensive irrigated agriculture; established widely diffused religious and artistic symbols spread all over Andean zone. (p. 189)

Huitzilopochtli   [wEE tsEE lO *pOch* tlEE] Aztec tribal patron god; central figure of cult of human sacrifice and warfare; identified with old sun god. (p. 375)

Hulegu Ruler of the Ilkhan khanate; grandson of Chinggis Khan; responsible for capture and destruction of Baghdad. (p. 290)

humanism Focus on humankind as center of intellectual and artistic endeavor; method of study that emphasized the superiority of classical forms over medieval styles, in particular the study of ancient languages. (p. 514)

Hundred Years' War Conflict between England and France from 1337 to 1453; fought over lands England possessed in France and feudal rights versus the emerging claims of national states. (p. 353)

hunting and gathering Means of obtaining subsistence by human species prior to the adaptation of sedentary agriculture; normally typical of band social organization. (p. 7)

Ibn Batuta Arab traveler who described African societies and cultures in his travel records. (p. 309)

Ibn Khaldun [i buhn kal *dUn*, KHUn] A Muslim historian; developed concept that dynasties of nomadic conquerors had a cycle of three generations—strong, weak, dissolute. (p. 284)

iconoclasm Religious controversy within the Byzantine Empire in the 8th century; emperor attempted to suppress veneration of icons; literally "breaking of images"; after long struggle, icon veneration was restored. (p. 332)

icons Images of religious figures that became objects of veneration within Christianity of the Byzantine Empire; particularly prevalent in Eastern monasticism. (p. 332)

ideographic writing Pictographic characters grouped together to create new concepts; typical of Chinese writing. (p. 62)

Ifriqiya [if ree *ki* uh] The Arabic term for eastern north Africa. (p. 306)

Iliad Greek epic poem attributed to Homer but possibly the work of many authors; defined gods and human nature that shaped Greek mythos. (p. 103)

Inca Group of clans centered at Cuzco that were able to create empire incorporating various Andean cultures; term also used for leader of empire. (p. 191)

Inca socialism A view created by Spanish authors to describe Inca society as a type of utopia; image of the Inca Empire as a carefully organized system in which every community collectively contributed to the whole. (p. 382)

Indian Misnomer created by Columbus referring to indigenous peoples of New World; implies social and ethnic commonality among Native Americans that did not exist; still used to apply to Native Americans. (p. 371)

Indra Chief deity of the Aryans; depicted as a colossal, hard-drinking warrior. (p. 55)

Indus River valley River sources in Himalayas to mouth in Arabian Sea; location of Harappan civilization. (p. 49)

investiture Practice of state appointment of bishops; Pope Gregory VII attempted to ban the practice of lay investiture, leading to war with Holy Roman Emperor Henry IV. (p. 355)

Ionic Along with Doric and Corinthian, distinct style of Hellenistic architecture; more ornate than Doric but less than Corinthian. (p. 116)

Islam Major world religion having its origins in 610 C.E. in the Arabian peninsula; meaning literally submission; based on prophecy of Muhammad. (p. 253)

Jericho Early walled urban culture site based on sedentary agriculture; located in modern Israeli-occupied West Bank near Jordan River. (p. 22)

Jesuits A new religious order founded during the Catholic Reformation; active in politics, education, and missionary work; sponsored missions to South America, North American, and Asia. (p. 516)

Jesus of Nazareth Prophet and teacher among the Jews; believed by Christians to be the Messiah; executed c. 30 C.E. (p. 163)

jihad Struggle often used for wars in defense of the faith. (p. 264)

Jin Kingdom north of the Song Empire; established by Jurchens in 1115 after overthrowing Liao dynasty. (p. 406)

jinshi [chin shEE] Title granted to students who passed the most difficult Chinese examination on all of Chinese literature; became immediate dignitaries and eligible for high office. (p. 399)

jizya [*jiz* yuh] Head tax paid by all nonbelievers in Islamic territories. (p. 266)

Jomon culture Created by early migrants to Japan after 3000 B.C.E.; hunting-and-gathering people, produced distinctive pottery form. (p. 216)

junks Chinese ships equipped with watertight bulkheads, sternpost rudders, compasses, and bamboo fenders; dominant force in Asian seas east of the Malayan peninsula. (p. 407)

Jurchens Founders of the Qin kingdom that succeeded the Liao in northern China; annexed most of Yellow River basin and forced Song to flee to south. (p. 406)

juula [jUlä] Malinke merchants; formed small partnerships to carry out trade throughout Mali Empire; eventually spread throughout much of west Africa. (p. 309)

Ju Yuanzhang [jU yU *än jäng, yYän*] Chinese peasant who led successful revolt against Yuan in 14th century; founded Ming dynasty. (p. 463)

Ka'ba Most revered religious shrine in pre-Islamic Arabia; located in Mecca; focus of obligatory annual truce among bedouin tribes; later incorporated as important shrine in Islam. (p. 258)

Kabir Muslim mystic during 15th century; played down the importance of ritual differences between Hinduism and Islam. (p. 295)

Kamasutra Written by Vatsayana during Gupta era; offered instructions on all aspects of life for higher caste males, including grooming, hygiene, etiquette,

selection of wives, and instruction on lovemaking. (p. 144)

Kamehameha I [kä *mAϒ* hä *mAϒ* hä, kuh *mAϒ* uh *mAϒ* uh] Fought series of wars backed by British weapons and advisors resulting in unified Hawaiian kingdom by 1810; as king he promoted economic change encouraging Western merchants to establish export trade in Hawaiian goods. (p. 222)

kapu Complex set of social regulations in Hawaii which forbade certain activities and regulated social discourse. (p. 222)

Karakorum Capital of the Mongol Empire under Chinggis Khan. (p. 452)

Karbala Site of defeat and death of Husayn, son of Ali; marked beginning of Shi'a resistance to Umayyad caliphate. (p. 265)

karma The sum of merits accumulated by a soul at any given point in time; determined the caste to which the soul would be assigned in the next life. (p. 130)

Kautilya Political advisor to Chandragupta Maurya; one of the authors of *Arthashastra*; believed in scientific application of warfare. (p. 136)

Khadijah First wife of the prophet Muhammad, who had worked for her as a trader. (p. 259)

khagan Title of the supreme ruler of the Mongol tribes. (p. 450)

khanates Four regional Mongol kingdoms that arose following the death of Chinggis Khan. (p. 445)

Khitans Nomadic peoples of Manchuria; militarily superior to Song dynasty China but influenced by Chinese culture; forced humiliating treaties on Song China in 11th century. (p. 404)

Khmers Indianized rivals of the Vietnamese; moved into Mekong River delta region at time of Vietnamese drive to the south. (p. 435)

Kiev Trade city in southern Russia established by Scandinavian traders in 9th century; became focal point for kingdom of Russia that flourished to 12th century. (p. 337)

kiva Circular pit in Anasazi communities used for religious meetings by the men in the society. (p. 185)

Koguryo Tribal people of northern Korea; established an independent kingdom in the northern half of the peninsula; adopted cultural Sinification. (p. 431)

Kongo Kingdom, based on agriculture, formed on lower Congo River by late 15th century; capital at Mbanza Kongo; ruled by hereditary monarchy. (p. 320)

Kubilai Khan Grandson of Chinggis Khan; commander of Mongol forces responsible for conquest of China; became khagan in 1260; established Sinicized Mongol Yuan dynasty in China in 1271. (p. 457)

Kumbi Saleh Capital of empire of Ghana; divided into two adjoining cities—one for the king, court, and indigenous people, one for the merchants, scholars, and religious leaders. (p. 206)

kuriltai Meeting of all Mongol chieftains at which the supreme ruler of all tribes was selected. (p. 450)

Kush An African state that developed along the upper reaches of the Nile c. 1000 B.C.E.; conquered Egypt and ruled it for several centuries. (p. 42)

Laozi Also known as Lao Tsu; major Chinese philosopher; recommended retreat from society into nature; individual should seek to become attuned with Dao. (p. 81)

legions The basic military unit of the Roman military; developed during the republic. (p. 152)

Lepanto Naval battle between the Spanish and the Ottoman Empire resulting in a Spanish victory in 1571; demonstrated European naval superiority over Muslims. (p. 499)

Liao dynasty Founded in 907 by nomadic Khitan peoples from Manchuria; maintained independence from Song dynasty in China. (p. 404)

Li Bo Most famous poet of the Tang era; blended images of the mundane world with philosophical musings. (p. 415)

Liu Bang Founder of the Han dynasty in 202 B.C.E. (p. 87)

Livy Roman historian who linked empire to traditions of republican past; stressed republican virtues popular in early empire. (p. 157)

Li Yuan Also known as Duke of Tang; minister for Yangdi; took over empire following assassination of Yangdi; first emperor of Tang dynasty; took imperial title of Gaozu. (p. 398)

llamas Along with alpacas, domesticated animals of the Americas; basis for only form of nomadic pastoralism in the New World until European importation of larger animals in 15th century C.E. (p. 187)

Locke, John English philosopher during 17th century; argued that people could learn everything through senses and reason; argued that power of government came from the people, not divine right of kings; offered possibility of revolution to overthrow tyrants. (p. 522)

loess [*lO* es, les, lus] Fine grained soil deposited in Ordos region in China bent by winds from central Asia; created fertile soil for sedentary agricultural communities. (p. 58)

long count Mayan system of dating from a fixed date in the past, 3114 B.C.E.; marked the beginning of a great cycle of 5200 years; allowed precision dating of events in Mayan history. (p. 178)

Louis XIV French monarch of the late 17th century who personified absolute monarchy. (p. 523)

Loyang Along with Xian, capital of the Zhou dynasty. (p. 63)

lunar cycle One of the principal means of establishing a calendar; based on cycles of moon; differed from solar cycles and failed to provide accurate guide to round of the seasons; required constant revision or intercalation. (p. 184)

Luther, Martin German monk; initiated Protestant Reformation in 1517 by nailing 95 theses to door of Wittenberg church; emphasized primacy of

faith over works stressed in Catholic church; accepted state control of church. (p. 516)

Macedon Kingdom located in northern Greece; originally loosely organized under kings, became centralized under Philip II; served as basis for unification of Greece and later Macedonian Empire. (p. 110)

Machiavelli, Niccolo [mak EE uh *vel* EE] Author of *The Prince* (16th century); emphasized realistic discussions of how to seize and maintain power; one of most influential authors of Italian Renaissance. (p. 514)

Magellan, Ferdinand Spanish captain who in 1519 initiated first circumnavigation of the globe; died during the voyage; allowed Spain to claim Philippines. (p. 495)

Maghrib [*mug* ruhb] The Arabic word for western north Africa. (p. 306)

Magna Carta Great Charter issued by King John of England in 1215; confirmed feudal rights against monarchical claims; represented principle of mutual limits and obligations between rulers and feudal aristocracy. (p. 352)

Mahabharata [muh *hä bär* uh tuh] Indian epic of war, princely honor, love, and social duty; written down in the last centuries B.C.E.; previously handed down in oral form. (p. 130)

Mahayana Chinese version of Buddhism; placed considerable emphasis on Buddha as god or savior. (p. 238)

Mahmud of Ghazni Third ruler of Turkish slave dynasty in Afghanistan; led invasions of northern India; credited with sacking one of wealthiest of Hindu temples in northern India; gave Muslims reputation for intolerance and aggression. (p. 293)

maize One of the staple crops of sedentary agriculturists in the Americas; domesticated by 4000 B.C.E. in central Mexico. (p. 173)

Malacca Portuguese factory or fortified trade town located on the tip of the Malayan peninsula; traditionally a center for trade among the southeastern Asian islands. (p. 297)

Mali Empire centered between the Senegal and Niger rivers; creation of Malinke peoples; broke away from control of Ghana in 13th century. (pp. 206, 309)

Mamluks Muslim slave warriors; established a dynasty in Egypt; defeated the Mongols at Ain Jalut in 1260 and halted Mongol advance. (p. 290)

mana Power of Hawaiian ali'i; emanated from their lineages and enabled them to extract labor or tribute from their subjects. (p. 222)

Mandate of Heaven The divine source for political legitimacy of Chinese rulers; established by Zhou to justify overthrow of Shang. (p. 64)

manioc One of staple crops of sedentary agriculturists in the Americas; principal crop of peoples of the lowlands of South America and the islands of the Caribbean. (p. 173)

manorialism System that described economic and political relations between landlords and their peasant laborers during the Middle Ages; involved a hierarchy of reciprocal obligations that exchanged labor or rents for access to land. (p. 347)

Maori Residents of New Zealand; migrated to New Zealand from Society Islands as early as 8th century C.E. (pp. 221, 223)

Marius Successful Roman general during the last century B.C.E.; introduced the concept of using paid volunteers in his army rather than citizen conscripts; created military force with personal loyalties to commander. (p. 154)

Martel, Charles Carolingian monarch of Franks; responsible for defeating Muslims in battle of Tours in 732; ended Muslim threat to western Europe. (p. 348)

matrilineal Family descent and inheritance traced through the female line. (p. 13)

matrilocal A culture in which young men upon marriage go to live with the brides' families. (p. 13)

Mauryas Dynasty established in Indian subcontinent in 4th century B.C.E. following invasion by Alexander the Great. (p. 136)

mawali Non-Arab converts to Islam. (p. 266)

Maya Classic culture emerging in southern Mexico and Central America contemporary with Teotihuacan; extended over broad region; featured monumental architecture, written language, calendrical and mathematical systems, highly developed religion. (p. 178)

Mecca City located in mountainous region along Red Sea in Arabian peninsula; founded by Umayyad clan of Quraysh; site of Ka'ba; original home of Muhammad; location of chief religious pilgrimage point in Islam. (p. 257)

Medina Also known as Yathrib; town located northeast of Mecca; grew date palms whose fruit was sold to bedouins; became refuge for Muhammad following flight from Mecca (hijra). (p. 258)

Mencius Also known as Meng Ko; follower of Confucius; stressed consent of the common people. (p. 81)

mercantilism Economic theory that stressed governments' promotion of limitation of imports from other nations and internal economies in order to improve tax revenues; popular during 17th and 18th centuries in Europe. (p. 499)

Mesoamerica Mexico and Central America; along with Peru, site of development of sedentary agriculture in Western hemisphere. (p. 173)

Mesopotamia Literally "between the rivers"; the civilizations that arose in the alluvial plain of the Tigris–Euphrates river valleys. (p. 27)

mestizos People of mixed European and Indian ancestry in Mesoamerica and South America; particularly prevalent in areas colonized by Spain; often part of forced labor system. (p. 500)

Methodius Along with Cyril, missionary sent by Byzantine government to eastern Europe and the Balkans; converted southern Russia and Balkans to Orthodox Christianity; responsible for creation of written script for Slavic known as Cyrillic. (p. 335)

Middle Ages The period in western European history from the decline and fall of the Roman Empire until the 15th century. (p. 345)

Minamoto Defeated the rival Taira family in Gempei Wars and established military government (bakufu) in 12th-century Japan. (p. 425)

Ming dynasty Succeeded Mongol Yuan dynasty in China in 1368; lasted until 1644; initially mounted huge trade expeditions to southern Asia and elsewhere, but later concentrated efforts on internal development within China. (p. 463)

Ministry of Rites Administered examinations to students from Chinese government schools or those recommended by distinguished scholars. (p. 399)

Minoan A civilization that developed on the island of Crete c. 1600 B.C.E.; capital at the palace complex of Knossos. (p. 45)

Mira Bai Celebrated Hindu writer of religious poetry; reflected openness of bhaktic cults to women. (p. 295)

miscegenation [mi se juh *nAY* shuhn, misi juh-] Practice of interracial marriage or sexual contact; found in virtually all colonial ventures. (p. 56)

Mississippian culture Last of the mound-building cultures of North America; flourished between 800 and 1300 C.E.; featured large towns and ceremonial centers; lacked stone architecture of Central America. (p. 183)

mita Labor extracted for lands assigned to the state and the religion; all communities were expected to contribute; an essential aspect of Inca imperial control. (p. 386)

moa Large, wingless birds native to New Zealand; hunted to extinction by early settlers; extinction established need to develop new sources of protein. (p. 223)

Mochica state Flourished in Andes north of Chavín culture in Moche valley between 200 and 700 C.E.; featured great clay-brick temples; created military chiefdom supported by extensive irrigated agriculture. (p. 189)

Mohenjo Daro Along with Harappa, major urban complex of the Harappan civilization; laid out on planned grid pattern. (p. 50)

moldboard Heavy plow introduced in northern Europe during the Middle Ages; permitted deeper cultivation of heavier soils; a technological innovation of the medieval agricultural system. (p. 347)

Mongols Central Asian nomadic peoples; smashed Turko-Persian kingdoms; captured Baghdad in 1258 and killed last Abbasid caliph. (p. 290)

monotheism The exclusive worship of a single god; introduced by the Jews into Western civilization. (p. 44)

monsoons Seasonal winds crossing Indian subcontinent and southeast Asia; during summer bring rains. (p. 50)

montaña Located on eastern slopes of Andes mountains; location of cultivation and gathering

of tropical fruits and coca leaf. (p. 187)

Monte Alban Chief center of Zapotec culture in southern Mexico during preclassic period; contemporary with Olmec culture; based on irrigated agriculture and calendrical and writing systems. (p. 176)

Mu'awiya [mU *ä* wEE ä] Leader of Umayyad clan; first Umayyad caliph following civil war with Ali. (p. 265)

Muhammad Prophet of Islam; born c. 570 to Banu Hashim clan of Quraysh tribe in Mecca; raised by father's family; received revelations from Allah in 610 C.E. and thereafter; died in 632. (p. 253)

Muhammad ibn Qasim Arab general; conquered Sind in India; declared the region and the Indus valley to be part of Umayyad Empire. (p. 292)

Muhammad of Ghur Military commander of Persian extraction who ruled small mountain kingdom in Afghanistan; began process of conquest to establish Muslim political control of northern India; brought much of Indus valley, Sind, and northwestern India under his control. (p. 294)

Muhammad Shah II Turkic ruler of Muslim Khwarazm kingdom; attempted to resist Mongol conquest; conquered in 1220. (p. 451)

Muhammad the Great Extended the boundaries of the Songhay Empire; Islamic ruler of the mid-16th century. (p. 312)

mummification The act of preserving the bodies of the dead; practiced in Egypt to preserve the body for enjoyment of the after-life. (p. 38)

Muslim   Follower of Islam. (p. 253)

Nahuatl   [*nä* wät l] Language spoken by the Toltecs and Aztecs. (p. 182)

Nara   Along with Heian, capital of the Yamato emperors; patterned after ancient imperial centers of China; never fully populated. (p. 218)

Narmer   First pharaoh of Egyptian Old Kingdom; ruled c. 3100 B.C.E. (p. 36)

Natufian complex Preagricultural culture; located in present-day Israel, Jordan, and Lebanon; practiced the collection of naturally present barley and wheat to supplement game; typified by large settlement sites. (p. 11)

Neanderthals   Species of genus *Homo* that disappeared at the end of the Paleolithic period. (p. 8)

neo-Confucians   Revived ancient Confucian teachings in Song era China; great impact on the dynasties that followed; their emphasis on tradition and hostility to foreign systems made Chinese rulers and bureaucrats less receptive to outside ideas and influences. (p. 405)

Neolithic Age   The New Stone Age between 8000 and 5000 B.C.E.; period in which adaptation of sedentary agriculture occurred; domestication of plants and animals accomplished. (p. 7)

Neolithic revolution   The succession of technological innovations and changes in human organization that led to the development of agriculture, 8500–3500 B.C.E. (p. 14)

Nestorians   A Christian sect found in Asia; tended to support Islamic invasions of this area in preference to Byzantine rule; cut off from Europe by Muslim invasions. (p. 264)

New France   French colonies in North America; extended from St. Lawrence River along Great Lakes and down Mississippi River valley system. (p. 503)

Newton, Isaac   English scientist during the 17th century; author of *Principia;* drew the various astronomical and physical observations and wider theories together in a neat framework of natural laws; established principles of motion; defined forces of gravity. (p. 521)

Nezhualcoyotl   [nez wät l coiOt l] Leading Aztec king of the 15th century. (p. 375)

Nguyen   [ngI *en, ngu yen*] Rival Vietnamese dynasty that arose in southern Vietnam to challenge traditional dynasty of Trinh in north at Hanoi; kingdom centered on Red and Mekong rivers; capital at Hue. (p. 441)

nirvana   The Buddhist state of enlightenment, a state of tranquility. (p. 134)

Nok   Culture featuring highly developed art style flourishing between 500 B.C.E. and 200 C.E.; located in forests of central Nigeria. (pp. 202, 318)

nomads   Cattle- and sheep-herding societies normally found on the fringes of civilized societies; commonly referred to as "barbarian" by civilized societies. (p. 10)

Northern Renaissance Cultural and intellectual movement of northern Europe; began later than Italian Renaissance c. 1450; centered in France, Low Countries, England, and Germany; featured greater emphasis on religion than Italian Renaissance. (p. 515)

nuclear families   Consisted of husband and wife, their children, and perhaps a grandmother or orphaned cousin; typical of Chinese peasantry. (p. 60)

Odyssey   Greek epic poem attributed to Homer but possibly the work of many authors; defined gods and human nature that shaped Greek mythos. (p. 103)

Ogedei   Third son of Chinggis Khan; succeeded Chinggis Khan as khagan of the Mongols following his father's death. (p. 452)

Olmec culture   Cultural tradition that arose at San Lorenzo and La Venta in Mexico c. 1200 B.C.E.; featured irrigated agriculture, urbanism, elaborate religion, beginnings of calendrical and writing systems. (p. 176)

Olympic games   One of the pan-Hellenic rituals observed by all Greek city-states; involved athletic competitions and ritual celebrations. (p. 107)

oracle at Delphi   Person representing the god Apollo; allegedly received cryptic messages from the god that had predictive value if the seeker could correctly interpret the communication. (p. 108)

oracles   Shamans or priests in Chinese society who foretold the future through interpretations of animal bones cracked by heat; inscriptions on bones led to Chinese writing. (p. 60)

Ordos bulge Located on Huanghe River; region of fertile soil; site of Yangshao and Longshan cultures. (p. 58)

Ottoman Empire Turkic empire established in Asia Minor and eventually extending throughout Middle East; responsible for conquest of Constantinople and end of Byzantine Empire in 1453; succeeded Seljuk Turks following retreat of Mongols. (p. 283)

Ovid Roman poet exiled by Augustus for sensual poetry considered out of touch with the imperial policies stressing family virtues. (p. 157)

Pachacuti Ruler of Inca society from 1438 to 1471; launched a series of military campaigns that gave Incas control of the region from Cuzco to the shores of Lake Titicaca. (p. 384)

Paekche Independent Korean kingdom in southeastern part of peninsula; defeated by rival Silla kingdom and its Chinese Tang allies in 7th century. (p. 431)

pahi Double canoes used for long-distance voyaging; carried a platform between canoes for passengers or cargo. (p. 221)

Paleolithic Age The Old Stone Age ending in 12,000 B.C.E.; typified by use of crude stone tools and hunting and gathering for subsistence. (p. 7)

parliamentary monarchy Originated in England and Holland, 17th century, with kings partially checked by significant legislative powers in parliaments. (p. 526)

parliaments Bodies representing privileged groups; institutionalized feudal principle that rulers should consult with their vassals; found in England, Spain, Germany, and France. (p. 352)

pastoral nomads An intermediate form of ecological adaptation dependant on domesticated animal herds that feed on natural environment; typically more populous than shifting cultivation groups. (p. 208)

pastoralism A nomadic agricultural lifestyle based on herding domesticated animals; tended to produce independent people capable of challenging sedentary agricultural societies. (p. 15)

patriarchal [*pAY* trEE är k'l] Societies in which women defer to men; societies run by men and based on the assumption that men naturally directed political, economic, and cultural life. (p. 41)

patrilineal Family descent and inheritance traced through the male line. (p. 57)

Paul One of the first Christian missionaries; moved away from insistence that adherents of the new religion follow Jewish law; use of Greek as language of Church. (p. 159)

Peloponnesian Wars Wars from 431 to 404 B.C.E. between Athens and Sparta for dominance in southern Greece; resulted in Spartan victory but failure to achieve political unification of Greece. (p. 107)

Pericles Athenian political leader during 5th century B.C.E.; guided development of Athenian Empire; died during early stages of Peloponnesian War. (p. 106)

Persian Wars Two wars fought in early 5th century B.C.E. between Persian Empire and Greek city-states; Greek victories allowed Greek civilization to define identity separate from the Asian empire. (p. 108)

pharaoh Title of kings of ancient Egypt. (p. 36)

Philip II Ruled Macedon from 359 to 336 B.C.E.; founder of centralized kingdom; later conquered rest of Greece, which was subjected to Macedonian authority. (p. 110)

Phoenicians Seafaring civilization located on the shores of the eastern Mediterranean; established colonies throughout the Mediterranean. (p. 45)

Pisastratus Athenian tyrant of the 6th century B.C.E.; gained popular support against traditional aristocratic councils of Athenian government. (p. 105)

Pizarro, Francisco Led conquest of Inca Empire of Peru beginning in 1535; by 1540, most of Inca possessions fell to the Spanish. (p. 502)

Plato Greek philosopher; knowledge based on consideration of ideal forms outside the material world; proposed ideal form of government based on abstract principles in which philosophers ruled. (p. 113)

plebeians Ordinary citizens; originally those Roman families that could not trace their relationship to one of the major Roman clans. (p. 151)

pochteca [poKH tAY cä] Special merchant class in Aztec society; specialized in long-distance trade in luxury items. (p. 378)

polis City-state form of government; typical of Greek political organization from 800 to 400 B.C.E. (pl. poleis). (p. 20)

Politburo Executive committee of the Soviet Communist party; 20 members. (p. 876)

polyandry [*pol* EE an drEE, pol EE *an-*] Marriage practice in which one woman had several husbands; recounted in Aryan epics. (p. 57)

polygamy Marriage practice in which one husband had several wives; practiced in Aryan society. (p. 57)

Polynesia Islands contained in a rough triangle whose points lie in Hawaii, New Zealand, and Easter Island. (p. 221)

pope Bishop of Rome; head of the Christian Church in western Europe. (p. 239)

potter's wheel A technological advance in potterymaking; invented c. 6000 B.C.E.; encouraged faster and higher-quality ceramic pottery production. (p. 27)

Prester John Name given to a mythical Christian monarch whose kingdom had supposedly been cut off from Europe by the Muslim conquests; Chinggis Khan was originally believed to be this mythical ruler. (p. 455)

proletariat Class of working people without access to producing property; typically manufacturing workers, paid laborers in agricultural economy, or urban poor; in Europe, product of economic changes of 16th and 17th centuries. (p. 519)

Protestantism General wave of religious dissent against Catholic church; generally held to have begun with Martin Luther's attack on Catholic beliefs in 1517; included many varieties of religious belief. (p. 516)

Ptolemies One of the regional dynasties that followed the death of Alexander the Great; founded in Egypt. (p. 111)

puna High valleys and steppes lying between the two major chains of the Andes mountains; site of South American agricultural origins, also only location of pastoralism in Americas. (p. 186)

Punic Wars Fought between Rome and Carthage to establish dominance in the western Mediterranean; won by Rome after three separate conflicts. (p. 152)

pure land Buddhism Emphasized salvationist aspects of Chinese Buddhism; popular among masses of Chinese society. (p. 400)

Pygmies One of few pure hunting societies left in Africa following Bantu migration. (p. 203)

pyramids Monumental architecture typical of Old Kingdom Egypt; used as burial sites for pharaohs. (p. 37)

Qin dynasty [chin] Established in 221 B.C.E. at the end of the Warring States period following the decline of the Zhou dynasty; fell in 207 B.C.E. (p. 77)

Quetzalcoatl [ket säl kO *ät* l] Toltec deity; Feathered Serpent; adopted by Aztecs as a major god. (p. 372)

quipu System of knotted strings utilized by the Incas in place of a writing system; could contain numerical and other types of information for censuses and financial records. (p. 388)

Qur'an [koo *rän, -ran*] Recitations of revelations received by Muhammad; holy book of Islam. (p. 253)

Quraysh [koor *Ish*] Tribe of bedouins that controlled Mecca in 7th century C.E. (p. 257)

Qutb-ud-din Aibak [kUt bUd *dEEn* I *bäk*] Lieutenant of Muhammad of Ghur; established kingdom in India with capital at Delphi; proclaimed himself Sultan of India. (p. 294)

Rajput [*räj* pUt] Regional princes in western India; emphasized military control of their regions. (p. 232)

Rama Major figure in the popular Indian epic *Ramayana*. (p. 130)

Ramadan Islamic month of religious observance requiring fasting from dawn to sunset. (p. 262)

Ramayana One of the great epic tales from classical India; traces adventures of King Rama and his wife, Sita. (p. 130)

reincarnation The successive attachment of the soul to some animate form according to merits earned in previous lives. (p. 130)

Renaissance Cultural and political movement in western Europe; began in Italy c. 1400; rested on urban vitality and expanding commerce; featured a literature and art with distinctly more secular priorities than those of the Middle Ages. (p. 472)

Ridda Wars Wars that followed Muhammad's death in 632; resulted in defeat of rival prophets and some of larger clans; restored unity of Islam. (p. 263)

Romance of the West Chamber Chinese novel written during the

Yuan period; indicative of the continued literary vitality of China during Mongol rule. (p. 461)

Roman republic   The balanced constitution of Rome from c. 510 to 47 B.C.E.; featured an aristocratic Senate, a panel of magistrates, and several popular assemblies. (p. 150)

Rurik   Legendary Scandinavian, regarded as founder of the first kingdom of Russia based in Kiev in 855 C.E. (p. 337)

Russian Orthodoxy   Russian form of Christianity imported from Byzantine Empire and combined with local religion; king characteristically controlled major appointments. (p. 338)

Sahara   Desert running across northern Africa; separates the Mediterranean coast from southern Africa. (p. 197)

sahel   The extensive grassland belt at the southern edge of the Sahara; a point of exchange between the forests to the south and northern Africa. (pp. 197, 308)

saints   Holy men and women, often martyrs, who were revered in Christianity as models of Christian lifestyles; built up treasury of merit that could be tapped by more ordinary Christians. (p. 238)

Saladin   Muslim leader in the last decades of the 12th century; reconquered most of the crusader outposts for Islam. (p. 283)

samurai   Mounted troops of Japanese warrior leaders (bushi); loyal to local lords, not the emperor. (p. 424)

Sanskrit   The sacred and classical Indian language. (p. 55)

Sargon I   Ruler of city-state of Akkad; established the first empire in Mesopotamian civilization c. 2400 B.C.E. (p. 32)

sati   Ritual in India of immolating surviving widows with the bodies of their deceased husbands. (p. 295)

savages   Societies engaged in either hunting and gathering for subsistence or in migratory cultivation; not as stratified or specialized as civilized and nomadic societies. (p. 20)

scholar-gentry   Chinese class created by the marital linkage of the local land-holding aristocracy with the office-holding shi; superseded shi as governors of China. (p. 89)

scholasticism   Dominant medieval philosophical approach; so-called because of its base in the schools or universities; based on use of logic to resolve theological problems. (p. 357)

Scientific Revolution Culminated in 17th century; period of empirical advances associated with the development of wider theoretical generalizations; resulted in change in traditional beliefs of Middle Ages. (p. 520)

secret societies   Chinese peasant organizations; provided financial support in hard times and physical protection in case of disputes with local aristocracy. (p. 92)

Seleucids   [si *lU* sids, -cids] One of the regional dynasties that followed the death of Alexander the Great; founded in Mesopotamia. (p. 111)

Seljuk Turks   Nomadic invaders from central Asia via Persia; staunch Sunnis; ruled in name of Abbasid caliphs from mid-11th century. (p. 283)

Senate   Assembly of Roman aristocrats; advised on policy within the republic; one of the early elements of the Roman constitution. (p. 150)

sepukku   Ritual suicide or disembowelment in Japan; commonly known in West as hara-kiri; demonstrated courage and a means to restore family honor. (p. 425)

serfs   Peasant agricultural laborers within the manorial system of the Middle Ages. (p. 347)

Seven Years' War   Fought both in continental Europe and also in overseas colonies between 1756 and 1763; resulted in Prussian seizures of land from Austria, English seizures of colonies in India and North America. (p. 503)

Shah-Nama   Written by Firdawsi in late 10th and early 11th centuries; relates history of Persia from creation to the Islamic conquests. (p. 286)

Shang   First Chinese dynasty for which archeological evidence exists; capital located in Ordos bend. (p. 59)

Sharia   [shä *rEE* ä] Islamic law; defined among other things the patrilineal nature of Islamic inheritance. (p. 313)

shaykhs   [shAYks] Leaders of tribes and clans within bedouin society; usually men with large herds, several wives, and many children. (p. 255)

shi Probably originally priests; transformed into corps of professional bureaucrats because of knowledge of writing during Zhou dynasty in China. (p. 63)

Shi Huangdi [*shOE hwäng dEE*] Founder of the brief Qin dynasty in 221 B.C.E. (p. 77)

Shi'a Also known as Shi'ites; political and theological division within Islam; followers of Ali. (p. 265)

shifting cultivation An intermediate form of ecological adaptation in which temporary forms of cultivation are carried out with little impact on the natural ecology; typical of rainforest cultivators. (p. 15)

Shinto Religion of early Japanese culture; devotees worshipped numerous gods and spirits associated with the natural world; offers of food and prayers made to gods and nature spirits. (p. 216)

Shiva Hindu, god of destruction and reproduction; worshipped as the personification of cosmic forces of change. (p. 140)

shoguns Military leaders of the bakufu (military governments in Japan). (p. 426)

Shrivijaya [srEE wi *jô* yuh] Trading empire centered on Malacca Straits between Malaya and Sumatra; controlled trade of empire; Buddhist government resistant to Muslim missionaries; fall opened up southeastern Asia to Muslim conversion. (p. 297)

Signet Ring of Rakshasa One of great Sanskrit dramas produced during the Gupta Empire; dramatized authority of Brahmans. (p. 141)

Silk Roads The most famous of the trading routes established by pastoral nomads connecting the European, Indian, and Chinese civilizations; transmitted goods and ideas among civilizations. (p. 98)

Silla Independent Korean kingdom in southeastern part of peninsula; defeated Koguryo along with their Chinese Tang allies; submitted as a vassal of the Tang emperor and agreed to tribute payment; ruled united Korea by 668. (p. 431)

Sinification Extensive adaptation of Chinese culture in other regions; typical of Korea and Japan, less typical of Vietnam. (p. 431)

Skanda Gupta Last of the able rulers of the Gupta dynasty; following his reign the empire dissolved under the pressure of nomadic invasions. (p. 146)

slash and burn agriculture A system of cultivation typical of shifting cultivators; forest floors cleared by fire are then planted. (p. 178)

Smith, Adam Established liberal economics (*Wealth of Nations*, 1776); argued that government should avoid regulation of economy in favor of the operation of market forces. (p. 527)

Socrates Athenian philosopher of later 5th century B.C.E.; tutor of Plato; urged rational reflection of moral decisions; condemned to death for corrupting minds of Athenian young. (p. 113)

solar cycle Calendrical system based on solar year; typical of all civilizations; variations of solar calendars in Western civilization are Julian and Gregorian calendars; Mayas also constructed solar calendar. (p. 184)

Solon Athenian reformer of the 6th century; established laws that eased burden of debt on farmers, forbade enslavement for debt. (p. 105)

Songhay Successor state to Mali; dominated middle reaches of Niger valley; formed as independent kingdom under a Berber dynasty; capital at Gao; reached imperial status under Sunni Ali (1464–1492). (p. 312)

Sophocles Greek writer of tragedies; author of *Oedipus Rex*. (p. 114)

Southern Song Rump state of Song dynasty from 1127 to 1279; carved out of much larger domains ruled by the Tang and northern Song; culturally one of the most glorious reigns in Chinese history. (p. 407)

split inheritance Inca practice of descent; all titles and political power went to successor, but wealth and land remained in hands of male descendants for support of cult of dead Inca's mummy. (p. 384)

stateless societies African societies organized around kinship or other forms of obligation and lacking the concentration of political power and authority associated with states. (p. 305)

stelae Large memorial pillars erected to commemorate triumphs and events in the lives of Maya rulers. (p. 178)

Stoics Hellenistic group of philosophers; emphasized inner moral independence cultivated by strict discipline of the body and personal bravery. (p. 113)

stupas Stone shrines built to house pieces of bone or hair and personal possessions said to be relics of the Buddha; preserved Buddhist architectural forms. (p. 137)

Sudanic states Kingdoms that developed during the height of Ghana's power in the region; based at Takrur on the Senegal River to the west and Gao on the Niger River to the east; included Mali and Songhay. (pp. 206, 308)

Sufis Mystics within Islam; responsible for expansion of Islam to southeastern Asia and other regions. (p. 288)

Sui Dynasty that succeeded the Han in China; emerged from strong rulers in northern China; united all of northern China and reconquered southern China. (p. 231)

Sulla Conservative military commander during last century B.C.E.; attempted to reinforce powers of the Senate and to undo influence of Marius. (p. 154)

Sumerians People who migrated into Mesopotamia c. 4000 B.C.E.; created first civilization within region; organized area into city-states. (p. 29)

Sundiata The "Lion Prince"; a member of the Keita clan; created a unified state that became the Mali Empire; died about 1260. (p. 309)

Sunnis Political and theological division within Islam. (p. 265)

Sunzi [hsun tzu, shUn] A 4th century B.C.E. advisor to Chinese monarch, who wrote the classic treatise *The Art of War*. (p. 81)

Taika reforms [*tI* kä] Attempt to remake Japanese monarch into an absolute Chinese-style emperor; included attempts to create professional bureaucracy and peasant conscript army. (p. 420)

Taira Powerful Japanese family in 11th and 12th centuries; competed with Minamoto family; defeated after Gempei Wars. (p. 425)

tambos Way stations used by Incas as inns and storehouses; supply centers for Inca armies on move; relay points for system of runners used to carry messages. (p. 386)

Tang Dynasty that succeeded the Sui in 618 C.E.; more stable than previous dynasty. (p. 231)

Tangut Rulers of Xi Xia kingdom of northwest China; one of regional kingdoms during period of southern Song; conquered by Mongols in 1226. (p. 406)

Tatars Mongols; captured Russian cities and largely destroyed Kievan state in 1236; left Russian Orthodoxy and aristocracy intact. (p. 340)

Tatu Mongol capital of Yuan dynasty; present-day Beijing. (p. 458)

Temple of the Sun Inca religious center located at Cuzco; center of state religion; held mummies of past Incas. (p. 385)

Tenochtitlan [tAY nôch tEE *tlän*] Founded c. 1325 on marshy island in Lake Texcoco; became center of Aztec power; joined with Tlacopan and Texcoco in 1434 to form a triple alliance that controlled most of central plateau of Mesoamerica. (p. 374)

Teotihuacan [tAY O tEE wä *kän*] Site of classic culture in central Mexico; urban center with important religious functions; supported by intensive agriculture in surrounding regions; population of as much as 200,000. (p. 177)

The Tale of Genji Written by Lady Murasaki; first novel in any language; relates life history of prominent and amorous son of the Japanese emperor; evidence for mannered style of Japanese society. (p. 422)

Thirty Years' War War within the Holy Roman Empire between German Protestants and their allies (Sweden, Denmark, France) and the emperor and his ally, Spain; ended in 1648 after great destruction with Treaty of Westphalia. (p. 517)

three-field system System of agricultural cultivation by 9th century in western Europe; included one-third in spring grains, one-third fallow. (p. 347)

Tian Heaven; an abstract conception in early Chinese religion; possibly the combined spirits of all male ancestors; first appeared during Zhou dynasty. (p. 66)

Tihuanaco [*tEE* uh wuh *nä* kO] Along with Huari, large center for regional chiefdoms between 300 and 900 C.E.; located in southern Peru; featured large ceremonial center supported by extensive irrigated agriculture; established widely diffused religious and artistic symbols spread all over Andean zone. (p. 189)

Timbuktu   Port city of Mali; located just off the flood plain on the great bend in the Niger River; population of 50,000; contained a library and university. (p. 311)

Timur-i Lang   Also known as Tamerlane; leader of Turkic nomads; beginning in 1360s from base at Samarkand, launched series of attacks in Persia, the Fertile Crescent, India, and southern Russia; empire disintegrated after his death in 1405. (p. 463)

Tlaloc   [tlä *lOk*] Major god of Aztecs; associated with fertility and the agricultural cycle; god of rain. (p. 374)

Toltec culture   Succeeded Teotihuacan culture in central Mexico; strongly militaristic ethic including human sacrifice; influenced large territory after 1000 C.E.; declined after 1200 C.E. (p. 372)

Toltecs   Nomadic peoples from beyond the northern frontier of the sedentary agricultural area in Mesoamerica; established capital of Tula following migration into central Mesoamerican plateau. (p. 182)

Topiltzin   Religious leader and reformer of the Toltecs; dedicated to god Quetzalcoatl; after losing struggle for power, went into exile in the Yucatan peninsula. (p. 372)

Trajan   Emperor from 101 to 106 C.E.; instituted more aggressive imperial foreign policy resulting in expansion of empire to its greatest limits. (p. 158)

transhumant   A form of pastoralism common to the Mediterranean basin and the Sahara; involves moving from one region to another according to the season. (p. 199)

Treaty of Paris   Arranged in 1763 following Seven Years' War; granted New France to England in exchange for return of French sugar island in Caribbean. (p. 504)

Treaty of Westphalia   Ended Thirty Years' War in 1648; granted right to individual rulers within the Holy Roman Empire to choose their own religion—either Protestant or Catholic. (p. 517)

tribunes   Plebeian representatives in the Roman republic; elected in the Concilium Plebis Tributum on an annual basis. (p. 151)

Trinh   Dynasty that ruled in north Vietnam at Hanoi; rivals of Nguyen family in south. (p. 441)

Trung sisters   Leaders of one of the frequent peasant rebellions in Vietnam against Chinese rule; revolt broke out in 39 C.E.; demonstrates importance of Vietnamese women in indigenous society. (p. 438)

tsetse fly   [*tset* sEE, *tet-*, *tsEE* tsEE] Flourished in wet lowlands; carried sleeping sickness that severely limited pastoralism in western and central Africa. (p. 199)

tumens   Basic fighting units of the Mongol forces; consisted of 10,000 cavalrymen; each unit was further divided into units of 1000, 100, and 10. (p. 450)

Twantinsuyu   [twän tin sUyU] Word for Inca Empire; region from present-day Colombia to Chile and eastward to northern Argentina. (p. 383)

ulama   Orthodox religious scholars within Islam; pressed for a more conservative and restrictive theology; increasingly opposed to non-Islamic ideas and scientific thinking. (p. 288)

Umayyad   [U *mI* yad] Clan of Quraysh that dominated politics and commercial economy of Mecca; clan later able to establish dynasty as rulers of Islam. (p. 257)

umma   Community of the faithful within Islam; transcended old tribal boundaries to create degree of political unity. (p. 261)

untouchables   Outcaste in Hindu society; performed tasks that were considered polluting—street sweeping, removal of human waste, and tanning. (p. 130)

Upanishads   [U *pan* i shad, U *pä* ni shäd] Later books of the Vedas; contained sophisticated and sublime philosophical ideas; utilized by Brahmans to restore religious authority. (p. 140)

Urban II   Called First Crusade in 1095; appealed to Christians to mount military assault to free the Holy Land from the Muslims. (p. 353)

Uthman   Third caliph and member of Umayyad clan; murdered by mutinous warriors returning from Egypt; death set off civil war in Islam between followers of Ali and the Umayyad clan. (p. 264)

varnas   Clusters of caste groups in Aryan society; four social castes—Brahmans (priests), warriors, merchants, and peasants; beneath four Aryan castes was group of socially untouchable Dasas. (p. 129)

vassal retainers   Members of former ruling families granted control over the peasant and artisan populations of areas throughout Shang kingdom; indirectly exploited wealth of their territories. (p. 60)

vassals   Members of the military elite who received land or a benefice from a lord in return for military service and loyalty. (p. 351)

Vedas   Aryan hymns originally transmitted orally but written down in sacred books from the 6th century B.C.E. (p. 55)

Vergil   One of greatest of Roman poets during "Golden Age" of Latin literature; patronized by Augustus; author of *Aeneid*. (p. 156)

Vikings   Seagoing Scandinavian raiders from Sweden, Denmark, and Norway who disrupted coastal areas of western Europe from the 8th to the 11th centuries. (p. 346)

Vishnu   The Brahman, later Hindu, god of sacrifice; widely worshipped. (p. 140)

Vivaldis   Two Genoese brothers who attempted to find a Western route to the "Indies"; disappeared in 1291; precursors of thrust into southern Atlantic. (p. 475)

Vladimir I   Ruler of Russian kingdom of Kiev from 980 to 1015; converted kingdom to Christianity. (p. 337)

Völkerwanderungen   [*fölk* er van der Ungen] Movement of Germanic peoples southward into the Roman Empire; resulted from population growth, pressure of Asian groups on eastern flanks of Germanic regions. (p. 214)

Wang Anshi   Confucian scholar and chief minister of a Song emperor in 1070s; introduced sweeping reforms based on Legalists; advocated greater state intervention in society. (p. 406)

Wang Mang   Member of one of the powerful families related to the Han emperors through marriage; temporarily overthrew the Han between 9 and 23 C.E. (p. 96)

wazir   Chief administrative official under the Abbasid caliphate; initially recruited from Persian provinces of empire. (p. 270)

Wendi   Member of prominent northern Chinese family during period of Six Dynasties; proclaimed himself emperor; supported by nomadic peoples of northern China; established Sui dynasty. (p. 396)

White Lotus Society   Secret religious society dedicated to overthrow of Yuan dynasty in China; typical of peasant resistance to Mongol rule. (p. 461)

William the Conqueror   Invaded England from Normandy in 1066; extended tight feudal system to England; established administrative system based on sheriffs; established centralized monarchy. (p. 352)

witchcraft persecution   Reflected resentment against the poor, uncertainties about religious truth; resulted in death of over 100,000 Europeans between 1590 and 1650; particularly common in Protestant areas. (p. 520)

Wollstonecraft, Mary   Enlightenment feminist thinker in England; argued that new political rights should extend to women. (p. 529)

world economy   Established by Europeans by the 16th century; based on control of seas, including the Atlantic and Pacific; created international exchange of foods, diseases, and manufactured products. (p. 491)

Wu   First of the Zhou to be recognized as king, 1122 B.C.E. (p. 63)

Wuzong   Chinese emperor of Tang dynasty who openly persecuted Buddhism by destroying monasteries in 840s; reduced influence of Chinese Buddhism in favor of Confucian ideology. (p. 402)

Xia   [*shEE ä*] China's first, possibly mythical, kingdom; no archeological sites have been connected to it; ruled by Yu. (p. 59)

Xian   [*shEE än*] Along with Loyang, capital of the Zhou dynasty. (p. 63)

Xi Xia   Kingdom of Tangut people, north of Song kingdom, in mid-11th century; collected tribute that drained Song resources and burdened Chinese peasantry. (p. 406)

Xuanzong   [*shU än jonh,* shwantsong] Leading Chinese emperor of the Tang dynasty who reigned from 713 to 755 though he encouraged overexpansion. (p. 403)

Yamato   Japanese clan that gained increasing dominance in the 4th and 5th centuries C.E.; created imperial cult around Amaterasu and Shinto; brought most of the lowland plains of the southern islands under control. (p. 217)

yanas A class of people within Inca society removed from their ayllus to serve permanently as servants, artisans, or workers for the inca or the Inca nobility. (p. 387)

Yang Guifei [*yäng gwä fä*] Royal concubine during reign of Xuanzong; introduction of relatives into royal administration led to revolt. (p. 403)

Yangdi Second member of Sui dynasty; murdered his father to gain throne; restored Confucian examination system; responsible for construction of Chinese canal system; assassinated in 618. (p. 397)

Yaroslav Last of great Kievan monarchs; issued legal codification based on formal codes developed in Byzantium. (p. 338)

Yayoi epoch [ya yU] Last centuries B.C.E. in Japan; featured introduction of wet-rice cultivation, iron working; produced wheel-turned pottery and sophisticated bronzeware. (p. 216)

Yellow River Also known as the Huanghe; site of development of sedentary agriculture in China. (p. 58)

Yellow Turbans Chinese Daoists who launched a revolt in

184 C.E. in China promising a golden age to be brought about by divine magic. (p. 228)

Yi Korean dynasty that succeeded Koryo dynasty following period of Mongol invasions; established in 1392; ruled Korea to 1910; restored aristocratic dominance and Chinese influence. (p. 434)

Yoruba City-states developed in northern Nigeria c. 1200 C.E.; Ile-Ife featured artistic style possibly related to earlier Nok culture; agricultural societies supported by peasantry and dominated by ruling family and aristocracy. (pp. 202, 318)

Yu A possible mythical Chinese ruler revered for the construction of an effective system of flood control along the Huanghe River valley; founder of the Xia kingdom. (p. 59)

zakat Tax for charity; obligatory for all Muslims. (p. 261)

Zen Buddhism Known as Chan Buddhism in China; stressed meditation and the appreciation of natural and artistic beauty. (p. 400)

Zenj Arabic term for the east African coast. (p. 315)

Zhao Kuangyin [jaoo *kwän yin*] Founder of Song dynasty;

originally a general following fall of Tang; took title of Taizu; failed to overcome northern Liao dynasty that remained independent. (p. 404)

Zhenghe Chinese Muslim admiral who commanded series of Indian Ocean, Persian Gulf, and Red Sea trade expeditions under third Ming emperor, Yunglo, between 1405 and 1433. (p. 469)

Zhou Originally a vassal family of Shang China; possibly Turkic in origin; overthrew Shang and established second historical Chinese dynasty. (p. 63)

Zhu Xi [tsU shEE, ju shEE] Most prominent of neo-Confucian scholars during the Song dynasty in China; stressed importance of applying philosophical principles to everyday life and action. (p. 405)

ziggurats Massive towers usually associated with Mesopotamian temple complexes. (p. 31)

Zoroastriansim [zôr O *as* trEE uh niz uhm, zOr-] Animist religion that saw material existence as battle between forces of good and evil; stressed the importance of moral choice; righteous lived on after death in "House of Song"; chief religion of Persian Empire. (p. 102)

CREDITS

Literary Credits

PART I

Chapter 1
From *A History of Human Community, Third Edition* by W.H. McNeil, copyright © 1990. Reprinted by permission of Prentice-Hall, Inc., Upper Saddle River, NJ.

Chapter 2
Excerpts from *The Babylonian Laws*, edited and translated by G.R. Driver and John C. Miles. Copyright © 1955 Oxford University Press. Reprinted by permission of Oxford University Press.

Chapter 3
From A. L. Bashman, *The Wonder That Was India* by A.L. Bashman. London Sidgwick and Jackson Ltd., 1954.

PART II

Chapter 5
Excerpts from *The Greek Way* by Edith Hamilton. Copyright 1930, 1943 by W. W. Norton & company, Inc., renewed © 1958, 1971 by Dorian Reid. Used by permission of W. W. Norton & Company, Inc.

Chapter 10
Excerpt from *Chinese Civilization and Society: A Sourcebook* edited by Patricia Buckley Ebrey. Copyright © 1981 by The Free Press. Reprinted with the permission of The Free Press, a Division of Simon & Schuster Adult Publishing Group.

PART III

Chapter 12
From Rosenthal, Franz; *The Mudquaddimah: An Introduction to History, Vol. 1.* Copyright © 1958 by Princeton University Press. Reprinted by permission of Princeton University Press.

Chapter 15
From *The Goodman of Paris*, translated by Eileen Power. London: George Routledge and Sons, 1929.

Chapter 16
Map of Inca Empire from *Atlas of Ancient America* by Coe, Snow and Benson, copyright © 1986, p. 196. Reprinted by permission of Andromeda Oxford Ltd., Abington, UK.

Chapter 18
Poem by Ki no Tsurayuki from *Japanese Culture*, © 1977 by H. Paul Varley. Reprinted by permission of Henry Holt and Company, LLC.

From *Cultural Atlas of Japan* by M. Collcutt, copyright © 1988. Reprinted by permission of Andromeda Oxford Ltd., Abington, UK.

Chapter 19
Abridgment of "The Mongols in the Eyes of the Europeans" from *History of the Mongols* by Bertold Spuler, translated by Helga and Stuart Drummond, copyright 1988. Copyright © 1972 by Routledge Kegan Paul. Reprinted with permission of the The Regents of the University of California.

Photo Credits

PART I

Chapter 1
Chapter Opener 01 Douglas Mazonowicz/Art Resource, NY; **Figure 01.01** Reprinted from *Life: Introduction to Biology*, 3rd ed., by Beck, Liem & Simpson ©1991/Reprinted by permission Harper-Collins Publishers, Inc.; **01.02** Musée de l'Homme, Paris; **Document** Ralph Morse; **01.03** *From Past Worlds: Archaeology*, Time Books, London; **01.04** Robert Harding Picture Library; **Visualizing the Past Image 1** *Encyclopedia Universalis*, **Image 2** Dr. P. G. Bahn, Hull, England

Chapter 2
Chapter Opener 02 Robert Frerck/Odyssey Productions, Chicago; **Figure 02.01** University of Pennsylvania Museum (neg.#S4-13970); **02.03** Directorate General of Antiquities, Baghdad, Iraq; **02.04** Hirmer Fotoarchiv, Munich; **02.05** Corbis; **02.06** Erich Lessing/Art Resource, NY; **02.07** Lepsius, *Denkmaler*; **02.08** Jewish Museum/Art Resource, NY

Chapter 3
Chapter Opener 03 National Museum of Pakistan, Karachi, Pakistan/Borromeo/Art Resource, NY; **Figure 03.01** Alan Sorrell/Bridgeman Art Library/Mark Sorrell; **03.02** Baldwin H. Ward/Corbis; **03.03** National Museum of Pakistan, Karachi, Pakistan/Borromeo/Art Resource; **03.04** The Granger Collection, New York; **03.05** Musée Cernuschi, Musée des Arts de l'Asie de la Ville de Paris; **03.06** Werner Forman/Art Resource, NY; **03.07** Photosearch, Inc.

PART II

Chapter 4
Chapter Opener 04 Robert Harding Picture Library; **Figure 04.01** The Field Museum, #CSA35933; **04.02** N. Durrell McKenna/Photo Researchers, Inc.; **04.03** Bridgeman Art Library; **04.04** The Nelson-Atkins Museum of Art, Kansas City, Missouri (Purchase: Nelson Trust); **04.05** Wan-go Weng Archive; **04.06** *From Five Tracts of Hasan al-Banna: A Section from the Majmu 'At Rasa" Il Al-' Imam Al-Shahid Hasan Al Banna'*, translated and edited by Charles Wendell, University of California Press/Berkeley, 1978. Copyright © 1978 The Regents of the University of California; **04.07** Bridgeman Art Library

Chapter 5
Chapter Opener 05 Courtesy of the Trustees of the British Museum, London (PS112376); **Figure 05.01** Courtesy of the Oriental Institute of the University of Chicago; **05.02** The Granger Collection, New York; **05.03** Alinari/Art Resource, NY; **05.04** Raymond V. Schoder/Loyola University; **05.05** Hirmir Fotoarchiv, Munich; **05.06 Image 1** Alison Frantz Collection, American School of Classical Studies at Athens; **Image 2** Hirmer Fotoarchiv, Munich; **05.07** Alinari/Art Resource, NY; **Visualizing the Past** Bibliothèque Nationale de France, Paris

Chapter 6
Chapter Opener 06 Robert Ivey/Ric Ergenbriet Photography; **Figure 06.01** Cleveland Museum of Art, Purchase from the J. H. Wade Fund, 30.331; **06.02** From Percy Brown's *Indian Architecture: Buddhist and Hindu Period*. Published by D. B. Taraporevala Sons & Co. Ltd., Bombay; **06.04** Government of India Tourist Office

Chapter 7
Chapter Opener 07 Alinari/Art Resource, NY; **Figure 07.01** Alinari/Art Resource, NY; **07.02** Shell Photographic Unit, London; **07.03** Alinari/Art Resource, NY; **07.04** Musée de l'Arles et de la Provence Antiques (Cl. M. Lacanaud)

Chapter 8
Chapter Opener 08 Doug Bryant/D. Donne Bryant Stock; **Figure 08.02** Courtesy of Cahokia Mounds Historic Site;

INDEX

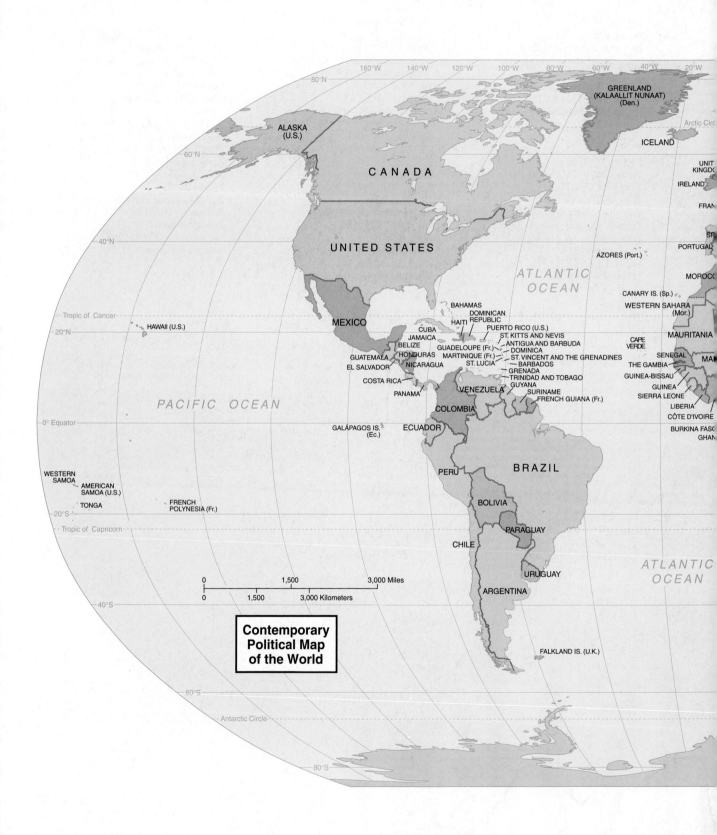

GREENLAND
(KALAALLIT NUNAAT)
(Den.)

ICELAND

Arctic Circle

ALASKA
(U.S.)

80°N

60°N

UNIT
KINGD

IRELAND

C A N A D A

FRAN

40°N

SP

PORTUGAL

UNITED STATES

AZORES (Port.)

ATLANTIC
OCEAN

MOROCCO

CANARY IS. (Sp.)

Tropic of Cancer

WESTERN SAHARA
(Mor.)

HAWAII (U.S.)

20°N

MEXICO

BAHAMAS

DOMINICAN
REPUBLIC

HAITI

PUERTO RICO (U.S.)

CUBA

ST. KITTS AND NEVIS

MAURITANIA

JAMAICA

CAPE
VERDE

ANTIGUA AND BARBUDA

BELIZE

GUADELOUPE (Fr.)

DOMINICA

SENEGAL

MA

HONDURAS

MARTINIQUE (Fr.)

ST. VINCENT AND THE GRENADINES

GUATEMALA

THE GAMBIA

ST. LUCIA

BARBADOS

EL SALVADOR

NICARAGUA

GRENADA

GUINEA-BISSAU

COSTA RICA

TRINIDAD AND TOBAGO

GUYANA

GUINEA

PANAMA

VENEZUELA

SURINAME

SIERRA LEONE

FRENCH GUIANA (Fr.)

LIBERIA

COLOMBIA

CÔTE D'IVOIRE

PACIFIC OCEAN

GALÁPAGOS IS.
(Ec.)

ECUADOR

0° Equator

BURKINA FASO

GHAN

WESTERN
SAMOA

PERU

BRAZIL

AMERICAN
SAMOA (U.S.)

FRENCH
POLYNESIA (Fr.)

20°S

BOLIVIA

TONGA

Tropic of Capricorn

PARAGUAY

CHILE

ATLANTIC
OCEAN

URUGUAY

| 0 | | 1,500 | | 3,000 Miles |

| 0 | 1,500 | 3,000 Kilometers |

ARGENTINA

40°S

**Contemporary
Political Map
of the World**

FALKLAND IS. (U.K.)

60°S

Antarctic Circle

80°S

160°W 140°W 120°W 100°W 80°W 60°W 40°W 20°W